D0930167

Treasury of Great Books

Reader's Digest

Treasury of Great Books

THE READER'S DIGEST ASSOCIATION, INC.
Pleasantville, New York • Montreal

Editor: Charles S. Verral
Art Director: Robert Grant

The stories in this book previously appeared in *Reader's Digest,* as listed in the Acknowledgments and Credits on pages 639–640, which are hereby made a part of this copyright page.

Library of Congress Catalog Card Number 80-50421
ISBN 0-89577-084-9

Printed in the United States of America

Contents

MADAME SARAH

CONDENSED FROM THE BOOK BY

CORNELIA OTIS SKINNER

PAINTING BY GEORGES CLAIRIN, 1876

She was the greatest actress of her era, the darling of royalty, the playmate of the rich and the powerful. Everywhere she went adoring crowds thronged to see her.

Although she was no beauty, she could create the illusion of great beauty. A painter who knew her well said that he had no idea whether or not she was even passably good-looking. Beauty with her, he said, was a garment she could put on or take off as she pleased.

A poet once declared: "She is the Muse of Poetry herself. She recites as a nightingale sings, as the wind sighs, as the water murmurs."

Yet she could be vindictive, petty and cruel. Her love affairs across two continents were numerous and scandalous, her financial dealings precarious.

In *Madame Sarah* Cornelia Otis Skinner, herself a distinguished actress and author, has written a vivid biography that brings to life the turmoil and eccentricities, the wit and the genius that were all part of the amazing Sarah Bernhardt.

1. THE GREAT BERNHARDT

SHE WAS HAILED as the Eighth Wonder of the World, the greatest personality France had produced since Joan of Arc. Emperors knelt at her feet, crowned heads showered her with jewels, and adoring mobs collected wherever she went. Stories about her numerous lovers, her vast fortunes, wild expenditures and bankruptcies survive to this day.

No actress ever had more written about her, more gossip told about her, more ecstatic praise or vicious censure showered upon her. Once she wailed in the tones of a martyr: "I am the most lied-about woman in the world!"

Sarah Bernhardt was a genius, and a colossal egoist. She accepted the fact that she was the greatest actress of her era as logically as Victoria accepted the fact that she was Queen of England. On her first visit to America, when the crowds went wild over her, one reporter exclaimed: "Why, New York didn't give Don Pedro of Brazil such an ovation!"

"Yes," replied Sarah serenely, "but he was only an emperor."

Throughout her fabulous career, which lasted for more than 60 years, she passed as a beauty. But her looks by themselves could not have been a major factor in Sarah's success. Her hair was a reddish-blond mop, thick, fuzzy and completely unruly. Her body was that of a consumptive wraith. Her face was hollow-cheeked and colorless, and she emphasized its pallor with slathers of white rice powder.

Her eyes were shaped like a cat's, blue as star sapphires when she was in a good mood. When she was angry, they deepened into a brooding slate color, with threatening flashes of green. Her nose was straight and Hebraic. Her mouth could be passionately expressive one moment and slyly prim the next. The author-painter W. Graham Robertson wrote that he had no idea whether or not Sarah Bernhardt was even passably good-looking. Beauty with her, he said, was a garment she could put on or take off as she pleased. When she put it on, "her face became a lamp through which glowed pale light, her hair burned like an aureole, she grew tall and stately; it was transfiguration."

But if Sarah Bernhardt was no true beauty, she could create the illusion of great beauty. Watching her, said one critic, was as fascinating as watching a wild animal in a cage. She acted with unerring instinct and with no intellectual approach to any role, but with emotional concentration and a fervor that was almost fanatic. Her sense of timing was perfect, and at the sound of her Golden Voice, critics forgot to criticize and went into almost mawkish rhapsodies. The poet Theodore de Banville declared: "She is the Muse of Poetry. She recites as the nightingale sings, as the wind sighs, as the water murmurs . . ."

That voice is forever silenced, and the acting of Sarah Bernhardt lies buried with her body in the Parisian cemetery of Père Lachaise. Her legend, however, lives on.

SARAH BERNHARDT WAS BORN in Paris in 1844, the illegitimate daughter of Judith van Hard, a Dutch Jewess. Her father, reputedly a law student named Edouard Bernhardt, settled 100,000 francs on the child as a dowry and then disappeared, leaving Judith to fend for herself. In the Paris of the 1840's a middle-class young woman without a husband, family or fortune had just three ways of making a living: by being a milliner, by being a governess or by being kept. Judith, who now called herself Madame Bernhardt, chose the last of these and soon prospered.

There was no place for a child in such a life, and for her first four years Sarah was farmed out to a wet nurse. Eventually the woman married and moved from the country to Paris, where her husband was the concierge of a run-down apartment house. She could not locate the mother to return the child, so the newly married couple had to share their damp, dingy single room with the little girl. Under these dismal conditions Sarah was very unhappy and became painfully thin.

It was only by a farfetched coincidence that Sarah escaped this environment. She happened to be sitting on the curb one day when a coachman stopped his horses to fix the harness. Getting out of the carriage was her Aunt Rosine, who followed the same dubious profession as Sarah's mother. Before anyone could stop her, Sarah dashed into the street, and threw her arms around her aunt.

"I'm a prisoner here!" she cried. "If you don't take me away I'll die!"

Sarah's pleas fell on deaf ears. Rosine was only embarrassed by her filthy little niece and was visibly relieved when the concierge and his wife rushed out and yanked her away from the carriage. They locked her in their quarters, but before the coachman could drive away, Sarah flung herself out a window to the street below. As a result of this, her first big dramatic scene, she suffered a dislocated shoulder, a slight concussion and a shattered kneecap; but she was taken to her mother's elegant apartment.

When she was eight Sarah was sent off to school, first to a fashionable pension for young ladies and after that to a Catholic convent. But by 15 her education was considered complete and she was summoned home again, this time for a "family conference" to decide her future. Among those present were her mother, two aunts, a notary from Le Havre and four gentlemen friends, among them the fashionable Duc de Morny. Sarah quickly announced that she had already made up her mind to become a nun, a decision which evoked gales of laughter. When her mother protested that money was needed to join a religious order, Sarah reminded her of the 100,000-franc legacy from her father.

"But that is for your dowry when you marry!" said the notary.

Sarah, raising her eyes to heaven, replied in the voice of a child martyr, "I shall marry God."

This was too much for the notary from Le Havre. "The silly fool should be sent to a house of correction!" he snorted. At that, Sarah threw a tantrum. With the yowl of an infuriated animal, she sprang at the notary, pummeled his chest, scratched his face and tore out a fistful of hair. When order had been restored, the Duc de Morny remarked with amused prescience, "The girl's a born actress. She ought to be sent for training at the Conservatoire."

Sarah was horrified at this proposal. "An actress?" she exclaimed. "Never!" She had been taught by the sisters at her convent that acting was a wicked profession.

To dispel this illusion, she was taken that evening to the Comédie Française, where her mother and her friends occupied a box as the guests of Alexandre Dumas, the famous author of *The Three Musketeers.* The girl had never seen a play before and, with her preconceived notions about the horrors of theatrical life, she had little desire to go. But with the rise of the red curtain her baleful mood vanished, to be replaced first by wonder, then rapture, then raw uncontrollable emotion. Sarah experienced every mood of every character on the stage. The sad passages reduced her to tears, which in time gave way to embarrassingly loud sobs. When warning "Sh's!" began to come from the audience, her mother turned purple with shame, and one guest stormed out of the box, slamming the door behind him. Only Dumas came to the girl's aid. He moved his chair next to hers and put an arm around her.

Sarah was still in a highly emotional state when she returned home. Her mother, outraged, dispatched her immediately to bed. But Dumas, who had agreed with Morny that the girl did indeed seem destined for the stage, saw her to her room. At the door he bent his handsome head over Sarah's hand, kissed it and spoke the prophetic words, *"Bonsoir, petite étoile!"* (Good-night, little star!)

2. TALK OF THE BOULEVARDS

ONCE SHE HAD MADE UP her mind to become an actress, Sarah was determined to be the world's greatest. At the Conservatoire, with the help of Dumas and Morny, she successfully passed her audition. She studied zealously, practiced her diction exercises hours at a time and memorized many more roles than were assigned her.

After she graduated two years later, the politically powerful Morny secured her a junior member's post at the Comédie Française. In August 1862 the celebrated theater announced the debut of Mlle. Sarah Bernhardt in the title role of Racine's *Iphigénie.* But on opening night she was seized by an attack of stage fright and she simply rattled off her lines. At the end of the performance, all her coach from the Conservatoire could find to say was, "Why? Why?" Shattered with shame, Sarah asked if he could ever forgive her. "Yes, I can forgive you," he said. "But Racine in his grave never will."

During the ensuing weeks, Sarah appeared in several other plays, but without distinction, and most people agreed that the Comédie had made a mistake in hiring her.

Her offstage performances, however, were vivid and compelling. The story goes that once, objecting when the stage doorkeeper addressed her as "Little Bernhardt," she wrathfully broke her parasol over his head. The blow opened his scalp, which bled so profusely that Sarah, in dramatic remorse, tore off strips of her petticoat to bandage the wound. (Twenty years later, when the doorkeeper retired, she purchased a cottage for him and set him up with a trust fund for life.)

More serious consequences resulted from a flare-up which occurred when she took her nine-year-old sister Regina (also illegitimate) backstage to watch the annual ceremony honoring Molière's birthday. Unfortunately, Regina halted the entrance of a senior actress by standing on her train. The actress, a monumental lady named Madame Nathalie, pushed the child aside roughly, causing her to cut her forehead on a stucco pillar. The little girl, pointing accusingly at the actress, screamed the insulting, *"Vache! Vache!"* at the top of her lungs. Incensed, Madame Nathalie turned her wrath on Sarah, but Sarah silenced her with a slap which sent the actress into a dramatic faint.

The blow not only felled Madame Nathalie, it rocked the Comédie to its foundations. Never before had a first-year probationer dared to defy a senior member of the troupe, let alone use physical violence. But if her fellow troupers were outraged, the Paris newspapers were delighted. Sarah became the talk of the boulevards.

While she was rehearsing for her next appearance, Madame Nathalie descended upon the theater manager and demanded that he withhold any further appearances of this violent upstart until she had made a public apology. Sarah refused, and the manager had no choice but to request her resignation. She was not to reappear at the Comédie Française for another ten years.

For all Sarah Bernhardt's stubborn pride, her enforced resignation from the leading theater of France was a bitter blow. Other managers were reluctant to hire her, and it was only through some wire-pulling that she was finally able to land a job at the Gymnase, a popular boulevard theater which was presenting a series of highly successful, lightweight comedies. But such plays were never Sarah's forte, and her performances were so bad that she was driven to the brink of suicide.

It was at this point that Dumas again walked into her life. He was present at one of her lamentable stage performances, sensed her desperation and felt a sudden compulsion to talk to her before she did anything rash. Realizing she was on the verge of a complete emotional breakdown, he told her that she must cut her stakes for the time being and start off immediately for some other country. Within a few hours, she was on a train bound for Brussels, armed with an introduction to some of Dumas' friends there.

Apparently Dumas' prescription was the right one, because a few weeks later he received word that Sarah had conquered not only Brussels, but also the heart of Prince Henri de Ligne, scion of a noble Belgian family. Unhappily, this idyll was cut short by a dispatch from Paris saying that her mother was seriously ill with a heart attack. Sarah took the next train home, only to discover upon her arrival that Judith was well on her way to recovery. She also found, after a few weeks, that she herself was pregnant. She told no one, not even her lover, for fear he'd feel trapped into sharing the responsibility.

For five months she was jobless. Eventually her pregnancy became so apparent that she was forced to tell her mother. Judith, with all the bourgeois respectability of a retired courtesan, was outraged. "I won't have any little bastard born under my roof!" she screamed, ignoring the fact that by this time she herself had had three bastards, each by a different father.

Ordered from her mother's home, Sarah found a small flat elsewhere in Paris, and there, on December 22, 1864, she gave birth to a son, Maurice Bernhardt.

Almost at once she again started forth to find work for the support of the baby she adored. So desperate was Sarah that she was willing to play parts that were practically walk-ons at the Porte-Saint-Martin, a theater specializing in melodramas.

Fortunately her financial problems were solved for a time by the arrival in Paris of the Prince de Ligne. Through the theater he found her and immediately moved in with her. Far from being horrified over the arrival of her infant son, he was filled with happiness, and proposed marriage. But his family would have none of it. When he announced that he wanted to marry an unknown half-Jewish actress by whom he had had an illegitimate child, his father threatened to disown him.

A distinguished uncle, General de Ligne, was sent to Paris to break up his nephew's shocking liaison, and even though he himself was personally captivated by Sarah, he left with her heartbroken promise to give up her lover. That evening Sarah told the Prince that, much as she adored him, she could not allow him to give up his inheritance for her.

When he protested, she silenced him by saying her only aim in life was to be a great and successful theatrical star, and she added that she had already received an offer to appear at the Odéon, a state theater, second only to the Comédie Française. The young man listened with incredulity which changed to fury. He called her everything from a ham actress to a vulgar harlot, and then stormed from the room and out of her life forever.

Sarah had indeed had an offer from the Odéon, and her big break came there in 1868 with the revival of *Kean*, a drama by her old friend and mentor, Alexandre Dumas. On opening night, anti-royalist students who regarded Victor Hugo as their champion staged a riot to protest the fact that a state theater should be giving them Dumas instead of Hugo. To add to their indignation, Dumas himself appeared in a box, accompanied by his current mistress.

The rising of the curtain didn't quiet the uproar, nor did Sarah's entrance. Trembling with fright, she was unable to make herself heard by the demonstrators, who continued to whistle, stamp and demand their author. But then terror gave way to defiance. She stepped down to the footlights and held out her hands in a gesture of disarming appeal.

The audience grew quiet, and in a clear tone she said, "Friends, you wish to defend the cause of justice. Are you doing it by making Monsieur Dumas responsible for the banishment of Monsieur Hugo?"

It did the trick. The audience broke into good-natured laughter and applause. The rioting stopped, and the play proceeded without further interruption except for occasional bursts of spontaneous appreciation for the remarkable performance Sarah gave. Afterward, students unharnessed her horses and, taking the shafts of her carriage, ran through the streets of Paris shouting, "Make way for our Sarah!"

3. PARIS UNDER SIEGE

FROM 1869 ON SARAH was one of the most popular actresses of the Odéon, and when her name appeared on the bill the theater was usually sold out. Her health, always precarious, never interfered with her dedication to work or her exuberant way of living until the summer of 1870, when an oral hemorrhage so depleted her strength that she was ordered to rest for a couple of months at a spa in southern France.

In July of that year the Franco-Prussian War broke out, and by the end of September 160,000 Germans were encamped in the immediate suburbs of Paris. The Great Siege had begun.

At the news of the French army rout, Sarah tossed to the winds all prospects of completing her cure and, against the orders of her doctors, rushed home. She managed to send her small son and other relatives from the city, and then settled in her apartment to face what might come. She was completely alone except for her cook and Madame Guérard, an old friend of her mother's who had attended her at the birth of her baby and then stayed on as her personal secretary.

Most theaters were shut down, but when the Comédie Française was opened as an emergency military hospital, Sarah made up her mind that the Odéon must also care for the wounded, and that she herself would organize the enterprise. The prefect of police gave her permission to install 32 hospital beds in the foyer and lobby of the theater.

She opened her hospital, then returned to ask the prefect for further favors. The weather was bitterly damp and chill, and she found him in his unheated office trying to keep warm in a fur-lined overcoat. At the finish of the interview, Sarah not only had his promise of food and medical supplies, she also had his overcoat. She wanted it, she explained, for one of her ambulatory cases whose bed was needed for the more seriously wounded.

The frail 26-year-old actress now worked with the vigor of ten peasants. She staunchly held a basin while doctors amputated a limb or probed for shrapnel, and herself unflinchingly dressed wounds which reeked of infection and gangrene. As winter set in, one of the severest on record, and the city became more desperate, she and her co-workers often went without food in order to feed their patients.

One day a captured Prussian officer was brought in. Although seriously wounded, he had all the arrogance of a Teutonic conqueror.

"In less than 48 hours Paris will capitulate," he boasted. "We know you have been reduced to eating rats and mice."

That evening Sarah herself brought the German his supper, saying, "This is how we are starving, my man."

On the tray was a breast of excellent chicken. It came from a small barnyard of fowl and geese she'd bought at the beginning of the Siege and housed in her boudoir.

In the 19th and final week of the Siege, conditions became so bad that Sarah was finally forced to shut down her hospital. By that time the continual bombardment of the city had made it necessary for her to move her patients down into the cellars, where the poor wretches had to suffer the horrors of burst water pipes, flooding sewage, and rats that ran over the beds and even tried to gnaw at open wounds. When it closed its doors shortly before Paris fell, Sarah's improvised hospital had cared for 150 patients.

AFTER THE WAR, SARAH RESUMED her acting career at the Odéon, finally becoming a full-fledged star with her performance as the Queen in Victor Hugo's *Ruy Blas.* At the finish she took a solo curtain call and heard for the first time the intoxicating thunder of a personal ovation.

"Back in my room that night," Sarah wrote later, "I felt so rich I was afraid of robbers."

It was almost inevitable after this that she should be invited to rejoin the Comédie Française. The offer came while she was having an altercation with the Odéon authorities because her dog, a toy griffon named Hamlet, had one day escaped from her dressing room and appeared onstage. The manager blamed the actress for the incident and slapped a fine on her, but she refused to pay it.

"Have you taken leave of your senses?" he shouted, when she announced her defiance. "What other theater in Paris could offer you the advantages you have here?"

"Perhaps the Française?" Sarah replied.

The manager, recalling her past difficulties with that institution, simply laughed in her face. Whereupon Sarah stormed from his office, hailed a carriage and in tones of Racinian fury thundered at the startled coachman, "To the Comédie Française!"

Once there she was beset by misgivings. These were heightened when she dripped ink on the contract as she was preparing to sign it.

"Wait!" she cried with childish superstition. "Let me fold the paper and see what comes out. If I make a 'butterfly,' I'll sign the contract. If it's just a smear, you can tear it up."

Painstakingly she made a fold. When she opened it there appeared the silhouette of a perfect butterfly, complete with antennae.

Sarah spent the next seven and a half years with the Comédie, enjoying one success after another. She seems to have had a genius for both fascinating and infuriating the public, for she was adored one moment, bitterly resented the next. Her thinness was always a gold mine for caricaturists and wits. One columnist declared that Sarah never needed an umbrella because she was so skinny she could walk between the raindrops. Wrote another: "An empty carriage pulled up and Sarah Bernhardt got out." Stories of her eccentricities were on every tongue. One told of an elderly Parisian whose dying words were, "I depart this life willingly, for I shall hear no more about Sarah Bernhardt."

Her circle of friends included many leading figures of the day, among them Victor Hugo and Emile Zola. She also entertained Ferdinand de Lesseps, the builder of the Suez Canal, the poet d'Annunzio and Oscar Wilde. Theodore Roosevelt visited her whenever he came to Paris, and Sarah's admiration for him was boundless. "That man and I," she once told a group of friends, "together we could rule the world!"

She was also on intimate terms with the British Prince of Wales, and on one occasion this genial monarch-to-be doubled for a corpse in one of her plays.

In spite of her fame, Sarah was never altogether happy at the Comédie Française. She continually chafed against the restrictions of that tradition-bound institution, which in turn found her high jinks a source of embarrassment. One day when the company was playing a London engagement, Edward Jarrett, England's most celebrated entrepreneur, came backstage and asked pointblank if she would like to make a fortune. Never averse to such a possibility, she inquired how, and he proposed a six-month tour of the United States.

"But I can only act in French," Sarah protested.

"My dear, you could act in Chinese and the Americans would still turn out in droves to see you," he replied.

She did not then leave the Comédie Française, but the seed had been sown. The break finally occurred when the management forced her to appear in a play for which she felt she was ill-suited and under-rehearsed. After reading her notices, the most disastrous of her career, Sarah immediately sat down and wrote her resignation. The Française dignitaries first sued her, then implored her to come back, but she turned a deaf ear to their entreaties. The road to her future now led westward across the Atlantic.

4. IN AMERICA

AS SOON AS HE LEARNED SARAH was free, Edward Jarrett hastened over from London, contract in hand. He proposed that she tour the United States in a repertory of eight plays of her own selection, with a company which she herself would assemble and direct. The financial terms, considering the buying power of the dollar in that era, were downright staggering. He guaranteed her 100 engagements over a four-month period at $1000 a performance, plus 50 percent of the gross if the night's receipts went over $4000. She would receive an additional $200 weekly for hotel expenses, and would travel in her own private railroad car with a personal entourage of two maids, two cooks, a waiter, her maître d'hôtel and her companion and secretary Madame Guérard—all of their salaries to be paid by the management.

On October 15, 1880, Madame Sarah's troupe, shepherded by Jarrett, set out for the New World on a battered old tub, part steam, part sail, called the *Amérique.* Twelve days later, after a remarkably rough crossing, the ship dropped anchor in New York harbor.

It was 6:30 a.m., freezing cold, and the river was clogged with ice. A tugboat came alongside bearing a thoroughly chilled but intrepid welcoming committee of officials, consular delegates and important citizens. Close in its wake steamed a tender weighted down with newspapermen and a brass band. This overwhelming boarding party alarmed the whole French troupe, and Madame Bernhardt, theatrically dying of seasickness, locked herself in her cabin and refused to budge.

It was only when Jarrett pounded on the door and reminded her that he had staked not only his entire fortune but also his reputation on the success of their joint venture that she finally tottered forth to face the waiting mob. Clinging dramatically to Jarrett's arm, she dragged herself up the stairs to the main ballroom. When the band struck up the "Marseillaise," however, Sarah's attitude of not-long-for-this-world frailty turned into one of passionate patriotism. Raising her head high, she stood as though the French tri-color had suddenly been unfurled behind her. The act, as was to be expected, electrified the gathering.

After she had been presented with flowers, speeches had been made, and a line of important New Yorkers had filed past to shake her hand and attempt a word or two in French, the reporters were let loose like hounds released for the kill. They mobbed their prey, hurling questions until finally Sarah could bear no more and put on such an effective fainting act that even Jarrett was fooled.

Hastily informing the gentlemen of the press that they could continue their interviews later in Madame's hotel suite, he lifted his swooned star up over his shoulder and carried her back to her cabin. There she instantly recovered, went into shrieks of laughter and, grabbing Jarrett by both hands, whirled him about in a mad waltz.

At her opening performance the house was packed, although tickets cost up to $40 each. Since the majority had come mainly out of curiosity because of her scandalous reputation, her very appearance came as a shock. They were unprepared for this miracle of delicacy, for her feline grace, for the incandescent, shimmering aura she gave forth.

When Sarah started to speak, in French, there was no need for translation. The audience sat hushed and transfixed at the sound of her incredible voice. Complete silence prevailed throughout the performance. It was only after the final scene in which she died most effectively from poisoning that the spectators broke into roaring applause. The pandemonium did not quiet down until she had taken 27 curtain calls.

Almost overnight "The Bernhardt," as she was called in America, became all the rage. Her every move was reported in the papers, while the women's pages published daily accounts and sketches of her gowns, furs and jewelry. Sarah Bernhardt perfume, Sarah Bernhardt candy, Sarah Bernhardt cigars and even Sarah Bernhardt eyeglasses appeared on the market, as eager entrepreneurs rushed to take full advantage of the fad.

In Boston, Sarah's reception was even more hysterical than in New York, and the doors of the most exclusive homes were opened to her. When she asked to meet Henry Wadsworth Longfellow, the 73-year-old poet was delighted, but implored a friend with hasty caution, "Be sure to come along as I'll need a chaperon." Longfellow spoke excellent French, and the little gathering, attended also by Mrs. William Dean Howells and Dr. Oliver Wendell Holmes, went off swimmingly. Sarah rapturously announced that her favorite poem was *Hiawatha,* which she pronounced "Ee-ah-vah-tah." Longfellow was naturally pleased, but his pleasure turned to acute embarrassment when, as he was seeing her to her carriage, Sarah suddenly cried out, *"Ah, que je vous admire!"* and, flinging her arms around his neck, kissed him resoundingly on both of his cheeks.

During her Boston stay the actress was also invited to inspect a captured whale, which was tied up to a pier in a moribund state. For the benefit of reporters, she posed on the creature's back, then drew forth a small bone planted in its massive hide. Whereupon imaginative drawings of this incident appeared in all the papers under the caption, "How Sarah Bernhardt gets the whalebone for her corsets"—although Sarah had never in her life worn a corset.

After this the owner of the whale (which had by now expired) turned his pitiable behemoth into a traveling tent show, admission 25 cents. He ballyhooed it with a horse-drawn calliope which blared through the streets with a billboard in horrendous colors portraying the actress in her deboning act under the caption, "Come see the gigantic whale killed by Sarah Bernhardt to furnish bones for her corsets."

The frenzy which surrounded Sarah was now so great that, before she left for Chicago, Jarrett wrote the mayor asking for a bodyguard of extra police. The mayor considered the request absurd, for somehow he had never heard of "The Bernhardt." He soon heard a great deal about her. When Sarah arrived she was all but annihilated by mobs of greeters. She was rescued by an unknown admirer who lifted her on his shoulders, bore her safely through the crowd to a cab and deposited her at the Palmer House.

Her performances were sellouts, as usual, because of a vast amount of unsolicited publicity. The Episcopal bishop of Chicago had denounced her so eloquently in his sermons that Jarrett's partner wrote the bishop a letter, which was reprinted in the newspapers:

Your Excellency:

I am accustomed when I bring an attraction to your town to spend $500 on advertising. As you have done half the advertising for me, I herewith enclose $250 for the poor of your parish.

From Chicago the troupe was launched into a backbreaking tour of one-night stands. Wherever Sarah appeared, she was besieged by reporters who asked the most impertinent questions. "Is it true," one inquired, "that you have had four children and never any husband?"

"Certainly not!" Sarah replied. "But at least that would be better than the case of some of your American women, who have had four husbands and never any children!"

Throughout her entire American tour, as indeed throughout her life, Sarah insisted upon being paid in gold coins, which she carried with her in a small chamois bag. Out of this she paid her creditors, doling out the coins like a miser. When her fortunes were at a high peak, she put the golden overflow in a metal-bound chest which she kept under her bed.

By the time Sarah returned to New York, she had given 157 performances in 51 cities. On May 3 she gave a farewell matinee, and then a few days later she set sail for France. Upon her departure she had $194,000 in gold coins stashed in her metal-bound chest.

5. WORLD APPEARANCES

As a result of her American tour, Sarah developed wanderlust. Throughout the rest of her life, whenever she needed money she took to the road. Paris was always home to her, but, interspersed with her theatrical appearances there, she traveled through all of Europe, North and South America, and even to such distant places as Samoa, Honolulu, Auckland and Australia. There were to be nine American tours in all, four of them "farewell appearances." Her memories of the Franco-Prussian War were so vivid that she avoided Germany until 1902, when she was persuaded to perform in several cities there.

On her first trip to Russia, in the winter of 1881, her success in St. Petersburg was spectacular. Every night a red carpet was unrolled over the snow from the curb to the stage door, and after each performance crowds ran behind her sleigh and fought to pick up the flowers she threw to them. She was invited to the Winter Palace, and when Czar Alexander III stepped forward to meet her, he would not permit her to curtsy. "No, Madame," he said. "It is I who must bow to you."

It was in Russia that Sarah met the man she was to marry. His name was Jacques Damala, he came from a prominent Athens family, and he was stationed in St. Petersburg as an attaché with the Greek legation. Eleven years Sarah's junior, handsome, insolent and vain, he had a reputation as a notorious Don Juan. Wherever he went women lost their heads over him, but he boasted that no one of them had ever meant anything in his life.

For Sarah, such indifference was an obvious challenge. She turned on the full battery of her wiles, which heretofore had made an adoring slave of any man she cared to conquer, but this time with no success. Damala was playing a game, and it amused him to realize that the most celebrated woman in Europe could be his at the wink of an eyelash. In a rash move, the actress prevailed upon him to resign his diplomatic post and become an actor in her company. He had no qualifications beyond his good looks, but Sarah kept insisting that he'd prove to be one of the most brilliant newcomers in the theater.

From Russia, the tour continued southward. When Damala, who could not remain faithful to any woman for more than a few weeks, began casting his eye over some of the younger actresses in the company, Sarah completely lost her head. Thinking it a means of holding her vacillating man, she proposed marriage, and Damala accepted. During a five-day holiday between engagements in Naples and Nice, the couple skipped off to London, and there, on April 4, 1882, Sarah Bernhardt became Madame Jacques Damala.

Upon her return to Paris the following May, the bride's first ordeal was to confront her son.

"Maurice, dear," she said. "I have news for you."

"I know, *Maman,*" the boy said coldly. "You have married *Monsieur* Sarah Bernhardt."

This was precisely the role that Damala was to play during the seven years of their stormy marriage and, like many other husbands of famous wives, he bitterly resented it. With Sarah's expert coaching he became a passable performer, and for a time there was a certain novelty for audiences in seeing him as her leading man. But this soon wore off, and when the opportunity came for her to appear in a new play called *Fedora,* the author refused pointblank to hire Damala. To appease her husband, Sarah rented a theater for him, but though the press was lenient, even kind, when he opened there in his first starring role, his success was completely overshadowed by hers.

Sarah's triumph in *Fedora* so enraged Damala that a few nights after the opening he provoked a quarrel in which he accused his wife of everything from double-crossing him to deliberately trying to ruin his career, and then stormed out of the house. The next morning, without notice, he departed for Africa, leaving Sarah with an empty theater on her hands and an enormous financial loss.

But this was not the end of him. A few months later he was back, having by this time become a confirmed morphine addict. Sarah did everything in her power to stop him. She ransacked his room, threw out all the phials of the stuff she could find and threatened the pharmacist from whom he got his supply. But nothing helped, and at last Sarah could put up with her husband's behavior no longer. She arranged for him to enter a sanitarium, then secured a legal separation. Being a Catholic, she never considered getting a divorce.

After this Damala drifted aimlessly in a daze of drugs, sinking lower and lower until, several years later, he was found living in a shabby furnished room. When news of his hopeless state was brought to Sarah, she rushed to his bedside and had him sent to her house. There she nursed him herself but, in spite of her efforts, he went into physical collapse and had to be sent to a hospital, where he finally died.

Sarah had his body shipped back to Greece, and in later years, whenever a tour took her to Athens, she made a pilgrimage to his grave. For several months she wore mourning and signed any legal or financial document "Sarah Bernhardt Damala, widow."

"If there is anything more remarkable than watching Sarah act," declared Victorien Sardou, who wrote many of her biggest hits, "it is watching her live!"

No project struck her as impossible. At one time or another during her restless life she took up sculpture (some of her works won awards), painting, the piano, pistol shooting, fishing and alligator hunting. She once played *Hamlet* in French to London audiences. Although the public was receptive to the production, some critics were not over-polite. Max Beerbohm headed his review: "Hamlet, Princess of Denmark."

All her life Sarah hated any form of tyranny and, when the Dreyfus case exploded, triggering a wave of anti-Semitic hysteria, she had the courage to take a stand in favor of the French army captain, even when it came to open rupture with her nearest and dearest. After Dreyfus was sentenced to Devil's Island, she went to see Emile Zola, and it was said that it was she who persuaded him to write *J'Accuse,* the celebrated outcry for Captain Dreyfus' vindication.

Despite this unpopular offstage role, she remained unrivaled as a star. In 1898 she moved her troupe to the Théâtre des Nations, a great barn of a building with a huge seating capacity. She was 55 at the time, but confidently signed a 25-year lease. Her first move was to rename the place the Théâtre Sarah Bernhardt, a title which was changed during the occupation of Paris in World War II when Nazi officials learned that the actress had been half-Jewish. The theater is still in operation today, and once again under Sarah's name.

By now she had complete control of her productions, and she ran her theater with the efficiency of a field marshal and the lavishness of a Croesus. Her personal backstage quarters consisted of a five-room suite, including a kitchen and a richly decorated salon where a fire burned all winter and much of the summer. Equally overheated was her private dressing room, which was always filled with masses of flowers sent by admirers. Here, before each performance, Sarah waited in regal majesty for the callboy to knock on her door and announce, "Madame, it will be eight o'clock when it suits you."

No other actress ever approached her profession with more study or more hours of relentless work. She rose at seven, conferred at eight with costume and scene designers, then rehearsed her company for three hours. After lunch in her dressing room, she would sometimes play a matinee and return to her home. She was back at the theater for an evening performance, and after supper with friends she would often study a new role until three in the morning.

Her home, a small ornate residence at 56 Boulevard Péreire, became a Paris landmark, and it had the same hothouse atmosphere as her backstage quarters. A Bernhardt interior was always a confusion of the good, the picturesque and the dreadful. Dominating the main salon was a canopied divan, strewn with immense satin pillows and furs, from which she held court. The floors were covered with Persian carpets and tigerskin rugs, while the walls hardly showed through a jumble of Japanese fans, antique weapons, paintings and brocades.

One of her favorite pieces of furniture was a satin-lined rosewood coffin. During her sickly adolescence, Sarah had developed a morbid fear that she was dying, and she persuaded her mother to buy this macabre object. She kept it in her bedroom and even slept in it occasionally in order, she said, to get used to her final resting place. By the time her illness had passed she had acquired a bizarre fondness for the coffin, and she kept it for the rest of her life.

Each year Sarah became more attached to her summer-holiday

home, a converted 17th-century fort on the wild, rocky island of Belle-Ile off the Brittany coast. There, in the clean salt air, she shed her eccentricities and became as happy and unaffected a woman as it was ever possible for her to be.

Belle-Ile could be reached only by ferry, but it was always swarming with visitors: authors, artists, musicians and politicians. Once the British royal yacht anchored offshore, and Sarah's old friend, by then King Edward VII, came across in a launch to pay a visit.

The island folk adored "La Bonne Dame," as they called Sarah, and whenever she drove through the small village they came out in crowds to greet her. She was always laden with cakes and preserves to distribute, and large bags full of candy for the children. She chatted with the farmers and fishermen and inquired after their welfare. Her concern was genuine. She had only to hear of a ship's master whose cargo had been ruined in a storm, or a fisherman who had lost his nets, and she'd dive into her purse to help him out. She paid visits of condolence to every family who lost a man at sea.

At Belle-Ile, and wherever Sarah Bernhardt lived, she kept a menagerie of pets. Wild animals, especially the big cats, fascinated her. She once told a group of dinner guests that she had consulted an eminent surgeon to see if it would be possible for him to graft a living tiger's tail to the end of her spine. It would be so satisfactory, she explained, to lash it about when she was angry.

At various times she kept a tame lion, a baby tigress, a wildcat, an ocelot, a lynx, a cheetah and four pumas. She also owned dogs, chameleons, turtles, parrots, monkeys and a crocodile. She once claimed she had a pet boa constrictor ("To rest my feet on after meals," she explained).

Sarah always insisted that her creatures were tame, but her visitors were not so sure. Alexandre Dumas the younger was introduced to the Bernhardt zoo on the first day he came calling with a copy of a new play. While waiting for his hostess, he heard a curious crunching sound behind him. Looking about, he beheld a puma serenely eating his straw boater.

A moment later the beast bounded from the room, but Dumas' relief was short-lived. A parrot suddenly landed on his shoulder and began biting off the buttons on his waistcoat. It was stopped by the leaping entrance of two gigantic collies, one of whom grabbed the script of the play. The other, with its paws on Dumas' chest, began licking his face with such ferocity that the novelist fell backward onto the divan, knocking over a large vase filled with water and peonies. At that moment Sarah appeared. Seeing the wreck her pets had made of her caller, she began to laugh so uncontrollably that she toppled onto the couch beside him. Thus began the long friendship between Bernhardt and the author of her greatest success, *La Dame aux Camélias.*

6. TWILIGHT

DURING THE FINAL YEARS of her life, Sarah was regarded almost as a French national institution. Her tours had made her one of her country's best ambassadors, and on March 6, 1914, she was made a Chevalier of the Légion d'Honneur, France's most coveted award.

By August of that same year France was again at war with Germany. Sarah was at Belle-Ile at the time but, just as in the Franco-Prussian War, she immediately returned to Paris.

During the next month the Germans advanced steadily, and soon the occupation of the city seemed inevitable. Sarah's friends implored her to leave, but she flatly refused. Only after her name was discovered on a list of hostages the Kaiser wanted brought to Germany was an official from the War Ministry able to convince her that it was her patriotic duty to move to a safer part of the country.

Sarah spent the next five months in a pine-surrounded villa overlooking the tranquil Bay of Arcachon in southwest France. Far from being tranquil for Madame Sarah, they were months of agony. Coming back from one of her American tours, she had suffered a bad fall on her right knee and had been in pain ever since. Recently the pain had become so severe that, at the villa, her entire leg was kept permanently immobilized in a plaster cast. When the pain increased, an eminent surgeon was summoned from Paris. He removed the cast, and for a while this brought relief. But soon the pain grew worse, and Sarah asked to have her leg amputated.

In the bleak early morning of February 22, 1915, Sarah was carried on a stretcher into a hospital in Bordeaux. As she passed by the waiting room she waved cheerfully to her son Maurice and a group of close friends. "Courage, my children!" she called out, and then with mock bravado hummed the opening bars of the "Marseillaise" as she was wheeled to the operating room.

News of the calamity flashed about the globe, and messages of condolence swamped the Bordeaux telegraph office. One gruesome communication came from the P.T. Barnum freak show, which offered $10,000 to display the severed leg.

Sarah was past 70 when her leg was amputated. Convalescence was long and critical, and for a time her life hung in the balance. Slowly, however, her strength returned and she was able to try on a wooden leg. Her own had been taken off halfway up the thigh, and the new contrivance had to be attached by means of a heavy girdle. Her feminine vanity rebelled at the idea of wearing a corset, and she tried to attach the contraption by other means. When every attempt failed, she flew into a rage and ordered the thing to be thrown into the fire.

The public speculated as to how Madame Sarah would get about now. Some thought she would use crutches, others a wheelchair.

"What do they take me for," she snorted, "an invalid?"

Her solution was a specially designed litter chair with two horizontal shafts by which she could be borne about. She stipulated that it be finished in Louis XV style, painted white and ornamented with gilt carving at the sides. Naturally, she dramatized the situation wherever she was carried, assuming the attitude of an empress in a procession.

If people had any idea that Sarah Bernhardt was finished as an actress, they were quickly undeceived. She returned to Paris in October 1915, after the Germans had fallen back, reducing the risk of her being taken hostage. Soon after, she put on a bill of three one-act plays, appearing in the final one herself. Then, when she heard that a Théâtre aux Armées had been organized for the purpose of sending performers behind the lines to entertain the troops, she immediately volunteered. The authorities were aghast, but finally agreed to send her.

In three days she performed in seven villages, some of them less than a half mile from the Argonne and Verdun. The first appearance was in an open marketplace where a crude stage had been set up. Makeshift floodlights flickered and a flimsy curtain flapped in the gusts of damp wind. When the audience of 3000 battle-weary men heard that they were about to see Madame Sarah Bernhardt, the announcement met with dead silence. The flimsy curtain fluttered open to reveal the fragile, aging actress propped against pillows in a shabby armchair.

Then this wisp of a woman began to speak the lines of a patriotic piece she had selected, and once again the miracle of Sarah Bernhardt took place. When she wound up her recitation with the clarion "To arms!" the men rose to their feet cheering and some of them sobbing.

In 1916 Sarah was again short of funds. As always, her El Dorado lay in the United States, and so once again she crossed the Atlantic for another "Farewell American Tour" that was to last for 18 months.

The *Lusitania* had been sunk the previous spring, and people were wondering how long it would be before America entered the war. To the utmost of her capacity Sarah became a rabble-rouser. Her arrival in most cities was greeted by brass bands that alternated "Tipperary" with "Madelon" and "The Stars and Stripes Forever." In her off-theater hours she spoke at Red Cross rallies, and recited the "Marseillaise" at benefits for French war widows, Belgian orphans and starving Serbians. When the United States finally declared war on April 6, 1917, Sarah sent off a cable to her son which said simply, "Hip, hip, hurray."

Throughout the tour she had intermittent attacks of uremia, and upon reaching New York she was rushed to Mt. Sinai Hospital for a kidney operation. She took the fresh disaster in stride. "They can cut out everything," she said, "as long as they leave me my head."

After a slow recovery she completed an extensive vaudeville-circuit tour. Then, in the autumn of 1918, she decided to return to France. News from Europe was much more hopeful. The big Allied offensive was on and enemy forces were at last retreating. But German U-boats still menaced North Atlantic shipping, and friends begged her not to risk the crossing. She brushed aside warnings and waved gaily from her litter as she was carried aboard the steamer. The captain wanted to delegate two seamen to be on hand in case they were torpedoed and had to abandon ship, but she refused. "They'll be needed elsewhere," she said. "Young lives are more important than my old one."

When the ship docked at Bordeaux on November 11, flags were flying and bands were playing. As soon as the gangplank had been secured, Maurice sprang aboard and burst into her cabin.

"The Armistice has been signed!" he shouted. "The war is over!"

But Sarah's personal war against ill health and old age continued. Ill health she ignored. Old age she would not admit. "That's me ten years from now," she remarked after seeing an old acquaintance who was not yet 60. Sarah was then 76. In the same year she played the lead in a drama called *Daniel,* but objected when she learned that the man who was to play her brother was an actor in his 50's.

"Why, he's too old!" she complained. "He'll look like my father!"

Actually, she did seem to remain ageless. In 1909, when she was 65, she had appeared as Joan of Arc in a play by Emile Moreau. The critics were prepared to scoff, but when the Grand Inquisitor asked Joan how old she was, Sarah turned calmly to the audience and answered, "Nineteen." There was a gasp of wonder and admiration from the house, then thunderous applause, for somehow she did convey the impression of being both naïve and touchingly young.

Soon she was off on a European tour, appearing in Italy and England. She and Queen Mary had known each other for years, and, after Sarah's performance at the London Music Hall, the two met and chatted. At one point the Queen asked her how she was able to bear up under the strain of acting every day. "Madame," Sarah replied, "I shall die on the stage; it is my battlefield."

In the autumn of 1922 she began rehearsing a new play, but on the night of dress rehearsal, while starting to make up, she suddenly collapsed into a coma which lasted about an hour. Her first words on coming to were, "When do I go on?"

But she never went on again. The opening was postponed and another actress took the part. Sarah was heartbroken. She kept the script of the play by her bed and every evening she went over it, timing her lines to coincide with those spoken by her replacement.

For a month she lay in bed desperately ill. Then she took a turn for the better and, with characteristic zest, she accepted a small part in a film. As she was too ill to work in a studio, it was decided to shoot her scenes in her house. Klieg lights, scenery and photographic equipment were installed, and she set to work. She told a caller, "They're paying me 10,000 francs a day. It's as good as going to America." Then she added brightly, "I wonder when my next tour will be."

But on March 21 she collapsed and returned to bed, never to get up again. For five days she was in a state of semi-consciousness. The weather was mild and clear. "It will be a beautiful spring," she murmured. "There will be lots of flowers." And she requested Maurice to see that she was covered with lilacs.

To the people of Paris, the Great Sarah had seemed as indestructible as Notre-Dame. When word spread that she was dying, they gathered in silent groups outside her house like the subjects of an ailing monarch. On March 25 she asked if there were any reporters among them.

"All my life reporters have tormented me," she said, smiling. "I can tease them now a little by making them cool their heels."

These were her final words. At eight o'clock the next evening her doctor opened the windows, stepped out on the balcony and announced: "Madame Sarah Bernhardt is dead."

The stark finality of this news, expected though it was, came as a shock. As one Parisian commented, "Bernhardt is gone. How dark it seems all of a sudden."

KING TUT'S TOMB:

THE UNTOLD STORY

CONDENSED FROM THE BOOK
"TUTANKHAMUN: THE UNTOLD STORY" BY

THOMAS HOVING

ILLUSTRATED BY MICHAEL HERRING

HERRING

When Thomas Hoving was director of New York City's Metropolitan Museum of Art, he headed the team that organized the exhibition "Treasures of Tutankhamun" for its American tour. Sent here by the government of Egypt in honor of the U.S. Bicentennial, the showing attested to the enduring allure of the boy-King whose tomb was uncovered in November 1922. In the 16 weeks that the 55 masterpieces were at the National Gallery of Art in Washington, D.C., they were viewed by nearly a million visitors. In Chicago the million mark was reached in 13 weeks. In New York the show was a sellout.

While Hoving was researching historical data for the exhibition, he first became suspicious of discrepancies in the official accounts of the unearthing of Tutankhamun. Ferreting about in the Metropolitan Museum, he stumbled onto hundreds of original documents dusty with disuse—letters, drawings and diaries in the handwriting of the excavators.

Here in his book, the author tells for the first time the true story of the richest find in archeological history—a story of mystery and suspense and one, too, of shadowy intrigue, lies and skulduggery.

1. VALLEY OF THE KINGS

THE DISCOVERY IN THE LATE EVENING of November 26, 1922, of the tomb of King Tutankhamun, and the removal over ten years of nearly 5000 dazzling works of art caused a worldwide sensation. It was, and remains, the richest discovery in the history of archeology.

Tutankhamun, a pharaoh who ruled nine years and died under mysterious circumstances at the age of 18 in 1350 B.C., instantly became a prime celebrity. The discoverers of the tomb—British Egyptologist Howard Carter and his wealthy patron, Lord Carnarvon—became unwilling celebrities at the same time. After the shattering years of World War I, the events in Egypt's Valley of the Kings seemed extraordinarily appealing. In the wake of thousands of news stories, one would think that today there would be little new to relate about Tutankhamun and the dramatic find. Not so.

In all the accounts published up to now, as a matter of fact, some of the most important facts were not revealed. And the full story is not altogether the noble, proper and triumphant tale usually told. The truth is full of intrigue, skulduggery, lies, dashed hopes and sorrow, a story quite as astounding as the noble discovery itself.

In 1907—the year that brought Carnarvon and Carter together—few people outside his own set had ever heard of George Edward Stanhope Molyneux Herbert, Lord Porchester, the fifth Earl of Carnarvon. If they had bothered to inquire, they would have discovered that Lord Carnarvon ("Porchy" to his intimates) was an aristocrat who had, in the 41 years since his birth, accomplished virtually nothing of note.

In his youth, Lord Carnarvon had a strong profile, was elegant and a bit dashing. But by 1907 his face was haggard, his body frail. Contemporary photographs show him with a cane in one hand, his other hand thrust into a jacket pocket, holding himself as if he had been wounded.

Idle in scholastic achievement, Porchy dropped out of Trinity College, Cambridge, in 1887, and embarked on travels that lasted for seven years. His itinerary, even in terms of today's air age, was phenomenal. He first sailed three-quarters of the way around the world, then went to South Africa, and followed that with trips to Australia, Japan, France, Turkey, Sweden, Italy, Germany and the United States, which he covered coast to coast. On his 29th birthday, Carnarvon married Almina Wombwell, a pretty and intelligent woman. In four years they had two children—a son Henry, Lord Porchester, and a daughter, Evelyn, who was to become her father's close companion.

A few years after the birth of the children, Lord Carnarvon suffered an automobile accident that completely changed his destiny. He was fortunate to have survived, sustaining a severe concussion and crushed chest. From that moment, he was never well again. But he emerged mellowed, thoughtful, determined.

On his physician's recommendation, he went to Egypt in 1903 and was at once captivated. Carnarvon had, in fact, been interested in archeology for some years, and now he took it up as a hobby. He obtained a concession, or license, in 1906 from the Ministry of Public Works and its Antiquities Service to work in the Valley of the Tombs of the Kings.

Today, the idea that an English "Lordy" (as he was known to Egyptians) could descend upon Egypt and almost at once obtain official permission to flail away in the sacred precincts of the Pharaonic Age without training or supervision is appalling. But then a private citizen had only to be rich and alert enough to find an "in" with the appropriate Frenchman in the Antiquities Service to obtain a license to dig. The French had almost exclusive control over all matters concerning antiquities on behalf of the Egyptian government—a legacy from Napoleon's Egyptian expeditions.

At that time, a concession to excavate was a simple agreement. The undertakings had to be conducted under the supervision of the Antiquities Service, a condition only casually enforced. If the digger found a tomb, Antiquities had to have instant notice. But the discoverer did have the right to enter the tomb first, provided he was accompanied by an Inspector of Antiquities.

The critical issue—division of the spoils—was handled most offhandedly. The unwritten rule was that mummies, together with coffins and sarcophagi, were to remain the property of the state, but objects in tombs found not intact—that is, tombs which had already been "searched in ancient times"—would be divided equally between the digger and the Antiquities Service. Treasures from an intact tomb would all revert to the state, but no one had ever found a tomb not substantially plundered by ancient robbers.

When Lord Carnarvon obtained his concession, he started digging in a highly undisciplined manner. For six weeks, enveloped in clouds of dust, he stuck to it day after day. The more dust he sent up, the more he became convinced that he needed an expert to assist him. That expert was to be a curious individual named Howard Carter

CARTER'S ORIGINS WERE HUMBLE. He was born in 1874, in Kensington, England. His father, a draftsman and watercolorist whose specialty was painting portraits of animals belonging to the aristocracy, was too poor to send the boy to school. So Carter was tutored at home. Taught by his father, he too became a watercolorist, fated, it seemed, to continue his father's career as a painter of animals and banal village scenes.

But, in the summer of 1891, his life totally changed. Prof. Percy E. Newberry of the Cairo Museum happened to show an old acquaintance, Lady Amherst of Hackney, some pencil tracings of hieroglyphs on ancient monuments. What he needed, he explained, was someone to help finish the drawings. Lady Amherst suggested Howard Carter, then 17, who lived nearby.

Carter was hired and worked at the British Museum for three months, then joined the staff of a private organization linked to the museum that carried out excavations in the land of the Nile. Eventually he became an assistant to one of the greatest Egyptologists who ever lived, Sir William Flinders Petrie, and from 1891 to 1898 he patiently recorded in watercolor the paintings and reliefs from the walls of the great funerary temple at Deir-el-Bahri.

Carter, a short, stocky man of great physical strength, kept fairly well to himself during his apprenticeship. He was a humorless, rather dour individual of driving energy. Despite his lack of formal schooling, he learned archeology quickly. He apparently had a streak of obstinacy and an explosive temper, but his dedication and enthusiasm won him the respect of his superiors. In 1899, at the age of 25, he was appointed by Sir Gaston Maspero, a genial Frenchman who was director of the Antiquities Service, to the post of Inspector of Monuments in Upper Egypt and Nubia.

Carter's career in the Antiquities Service flourished until 1903, when it ended forever. Petrie, accompanied by his wife and three young women apprentices, had been recording hieroglyphs in a tomb at Saqqara. According to Petrie, several drunken Frenchmen entered their camp one evening, demanded a guided tour, then tried to make a forced entry into the women's quarters. Petrie sent word to Carter, who arrived with a squad of Egyptians attached to the Antiquities Service. There was a struggle and a Frenchman was knocked down.

The French complained bitterly to Maspero, and the French consul general demanded a formal apology. Carter refused. Maspero, who had great affection for the headstrong Carter, tried to persuade him to make a routine apology for the sake of Anglo-Gallic amity. But Carter, insensitive to the exigencies of petty politics, would have none of it. Sorrowfully, Maspero dismissed him.

For the next four years, Carter barely survived. He conducted guided tours, sold his watercolors to tourists and apparently also dealt occasionally in *antikas,* as Egyptians called antiquities. When he was introduced to Lord Carnarvon by a solicitous Maspero and asked to become Carnarvon's archeological expert, he readily accepted. It was an excellent arrangement for both, for Howard Carter was a professional, and eminently and cheaply available.

2. SEATS OF ETERNAL SILENCE

THE SETTING FOR THE DRAMA that was to involve Tutankhamun, Lord Carnarvon and Howard Carter is an awesome one—the Valley of the Tombs of the Kings. The very name is full of romance. But one can hardly imagine a more remote, unpleasant, hot, lonely place.

In ancient days, as now, one traveled to the Valley from Thebes, today the city of Luxor, situated on the Nile about 450 miles south of Cairo. Across the river, stretching for three or more miles, was a plain made lush by seasonal flooding. The point of transition from arable land to desert has varied only a few yards in thousands of years. From that point, the wasteland rises up, at first gradually, and then in a dynamic crescendo to a great cliff known as Deir-el-Bahri. At the base of the cliff is the Valley of the Kings.

To the ancient Egyptian it was vital that his body should be fully equipped for every need in the afterlife and should rest inviolate in the place constructed for it. The earliest kings sought to ensure this by erecting pyramids over their bodies, veritable mountains of stone. Everything that ingenuity could suggest or wealth could buy was tried.

The entrance was plugged with granite monoliths weighing tons. False passages were constructed. Secret doors were contrived. It was all in vain. For in that timeless struggle between those who sought to conceal their treasures for eternity and those who sought them for themselves, those who yearned for secrecy were inevitably vanquished.

By the beginning of the 18th Dynasty, around 1580 B.C., there was hardly a king's tomb in Egypt that had not been rifled. In a drastic break with tradition, Thutmose I, one of Egypt's greatest rulers, decided to construct a totally hidden, below-ground burial chamber. He selected a valley beneath the great cliff that loomed across the Nile from his capital city, Thebes.

All the succeeding monarchs of the 18th Dynasty followed his lead, and during the 500-year course of the empire very few robberies were known. But in the 19th and 20th dynasties (approximately 1320 to 1200 B.C.), tomb plundering became a plague. In time, all the great monarchs were defiled.

Carter had fallen in love with the solitary character of the Valley, its history and what he called a "religious feeling emanating from it so profoundly that it appears almost imbued with a life of its own." He often liked to ride there alone, on a donkey, moved by the solemn character of endless "savage rocks" around him. All was dead and mute. It was sometimes almost terrifying to pass through the winding, trackless desert's rocky defiles to the tombs themselves, called in ancient times the "Great Seats" of eternal silence.

Over the years Carter had kept careful track of every archeological discovery, no matter how insignificant, and accounted for every king's tomb or mummy. He began to believe early in his career that the Valley had not given up all its secrets, although each succeeding scientist or treasure seeker was convinced that he had totally investigated the area.

In 1875 the most curious discovery of all took place, at Deir-el-Bahri. A family of professional tomb robbers by the name of Abd-el-Rasul found a rock-cut chamber containing the mummies of no fewer than 40 kings of the 18th through the 21st dynasties who had been gathered up and put in one common chamber in a frantic attempt to foil thieves.

The leader of the Abd-el-Rasul family, seeing the unprecedented treasure, swore all to secrecy. But greed got the best of him, and soon rich royal artifacts began coming on the *antika* market. The case came to the attention of the governor of the province, Daoud Pasha.

Daoud had a unique system of interrogation; he simply riveted a suspect with the coldest, most malevolent eyes in Egypt. One of Carter's workmen, who had been a thief in his youth, had once been dragged before him. Daoud was sitting up to his neck in a large jar filled with water. To see only a great bullet head cut off by the water, and a pair of cruel, black eyes, was upsetting right at the start—then, as Carter described the scene:

> From this unconventional seat of judgment Daoud had looked at him—just looked—"and as his eyes went through me I felt my bones turning to water within me. Then very quietly he said: 'This is the first time you have appeared before me. You are dismissed, but—be very careful that you do not appear a second time,' and I was so terrified that I changed my trade."

Daoud gazed at one member of the Abd-el-Rasul family, who confessed and led authorities to the ancient chamber. There in a shallow grave lay, tattered but intact, the remains of the most powerful monarchs of ancient Egypt. On their wooden coffins (the rich trappings had long since been plundered) and on the linen wrappings of the mummies themselves, the priests had composed a precise travelogue of their wanderings. Each king was specifically identified, a point of particular interest to Carter, who many years later knew just who was still missing in the royal succession. This phenomenal discovery convinced historians that this time the Valley really had been exhausted. Nonetheless, in 1902, American millionaire Theodore Davis obtained a concession for the area, and in 1907 came across a number of items that pointed directly to the presence of King Tutankhamun.

The following year he found a crude pit on a hill near two other known tombs. There were no markings on it and the contents—about 40 pottery jars filled with linen, a number of clay cups and the like—were disappointing. That these unprepossessing leavings had something to do with Tutankhamun, Davis had no doubt. He had found that "the cover of one of these jars had been broken, and wrapped around it was a cloth on which was inscribed the name of Tutankhamun." But the leavings were of such modest character that no one gave them much thought.

Finally, Davis also proclaimed the Valley exhausted, relinquished his rights, and Lord Carnarvon and Howard Carter received the concession. At the time it was signed, Maspero told the pair that he didn't consider the number of finds they might unearth would repay the costs of their excavations. But Carter had become convinced that the tomb of one more pharaoh lay in the Valley of the Tombs of the Kings, and that this pharaoh was Tutankhamun.

The conventional view of the discovery of Tutankhamun's tomb holds that Carter blundered upon it in a monumental act of serendipity. It was exactly the opposite. Precise, calculating, Carter had been thinking for years of almost nothing but Tutankhamun. As he and Carnarvon were in the process of completing plans for an elaborate campaign to start in October 1914, World War I broke out. For the time being, all had to be held in abeyance.

In the fall of 1917 their campaign resumed. Carter decided to concentrate on a triangular plot defined by the unearthed tombs of Ramesses II, Merenptah and Ramesses VI. It was an area he had judged from earlier researches to be the likeliest place for the site of the tomb of Tutankhamun.

To be absolutely certain that the work would be methodical, Carter devised a grid system based upon the devastating, step-by-step artillery barrages of the war. He planned to faithfully follow each square on his grid without variation.

The triangular plot was only about 2½ acres, but the work was prodigious. Hundreds of thousands of cubic meters of sand, rock chips and boulders had to be removed. In those days there was no mechanical equipment. Young boys and men worked with picks, hoes and small baskets, filling and emptying endlessly.

In the first season, Carter descended to the foot of the entrance to the tomb of Ramesses VI. Ten or 15 yards away, he came across the ancient foundations of workmen's huts, constructed above a mass of flint boulders. The presence of these boulders was normally a sure sign of the proximity of a tomb, yet he abruptly stopped and instructed his work force to go to the opposite end of the triangle.

It is extremely puzzling that he did. Perhaps he thought that the huts belonged to the time of Ramesses VI, 200 years after Tutankhamun. In any event, he started at the other end of the triangle. In the next two months he found nothing much beyond dust, sand and rocks.

The second season, commencing in October 1918, was little better. Carter's thought was to clear the whole of the remaining part of the triangle. It took six months simply to clean the top debris before they could begin to penetrate to virgin rock. Just as Carnarvon arrived with his wife on her first visit, they found 13 alabaster jars with the names of Ramesses II and Merenptah—the nearest thing to a discovery of significance in almost two years.

The third, fourth and fifth seasons, from 1919 to 1922, produced nothing but months of backbreaking labor with a large, expensive crew.

Lord Carnarvon began to lose interest. His health was fading, even though he was only 47.

His disposition had also been soured by the new mood of the Antiquities Service. At this moment in the drama, it is important to introduce a character who would have a fundamental impact on the undertakings surrounding Tutankhamun. This is Pierre Lacau, who in 1917 had succeeded Sir Gaston Maspero. Lacau was a handsome, extremely capable archeologist who prided himself on his administrative abilities. He could discourse volubly, brilliantly, on dozens of subjects, yet was so precise that it was said "he kept lists of lists."

Maspero had personally chosen Lacau to follow him. But whereas Maspero had been staunch in his conviction that foreign explorers had to be encouraged by the promise of at least half of any finds, Lacau insisted that in all discoveries the head of the Antiquities Service should have the right to pick any or all objects he wanted for Egypt. Howard Carter, a proponent of total laissez-faire regarding the rights of an excavator, loathed Lacau.

Then, in 1921, in a storeroom of New York's Metropolitan Museum of Art came a monumental discovery. Herbert Winlock, later director of the museum, had acquired for it some of the unpromising objects dug up by Theodore Davis. Now, finally, he had got around to examining them. When he did, he saw things no one had seen before. Eventually he was able to prove that some materials pertained to the ceremony of the mummification of Tutankhamun. Others were implements used in the final, ritual funerary banquet held within the tomb just before it was sealed for the last time—absolute evidence that Tutankhamun was buried in the Valley.

Winlock at once informed Carter, who was elated. And Lord Carnarvon agreed to underwrite the expedition for one more season.

3. THE GOLDEN BIRD

CARTER ARRIVED IN THE Valley of the Kings on October 28, 1922, for the "last" season. He spent a few days hauling in equipment, going over the work plans with his three foremen, and hiring crews. Not all the equipment was purely archeological; there was a wealth of tinned meats, boxes of special crackers and an abundance of the finest wines, carefully selected by Carnarvon from Fortnum & Mason, world-famous purveyors to the aristocracy. A casual visitor might have thought that he had walked into Fortnum & Mason-on-the-Nile, so numerous were the distinctive wooden crates bound up in bands of steel, each punctiliously identified as to its contents.

Carter had also brought a canary to brighten his lonely home. It became an object of great affection to the workers and foremen. They called it the "Golden Bird" and believed it was a sign of success.

On November 1, Carter began on the spot where five years before he had probed and then backed off: the foundations of workers' huts. By the evening of November 3, he could see that there was still about three feet of ancient soil underneath the huts and above bedrock. That would be the place to work the following day.

When Carter arrived next morning, he was surprised by an unusual silence among the workers, who normally jabbered through the day. His first thought was that there had been an accident. Then one of his foremen announced that a step cut in the rock had been found. After a little more clearing had been done, Carter could see that he was in the entrance to a steep cut in the rock and recognized that the manner of cutting was precisely that of a sunken stairway to a royal tomb.

The work continued at fever pitch through that day and the next. The style of the steps signified a tomb entrance of the 18th Dynasty, the era of Tutankhamun. Everyone was intensely excited. Some of the workmen began to speak of it as "the tomb of the Golden Bird," crediting Carter's canary for such good fortune.

The stairway, entirely rock-cut, descended at a 45-degree angle into a hillock. As step after step emerged, the western edge gradually became roofed in and the stairs became a stepped tunnel. At the level of the 12th step, toward sunset, Carter came across the upper part of a door, constructed of large stones, plastered over and stamped with seals and hieroglyphs. In a fever of expectancy, he searched the seals—each about the size of his hand—for the name of the owner of the tomb. There had to be the owner's name; that was sacred procedure in the Valley. Finding no name, Carter deduced that the tomb was not that of a king.

If Carter had dug down just a few more inches, he would have found seals bearing the ellipitcal cartouche of Nebkheperura, the throne name of Tutankhamun—and thus, as he said, would have spared himself more than three weeks of anxiety. He didn't, for the practical reason that it had become late; electric lights were not yet available in that part of the Valley. He needed to devote the remaining hours of sun to refilling the cleared part of the stairway, protecting it as fully as possible. And there was a gentlemanly reason, too. Carter decided not to

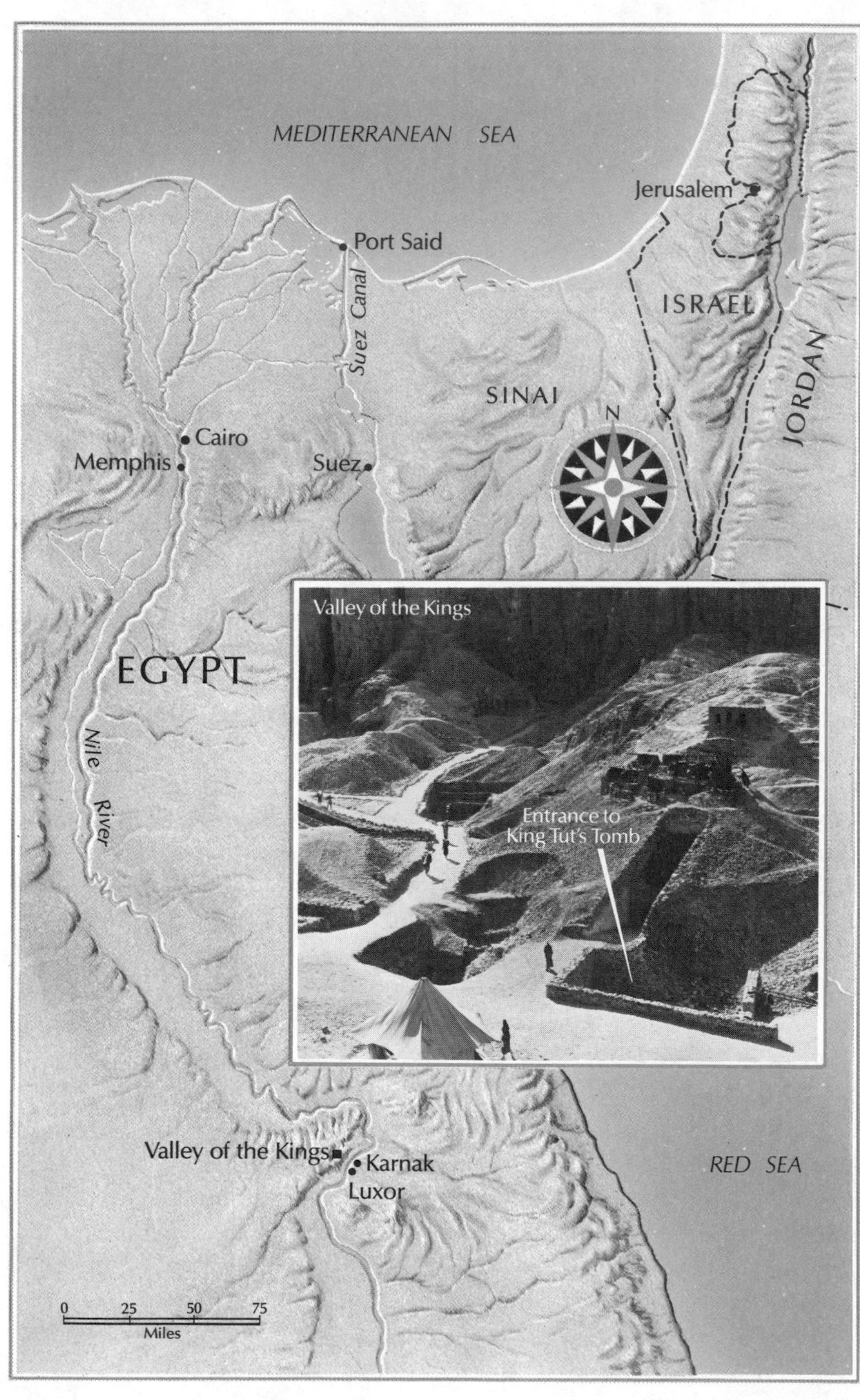
MEDITERRANEAN SEA
Jerusalem
Port Said
Suez Canal
ISRAEL
JORDAN
SINAI
N
Cairo
Memphis
Suez
Valley of the Kings
Entrance to King Tut's Tomb
EGYPT
Nile River
Valley of the Kings
Karnak
Luxor
RED SEA
0 25 50 75
Miles

proceed until his patron could arrive from England. It was only fair.

So, reluctantly, he filled in the excavation. He chose the most trustworthy workmen, established an orderly system of watches, day and night, and went back down the Valley.

On the next day he dispatched a cable to Carnarvon, and also enlisted the aid of British archeologist A. R. "Pecky" Callender. Callender could do anything on a dig and was, as Winlock noted, "one of the few colleagues who could actually be with Carter for any length of time without going clear out of his head." While awaiting Carnarvon's arrival, Carter purchased equipment to provide electric lighting for forthcoming explorations. The work went smoothly.

And then something happened that deeply disturbed the workmen: the "Golden Bird," harbinger of good luck, perished under strange circumstances. Winlock later described the event in a letter to an associate: "Carter went to Cairo to meet Carnarvon. Callender was living alone in Carter's house with the bird consigned to his care. One afternoon, he heard a fluttering and squeaking and there in the cage with the bird was a cobra just in the act of gulping the canary down.

"Now cobras, as every native knew, grow on the heads of the Old Kings. The conclusion was obvious. The King's serpent had struck at the mascot who had given away the secret of the tomb. And the sequel was obvious—that before the winter was out someone would die."

On November 23, Lord Carnarvon and his lively daughter, Evelyn Herbert, arrived with Carter at Luxor. After lunch, the three inspected the entrance to the tomb, which Callender had been clearing.

Next morning, workers removed the debris from the remaining steps. Only then were the excavators able to examine the entire sealed doorway. On the lower part, the seal impressions were relatively clear. On several of them they could make out the name Tutankhamun.

There was a moment of jubilation. They had, after all, grasped their most cherished dream. But, as the inspection progressed on November 25, evidence of at least two consecutive openings and closings of part of the door was discovered. The tomb, then, was not intact. Plunderers had entered it. But the thievery could not have happened later than the construction of the tomb of Ramesses VI, some 200 years after Tutankhamun's reign. Carter and Carnarvon found hope in the fact that the tomb had twice been carefully resealed, for this suggested the thieves had not rifled everything.

The chief inspector of the Antiquities Service, Rex Engelbach, was present that day at Lacau's insistence. Carter took pains to point out to

Engelbach the evidence of ancient openings and re-closings—he wanted it clear that the tomb had been penetrated illicitly in antiquity.

Throughout the morning of November 26, excavation went on, basket by basket. Thirty feet beyond the first doorway, the party encountered a second door, carrying the seals of Tutankhamun's throne name.

The unbelievable moment had arrived. Carter's hands trembled as, taking an iron rod from Callender, he made a tiny hole in the upper lefthand corner of the door. Whatever lay beyond had not been filled in like the passage between the doors. Carter lit a candle and brought its flame close to the aperture to test for foul gases. He widened the hole and looked in.

Then, in one of the most dramatic and famous passages of archeological literature, Carter described what he saw:

> I inserted the candle and peered in, Lord Carnarvon, Lady Evelyn and Callender standing anxiously beside me. At first I could see nothing, the hot air escaping from the chamber causing the candle flame to flicker. But presently, as my eyes grew accustomed to the light, details of the room within emerged slowly from the mist, strange animals, statues and gold—everywhere the glint of gold. For the moment—an eternity it must have been to the others standing by—I was struck dumb with amazement, and when Lord Carnarvon, unable to stand the suspense any longer, inquired anxiously, "Can you see anything?" it was all I could do to get out the words, "Yes, wonderful things."

Carter's own published account and all the dozens, even hundreds, that have described those magical minutes report that the four discoverers simply looked into the tomb's first room, which would be called the Antechamber, re-closed the hole and left. In fact, Carter's account is a lie. The actual events are revealed in materials in the Egyptian Department of the Metropolitan Museum of Art and in three obscure notes published in a scholarly journal in 1945 and 1947 by Alfred Lucas, an Englishman who had participated in the excavation.

First, Carter wrote a hasty note to Engelbach, advising him of the clearing of the inner doorway and asking for an official inspection. The note was delivered to the Antiquities Service at Luxor too late in the evening for Engelbach to respond. Then Carter returned to the door.

After all the depressing years of barren labor, this most magnificent discovery brought on euphoria. It may have been Lord Carnarvon or Lady Evelyn who first suggested climbing into the tomb. We will never know. But in a draft of an article describing the first impressions of the party, written by Carnarvon but never published, his Lordship stated that Carter made an opening in the door large enough for them to jump down into the Antechamber. Being the smallest, Evelyn was the only one who could get through at first, but the others followed eventually.

The Antechamber was not large; it measured 12-by-26 feet, with a ceiling about $7\frac{1}{2}$ feet high. Against each wall was stacked—"in confusion, but orderly confusion," as Carter recalled—a treasure of objects. Everything appeared so incredibly fresh—a bowl of mortar used in the plaster for the door, a lamp seemingly just extinguished, a finger mark

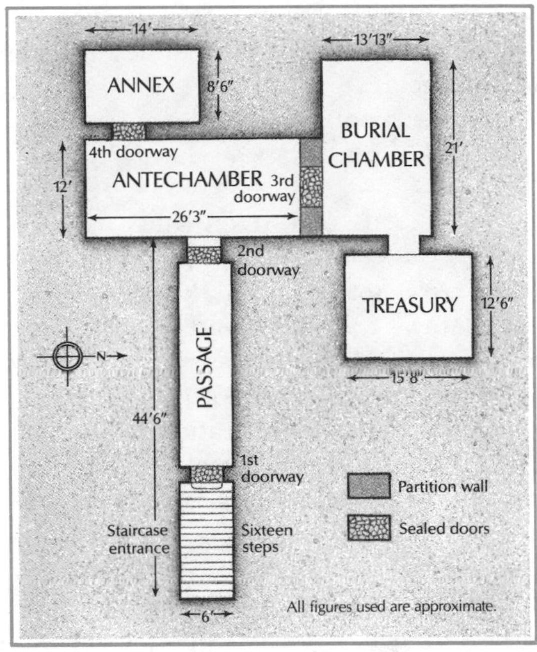

Plan of Tutankhamun's tomb

still visible on the painted surface, remarkably preserved flowers left at the threshold. The intimacy of it all, the penetrating sense of life still clinging to the ancient room, made them feel like trespassers.

Highlighted by the flashing beams of their lights, some of the objects terrified the searchers. Along the western wall were three phantasmagorical gilded couches, their sides carved into monstrous animals throwing grotesque shadows. Directly right from the entrance were two life-sized sculptures in black of the King, facing each other like sentinels, dressed in gold kilts and carrying staffs and maces of gold. The figures were majestic, and in excellent condition.

These were the first things that captured the searchers' attention. But surrounding the dominant objects, piled above them, were hundreds of others—fabulous caskets, painted and inlaid; vases in alabaster; peculiar black shrines, closed and sealed; a haphazard group of white boxes, shaped like giant eggs; chariots, overlaid in gold; and, partly hidden among them, a portrait of the pharaoh.

Despite his fascination, Carter was looking for something far more important to him—evidence of other chambers. He found it, in the southwest wall, where he detected a tiny hole. Peering in, he saw yet another room crammed with objects. Carter was convinced the thieves had used this room, which he called the Annex, to examine the treasures and strip off the gold.

But where were the sarcophagus and the mummy?

4. THE BURIAL CHAMBER

APART FROM THE ENTRY to the Annex, there was only one other possible door. That was a plastered and sealed partition between the two black and gold sentinels. Carter was shocked to discover that here, too, thieves had made a penetration. At the bottom, almost exactly in the middle, was semicircular discoloration in the plaster similar to those on the outer doorways. On the resealed part appeared a cluster of the necropolis seals, a sure sign that priests had closed the hole after the thieves' departure. But the plastering had been done hastily; there were large cracks on the bottom, through which irregular blocks of stone could be seen.

Carter pried a few of them away. As he pointed his flashlight into the opening he saw a narrow corridor ending with a blank wall. The thieves, it seemed, must have ransacked everything.

Carter and Callender removed more stones until they had opened a hole large enough to squeeze through. As the others watched, Carter entered. The corridor was some three feet below the level of the Antechamber, and for a few seconds he simply disappeared.

When he found his footing, he played his flashlight onto the west wall of the passageway and discovered two massive doors of an outer shrine, bolted but not sealed, decorated with gold and blue faïence of the most breathtaking beauty. It was not a corridor at all. He was standing in the Burial Chamber itself.

Both Lord Carnarvon and Evelyn Herbert managed to squeeze

through the hole, but Callender, a heavy-set man, could not. Carter apparently decided not to try to make the opening bigger. It probably occurred to them all that they were about to embark upon an adventure wholly unauthorized by their concession.

They examined the doors of the great blue and gold shrine. Should they open them? They had no right to do so. But they were, after all, archeologists—and human.

So the two ebony bolts were drawn back. Slowly Carter pulled, at first gently and then, when the great double door would not budge, with increasing force. There was a sudden, abrupt movement, and the door swung back. The flashlight revealed a gossamer hanging of linen, so diaphanous that it seemed to be made of the very motes in the air. Suspended on the shroud were dozens of bronze-gilded rosettes, each the size of a coin. As Carter touched one, it fell into his hand as if waiting 3200 years to be plucked; he put it into his pocket. Ever so cautiously, he pushed back the linen to reveal the doors of another shrine—this one magnificently gilded and covered with hieroglyphs. And there in the center, upon two large bronze staples, was a neatly coiled and braided rope stamped with a perfectly intact seal of the royal necropolis. So, Carter observed in a hushed voice, the King had not been disturbed. That moment, he was to remark later, was easily the most thrilling of his entire life.

Between the doors of the outer and second shrines was a treasure-trove. Every nook and cranny had been stuffed with works of art. After examining several, including an exquisite perfume box that Carter pocketed, and after touching the tightly coiled rope and its intact seal, the searchers carefully replaced the doors of the shrine and returned the bolts to their original position.

The party then walked north in the area between the front of the Burial Chamber. At the northeast corner of the room was an open door. Carter flashed his light inside to find another room, almost square. Just inside was a large sculpture in black wood of the jackal god Anubis lying upon a pedestal. It was almost shocking in its majestic beauty. The head was held high, watchful; the ears were erect, listening.

The flashlight illuminated the rest of the square chamber, which Carter christened the Treasury. Chests, caskets and tall, thin, black boxes, closed and sealed, were all around the room. And on top of them were several dozen boats, as if the room were somehow the surface of the Nile itself, with a flotilla ready to set sail.

Hours had now passed. They dared not examine too many of the works of art for fear that the Antiquities Service might discover their illicit presence. They carefully made their way back through the Burial Chamber. The stone blocks were replaced, and Carter picked up the lid of a large reed basket near one of the twin sentinels and leaned it, with a bundle of loose reeds, against the wall to disguise the breach.

Then they left, re-closed the outer hole, mounted their donkeys and rode home down the Valley, strangely silent and subdued.

On November 27, Engelbach was occupied with official duties, and around noon the local Antiquities Inspector came in his stead. By then all traces of entry on the night before had been obliterated.

Word of the discovery spread almost instantly throughout Egypt. Rumors began to crop up, including one that three airplanes had landed in the Valley and made off with loads of treasure. To quell these reports, Carnarvon and Carter staged an official opening of the tomb on November 29, without asking the Antiquities Service for permission.

They compounded this blunder by inviting only one member of the press, Arthur Merton, head of the London *Times* bureau in Egypt and a friend of Carter's. No member of the Egyptian press or anyone representing Europe or America was allowed in on the discovery. Thus, in a monumental example of insensitivity, Carnarvon and Carter alienated the very people whom they would need as friends in the future.

From the moment the first newspaper stories appeared, telegrams and messages inundated the excavators. Congratulations came first, followed by offers of assistance, requests for souvenirs, contracts for movie rights. An unruly throng of visitors arrived at all hours with all sorts of demands. As the hordes grew, any visitor Carter did not personally approve he snubbed. He would, in time, pay a heavy price for this.

Carter soon came to realize that years of the most delicate work lay before him. To repair just one royal robe embellished with hundreds of gold sequins would take two months. There were countless things to be accomplished before he could remove even the smallest object from the Antechamber. Preservatives and packing materials had to be obtained, experts in conservation enlisted.

He dismissed the idea of calling upon members of the Antiquities Service. Their competence was questionable, and their point of view incompatible with his. He never considered seeking help from the British Museum. The obvious choice was the Metropolitan Museum of Art in New York. The Metropolitan had an exceptional Egyptological staff—among them Winlock, who had supplied Carter with the invaluable clue to the presence of the tomb.

But, this factor aside, Carter and Carnarvon had for years been involved in a special financial relationship with the Metropolitan, which until today has been one of the best-kept secrets of the institution. Indeed, one of the finest collections of Egyptian artifacts in the Museum's possession—stolen items that had eluded the investigations of the Antiquities Service—was clandestinely purchased by the Museum directly through Carter, who bought it from an Egyptian dealer with funds deliberately supplied by Carnarvon so that Carter could profit from the sale. These transactions had started in 1917 and were concluded in 1922. The Museum eventually paid the unheard-of sum of $256,305 (equivalent to more than $2.5 million today). With his profit and commission, Carter received nearly $40,000.

Moreover, both Carnarvon and Carter knew that Winlock and Albert Lythgoe, the Metropolitan's curator of the Egyptian Department, had been doing everything in their power to thwart Lacau's attempt to upset the standard 50-50 split of treasures, a matter which was of deep concern to them both.

Carter now sent a telegram to Lythgoe, who was in London. Lythgoe's reply gave Carter virtual carte blanche to use every member of the Metropolitan's Egyptological staff "in any way he saw fit."

Everyone who has described this arrangement seems to have praised it as selfless and coöperative. On one level it was, but it was also a pact of mutual self-interest, coldly calculated by both sides to achieve the greatest financial and artistic gain. In secret, Carnarvon confided to Lythgoe, "I shall have to give something to the British Museum, but I intend to see that the Metropolitan is well taken care of."

While the team was being assembled, Carter closed the tomb. A detachment of Egyptian soldiers was placed on round-the-clock guard duty. To look after *them,* Carter hired his own guardians. Carnarvon and Lady Evelyn left for England for the Christmas holidays, and Carter went to Cairo to purchase equipment, including a gate of steel bars for the inner doorway. Callender remained, most of the time sitting near the entrance to the treasure with a loaded rifle on his knees.

On January 10, Carnarvon signed an exclusive contract with the London *Times* for world rights to all news of the tomb. The agreement produced a storm of protest from virtually every major newspaper in the world. In Cairo, Lacau was beleaguered on all sides. Egyptian newsmen, goaded by the foreign press, complained bitterly that they had been refused entry to an Egyptian tomb. In addition, thousands of would-be visitors streamed into his offices, outraged that Carter was turning *everyone* away, even those people who had official permits.

Lacau met privately a number of times with Carter, beseeching him to give Egyptian reporters news releases. Carter refused. Lacau also begged him to allow the Antiquities Service to send visitors into the tomb, along with those Carter was daily guiding through. Carter refused this request, too, saying that *his* visitors were all archeologists and had every right to enter.

Meanwhile, Carter was attempting to proceed with the delicate scientific enterprise. He obtained a darkroom for his photographer, Harry Burton of the Metropolitan Museum, and received permission to use a nearby tomb for a conservation laboratory and storeroom.

The excavators established an unvarying procedure to record the treasures. First, Burton would take an on-site photograph. Then Carter would make a line drawing on a five-by-eight card, write a precise description and record all measurements, noting the damage or loss of any part of the material. After this, Burton would take another series of photographs, placing a numbered card in front of the object. Following this, two draftsmen located the object in a set of master drawings which showed, from above, the juxtaposition of each item. The treasure would then be transported to the laboratory where Burton would take additional photographs showing the varying stages of repair. Never before had such an exacting record been made of the clearing of a tomb.

In this delicate, nerve-racking work, Carter was fabulous. He spoke of the objects as "direct legacies from the past" and described himself as the privileged but temporary intermediary through whom they had happened to come. "If, by slackness or ignorance, an excavator diminished the knowledge that might have been derived from the treasure," he observed, "he knows himself to be guilty of an archeological crime of the first magnitude."

Carter continually complained about the spectators, but he was clearly ambivalent about them. Though furious at their being there, he tolerantly ordered his workmen to carry the more spectacular finds unwrapped past the crowds lining the path to the laboratory. Lesser objects, all bandaged up and transported with tender care on stretcher-like trays, looked like casualties being brought out of the trenches.

By the time Carnarvon and Lady Evelyn returned in late January, 60 objects had been removed from the Antechamber, and on February 17 Carnarvon presided over the official opening of Tutankhamun's Burial Chamber. Two days before the sealed door was to be breached, Luxor had become the center of the globe. Hundreds of press reports clattered daily over the recently installed wire service to Cairo. Celebrities, notables, sultans and pashas arrived by the trainload. A makeshift theater had been constructed for the exciting event. Carter would open the partition for a select audience of about 20, then be permitted two full days for an examination of the contents. After that, for two additional days, the world press and visitors would view the discovery.

Carter personally hefted out each stone in the door and handed it to one of his assistants. When the hole was large enough, he entered and dropped into the chamber. Lord Carnarvon followed. After about 20 minutes, they re-emerged. They uttered not a word, but simply lifted their hands in a gesture of amazement. Then the rest of the select party went in, two by two.

The resultant reports were almost unanimously ecstatic. Royalty, nobility and scientists praised the discovery and the painstaking manner in which the preservation work was being carried out. Carnarvon and Carter fully believed that they had overcome the criticisms voiced by the Egyptians and the world press.

On February 26, the two men closed the tomb for the season, refilled the shaft and the stairs, and retreated to the laboratory, where the behind-the-scenes work was intensified. Carnarvon's health was now visibly affected by the heat. The average temperature in the lab was 100 degrees F. Dust storms clogged the air outside.

5. THE CURSE

In early March, Carnarvon left for Cairo to attempt to obtain from Lacau assurances of a "proper" division of objects found in the tomb. Evelyn wrote Carter every two days, informing him how things were going. Then, on March 16, she dispatched an alarming message: "Yesterday quite suddenly all the glands in his neck started swelling and last night he had a high temperature and still has today. He feels just *too* rotten for words."

By the next week, Carnarvon was terminally ill. He died on April 5. It was said that at the moment of his death all the lights in Cairo blacked out and that a subsequent investigation could not uncover any explanation. To compound the mystery, his son and heir, Lord Porchester, claimed that at the family's home, at the instant of his father's death, his father's favorite dog howled and dropped dead.

Newspapers around the world ascribed Carnarvon's death to a curse from the tomb. Despite the fact that no real curse had been or would be found in Tutankhamun's grave, the "curse" is today probably as well known as Tutankhamun himself and his unique treasures. When the current Lord Carnarvon was asked about it in a television interview in New York on July 14, 1977, he replied that he "neither believed it nor disbelieved it." But he assured his interviewer that he would "not accept a million pounds to enter the tomb of Tutankhamun in the Valley of the Kings."

"ALL WE HAVE TO DO is to peel the shrines like an onion," Carter told Winlock at the end of the first spectacular season, "and we will be with the King himself."

From Carter's own account of the second season one gains the impression that the excavation proceeded fairly smoothly. But in reality it would take Carter 80 days to dismantle the shrines before he could examine what lay inside, a delay that often caused his temper to flare. After that, a full ten months would pass before the mummy was revealed—ten months involving negotiations of the utmost delicacy, many outbursts and arguments, lawsuits, a suppressed scandal and political dissension.

The initial difficulty arose over the exclusive contract with the London *Times.* To circumvent the demand that all reporters be allowed in the tomb whenever any single member of the press entered, Carter had decided to appoint the *Times* correspondent, Arthur Merton, an official member of the excavation staff. By this means Merton could enter the tomb any time Carter wished. As for the problem of requests to Antiquities to see the tomb, Carter said that scientific work would be impeded by visitors—any visitors.

Lacau prided himself on being an excellent administrator. As such he was tactful and conciliatory. Yet in the complex relationship he was to have with Howard Carter, tact became a weakness. His inability or his unwillingness to be completely frank—attributable in part to his not wanting to offend—would be interpreted by Carter as vacillation, insincerity and, on occasion, outright duplicity. Lacau and his colleagues finally agreed to Carter's proposals regarding Merton and the visitors. No one told Carter that there had been a bitter difference of opinion among the Egyptian members of the group. Thus Carter returned to the Valley on October 18, 1923, believing all was well.

But the unrelenting pressure of the press and Egyptians soon necessitated more talks with Lacau. Indeed, Carter was to complain that of the first 50 working days of the season, a third had been "frittered away through departmental interference." In the course of these extended conversations and in several public statements, Carter managed to insult Lacau. His feeling that he and the Carnarvon estate really did "own" the tomb was a factor. His personal dislike for Lacau must also have had a bearing. But, above all, Carter was exhausted, his mind in turmoil. The slightest setback, the smallest irritation, seemed to drive him either into rage or into brooding silence.

Lacau was being urgently advised to annul the concession and throw Carter out of the tomb. Lacau decided on another course. By "going by the book," by enforcing his administrative rights to the letter, he just might get Carter to do something rash. Lacau began by instructing Engelbach to drop the word to Carter, casually, that the Antiquities Service wanted a list of his co-workers, a request that Carter found "outrageous." This was followed over the next weeks by a series of demands that to Carter and his colleagues seemed deliberately to encroach on the rights of the concession.

Lacau was aided in his campaign by a political event of tremendous magnitude. In the elections of 1923, the incumbent government, sympathetic to the British Protectorate, was swept out of office and a profoundly nationalistic regime took its place. The Minister of Public Works, to whom Lacau reported, was to be Morcos Bey Hanna, a stolid bear of a man who had once been tried, convicted and imprisoned by the British for treason. His suspicion of foreigners, particularly the British and specifically Carter, made him sympathetic to any scheme that might force them out of the tomb, the region, Egypt.

The matter came to a head on February 13, 1924. By this time Carter had successfully penetrated to the sarcophagus itself, though it is a wonder that he found time to conduct the excavation at all. He had first to dismantle the outer shrine or canopy. Beyond that lay the doors of the second shrine. When these were opened, the doors of a third shrine broke into a golden blaze, and beyond them yet a fourth, marked by a prominent group of hieroglyphs that appeared to be the words of the King himself: "I have seen yesterday; I know tomorrow."

Beyond the fourth shrine lay a beautiful crystalline sandstone sarcophagus with a granite lid. Finally, on February 12, in the presence of Lacau and various dignitaries, the two-ton lid was raised with a system of ropes. There, filling the interior of the sarcophagus, glowing in full glory from the reflection of the lights, was a golden effigy of the boy-King. It was of the most magnificent workmanship, fashioned out of gilded wood, and inlaid with faïence, glass and semiprecious stones.

Before the officials departed that day, Carter discussed with them arrangements for a press conference the next day. He asked casually if it was acceptable to allow the excavators' wives to visit the tomb. No objections were raised then. But the next morning a letter arrived, informing Carter that the Minister of Public Works had refused. Carter rushed to the tomb and showed the "insulting" communication to his colleagues. They were as astonished and angry as he. They at once drafted a notice to be sent to Lacau, Morcos Bey Hanna and the public at large, stating that they would close the tomb and walk off the job. And they did just that. Carter locked both tomb and laboratory, and took with him the only existing set of keys, leaving tons of stone suspended—dangerously—over the golden effigy.

How so many intelligent individuals could so grievously have miscalculated is difficult to comprehend. They misunderstood the mood of the new regime. They failed to realize that the notion of allowing foreign women special entry into the tomb, long before any Egyptian, would enrage all of Egypt. They were locked in positions rooted in outmoded concepts of colonialism, elitism and scientific privilege.

The government was swift to react. Two days after the beginning of the "strike," as the newspapers branded it, Carter went to the tomb and was refused entry by government troops. Shortly afterward, locksmiths cut through the padlocks of the steel gate and government forces gingerly lowered the granite lid back upon the sarcophagus. At the same time, Morcos Bey Hanna informed Carter that the concession for the current season had been canceled.

Carter thereupon commenced proceedings in the Mixed Courts of Cairo. Under the British Protectorate, a case involving a foreigner was heard by a mixed panel of foreign and Egyptian judges with a foreigner as chief judge. Carter retained as his lawyer an Englishman, F. M. Maxwell. The choice was unfortunate. Maxwell had acted as the British prosecutor in the treason trial of Morcos Bey Hanna. Summing up his arguments after a long day in court, Maxwell was explaining to the court that Carter had still been in legal possession when he closed the tomb and sued, but that the government had then come in "like a pack of bandits and forced him out of possession by violence."

There was an uproar in the court. In Arabic the word "bandit" is one of the vilest things one can call anyone. The Egyptian press made the most of it, suggesting that not only Maxwell but Carter and all his collaborators had called the cabinet minister a thief and, by extension, had insulted all Egyptians. Morcos Bey Hanna issued a statement announcing that the Ministry of Public Works would never negotiate with Carter, even if directed to do so by the court.

Meanwhile, Carter decided to approach the British vice consul in the hope that strong political pressure might be brought to bear on the Egyptian regime.

Carter arrived for the meeting in a quarrelsome and cantankerous state of mind, and rapidly lost control of himself. One hot word followed another until Carter abandoned all reserve and commented acidly on the inadequacy of the Antiquities Service and the imbecility of the vice consul. The vice consul lost his temper and let fly at Carter's head with an inkwell. The enraged pair had to be calmed by others.

Trying at the court's behest to mediate the dispute, Herbert Winlock was profoundly disturbed when he got wind of the story. He decided to get Carter out of the country. Carter had been scheduled to make a lecture tour in America and, though he now talked of canceling it, Winlock convinced him he had to stand by the commitment. So, on March 21, Carter left Cairo, not knowing whether he would ever see Egypt again.

But the affair was not finished. A special commission of Egyptians headed by Lacau had been making an inventory of the tomb and storerooms. They discovered that all the objects had been dutifully labeled and numbered personally by Carter in three separate places: on the outside of each box, again on the inside, and yet a third time in an entry booklet set on a table nearby. They were visibly impressed with Carter's precise methods.

Then, far back in the storage area, near a stack of empty Fortnum & Mason crates, they came across one crate marked "Red Wine." They almost neglected to open it. But Lacau instructed them to do so. There was a near-life-size wooden head, painted so delicately that the figure seemed almost to breathe. The head emerged from a small pedestal carved with the petals of the sacred blue lotus of the Nile.

An astonished Lacau attempted to preserve order among his colleagues, insisting over and over that there had to be a logical explanation for Carter's storing the head in so curious a place, without the notes and numbers he had used with all the other pieces. But the Egyptians demanded that a telegram of outrage be sent at once to the Egyptian Prime Minister himself.

Winlock soon had a visit from Engelbach. The Egyptians, in his words, "had gone completely off their heads," shouting that there was no doubt the sculpture had been stolen from the tomb. Lacau had told the Egyptians that the lotus head had been purchased by Carter on the art market. Engelbach was not certain that they believed the story, but they seemed to be leaning to it, knowing Carter's "methodical ways." Could Winlock obtain confirmation from Carter?

Winlock sent word to Carter by means of a numerical code that had been concocted some years before in case of an emergency. Carter answered that the piece was part of the material he had discovered in the debris of the entrance passage. All such objects were noted in "group numbers," but were "not yet fully registered in the Index." His alibi was unconvincing. The first volume of his *The Tomb of Tutankhamun* had been published six months earlier, in which he had given a detailed description of the objects found in the rubble of the stairway. The lotus head was not among them.

Nonetheless, the Egyptian commission accepted his story and, as Winlock wrote, Lacau "was perfectly delighted with it, partly because it meant there was no question that the piece belonged to the Cairo Museum." By mid-April, Winlock had begun to hope that Tutankhamun's malignant aura was waning and that he could persuade "all lawyers to retire and let the only two archeologists left in the case"—Lacau and himself—resolve the bitter controversy.

WINLOCK'S EFFORTS TO RENEW the concession—on much different terms—had been nearly capped with success when early in June, toward the conclusion of his immensely successful U.S. tour, Carter received from his publishers the first five copies of a pamphlet he had been writing clandestinely. Ostensibly for "Private Circulation Only," the booklet was a scathing indictment, written in the third person, assaulting the Egyptian government, the Antiquities Service and Lacau, whose methods Carter described as "a menace to the whole future of archeology in Egypt."

Winlock received his copy out of the blue on July 1, 1924, the very morning he was to receive Carter in his office at the Metropolitan. They had not seen one another in months. Winlock leafed through the document rapidly, disgusted to see that Carter had included *everything*—coded telegrams, confidential letters and notes—about Winlock's role in suppressing the scandal over the sculpture found in the wine case. It was a shattering blow to his reputation as an archeologist.

When Carter arrived, he was genuinely taken aback to find his friend so outraged. Winlock informed Carter that, with the appearance of the booklet, he was no longer willing to be associated with him in any way. He told Carter coldly that he believed his conduct throughout the entire affair had been unbalanced and stubborn, and the confounded pamphlet was the last straw. In his view, Carter would never again be allowed to dig in Egypt unless he surrendered to Egyptian demands. Carter was at a loss for words.

Winlock cut short the meeting and immediately informed the Museum's director, Edward Robinson, what he thought of Carter's most recent act of impetuosity. Carter, he warned, would undoubtedly give Robinson a copy of the "disgusting" booklet on the steamer—for they were booked on the same ship to England—and attempt to drag the director into Carter's campaign against the Egyptians. Winlock cautioned Robinson not to be taken in.

Yet Carter had been profoundly shaken by the anger of his old friend. It had apparently never occurred to him that Winlock would feel betrayed by the publication of the incriminating information regarding the concealed lotus head. But he quickly made efforts to halt further distribution of the pamphlet, and thereafter remained in his hotel room until he could board the *Mauretania* for his return home. When he and Robinson talked aboard ship, Carter admitted "that he had done and said many foolish things which he deeply regretted—some of which were due to bad advice, others to the strain he was under, that had prevented his thinking clearly or calmly." Robinson, seeing that Carter was in an astoundingly receptive mood, advised him to give the Egyptian government "any apology they wanted" so that he could finish his work in the tomb.

And so, as the ship steamed toward England, Carter finally decided to abandon his long struggle. Exhausted, he drafted a message to Lacau renouncing "definitively any action, claim, or pretension whatsoever, both as regards the Tomb of Tut-Ankh-Amun and the objects therefrom. . . . I declare that I withdraw all actions pending."

When Howard Carter returned to the Valley on January 25, 1925, he was ceremoniously handed a duplicate set of keys to the tomb and laboratory. He immediately made an inspection of the contents of the Burial Chamber with Pierre Lacau. Nothing had been moved; nothing changed. He expressed his satisfaction to Lacau, who in a low voice told Carter how pleased he was to have him back. It was a brief, private, emotional reconciliation.

From that day on, through eight full years of painstaking work, carried out, as before, in the debilitating heat, wind and dust of the Valley,

Carter seldom manifested the dark, impulsive side of his character. Immersed once more in the systematic duties of pure archeology, his attentive and sensitive nature became dominant.

Carter's first task was to raise the lid of the gilded coffin he had discovered a year before. He found, within, what looked like a second coffin, covered with fine linen shrouds and decked with garlands of flowers. The shrouds were rolled back, and Carter gazed upon "the finest example of the ancient coffinmaker's art ever yet seen." The lid of the second coffin, like the first, depicted the young King as the god Osiris. But it was far more splendid in quality.

When the lid of the second coffin was plucked off, yet another human image came to Carter's excited eyes. This, too, was obscured by a film of gossamer linen shrouds. When he folded back the fabric and the elaborate bead and floral collar surrounding the neck, a breathtaking sight came to view. The third coffin, over six feet in length, was fashioned from solid gold—half-an-inch thick in parts. It was, to Carter, an "absolutely incredible mass of pure bullion."

Carter removed the lid of the third coffin, and there lay the mummy of the King, bound up by a corselet of gold and inlay. Shining against the somber background of linens was a life-size gold mask of the King—surely one of the most beautiful portraits in the history of mankind.

Once the mummy had been revealed, Carter embarked upon a most unusual journey—a sort of dig within a dig through layer after layer of wrappings. With scalpels honed to the sharpest edge, Carter, assisted by the professor of anatomy at Cairo's Egyptian University, painstakingly sliced through the stiffened linen of the first layer to reveal a virtual treasure of gold—the royal diadem, a golden pectoral, a knife and scabbard of pure gold. On the two desiccated arms, crossed one on top of the other, lay 13 bracelets. After cutting through all the layers of wrappings he unearthed no less than 143 magnificent pieces of jewelry, ornaments, amulets and implements.

With fine sable brushes, the last few fragments of decayed fabric were brushed aside. The face of Tutankhamun himself was finally revealed. The King must have been handsome beyond belief. As he held the head in his hands, Carter was transported back to the time when the young King still lived. He was profoundly shaken by the experience.

By the end of February 1932, Howard Carter had removed the last objects from the tomb and supervised their transfer to the Egyptian Museum in Cairo. Less than ten years had elapsed from the day he made history's most remarkable archeological discovery.

That spring, he returned to England. Within a year, he fell sick, and never seemed to regain his health. Although he returned to Egypt several times, he never again embarked upon an excavation. On March 2, 1939, in his mid-60s, he died. Only a handful of people attended his funeral, among them Lady Evelyn Herbert Beauchamp.

Carter never turned up any documents or papyri that would dispel the mystery of why Tutankhamun died so young. Yet in some unexpected place, hidden in the Valley of the Kings and still to be discovered by some heir to Howard Carter's dreams and ambition, further revelations may emerge. Until then, there will always be doubts, always be questions.

The gold mask covering the face of the King's mummy

Shrouded in silence, surrounded by profound mystery, Tutankhamun has ensured himself a more compelling fascination than most rulers of ancient times. And he has achieved the ultimate victory—a continuing and secure afterlife.

King Tutankhamun's confident words, written upon the last shrine surrounding his great sarcophagus, ring true: "I have seen yesterday; I know tomorrow."

My Friend Flicka

CONDENSED FROM THE ORIGINAL SHORT STORY

by Mary O'Hara

ILLUSTRATED BY DAVID BLOSSOM

This is a warm, sensitive story set against Wyoming's picturesque rangeland. It concerns a nine-year-old boy and a horse.

Young Ken McLaughlin had set his heart on one thing—a horse of his own. Not just any horse, but the fastest and wildest filly on his father's 3000-acre ranch. What happened when Ken tried to tame the savage, stormy Flicka makes one of the best loved animal stories ever written.

My Friend Flicka first appeared in story form in 1941. It was so popular that the author expanded the story into a book that quickly became a best-seller.

"It combines deep understanding with a hard sense of reality," wrote author Oliver La Farge at the time. "I shall not be surprised if *My Friend Flicka* becomes an American classic."

La Farge's prediction has come to pass, and Mary O'Hara's beloved book is still popular and widely read. It was made into a motion picture with Roddy McDowall in 1943.

1. THE COLT

REPORT CARDS FOR THE SECOND SEMESTER were sent out soon after school closed in mid-June.

Kennie's was a shock to the whole family.

"If I could have a colt all for my own," said Kennie, "I might do a lot better."

Rob McLaughlin glared at his son. "Just as a matter of curiosity," he said, "how do you go about it to get a *zero* in an examination? Forty in arithmetic; seventeen in history! But a *zero?* Just as one man to another, what goes on in your head?"

"Yes, tell us how you do it, Ken," chirped Howard.

"Eat your breakfast, Howard," snapped his mother.

Kennie's blond head bent over his plate until his face was almost hidden. His cheeks burned.

McLaughlin finished his coffee and pushed his chair back.

"You'll do an hour a day on your lessons all through the summer," he said to Kennie.

Nell McLaughlin saw Kennie wince as if something had actually hurt him.

Lessons and study in the summertime, when the long winter was just over and there weren't hours enough in the day for all the things he wanted to do!

Kennie took things hard. His eyes turned to the wide-open window with a look almost of despair. The hill opposite the house, covered with arrow-straight jack pines, was sharply etched in the thin air of the 8000-foot altitude. Where it fell away, vivid green grass ran up to meet it; and over range and upland poured the strong Wyoming sunlight that stung everything into burning color.

Ken had to look at his plate and blink back tears before he could turn to his father and say carelessly, "Can I help you in the corral with the horses this morning, Dad?"

"You'll do your study every morning before you do anything else." And McLaughlin's scarred boots and heavy spurs clattered across the kitchen floor. "I'm disgusted with you. Come, Howard."

Howard strode along after his father, nobly refraining from looking at Kennie.

At supper that night Kennie said, "But Dad, Howard had a colt all of his own when he was only eight. And he trained it and schooled it all himself; and now he's eleven, and Highboy is three, and he's riding him. I'm nine now and even if you did give me a colt now I couldn't catch up to Howard because I couldn't ride it till it was a three-year-old and then I'd be twelve."

Nell laughed. "Nothing wrong with that arithmetic."

But Rob said, "You'll notice that Howard never gets less than seventy-five average at school."

Kennie didn't answer. He couldn't figure it out. He tried hard; he spent hours poring over his books. That was supposed to get you good marks, but it never did. Everyone said he was bright. Why was it that when he studied he didn't learn? He had a vague feeling that perhaps he looked out the window too much, or looked through the walls to see clouds and sky and hills and wonder what was happening out there. And then the bell would ring, and study period would be over.

If he had a colt . . .

WHEN THE BOYS HAD GONE TO BED that night Nell McLaughlin sat down with her overflowing mending basket in her lap and glanced over at her husband.

He was at his desk as usual, working on account books and inventories. There was a worried line between his eyes, and a grim look on his weathered face.

Rob, thought Nell, was a lot like Kennie himself. He set his heart. Oh, how stubbornly he set his heart on just some one thing he wanted above everything else. He had set his heart on horses and ranching way back when he had been a crack rider at West Point; and he had resigned his army career just for the horses. Well, he'd finally got what he wanted. . . .

She drew a deep breath and snipped her thread. To get what you want is one thing, she was thinking. The 3000-acre ranch and the hundred head of horses. But to make it pay—for a dozen or more years they had been trying to make it pay. People said ranching hadn't paid since the beef barons ran their herds on public land; people said the only prosperous ranchers in the state of Wyoming were the dude ranchers; people said . . .

But suddenly she gave her head a little rebellious, gallant shake. Rob would always be fighting and struggling against something, like Kennie; perhaps like herself too. Even those first years when there was no water piped into the house, when every day brought a new difficulty or danger, how she had loved it! How she still loved it!

She ran the darning ball into the toe of a sock, Kennie's sock. The length of it gave her a shock. Yes, the boys were growing up fast, and now Kennie—Kennie and the colt . . .

After a while she said, "Give Kennie a colt, Rob."

"He doesn't deserve it." The answer was short. Rob pushed away his papers and took out his pipe.

Nell put down her sewing. "He's crazy for a colt of his own," she said quietly. "He hasn't had another idea in his head since you gave Highboy to Howard."

"I don't believe in bribing children to do their duty."

"Not a bribe." She hesitated.

"No? What would you call it?"

She tried to think it out. "I just have the feeling Ken isn't going to pull anything off, and"—her eyes sought Rob's—"it's time he did. It isn't the school marks alone, but I just don't want things to go on any longer with Ken never coming out at the right end of anything."

"I'm beginning to think he's just dumb."

"He's not dumb. Maybe a little thing like this—if he had a colt of his own, trained him, rode him. . . ."

Rob interrupted. "But it isn't a little thing or an easy thing to break and school a colt. I'm not going to have a good horse spoiled by Ken's careless ways. He goes woolgathering. He doesn't stick at anything."

"But he'd *love* a colt of his own, Rob. If he could do it, it might make a big difference in him."

"*If* he could do it! But that's a big if."

At breakfast next morning Kennie's father said to him, "When you've done your study come out to the barn. I'm going up to section twenty-one this morning to look over the brood mares. You can go with me if you like."

"Can I go, too, Dad?" cried Howard.

McLaughlin frowned at Howard. "You turned Highboy out last evening with dirty legs."

Howard wriggled. "I groomed him . . ."

"Yes, down to his knees."

"He kicks."

"And whose fault is that? You don't get on his back again until I see his legs clean."

The two boys eyed each other, Kennie secretly triumphant and Howard chagrined. McLaughlin turned at the door, "And, Ken, a week from today I'll give you a colt. Between now and then you can decide what one you want."

Kennie shot out of his chair and stared at his father. "A—a spring colt, Dad, or a yearling?"

McLaughlin was somewhat taken aback, but his wife concealed a smile. If Kennie got a yearling colt he would be even up with Howard.

"A yearling colt, your father means, Ken," she said smoothly. "Now hurry with your lessons."

Kennie found himself the most important personage on the ranch. Prestige lifted his head, gave him an inch more of height and a bold stare, and made him feel different all the way through. Even Gus and Tim Murphy, the ranch hands, were more interested in Kennie's choice of a colt than anything else.

Howard was fidgety with suspense. "Who'll you pick, Ken? Say—pick Doughboy, why don't you? Then when he grows up he'll be sort of twins with mine, in his name anyway. Doughboy, Highboy, see?"

The boys were sitting on the worn wooden step of the door which led from the tack room into the corral, busy with rags and polish, shining their bridles.

Ken looked at his brother with scorn. Doughboy would never have half of Highboy's speed.

"Lassie, then," suggested Howard. "She's black as ink, like mine. And she'll be fast."

"Dad says Lassie'll never go over fifteen hands."

NELL MCLAUGHLIN SAW THE CHANGE in Kennie, and her hopes rose. He went to his books in the morning with determination and really studied. A new alertness took the place of the daydreaming. Examples in arithmetic were neatly written out, and as she passed his door each morning before breakfast she heard the monotonous drone of his voice as he read his American history aloud.

Each night, when he kissed her, he flung his arms around her and held her fiercely for a moment, then, with a winsome and blissful smile into her eyes, turned away to bed.

He spent days inspecting the different bands of horses and colts. He sat for hours on the corral fence, very important, chewing straws. And when the week was up he announced his decision.

"I'll take that yearling filly of Rocket's. The sorrel with the cream tail and mane."

His father looked at him in surprise. "The one that got tangled in the barbed wire? That's never been named?"

In a second all Kennie's new pride was gone. He hung his head defensively. "Yes."

"You've made a bad choice, son. You couldn't have picked a worse."

"She's fast, Dad. And Rocket's fast. . ."

"It's the worst line of horses I've got. There's never one amongst them with real sense. The mares are hellions and the stallions outlaws; they're untamable."

"I'll tame her."

Rob guffawed. "Not I, nor anyone, has ever been able to really tame any one of them." Kennie's chest heaved. "Better change your mind, Ken. You want a horse that'll be a real friend to you, don't you?"

"Yes." Kennie's voice was unsteady.

"Well, you'll never make a friend of that filly. She's all cut and scarred up already with tearing through barbed wire after that hellion mother of hers. No fence'll hold 'em. . ."

"I know," said Kennie, still more faintly.

"Change your mind?" asked Howard briskly.

"No."

Rob was grim and put out. He couldn't go back on his word. The boy had to have reasonable help in taming the filly, and he could envision precious hours, whole days, wasted in the struggle.

Nell McLaughlin despaired. Once again young Ken seemed to have taken the wrong turn and was right back where he had begun; stoical, silent, defensive.

But there was a difference that only Ken could know. The way he felt about his colt. The way his heart sang. The pride and joy that filled him so full that sometimes he hung his head so they wouldn't see it shining out of his eyes.

He had known from the very first that he would choose that particular yearling because he was in love with her. The year before, he had been out working with Gus, the big Swedish ranch hand, on the irrigation ditch, when they had noticed Rocket standing in a gully on the hillside, quiet for once, and eying them cautiously.

"Ay bet she got a colt," said Gus.

They walked carefully up the draw. Rocket gave a wild snort, shook her head wickedly, then fled away. And as they reached the spot they saw standing there the wavering, pinkish colt, barely able to keep its feet. It gave a little squeak and started after its mother on crooked, wobbling legs. "Yee whiz! Luk at de little *flicka!*" Gus had said.

"What does *flicka* mean, Gus?"

"Swedish for little gurl, Ken."

Ken announced at supper, "You said she'd never been named. I've named her. Her name is Flicka."

2. A WILD ONE

THE FIRST THING TO DO WAS TO GET her in. She was running with a band of yearlings on the saddleback, cut with ravines and gullies. They all went out after her, Ken, as owner, on old Rob Roy, the wisest horse on the ranch.

Ken was entranced to watch Flicka when the wild band of youngsters discovered that they were being pursued and took off across the mountain. Footing made no difference to her. She floated across the ravines, always two lengths ahead of the others. Her cream mane and tail whipped in the wind. Her long delicate legs had only to aim, it seemed, at a particular spot, for her to reach it and sail on. She seemed to Ken a fairy horse.

He sat motionless, just watching and holding Rob Roy in, when his father thundered past on Sultan and shouted, "Well, what's the matter? Why didn't you turn 'em?"

Kennie woke up and galloped after. Soon they had brought in the whole band. The corral gates were closed, and an hour was spent shunting the ponies in and out and through the chutes, until Flicka was left all alone in the small round corral in which the baby colts were branded. Gus drove the others away, out through the gate, and up the saddleback.

But Flicka did not intend to be left. She hurled herself against the poles which walled the corral. She tried to jump them. They were seven feet high. She caught her front feet over the top rung, clung, scrambled, while Kennie held his breath for fear the slender legs would be caught between the bars and snapped. Her hold broke; she fell over backward, rolled, screamed, tore around the corral. Kennie had a sick feeling in the pit of his stomach, and his father looked disgusted.

She hurled herself again. One of the bars broke, then another. She saw the opening and, as neatly as a dog crawls through a fence, inserted her head and forefeet, scrambled through, and fled away, bleeding in a dozen places.

As Gus was coming back, just about to close the gate to the upper range, the sorrel whipped through it, sailed across the road and ditch with her inimitable floating leap, and went up the side of the saddleback like a jack rabbit.

"Yee whiz!" said Gus, and stood motionless and staring.

Rob McLaughlin gave Kennie one more chance to change his mind. "Last chance, son. Better pick a horse that you have some hope of riding one day. I'd have got rid of this whole line of stock if they weren't so damned fast that I've had the fool idea that someday there might turn out one gentle one in the lot—and I'd have a race horse. But there's never been one so far, and it's not going to be Flicka."

"It's not going to be Flicka," chanted Howard.

"Perhaps she *might* be gentled," said Kennie; and Nell, watching, saw that although his lips quivered, there was fanatical determination in his eye.

"Ken," said Rob, "it's up to you. If you say you want her we'll get her. But she wouldn't be the first of that line to die rather than give in. They're beautiful and they're fast, but let me tell you this, young man, they're *loco!*"

Kennie flinched under his father's direct glance.

"If I go after her again I'll not give up, whatever comes; understand what I mean by that?"

"Yes."

"What do you say?"

"I want her."

They brought her in again. They had better luck this time. In trying to get free she jumped over the Dutch half door of the stable and crashed inside. The men slammed the upper half of the door shut, and she was caught.

The rest of the band were driven away, and Kennie stood outside the stable, listening to the wild hoofs beating, the screams, the crashes. His Flicka inside there! He was drenched with perspiration.

"We'll leave her to think it over," said Rob, when dinnertime came. "Afterward we'll go up and feed and water her."

But when they went up afterward there was no Flicka in the barn. One of the windows, higher than the mangers, was broken.

The window opened into a pasture fenced in barbed wire six feet high. Near the stable stood a wagon-load of hay. When they went around the back of the stable they found Flicka hidden behind the hay wagon. At their approach she leaped away, then promptly headed east across the pasture.

"If she's anything like her loco mother," said Rob, "she'll go right through the wire."

"Ay bet she'll go over," said Gus. "She yumps like a deer."

"No horse can jump that," said McLaughlin.

Kennie said nothing because he could not speak. It was, perhaps, the most terrible moment of his life. He watched Flicka racing toward the eastern wire.

A few yards from it she swerved, turned, and raced diagonally south.

"It turned her! It turned her!" cried Kennie, almost sobbing. It was the first sign of hope for Flicka. "Oh, Dad! She has got sense. She has! She has!"

Flicka turned again as she met the southern boundary of the pasture; again at the northern; she avoided the barn. Without abating anything of her whirlwind speed, she investigated every possibility. Then, seeing that there was no hope, she raced south toward the range where she had spent her life, gathered herself, and shot into the air.

The three men watching had the impulse to cover their eyes, and Kennie gave a sort of a howl of despair.

Twenty yards of fence came down with her as she hurled herself through. Caught on the upper strands, she turned a complete somersault, landing on her back, her four legs dragging the wires down on top of her, and tangling herself in them beyond hope of escape.

"Damn the wire!" cursed McLaughlin. "If only I could afford decent fences . . ."

Kennie followed the men miserably as they walked to the filly. They stood in a circle watching, while she kicked and fought and thrashed until the wire was tightly wound and knotted about her, cutting, piercing, and tearing great three-cornered pieces of flesh and hide.

At last the fight left her and she lay unconscious, streams of blood running on her golden coat, and pools of crimson widening and spreading on the grass beneath her. With the wire cutter which he always carried Gus cut all the wire away, and they drew her into the pasture, repaired the fence, placed hay, a box of oats, and a tub of water near her, and called it a day.

"I don't think she'll pull out of it," said McLaughlin.

Next morning Kennie was up at five, doing his lessons. At six he went out to Flicka.

She had not moved. Food and water were untouched. She was no longer bleeding, but the wounds were swollen and caked over.

Kennie got a bucket of fresh water and poured it over her mouth. Then he leaped away, for Flicka came to life, scrambled up, got her balance, and stood swaying.

Kennie sat down to watch her. When he went in to breakfast she had drunk deeply of the water and was mouthing the oats.

There began then a sort of recovery. She ate, drank, limped about the pasture, stood for hours with hanging head and weakly splayed out legs under the clump of cottonwood trees. The swollen wounds scabbed and began to heal.

Kennie lived in the pasture too. He followed her around; he talked to her. He, too, lay snoozing or sat under the cottonwoods; and often, coaxing her with hand outstretched, he walked very quietly toward her. But she would not let him come near her.

Often she stood with her head at the south fence, looking off to the mountain. It made the tears come to Kennie's eyes to see the way she longed to get away.

Still Rob said she wouldn't pull out of it. There was no use putting a halter on her. She had no strength.

One morning, as Ken came out of the house, Gus met him and said, "De filly's down."

Kennie ran to the pasture as fast as he could, Howard close behind him. The right hind leg which had been badly swollen at the knee joint had opened in a festering wound, and Flicka lay flat and motionless, with staring eyes.

"Don't you wish now you'd chosen Doughboy?" asked Howard.

"Go away!" shouted Ken.

Howard stood watching while Kennie sat down on the ground and took Flicka's head on his lap. Though she was conscious and moved a little she did not struggle or seem frightened. Tears rolled down Kennie's cheeks as he talked to her and petted her. After a few moments Howard walked away.

"Mother, what do you do for an infection when it's a horse?" asked Kennie when he went to the house.

"Just what you'd do if it was a person," his mother said. "Wet dressings. I'll help you, Ken. We mustn't let those wounds close or scab over until they're clean. I'll make a poultice for that hind leg and help you put it on. Now that she'll let us get close to her, I'm sure we can help her a whole lot."

"The thing to do is see that she eats," said Rob. "Keep up her strength." But he himself would not go near her. "She won't pull out of it," he said. "I don't want to see her or think about her."

Kennie and his mother nursed the filly. The big poultice was bandaged on the hind leg. It drew out much poisoned matter, and Flicka felt better and was able to stand again. She watched for Kennie now and followed him like a dog, hopping on three legs, holding up the right hind leg with its huge knob of a bandage in comical fashion.

"Dad, Flicka's my friend now; she likes me," said Ken.

His father looked at him. "I'm glad of that son. It's a fine thing to have a horse for a friend."

Kennie found a nicer place for her. In the lower pasture the brook ran over cool stones. There was a grassy bank, the size of a corral, almost on a level with the water. Here she could lie softly, eat grass, drink fresh running water.

Kennie carried her oats morning and evening. She would watch for him to come, eyes and ears pointed to the hill. And one evening Ken, still some distance off, came to a stop and a wide grin spread over his face. He had heard her nicker. She had caught sight of him coming and was calling to him!

"You'll be well soon, Flicka," he whispered as she ate her oats and he played with her cream-colored mane. "You'll be so strong you won't know I'm on your back, and we'll fly like the wind. . . ."

This was the happiest month of Kennie's life.

3. THE VERDICT

THEN ONE DAY ALL THE WOUNDS were swollen again. Presently they opened, one by one; and Kennie and his mother made more poultices. Still the little filly ran about on three legs, but she began to go down in flesh and almost overnight wasted away to nothing. Every rib showed; the glossy hide was dull and brittle and was pulled over the skeleton as if she was a dead horse. Gus said, "It's de fever. It burns up her flesh. If you could stop de fever she might have de chance to get vell, Ken."

McLaughlin was standing in his window one morning and saw the little skeleton hopping about three-legged in the sunshine, and he said, "That's the end. I won't have a thing like that on my place."

Kennie had to understand that Flicka had not been getting well all this time; she had been slowly dying.

"She still eats her oats." he said mechanically.

They were all sorry for Ken. But Nell McLaughlin stopped disinfecting and dressing the wounds.

"It's no use, Ken," she said gently; "you know Flicka's going to die, don't you?"

"Yes, Mother."

Ken stopped eating. Howard said, "Ken doesn't eat anything any more. Don't he have to eat his dinner, Mother?"

But Nell answered, "Leave him alone."

Because the shooting of wounded animals is all in the day's work on the western plains, and sickening to everyone, Rob's voice, when he gave the order to have Flicka shot, was flat and unemotional.

"Here's the Marlin, Gus. Pick out a time when Ken's not around and put the filly out of her misery."

Gus took the rifle. "*Ja,* boss. . . ."

Ken knew what had to happen, and he kept his eye on the rack which held the firearms. His father allowed no firearms in the bunkhouse. The gun rack was outside the dining room, and three times a day, on his way to meals, Ken's eye scanned the weapons to make sure that they were all there.

That night they were not all there. The Marlin rifle was missing.

When Kennie saw that, he stopped walking. He felt dizzy. He kept staring at the gun rack, telling himself that it surely was there—he counted again and again—he couldn't see clearly. . . .

Then he felt an arm across his shoulders and heard his father's voice. "I know, son. Some things are awful hard to take. We just have to take 'em. I have to too."

Kennie got hold of his father's hand and held on. It helped steady him. Finally he looked up. Rob smiled down at him, and gave him a little shake and squeeze. Ken managed a smile too.

"All right now?"

"All right, Dad."

They walked in to supper together.

Ken even ate a little. But Nell looked thoughtfully across the table at the ashen color of her son's face and at the little pulse that was beating in the side of his neck.

After supper Kennie carried Flicka her oats, but he had to coax her and she would only eat a little.

She stood with her head hanging but when he stroked it and talked to her she pressed her face into his chest and was content. He could feel the burning heat of her body. It didn't seem possible that anything so thin could be alive.

Presently Kennie saw Gus come into the pasture carrying the Marlin. When he saw Ken he changed his direction and sauntered along as if he was out to shoot some cottontails.

Ken ran to him. "When are you going to do it, Gus?"

"Ay was goin' down soon now, before it got dark. . . ."

"Gus, don't do it tonight. Wait till morning. Just one more night, please, Gus."

"Vell, in de morning den, but it got to be done, Ken. Yer fader gives de order."

"I know. I won't say anything more."

AN HOUR AFTER THE FAMILY had gone to bed Ken got up and put on his clothes. It was a warm moonlit night. He ran down to the brook, calling softly. "Flicka! Flicka!"

But Flicka did not answer with a little nicker; and she was not hopping about the pasture. Ken hunted for an hour.

At last he found her down the creek, lying in the water. Her head had been on the bank, but as she lay there the current of the stream had sucked and pulled at her, and she had had no strength to resist; and little by little her head had slipped down until when Ken got there only the muzzle was resting on the bank, and the body and legs were swinging in the stream.

Kennie slid into the water, sitting on the bank, and hauled at her head. But she was heavy, and the current dragged like a weight. He began to sob because he had no strength to draw her out.

Then he found a leverage for his heels against some rocks and pulled till her head came up onto his knees, and he held it cradled in his arms.

He was glad that she had died of her own accord, in the cool water, under the moon, instead of being shot by Gus. But then, looking searchingly at her, he saw that she was alive.

And then he burst out crying.

The long night passed.

The moon slid slowly across the heavens.

The water rippled over Kennie's legs and over Flicka's body. And gradually the heat and fever went out of her. And the cool running water washed and washed her wounds.

When Gus went down in the morning with the rifle they hadn't moved. There they were, Kennie sitting partially in water, with Flicka's head in his arms.

Gus seized Flicka by the head and hauled her out on the grassy bank and then, seeing that Kennie was stiff and half-paralyzed, lifted him in his arms and carried him to the house.

"Gus," said Ken through chattering teeth, "don't shoot her, Gus."

"It ain't fur me to say, Ken. You know dat."

"But the fever's left her, Gus."

"Ay wait a little, Ken. . . ."

Rob McLaughlin drove to Laramie to get the doctor, for Ken was in violent chills that would not stop. His mother had him in bed wrapped in hot blankets when they got back.

Kennie looked at his father imploringly as the doctor shook down the thermometer.

"She might get well now, Dad. The fever's left her. It went out of her when the moon went down."

"All right, son. Don't worry. Gus'll feed her, morning and night as long as she's . . ."

"As long as I can't do it," finished Kennie happily.

The doctor put the thermometer in his mouth and told him to keep his mouth shut.

All day Gus went about his work, thinking of Flicka. He had not been back to look at her. He had been given no more orders. If she was alive the order to shoot her was still in effect. But Kennie was ill, and maybe the boss had forgotten about Flicka.

After their supper in the bunkhouse Gus and Tim walked down to the brook. They did not speak as they approached the filly, lying stretched out flat on the grassy bank, but their eyes were straining at her to see if she was dead or alive.

She raised her head as they reached her.

"By the powers!" exclaimed Tim. "There she is!"

She dropped her head, raised it again, and moved her legs and became tense as if struggling to rise.

"Yee whiz!" said Gus. "She got plenty strength yet."

He took his pipe out of his mouth and thought it over. Orders or no orders, he would try his best to save the filly. Ken had gone too far to be let down.

"Ay'm goin' to rig a blanket sling fur her, Tim, and get her on her feet, and keep her up."

There was bright moonlight to work by. They brought down the posthole digger and set two aspen poles either side of the filly, then, with ropes attached to the blanket, hoisted her by a pully.

Not at all disconcerted, she rested comfortably in the blanket under her belly, touched her feet on the ground, and reached for the bucket of water Gus held for her.

4. MIRACLE

KENNIE WAS SICK A LONG TIME. He nearly died. But Flicka picked up. Every day Gus passed the word to Nell, who carried it to Ken.

"She's cleaning up her oats."

"She's out of the sling."

"She bears a little weight on the bad leg."

Tim declared it was a real miracle. They argued about it, while eating their supper.

"Na," said Gus. "It was de cold water, washin' de fever outa her. And more dan dot—it was Ken—you tink it don't count? All night dot boy sits dere and says, 'Hold on, Flicka, Ay'm here wid you. Ay'm standin' by, two of us togedder' . . ."

Tim stared at Gus without answering, while he thought it over. In the silence a coyote yapped far off on the plains; and the wind made a rushing sound high up in the jack pines on the hill.

Gus filled his pipe.

"Sure," said Tim finally. "Sure. That's it."

Then came the day when Rob McLaughlin stood smiling at the foot of Kennie's bed and said, "Listen! Hear your friend?"

Ken listened and heard Flicka's high, eager whinny.

"She doesn't spend much time by the brook any more. She's up at the gate of the corral half the time, nickering for you."

"For me!"

Rob wrapped a blanket around the boy and carried him out to the corral gate.

Kennie gazed at Flicka. There was a look of marveling in his eyes. He felt as if he had been living in a world where everything was dreadful and hurting but awfully real; and *this* couldn't be real; this was all soft and happy, nothing to struggle over or worry about or fight for any more. Even his father was proud of him! He could feel it in the way Rob's big arms held him. It was all like a dream and far away. He couldn't, yet, get close to anything.

But Flicka—Flicka—alive, well, pressing up to him, recognizing him, nickering . . .

Kennie put out a hand—weak and white—and laid it on her face. His thin little fingers straightened her forelock the way he used to do, while Rob looked at the two with a strange expression about his mouth and a glow in his eyes that was not often there.

"She's still poor, Dad, but she's on four legs now."

"She's picking up."

Ken turned his face up, suddenly remembering. "Dad! She did get gentled, didn't she?"

"Gentle—as—a kitten. . . ."

They put a cot down by the brook for Kennie, and the boy and the filly, Flicka, got well together.

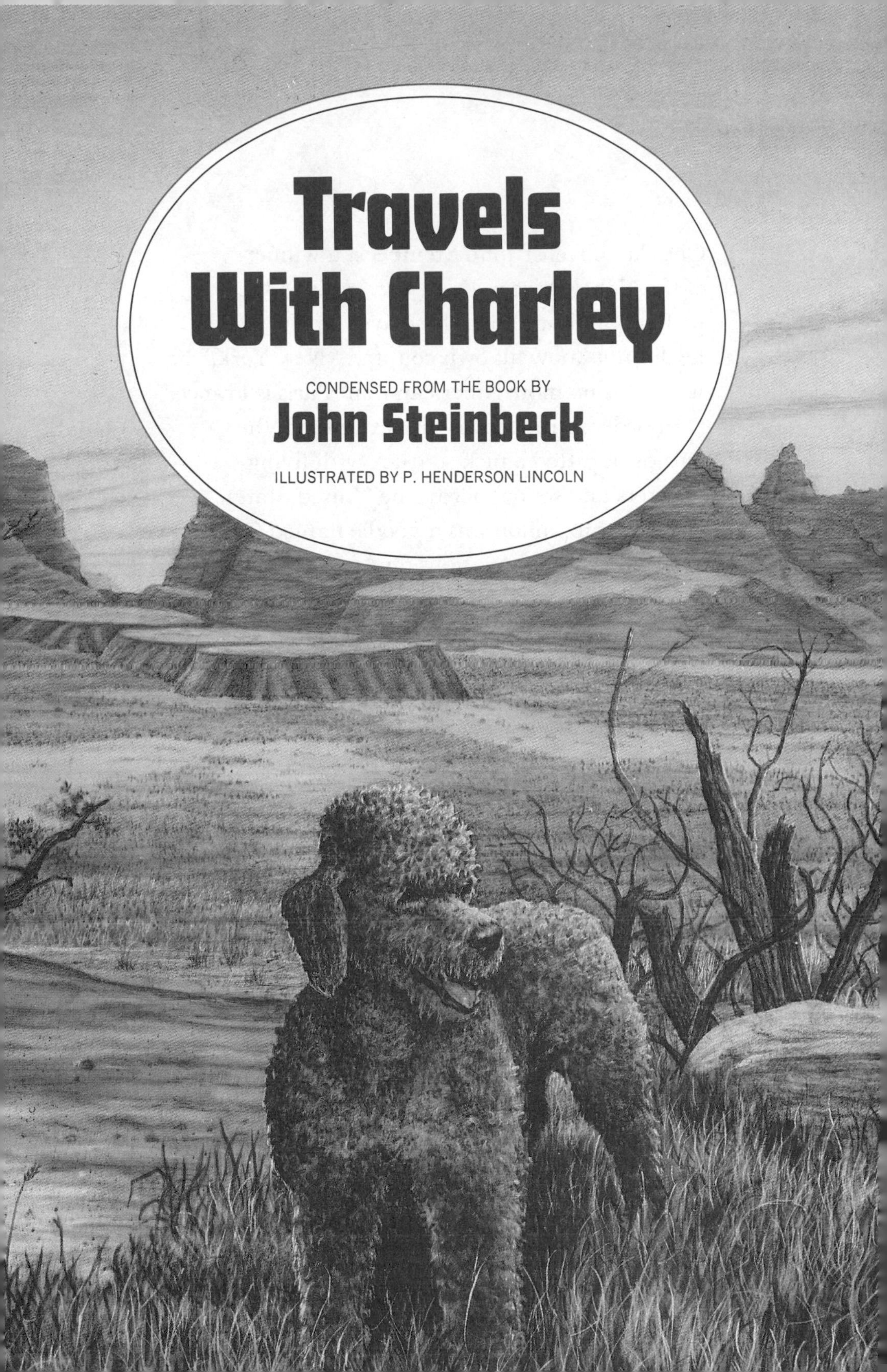
Travels
With Charley
CONDENSED FROM THE BOOK BY
John Steinbeck
ILLUSTRATED BY P. HENDERSON LINCOLN

One day novelist John Steinbeck, a winner of the Nobel Prize in literature, came to the realization that although he lived in New York, he did not know his own country. "New York," he wrote, "is no more American than Paris is France."

In order to rediscover his native land, the author outfitted a pickup truck with living quarters and set out across the United States. His sole companion was a poodle named Charley.

Steinbeck's observations on America—shrewd and witty—were recorded in this book, which *The New York Times Book Review* characterized as "pure delight."

1. DEPARTURE

MY PLAN WAS CLEAR, concise and reasonable, I think. For years I have traveled in many parts of the world. In America I live in New York, but New York is no more America than Paris is France or London is England. Thus I discovered that, as a writer, I was working from memory; I did not know my own country. So I determined to try to rediscover this monster land.

I wrote to a great corporation which manufactures trucks, and specified my needs. I wanted a three-quarter-ton pickup truck, capable of going anywhere, and on this truck I wanted a little house built like the cabin of a small boat. In due time, exactly what I wanted came through—a tough, fast vehicle with double bed, four-burner stove, a heater, refrigerator and lights operating on butane, a chemical toilet, storage space, windows screened against insects. I named it Rocinante, after Don Quixote's horse.

As the morning of my departure approached, I decided to take one companion—an old French gentleman poodle known as Charley. Charley is a born diplomat. He prefers negotiation to fighting, and properly so, since he is very bad at fighting. But he is a good watchdog, and has a roar like a lion. He is a good friend and companion, and would rather travel than anything he can imagine. He contributed much to the trip.

The morning came, a clear bright one with the tawny look of autumn in the sunlight. My wife and I parted very quickly, since both of us hate good-bys.

As Charley and I headed north through Connecticut, I thought it might be nice if I could invite people I met along the way to my home for a drink, but I had neglected to lay in liquor. I found a small store set back from the road in a grove of sugar maples. It had a well-kept garden and flower boxes. I ordered bourbon, scotch, gin, vermouth, brandy, applejack and a case of beer—a big order for a little store. The owner, a young-old man with a gray face, was impressed.

"Must be quite a party."

"No—it's just traveling supplies."

He helped me to carry the cartons out of the store, and I opened Rocinante's door.

"You going in that?"

"Sure."

"Where?"

"All over."

And then I saw what I was to see so many times on the journey—a look of longing. "Lord! I wish I could go."

"Don't you like it here?"

"Sure, it's all right. But I wish I could go."

"You don't even know where I'm going."

"I don't care. I'd like to go anywhere."

Eventually I had to come out of the tree-hidden roads and do my best to bypass the big cities, bustling with manufacturing, lousy with traffic. American cities are like badger holes, ringed with trash—all of them—surrounded by piles of wrecked and rusting automobiles, and almost smothered with rubbish. Everything we use comes in boxes, cartons, bins, the packaging we love so much. The mountains of things we throw away are much greater than the things we use. In this, if in no other way, we can see the reckless exuberance of our production.

Driving along, I thought how in France or Italy every item of these thrown-out things would have been saved and used for something. This is not said in criticism of one system or the other, but I do wonder whether there will come a time when we can no longer afford our wastefulness—wastes everywhere.

I pulled Rocinante into a small picnic area and got out my book of maps. Suddenly the United States became huge beyond belief and impossible ever to cross. I wondered how I'd got myself mixed up in a project that couldn't be carried out. It was like starting to write a novel. When I face the desolate impossibility of writing 500 pages, a sick sense of failure falls on me and I know I can never do it. Then gradually I write one page and then another. One day's work is all I can permit myself to contemplate, and I eliminate the possibility of ever finishing. So it was now, as I looked at the bright-colored projection of America.

Charley put his nose close to my ear and said, "Ftt." He is the only dog I ever knew who could pronounce the consonant *F*. This is because his front teeth are crooked, a tragedy which keeps him out of dog shows. The word "Ftt" usually means he would like to salute a bush or a tree. I opened the cab door and let him out, and he went about his ceremony.

We drove on in the autumn afternoon. My route went north in Vermont, then east in New Hampshire in the White Mountains. The roadside stands were piled with golden pumpkins and russet squashes and baskets of red apples so crisp and sweet that they seemed to explode with juice when I bit into them. The villages, neat and white-painted, are the prettiest, I guess, in the whole nation.

The climate changed quickly to cold, and the trees burst into color—the reds and yellows you can't believe. I got high in the mountains before dusk.

A sign beside a stream offered fresh eggs for sale, and I drove up a farm road and bought some eggs and asked permission to camp beside the stream and offered to pay.

The farmer was a spare man, with what we think of as a Yankee face and the flat vowels we consider Yankee pronunciation.

"No need to pay," he said. "The land's not working. But I would like to look at that rig you've got there."

I said, "Let me put it in order, then please come down for a cup of coffee—or something."

I backed and filled until I found a level place where I could hear the eager stream rattling. It was getting dark and bitterly cold, but the lamp and the gas burners of the stove warmed my little house cozily.

Charley ate his supper and retired into a corner under the table. The coffee was barely ready when Charley let out his lion roar. I can't say how comforting it is to be told that someone is approaching in the dark.

The farm owner knocked on my door, and I invited him in. "You've got it nice in here," he said. "Yes, sir, you've got it nice." He slipped in the seat beside the table. I poured him a cup of coffee. It seems to me that coffee smells even better when the frost is in. "A little something on the side?" I asked. "Something to give it authority?"

"No—this is fine."

"Not a touch of applejack? I'm tired from a day's driving, I'd like a spot myself."

He looked at me with the contained amusement that is considered taciturnity by non-Yankees. "Would you have one if I didn't?"

"No, I guess not."

"I wouldn't rob you then—just a spoonful."

So I poured each of us a good dollop of 21-year-old applejack and slipped in on my side of the table.

There's a gentility on the road. A direct or personal question is out of bounds. He did not ask my name nor I his.

I asked, "Have you listened to the radio today?"

"Five-o'clock report."

"What happened at the U.N.?"

"You wouldn't believe it," he said. "Mr. K. took off his shoe and pounded the table."

"What for?"

"Didn't like what was being said."

"Seems a strange way to protest."

"Well, it got attention." He slowly sipped the applejack with a deep appreciation.

"How do folks around here feel about talking back to the Russians?"

"I don't know about other people. But I think if you're talking back, it's kind of like a rear-guard action. I'd like to see us do something so they had to talk back to us."

I refilled the coffee cups and poured a little more applejack for both of us. "You think we should attack?"

"I think we should at least take the ball sometimes. No thanks, no more. I can smell your supper's nearly ready. I'll step along. Thanks for the—coffee. Good-night."

I ate my corned-beef hash, then made my bed, but found I couldn't sleep. The clattering stream on the rocks was a good reposeful sound, but the conversation of the farmer stayed with me—a thoughtful, articulate man he was.

Roosters were crowing before I went to sleep. Charley likes to get up early, and he likes me to get up early, too. Perhaps his most irritating method of arousing me is to sit quietly beside the bed and stare into my face with a sweet, forgiving expression; I come out of deep sleep with a feeling of being looked at.

I SOON DISCOVERED THAT if a stranger wishes to eavesdrop on a local population the places for him are bars and churches. But some New England towns don't have bars, and church is only on Sunday. A good alternative is the roadside restaurant. To find these places inhabited, one must get up very early. But early-rising men not only do not talk much to strangers; they barely talk to one another. The natural New England taciturnity reaches its glorious perfection at breakfast.

I fed Charley and hit the road. At the first restaurant I pulled in and took my seat at a counter. The customers were folded over their coffee cups like ferns. A normal conversation is as follows:

Waitress: "Same?"

Customer: "Yep."

Waitress: "Cold enough for you?"

Customer: "Yep."

(Ten minutes.)

Waitress: "Refill?"

Customer: "Yep."

This is a really talkative customer. Some reduce it to "Burp," and others do not answer at all.

I wanted to see Aroostook, the big northern potato-raising county of Maine. I've seen many migrant crop-picking people about the country: Hindus, Filipinos, Mexicans, Okies away from their states. Here in Maine a great many were French Canadians who came over the border for the harvest season. Some of their tents and trucks and trailers were settled on the edge of a clear and lovely lake, and the smells that came from their cooking fires indicated that they had not lost their French genius for making soup. I parked Rocinante about 95 yards away, then put on coffee to boil.

In establishing contact with strange people, Charley is my ambassador. I release him, and he drifts toward the objective. I retrieve him so that he will not be a nuisance to my neighbors—*et voilà!*

I sent out my ambassador and drank a cup of coffee while I gave him time to operate. Then I strolled to the camp to relieve my neighbors of the inconvenience of my miserable cur. They were nice-looking people, a dozen of them, not counting children. The women wore corduroy pants and bright-colored scarves. The operating chieftain was a fine-looking man of about 35, broad-shouldered and lithe.

The dog had caused no trouble, he said. The truth was that they had remarked that he was a handsome dog. I, of course, found myself prejudiced, being his owner, but the dog had one advantage over most dogs. He was born and raised in France.

Was that the truth? Where in France?

In Bercy, on the outskirts of Paris—did they know it?

No, unfortunately they had never been to the fatherland.

I hoped they might remedy that.

They had observed my *roulotte* with admiration.

If they found it convenient, I should be pleased to show it to them. Might I expect them after their supper?

They would be honored.

I set my cabin in order, heated and ate a can of chili con carne, made sure the beer was cold. Then Charley barked them in. Six people can squeeze behind my table, and they did. Two others beside me stood up, and the back door was wreathed with children's faces. I opened beer for the big ones and pop for the outsiders.

In due course these people told me quite a bit about themselves. This clan, having put their own small farm to bed for the winter in the Province of Quebec, came over the border to make a small nest egg. They were a hardy and self-sufficient people, quite capable of taking care of themselves.

I reached under my sink, lifted out a bottle of very old and reverend brandy and handed their chieftain John a corkscrew while I laid out the crystal—three plastic coffee cups, a jelly glass, a shaving mug and several wide-mouthed pill bottles.

The cognac was very, very good, and from the first muttered *"Santé"* you could feel the Brotherhood of Man growing until it filled Rocinante. They refused seconds, and I insisted. The division of thirds was put on the basis that there wasn't enough to save. And with the few divided drops of that third there came into Rocinante a triumphant human magic that can bless a house, or a truck for that matter. Rocinante took on a glow it never quite lost.

The adieus were short and formal. Then the visitors went home, their way lighted by John carrying a tin kerosene lantern.

I slept until in the dim false dawn Charley looked into my face and said, "Ftt." While I heated my coffee, I made a little sign on cardboard and stuck it in the neck of the empty brandy bottle. Then, passing the sleeping camp, I stopped and stood the bottle where they would see it. The sign read: *"Enfant de France, Mort pour la Patrie."*

2. EN ROUTE

SUNDAY MORNING IN A VERMONT town, my last day in New England, I shaved, dressed in a suit, polished my shoes, whited my sepulcher, and looked for a church to attend. On seeing a John Knox church, I drove into a side street and parked Rocinante out of sight, then took my seat in the rear of the spotless, polished place of worship.

The service did my heart and I hope my soul some good. It is our practice now, at least in the large cities, to find from our psychiatric priesthood that our sins aren't really sins at all but accidents that are set in motion by forces beyond our control. There was no such nonsense in this church. The minister, a man of iron with tool-steel eyes and a delivery like a pneumatic drill, opened up with prayer and reassured us that we were a pretty sorry lot. We didn't amount to much to start with, and because of our own tawdry efforts we had been slipping ever since.

Then, having softened us up, he went into a glorious fire-and-brimstone sermon. Having proved that we, or perhaps only I, were no damn good, he painted with cool certainty what was likely to happen to us if we didn't make some basic reorganizations for which he didn't hold out much hope.

He spoke of hell as an expert, not the mush-mush hell of these soft days, but a well-stoked, white-hot hell served by technicians of the first order. This reverend brought it to a point where we could understand it, a good hard coal fire, plenty of draft, and a squad of open-hearth devils who put their hearts into their work, and their work was me. I began to feel good all over.

For some years now God has been a pal to us, practicing togetherness, and that causes the same emptiness a father does playing softball with his son. But this Vermont God cared enough about me to go to a lot of trouble kicking the hell out of me. He put my sins in a new perspective. Whereas they had been small and mean, this minister gave them size and bloom and dignity.

I felt so revived in spirit that I put five dollars in the plate, and afterward, in front of the church, shook hands warmly with the minister and as many of the congregation as I could. All across the country I went to church on Sundays, a different denomination every week, but nowhere did I find the quality of that Vermont preacher. He forged a religion designed to last.

From the beginning of my journey, I had avoided the great high-speed slashes of concrete and tar called "thruways," or "super-highways." But I had dawdled in New England; the winter grew apace, and I had visions of being snowbound in North Dakota. I sought out Interstate 90, a wide gash of a super-highway, and sent Rocinante bucketing along.

These great roads are wonderful for moving goods, but not for inspection of a countryside. You are bound to the wheel and your eyes to the car ahead and to the rearview mirror for the car behind and the side mirror for the car or truck about to pass, and at the same time you must read all the signs for fear you may miss some instructions or orders. When we get these thruways across the whole country, it will be possible to drive from New York to California without seeing a single thing.

I drove this wide, eventless way past Buffalo and Erie to Madison, Ohio, and then found the equally wide and fast U.S. 20 past Cleveland and Toledo. On these roads out of the manufacturing centers there moved many mobile homes, pulled by specially designed trucks. Early in my travels I had become aware of these new things under the sun, and since they occur in increasing numbers all over the nation, perhaps some speculation is in order.

Mobile homes are not trailers to be pulled by one's own car but shining cars as long as pullmans. They are wonderfully built homes, sometimes as much as 70 feet long, with two to five rooms, and complete with air-conditioners, toilets, baths and television.

From the beginning of my travels I had noticed the lots where they were sold, but then I began to be aware of the parks where they sit in uneasy permanence. A mobile home is drawn to the park and installed on a ramp, a heavy rubber sewer pipe is bolted underneath, water and electric power are connected, the television antenna is raised, and the family is in residence. The park men charge a small ground rent. Telephones are connected simply by plugging in a jack. Several park managers agreed that last year one in nine new housing units in the whole country was a mobile home.

The fact that these homes can be moved does not mean that they do move. Sometimes their owners stay for years in one place, plant gardens, build little walls of cinder blocks, put out awnings and garden furniture. The owners were proud to show their homes to me.

"How are they purchased?" I asked one man.

"On time, just like an automobile. It's like paying rent."

And then I discovered the greatest selling appeal of all—one that crawls through nearly all American life. Improvements are made on these mobile homes every year. If you are doing well, you turn yours in on a new model just as many do with an automobile. And the turn-in value is higher than that of automobiles because there's a ready market for used homes. They are easy to maintain, need no paint since they are usually of aluminum, and are not tied to fluctuating land values.

One of the dinners I shared in a mobile home was cooked in an immaculate kitchen, walled in plastic tile, with stainless-steel sinks and ovens and stoves flush with the wall. The husband worked as a garage mechanic about four miles away and made good pay. Two children were picked up every morning by a yellow school bus.

After dinner I brought up a question that had puzzled me. "One of our most treasured feelings concerns roots, growing up rooted in some soil or some community." How did they feel about raising their children without roots?

"How many people today have what you are talking about?" the father answered. "What roots are there in an apartment 12 floors up? What roots are in a housing development of thousands of small dwellings almost alike?

"My father came from Italy," he said. "He grew up in Tuscany in a house where his family had lived maybe a thousand years. That's roots for you. No running water, no toilet, and they cooked with charcoal or vine clippings. They had just two rooms, a kitchen and a bedroom where everybody slept—grandpa, father and all the kids; no place to read, no place to be alone. Was that better? I bet if you gave my old man the choice, he'd cut his roots and live like this."

DRIVING THE BIG HIGHWAY near Toledo, I had a conversation with Charley on the subject of roots. Could it be that Americans are a restless people, a mobile people, never satisfied with where they are? The pioneers who peopled the continent were the restless ones from Europe. Wouldn't it be unusual if we had not inherited this tendency?

I came upon the Missouri River in amazement. Here is the boundary between east and west. On the Bismarck, N.D., side it is eastern landscape, eastern grass, with the look and smell of eastern America. Across the Missouri it is pure west, with brown grass and water scorings and small outcrops. The two sides might well be a thousand miles apart.

As I was not prepared for the Missouri boundary, so I was not prepared for the Badlands. They deserve this name. They are like the work of an evil child. Such a place the Fallen Angels might have built as a spite to Heaven, dry and sharp, desolate and dangerous, and for me filled with foreboding. A sense comes from it that it does not like or welcome humans. I turned off the highway on a shaley road and headed in among the buttes. The road surface tore viciously at my tires, and made Rocinante's overloaded springs cry with anguish. I went into a state of flight, running to get away from the unearthly landscape. And then the late afternoon changed everything.

As the sun angled, the buttes and coulees, the cliffs and sculptured hills and ravines lost their burned and dreadful look, and glowed with yellow and rich browns and a hundred variations of red and silver-gray, all picked out by streaks of coal-black. It was so beautiful that I stopped near a thicket of dwarfed and wind-warped cedars and, once stopped, I was caught, trapped in color and dazzled by the clarity of the light.

Against the descending sun the battlements were dark and clean-lined, while to the east, where the light poured slantwise, the strange landscape shouted with color. And the night, far from being frightful, was lovely beyond thought, for the stars were close, and although there was no moon, the starlight made a silver glow in the sky.

The air cut the nostrils with dry frost. For pure pleasure I collected a pile of dead cedar branches and built a small fire just to smell the perfume of the burning wood and to hear the excited crackle of the branches. My fire made a dome of yellow light over me, and nearby I heard a screech owl hunting and a barking of coyotes.

That night was so cold that I put on my insulated underwear for pajamas, and when Charley curled up in his place under the bed, I dug out an extra blanket and covered him—all except the tip of his nose. He sighed and wriggled and gave a great groan of pure ecstatic comfort. I thought how every safe generality I gathered in my travels was canceled by another. In the night the Badlands had become Goodlands.

I AM IN LOVE WITH MONTANA. For other states I have admiration, respect, recognition, even some affection, but with Montana it is love. Montana is a great splash of grandeur. The scale is huge but not overpowering. The land is rich with grass and color, and the mountains are the kind that I would create if mountains were ever put on my agenda.

Here for the first time I heard a definite regional accent unaffected by TV-ese, a slow-paced warm speech. It seemed to me that the frantic bustle of America was not in Montana. The calm of the mountains and the rolling grasslands had got into the inhabitants. The towns were places to live in rather than nervous hives. People had time to pause in their occupations to undertake the passing art of neighborliness.

I found I did not rush through the towns to get them over with. I even found things I had to buy to make myself linger. In Billings I bought a hat, in Livingston a jacket, in Butte a secondhand rifle I didn't particularly need. Then I found a telescope sight I had to have, and waited while it was mounted on the rifle, and in the process I got to know everyone in the shop and any customers who entered. I spent the good part of a morning at this, mostly because I wanted to stay.

But I see that, as usual, love is inarticulate. Montana has a spell on me. It is grandeur and warmth. If Montana had a seacoast, or if I could live that far from the sea, I would instantly move there and petition for admission. Of all the states it is my favorite and my love.

3. RETURN

I FIND IT DIFFICULT TO WRITE about my native place, northern California. It should be the easiest, because I knew that strip angled against the Pacific better than any other place in the world.

This four-lane concrete highway I remember as a narrow, twisting mountain road where the wood teams moved, drawn by steady mules. This was a little, little town, a general store under a tree and a blacksmith shop and a bench in front on which to sit and listen to the clang of hammer on anvil. Now little houses, each one like the next, spread for a mile in all directions. That was a woody hill with live oaks dark green against the parched grass where the coyotes sang on moonlit nights. Today the top is shaved off, and a television relay station lunges up at the sky.

Before I left California I did one formal and sentimental thing. I drove up to Fremont's Peak and climbed the last spiky rocks to the top. Here among these blackened granite outcrops General Fremont made his stand against a Mexican army, and defeated it. When I was a boy, we occasionally found cannon balls and rusted bayonets in the area.

This solitary stone peak overlooks the whole of my childhood and youth, the great Salinas Valley stretching south for nearly a hundred miles, the town of Salinas where I was born now spreading like crab-grass toward the foothills. I felt the wind blow up from the long valley. Charley sat at my feet, his fringed ears blowing like laundry on a line.

"You wouldn't know, my Charley, that right down there, in that little valley, I fished for trout with your namesake, your Uncle Charley. And over there—see where I'm pointing—my mother shot a wildcat.

"Can you see that darker place? Well, that's a tiny canyon with a clear and lovely stream bordered with wild azaleas and fringed with big oaks. And on one of those oaks my father burned his name with a hot iron, together with the name of the girl he loved. In the long years the bark grew over the burn and covered it. And just a little while ago, a man cut that oak for firewood and his splitting wedge uncovered my father's name and the man sent it to me. In the spring, Charley, when the valley is carpeted with blue lupines like a flowery sea, there's the smell of heaven up here, the smell of heaven."

I printed it once more on my eyes, south, west and north, and then we hurried away from the permanent and changeless past where my mother is always shooting a wildcat and my father is always burning his name with his love.

Texas, a nation in every sense of the word, is always threatening to secede from the Union. We have heard them threaten this so often that I formed an enthusiastic organization—The American Friends for Texas Secession. This stops the subject cold. They want to be able to secede, but they don't want anyone to want them to.

The tradition of the frontier cattleman is tenderly nurtured in Texas. When a man makes his fortune in oil or government contracts, in chemicals or wholesale groceries, his first act is to buy a ranch, the largest he can afford, and to run some cattle. A candidate for public office who does not own a ranch is said to have little chance of election. Businessmen wear heeled boots that never feel a stirrup, and men of great wealth who have houses in Paris and regularly shoot grouse in Scotland refer to themselves as "little old country boys."

It would be easy to make sport of their attitude if one did not know that in this way they try to keep their association with the strength and simplicity of the land. Instinctively they feel that this is the source not only of wealth but of energy. And the energy of Texans is boundless and explosive. The successful man with his traditional ranch, at least in my experience, is no absentee owner. He works at it, oversees his herd and adds to it. The energy, in a climate so hot as to be staggering, is also staggering. And the tradition of hard work is maintained whatever the fortune or lack of it.

I have moved over a great part of Texas, and within its borders I have seen about as many kinds of country, contour, climate and conformation as there are in the world, saving only the arctic, and a good north wind can even bring the icy breath down. The stern horizon-fenced plains are foreign to the wooded hills and sweet streams in the Davis Mountains. The rich citrus orchards of the Rio Grande Valley do not relate to the sagebrush grazing of West Texas. The hot and humid air of the Gulf Coast has no likeness whatsoever in the cool crystal in the northwest of the Panhandle.

Most areas in the world may be placed in latitude and longitude, described chemically in their earth, sky and water. Then there are others—like Greece, and those parts of England where King Arthur walked—where fable, myth, love or prejudice step in and so distort a cool, clear appraisal that a kind of high-colored magical confusion takes permanent hold. Surely Texas is such a place.

Who has not known a journey to be over before the traveler returns? I know exactly where and when mine was over. Up to Abingdon, Va., I can reel back the trip like film. I have almost total recall: every face is there, every hill and tree and color. After Abingdon—nothing. There my journey went away and left me stranded far from home. I bulldozed blindly through West Virginia, Pennsylvania, New Jersey. I must have stopped to fill my gas tank, to walk and feed Charley, to eat, to telephone, but I don't remember any of it.

THEN MAGICALLY I WAS ASHORE ON MANHATTAN, far downtown with the daily panic rush of commuters. I made a turn and then another, entered a one-way street the wrong way and had to back out, got boxed in the middle of a crossing by swirling rapids of people.

Suddenly I pulled to the curb in a no-parking area, cut my motor, and leaned back in the seat and laughed, and I couldn't stop. My hands and arms and shoulders were shaking with road jitters. An old-fashioned cop with a fine red face and a frosty blue eye leaned in toward me. "What's the matter with you, Mac?"

I said, "Officer, I've driven this thing all over the country—mountains, plains, deserts. And now I'm back in my own town, where I live—and I'm lost."

He grinned happily. "Think nothing of it, Mac," he said. "I got lost in Brooklyn only Saturday. Now where is it you want to go?"

And that's how the traveler came home again.

It would be pleasant to be able to say of my travels with Charley, "I went out to find the truth about my country, and I found it." I wish it were that easy.

If an Englishman or a Frenchman or an Italian should travel my route, see what I saw, hear what I heard, their stored pictures would be not only different from mine but equally different from one another. If other Americans reading this account should feel it true, that agreement would only mean that we are alike in our Americanness.

From start to finish I found no strangers. If I had, I might be able to report them more objectively. But these are my people and this is my country. If I were to prepare one immaculately inspected generality, it would be this: For all of our enormous geographic range, for all of our sectionalism, for all of our interwoven breeds drawn from every part of the ethnic world, we are a nation, a new breed.

Americans are much more American than they are Northerners, Southerners, Westerners or Easterners. This is not patriotic whoop-de-do; it is carefully observed fact. California Chinese, Boston Irish, Wisconsin Germans, yes, and Alabama Negroes, have more in common than they have apart. It is astonishing that this has happened in a little more than 200 years, and most of it in the last 50. The American identity is an exact and provable thing.

CONDENSED FROM THE BOOK

"I Will Be Called John"

by Lawrence Elliott

PHOTOGRAPH FROM
PICTORIAL PARADE

There was something about the man that radiated goodness. His smile alone conveyed a blessing.

He was John XXIII, the Supreme Pontiff of the Roman Catholic Church, yet he welcomed people of every faith to a universal brotherhood of peace and goodwill. At the same time, he imbued his own church with a fresh sense of freedom.

In this well-written biography, Lawrence Elliott carefully traces the life of Angelo Giuseppe Roncalli from humble peasant beginnings in northern Italy, through seminary life and the gradual rise in the hierarchy of the church, to his elevation as Pope at the age of 77.

In *Good Pope John* the author has caught the qualities that set the man apart—the warmth, the wit and laughter, and the deep humanity that won so many hearts.

1. THE DECISION

IT BEGAN, AS THINGS often do, with an ending. For three centuries the Popes had gone to Castel Gandolfo, in the hills southeast of Rome, to escape the summer heat. There, on October 9, 1958, Pope Pius XII died, worn out by years and the burdens of holy office.

The following day, his mortal remains were returned to the Vatican. By the time the procession reached Rome it was two miles long, and hundreds of thousands of mourners lined the streets. It moved slowly past the Colosseum to the Basilica of St. Peter, where a Swiss Guard contingent led the way to a bier at the papal altar. The funeral chant rose to the soaring dome, echoing hauntingly against the silent stone. Three days later, the body of Pius was laid to rest in the grottos beneath the Basilica, close to the tomb of St. Peter.

The cardinals of the Church, posted in 21 countries on five continents, came to Rome to bury the Pope and choose his successor. Over the years, death had cut their ranks from 70 to 55; now their age and frailty were sadly emphasized when two died as the conclave was about to begin. (Two others were detained behind the Iron Curtain.)

In early conclaves, the College of Cardinals was often at the mercy of imperious sovereigns or a rioting populace. But since 1276 the papal electors have locked themselves away from the world to make their decision. Thus, at 5:30 p.m. on October 25, a great bell in the courtyard rang out three times, warning all unauthorized persons to leave the 200-room conclave enclosure. Walls and passages had been sealed off, telephones disconnected, radios removed.

Though in an imposing and celebrated part of the Vatican, the enclosure was quite short of sleeping and bathing facilities. Journalists shown through it had jauntily noted that the cooking for Their Eminences would be done in improvised kitchens by the Sisters of Santa Marta, an order not noted for culinary excellence, and predicted that the conclave would be brief. At 6:08 p.m., the last entryway was locked from the outside. The cardinals were alone. They would not come out until one of them was elected Pope.

The immense piazza in front of St. Peter's was never empty, day or night. Priests came to pray, nuns to sing hymns, the people of Rome to exchange rumors and wait. Four times each day, for a moment, all fell still, every eye fixed on the slender stovepipe over the Sistine Chapel and the wisp of slate-colored smoke winding out of it. In accordance with tradition, the cardinals burned each of their ballots, adding damp straw to produce black smoke if a Pope had not been chosen.

Sunday passed, and Monday, and the guessing game intensified. Some said the cardinals were seeking an interim Pope, a Pope of transition; others that a young Pope was favored, one who could adapt the ancient traditions of the Church to the 20th century. No one knew.

On Tuesday, at a few minutes past 5 p.m., white smoke puffed up from the chimney. A Pope had been elected! *"Viva il Papa!"* some people cried, and it was taken up, a joyous, roaring wave of sound. The news spread, and from the farthest corners of the city people started converging on St. Peter's, turning the great piazza dark with their numbers, all waiting to hear the name of the new Pope.

The band of the *carabinieri* honor guard crossed the piazza, red plumes bobbing on their ceremonial bicorns. On the steps of the church the Vatican Palatine Guard was forming, ready to present arms at the appearance of the Pontiff. The triple-barred golden papal cross was carried out to the central balcony of the Basilica, and the 84-year-old senior cardinal deacon appeared at the railing. He cleared his throat and began to speak in Latin, his voice so charged with emotion that it broke in the middle of the pronouncement.

"*Annuntio vobis gaudium magnum. Habemus Papam!* (I announce to you a great joy. We have a Pope!)" There were cheers and hand-clapping. But the real question was: Who?

"He is my most eminent and reverend lord, Angelo Cardinal Guiseppe Roncalli."

There was a moment of astonishment. If Roncalli's name appeared on the lists of possibilities at all, it was always near the bottom, a sort of afterthought. But no matter—*Habemus Papam!* A thundering roar broke from the crowd.

Now the cardinal announced the name by which the new Pope had chosen to be known henceforth: "Iohannes XXIII." John XXIII.

Again a pause of surprise—no Pope had been called John since the Middle Ages. Then almost unexpectedly he was there, a solid, thickset figure in white. Other Popes had been borne to the balcony in portable thrones amid the full splendor of the Vatican Court. John XXIII came alone and on foot, and he stood so still that seconds passed before those below were aware he was there. Then they raised the mightiest cheer and waved their handkerchiefs.

The Pope smiled with unconcealed pleasure, lifted his hands in benediction and began to intone the time-honored *Urbi et Orbi,* the Apostolic blessing on the city and the world. Thousands crossed themselves and dropped to their knees. "May Almighty God bless you; the Father, the Son and the Holy Spirit."

For a long last moment the Pope stood there, arms still extended to the people of Rome. Then he turned and disappeared behind the curtains. The crowd began to break up, slipping through the colonnade to side streets that would lead them home. They spoke of this John XXIII. Whoever thought they would pick *that* one? He is so old—what, 77?

And again and again: Will he be good?

In the yellow hills that rise above the Po River valley in northern Italy is a gathering of earth-and-plaster houses called Sotto il Monte—Under the Mountain. Its people have tilled the stony soil for centuries. In summer the vineyards and little plots of corn languish in the heat; in winter a bitter wind sweeps down from the Alps.

On the morning of November 25, 1881, a child was born to Giovanni Battista Roncalli and his wife Marianna—the first son, after three daughters. By midafternoon the mother had risen from her bed and, with her husband, set out to the parish church to have the child baptized. The priest was on sick call, so they sat down and waited.

Giovanni was dark and wiry with a great black mustache and the arched nose and prominent ears that, in manhood, would characterize the new baby. Marianna, at 27, was ample in shape. She had a warm open face that would be her son's. Tenant farmers, the Roncallis labored in the fields from daybreak to dusk, trying to put a few lire aside.

It was late in the evening when the priest, Don Francesco, returned. Marianna thrust the baby toward him.

"We came for the baptism," Giovanni said.

The priest sighed, and led them into the chapel. The wind howled and rain clattered against the shutters as he read the service. And so

Angelo Giuseppe Roncalli was received into the Church that day.

The Roncallis lived in a 300-year-old farmhouse near the piazza of Sotto il Monte, with grandparents, uncles and aunts and *their* children all under the same roof. There were 28 mouths to feed. As soon as he could, young Angelo went to work in the fields with his parents.

Angelo was nearly six when he was enrolled in the town's only school, a one-room building with three benches, one for each grade. His younger brother Zaverio, who joined him the following year, said, "I knew he was cut out for important things. He *wanted* to go to school. I only went when it rained."

When Angelo had completed the three primary grades, Don Francesco sent him with his father to a neighboring parish where the priest was said to be an excellent teacher of Latin.

"He is not stupid," Giovanni said. "So if he falls behind, beat him."

The priest needed no encouragement. Angelo learned Caesar, as he himself put it, "at the rate of one word per clout."

The next year he entered a secondary school at Celana, five miles across the mountain. His father was doubtful that he needed all that education, but Don Francesco said he was a bright boy and must learn geography and arithmetic. So from home he walked to school each day, his shoes most often slung over his shoulders to preserve them, a slice of cold *polenta*—a cornmeal dish—for lunch. At night he hadn't the energy to do more than eat and fall into bed.

Religious faith had come to the boy as spontaneously as breathing. God was real. Angelo felt His presence. He thought there could be no nobler calling than to serve God as a parish priest. He did not speak of his aspiration, feeling it presumptuous for a farmer's son, but somehow Don Francesco knew.

"Don't ever become a priest," he teased Angelo. "Look how we sweat in this clothing and how the collar hurts." But in the autumn of 1892 he managed, despite Angelo's poor showing at Celana, to have him accepted at a seminary in Bergamo, near Milan.

This did not commit Angelo to the priesthood, but Giovanni knew what path his boy would take. "He's the son of a poor farmer," he said. "He'll become an impoverished priest." But, much as most fathers look forward to the help of their firstborn son in the fields, he gave his assent.

Thanks to Don Francesco's intercession, the brother of the Roncallis' landlord agreed to help pay the tuition. But Marianna said that a boy so far from home needed a few lire in his pocket. She and Giovanni had nothing. Their family had grown to 12, and whenever there was any cash it went for shoes or a warm coat. So she set out one morning to petition each of her relatives for a little money. When she returned, she sagged down at the kitchen table, weeping bitterly.

"What is it, Mama?" Angelo asked.

Unable to speak, she shook open her worn purse. Some small coins clattered onto the table. They added up to two lire—about 40 cents.

With that sum, and a heart full of youthful hope, Angelo Roncalli, almost 11 years old, set out to become a priest.

2. THE SEMINARY

BERGAMO, THOUGH ONLY EIGHT MILES from Sotto il Monte, was another world, pulsing with urbanity and life. Its shops were full of finery such as a country boy hadn't even imagined, and peering into the cafés he saw coolly elegant men and women who bore no resemblance to anyone he had ever known.

At the seminary Angelo had trouble with science and mathematics. He read widely in history and theology, however, and while other boys were undone by the rigorous routine—the long hours of study and devotions beginning at six every morning—young Roncalli's peasant stamina saw him through. At the end of two years his grades were satisfactory, if unspectacular.

In the spring of 1895, 13-year-old Angelo acquired a notebook with a stiff black cover. On the inside front cover he wrote a Latin motto: "Faults which are trifles in the mouths of lay people are blasphemies in the mouths of priests." Then he copied out a long list of precepts he meant to follow each day: "Devote at least a quarter-hour to mental prayer before you get out of bed." "Beware of praising yourself and of wishing to be esteemed more than, or even as much as, others."

These were the first entries in a spiritual diary that Angelo Roncalli would keep faithfully for the rest of his life. Wherever he went, it went with him. He came to call it his journal, the journal of a soul, and it grew eventually to 38 notebooks and folders.

In those early entries, it is not hard to see the stocky, dark-eyed boy earnestly scolding himself, struggling against countless misdemeanors:

"I will be less of a chatterbox during recreation and will not let myself become too merry."

"I must not doze during meditation, as I did this morning."

"Another thing—I am really very greedy about fruit."

He cautioned himself about the temptations of the opposite sex: "As regards purity, I do not have any strong temptation contrary to this virtue—yet I must confess that I have two eyes in my head which want to look at more than they should."

He was happy in Bergamo. His mind was stirred, his spirit uplifted, and he moved purposefully past the milestones. At 14 he received the sacred tonsure, a ceremonial shaving of the head which at that time signified admission to the ecclesiastical state. Three years later he took minor orders. Suddenly he was absorbed in his studies. His scholastic record, once indifferent, now put him near the top of his class.

The diocese of Bergamo had long maintained places at a papal college in Rome, the Apollinare, for its most promising seminary students. In 1900, three were chosen, among them Angelo Roncalli. He arrived in Rome in the dark of a winter dawn. The Apollinare looked forbidding, a gloomy stone building turned gray by the centuries. His room had a single barred window, high on the wall. The ancient stone floor never seemed quite dry. Yet in his first letter home he wrote:

"I could never have imagined I would be so fortunate. The food here is different: we live like lords!"

At the end of his first year in Rome, his studies were interrupted. The Italian government, antagonistic toward the Church, did not exempt seminarians from military service. So in November 1901, Roncalli had to present himself for duty in Bergamo with the 73rd Infantry Regiment of the Lombardy Brigade. He dutifully served a year and was discharged as a sergeant.

Back at the Apollinare, Angelo lost himself in study and prayer. His investiture as a priest was not far off. "What shall become of me?" he wrote. "Shall I become a good theologian, or just a simple country priest? What does all this matter to me? . . . After all, it is easy for Jesus to scatter to the four winds my dream of cutting a brilliant figure in the eyes of the world."

This idea that his aspirations were too worldly continued to trouble him. He feared that even his zest for learning, and wanting to do well on his examinations, were sins of pride. "Mind and memory are gifts from God," he wrote in his journal. "Why should I lose heart if others have more of these gifts than I?"

Ordained a priest in August 1904, he started for home, and finally on August 15, the Feast of the Assumption, was back in Sotto il Monte. "I count that day among the happiest of my life," he wrote.

The weathered little church where he had been baptized 23 years before was crowded with Roncalli relatives, expectant and proud, dressed in somber Sunday black despite the summer heat. After the Mass, Don Angelo preached his first sermon. "Dear brothers," he said, "my dear real brothers . . ." There was open weeping, and at one point the young priest himself became a little undone, and his voice broke.

Afterward they swarmed around him with congratulations. An elder offered the traditional commendation to a new priest: "Now you must work hard and become Pope." They both laughed.

SOON HE WAS OFFERED THE POST of secretary to the new Bishop of Bergamo, Msgr. Giacomo Maria Radini-Tedeschi. The appointment had an incalculable impact on the young priest and on the distant future of the Church. The two men could not have been more dissimilar. Radini-Tedeschi was of the nobility, a tall regal man, gifted with grace and great eloquence. Roncalli, of poor peasant stock, was a head shorter, already inclining to stoutness. His Italian still rang with the jarring accents of the Lombard country people.

They had hardly settled in Bergamo when they were off on a series of canonical visits to holy sites in Italy and France. Later they also visited Spain, Palestine, Germany, Austria, Hungary, Poland and Switzerland. Soon Don Angelo was at ease in the French language and had come to know a goodly number of foreign prelates.

At Bergamo he found himself in the very mainstream of the Church. To the ecclesiastical palace, to confer with the bishop, came the churchmen and lay leaders of a resurgent Catholic social movement. The question was how deeply the Church should become involved in wholly temporal matters—especially in the adversities wrought by the Industrial Revolution. Poverty and deprivation, some said, were God's will. But certain activists, Monsignor Radini-Tedeschi among them, believed otherwise. The struggle for social justice, they held, was an indivisible part of the Christian ethic.

Thus in the very beginning of his priesthood, Don Angelo was exposed to a stimulating ferment of ideas and to their practical applications. And later he would call the bishop "the polar star of my priesthood."

Together Radini-Tedeschi and Roncalli organized an emigration office, to assist the thousands of Italians going to foreign countries in search of employment. Then the monsignor turned his attention to the needs of working women—first high-ranking churchman in all Italy to do so. He created the League of Women Workers, the Association for the Protection of Young Women and, perhaps most important, the

Cassa di Maternita, which provided a broad range of assistance to expectant mothers and the newborn.

In 1909 there was a strike at the textile factory in Ranica, just outside Bergamo. The workers wanted a reduction in the 63-hour workweek and an increase in wages. As the strike stretched into weeks, Radini-Tedeschi and Don Angelo pledged money to a relief fund, organized soup kitchens and assisted strikers' families. The bishop's open advocacy of the workers' cause inflamed the opposition, and Roncalli noted: "Less than benevolent reports were sent off to his superiors in Rome."

The strike ended after 50 days, with the employers acknowledging defeat. Bishop Radini-Tedeschi was vindicated. He received a handwritten letter from the Pope. "We cannot disapprove of what you have thought prudent to do," said the Holy Father, "since you are fully acquainted with the place, the persons involved and the circumstances."

Prudent. It was a word greatly emphasized within the Catholic clergy, and now Angelo Roncalli understood it more clearly. "Prudent," Radini-Tedeschi said, holding out the Pope's letter. "As I have told you many times, prudence doesn't mean doing nothing. It means to act, and to act well."

Then came World War I. Italy declared war on Austria-Hungary in May 1915, and the next day Roncalli was called up. He was assigned to the military hospital in Bergamo.

To the north, Italian divisions commenced a drive against the Austrians on a narrow front that gave onto the southern slopes of the Alps. It was back-breaking terrain, the way always upward, with mud and rock underfoot, and later snow, and the Austrian artillery raining death from above. On the eastern front, conditions were no better. In the first eight months of fighting the Italians suffered 66,000 killed and 190,000 wounded or missing. Over the next 18 months they made only pathetic gains from the enemy at the cost of hundreds of thousands of men.

Bergamo became a major receiving center for the unending stream of casualties. Sergeant Roncalli served as both medical orderly and priest, and rarely slept more than five hours a night during this time.

In October 1917, the Austrians, reinforced by seven German divisions, launched an offensive to break the bitter stalemate. Within days that powerful force had torn the front open, and the shattered Italian armies began a headlong retreat. Only the quick dispatch of the French and British reinforcements from the Western Front enabled the Italians to regroup and hold, but they suffered 70,000 killed and wounded, and 290,000 taken prisoner.

Battle victims overflowed every facility in Bergamo and had to be carried to the almshouse and several public buildings. There they lay on the floor, waiting for one of the meager number of overworked doctors or nurses. Among them, often working all night, went Roncalli and a cluster of aides, bringing what medical help he could.

Years later, Roncalli would say, "I thank God that I served as a sergeant and army chaplain in the first World War. How much I learned about the human heart during this time, how much experience I gained, what grace I received." But at the time, his sensitive spirit was sickened by the brutality and waste.

Two qualities invariably characterized Roncalli's ministry: great warmth, and a deep concern for his parishioners. Always aware of his ambition to succeed, he still ignored Church politics and directed his attention to the people. It was fortunate he was able to do so; because for 20 years following the war he was assigned to the backwaters of the Church—first to Bulgaria, which had only 50,000 Roman Catholics, then to Turkey, which had even fewer.

In 1925, when he had been in Bulgaria scarcely three weeks, Roncalli set out on a tour that took him to each of the Catholic enclaves. He journeyed through the land all that spring and summer, and encouraged the saying of prayers in Bulgarian. In an automobile he bounced along mountainous sun-seared tracks meant for goats, and when the car could go no farther he climbed onto a spavined mare. He was now nearly 45 years old and accustomed to a less rigorous life, but there was no other way to reach these isolated communities and come to know the local priests.

Wherever he went, people poured from huts and simple stone houses: sheepherders, peasants, refugees, all astonished that so exalted a personage—he was a bishop now—would have crossed the mountains to see them. In fact, not in centuries had Rome sent to inquire after this isolated handful who clung to the faith.

As a result of his travels he made many constructive suggestions, but his ideas brought little action from Rome. "This is a form of mortification and humiliation," he wrote, "that I did not expect."

Whenever there was an opportunity, he attended services conducted by the Eastern Orthodox church, the primary religion in Bulgaria. One day he turned up at the Orthodox monastery of Rila, a shrine outside Sofia. Surprised by the sudden appearance of the Roman bishop, the monks nonetheless politely showed him through the beautiful old church, and were deeply moved when he knelt to pray at their altar.

Someone dubbed him, "The monsignor whose approach is: 'Let us have goodwill for one another.'"

The years slipped by without promotion or encouragement, and he struggled against his frustrations, which were usually rubbed raw in the course of his periodic visits to Rome. Once, he uncharacteristically revealed the depth of his feelings in a letter to his sisters: "I must tell you that I was glad to get away from Rome where the sight of so much petty meanness got on my nerves. Everyone is busy maneuvering for a career. Ah! How wretched a priestly life becomes when one is more anxious for one's own comfort than for the glory of the Lord."

Throughout his 20-year sojourn in the Balkans, Roncalli's letters home reveal him more sharply than do the biographers' portraits. Shining through them are the humor and gentle wisdom by which all the world would someday know him. Thus, writing one Christmas that he planned to celebrate the Solemn Mass with the Capuchin Fathers, he said, "I hope to preach in Bulgarian"; then added, poking fun at himself, "the sermon will be short." In 1934 he was reassigned to Istanbul, a post even farther removed from Rome. However, his new responsibilities included the small Roman Catholic population of Greece, and this soon became a vital constituency.

WITH THE RISE OF ADOLF HITLER, skies were beginning to darken over Europe. In October 1940, Italy invaded Greece, followed by massive German reinforcements. In April 1941, the Greek army capitulated, and during the years of occupation over 400,000 Greeks perished and homeless millions wandered, starving, through the ruined land.

Roncalli visited Greece several times in 1941–42 and, with funds provided by the Vatican, established a few food depots. Still, in that terrible winter, a thousand people were dying every day from hunger. The British had blockaded Greek ports so that supplies would not reach the Germans and Italians. Roncalli's intercession with both sides, Allied and Axis, helped to work out an agreement, and shiploads of provisions began coming in—saving hundreds of thousands of lives.

Headquartered in neutral Turkey, Roncalli was also able to save countless Jews from the Nazi terror. His greatest feat came in 1944. Ira Hirschmann, an envoy of President Roosevelt and special representative of the American War Refugee Board, requested an interview with him in Istanbul. Hirschmann, armed with statistics and eyewitness accounts of the Jews' desperate plight in Hungary, pleaded for help. Roncalli asked whether he had any direct contacts with the Hungarian

Jews. Hirschmann did. Whereupon Roncalli proposed a plan worthy of the years he had spent in intrigue-ridden Turkey.

He had heard that certain nuns in Budapest had given baptismal certificates to some Jews, mainly children, and that the Nazis had left these certificate holders unmolested. Now, said Roncalli, he was ready to make available as many such certificates as necessary, without regard to whether the Jews actually received the sacrament or stayed in the Church when the war ended. So Operation Baptism was launched.

In Budapest that autumn and winter, there was virtually no Catholic church where Jews did not find refuge. And when the Russians took the city in February 1945, thousands of Jews had been spared by Roncalli's stratagem and the assistance of the American underground.

3. CARDINAL

LATE IN 1944 CAME THE NEWS that he had been appointed the papal nuncio in Paris, the Vatican's most eminent diplomatic post. It seemed almost unbelievable—he who had never been more than a semi-official papal representative in obscure places, and who at 63 had come to feel that only the grave lay ahead.

Roncalli harbored no illusions about his appointment. A number of more logical candidates for the post had been passed over because they were needed where they were, or because they were *persona non grata* with the provisional president of France, Gen. Charles de Gaulle, for service in countries politically inimical to France. Roncalli himself noted, "When the horses break down, they trot out an ass."

On the first day of the new year, Roncalli presented his credentials to the president at the Elysée Palace. General de Gaulle, towering over the stout little bishop, stood rigid and unsmiling. He had not forgotten Italy's heinous attack on France in 1940, or the Vatican's acquiescence in the German occupation. With a devout prayer for guidance, Roncalli began reading a carefully prepared speech: "With sincere affection I come to this dear nation over which war has passed with all its devastations and destruction . . ."

No one could listen to Roncalli speak, not even the high-flown phrases of diplomacy, without knowing that the words came from his heart. And his French was good. It is said that there was some response, that the General's glare thawed a little.

All his skills and sensibilities, as well as inexhaustible patience, were unsparingly tested during his mission to France in the churning wake of the war. But before long the nunciature on Avenue Président Wilson had become a gathering place for the diplomatic corps, for mainstays of the French cabinet and visiting dignitaries. They came not for the excellent food and wine but because of the nuncio himself. Robert Schuman, French minister of foreign affairs, said, "He is the only man in Paris in whose company one feels the physical sensation of peace."

Complimented once for his adroitness at representing the Vatican's interests, Roncalli said, "I deserve no credit. It is just that my friends in government are accustomed to diplomatic indirection. When they discover that I am telling only the simple truth, they say, 'How clever!'"

He did not believe that God penalized anyone for not being Catholic. He even went so far as to include non-believers in his prayers. And he struck up some remarkable friendships. The Turkish ambassador, coolly aloof in his native country, was free to express his real feelings in Paris. "What we could not do for you, Excellency, in Turkey, we do here in France," he told Roncalli at the very outset. They were particularly close thereafter, Roncalli once referring to the ambassador as "my favorite infidel."

His wit endeared him to everyone. At a diplomatic reception he was engaged in conversation with the Chief Rabbi of Paris. As they started into the dining room, the rabbi said, "After you, Excellency."

"No, no," replied Roncalli, gently steering the rabbi forward. "The Old Testament before the New."

As before, he traveled widely, going to every corner of France, keeping an exhausting schedule. He noted in his diary that he still felt "young, eager, agile and alert." Yet he was increasingly conscious of his age. His parents had died before the war, and he had not been able to leave his post in Turkey to attend their funerals. Now the bishop could again vacation regularly in Sotto il Monte with his large family—brothers, sisters, nephews, nieces. His roots in the stony soil of Lombardy were more precious to him than all the glitter of Paris.

Once he wrote home that the company of kings and princes, statesmen and ecclesiastics, only put him in mind of the "simplicity of our fields." Amid the splendor of the Elysée Palace, he told his brother Zaverio, he had thought of their mother: "It was just as though I could see her, popping out of some corner and saying with her usual simplicity, 'Madonna! Where on earth has my Don Angelo got to?'"

All his life he had sent money to his family, even borrowing to cover their needs. "The bishop may look rich, but is really poor," he said.

"But there is not much satisfaction in doing good if there is no difficulty about it." Although his stoutness was almost a trademark, he ate remarkably little. He had suffered a stomach disorder in Bulgaria and ever since had restricted his diet. His cook in Paris lamented, "For a man who is fat as a curate, he eats like a bird. It must be those books and newspapers he devours that fill him out."

In November 1952, a message arrived from the Vatican: the Patriarch of Venice was incurably ill and the Pope had chosen Roncalli, 71 years old, to replace him when the See became vacant. Two weeks later the Vatican announced that his name was on the list of cardinals soon to be nominated. A month later the ailing monsignor died.

Roncalli received the news of his advancement with typical humility and grace. Writing to a nephew who was studying for the priesthood, he cautioned him against daydreams animated by his uncle's new circumstances: "Even in our prayers we ask for our daily bread, not for tomorrow's trimmings." Then, a few days before the boy was to receive the sacred tonsure, he wrote again: "The Lord blesses dawns and sunsets. You are going forward toward the dawn of your priesthood; I am turned toward the sunset. But we must bless the Lord together as we both draw strength from the same light."

It had long been a privilege of the heads of state of Catholic countries to confer the red biretta on cardinal-nuncios. Roncalli accepted the honor from his good friend Vincent Auriol, then president of France. Roncalli knelt and Auriol stood gazing down on the bent head, then gently put the biretta on it. "I saw his friends weep for joy," he said later. "And I was not ashamed to join them."

The people of Venice welcomed their new patriarch with tumultuous warmth, turning out in every available launch and gondola to meet him. The flotilla then fell into procession behind the vessel carrying Roncalli to the Piazza San Marco and the 1000-year-old basilica, a glory of Byzantine architecture.

The Venetians were delighted with him, and he returned their affection. In his first address he declared, "I have never aspired to any role other than to be a simple pastor in my native Bergamo, but until this day Providence has deemed otherwise. Now that I am a shepherd at last, your shepherd, my first desire is to count the sheep, one by one."

Soon he was the first citizen of the city. The people grew accustomed to seeing his rotund figure striding along the streets looking, except for the red and gold band on his broad-brimmed hat and a flash of red socks beneath the cassock, like an ordinary parish priest. He owned neither a gondola nor a private motor launch, hiring them as needed or, more often, riding the *vaporetto,* the community boat bus. Recognizing their cardinal-patriarch, other passengers bustled to make room. But he wanted them close. "Come and sit by me," he encouraged them. "You pay the same fare as I. Come, we'll talk."

Often, when spring tides flooded the great square in front of St. Mark's, Roncalli cut through a café called the Beer Hall of the Little Lions. At first his appearance signaled an uneasy silence among patrons and proprietor. Then "Want to wet your throat, Eminence?" someone would call out. "No, nor my feet either," was the patriarch's reply as he scurried through.

In retrospect these were probably his happiest days, but in the midst of happiness came sorrow, too. During his years in Venice two of his sisters, Ancilla and Maria, died of cancer. They were the closest members of his family—"we three are like three candles burning on the same altar." Another sister, Teresa, died. A nephew was killed in an accident. A brother, Giovanni, succumbed to an intestinal malignancy.

Death was much in his thoughts. He had ordered a lot of work done on the patriarchal palace, and as the construction dragged on he told the concierge of the building, "You will see, Bruno, when the nest is finally built, the bird will have died."

Yet he worked from 4 a.m. until 10 p.m. and his energy was undiminished. When restoration work on the angel atop the bell tower of St. Mark's was completed, Roncalli climbed the narrow stairway to bless it, his secretary, Loris Capovilla, doggedly following. Teetering on a narrow landing 300 feet high, he leaned out and conferred his blessing. Then —"as long as we are here"—he hoisted himself onto a scaffolding, and blessed the entire city.

Like the Parisians, the Venetians appreciated the Roncalli wit and style. One piercing shaft was directed at the tourists who engulfed Venice in summer and, exposing more bare flesh than they would dream of showing in a church at home, made straight for St. Mark's. "Italy, after all, is not on the equator," said the cardinal. "And even there, lions wear their coats and crocodiles are covered by their valuable hides."

But his stay in Venice—five years—was not long. In October 1958 there were disturbing hints of Pope Pius XII's growing incapacity. As medical reports of the Pontiff's condition became increasingly alarming, each member of the College of Cardinals throughout the world knew he must hold himself in readiness for the journey to Rome.

On the morning of October 9, shortly before dawn, Roncalli was listening to his radio and praying for the man with the gaunt face and good heart who had personally chosen him to be papal nuncio in Paris. Then there was the familiar phrase of the Vatican Radio, *"Laudetur Jesus Christus,"* and a flat, tired voice read a bulletin: "The Supreme Pontiff is dead." Roncalli rose heavily and went alone to his chapel.

He left for Rome on the 12th. Though it was raining, the Venetians had gathered to wish him farewell. There is a last photograph of him standing in the open window of a railroad car, smiling down at his friends on the platform. But there is a certain sadness to the smile, a reflection of the moment, surely, but also of his most private thoughts. The past was behind him now. Ahead lay his ultimate destiny.

Each of the 51 cardinals who entered the Vatican conclave area on October 25 was permitted to bring with him two aides. There was also a small work force—two doctors, a clerical staff, firemen, barbers, plumbers, carpenters and cooks. In all, perhaps 250 people were confined in the sealed-off section of the Apostolic Palace. Roncalli arrived at the Vatican, along with his assistant, Capovilla. The office of the Commandant of the Noble Guard, Cell No. 15, had been designated as his quarters, a small, modestly furnished room.

With the conclave area locked from within and without, the cardinals sat down to a simple meal, then went to their quarters. The following morning, at ten o'clock, they assembled in the Sistine Chapel to begin the voting. Chairs of purple damask were arranged around the walls, a canopy above each one. On the altar stood a silver chalice into which the cardinals would drop their paper ballots and, nearby, a stove in which the ballots would be burned. The lofty vaulted ceiling and the golden light that falls on its frescoes—on Michelangelo's incomparable "Last Judgment" at the end wall—make the chapel eminently appropriate as the place to elect the Supreme Pontiff of the world's 500 million Roman Catholics.

Four ballots were taken on Sunday, and the smoke was black. Monday it was the same. Late that day, the contending forces had reached an impasse. Although a pledge of secrecy surrounds all conclaves, making all supposed inside information mere conjecture, the cardinals were roughly split into two groups: those who tended to oppose change, and those who saw an urgent need for the Church to modernize.

One by one the candidacies of the favorites collapsed. Some of them were considered too rigidly conservative; others too modern or flamboyant. Then a group of French cardinals clustered their vote on someone they had reason to believe amenable to change—Angelo Roncalli.

And they began to win others to their side. Because of the strongly differing views, his advanced age was a factor in favor of his candidacy.

Later, Roncalli would say of that night, "When from certain signs I learned that I might become elected, I placed myself in God's hands." And he went quietly to sleep.

On Tuesday morning the voting still wavered, but Roncalli had gained the votes of moderates as well as a few of the more conservative. That afternoon there was a sense of anticipation in the chapel as the eleventh ballot began, with each of the cardinals saying aloud: "I call to witness Christ the Lord, my judge, that I am electing him who I believe should be elected by God's will." When all had voted, three cardinals read out the name on each ballot as the others kept count. Time after time, the name called out was, "The most reverend Cardinal Roncalli." When they had finished, the Patriarch of Venice had many more than the required 35 votes.

Cardinal Tisserant of France, dean of the Sacred College, walked slowly to where Roncalli sat, pale and silent and, in the midst of all the others, already alone. "Do you accept your election, which has been performed canonically?" he asked.

Roncalli replied, "Listening to your voice 'I tremble and am afraid,' and what I know of my own poorness and insignificance is enough to explain my confusion. But seeing in the votes of my brother cardinals the sign of God's will, I accept the choice they have made."

In the instant he spoke the words "I accept," he became the Pope. Attendants pulled the cords that lowered the canopies over the chairs of the other cardinals to signal that they were no longer his equals.

"My children," he said, "love one another, because this is the greatest commandment of the Lord."

The white zucchetto, or skullcap, was placed on his head and he went alone to the main altar to pray, then to the sacristy to change into papal vestments. Although the official tailors had provided pontifical habits in various sizes, Roncalli's more than 200 pounds defied the largest of them. "I feel trussed up and ready for delivery," he said as an attendant tugged at the cassock.

Summoned by the thunderous applause, he made his way to the balcony of St. Peter's. Then he stepped into the glare of the lights and into the gaze of the whole world.

In Sotto il Monte, the Pope's sister Assunta was out buying bread when the news came over the baker's radio. "My God!" she gasped aloud. "Little Angelo."

Angelo Roncalli also found it hard to believe. "Today they made me Pope," he wrote in his diary, and there welled up in him the black doubt, the inability to grasp so stunning a fact: that he, Angelo Giuseppe Roncalli—"the poor son of Giovanni and Marianna, certainly both good Christians, but so modest and humble!"—was now Pope.

The next morning he said Mass for the cardinals in the Sistine Chapel, then delivered over the Vatican Radio a moving appeal for peace. Later that day his diary notes expressed a plaintive cry for the spiritual support of departed loved ones: "O Mama, O Father, Grandfather Angelo, Uncle Zaverio, where are you? Who brought us to such honor? Pray for me!"

4. SPIRIT OF ECUMENISM

THE VATICAN, ALTHOUGH IT IS the nerve center and beating heart of the Church, is a tiny kingdom of not quite 110 acres. John, who had never lived or worked there before his election, was curious about all of it, and turned up in the most unexpected places.

One day a visitor, lost in the Vatican's maze of corridors and courtyards, wandered into a splendid chamber of mirrored walls. Once he had closed the ornate door behind him, he found himself staring at his own reflection wherever he looked. Then, to his horror, one of the great mirrors slowly swung toward him, and into the room stepped the Pope. Evaluating the situation at a glance, John put a finger to his lips and whispered, "Shh. I'm lost, too."

Immediately he began dispensing with some of the rigorous protocol to which Popes had been heir for centuries. After suffering through a week of solitary meals, and searching all through the Scripture for "whatever it is that requires the Pope to eat alone," he began inviting people to eat with him. It also bothered him to have even his closest aides genuflect every time they came into his presence. He insisted that they limit this to once in the morning and once in the evening.

When he was first carried aloft in the *sedia gestatoria,* the golden throne chair, he looked down on the people below and remarked wistfully, "It's windy up here."

Unlike other 20th century Popes, John made frequent forays beyond the Vatican walls. Every Pope in living memory had worn slippers of red velvet, but they would hardly do for these excursions. So he had a shoemaker fashion a stout leather sole on the papal slippers, and set out to explore the 180 parishes of Rome. The Romans were enchanted. With affectionate reverence they dubbed him "Johnnie Walker."

On the day after Christmas in 1959, he made a memorable visit to the Regina Coeli prison. "You could not come to see me, so I have come to see you," he told the prisoners with a broad smile.

"Viva il Papa!" they yelled back.

When he came to a section reserved for incorrigibles, sealed off from the rest of the prison, he asked that the gate be opened. "Do not bar me from them—they are all children of the Lord." Inside, a convicted murderer knelt and begged, "Can there be forgiveness for such as me?" In answer, John raised the convict and embraced him.

By the end of the first year of his papacy, he had received in audience more than 240,000 people. Before the wife of President John F. Kennedy came, he wondered whether she should be addressed as Madame President. Advised that simply Madame, or Mrs. Kennedy, was proper, he worried the choice around in his mind until she appeared in his doorway. Then he rushed toward her with extended arms and exclaimed, "Jacqueline!"

What he said on such occasions did not matter so much as the glow of his presence. He was interested in everyone, welcomed everyone, not in a detached, protocol-ridden manner, but in a human way.

At the outset, John had no conscious plan to revolutionize the Church, but it was not long before several traditions lay shattered about him. Two weeks after his coronation he announced that he would create 23 new cardinals—stunning news, since the total would exceed the limit of 70 cardinals set in 1586. On his first Good Friday as Supreme Pontiff, John expunged from the traditional prayer the reference to "perfidious Jews and infidels."

He was not a revolutionary, and he stood firm against any impulse to discard 2000 years of dogma and doctrine. But he did believe that the Church needed to be brought into the 20th century. The world had changed. More than a third of mankind was under communist rule. Even in France and Italy, barely one Catholic in three attended Mass with any regularity. Everywhere, commitments to the priesthood were on the decline. Some changes in Church administration and liturgy were obviously needed.

Just three months after his election, John was discussing these matters with Cardinal Tardini. Suddenly, as John later described the moment, "an inspiration sprang up within us as a flower that blooms . . . a Council!" Five days later he proposed to 17 members of the Sacred

College of Cardinals that an Ecumenical Council be convened.

The response was a stony silence. In 1870, at Vatican Council I, the doctrine of papal infallibility had produced a single answer to every question: Rome has spoken; the case is closed. What earthly—or heavenly—purpose could a Council, a summoning of church fathers from all over the world, now serve?

When someone put this question to John, he threw the window of his study open. "We expect the Council to let some fresh air in here."

For him that was enough. He imposed no program—but it soon became quite clear that Vatican Council II was to be a forum free to reexamine almost every aspect of Catholic life. Within the Church, modification of everything from the liturgy to fish on Friday became possible. And in a larger sense, the Church prepared to study itself in the context of a new and bewildering world.

Voices of opposition were soon snapping along Vatican corridors, but John went serenely on his way. When a curial elder protested the impossibility of organizing a Council by 1963, John replied, "Good. Then we will have it in 1962."

Actually, the Council was to be 45 months in preparation. As it progressed, John issued a towering encyclical letter, *Mater et Magistra* (Mother and Teacher), on the subject of Christianity and social progress. It voiced the Church's deep concern for the exploited poor of the industrialized as well as the underdeveloped nations. John had never forgotten the textile workers' strike of 1909, or the moral: "Prudence doesn't mean doing nothing. It means to act, and to act well."

The Council began on October 11, 1962, with a solemn procession of white-robed bishops marching through St. Peter's piazza to the great bronze doors of the largest church in Christendom. Pope John insisted on walking among them. Only a few knew that he was already fatally ill, but the effort was clearly a test of his strength and courage.

After a welcoming sermon, John allowed the Council to proceed without his interference. Quoting Pius IX, he remarked, "There are three periods in a Council: that of the devil, who tries to mix up the papers; that of man, who contributes to the confusion; and that of the Holy Ghost, who clears up everything."

After nearly a month of intense debate, the Council approved certain limited liturgical reforms, among them the right of the bishops to decide whether parts of the Mass could be said in the language of their own countries. The vote was 1922 to 11. It was an emphatic sign that change *was* possible.

The spirit of ecumenism also gained ground. No ringing decrees of universality were proclaimed, but the Council spoke out in the name of "holy liberty," and it was planned that it would convene again in September 1963.

The bishops had come to know each other and their strength. They had dealt a death blow to the creaky dictum, "Rome has spoken; the case is closed." In its place a certain optimism, a divine audacity was in the air, and would haunt the Vatican and inspirit the world.

Some windows, once opened, can never be closed again.

It had begun around the time of his 80th birthday, November 1961. "I notice in my body the beginning of some trouble," he wrote in his journal. "It is not pleasant to think too much about this; but once more I feel prepared for anything."

When he was told by doctors that he had a "gastropathic condition," he smiled and said, "That is because I am Pope. Otherwise you would call it a stomachache." He gave the impression he did not realize the gravity of his illness. But it is hard to believe that a man who had lost a brother and two sisters to cancer would be taken completely unaware by the onset of the disease in his own body.

In October 1962, following a series of tests, the diagnosis became unmistakable: inoperable cancer. His doctor told John that he was suffering from a tumor. "A tumor," the old man repeated, full of concern for his friend. "*Ebbene* (very well)—let God's will be done. But don't worry about me, because my bags are packed. I'm ready to go."

That fall, as the Council weighed the future course of the Church, John had followed its deliberations from his quarters. Although pale and perceptibly weaker, he maintained a regular schedule of audiences and conferences. Now, as winter softened into the final spring of his life, the quest for a just and lasting peace in a world sown with the seeds of its own destruction became his most tormenting concern. On April 11, 1963, he put his name to the *magnum opus* of his pontificate. It was his eighth and last encyclical letter, *Pacem in Terris*—Peace on Earth—the first papal encyclical to be addressed not only to the bishops and Catholic faithful but to "all men of goodwill."

Boldly conceived, it offered a blueprint for a world community in which men of different religious and political persuasions could live in harmony, justice, security and freedom. The New York *Times* labeled it one of the "most profound and all-embracing formulations of the road toward peace that has ever been written."

In May, Pope John was awarded the Balzan Peace Prize. Despite almost constant pain, he insisted on leaving the Vatican the next day to attend the ceremony for other award winners. "Why not?" he said. "What could be finer than for a father to die in the bosom of his assembled children?"

By May 30 what he had reverently spoken of as Sister Death was close at hand. His stomach would tolerate no food, now, and he had to be fed intravenously. That night he suffered a hemorrhage and inflammation of the abdominal lining: peritonitis.

In the morning he lay spent and gaunt, his white-linen nightshirt hanging slackly on his shrunken frame. He gazed out the window at the spring sky. Then he turned his eyes to the crucifix on the wall opposite his bed, placed "so I can see it with the first glimpse in the morning and the last one at night."

He made his confession and received communion and extreme unction. Again and again he whispered the words of Jesus after the Last Supper, "*Ut unum sint* (That they may be one)." Slowly, the room began to fill with cardinals and monsignori, and by evening his family had arrived from Sotto il Monte.

Beyond the bedroom window, television lights swept across the great piazza, packed with people waiting, grieving, many on their knees. And beyond the piazza, the world waited and grieved, too. They had their answer now—he had been a good Pope.

Other Popes had decried war and defended peace, praised virtue and condemned evil. But in the experience of living men, none before John XXIII had ever moved the Church toward the mainstream of human endeavor or welcomed all men and all creeds to the good fight. Even more deeply, the world's millions were caught up with the man who had lived beneath the robes of the Supreme Pontiff of the Universal Church, Bishop of Rome, Vicar of Jesus Christ and Sovereign of Vatican City. To the multitudes, some devout, some disaffected, the peasant face with its undisguised warmth meant more than all the weighty titles, and as Pope John struggled toward death, they mourned with a sense of personal loss.

On Monday, June 3, he lost consciousness for the last time, and lay gulping for air. That evening, Luigi Cardinal Traglia celebrated an outdoor Mass for the thousands in St. Peter's Square. The spring breeze was so soft that the altar candles barely flickered. A little before eight, Cardinal Traglia spoke the traditional words of dismissal, "*Ite, missa est* (Go, the Mass is ended)." At that moment, the man born Angelo Roncalli, and now a candidate for sainthood, took a last breath and died.

In One Era and Out the Other

CONDENSED FROM THE BOOK BY

Sam Levenson

ILLUSTRATED BY TED LEWIN

Sam Levenson was raised in an impoverished Jewish neighborhood in New York City, and he has never forgotten the strict, sometimes harsh, aspects of his early years. But mostly he remembers the funny things that happened to him and to his family.

As a television comedian, Sam Levenson has entertained millions with recitals of these homey anecdotes. *In One Era and Out the Other* is the story of his return to scenes of his youth to reassess, and reaffirm,the values instilled in him then.

Typical of Levenson, it is a tale that blends bittersweet memories with the effervescent humor of a man who loves to laugh—especially at his own jokes. That's because, he says, of a bit of advice from his father: "Never depend on strangers."

1. GROWING UP

On my fifth birthday, Papa said, "Remember, son, if you ever need a helping hand, you'll find one at the end of your arm." So I took my arm by the hand, and off we went to seek my fortune. Show business was the last place I expected to find it.

I almost made it as a child star, but it was not yet to be. My stage debut was in a kindergarten play at Public School 86, Manhattan. It was on the eve of Chanukah that I brought home the glad tidings. "Ma, tomorrow I'm gonna be the last 's' in Merry Christmas."

"Oy," Mama groaned gratefully.

Mama and I dreamed of my becoming a great violinist. We saw me in Carnegie Hall, delivering a brilliant performance to 3500 cheering and swooning Mama Levensons. My brothers found me less inspiring. "Sammy has such a wonderful memory," they said. "He makes the same mistakes over and over again."

They compared me with Heifetz. "A Heifetz he ain't!" They appointed me "company violinist." If company stayed too long, they said to me, "Sammy, play the violin."

As in all my careers (I think I'm now in my fourth), I was a late bloomer in music. In high school I fiddled well enough to earn spending money with my own dance band, Sam's Snazzy Syncopators. But by the time I graduated, the Depression had set in (I never noticed the change), and unemployed symphony men were underbidding me for jobs. I gave up the dream of Carnegie Hall and took up the next dream—college and schoolteaching.

My first class of teen-agers was described by the principal as "a challenge to a young teacher." I found out soon enough what that meant.

"How do you spell 'Levenson,' Levenson?"

"My name is not Levenson. It is *Mr.* Levenson."

"Oh, *'Mr.'* Levenson? You mean you're married?"

The latecomers arrived one by one. "Why are you late?" I asked one. (Only a new teacher does that.)

"I'm not late; the bell is early. This is the earliest I ever came late."

"Why are you late?"

"It was late when I left home."

"Why didn't you start earlier?"

"It was too late to start out earlier."

I met all the challenges so well that the principal moved me to the Guidance Department. My first challenge occurred on the first day of my new assignment. A young girl told me that a friend of hers was "in trouble." She didn't mean her friend had lost her report card.

I was too scared to face this challenge alone, so I talked to the head of the department. She immediately sent for the girl, whom she proceeded to interrogate.

"Is it one of our boys?"

"Yes, ma'am."

"Did you talk to him about the condition you're in, my dear?"

"Yes, ma'am."

"And what did he say?"

"He said, 'I apologize.'"

I used to gather all the school humor I could for the faculty luncheons at which I would "play back" the funny incidents of our academic life. But it never dawned on me that anyone would give me money to be funny until the faculty of a neighboring school offered me $5 to talk to them. After that I went from one luncheon to another. The luncheons provided me with humorous material about luncheons.

"Our only speaker today is Sam Levenson," it was announced on one occasion. "The rest of the program is entertainment."

On another occasion, I was asked to follow two minutes of silence "in memory of our vice president, who passed away this morning. And now for some real laughs from Sam Levenson."

At an end-of-term party, a colleague made me an offer: "Sam, we've got together an all-teachers dance band. We've been booked at a summer resort, and we need a master of ceremonies. It's a real challenge. How about it?"

I agreed. On show nights I filled the interval between acts in front of the curtain with local jokes. I would run off, open the curtain, work the lights, close the curtain, run out, play the violin, tell another joke. By the following year I had an act. I tried it out for a few years, then asked the Board of Education for a leave of absence. My family was stunned.

"You crazy or something? You're gonna quit schoolteaching?"

"Yep, I'm going to seek my fortune in show business."

"But what are we gonna tell the neighbors? Sammy the comedian? For this you went to college?"

Later, I wrote my first book, *Everything But Money.* It did so well that I changed my listing in the Yellow Pages from Comedian to Humorist and raised my fees. I had got the family off the hook. They could now face the neighbors with: "He's a humorist."

Along with Papa's "if you ever need a helping hand" advice, he often threw in, "And, if you want your dream to come true, don't sleep."

Well, my dreams did come true. I met all the challenges, reaped the rewards, and found myself with everything a man could ask for—including an outstanding collection of doubts, misgivings and ambivalences in all sizes.

It's this way. I started out in one era and arrived in another. The trip took half a lifetime. By the time I got to my dream castle at the end of the rainbow, it had been condemned and replaced by something more up-to-date. The times had changed. I'm not sure whether I got here too late for the old world or too soon for the new one. I am hung up between two eras. My hair is getting gray, some of it from aging, some of it from the falling plaster of venerable institutions crumbling over my head. Take, for instance, the institution of money . . .

Having no money to leave me, my parents left, instead, a rich legacy of attitudes toward money. Frugality was not just a good habit; it assured a good life. A frugal boy would become a prosperous man. The American way was to frugal your way up the ladder of success.

You started by collecting rare coins—pennies, for instance. "A penny is a lot of money if you haven't got a cent," Mama said.

In school we learned one kind of arithmetic, at home another. $1 + 1 = 2$ was fine with our teacher, but not good enough for Mama. She demanded to know $1 + 1 = 2$ what? Mama's method was aimed at remedying our poverty by judicious spending. It worked something like this: 1 pair of skates = 12 violin lessons. Cancel out the skates and carry over the lessons.

1 phone call = 1 carfare to a museum
4 movies = 1 shirt
1 bicycle = 10 pairs of eyeglasses
5 ice-cream sodas = 2 pairs of socks

It was a form of reverse budgeting, planning not only for what not to buy but for buying the instead of, which she could not afford not to own. She knew the world would never examine her books, but it would examine her children. (She had only one set of these.)

I must admit that survival through saving sometimes dulled the conscience. If children through the age of five could ride free on the trolley, what father's child would ever turn six?

"When will I be six, Pa?"

"When you get off the trolley."

There were conspiracies of silence between fathers and kids. "You mustn't lie, but you don't have to tell the truth either. Just keep your mouth shut."

"How old are you, son?" the conductor would ask.

No answer.

"How old could he be?" said Papa. "He can't even talk yet."

It was possible to ask Papa for a penny if you had plenty of time to listen to his questions.

"You mean I have to pay you for living with us?"

"You want your inheritance now? You can't wait for me to die?"

Asking was not only unproductive, but in bad taste.

"Just because you asked you're not gonna get."

"Papa, I'm not asking."

"Good. If you're not asking, I guess you don't need it."

Moral support was all Papa could afford to give. "I'd like to go to college," brother Joe said to Papa, and Papa answered, "Somebody's stopping you?" When Jack told Papa he wanted to become a dentist, Papa said, "Good, I could use one."

Papa had never heard of the Horatio Alger superboy hero, that all-American, shoulder-to-the-wheel surmounter of obstacles, so we told him. "He started by shining shoes, Papa, and in one year he made a million dollars."

"A million dollars? He must have used very little polish."

When I got to be a teacher, I was assigned to the neighborhood in which I had spent much of my early life. I was shocked when I walked into the school Lost and Found office for the first time and came upon a treasure of eyeglasses, pens, pencils, purses, sweaters, sneakers, skates, belts, ties—all unclaimed.

According to my puritan Jewish upbringing, dissipation of earthly goods was a sin against man and God. I saw (and, in fact, still see) the luminescent finger of God pointing down at me through a break in the clouds and heard (and still hear) the awful indictment reverberating through the heavens: "Hey you, Sammy. What's that you're throwing away? Wait till I tell your mother! Will you get it!"

We lived not only on borrowed time but on borrowed shoes, sweaters, coats, food.

"Why are you wearing my raincoat?"

"You wouldn't want me to get your suit wet, would you?"

One brother would say, "Look who came in." I would turn my head, and my meatballs would be gone.

When brother Bill's appendix kicked up and he was taken to the hospital in the middle of dinner, we ran after the ambulance shouting, "Bill! Bill! Who gets your strudel?"

When brother David gazed on the immense dinosaur skeleton at the Museum of Natural History his reaction was: "Boy! What a soup Mama could make out of that!"

"Liver for the cat" was a common ruse. Everybody knew it, including the butcher.

"Mr. Butcher, the liver you threw into the order yesterday for the cat was not fresh."

"Did it make the cat sick?"

"Sick! He couldn't go to school for two days!"

But the penny I saved for a rainy day has come upon bad times. The truth is that pennies are hardly worth pinching anymore. And if the doctor tells you you're sound as a dollar, you're really in trouble. In fact, if I had to do it all over again today, I couldn't afford it. I spent years of my life learning how to make ends meet—and now that I have the means, they have moved the ends farther apart.

2. FINANCES

TODAY'S SUPERMARKET IS TOO MUCH for me. I do not believe that "super" equals "superior" or that man became superman in the supermarket. I remember that Mama's groceryman used to add up the bill right on the brown paper bag with a heavy black pencil. The lady would then check his addition, item for item.

"What's this nine cents?"

"I'm sorry, it's a mistake. It's supposed to be a seven."

"So make another mistake and make it a six."

The supermarket cashier clicks off each item on a register. Gears hum and numbers appear on a ticker tape. It comes to about $5 per inch of tape. Before milady can even think, "What's this nine cents for?" she is handed several strips of trading stamps. This act of super-generosity leaves her limp with gratitude. As she goes out, she counts her stamps instead of her change.

Once she gets home she takes stock. "Let's see if I have everything. I got my stamps, my stamp catalogue, the stamp contest forms—now what did I forget? My God! I forgot Georgie!"

"Hello, is this the supermarket? If you have a kid named Georgie around there, send him home."

"Sorry, we don't deliver."

One day I heard the voice of Mama's old groceryman on the check-out line at the supermarket. He seemed to have come back from the dead to speak up for all the meek who have inherited efficiency but lost their democratic right to talk, question, complain or haggle. He had got about halfway home when he realized he had been given the wrong change. He rushed back, went to the end of the line, waited his turn and finally got his chance: "I'm sorry, but you gave me the wrong change."

"When did this happen?"

"About 20 minutes ago."

The check-out man rose to his full national-chain height, pointed imperiously to a sign on the wall and declaimed. "All errors in change must be reported at time of check out or they will not be rectified. Signed: The Management!"

"You mean it's too late?"

"I'm afraid so."

"All right," the groceryman said as he walked out, "too late is too late. I just wanted you to know you gave me three dollars too much."

I REMEMBER MY FIRST ENCOUNTER with the Internal Revenue Service. A man from the government came to Papa's tailor shop to investigate him. Washington could not believe that a man with so many kids could live on so little. We knew that Papa had not evaded the income tax: he and the income had evaded each other.

I saw poor Papa's face go white. I understood (I was in college at the time). Papa had never lost his fear of "government." His memory went back to when government meant czarist officers, cossacks and pogroms. Papers and investigations meant trouble. This man in his dark blue suit (Papa could recognize government cloth), carrying papers was enough to make Papa quiver. But, of course, things had changed. In the old country, Papa had had no alternative but to answer questions. In America he could refuse.

Seeing Papa in his skullcap, the government man turned to me and asked, "Does your father speak English?" I answered simply that I had better act as an interpreter. Papa knew enough English to get along, but he had no intention of getting along with this man. There was no point in explaining Papa's ethnic resistance to giving up his ways for "their" ways. "Let them learn Yiddish! How could anybody live in this country so many years and not know Yiddish?"

The government opened its case with, "How much does your father earn a week?"

Papa never even told Mama. He was going to tell this stranger? Why does *he* have to know how this poor Jew is doing? What business was it of *his?* I translated the question into Yiddish, and got an answer in Yiddish, which I retranslated into English for the government.

"My father says that his worst enemies should earn what he earns."

The investigator tried again: "Ask him how much rent he pays."

I went through the process of translation again, with this result: "My father says the landlord should have so many boils on his neck how much too much he pays."

I could see the beads of sweat collecting on the government's forehead. He stepped outside and checked the number on the door, obviously wondering whether he was in the right place.

"Just one more question, son. Ask your father who owned this store before him."

"Papa, the man wants to know who owned this store before you."

"Tell him some other poor shnook with a house full of loafers."

By the time I turned around to deliver the translation the man was heading for the door mumbling in what sounded like Yiddish. Papa was beaming. He had defended the Bill of Rights.

"It's a good country," Papa said in perfect English.

3. LOVE

MY APPRENTICESHIP FOR MARRIAGE was long and arduous. Like all other normal boys, I started at about the age of six by dipping girls' pigtails into school inkwells, but by the age of 13 I was writing real live love letters, committing myself to climb the highest mountains, swim the deepest rivers and see you Saturday if it doesn't rain. Walking down the street with a girl, however, took courage. It meant you had turned traitor to the gang, and they let you know about it publicly. They lined the sidewalk as you passed.

"Hey, get a load of him! Look who's got a girl!"

They made it clear, from the way they put their hands on their hips and wiggled their elbows and fannies, your masculinity was suspect.

You could always save face by announcing, "It's my cousin." It was permissible for a boy to be seen in the company of a girl cousin. Girl cousins weren't really girls; they were just cousins. They didn't even look like girls; they were neuter. It could work the other way, too. A girl was considered safe with a boy cousin. My mother once ordered me to take Cousin Sophie to a school dance because her date had conked out. "Remember," Sophie warned me when we got there, "if anybody asks you, you're not a cousin, you're a boy. And don't forget, you're not here to enjoy yourself—you're here to dance with me."

From about the age of 18 on, we courted in the damp hallways of tenements, where love radiated more heat than radiators. Our fiery breath sent up clouds of steam, but never enough to defrost us.

We practiced mass courting; privacy was unheard of. Each couple stood wrapped up in themselves about three feet away from the next couple. Non-lovers and other transients maneuvered their way around us, discreetly ignoring our presence. It was not the normal flow of traffic that concerned us; it was the girls' irate fathers. Ten o'clock was curfew time. One second later, a door would be flung open and the voice of Father Time would reverberate through the halls: "It's ten o'clock! Ruthie!" Ruthie cleared out so fast her beau would be left kissing the letter boxes good-night.

For serious romances, the kitchen was set aside as love quarters, a warm place where lovers could cook up large dreams on a small flame, a place where they were allowed to be together, but hardly alone. All around them were beds, beds, beds, occupied by people, people, people—mothers, fathers, brothers, sisters, snoring, moaning, muttering, tossing, but mostly listening, and they let you know they were listening.

"One little kiss, just one kiss."

"Give him a kiss and let's get some sleep around here!"

"How can I ever leave you?"

"How's about a trolley?"

"I'd go through anything for you."

"How's about the door?"

We wooers were used to the heckling. What these wise guys were doing to their sister at their house we were doing to our sister at our house. When my sister Dora walked into the kitchen with a suitor, seven brothers hidden under quilts would sing out the Lohengrin "Wedding March"—*"Ta,* ra, ra, *ra!"* If he kissed her, we passionately kissed the backs of our hands—*chmuck, chmuck, chmuck.*

Papa was the least coöperative of all. Every 15 minutes, like a cuckoo clock, Papa's head would pop out: "What time is it?" followed at intervals with: "He's here yet? . . . He ain't got no home? . . . He's an orphan? . . . Whatsamatter it's so quiet? I don't like so quiet! . . . You're showing him the family pictures? Show him better the gas bills!"

All mothers wanted their children to get married, but they set up a different timetable for each sex. Sons were always asked, "What's your rush?" and daughters, "What are you waiting for?"

Mothers never said they didn't like the girl. "I like that girl, Julius. She's a nice girl, a good girl, a sweet girl, a darling girl, but not for you. There are millions of girls who are for you. She's not one of them."

While in theory he could choose the girl of his heart and she the boy of her heart, custom required that each had to please the hearts of his/her mother/father and brothers/sisters, and relatives/friends on his/her side. The choice was free if ratified by the tribe.

It was not easy for a suitor to suit. If the papa liked him, the mama didn't; if the mama liked him, the papa didn't; if the mama and the papa liked him, the children didn't. By this time it was also possible that he hated their whole gang.

One of the cleverest devices for silencing parental opposition was to label the choice as either "a girl like Mama" or "a boy like Papa." "A girl like Mama" conjured up an image of an immaculate Queen Mother and housekeeper. A "boy like Papa" meant that he could be depended upon to be outwardly grouchy but good, tender and noble on the inside. At least our Papa was. So Dora knew that Papa was joking when he said: "You don't want to get married because you're our only daughter? You don't want to leave Mama to take care of such a large family by herself? Who are we to stand in the way of your happiness? You can take Mama."

It was hard to tell whether the papas and mamas of that era were happily married. The subject was not open for discussion.

"Are you happy, Ma?"

"I got nothing else to think about?"

"Love, shmove!" Papa used to say. "I love blintzes; did I marry one?" The word "love" embarrassed them. It was an unmentionable, like "brassiere," "hernia" and "miscarriage." Not that they didn't believe in love. They felt it, but avoided the precise definition that young people demand.

To Mama, love was not passion or infatuation or compatibility. She had given birth to ten kids without any of those. Love was made up of satisfaction ("Ten kids, thank God, is plenty"), sharing ("If he can take it, I can take it") and optimism ("Worse it couldn't get!").

I knew my parents valued each other, because Papa told me always to listen to Mama and Mama told me always to listen to Papa; because Mama always watched at the window when Papa left for work and whispered to herself about his being "a good man, a learned man—to work so hard in a shop, it's a pity"; because at lunchtime she had me deliver a pot of hot soup two miles in the snow to Papa's shop so "he should know"; because Papa wouldn't spend a penny on himself unless Mama spent on herself. Share and share alike. So the day Mama had all her teeth pulled, Papa bought a suit.

If papas were at all romantic before marriage, they quickly shed "the foolishness" soon after. My father never took my mother out before they were married, and afterward only if they were headed for the maternity hospital, which in Mama's case was often enough to give her rosy cheeks: "If it's nice out, we'll walk. If it's raining, we'll take an umbrella." They had never had a honeymoon.

Every night, after we kids were in bed and supposedly asleep, I could hear Mama and Papa in the kitchen, not making love, no, but reading about it. Papa would read aloud the daily installment of a romantic novel that ran forever in the Yiddish newspaper. He read in a dull, monotonous voice, perhaps to avoid betraying any emotional involvement in the subject matter, while Mama pressed his shirts. The hissing of her iron seemed to become more urgent as the hero pressed his passion on the girl: ". . . and he drew her toward him, looking into the pupils of her wide blue eyes and kissed her on her trembling lips—"

"Again?" said Mama, her iron coming to a dead stop. "He kissed her only yesterday!" Papa took a closer look at the paper and hurled it against the wall. "You're right! It's yesterday's paper!"

The secret of an enduring marriage was no secret. They quarreled. We saw nothing paradoxical about it. Married people exercised their marriages the way babies exercise their lungs by yelling.

Like the sounds of slamming of doors, banging of pots and beating of rugs, the bickering of estranged bedfellows was an accepted household noise. Sometimes it was Mama who talked first: "I don't understand you. Monday you liked fried herring, Tuesday you liked fried herring, Wednesday you liked fried herring, now all of a sudden Thursday you don't like fried herring!"

"Herring! Herring! It's not the herring! It's the last 20 years!"

Sometimes he talked first: "You can always leave me!"

"I'm gonna leave you and make you happy?"

It would seem that our constant exposure to the quarreling might have turned us prematurely cynical. On the contrary, we came to realize that every man and woman has something to say in his or her own defense; that there are not two sides to an argument, but dozens; that one of the reasons God said, "Thou Shalt Not Kill," was that you might not yet have heard all sides of the story; that in human relations there is no perfect and final answer; that the dialogue, whispered or shouted, is eternal, and that the seeking of the answer is the answer.

4. FOR LIFE!

I WAS 25 YEARS OLD before I had both job enough and courage enough to propose to Esther: "Marry me and you'll make me the happiest man on Saratoga Avenue." She came back with: "Sam, I've already been asked."

My heart fell. "You have? By whom?"

"By my mother and father—lots of times. I was just waiting for somebody besides them to ask me."

Our wedding was on December 27. The ceremony started late, but the crying started early. It was traditional to cry at joyous occasions, especially for women. Mostly the tears came from a disbelief in the possibility of pure joy in human life, a belief, in fact, that life and death are one. Besides, they loved us. What better way to show love than to cry, not near us, but on us, unashamedly letting their hot teardrops run down our necks—literally pouring affection upon us. What's a wedding without tears? A dehydrated affair at best.

Everybody participated in the ceremony, either by marching down the aisle or by crying on either side of it. The elders were given the privilege of walking down the aisle first, in twos in the style of the guests in Noah's Ark, a grandpa and a grandma, a father and a mother, an uncle and an aunt. Anybody coming down the aisle was greeted with a mass clearing of sinuses.

The major celebrants of the ritual gathered under a canopy. The rabbi read the marriage certificate first in Aramaic, then in English, welcomed us unto the House of Israel, had me say the Hebrew equivalent of "With this ring I thee wed," told us to go forth and multiply, had me offer to share my worldly goods (my worldly what?) with my bride, had us sip wine from the same goblet and pronounced the ancient priestly blessing upon us: "May the Lord bless you and keep you, may the Lord let his countenance shine upon you and be gracious unto you, and bring you peace."

Then he went on, "O God, full of compassion, Thou who dwellest on high! Grant perfect rest beneath the sheltering wings of Thy presence unto the soul of the departed Rebecca Levenson, who has gone into eternity. Lord of mercy, bring her under the cover of Thy wings, and let her soul be bound up in the bond of eternal life. Amen."

I didn't know whether tradition or Papa had called for it, but there it was, a prayer of mourning for Mama, who was no longer with us. My brothers and sister knew that Mama was the bond that tied us all together. Yet none of us, not even Papa, had the courage to mention the word "Mama" that day. It was Papa who had asked for the prayer. Was it possible that after all these years he was openly declaring his love for Mama, that his public "love-shmove" was only a cover-up for his private embarrassment? I left my bride, walked over to Papa and put my arms around him. He kissed me for the first time in my life, and we broke into tears.

I left Papa still crying, and went back to complete the wedding ceremony which, from this point on, became inaudible because of the mass lamentation in the hall. There was only one more ritual act left for me to perform—to smash a small wineglass under my heel as a reminder again of the fragility of human happiness. I pulverized the glass with one loud scrunch, the drummer hit the cymbal, and joy took over. *Mazel tov!* (Good luck!) *Mazel tov! Mazel tov! . . .*

The musicians caught the beat, and the crowd was off and dancing in the aisle. It was not the young but the old who were the first to kick up their heels, reverting instinctively to the dances of their youth. Off they went in a mad whirl. While the young clapped for them, they polka'd, mazurka'd, czardas'd, waltzed, hora'd or just held on to each other for dear life, for sweet life, for good life, for life, for life!

People are still marrying for better or for worse, for richer or poorer, but not for long. It is still true that lots of people can't live without each other—until they get married. Then they can. "I do" and "Adieu" are running neck and neck.

In fact, for many of our young marriageables, wedlock is on the way out. Even a simple wedding band may cut off the circulation.

Papa said, "love-shmove," but got married. His grandson prefers unbridaled, free-lance love.

He loudly proclaims his affection for girls and his disaffection for marriage. He wants all the fringe benefits, but won't join the union. "I don't want a marriage license," he says (and she nods)—"your hypocritical scrap of paper, the lease you matrimonial slumlords want me to sign so I can live in a decrepit institution unfit for human habitation." (She nods again.) "Either you renovate, remodel or rebuild, or we don't move in." (Nod, nod, nod.)

The new marriage mores seem like home movies of the old ways run off backward. Everybody seems to be backing down the aisle, away from the altar rather than toward it.

"Yes, Mother, we're living together. You wouldn't want us to be dishonest, would you? We love each other. If you love each other and don't live together, that's dishonest. We're not ready to be married; we're only ready to be honest."

Parents who cannot honestly take all this honesty are left with two alternatives: (1) to make a scene, which ends in the child's moving out, or (2) not to make a scene, which also ends in the child's moving out. Then, while the children are away premaritalizing, the parents have a chance to discuss things in the kid's empty bedroom.

"Let's talk it over, darling. They're gonna do it anyhow. If anybody asks us, we'll say they're engaged. If they ask, 'Engaged in what?' we can say they are studying together, sort of cramming for their Wassermann test.

"You never say they are having an affair. That's old-fashioned. They are having a relationship. He's a sort of sleep-in friend. No, we can't call him our son-in-law. He's our friend-in-law."

Patiently, lovingly, mothers plead for tradition while their children beg to bypass it.

"How about a rabbi?"

"Only if he has no religious hang-ups."

"And a ring?"

"Slave symbolism, Mother."

"At least you're going to break the glass!"

"In my bare feet?"

"Are you going on a honeymoon?"

"Yes, to Russia."

"What a coincidence. That's where your grandfather ran away from when he was your age."

Marriage isn't the only institution where mores are changing. In the theater, the classic formula for a three-act play used to be:

Act I: He wants to; she doesn't.

Act II: She wants to; he doesn't.

Act III: They both want to, so they drop the curtain and the audience politely goes home.

In today's theater, he wants to and she wants to before the play starts, but they wait until the curtain goes up, then proceed to do it.

In the old movies, intimations of intimacy were handled with the greatest subtlety. "It" was implied but never shown. If the couple went into the woods and birds began flying madly in circles, that was "it"; a bee drawing honey out of a flower was "it." Two cigarettes left to burn out in an ashtray, or a record that kept playing in the last groove, was "it." Modern camera techniques make imagination unnecessary. The zoom lens can give a loving couple a physical that would take six days at the Mayo Clinic.

When my daughter Emily started to date, we talked about being beautiful. I suggested to her that the truly "beautiful people" are not necessarily in the jet set, the money set or the sex set, but in the soul set. I even suggested several time-tested and inexpensive beauty hints:

For attractive lips, speak words of kindness.

For lovely eyes, seek out the good in people.

For a slim figure, share your food with the hungry.

For beautiful hair, let a child run his fingers through it.

For poise, walk with the knowledge that you never walk alone.

Children today have many more freedoms than I did in my era. They want to "liberate" me, but their conception of freedom is different from mine. Freedom for me means the right to choose to be somewhat less than free, or not free at all, on behalf of some other equally precious human value, such as sacrifice or devotion, given freely for the good of some other person.

On my Bar Mitzvah, I came into my ethical inheritance. I was presented with the rights of manhood. I had to accept these rights in a speech written not by me, nor by my elders, but by tradition:

"I now have the right to do right, to do justice, to do good, to serve humanity, to help the needy, to heal the sick, to look after my country, to strive for peace, to seek after truth, to liberate all mankind from bondage . . ."

As I read, I realized that I had fallen into a moral trap. What rights? These rights were really obligations, commitments, responsibilities. I began to catch on. What tradition was telling me was that responsibilities exercised by all guaranteed the rights of all.

When I finished the speech, I was pelted with little bags of candy. That was the custom. The symbolism was clear. My manhood was going to be full of responsibilities—but they could be sweet.

The "new consciousness" my children's generation talks about is actually ancient. They have rediscovered simplicity, the sanctity of life, nature, peace. They are going back to the past, to the earth, to working with their hands, mastering ancient handicrafts, to small shops and street vending. They give birth naturally, nurse their babies and carry them on their backs. They bake bread and eat organic foods, and, like Grandma, have long lists of edibles that are kosher or not kosher according to the new ecological rules. They are nostalgic for a past they never knew. They have not come to the end but to the very beginning of tradition.

WHILE I WAS WRITING THIS BOOK, our first grandchild arrived—Georgia, daughter of our son, Conrad, and Isabella. When I first heard her cry, I remembered my own firstborn's first night at home with us. He cried all night, and we didn't know what to do about it. Esther read through pages and pages of Dr. Spock, trying to find out what makes babies cry. Esther's mother was standing in the doorway. We wouldn't allow her in the room because she might spread germs. She reluctantly kept her distance but tossed us the best advice on child-rearing we ever had: "Put down the book and pick up the baby." That's just what I am going to do after I finish this little note to Georgia:

Georgia baby: We leave you a tradition with a future. The tender loving care of human beings will never become obsolete. People, even more than things, have to be restored, renewed, revived, reclaimed, and redeemed, and redeemed, and redeemed. . . . Never throw out anybody. Remember, if you ever need a helping hand, you'll find one at the end of your arm. As you grow older, you will discover that you have two hands. One for helping yourself; the other for helping others. While I was growing up, I took as many hands as I gave. I still do.

Your good old days are ahead of you. May you have many of them.

At our age we doubt whether we will make it to your wedding; but if you remember us on that day, we shall surely be there.

Mazel tov!

The Epic Battle That Launched the U.S. Navy

CONDENSED FROM THE BOOK BY

JOHN EVANGELIST WALSH

NIGHT ON FIRE

PAINTING BY JAMES HAMILTON, 1854

John Paul Jones's place on the honor roll of American heroes stems in large part from the thunderous encounter between his ship, the *Bonhomme Richard,* and the British frigate *Serapis.* The 1779 engagement, fought less than three miles from the eastern coast of England and won by the young American captain, was the most spectacular sea battle of the Revolution.

The American victory, and the fierce determination displayed by John Paul Jones, were vital first steps in the transformation of America's puny collection of warships into a force which would later girdle the globe.

John Evangelist Walsh has turned to original sources to re-create, with a vigor Jones himself would have applauded, that furious and crucial engagement. The late historian Samuel Eliot Morison called it "a naval combat the like of which has never been fought before or since."

1. THE CONVOY

STANDING ON THE scrubbed quarterdeck of His Majesty's frigate *Serapis,* Capt. Richard Pearson trained his telescope on the Yorkshire coast, some two miles to starboard. If enemy activity had been reported in these waters, red flags would be flying ashore. Towering above Pearson's head there rose an immense cloud of sail, but the wind, very light, was directly against the *Serapis* and the ship was now on a port tack, heading inshore.

Eight days before, Pearson had departed Christiansund, Denmark, as escort for a convoy of 70 ships, laden mostly with stores for the Royal Navy. It had been an anxious eight days, for he had only one other warship to support him, a lightly armed sloop, the *Countess of Scarborough.* But the passage across the North Sea had been uneventful, with no sign of the Yankee privateersmen who, since the start of the American Revolution, had plagued English waters.

Some five hours before, at daybreak on September 23, 1779, he had made his landfall, and part of the convoy had broken off and turned north for Scotland, leaving Pearson to continue south for London with 41 vessels in his care. Depending on the winds, the capital was still about three days away.

By 11 a.m. the foremost ships of the strung-out convoy were starting to come up on jutting Flamborough Head, a lofty chalk promontory on the British coast. It was about this time that Pearson's telescope picked up the mottled gray ramparts of ancient Scarborough Castle, just north of the Head, and he quickly spotted the large red flag waving from a staff. In the waters below the castle a small cutter, also flying a red flag, was setting out. Within a half hour, after threading its way through the convoy, the boat was alongside.

On deck, a messenger presented a letter from the bailiff of Scarborough. Reading it, Pearson saw in dismay that his arrival home could not have been more badly timed. The American raider, John Paul Jones, was reported to be cruising the English coast with at least four ships, three of them large.

Captain Pearson did not have to inquire who John Paul Jones was. In the last year nearly all of England had become familiar with the name. During one sensational three-day period in April 1778, Jones had engaged in a series of actions round the north of England that had sent a shock through the populace.

First, at the port of Whitehaven, he had personally led a large raiding party ashore at dawn. Holding the townspeople at bay, the raiders had spiked cannon and set fire to shipping, escaping back to their own vessel without a casualty. It had been a very small and brief invasion but it it had been the first time in memory that an enemy had landed with hostile intent on an English shore.

It had brought home to the ordinary British citizen, as nothing else could have done, the reality of the Revolution then raging in the far-off American colonies.

The day after that, Jones had calmly landed another party at St. Mary's Isle in order to kidnap the Earl of Selkirk and hold him hostage for the release of American naval prisoners in English jails. The earl had been absent from home, so Jones's party had confiscated the treasure of the house, 160 pounds of silver plate. Then, incredibly, on the next day, while ships of the Royal Navy were rushing to intercept him, Jones enticed into battle His Majesty's sloop of war *Drake.* After an hour's murderous broadsiding, the Englishman had struck his colors and Jones had sailed serenely away, his hold full of prisoners, the battered sloop his prize.

Since then, in gossip, news accounts and even in street ballads, rumor had shaped a legend around the figure of John Paul Jones, not as an intrepid naval officer but as a hated pirate. Lurid stories were told about his cruelties toward his foes, his ruthlessness toward his own men, his evil visage and his cutthroat heart.

On finishing the bailiff's letter, Pearson did not hesitate. If Jones's rapacious eye should fall on this large convoy, protected only by a frigate and a sloop, there could be no doubt of the action he would take. It was now past noon and the forward ships of the convoy were almost abreast of Flamborough Head.

Pearson gave swift orders: hoist signal flags calling all ships to bear down under the lee of *Serapis*—to get north of their escort—and fire off two guns to reinforce the command. By this time a half-dozen more of the merchantmen were already far south, stretching for the Head, and that meant they would have to come round and run back before the wind. As the sound of the cannon boomed over the water—once, twice—Pearson held his own course southward, awaiting the return of the leaders.

Suddenly, from the two or three lead ships—those that had already begun the long pull round the Head—there came the repeated firing of guns. Peering through his telescope, Pearson saw that these vessels had let fly their topgallant sheets and were frantically tacking in an effort to turn back north.

The alarm, Pearson knew, could mean only one thing: strangers had been sighted. If the unidentified ships were indeed those of Jones, then he must hurry to place the *Serapis* squarely between the Americans and the scurrying convoy.

To increase speed he ordered out all studding sails—hanging at the outer ends of the yardarms on both sides, they made the ship appear almost as if it had wings—then instructed his lieutenant to announce, "Clear ship for action!"

2. CAPTAIN JONES

TWENTY MILES SOUTH-SOUTHWEST of Flamborough Head rode the American armed vessel *Bonhomme Richard* under full sail. Standing on its high poop deck were several officers, each attired in a blue uniform coat, white knee britches and black tricorn hat. The eyes of all were turned south, beyond the *Richard's* bow, fixed on a small brigantine that was straining against the wind a mile or so away. Trailing behind the *Richard* were the other ships of the squadron: frigate *Alliance,* frigate *Pallas* and the *Vengeance,* a small corvette.

For more than two hours, since about 11 that morning, the *Richard* had been chasing the brig, anticipating an easy capture. But the little vessel had repeatedly managed to skip away, frantic to reach safety at the entrance to the Humber River.

In command on the *Richard's* quarterdeck was John Paul Jones. Slightly smaller in stature than the other officers, he was neatly dressed in the same blue-and-white uniform, with extra gold on the buttonholes and piping, and two shoulder epaulets, indicating his rank as commodore of the squadron. At the age of 32, Jones was an impressive figure, with a slim, athletic build and a straight-backed carriage that hinted at unusual stores of energy. Under the tricorn hat the deeply tanned clean-shaven face was lean, the long hair gathered at the back into a queue, sailor fashion.

As the little brig tacked sharply in a last effort at escape, from high in the *Richard's* mainmast a call came from the lookout: "Large ship, standing south round the Head, bearing north-northeast."

Reacting promptly, Jones dispatched a small pilot boat to pursue the brig, while he came round and made north toward the lone sail. He felt, however, no particular relish at the prospect of yet another capture. On this cruise he had already taken numerous prizes, many with valuable cargoes. But, as he was only too well aware, he had not been given his command to seek out single ships, like any common privateer.

Departing from France with an open commission to repeat and, if possible, surpass the sensational deeds of his last year's cruise, he had solemnly promised, as he expressed it, "to go in harm's way," and had vowed to return with laurels, "if I survive." Yet in six weeks of prowling round the British Isles he had accomplished little. And very shortly, in a week at most, John Paul Jones would have to return with his squadron to his base in France.

Impetuous by nature, fretful of control, sharply aware of his superior abilities, Jones welcomed danger, because it was only out of such ultimate hazard that "glory" was born—and he never made a secret of his unbounded thirst for that most elusive of distinctions. It was a dream in which wealth and comfort played no part. "I have never served but for honor," he once proudly insisted. "I have never sought but glory."

Unusual ambition had been a part of Jones's character from his youth. Born in Scotland in 1747, he was the son of John Paul, a gardener. When only 12 years old he went to sea as an apprentice in the West Indies trade, and at 17 he became third mate on a slaver. At 21 he was master of a 60-ton merchantman, and three years later he became both captain and part owner of a large, three-masted square-rigger.

During his decade at sea he had frequently called into American ports, especially in Virginia, where he was able to visit an older brother who had settled at Fredericksburg. Fascinated by the bustling freshness of the colonies, Jones soon decided to follow his brother's lead, and in 1773 he made the move—though under circumstances that are still not clear. This much is known: in the West Indies, at the port of Tobago, where Jones had just arrived with a cargo from England, a violent disturbance arose among his crew. In quelling the riot he ran his sword through the ringleader, killing him. To avoid an inquiry, perhaps also to avoid vengeance from the dead man's friends, he fled Tobago incognito and soon afterward turned up in Virginia with the name of Jones added to the John Paul.

At the start of the Revolution he was among the first to offer himself for the Continental Navy, then a tiny struggling service employing a few old ships, insignificant when compared with England's ocean-dominating, 500-ship fleet. He threw himself into the task of learning, often studying far into the night, and his promotion was rapid. As acting captain of the sloop of war *Providence,* his unique talents were given their first true display. During a six weeks' cruise, in addition to destroying part of the English fishing fleet in Canadian waters, he captured no less than 16 prizes and gave abundant proof of his genius at ship-handling.

In November 1777, he was dispatched to France, and his descents on Whitehaven and St. Mary's Isle, and his capture of the *Drake,* soon made him one of the most talked-about, most sought-after personalities in the court circles of Paris.

FROM THE *Richard's* POOP DECK Captain Jones observed with disgust that the lone ship in sight was no longer continuing southward, but instead appeared to be heading toward land. Long before the *Richard* could come up with her, she would be riding safely at anchor.

Then from aloft there came an excited shout, and Jones's heart soared. "Convoy ahead! Bearing north-northeast, about 15 miles." Ten, a dozen, 20 sails in sight!

His voice now far from soft, Jones started issuing orders. Signal flags were hoisted ordering the squadron into a General Chase. Two guns were shot off to recall the pilot boat, though Jones did not intend to lose precious time waiting.

There was now hardly enough wind to belly the *Richard's* sails, but it was blowing from the southwest, so Jones and his consorts were able to make the most of it. The four ships were running almost due north, with the fast-sailing *Alliance* gradually forging ahead on the *Richard's* starboard. During the first hour's run, more and more sails came into view, until it seemed to the lookout that there must be at least 30 of them.

Jones, with mounting elation, felt certain that he was at last in pursuit of one of England's Baltic convoys. If he could succeed in breaking it up, sending some of the ships to the bottom, taking others as prizes, then he could indeed return to France in triumph. All the frustrations of his six weeks' prowl would be wiped out. There would be an armed escort to encounter, but with two frigates in support, that should present no problem. Among the three, he had at his command over 100 guns. So girded, he headed into one of the fiercest engagements ever fought by two ships under sail.

3. FORMIDABLE FOE

FOR HIS FATEFUL RENDEZVOUS with Jones, Captain Pearson could at least be grateful that he had under him one of the newest and best-equipped frigates in His Majesty's service. Barely six months off the stocks, the *Serapis* was among the first of Britain's warships to be fitted with a copper bottom (the thin plates, nailed on, inhibited marine growth and increased a ship's speed by as much as a knot). Heavily armed for her size, she carried a total of 50 guns, throwing a 300-pound broadside.

On the upper gun deck (just below the open main deck) were 20 9-pounders. Below this, another deck held the main battery, 20 long-barreled 18-pounders. The *Serapis* was thus a two-decker, carrying two full batteries, each of which was protected by having a deck overhead. Lacking the now old-fashioned poop deck, her sleek hull, measuring 140 feet in length and 38 feet in the beam, had been constructed along new lines, increasing her maneuverability.

The *Serapis's* highly trained, well-disciplined crew of more than 300 (including officers and a detachment of Royal Marines), conscious of their navy's long tradition of valor, saw themselves as invincible in any fight on equal terms, standing a fair chance even against heavy odds. One good British tar, ran the confident boast, was worth three Yankee sailors any day.

Even so Captain Pearson was convinced it wouldn't be much of a battle, as he fixed his eyes on the tall sails growing against the slate-colored skies to the south. The three larger vessels were bows-on, concealing their armament, reason enough for suspicion. But assuming the least, Pearson reasoned, each of the large ships might be carrying 15 guns to a side, perhaps a mixture of 9s and 12s. If the enemy formed Line of Battle—one ship behind the other—as he almost certainly would, then the *Serapis* could expect to receive, on a single pass of the Line, the full force of at least 45 cannon, the three ships combined throwing perhaps 500 pounds in weight of metal. In this light breeze, the first pass of the Line might occupy, say, seven or eight minutes, allowing some two minutes for each ship to come up, deliver its broadside and pass on.

To the first ship Pearson could return a full broadside, but he probably would not be able to reload in time to retaliate fully on the second ship. When the third came alongside, the *Serapis's* firepower would have been much reduced, if the American gunners proved at all competent. A second pass by Jones's Line might very well put an end to the battle. The *Countess,* with her small battery of ten 6-pounders on a side, could make little or no difference in the outcome.

Pearson now performed one last act of preparation. He ordered the flagstaff at the ship's stern taken down, with its huge Red Ensign, and called for hammer and nails. When the staff was once more in place on the stern, the Red Ensign ruffling lazily in the slight breeze, word of the Captain's action went through the ship. No man had to ask what it meant. The flag had been nailed to the staff—no surrender.

Yet the situation was not quite as desperate as Pearson thought. The *Bonhomme Richard* squadron had been financed almost entirely by the French, and that fact had created a confused situation in the command structure. Though Jones was commodore, his authority was not absolute. At the insistence of the French, the captains of the two frigates, both of them French naval officers holding special American commissions, had retained some independence—the ships of the squadron, the agreement specified, were associated together by what was termed "common consent."

Even his own ship, the *Bonhomme Richard* (named as a compliment to Benjamin Franklin, then minister to France, whose *Poor Richard's Almanac* was popular among the French), was not quite the vessel he had hoped for. Thirteen years old and built as a merchantman for the East Indian trade, its brine-soaked planks had been worn and weathered by numerous voyages to China. Gunports had been cut in the lower decks to accommodate 14 12-pounders to a side. One deck below this, Jones had improvised, installing six 18-pounders, three to a side. But they were old guns that he had managed to pry loose from the French navy, and he was not happy with their age or their condition.

Moreover, the crew of the *Richard* had been recruited in France, where there existed no regular supply of American sailors, and consequently was polyglot in makeup. At the start of the cruise the working crew had numbered nearly 150 men, about one third American. But this total had been reduced by assignments to the various prizes captured along the way. The effective crew was now, perhaps, 120, plus 20 officers and 10 midshipmen—a number barely adequate in a fight to handle both guns and sails.

Among the non-Americans, there was a large group of English sailors, captured at different times by other vessels, who chose to serve rather than be imprisoned. Jones was not happy about having these men aboard, but they were good hands and little else was available. Most of the remainder was made up of Portuguese volunteers, along with a few from Scotland, Sweden, Norway and the East Indies.

Also aboard was a company of French marines, including 137 men and officers, some 40 apprentice boys, and a number of landsmen, such as clerks, cooks, stewards, coopers and tailors. And deep in the ship's dimly lighted hold, closely confined, were at least 100 English prisoners recently taken off captured vessels.

Making scarcely three knots in the fitful breeze, the *Richard* glided sluggishly ahead, and it was after five o'clock, with graying skies reducing visibility, before Jones was able to count the frigate's armament. Noting her two covered gun decks and her battery of 18-pounders in the lower tier, he finally became aware of the formidable opponent he was rushing to attack.

THE STACCATO ROLL OF WAR DRUMS rattled along the *Richard's* length, and all over the ship men began hurrying to battle stations. Up to the foretop, the fighting platform of the foremast situated some 40 feet above the deck, went 14 men under command of a midshipman. Another mixed force of 20 sailors and marines scrambled up the rigging to the mainmast platform, while yet another midshipman took nine men with him into the mizzen top. A squad of 20 French marines, with muskets and grenades, trooped to its station on the poop deck, other marines dispersed to the forecastle and amidships, while the rest stayed in reserve below.

Lt. Richard Dale, 22, who would command the main battery of 12-pounders, assembled the 70 men of his gun crews on the lower deck. Those who would serve the three big 18-pounders, about 20 men in all, gathered round the chief gunner, one deck below the 12s. The starboard gunports fluttered open and the muzzles of all 17 belowdecks guns slowly emerged through the ship's side as the men hauled on the tackle.

A short time later Jones ordered signal made to his consorts—a combination of blue and yellow flags on all three masts—to form Line of

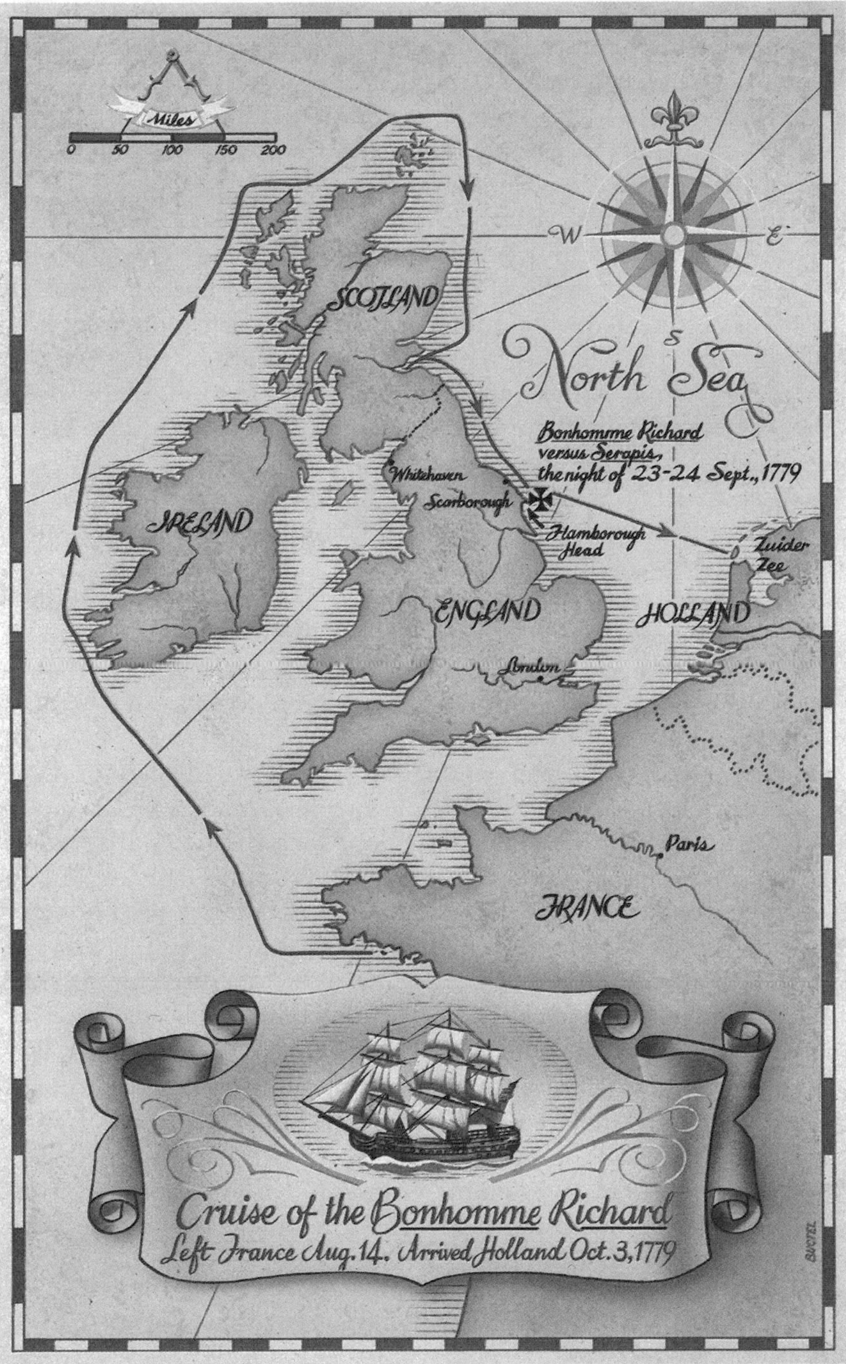
Miles
0 50 100 150 200
W
E
S
SCOTLAND
North Sea
Bonhomme Richard versus Serapis, the night of 23-24 Sept., 1779
Whitehaven
Scarborough
Flamborough Head
Zuider Zee
IRELAND
ENGLAND
HOLLAND
London
Paris
FRANCE
Cruise of the Bonhomme Richard
Left France Aug. 14. Arrived Holland Oct. 3, 1779

Battle. Obediently, the *Pallas* trailed in astern of the *Richard.* The *Alliance,* however, under the command of the French captain, Pierre Landais, instead of falling back to take her position at the rear of *Pallas,* acted in a way for which no one was prepared. She sheered off to the northeast, apparently heading for open water. (*Vengeance,* too small to have a place in the Line, kept her distance.)

Perplexed, his anger rising, Jones saw that Landais had either misunderstood or ignored his signals. Landais had already proved a source of serious discord, never giving wholehearted support to Jones, but there was nothing to be done about the apparent defection in these last critical moments. Then, in deepening consternation, Jones observed that the *Pallas,* too, had begun to drop off astern. In minutes she was out of the Line and had also altered course to the northeast. The *Richard,* within a half mile of its target, was on its own.

Jones wasted no time trying to fathom the motives of the two captains, nor did he give any thought to avoiding the powerful enemy frigate until he could form up his Line again. He would initiate the attack himself, trusting that the others would join in when able. If necessary, he was ready to engage entirely on his own—though it was soon evident to even the rawest seaman aboard the *Richard* that the English ship held superiority not only in firepower but in her sailing qualities as well.

It was now about 7 p.m. and the gap between the two ships was steadily diminishing. In the fast-gathering dusk, land, sea and sky were sweepingly blended in one leaden hue. Along the two hulls the neat rows of square gunports glowed menacingly in the light of lanterns. Low to the north a brightening silver disk rose above the horizon. It would be a harvest moon.

The *Serapis* was sailing west—toward land. Jones took up the same heading. He could have chosen to open the battle on either side of the enemy, but he accepted the weather gauge—to windward—his usual preference in a fight. The position would give him a slight advantage in maneuvering, and the breeze, such as it was, would carry away from his ship the dense clouds of smoke thrown up by the guns.

Both vessels were now pointed straight for Flamborough Head, which lay some three miles distant. As the bow of Jones's ship drew even with the stern of the Englishman's, the two were about 50 yards apart and closing.

Captain Pearson, at his stern rail, noted the scattering of the three strangers—the two frigates far off his stern and standing north, the remaining ship rapidly drawing up—and was puzzled. Perhaps the first two had been sent in pursuit of the convoy, leaving only a single ship to engage the armed escort. But that hardly made sense, since the vessel now bearing down was essentially a one-decker whose main armament appeared to be 12-pounders. Of course, the other ships might easily return, but at the moment it seemed that the engagement was not to commence with a devastating Line of Battle. Or was it possible, after all, that these were not the ships of John Paul Jones? (The *Richard* was flying British colors.)

Pearson spoke to his first lieutenant, John Wright. Raising a speaking trumpet to his mouth and pointing it at the *Richard,* Wright hailed loudly, "What ship is that?"

The answer floated back over the water and was clearly heard: "The *Princess Royal.*"

Again Wright hailed, "Where from?"

In the fading light, Pearson and his officers waited, each man counting the seconds. Aloft on the fighting platforms, crowded along the bulwarks, below at the guns, over 300 other men also waited, straining to listen. But no answer came.

4. THUNDERING GUNS

IT WAS JONES HIMSELF WHO had refused to reply to the inquiry from the *Serapis.* Instead, he gave a midshipman two orders: break out American colors, and commence firing full broadsides.

Seconds later, as American flags blossomed at mainmast and stern, the *Richard's* starboard side erupted. A sharp reverberating roar, echoing over the water, shattered the evening calm as livid flame leaped from the cannon mouths and swirling billows of yellow-gray smoke rose on the breeze. Slowly the rising smoke blended into one large pall and drifted upwind to envelop the target.

Almost at the same moment that the *Richard* fired, the *Serapis's* broadside also thundered out in flame and smoke. Crashing and thudding against the hull, many of the larger shot plunged through the wood and exploded large, jagged splinters into the air, two or three of them blasting ragged holes just at or below the waterline. Throughout the ships, as the tension broke, exulting shouts and howls arose, and here and there, choking, shrieking men crumpled or were hurled, torn and bloodied, to the deck. In the topsails, rips and holes appeared and several of the lines parted and fell snake-like through the night air.

Again the guns of both ships thundered out, again almost simultaneously. Aboard the *Richard,* however, there was a second, echo-like explosion which followed immediately on its broadside—the bursting, on the second discharge, of two of the old 18-pounders. Sprawled on the deck lay a dozen men, some unmoving, others writhing and groaning with their wounds and burns. The devastating force of the blast, it was soon found, had also wrecked part of the deck overhead, dismounting two of the 12-pounders.

Jones unhesitatingly ordered the rest of the 18s abandoned and the ports closed. Though with some effort the remaining 18s could have been trundled across from the port side to replace the damaged ones, he had quickly judged that the risk of another accident with the aged cannon outweighed any possible gain.

Even as Jones was giving his orders, the *Serapis* delivered her third broadside. The shot crashed with devastating accuracy through the bulwarks, tearing up planking and killing and wounding men, especially among the marines on the exposed poop deck. The battle had barely begun, Jones thought, and already the enemy had made his superiority felt.

Looking over his stern, Jones saw that neither of his consorts was making an effort to rejoin. The *Pallas* appeared to be trying to close with the British sloop, but the smaller vessel was maintaining a safe distance. What Captain Landais in the *Alliance* might have in mind, Jones found it hard to discern—at the moment he was contentedly trailing after the *Pallas* as if enjoying an afternoon's excursion.

Jones had two choices. He could retire to a distance and wait for help, or he could boldly carry the fight to the enemy and try to take her by boarding.

To Sailing Master Samuel Stacey, standing close at hand, Jones gave his orders: place the *Richard* alongside the frigate, to starboard, in a position to grapple. They were going to board. To another aide he gave further instructions, to be relayed to the men on the fighting platforms: concentrate fire on the opposing topmen, not on the decks—clear out the enemy's sharpshooters so that the boarders would not be under a rain of musketry and grenades.

At a word from Stacey, the *Richard's* fore and main topsails were backed (turned so that the wind caught their fronts and acted as a brake) and the ship slowly dropped astern of the *Serapis.* Then, a few seconds later, as the English ship was cleared, Stacey called for the sails to be filled again. Her bow swinging to the right, so that the *Serapis's* black-and-yellow hull for a moment lay dead ahead, the *Richard* surged forward. Except for a few muskets, since neither ship could now bring a cannon to bear, all firing had ceased.

What followed was an intricate sailing duel between the two captains. As Jones began to draw up on the *Serapis's* starboard, Captain Pearson turned away; Jones, following him, rammed into his enemy's port side toward the stern.

The angle was such that neither ship's big guns could be brought to bear, and the point of contact was so narrow that Jones could not send over a boarding party.

Jones dropped back. Pearson saw a chance to cross the *Richard's* bow and send devastating fire through the American ship. But this time Jones turned and, as Pearson turned also, the two ships again hit, the *Richard's* bowsprit crashing into the *Serapis's* stern, smashing windows in the rear cabins.

Again the *Richard* backed off, then began slowly to draw abreast of the *Serapis's* port side, much as she had in the initial action.

Captain Pearson, impatient to bring the whole weight of his broadside into action, backed his topgallants in order to check his speed and allow his opponent to come up faster. In a matter of moments, the two ships were abeam with less than 100 feet of water between them. The English gunners, firing at will as fast as they could load, set up a relentless cannonading—a rain of devastation that no ship could bear for long.

On his quarterdeck Jones waited, eyes fixed on the other ship's bow which was still dropping back. Suddenly he felt the breeze freshening. This was an unexpected gift of fate which had come at precisely the right instant. To the sailing master he snapped an order: "Athwart hawse, Mr. Stacey. Lay the enemy on board!" His intention, if sails and helm responded smartly, was to send the *Richard* lengthwise in front of her opponent, able to deliver raking broadsides with the *Serapis* unable to return even one gun.

But the maneuver was carried out with not quite the precision that Jones had intended, and with speed unslackened, the British ship ran heavily into the *Richard's* side toward the stern. Both ships trembled violently in the collision, and high on the *Serapis's* fighting platforms the topmen held tight as the masts swayed wildly. "Well done, my brave lads," shouted Jones to those around him on the quarterdeck. "We have got her now!"

The position of the two ships, however, linked roughly as a broad V, was not the best possible one for the American. It exposed his whole side to the enemy's formidable starboard battery. These guns had not yet been used and the ports were still closed, but it was certain that Pearson was even now giving the order to unlimber them. And the point of contact, as before, was a narrow one, which would make very doubtful any attempt to board. Yet Jones, aware that he might not be given another chance, determined to hang on.

There would be no more backing off for either ship. One or the other must triumph. And if victory was to go to the Englishman, Jones vowed, it would be only with the surface of the North Sea washing over the deck of the *Bonhomme Richard.*

PEARSON'S FIRST MOVE WAS TO BACK his sails in an effort to pull himself free. While confident that he stood at least an equal chance in a hand-to-hand melee, he logically preferred to fight from a position of strength, standing off and cannonading until he had reduced his antagonist to a drifting hulk. But the *Serapis* would not pull clear. She was, apparently, fouled in the other ship's rigging.

Then Pearson noticed something else—the gap between the two ships was diminishing. The wind was pushing him sideways, closing the V. They would soon be touching, side to side.

The *Serapis's* starboard gunports were still unopened when her whole starboard length crunched roughly against the *Richard's* hull. The two floated apart a few feet, then pressed together again. Dozens of grappling hooks leaped out from the American vessel, tumbling and clattering, then catching, on the *Serapis's* bulwarks and in the rigging. Pearson shouted for them to be cast off or the lines cut, but every man who rushed to obey was peppered by musket fire and many fell. Bow to stern, the ships were locked inseparably.

The starboard guns of the English frigate were now primed and ready. But it was found that most of the gunports, blocked by the foe's hull, could not be opened.

Through the bedlam of noise came the shouted command: "Blow off the ports!"

Deep, echoing thunder and biting smoke filled the *Serapis's* gun decks as the 9s and 18s disintegrated their own gunport covers, the shot crashing on through to the *Richard.*

Less than three miles away rose the shadowy eminence of Flamborough Head. Its grassy level now accommodated more than 1000 spectators, and the crowd continued to swell with excited newcomers as news of the extraordinary sea fight, so close to land, spread through the surrounding towns. Congregating on the beaches, piers, any available hill or eminence, all gazed breathlessly through the night at the radiant sulfur cloud that painted the darkness with a myriad of glowing colors. It was now full dark and the glistening track of the harvest moon tinged with shifting silver the mountainous pall of flame-rent smoke that swelled around the combatants.

"Unremitting fury" were the words with which Captain Jones later described the fighting during the first hour or so after the *Serapis* and the *Richard* locked together. The phrase is no exaggeration.

So far, the Englishman had lost only one of the ten big guns in his main battery. He still had six or seven of the 9-pounders in service, and all five of the smaller guns on the open deck. The *Richard* had perhaps a dozen cannon still working, including three topside 9s. Each ship had some 40 men in the tops of her three masts; spread behind the bulwarks, shooting from what cover they could find, were dozens more. Over 500 fighting men were aboard both vessels, and every hand was wielding or serving a weapon.

As yet, Captain Jones had given no order to board. Wary of committing himself too soon, he had decided to hold back until his topmen had cleared both the foe's tops and open main deck. That task, he hoped, would not require too much time, for he was uncertain just how long he could continue to stand up under the massive pounding of the *Serapis's* main battery.

Firing at point-blank range—no more than a foot or two for most of the guns—with every discharge the Englishman's 18s tore away large chunks of the *Richard's* side and mowed down men. The two ships did not sit stationary in the water under this ferocious cannonading. They rolled and shuddered violently with the recoil of the guns, rocking apart for three or four feet. Then they would come together again, sides and gun muzzles bumping.

There was one unique circumstance connected with this stage of the battle that by itself makes vivid the extraordinary heroism the gun crews displayed. In order to position the long-handled sponges and rammers for insertion into the gun mouths, it was necessary to pass the bare end of the nine-foot handle out through the gunport. When the two ships were touching, frequently the outer tip of a handle actually, if momentarily, passed in through one of the enemy gunports opposite.

Even in the heat of battle, Jones had been able to keep the positions of the other ships fixed in his mind. The *Alliance,* he knew, was hove to about a mile off his stern and, along with everyone else on the *Richard,* he was infuriated by Landais's shameful dawdling. The Frenchman's failure to commit his ship, with its fresh 215-man crew and its 18-gun broadside, verged on dereliction of duty. It was with no little sense of relief that Jones now saw that the *Alliance* had begun to move.

Judging by his course, Jones estimated, Landais apparently intended to come up on the Englishman's free side. That approach would require him to sail in a wide semicircle around the two ships, to the north, a time-consuming maneuver. However, once Landais was in place they would have the *Serapis* pinned between them. But no one aboard the *Richard,* Jones least of all, was prepared for what happened next.

As the *Alliance* crossed the interlocked bow and stern of the main antagonists, a row of bright-red flashes suddenly blossomed along her darkened hull. Jones was appalled. A simultaneous raking broadside, fired at that short distance, would hit both ships, doing as much damage to friend as to foe.

A split second later a heavy shower of spreading grapeshot sliced through the *Richard's* bow, cutting down several men. One of these, Master's Mate Joshua Carswell, repeated over and over, while being carried to the cockpit, that he had been hit by American guns.

It was a blunder on Landais's part that would have been unforgivable even in a midshipman, and in his own mind the enraged Jones branded the French captain a coward. He had opened fire from a position that was entirely safe from the *Serapis's* idle port battery, and at a distance well beyond the range of muskets. Something had to be done to warn Landais off. The *Alliance,* however, again surprised everyone by veering north, away from the battle.

There was no leisure, just then, for Jones to worry further about the mad behavior of Landais. From below, two reports reached him which indicated that, for the *Richard,* the situation had become critical.

5. DARING EXPLOIT

LIEUTENANT DALE, DRENCHED in sweat and looking exhausted, appeared on the quarterdeck to announce that every one of the 14 starboard 12s had been disabled. Casualties, moreover, had been high, with about half of the gunners wounded or dead.

The second report came from the chief carpenter, John Gunnison.

Despite unflagging efforts to plug the holes in the ship's bottom, and the constant working of four pumps, the leaks were steadily gaining. Water in the hold was more than four feet deep.

Another three or four feet and the vessel would be in danger of sinking. The English prisoners, close to panic, were demanding to be taken higher or released.

Careful to conceal his anxiety, Jones ordered that the prisoners be left where they were until further notice. Then, sitting wearily on a piece of timber, he pondered whether he had waited too long to send out his boarders. For at last, the enemy's tops seemed to have been cleared; firing from the platforms on all three masts had ceased.

At this point occurred one of those daring exploits whose unforeseeable results would radically alter the tide of battle. A Scot named William Hamilton volunteered to take a bucket of grenades and crawl out along the main yardarm, the tip of which hung over the enemy nearly amidships. From there Hamilton could lob grenades practically straight down. His superior agreed, and the seaman, clutching the heavy bucket in one hand, and with a smoldering slow match clamped between his teeth, inched gingerly along the yardarm on his stomach, his presence hidden from below by the folds of the clewed-up mainsail just underneath.

At the yardarm's end, Hamilton began lighting and dropping the grenades, wherever the drifting shadows indicated there might be a group of men. Soon his eye was caught by a large hatch in the *Serapis's* waist. The cover was lying askew, leaving a corner of the hatchway open to the skies.

Carefully, Hamilton gauged the distance, then released a grenade. It missed the opening and exploded on deck. Lighting another, he tried again. This time the sputtering missile bounced off the combing of the hatch, then fell straight down through the narrow slit and into the darkness below.

Captain Pearson could hardly believe his good fortune. He had been under fire for more than two hours, had inflicted severe punishment on his foe, and still the rest of Jones's squadron had shown no inclination to join in. The single broadside, delivered from a distance by the wandering frigate some ten minutes before, had in fact done little damage to the *Serapis.* And, according to reports, Jones's main battery had been completely destroyed, while the *Serapis* was still working nine of her heavy guns, methodically tearing apart the enemy's hull and bottom.

Against that, the Americans had managed to silence his tops, and had practically cleared the main deck, undoubtedly as a prelude to boarding. But any such attempt, Pearson felt confident, would be quickly repulsed by the force he had in reserve just below.

The question now was how much longer Jones could continue to stand up under the pounding of the 18s. According to everything Pearson had learned during his three decades at sea, the pirate should have struck long ago.

To urge his men to greater effort, Pearson sent Sailing Master William Wheately below to deliver a message of encouragement: the enemy appeared close to surrender; remain cool and aim without haste; a glorious victory was theirs this day.

It was only a few minutes after Wheately's departure that the grenade thrown by Seaman Hamilton came bouncing onto the lower gun deck, the noise of its descent lost in the general uproar. It rolled to rest, its fuse nearly consumed, beside several powder cartridges just behind Gun No. 6. A second later a tremendous roar shook the whole interior of the lower gun deck, from the mainmast aft. An impenetrable pall of gray smoke boiled all along the deck, veiling the carnage among the gun crews. Those who were not killed or badly wounded groped about in a stupor. Unaware of the reason for the catastrophe, they imagined that the ship's powder magazine itself had been hit and that the whole ship was about to go up. A number jumped overboard.

About 40 men had been put out of action. As for the guns, five of the 18s had been lost. Carriages were overturned or smashed to splinters, the guns themselves strewn about as if they were toys. Weighing some two tons apiece, they were impossible to remount, even if the carriages could have been salvaged. That left the *Serapis* with only four heavy cannon, all of them forward.

Captain Pearson, pacing his quarterdeck, was stunned by the sudden worsening of his position. For the first time since the battle began, he was face-to-face with the likelihood that, in fighting on, he might only be fruitlessly increasing his casualties. With his main battery now halved, whenever one of the enemy frigates decided to come down on him, his only humane response would be to surrender.

Aboard the *Richard,* fire was now as much of a threat as the English guns. Men hauled water throughout the ship in tubs, buckets, jugs, anything that was handy. At one point, fire swept up the tar-encrusted rigging of the mainmast, setting ablaze not only the topsails but the fighting platform itself.

6. PREPARE FOR BOARDING

ALMOST EQUALLY THREATENING WAS the condition of the ship's hull, now battered to the point where it seemed miraculous that she was still afloat. Nearly the whole starboard side had been demolished, leaving the interiors of the two gun decks exposed. The shot from the *Serapis,* carrying across the ship, had also beaten out much of the opposite side, so that the shot thrown by her remaining 18s was now being wasted as it sped in at one side and out through the other, touching nothing and splashing into the water hundreds of yards beyond.

In the forward part of the ship, because the *Serapis's* after guns had been silenced, the *Richard* exhibited less damage, and it was here, in the waist and on the forecastle, that Jones was now hurrying back and forth in a feverish effort to prepare his boarders.

A loud exclamation from a nearby seaman brought Jones's head erect, his eyes searching past the *Serapis* and into the night beyond. The *Alliance* was again approaching, this time with her mainsails clewed up as if prepared to enter the fight.

"I now thought the battle at an end," wrote Jones later. The boarding attempt, he decided, would have to be delayed.

Moving slowly under its topsails, the *Alliance* curved south around the two ships, closing to about 50 yards. Then, to the shocked surprise of the watching Americans, her guns boomed out raggedly and a hail of grape and bar shot rained on both ships. As the echoes died away, a score of bellowing voices arose from the *Richard,* all shouting angrily that the damn Frenchman was firing on the wrong ship, and cursing Landais as a coward, a traitor, a madman.

Jones, anticipating that Landais would next cross his bow, sent two midshipmen to the forecastle with speaking trumpets. As the *Alliance,* a few minutes later, began bearing down, both officers shouted Captain Jones's orders to cease firing and go alongside the enemy, prepared for boarding. But as the dark shadow of the frigate swept past, her broadside again thundered out, the shot slicing as before into both ships.

Jones had the wounded taken below, then ordered the boarders formed up once more. There was no more time to waste, he said. Before Landais came on the scene again, the *Serapis* must be taken.

But while the *Alliance* had been creating havoc on the main deck, another drama, of even more threatening proportions, had been developing below. Chief Carpenter Gunnison, after his latest inspection of the hold, had reported anxiously to Lieutenant Dale that the water stood at a depth of nearly seven feet. The English prisoners, convinced that the ship was about to sink, were demanding their release. Dale had left to carry Gunnison's report to Jones, reaching the quarterdeck just about the time the *Alliance* made her second pass.

Within minutes, a dismaying rumor sped among the men belowdecks: both Jones and Dale had been hit, and were dead or dying. Gunnison quickly realized that no one remained who was qualified to command. In such a rare situation, he concluded, the highest-ranking petty officers should take charge.

Gunnison now sought out the ship's master-at-arms, John Burbank, and the chief gunner, Henry Gardner, and assured them that the ship was on the brink of going down. The prisoners must be released, he insisted, so they might save themselves. That meant that the *Richard* must surrender, for it was inconceivable that she could continue the battle with more than 100 of the enemy freely roaming her decks. Henry Gardner agreed; the time had come to strike the colors.

On the forecastle, Jones suddenly became aware of running men, saw others climbing hurriedly out of the hatchways or milling aimlessly on deck, glimpsed a few even leaping overboard. Instantly he knew that the prisoners had either broken free or been released, and that there was now a horde of angry Englishmen running loose on his crippled ship. Before he could take any action, however, he was startled to hear, from the direction of the poop deck, a clamor of voices bawling, "Quarter! Quarter! For God's sake, quarter!" Someone on the *Richard* was frantically offering to surrender!

"What damned rascals are they?" Jones shouted as he raced aft. "Shoot them! Kill them!"

He pulled a pistol from his belt as he ran, forgetting that he had earlier emptied the weapon. Bounding up the ladder onto the poop deck he spotted Gardner waving a lantern over the side and begging at the top of his lungs for "Quarter!" Beside him, also bellowing his willingness to surrender, stood Gunnison.

Happening to look around, Gunnison was shocked to see the captain he thought dead striding across the poop deck, his face a thundercloud. In a sudden panic, Gunnison broke from the railing and scampered down the ladder to the quarterdeck.

Ignoring Gunnison, Jones with great deliberation leveled his pistol at Gardner and pulled the trigger. There was only a click. Gardner turned, saw Jones brandishing the firearm, and he too made a dash for the ladder. Grasping the pistol by its barrel, Jones flung the weapon with all his strength at the fleeing gunner. It flew straight for Gardner's head and crunched dully against the back of his skull. Gardner sprawled on the deck below and lay still.

His fury still shaking him, Jones stood alone on the poop deck. Then a voice, faint but clear, arose from the *Serapis.* It was Captain Pearson, speaking through a trumpet from his quarterdeck.

"Sir, do you ask for quarter?"

Jones could just make out the form of the English captain, not 50 feet away, holding the trumpet.

"No, sir!" he replied loudly. "I do not ask for quarter."

He paused, his tired brain searching for words that would wipe out the distasteful memory of his subordinates' defection, some defiant words that might be hurled as if from a cannon. Raising his head high, he shouted so that every syllable would hit home: "I—have—not—yet—*begun*—to—fight!"

7. CEASE-FIRE

CAPTAIN PEARSON WAS beset by racking doubts. All his training and instincts told him that it was useless to continue the battle. The enemy commander, it appeared, was a man of unyielding will, who seemed ready to send every living soul aboard both ships to the bottom rather than accept defeat. But for Pearson to push the fight to that awful extremity would be an utterly savage waste of life.

He was now, he judged, in a position that left him, whatever happened, without the slightest hope of victory. Even if Jones, by some twist of fate, should be brought to strike his colors, there would still be the two remaining frigates. If only one of the two should engage, then the *Serapis,* severely damaged and bereft of the greater part of her armament, must soon haul down her flag.

Yet there did exist a last chance, even if a slim one, for salvation, and it was that single forlorn hope that now made Pearson hesitate. If the American were to strike, or if the *Serapis* could somehow be wrenched loose from that fanatic death grip, she might be able to make a run for the friendly shore.

Pearson's dilemma was solved for him in an unexpected way. Before they were able to act in concert, the British prisoners aboard the *Richard* had been set to manning the pumps under guard. Now one of them slipped away unnoticed and jumped easily across to the *Serapis.* Escorted hurriedly to Pearson, he insisted that it was only a matter of a very short time until Jones must strike or sink.

His hopes of escape suddenly soaring, Pearson ordered the fire of the 18s increased. He also decided to risk a boarding and sent some 30 men across to the *Richard,* waving pikes and cutlasses. They were met by a disciplined force of double their number, pouncing swiftly out of the shadows. Within a few minutes the Englishmen turned and fled.

Pearson knew that the end had come. To add to his conviction, the *Serapis's* mainmast, which for an hour had been under the remarkably accurate fire of the *Richard's* quarterdeck guns, had finally cracked. Its trembling, 140-foot length now began to tilt to port, away from the foe. It remained upright only by virtue of numerous braces and stays. Thus, even if Pearson could get his ship loose and into open water, there was little hope of reaching shore.

Having made his decision, Pearson wasted no further time. Stepping up to the railing, he lifted his trumpet and shouted: "Sir, I have struck! I ask for quarter!"

Captain Jones heard the call almost without emotion. Glancing at the *Serapis's* stern, he saw that her flag was still flying. "If you have struck," he shouted, "haul down your ensign."

Pearson walked aft, took hold of the fluttering lower edges of the huge flag, then ripped it nail by nail from its staff.

"Cease firing!" Jones called to those around him on the quarterdeck. "She has struck! Send word below."

As quiet gradually settled over the *Richard,* Lieutenant Dale asked Jones's permission to board the *Serapis* and bring Pearson back. This was done, and in the pale-yellow glow of several lanterns the English officer came face-to-face with his foe. They were introduced. Then Pearson removed his sword and held it toward his conqueror.

"Sir, you have fought like a hero," said Jones as he accepted the token of surrender, "and I make no doubt that your sovereign will reward you." He then returned the sword, saying Pearson was welcome to continue wearing it.

VICTORY BROUGHT NO REST for Jones and his men. There were the fires, large and small, still burning fiercely. And there was the steadily deepening water in the hold. In addition, there existed a third peril, only a little less pressing—the warships of the Royal Navy which, as every man aboard the *Richard* fully anticipated, must even then be racing toward Flamborough Head.

Jones sent orders to Lieutenant Dale on the *Serapis* to cut the two ships loose. The *Richard* would proceed easterly under light sail, putting as great a distance as possible between herself and the watching eyes ashore. The *Countess of Scarborough,* which had earlier surrendered to the *Pallas,* and the *Serapis* were to trail behind the *Richard.*

At about 5 a.m. the first murky streaks of light began to seep through the darkness over the eastern horizon; within an hour, Jones saw happily that heavy clouds hung low in the sky, a light fog rolled along the surface of the water, the haze in every direction reducing visibility to a mile or two. Pursuit under such conditions would be difficult.

Through the night the men toiling at the leaks had made little progress. Most were complaining openly that the effort was useless, that the ship was doomed. Half agreeing, yet wanting to return to France on his own quarterdeck, to possess the living proof of the extraordinary nature of the battle and of his victory, Jones gave orders to lighten ship, beginning with the six useless 18-pounders. Meanwhile, he had himself rowed to the *Serapis.* If, finally, the *Richard* must be abandoned, then he would transfer his command to the English vessel.

It was late afternoon when Jones returned to the *Richard* to be informed that it was doubtful whether the ship could ride out the night. The prisoners and wounded must be taken off immediately. Bowing to the inevitable, Jones ordered the evacuation begun. It was just before 8 p.m. when Jones took his last look around the *Richard* and then formally transferred his flag to the *Serapis.* A work party was left aboard to carry out Jones's final orders.

On each of the *Richard's* three masts sails were unfurled, and the jibs and staysails hoisted. All her pennants were run up and a new ensign was affixed at the stern, replacing the one shot off early in the fight. If the gallant old vessel was to be given to the sea, she would go down robed in all her ravaged grandeur.

Midshipman Nathaniel Fanning, performing a last chore, returned to the ship to bring off a box of valuable papers left in Jones's cabin. "I shaped my course for the poor old ship," Fanning recalled, "which was then about a mile from the *Serapis.* Arriving alongside, I found that she was on the point of sinking. Finding our situation very dangerous, we got off about four rods from her, when she fetched a heavy pitch into a sea and a heavy roll, and disappeared instantaneously."

Watching from aboard the *Serapis,* hundreds of men, including many

British, stared fascinated as the stricken vessel rolled under the boiling surface. Gunner John Kilby always afterward remembered that instant as "a most glorious sight!"

From his place on the *Serapis's* quarterdeck, Captain Jones, feeling "inexpressible grief," took his last glimpse of his stout old warship, his heart stirred by the picture of the full-rigged vessel heeling to port and disappearing head foremost, all her pennants snapping in the rush of wind. As the bow submerged, the high poop deck rose up, briefly thrusting the red-white-and-blue ensign toward the sky.

Then the *Bonhomme Richard* was gone, the foaming turbulence gradually calming to a smooth eddy as small birds, crying shrilly, swooped and darted over her grave.

On October 3, ten days after the sinking of the *Bonhomme Richard,* the American squadron reached Holland. Through a combination of bad weather and good fortune, and because a dozen Royal Navy ships had wasted their time in searching along Britain's coast, drawn on by rumors and false leads, the American squadron had never come close to being intercepted.

At his first opportunity, Jones sent a report of his operations to Benjamin Franklin in Paris. In it he accused Captain Landais of "highly criminal" conduct, involving cowardice, dereliction of duty and treason. Franklin, with the concurrence of the French authorities, promptly called Landais to Paris to make his reply in person, as a prelude to a court-martial.

As it turned out, because of other circumstances Landais was never brought to trial. A dearth of American naval officers in France at the time made it necessary to transfer the site of the court-martial to the United States, causing a long delay.

While crossing the Atlantic Ocean in the *Alliance,* Captain Landais apparently became mentally deranged. His behavior toward both crew and passengers, among whom were several American Congressmen, grew steadily more alarming, until there arose actual fears for the safety of the ship.

In a short, bloodless mutiny, arranged and led by the Congressmen, Landais was removed from his post and confined under guard. Afterward, as the result of an official hearing, he was dismissed from the Navy as unfit for command. He spent a good part of his later life denying Jones's charges, grandly claiming to have played the decisive role in the famous battle.

Capt. Richard Pearson did not lose by his defeat. Rather, he became for a while one of England's national heroes. He was returned home in a prisoner exchange in 1780, underwent a court-martial (required of captains who lost their ships), and was found to have acted well and honorably.

John Paul Jones, for his stunning triumph, was invested by Louis XVI as a Chevalier of the *Ordre du Mérite Militaire,* and was also presented with a gold-hilted ceremonial sword by the king. One of France's leading sculptors, Jean-Louis Houdon, was commissioned to do a bust. The U.S. Congress voted him its thanks for a victory "so brilliant as to excite general applause," and later awarded him a special gold medal. George Washington, in a personal letter, assured him he had won "the admiration of all the world."

Yet perhaps it was none of these things that brought Jones his greatest satisfaction. The knowledge that all of America and France, and a good part of Europe, was ringing with his name and deeds must have afforded him a pleasure deeper than that provided by even the most exalted title or medal. He knew, as well as anyone, that an imperishable legend was in the making.

ON HIGH STEEL

CONDENSED FROM THE BOOK BY

MIKE CHERRY

PHOTGRAPH COURTESY
BETHLEHEM STEEL CORPORATION

Ironworkers are the men who erect the steel skeletons of modern buildings. They are not talkative, and usually they don't write books. As a result, although there are about 175,000 ironworkers in the United States, they remain almost invisible to the average person—except occasionally as silhouetted figures perched high on some skyscraper-to-be. Far below, passersby are apt to shiver at what seems to be an utterly fearless disregard of height and of safety—and then go on their way.

Mike Cherry is both an ironworker and a writer. In *On High Steel* he takes the reader behind the plywood barriers and on up the soaring metal towers of some skyscraper in the making, for a look at a trade that is always fascinating and ever dangerous.

1. HIRED

THE SUMMER MY WIFE DIVORCED ME, I went up to Elmira, N.Y., because I didn't know anyone there, and rented a room. July and half of August passed in a daze. I took out a library card, using it a couple of times a week to check out great heaps of science fiction, mysteries, fantasy. There was a pizza shop two blocks from my room, and I stopped there periodically, buying three or four at once. They were stacked in my room and eaten over several days, washed down with warm quarts of beer. I had no refrigerator and didn't care whether the beer was warm or the pizza cold.

By the middle of August I realized I wasn't going back to my job, and spent two days writing a letter of resignation to the school. After nine years, I was through with teaching in general, and math in particular.

At the end of September I was about broke, and started looking for work. It felt strange, at first, being out on the street again, seeing other people, being forced to talk to them. But I began to get used to it, even stopping in from time to time at a bar in the neighborhood.

It was there that I became friendly with a young fellow named Patrick. He was about 28 and insufferably cheerful. He came in every afternoon about a quarter to five. He would burst through the door, stalk to the coat stand to hang up his hard hat and tool belt, leap astride a stool and holler, "Injun whiskey! And quick, for God's sake!" The bartender would bring him two glasses: one filled with tequila, the other with ginger ale.

We gradually became pretty regular drinking partners, and it eventually became clear that Patrick was an ironworker, employed for the moment in erecting the skeleton of a high-rise apartment house down the road.

We were barhopping one night when we came to a gin mill where there were a number of ironworkers whom Patrick knew. We stood at the front of the room with three or four, listening to their stories about their jobs, but Patrick kept glancing at a group of men in the back.

"You want a job?" he asked.

"Doing what?" I said.

"Ironworking."

"I don't know anything about it."

"So what? You can learn, can't you?"

"Yeah, sure. I guess so. . . . But I thought you practically had to be God's nephew to get a book in your union."

"You won't get a book. You'll work on permit. Have another beer. I'll talk to you later."

Patrick closeted himself with one of the men in the rear. They talked for several minutes, Patrick smiling broadly and nodding his head vigorously every so often. Eventually they went to sit at a table, and Patrick motioned me over.

The other man's name was Jack. He seemed about 40, had gray curly hair and no patience with small talk. "Are you a drunk?" he asked.

"No."

"Show up regular?"

"Yes."

"You know anything about the work?"

"No, but I learn . . ." He waved me off.

"You can follow orders, keep yourself safe?"

"Sure."

"Sure? Don't hand me that. Safe is a matter of working at it all the time." He stood up, and Patrick and I followed suit. "I'll put you on because Patrick asked me to and I trust his judgment, so that means you owe him. You understand that, of course." I nodded assent. "Be at the Nicholson shanty at the Frederick Building at 7:30 Tuesday. Nice to meet you." He didn't offer to shake hands. We all nodded at each other briefly, and the man left. (The actual names of persons, companies and places have been changed throughout this story.)

"You are now earning $7.63 an hour," said Patrick.

ON THE 23RD FLOOR OF THE Frederick Building there was a Chicago boom rigged, and my first job as an ironworker was to go out on the sunshade to push it around.

A Chicago boom is simply a pole that sticks out of the side of a building, rather like a fishing pole. It has a line dropping from its end, with a hook on the end, and it is used to raise things.

Its base is pivoted and hinged, so that it can be swung from side to side and tilted from the vertical to nearly horizontal. An engine takes care of moving the boom up or down, and of raising or lowering the load; but swinging the load is done manually. The man who does this takes his title from the system in which a horizontal pipe is attached to the boom. He is the "bullstick man." The "stick" part is self-explanatory; the "bull" part becomes so the moment you try to push. Old hands never tire of telling new men that the only two prerequisites of the ironworking trade are a size-18 shirt and a size-3 hat.

The super (big boss) introduced me to the pusher (little boss) and told him to put me on the bullstick. On the elevator I thought better of asking what a bullstick was. He hadn't seemed overjoyed to get me in his gang. The elevator stopped at 21, and we used stairs to get to 23. On the climb he asked me if it was my first job, and I nodded that it was. He made a face, but said nothing.

We picked our way through giant heaps of machinery and stopped as we came to an outside wall in which the glass was already installed. A short, dark fellow was standing by the window, holding a three button electrical box in one hand and a two-way radio in the other. "Julie," said the pusher, "this is your bullstick man. He's on permit, but he's what you get, so don't bitch." The man shrugged his shoulders.

"C'mere," the pusher said. He dropped to his hands and knees, opened a low casement window and swung himself outside. I followed him and found that we were standing on a panel of sheet-metal louvers some three feet wide, running like a horizontal venetian blind along the length of the building side. I could see down to the street through the slats, and all I could think of was, *What am I doing here?* I grabbed genteelly for the first piece of rigging I could reach. It was a manila line an inch thick, but to me it looked like a thread.

The pusher trotted off down the shades. When he turned and saw what I was holding onto, he jumped back to where I was and yanked the line out of my hands.

"For Chrissake, watch what you hold onto! You got the bitter end of a slipped hitch here; if you put any weight on it, it'll pull out and you'll be holdin' ten feet of slack." He gave the entire sunshade a glance of withering dismissal. "Besides, you don't need to hang onto anything out here. You could roller-skate on this thing!" He jerked the line, and it came free. "That was only a tieback, see?" I said I saw.

The boom, two stories high, was anchored to the base of the louvers a few feet along the wall. "Now, look. When Julie signals you to swing left, stand here and push on this pipe. When you have to swing right, come over here and pull. That's all you do." He gave me a patronizing thump on the helmet, danced along the louvers, ducked in a single motion through the low casement, and was gone.

I stood motionless, examining all the lines for safe holds. Julie's agitated knocking at the window went unheeded until I felt I knew where I could and could not go. Eventually I began to respond, but in spite of his repeated gestures of exasperation, I moved very slowly. I was functioning, but just barely.

That afternoon, when I was changing clothes, Jack came over to ask how things had gone. I said all right. He asked if the height had bothered me. I said no, but by the way how high was it? He said he didn't know exactly, but the floors were unusually high, so it was probably 320 feet, give or take a dozen.

I lay awake most of the night wondering what the hell I was doing and why people like me tell lies about whether or not they are scared.

I STAYED ON THE BOOM for about a week and, although I can't say that I learned to like it, I did get to where I wasn't terrified.

My first insight into the rigidity of union procedures occurred during that week. The boom was being used to lift glass for the glaziers on the 17th floor, but they weren't allowed to handle the whole operation. Control of the machinery that moves the boom and its load is the province of the operating engineers. Julie's bell box—the thing with three buttons—is Julie's, or a brother engineer's, alone. The Chicago boom is erected by ironworkers, and all its functions other than those that are electromechanical belong to them. The glass belongs to the glaziers, who are the only ones with the right to unload it.

I was unaware of all this, or that it mattered, until lunchtime that first day. At 11:15 Julie put his hand in front of his mouth with his fingers toward his nose and flapped them against his thumb. This, I realized, was the signal for lunch. By the time I completed a cautious scramble in from the sunshade, he was gone. I headed down, but found when I got to the shanty that none of the ironworkers were there, except for the super. "What're you doing here?" he demanded.

"I came down for lunch."

"Lunch is at 12."

"But Julie went to lunch."

"He goes at 11:30."
"Then why don't I?"
"Because ironworkers eat at 12."

And that is where the matter remained. Every day Julie and the glaziers started down at 11:25, to be on the ground by 11:30, and I stayed up top until 11:45. They came back at 12:00 and stood around until I got to the top at about 12:45.

Devotion to the literal terms of a union contract is categorically just this blind. It has its origins, however, in the fight for better conditions, and is not likely to lessen. Before the unions developed strength, the employers called all the shots. If the company told a gang to erect iron in the rain, it was erected in the rain. Erection is never a safe job, and in the rain it becomes more hazardous, but a man did it under whatever conditions prevailed, because if he didn't, someone else got his job. (Now, they work in all seasons, hot or cold, but not in the rain.)

In the dark, hungry days of the 1930s, gangs of out-of-work ironworkers hung about on the streets around job sites, so that when a man fell, they would be instantly available to take his place. The pay of a man who fell was stopped at the time of his fall. Today things are better: when a man falls now, his widow is paid for the full day, even if he fell at 8:15 in the morning.

It is also true that at one time one out of every 15 ironworkers was killed within ten years of entering the trade. Illness and accident benefits, union-sponsored life insurance, protection against overly hazardous working conditions—these are the results of constant struggle, and it is not greatly surprising that fights between the various unions over who is to be awarded what kind of work sometimes descend to the picayune. White-collar workers, and to a considerable extent the younger blue-collar workers, have no gut understanding of the incredible bitterness of that struggle, but times of near destitution are well within the memories of the older men.

So, during the days that I pushed that bullstick, the operation stopped at 11:15 and resumed at 12:45. There were on the street a truck driver, his helper and five glaziers. There were, on floor 17, where the glass was being landed, four more men. There was an engineer on top, and there was me. There was an operator for the engine. That's 14 men. The average cost to the company of these men—hourly pay, insurance, maintenance, medical services, bookkeeping—was around $20 per man per hour. It's considerably higher today.

At every lunch I did nothing for the half hour after the others were gone. Ten bucks. Thirteen men waited a half hour daily for my return. Another $130. It comes to $700 a week. There was nothing the least unusual about this loss of time; in fact, it was so slight that no one at any level paid the least attention to it, nor would they have given a damn if told about it.

The super summed it up for me neatly when I asked what I was expected to do between the time the gang went to lunch and the time I went to lunch: "Keep your ass out of the way." So I did.

2. THE BRIDGE

When the job was over, I went to the union hall and waited, along with everybody else whose job had come to an end, or who had got fired or quit.

Jobs out of many locals are to a large extent a matter of patronage and good reputation. Supers' in-laws get work, and good men get work, most of the time. The business agents who run the halls can punish men they feel need punishing, or get even with men who might have opposed them in the previous local elections, by not sending them out. There is less of this in the larger locals than the smaller, but there is always plenty. All locals are under the guidance of the International, but who goes out on what job is much too small a matter for International scrutiny.

So I had my first experience at sitting in the hall. It was a short one, because times were good. I've had some long ones. But this time, in the hour between 7 and 8, nearly everyone was sent out. By 8:30 there were just two of us left. I had about concluded that we must both have leprosy when the B.A. (business agent) stuck his head over the counter and yelled to the other guy, "What're you doin' here, Harry? You get fired up in Utica?"

"Naw," said the one called Harry, who had shiny new teeth in a yellow-leather face. "It was just a bad job."

"You layin' out a lot of drinkin'?"

"I never lost no time to it."

"Awright," the B.A. snorted. "You know Callahan?"

Harry nodded.

"Well, he's takin' out that railroad bridge on Sagamore. Go over there." He wrote on a slip of paper and handed it to Harry, whose thank-yous were cut off as the man yelled at me, "Whadda *you* want?"

It would have seemed entirely appropriate if his squash-like nose had suddenly flipped up to reveal a 105-mm. howitzer swiveling in the bald turret of his head. Everything about him was tank-like.

"A job," I said, trying to sound as guttural as he did.

"I don't know you." He looked at me appraisingly. "Are you an out-of-town book?"

"No, I'm on permit. I just finished up at the Frederick Building. I got the job through Ja . . ."

He waved me off. "I got nuttin' for you."

I was dismissed. He was right; I didn't know anything about ironworking. But once one of the guys had spent five minutes showing me how to work an oxyacetylene torch, and I decided I'd better say so.

"I can burn."

"You can burn," he muttered, sounding exactly like me but an octave or so lower. His gun turret revolved idly about the room. "*What* can you burn?"

"Anything that melts," I said.

We stood facing each other for a moment; then he looked away at the wall clock and finally down at the counter.

"Awright," he growled finally. "Go to this address. Go *burn.*" He wrote something on a slip of paper and handed it to me.

When I got to the parking lot, Harry with the shiny teeth was sitting in his car, drinking from a bottle in a brown paper bag. He called to me as I started by. "Hey, Mac! He send you out?" I nodded, looking at the slip for the first time. "Yes," I said. "I think it's the same place he's sending you."

"I thought so. You got wheels?" I nodded. "Okay, follow me."

We got there at 10:15, and I made my first mistake almost immediately. While dragging a length of torch hose across the ground, I knocked over another man's container of tea. His name was Timmy Shaughnessy, and he began to scream hideously. "You knocked over my iced tea! You knocked over my iced tea!" He was as skinny a man as I've ever seen, about six feet tall with red-gray thinning hair, large hands, and feet like canal boats.

"Well, for crying out loud," I said. "What's the big deal? I'll buy you another one."

"But it was *my* iced tea! Damn it, it was *my* iced tea!"

"What's so special about your iced tea?" I asked, and went over to pick up the plastic cup. I smelled it, then looked at him. He didn't really seem to be angry so much as unstrung. His hands were shaking. I handed him my car keys. "In the trunk," I said, "there's a whole bottle of iced tea. Help yourself."

Timmy went to the car and opened the trunk. When he saw the bottle of vodka he looked around in the gutter until he found an old coffee container. This he wiped out with his bandanna. Then he filled the cup with vodka and carried it back to work. His ill humor vanished immediately, and for the balance of the day both he and Harry went out of their way to help me figure out what I was doing. They were equally attentive to my car.

There were six of us in that gang: Callahan, who was the pusher, Harry, Timmy, two guys I've never seen since and me. As the man who knew the least, I became coffee boy on midmorning and midafternoon coffee breaks. I still have one of my lists, written on the back of a dues receipt. It's about average for that gang's needs: a pint of Schenley, a pint of vodka, a pint of V.O., six cans of beer, two Danish, one English and one coffee—light and sweet.

Technically, there was supposed to be no drinking. Some companies enforce this rule. Some companies make noises but are careful not to look too closely. Some, like the little upstate outfit for whom we were taking down the bridge, ask only that it doesn't show in front of inspectors. Pints were carried in hip pockets and beer was drunk from cans pushed inside gloves, and there was never any trouble. I never saw anybody behave stupidly on the job except Harry, once, and when he did Callahan merely sent him home to sleep it off. It was summer, the work was heavy, and a man using a cutting torch all day long can sweat out a lot of booze.

THE BRIDGE WAS 90 FEET LONG: two 45-foot spans supported in the center by a concrete piling. We worked from one shore to the center for three weeks, then moved the crane to the opposite shore and repeated the operation. The main spans were riveted, multilayer I-beams, five feet from the top flange to the bottom. There were so many rivets—one every four inches—that walking along the top of the beams was like walking on a pebble beach. Joining each of the main spans to its neighbor was a series of smaller beams, three to four feet deep, spaced about every ten feet or so. Over this entire assembly there was a grid of galvanized iron.

The crane operator was a short, hairy Italian named Angie. His machine was a 100-ton P&H with 90 feet of stick. "P&H" is a brand name The "100-ton" part is a size rating, but not a description of lifting capacity. This particular P&H was capable of handling a load of about 12 tons when boomed out far enough from its place on the bank of the canal to reach the pieces we were cutting loose. It was Callahan's responsibility to decidc where we should make those cuts. Cutting the bridge into unnecessarily small pieces would add to the length of time required to complete the job, but cutting loose something too large could put the crane into the canal.

When a section was ready for removal, the signalman would motion for Angie to swing his stick out over the load. Hand signals were used, since an operator cannot hear anything over the noise of his engine. Timmy was ordinarily the signalman: sometimes Harry; sometimes Callahan—but never me. The signalman's responsibility is too great to be taken on by a beginner.

The operator demonstrates his skill in a variety of ways, but most visible are the smoothness with which he gets up and down on a load, the effectiveness with which he damps the lateral motion (once a load begins to swing it keeps on indefinitely if unchecked), and the accuracy with which he can make small changes (he is often asked to move a load up or down distances as short as an inch or two).

The signalman, for his part, must direct the exact placement of the boom prior to the lift and see that the hooks are put in the proper spots for a horizontal pick. He must have some idea of the weight of the load being picked, since this affects the apparent center of gravity. If he puts the hook directly above the center of a heavy load, it will swing out, instead of coming straight up when lifted, because the crane will unavoidably tilt forward as it takes the weight. Knowing how far it will tilt is an important part of the signalman's job. He compensates for the tilt by placing the boom a little back toward the crane. This is called leaving the boom "high."

Callahan made one major gaffe on that job, but since no one was hurt, it didn't really matter. He had decided we could save one lift if we could pick one of the next-to-largest girders in one shot. (On the first side of the bridge we'd cut its twin in two before lifting it, but it had come up very light.) He asked Angie if he thought the P&H could handle it, and Angie said he thought it would be close. He agreed to try it if there were no men nearby: Callahan nodded and said he would make the last cut himself.

When Harry and I had cut away a section of grid from below, and the other men had cut it away from above, and it had been lifted out and put ashore, we all went to work cutting the beams themselves. We left a few inches at the top uncut, so that the beam remained attached at each end by just enough to hold it in place. Then two men walked to the center of the piece and waited for the crane to boom out over them, delivering the chokers. A choker is a length of wire rope with an eye at each end. They were taken off the hook, put in place around the beam, and rehooked. The signalman then had the operator take a careful strain on the piece—a strain, it was hoped, equal to the weight of the thing, so that when cut loose it would go neither up nor down. When the beam was completely free, it was lifted away and landed on shore for cutting into truck-size pieces.

When we tried to do this with the long piece, everything went all right until time to make the last cut. Callahan looked at Angie for his opinion, and Angie simultaneously shook his head and shrugged his shoulders, an indication of a marginal situation. So Callahan grabbed a torch, and called for Timmy.

"I'm gonna cut it from the bank; I don't want the thing to put me in the drink. You hold my legs."

Timmy put down his iced tea and stretched out in the dirt. Callahan got down on his stomach and wriggled downhill toward the beam, with Timmy holding him by the legs. He wisely placed himself somewhat over to one side of the piece, so that if it jumped up it wouldn't get him in the face.

As he finished the cut, the piece jerked up and inward, forcing Callahan to squirm back uphill as fast as he could. Then the piece began to swing outward. With 90 feet of stick above it, its motion was slow, almost stately. But as it moved outward, the back of the crane began to leave the ground—two feet, three feet, until the whole rig was balanced on its toes. I was convinced that everything was going into the canal. Angie still had an option, however. He could drop the load if he didn't wait until past the point of no return. In the end, this is what he did.

The P&H slammed back down on the bank with a noise that sounded as though it were disintegrating. The stick jerked about so wildly that I was sure all the bolts that held its sections together were going to shear at once. But when the dust settled, everything seemed to be still in one piece.

Angie leaned out of his cab, a sour expression splitting his face. "A little heavy, maybe," he said.

We then spent the rest of the afternoon dragging the beam slowly up the canal bank, the end of the crane sticking up in the air whenever there was a major strain taken. Angie seemed to know exactly how far he could push his rig, but he kept his cab door open—ready to jump clear, I guessed.

After the bridge job I spent $2\frac{1}{2}$ weeks in the union hall. When I was sent out again, the job was in a little two-acre industrial park, 30 miles down the road. There were seven buildings, all in the terminal stages of erection. I opened the door of a trailer marked Seneca Construction Company to find Jack sitting on a stool before a drafting table, looking at blueprints.

"Patrick's up on the fourth floor; he'll straighten you out."

"Patrick's here?"

"He's up welding bar joists. You can bum tools from him. Your partner's on permit, too, a kid named Dan. He's even greener than you are, so the both of you be careful." I started to speak, but he waved me off. "After you've seen Patrick, report to your pusher." He looked at his watch, sighed, then glared at me. "I hope you didn't pick up bad habits on your last job. We're behind here, and everybody has to put out. Work, and I'll keep you here as long as I can. Goof off, and I'll throw you out tonight."

The hole the building stood in was only one-story deep, and the columns ran in one piece for four floors from the footings to the roof. The principal horizontal members connecting the columns are called headers. Horizontal members running from one header to another are called beams. On a large building, after the beams are in place, heavy corrugated-iron sheets are spread out and tack-welded in place, wire mesh is spread over the sheets, and three to six inches of concrete are poured on top. On this job, however, the floor support was composed of bar joists—steel trusses welded at either end to the headers. Then the corrugated-iron sheets, called decking, are laid on top.

My partner, Dan, and I laid out bar joists for six days. Through the last two we had a hell of a time keeping ahead of Patrick, who was laying out and tacking decking at top speed and threatening to overrun us. Over a beer one night I asked Patrick if he always worked at such a rate of speed.

"Not exactly," he said reflectively. "I like to go fast, but that ain't the whole thing. This is a bad job. I'd like to get it over with."

"What's the matter with it?"

"It's just a rinky-dink job. The gear is too light. You didn't see the crane we used to set the iron, but you will. They're bringin' it back to set the cooling tower. It's too small, but it's all the company's got."

"Why don't you quit?"

"Can't. Promised Jack if he'd put you on, I'd stay to the end. You don't realize what was being done to you. If you stay with Callahan's gang any length of time, you'll get a rep. They're known as the Drunk Gang. Every one of 'em's lushes, from Callahan down to Timmy, who's a knock-down, drag-out rummy."

"He gets his job done."

"Some job. He used to be a connector. Now he works on the ground, when he works at all. You don't ever want to be in a raising gang if he's in it. At least, I don't. Timmy's scared."

When they brought the crane back, a 30-foot extension jib had been added to the 80-foot stick, so it could reach in far enough beyond the lip of the roof to place the tower. The tower was a cube-shaped frame of light iron about 16 feet square.

Placing the tower where it belonged involved being able to boom out at an extreme angle; and Jack, after an argument with the operator, had us drag over a couple of tons of stuff and hang it off the counterweight. With this additional counterbalancing, the operator agreed to make the lift. Patrick was stationed on the edge of the roof as the signalman, since the final placement of the tower was so far back that it would be out of the operator's sight.

The tower was hooked on, and the crane lifted it until it was nearly "two-blocked"—hoisted as far as it could go. Patrick then extended his arm with his fist clenched and his thumb pointing down. This means "boom out." The operator began easing the boom forward—all of this is ordinary procedure—when his rear-end cats began to leave the ground. He was no Angie, though, and things happened very quickly. The balance point shot past, and the crane continued going over. He let go the load, but it was too late. The boom struck the edge of the roof, bent and collapsed.

In a sequence that no one was ever able to agree on, the rig went over on its nose, the boom folded over the roof, the cooling tower tore through the rear outside header and plunged to the ground, and the cable that had hoisted it snapped.

My partner, Dan, was astride a back header on the third floor, shoving bar joists around to marks I had made. The flying cable snaked in a giant arc, took a turn around a column and whipped him over the side. He fell only 35 feet, but he landed on his head on a pile of rocks that had been removed from the hole. I took one look and threw up.

It is traditional to take up a collection for the family of a man who has been killed. In Dan's case, the money came to $212.

3. PLUMBING-UP

FROM A STRUCTURAL POINT of view, it's too bad buildings aren't made of triangles. A triangle doesn't wiggle. Rectangles do. And that is why there are ironworkers whose job it is to "plumb-up," which was one of the next things I learned. If nobody plumbed-up, all the tall buildings in our cities would lean crazily into each other, their elevators would scrape and bang against the shaft walls, and the glaziers would have to redress all the window glass into parallelograms.

Plumbers-up are responsible, first of all, for making sure the columns are vertical. This is done with a plumb bob (a length of string with a weight on the end), a gauge (a short metal strip with a notch a couple of inches along its length), a rule, and a collection of hooks, clamps, cables and turnbuckles.

One man climbs to the top of whatever portion of the building then exists and lowers the weighted line down to another man on the working floor (generally two stories below). When the line is hanging, the man on top pushes it a known distance from the side of the column by interposing his gauge. The notch receives the line. The man below measures the distance between the line and the column. If the measurements are different, the gang will rig a cable from near the top of the offending column to a spot rather away from the base of the column on the working floor, using their hooks, clamps and a turnbuckle. The turnbuckles are three or four feet long, and the dumbest man in the gang gets the job of doing the turning. He uses his wrench or a stick or a piece of reinforcing rod to turn the buckle round and round, thus shortening the cable and pulling the column over until the pusher decides it is "close enough."

In the end, somehow, what leaned an inch west on the 32nd floor is sucked back east on the 34th, and a column that refused to quit leaning south on 46 can generally be brought over on 48; and by the time the whole job is up, the top is directly over the bottom.

When the gang has finished plumbing-up a floor, or a pair of floors, actually, that part of the building is more or less inflexible. The dozens of cables they have strung have converted the rectangles, or columns and headers, into a series of triangles. These cables will stay in place until the concrete floors have been poured. It always strikes me as amusing to realize, in walking down the canyons of a city, that the giant buildings owe a good part of their verticality to a $1.98 fishing line and an 89-cent rule.

My next job, a hospital addition in Binghamton, N.Y., was an ordinary one (except that I was connecting for the first time), and we put it up in the ordinary way. The excavators dug a hole, the dock builders poured the retaining walls and foundations for our columns, and we stood the first columns, which were three stories tall. When the columns were up, we set the first three floors of horizontal iron. When that was done, we brought in fir slabs and spread them over what was at that point the roof. Then, with the plank floor as a work surface, we used a crane to stand the first of our two derricks.

A derrick is simply a hoisting device, analogous in its setting to a Chicago boom and a crane in theirs. What is unique about a derrick is that it can be used to raise itself. It is made of two principal members: a fixed mast and a movable boom. On this particular derrick, a small one, the mast stood 90 feet high, the boom 80. The boom is hinged to the base of the mast, and is swung toward or away from the mast (called up or down) by shortening or lengthening a cable which runs from the engine drum through the mast head to the boom head. With guy wires to support the mast, the whole affair looks like a giant Maypole.

When the derrick was in place, we were able to reach over the side with it to pick our iron directly from the delivering trucks. When the iron was on the plank floor, we "shook out" (separated the pieces and placed them around the floor in the general areas of their eventual installation) and stood up the columns. The columns were two stories tall, bolted and ultimately welded to the tops of the columns below. When the columns were in place, we set the "intermediate" floor, then the "top" floor. When the top floor was complete, we planked it over. The derrick was then "jumped," that is, raised two floors, by separating the boom from the mast, then "guying off" (temporarily supporting) the boom and using it to raise the mast to the next level. Once the mast is in place, it is used to pull up the boom. From that point, the process was repeated every two stories. It's a procedure which could, from a structural point of view, be carried on more or less indefinitely; steel is wonderfully elastic, its compression strength is truly remarkable, and it is light.

Frank Lloyd Wright some years ago designed a building a mile high. It's never been built and probably never will be—but not because the techniques don't exist. The limiting factors in a building's height are financial and psychological, not structural.

A leading financial consideration is usable volume. Additional floors require additional elevators, and there is no rental return on space occupied by elevator shafts. (The Empire State Building in New York City has seven miles of them.) Past a certain point, one is gaining negligible usable space because more and more of the lower floor space is filled by shaftways.

Psychologically, the public whimsy is beyond computation. "It sways in the wind" was a common criticism of the Empire State, implying that one of these days it is going to blow down. Flexing, of course, is common to all tall buildings. The Empire State has a maximum deflection of only about half an inch, and to detect it in a building that tall requires very sophisticated instruments. It was also said that "lightning will strike it and electrify it." Lightning does strike the building, as it strikes many tall buildings, harmlessly, a dozen or so times a year.

Compared to this giant, our hospital annex was an outhouse. Part of the building was to be but five stories, while a tower would be only 20; and at that, one side would be tied into the mother building.

The erection process, however, was exactly the same. If you saw photographs of the Empire State taken during its construction, you would note derricks virtually identical to the ones we used some 10 years later. We weren't using rivets, and the power for the derrick was updated, but everything else was pretty much the same.

The experience I'd gained at moving about on the iron while plumbing-up was useful when it came to connecting. I think now that I'd have fallen, through clumsiness or fright, without it. But none of it gave me the least clue to how much I'd need Patrick. Connectors get each piece into place and fasten it to the pieces already erected with just enough bolts to keep it there. (Bolters-up finish the job.) That means, of course, that connectors are always working on the highest part of the building.

Patrick spent the first days showing me one thing after another, and often continued his teaching, belligerently, over an end-of-the-day drink. "Damn it, man!" he'd shout, the moment he'd had the first swallow of his tequila. "Don't give the bell man a signal till you've cleared it with me! If I hadn't jumped off that lug this afternoon, you'd have had him land that piece on my foot. I *need* my feet."

I'd apologize, for whatever it was worth, and he'd go on: "When you get to where you know what you're doin', and when I know that you know what you're doin', *then* you can tell the man to come down. Not now." He looked sore as hell, but I soon learned that his true emotion was concern, not anger.

"You just don't see yet," he said one afternoon after the shouting period was finished, "how easy it is to kill a man. It's no trouble at all." I just looked at him.

"Let's say we're settin' a piece. Up it comes. I grab my end and walk along the header, pushin' and turnin' until I get your end to where you can grab it. If it's a big beam, or one end's a little heavy, you'll grab it with both hands. The moment you do that, I'm responsible for you. All I've got to do is give it a little push and you're over the side. Then what're you gonna hold onto? The only thing you've got is the damned beam, and if I let go, or if you're heavier than I am so that my weight won't stop it from seesawing, you're gone. It's as simple as that.

"And that's only *one* way. One guy went 12 floors onto the exhaust pipe of a diesel truck when his partner let a header bang against the empty column he was perched on. Shot him off like a catapult. An Indian kid I knew went off an apartment building when his partner cut loose the chokers before he'd got a bolt stuck. The partner landed on the plank floor, but the kid slid off the end and over the side."

He shook his head. "No, you don't see how it works, yet. You're busy learnin' the moves, and you're learnin' fairly quick, but it doesn't matter how fast you can climb, or how well you figure out a way to make a tough piece in a narrow space, if you don't learn that you never do *anythin'* without first makin' sure that your partner's all right."

By the time we had set everything on the low side up to the roof headers, I had begun to get some feel for the iron, and while I couldn't trot around as well as Patrick, I was at least not ashamed of myself. I had learned in those weeks that more practice produced less anxiety, and I had set standards for myself: I would never crawl across a beam that another man could walk; I would stand on the top flange when cutting a choker loose from the hook; I would never let Patrick have the easy end of a piece.

Patrick and I generally had our coffee (delivered by tagline) sent up to us, instead of coming down to the plank floor to sit with the rest of the gang. Even this—dangling my legs over the side of the job, coffee in one hand and doughnut in the other—I regarded as practice. It all seems pompous and silly to me now, but then, when it was all new, it was important. It was important for a number of reasons, but principally as a demonstration to myself that I was going to neither fall nor jump.

One of the frustrations of construction work in general, and of "booming around" (traveling from place to place) in particular, is that you are forced continually to give up old friends and make new ones.

Some people you seem to bump into every so often, but many you meet once and never see again. The foreknowledge we all have of this produces a certain shallowness in relationships.

The hospital was my first "big" job, employing a couple of hundred men (50 or 60 of whom were ironworkers), and I've no idea what's become of most of the ones I knew. We worked together, had a few drinks after work, but rarely socialized in other areas. People who saw this manuscript as I worked on it asked me why so many of the conversations seemed to take place in a bar, and the answer is merely that that is about the only kind of place in which we talk.

Patrick and I have known each other for several years now, on and off jobs. Coley, a young Irishman who taught me how to plumb-up, and I go sailing together regularly. Even Timmy Shaughnessy showed up on the hospital job. (He had gone upstate to dry out, and he stayed sober all the way through.) I haven't seen Callahan in five years; Harry was killed in 1971 when a building collapsed, but I hadn't seen him in some time and learned of his death by chance. Every man must wonder, sometimes, whatever became of so-and-so, but a construction worker can do it indefinitely.

By the time the hospital was up, things were very slow indeed, as we learned as soon as we were back in the union hall. The chairs were all filled, and there were men spilling outside, huddling in patches of December sunshine, or sitting in small, forlorn groups in their cars.

Christmas passed and January and most of February. I quit going every morning to the hall; no permit men were being sent out. Then I heard that there were jobs in New York City. I didn't want to go. I felt I'd had it with New York. Still, I'd been a long time out of work, and it didn't look as though there was much chance of things improving.

4. ALTITUDE RECORD

On that February morning drive down the length of Manhattan, the anxiety that I'd thought was conquered came running back at me all over again. The buildings that for years had been so familiar I suddenly saw in an entirely different and wholly disturbing light. I might as well have been a country boy gaping in disbelief at the height of everything. The city had never struck me as so *tall* before.

I remembered conversations with non-ironworkers in which they asked if I didn't get nervous working so far above the ground, to which

I'd replied, "Of course not; after the first 30 feet or so it doesn't matter how far you fall." And I tried now to make myself believe it. I had believed it before, and was now shocked to discover how weak was my faith. By the time I parked the car, I was almost ready to give up the whole project.

There was plenty of work, it turned out, and during what remained of that winter I carried plank. It is a boring job, and is tolerable at all only in cold weather, when by regulating his pace a man may avoid both heatstroke and freezing.

In the spring I went on a bullwheel, which controls the lateral motion of a derrick. For the first hour I turned the wheel with one hand, seated. The second hour I turned it with one hand, standing. By lunchtime I was using both hands—standing. By midafternoon I was convinced that my arms were permanently ruined. When the rest of the gang saw how much trouble I was having with the wheel, they responded in standard fashion.

"Sometime today, fella!" ("Sometime today" is standard construction argot for "hurry up.")

"Your sister gets around faster'n that!"

The ribbing continued all day and moved with me into the shanty after work. I would have smacked somebody, but it was all I could do just to button my shirt.

I celebrated the first warm day of spring by getting myself dangled over the side of a job on 48th Street, 32 floors above the traffic.

I was taglining—guiding a piece of steel on its way up, using a rope warped around one end. The piece being set was a heavy outside header which had to be snaked up through a congested area, requiring me to pull down on my line with all my modest weight. To get a better grip on the line, I took a half hitch (an upside-down loop) around my palm. That was a mistake. A half hitch can't be cast off a line when there is a strain on the load end—which I knew, but wasn't thinking about. The bell man came up with the header slowly until its opposite end cleared the adjacent iron, at which point the piece was lifted in a hurry, and I was yanked from the plank floor like a fish on a hook.

The bullwheel man, ignorant of my plight, began swinging the header toward its intended position between the two columns. However, without a grounded tagline man (in midair, I was of no use) pulling to keep the piece on its intended path, it slowly turned 90 degrees, coming to a standstill midway between the two columns but at right angles to them, with me holding to the outer end. Because my weight was upsetting the balance, it hung with its outer end—my end—considerably depressed. I was, in fact, scarcely above the level of the plank floor, since the header was well over 30 feet long and was tipped down at a 60-degree angle.

My attention was directed initially to the choker: if its grip on the piece slipped, I was gone. As soon as I began worrying about that, I began also wondering how well I'd tied the tagline to the header. Once I realized that there were two connections to worry about, I couldn't settle upon a choice of anxieties and gave the whole business up; there wasn't a thing I could do about either one of them, anyway.

At 32 floors times about 12 feet, I was nearly 400 feet above the ground, hanging by a thin piece of manila line. I was frightened.

While I was dangling there, the rest of the gang merely gaped where they stood. Into this idiotic tableau walked the super. "What in the name of the Holy Mother," said he, "are you doin' out *there?*"

"Gettin' gangrene of the hand," I replied. Derision, I noticed, has a way of making off with a man's fears.

"Boom him back, Tommy," said the super. The bell man came down on the load, depositing me back on the plank. "Lots of men," the super said to me, realizing exactly how the mishap had come about, "have tied half hitches in taglines and gone for little rides, but I think you now hold the altitude record."

In July, I spent some time as the only white man in an Indian gang, and I would like to use the experience to clear up some common misconceptions about Indian ironworkers.

The misapprehensions, which seem to be universally held by non-construction workers, are that (1) all men employed in the erection of steel buildings and bridges are Indians, and (2) all Indians have a special sense of balance ideally suiting them for this work.

The facts are that (1) a small minority of ironworkers (microscopic away from New York and the Canadian border states) are Indians; (2) there are no data to support any "balance theory." They take falls no more or less often than anybody else.

I worked with them only a short while and was then sent to a big hole in the ground on Sixth Avenue. I remained there for 11½ months, until the job was completed, and I still rather enjoy, when walking past that building, the sense of continuity which having seen a thing through from beginning to end produces. This feeling—the "I made that" syndrome—is, to me, the most rewarding part of the work. It's an over-grand attitude, obviously, since the labors of thousands of men are enclosed in any building. But the illusion persists. I doubt that assembly-line workers, after putting identical handles on identical doors of identical cars through identical workdays, feel like saying "I made that." Ironworkers, looking at buildings, do.

It was early July 1971 when we started, in a hole in the ground that was three stories deep, two thirds of a block long from east to west and a full block long from north to south. I was laid off 44 floors and 528 feet later, in late June 1972.

The first part of a job is always the slowest and most frustrating. The connectors are trying to make pieces that have to go right where the plumbers-up are trying to pull a column over to the vertical; every time you turn sideways you bump into a carpenter building forms for concrete or trip over the cables being strung out by the electricians.

Once a job has risen 30 feet or more above the ground, there are breezes to help dissipate the heat and there is none of the mud that gets between the treads of a man's boots to compromise his footing. But, best of all, things finally begin to move a little faster, and one's sense of accomplishment is thereby expanded.

In the shanty one Friday afternoon, the super, Crockett, told me my partner wanted to take a month off and, if I knew anybody upstate to replace him, I ought to bring him down over the weekend. "There's nobody down at the hall but scum," he said.

I hadn't intended driving up that weekend, but I immediately took off for Elmira to find Patrick. Later, Coley and Timmy joined us, too. Timmy was still on the wagon.

By the middle of November we were up around 18, at which height elevator waiting-time losses began to show. We had just one car, and you could die of boredom waiting for the damned thing. Some of us said to hell with it and walked up; some men carried lunch pails and never came down. On high jobs in warm weather, I've been able, by not coming down for lunch, to eat a homemade sandwich and take a 45-minute nap during the 35-minute lunch break.

There was, that fall and winter, a large turnover of personnel. New men arrived almost daily. The cold, rainy weather was the principal cause of this; everybody was disgusted with it, and some of the men who had money in the bank decided that traveling into midtown only to be sent home three days out of five just wasn't worth it.

Shortly after we got a fellow called Albert for our bell man, I decided that I wanted out myself. Not out of the job, but out of the raising gang.

"I don't think," I told Patrick and Coley, "that I want to be in the same gang with Albert. He's crazy."

"Yes," agreed Coley. "I've been studyin' on him, and he has got a definite rip in his seabag."

Patrick added, "Sooner or later Albert is goin' to hurt somebody."

It was sooner. And it was relatively minor and didn't cost Albert his job, because it was not his fault alone.

Patrick took a day off, and Crockett sent a beginner in his place. The boy was about 19 and had been on bullwheels and taglines, but had never been connecting. He probably wouldn't have been allowed to go up, but we had only an hour or so of connecting to do, and he begged persuasively, and Crockett let him have his way.

He did everything wrong, of course. A new man categorically does everything wrong. Nobody got sore at him for doing the wrong thing trying to get the iron in place, but everybody got sore at him for doing the wrong things with his body. He was forever on the wrong side of the pieces, and it still amazes me that he wasn't knocked over the side. He hurried too much and, in his eagerness to look good, took foolish chances. Several times I held pieces away from him and told him I wasn't going to let him have his end until he stopped bouncing around.

When a beam is reluctant to go where it belongs, various approaches to getting it there present themselves. If it is so tight that it can't be brought in with a lever, someone throws the connector a sledgehammer and he stands on the header and proceeds to try to beat the thing in. If an ordinary sledge won't move it, he'll ask for a Monday. "Mondays" are overgrown sledges, weighing 16 to 22 pounds. Swing one, and you feel like it's Monday. With such a heavy beater a man can strike a hell of a blow, if he can hit what he's aiming at.

I once saw a man miss entirely, and as the hammer swooshed past the target and continued on around, he was forced to let it go—if he had tried to hold onto it, he would surely have been carried off the column. It sailed out perhaps a hundred feet and down 24 floors and landed in the seat of a bulldozer. Had the driver been in his machine, cleaning him up would have been a hose job. As it was, the seat and all adjacent sheet metal were destroyed. Operators, and everyone else whose jobs are on the ground near a rising tower, develop a protective fatalism.

Sometimes, however, the piece has been so badly bent in shipment that even repeated mighty swats won't move it into place. When that is the case, the connectors ask for the weight ball that hangs at the end of the derrick cable just above the hook. It is swung over so that it hangs xt to the offending piece. A one-ton or even half-ton ball does not have to be moving very fast to develop considerable force, and the piece generally yields.

It behooves anybody involved in this sort of maneuver to be extremely careful of his hands. I yelled at the kid to be careful; so did others. Everybody cautioned him not to put his hands on the cable from which the ball was hanging.

We gave the piece two good raps, and it slid over. I dropped to the beam to wrench the holes around to their places and was sticking the second bolt when I heard the ball start up and the kid yell.

He had apparently been bracing himself with a hand on the load cable while watching me make up the piece, and Albert had raised the load. The sheave (pulley), running up the cable as it rose, sheared off the boy's thumb with surgical neatness.

Albert's defense was threefold: He said that since we had finished with the ball, we were aware that it would be taken away; he further insisted that he had yelled beforehand that he was getting up on the load (which no one recalled); he rightly contended that only a dope would stand with his hand on the cable. My response was that, yes, we knew the ball should be moved away, but that neither of us had given him a signal. (The kid should have given one, instead of standing around watching me, but hadn't.)

I went to the hospital with the boy, returned to the job to report to Crockett how it had happened, spent the night brooding, and the following morning told Crockett that when there was another man available, I wanted out of the gang.

A week after I'd asked out, a new man took my place, and I went plumbing-up with Coley's gang. Yet, when any of the connectors was out, I was sent in his place, thus keeping my hand in while not daily destroying my rapidly aging body trying to keep up with the kids and animals—the guys whose strength exceeded their good sense.

5. LAY OFF

BY THE MIDDLE OF FEBRUARY we were on the 30th floor. One of the connectors on the east derrick managed to get his leg caught in a bundle of iron while shaking out and broke it, and Crockett put Timmy up in his place.

Watching Timmy work was an amazing experience. I couldn't escape the feeling that I was looking at somebody I'd never seen before. He was up this column and down that one, flitting across this header and back on the next, tiptoeing across needle (small) beams so lightly that they didn't wiggle, even with 60 pounds of tools and bolts strapped to his body.

"That's not our old shaky Timmy," Coley said. "It can't be."

The other connector's name was Henry. He was a local man, about Timmy's age, and had been on the job since the beginning. He knew where all the iron went, and by all rights should have been the lead connector. But they hadn't worked together an hour before it was clear to both of them that Timmy should call the shots.

On April 4, the center derrick was jumped to the 38th floor, and we all began to sense that the end was coming. There was no longer the feeling of rising from the ground; we were so far above the street that changes were hard to see. Pedestrians were mere dots, and even large trucks appeared so tiny that they all looked alike. The horizon, which earlier had expanded significantly with every jump, had some floors ago taken on a static quality. I was sorry when this happened.

By mid-month, an anxious note had begun to enter into the men's conversations: The hall was rumored to be getting crowded, and work was said to be slowing down.

Crockett came to Patrick and me. "I'll keep you two and Coley and Timmy on as long as I can," he said. "But things are gettin' tight. I don't even know where I'm goin' myself, so there's nothin' I can do for you guys from out of town. If I were you, I'd run up home some weekend soon to put my name in the pot."

When he'd left, Patrick asked me what I was going to do. I said I'd make out one way or another. A slowdown couldn't last forever.

"True," he agreed. "It'll pick up, sooner or later. I got a friend runs a little snake outfit; we'll give him a call when this job's done." (A "snake" outfit is one that is non-union.) He made a fist and hit me a playful jab on the shoulder. Somehow I knew what was coming next—the universal, ritual speech of an ironworker who's just been laid off. "What of it, I was lookin' for a job when I found this one, right?"

We topped out on May 15. It was a beautifully clear, warm, spring day, which added appreciably to the number of dignitaries attending the ceremonies. In the middle of the morning a truck arrived bearing just one column. It came up with a giant American flag attached, and Patrick and his partner wrestled it into place. When they finished, various luminaries took turns standing beside it in what they imagined to be laboring poses, while lesser functionaries took their pictures.

After the back-patting was over, we went back to work. Plenty of iron remained to be set. The topping-out column is the first piece on the highest elevation, not the last. Standing it up doesn't mark the end of anything, but it does mark the beginning of the reduction of the labor force: as each operation is performed for the last time, the man who performed it is let go.

Timmy's derrick was the last to get all its iron up. He died before it was all in place. He and Henry had spread a few planks in a completed bay for the welders to sit on while working. Somehow, Timmy, in hurrying from one side of the area to the other, put his inside foot down an inch to the right of where he should have, and the plank, which had a slight warp in it, rocked. At least, that's Henry's analysis.

Coley and I were on the plank floor two stories beneath the connectors, and saw nothing until we looked up when we heard Henry yell, "Watch out!" The yell was instinctive and of course a waste of breath, since there was nothing to yell about until it was too late. Timmy tumbled over the side, passing by us almost close enough to touch. He fell in silence, and no sound from the impact of his body on the concrete reached up to us.

For a while the only sounds were Henry's repeated cries of "Oh, Jesus! Oh, Jesus!" Then, as what had happened dawned on the others in his gang, there were random shouts and calls and finally the scuffling noises of men rushing to the building's edge.

Coley and I just sat down where we were. I turned my head the opposite way, looking toward the western end of the job, and saw that Patrick was the only man there. He was standing on the top, on a header, his arms hanging loosely at his sides.

The man died because he made a mistake, and that's about all there is to it. These things happen. It's true that I can't walk near that building without seeing Timmy hurtle past me, and it's true that this vision produces a brief wave of nausea and sets me to wondering. *Why?* But I know that no answer will appear. It was an Accident. "Accident" is a short way of saying "Causes Permanently Concealed."

MANY MORE OPERATIONS REMAINED before our part of the job was done. After all the floors were poured, we still had eight floors of plumbing-up cables to cut loose. Minor alterations remained to be made in the cellar iron, and there were a few hundred-odd bolts yet to be stuck. Then there were a few bent beams that had to be heated and straightened.

All three derricks had to come down, also. One derrick is used to assist in the dismantling of the others. Their sections are lowered to the street with it; and then a Chicago boom lowers the rest.

When it's over, there is no sign that anything other than the building itself was ever there.

The final detail work was dull, but I stayed on despite the boredom, because I didn't know how long it might be before I could find another job. But the place had become strange. The shanty was practically empty. The nails that had held so many jackets and overalls and sweatshirts were nearly all unused. Patrick had gone when the raising gang was laid off, and Coley quit the following week.

On June 24, Crockett came over to me while I was making up a bundle of old cables and told me that it was my last day. He had to lay somebody off, he said, and the others were all local books. He sounded almost apologetic. This slowdown was temporary, he said, and perhaps we'd all get together again when things picked up. I told him that I couldn't see where I had any complaints coming. I'd been employed in the city without a significant break since the first day I'd come down, and had made pretty good money during that time.

"Well, there you are," he said and, after shaking hands, he walked off toward the stairs.

"Hey, Crockett!" I called after him. He turned. "You know, I was lookin' for a job when I found this one."

He laughed.

The Sergeant Who Opened the Door

CONDENSED FROM THE BOOK "KGB" BY

JOHN BARRON

ILLUSTRATED BY NOEL SICKLES

The U.S. Armed Forces courier center was located in a small concrete building in a remote corner of Orly Field near Paris. Inside the center, top-secret documents from Washington to NATO and the U.S. Sixth Fleet were decoded and stored in a steel vault before being sent on to their final destinations.

Because of the Army's security precautions, the center's secrets, priceless to an enemy power, had long eluded the KGB (the Soviet secret police). Then came the break-in-a-million and suddenly the treasures of the center's vaults were within the KGB's grasp.

1. THE SPY

IT WAS THE MORNING OF OCTOBER 2, 1964, and Sgt. Robert Lee Johnson was worried. "Lady," he pleaded with the receptionist at Walter Reed Army Hospital in Washington, D.C., "something ought to be done *today.*"

"I'm sorry, Sergeant," the receptionist replied. "Tuesday is the earliest a psychiatrist can see your wife. Since there's no emergency, why can't she wait a few days?"

Unable to confess the depth of his desperation, Johnson left the hospital and crossed the parking lot to where his Austrian wife waited in the car. At 41, Hedwig Pipek Johnson retained few vestiges of the beauty that had first attracted him 16 years before. Her face was sallow and puffy, her blue eyes were watery, her once shapely figure was lost in fat. As they started for their home in Alexandria, she regarded him with a malign leer that portended one of her mad outbursts.

"You filthy man, I hate you," she said in a husky voice. "You're a pervert, a gambler, a drunk, a rapist. You're a filthy Russian general."

"For God's sake, Hedy," Johnson interrupted. He was so shaken that he nearly rammed the car ahead, which had stopped for a traffic light.

"You know why I hate you most?" she continued in a whisper. "Because you're a spy."

Johnson tried to speak deliberately: "If you ever say that again, I'll beat hell out of you."

"Spy, spy, spy!" Hedy sang defiantly. "You're a spy. And you know what? If you don't do what I say, I'm going to tell the FBI."

"Go ahead, you lunatic!" Johnson shouted at her. "Go ahead! You're so crazy nobody'll believe anything you say. They'll put *you* away, not me."

Johnson could bear it no longer. Several times in the preceding three years Hedy had been released after psychiatric treatment, only to lapse into ever-worsening seizures of paranoia that left him in perpetual dread. He had lured her to the hospital today on the pretense of having a prescription filled, hoping to persuade Army doctors to commit her on the spot to an institution. Having failed in that, Johnson knew only that he must escape. Back home, he began drinking heavily and brooding about suicide.

At 2:45 p.m. he left the house, ostensibly to report for duty at the Pentagon, where he was a courier of secret documents. He never arrived. Six days later, a back-page story in the Washington *Post* reported his disappearance. "It's quite a mystery," a Pentagon spokesman told the newspaper.

It was far more than that. The missing sergeant was one of the most destructive spies Soviet Russia's KGB had ever implanted in the United States armed forces. The information he had already passed along to Moscow placed the defenses of all of Western Europe in utmost peril—and for as long as he remained at large, the Pentagon remained in the dark with no way of removing, or even realizing, the danger.

Johnson, his wife and another rogue sergeant formed perhaps the most bizarre and improbable trio in the history of modern espionage. Like his two partners, Johnson was distinguished only by disabling personal defects. He had no qualifications of intellect, character or spirit. He was not impelled by the classic motivations of espionage—greed, idealism, fear or adventure. Indeed, he first delivered himself to the KGB out of the pettiest of grievances.

Working as a military clerk in Berlin in the fall of 1952, Johnson lost a coveted promotion to a rival sergeant. To "punish" the Army, he decided to run away to the Russians. He imagined himself a celebrated defector whose propaganda broadcasts over Radio Moscow would be the despair of the Pentagon.

Uncertain about how to communicate with the Russians himself, Johnson turned to Hedy. She had lived with him first when he was stationed in Vienna in 1948, then joined him in Berlin on the chance that she could make him her husband. Johnson knew that above all else she craved the security of marriage, and so, on Christmas Day 1952, he proposed a bargain. "If you'll fix me up with the Russians," he told her, "I'll marry you."

But Hedy, who had witnessed the behavior of the first Soviet troops in Vienna, was terrified of Russians, and for weeks she walked the winter streets unable to gather enough courage to approach them. She invented excuses to justify her failures and sometimes feigned illness to avoid going out. Belatedly, Johnson saw through her pretenses and threatened to abandon her. Fearful of losing him, she finally went to the Soviet compound in the Karlshorst district of the city. It was easy enough in those days, before the Wall, to cross into East Berlin.

The Russians agreed to talk to Johnson, and on the morning of February 22, 1953—George Washington's Birthday—he and Hedy stepped from the elevated train at the Karlshorst station. They were met by two KGB officers, a stocky, baldish man and a big, buxom woman, who identified themselves as Mr. and Mrs. White. The four drove by a circuitous route to a large gray stone house, whose windows were covered on the outside by heavy wooden shutters and on the inside by thick curtains. In a darkened room, a middle-aged Russian at an oval table was introduced as Mr. Brown. Without bothering to rise or shake hands, he filled five glasses with cognac and mumbled a toast "to peace." Then he questioned Johnson about his intentions and motives.

After listening to the explanation, White commented, "I can recall times when I myself was unhappy in our army. But that was not reason enough to desert my country. Why don't you just leave the Army?"

"No, no, I want to get even," Johnson replied. "I can make propaganda, give press conferences, go on the radio—stuff like that."

Concealing their amusement, the Soviet officers continued questioning him about his past life, military experiences and current associates. Johnson accepted glass after glass of cognac, and by early afternoon was in an incoherent stupor. The Russians helped him out through the snow into a Soviet car.

The interrogation revealed him to be an utterly amoral man, bereft of any beliefs whatsoever. Beyond drinking, gambling and liaisons with prostitutes, he had few interests, and the prospects of his ever accomplishing anything important in espionage were slim.

Yet the KGB automatically made the decision to recruit him. Whatever face the Soviet Union chooses to present to the world at any given time, the KGB remains organized and deployed for clandestine warfare lasting beyond the foreseeable future. Thus, it constantly cultivates agents who, though of no discernible present use, may become of value five, ten, even twenty years hence. There was a chance that in time Johnson would drift into an exploitable position. It was a remote chance, but one that the KGB had no difficulty in electing to take.

Two weeks later, at a second meeting, White and Brown suggested that Johnson stay in the Army and supply them with information from time to time.

"You mean, be a spy!" Johnson exclaimed.

"A fighter for peace," White corrected him.

"Well," Johnson said hesitantly, "if you're willing to teach me, I guess I could give it a try."

Prodded by Hedy, Johnson kept his promise, and they were married on April 23, 1953. He arranged for a leave, telling the Army he planned to vacation in Bavaria. Instead, he and Hedy crossed into East Berlin, took a train to Brandenburg and spent their honeymoon as guests of the KGB. Russians came daily to instruct them in the rudiments of espionage. Hedy was trained as a courier, and given false identification papers and shoes with hollow heels in which film could be concealed.

Soon after Johnson and Hedy returned to Berlin, they met Paula, a 27-year-old KGB officer, who replaced the first three Russians. Paula was Vladimir Vasilevich Krivoshey, newly arrived in Germany on his first foreign mission. He was handsome, with deeply set dark eyes and curly black hair. He soon established himself as the master upon whom Johnson's new secret life depended, treating the sergeant as a patient animal trainer would handle a dog. He rewarded each act of obedience, but never lavishly, and he reprimanded the slightest deviation from instructions, but never too harshly. He avoided any attempt to motivate Johnson ideologically. Instead, he sought to engender in him the the idea that through the KGB he could become an important person.

Initially, Johnson reacted by doing his best to please his new masters. Guided by Paula, he obtained a transfer to a clerical job in the G-2 (intelligence) section of the Berlin Command. There he began indiscriminately photographing masses of unclassified papers, which he slipped out overnight. Soon he churned up such a blizzard of worthless material that the KGB had to order him to desist. "We admire your energy, but we want only secret documents," Paula told him.

Frustrated, Johnson considered severing ties with the Russians, and might have done so except for the arrival of a man who was destined to appear unexpectedly as an influence in his life again and again.

"How are you, Bob?" a voice quietly called to Johnson in the corridor outside his office one day. It was an old friend, Sgt. James Allen Mintkenbaugh, whom he had last seen three years before at Fort Hood, Texas. Mintkenbaugh, 35, was tall and strong, but he had a vacuous face and empty brown eyes that shifted away from a direct gaze.

In most respects the two were utterly dissimilar. Johnson was gluttonous and reckless; Mintkenbaugh was fastidious and cautious. Johnson drank heavily and slept with any woman he could. Mintkenbaugh disliked drunkenness, and was rarely, if ever, seen with women. Yet, in

Texas, each had become the other's best friend, perhaps because they were both outsiders, devoid of purpose or values.

Johnson now saw in Mintkenbaugh a means of enhancing his stature with the KGB. He reasoned that, with his friend serving as a lookout while he rummaged through offices during off-duty hours, he could increase his productivity as a spy.

Johnson broached the subject deviously over wine and *wurst* in a beer garden. He said he was making good money by selling the Russians false information, and offered to include Mintkenbaugh in the deal if he would help out. Mintkenbaugh wavered, but eventually agreed, probably out of curiosity and a desire to be accommodating. Before long, however, he sensed that Johnson actually was hunting valuable intelligence for the Russians. To his surprise, he found that he didn't care. In fact, the realization that he was helping betray the United States gave him a strange sort of gratification.

Meanwhile, the two sergeants joined in a scheme to produce pornographic movies to sell to fellow soldiers. While filming one night in Johnson's apartment, they raised such a commotion that neighbors called the police. The next day, Army agents interrogated both men and searched the apartment. They found nothing incriminating, because Johnson had loaded his camera improperly, and the film was blank. The men were dismissed after a lecture about respecting German civilians.

Johnson was convinced that the Army was actually searching for evidence of his espionage. That night, he parked his Volkswagen on a side street and sought to infect Mintkenbaugh with his own panic. He confessed that he had been giving the KGB accurate information and insisted that the only way to avoid prison was to defect to the Russians. Acting on this impulse, the two sergeants crossed into East Berlin.

Paula was outraged that Johnson had brought Mintkenbaugh along. And Johnson's defensive explanations of the circumstances that made them fear arrest did nothing to placate him.

"That's idiotic," Paula declared. "If they suspected you, they would have confronted you with accusations or left you alone. Pull yourself together and forget these insane notions of running away."

Turning to Mintkenbaugh, he commanded, "Tell me about yourself. What do you do in the Army? Why did you get involved in this?"

After listening for a while, Paula relaxed. He was quite interested in the new American, and his brusqueness gave way to politeness. Schooled to analyze character and behavior, Paula detected in

Mintkenbaugh the kind of weaknesses the KGB delights in exploiting.

Paula asked Mintkenbaugh to return to East Berlin by himself, and during the next few weeks ushered him to meetings with other Russians at KGB houses in Karlshorst. Their conversations assumed that he was under their command, and Mintkenbaugh passively acquiesced without really understanding why. It would be more than a decade before he could articulate the reasons behind his treason.

Meanwhile, Johnson continued to supply occasional information, including a few copies of the confidential weekly intelligence summaries prepared for the Berlin Command. Paula patiently sought to guide and encourage him. But, in time, the allure of espionage faded, and Johnson's interest waned. When he was transferred to an Army finance office near Rochefort, France, in April 1955, he skipped his last scheduled meeting with Paula and left Berlin without provision for further contact. The KGB, ascertaining the nature of his new post, was content to let him go for the time being.

In July 1956, still embittered with the Army, Johnson accepted a discharge. He was 36, poorly educated and unprepared for any particular civilian work. But he had a plan. He imagined that by gambling he could multiply his savings of some $3000 into a modest fortune. Then he would enroll in a correspondence course in creative writing and and become a famous author. So he took Hedy to Las Vegas, bought a mobile home, and moved into a trailer camp. During the day he worked on his correspondence course; at night he drank and gambled. As their money dwindled, Johnson urged his wife to go to work. But, late in 1956, Hedy became ill, and soon they were destitute.

On a Saturday morning in January 1957, Johnson groggily answered a knock at the trailer door. "Well, I'll be damned!" he shouted. "Hedy, get up. Fix some coffee. Look who's here."

Standing outside, smiling and as impassive as ever, was Mintkenbaugh. He told them that he, too, had left the Army in 1956, and since then had been working in a California ice-cream parlor. After a while, he also mentioned that he was just back from Berlin.

His fixed smile unchanging, Mintkenbaugh handed Johnson an envelope containing 25 musty $20 bills. "It's a present from Paula," he said. "They want you to go back into the service. You'll work with me, and they'll pay you $300 a month."

Johnson regarded both the money and the invitation as providential. Without deliberating further, or consulting Hedy, he agreed.

The immediate KGB objective in reactivating Johnson was to gather intelligence about American missiles, which were just beginning to be deployed in numbers. The Russians recognized that he probably could not gain a technical assignment, but they thought that from some peripheral billet he might photograph equipment and documents.

Turned down by the Air Force, which the KGB wanted him to join, Johnson was able to rejoin the Army and retain his former grade. As KGB luck would have it, the Army stationed him as a guard at a new Nike-Hercules missile site on the Palos Verdes Peninsula in California. In meetings with Mintkenbaugh between the springs of 1957 and 1958, Johnson transmitted photographs and diagrams of the Nike-Hercules missile, together with overheard comments about its characteristics. He also succeeded in siphoning off a sample of the rocket fuel. The KGB rewarded him with bonuses of $900 and $1200.

The Army eventually transferred Johnson to Fort Bliss, outside El Paso, Texas, where he continued to pass missile data and other secret information to Mintkenbaugh. After each rendezvous with Johnson at the El Paso airport, Mintkenbaugh flew to Washington to report to Pyotr Nikolaevich Yeliseev, a 35-year-old protocol officer at the Soviet embassy. Then, in September 1959, Mintkenbaugh disappeared.

Late in 1959, Johnson was again transferred, this time to a base in Orléans, France. Here, Mintkenbaugh suddenly reappeared. He had spent four months in Moscow, training in the use of letter drops, microdots, invisible writing, surveillance and various other espionage techniques. Now he was on his way to Washington, D.C., under orders to establish himself in business, while at the same time carrying out KGB missions. But first he had instructions for Johnson.

He found his friend and Hedy living in a seedy hotel near the Orléans railroad station. He stayed with them three or four days, departing for the United States only after assuring himself that Johnson understood how to meet a KGB officer in Paris. It was a simple task, but it turned out to be the most important Mintkenbaugh ever performed.

2. CITADEL FOR SECRETS

FOLLOWING MINTKENBAUGH's instructions, Johnson drove to Paris, and he and Hedy stood before a theater on the Rue d'Athènes studying the advertisements. A handsome young man in a black beret paused beside them.

"Excuse me, are you British?" he asked with a slight Russian accent.

"No, I am American," Johnson replied.

"I wonder if you have change for ten francs," the Russian went on.

Johnson presented a German five-mark coin that Mintkenbaugh had given him. The Russian in turn handed him a two-mark coin. Then he smiled, shook hands, and said, "My name is Viktor. Why don't we go and have a drink?"

Viktor was Vitaly Sergeevich Orzhurmov, then a 29-year-old attaché at the Soviet embassy in Paris. Like Paula, he belonged to the new breed of poised and polished officers whom the KGB began grooming for foreign operations in the 1950s. He moved easily among Westerners, who were charmed by the novelty of meeting a sophisticated Soviet representative, particularly one who hinted that he favored democratic reform of the Soviet system. His behavior toward Johnson and Hedy reflected a careful study of the KGB files and its judgment of them. From the moment they sat down in a little corner café, he devoted himself to Hedy, trying to make her comfortable and secure in the relationship he was inaugurating. And he confided to Johnson that he was now a very important man upon whom Moscow counted heavily.

After chatting with Hedy for a while, Viktor gave Johnson $500 tightly wadded in a cigarette package.

"It's a Christmas present," he said. "We are very glad to have you with us here. You bring a good record. It shows that we can rely on you to use your own initiative in discovering information of interest."

Thereafter Johnson, sometimes accompanied by Hedy, met Viktor on the first Saturday evening of each month in cafés near the Porte d'Orléans in Paris. But his assignment in France, with an ordnance battalion, gave him no access to important data, and by the summer of 1960 Viktor started urging him to request duty at Supreme Allied Headquarters (SHAPE) in Paris.

That fall, as luck would have it, Hedy suffered her first breakdown and entered an Army hospital near Paris. With the permission of a sympathetic commanding officer, Johnson asked for a transfer to the Paris area because his wife needed to live closer to the hospital.

After an unsuccessful interview at SHAPE in March 1961, he fell into conversation with a sergeant, who told him, "If you want to get to Paris, you might try the Armed Forces courier center out at Orly Airport."

"What's that?" Johnson asked.

"It's a sort of post office for top-secret materials," the sergeant explained. "They guard the hell out of it, so lots of times there are openings for guards."

The description was accurate as far as it went. The courier center was a small concrete building standing in a far corner of the airfield. All vital documents, cipher systems and cryptographic equipment sent from Washington to NATO, American commands in Europe and the Sixth Fleet in the Mediterranean were first delivered here to be sorted and re-routed to their final destination. All materials bearing top-secret or higher classification originating from commands in Europe were also housed in the center, pending shipment to Washington. It was, in fact, the European citadel of many of the most important military secrets the United States possessed.

The Army had devised a labyrinth of security barriers to make the little building physically inviolate. The only outside door opened into a front office where clerks processed the documents. Behind this office was a huge steel vault. To enter the vault, it was necessary to pass through two steel doors. The first was secured by a metal bar with combination locks at either end. The second, the door to the vault itself, had a complicated key lock.

Thus, no one could open the vault without the combination to two locks and a key to the third. No one, from general to private, was ever allowed in the vault alone. Regulations required the constant presence of at least one officer whenever it was opened. In addition, an armed guard was posted in the office 24 hours a day, 365 days a year. Seemingly, the vault was impenetrable.

Johnson had little difficulty in gaining an assignment as a guard. When he reported this to his KGB contact, Viktor slapped him on the back and exclaimed, "Fantastic!"

With this move, the miserable sergeant, who eight years before had drifted into the hands of the KGB like so much flotsam, was suddenly transformed into an agent of incredible potential. Much still stood between the KGB and the treasures of the vault. But with an agent unexpectedly stationed within a few feet of those treasures, the KGB was now closer than it had ever thought possible. Soon, all its ingenuity, imagination and technical resources were concentrated in a plan to span those last few feet.

VIKTOR INCREASED THE FREQUENCY of his meetings with Johnson, questioning him about the routine of the center, the rotation of guards and the methods of selecting personnel admitted to the vault itself. Relaying instructions from the KGB Center in Moscow, he eventually said, "As a first step, you must become one of the clerks who work inside."

"To do that I need a top-secret clearance," Johnson replied. "That means an investigation."

"That is a chance we must take," Viktor responded.

Johnson worried most about what the increasingly unpredictable Hedy might do or say. During her recurrent fits of irrationality, neighbors had heard her babble about espionage and accuse her husband of being a spy. So had the medical personnel who treated her. All dismissed her rantings as delusions. But Johnson could not be sure that some conscientious investigator might not pursue such clues and discover the truth.

However, circumstances were to spare Johnson the thorough background investigation that is supposed to precede the granting of a top-secret clearance. The agreement by which France permitted American troops on its soil prohibited Army investigators from interrogating French citizens, and so no interviews of Johnson's neighbors were attempted. A cursory review of his past service and a routine written inquiry to his commanding officer cast no disqualifying doubts upon him. The check did not even note Hedy's mental illness, because Johnson, on the pretext of verifying some dates, had asked for his personnel folder and removed all references to her condition. Late in 1961, he received top-secret clearance and was admitted to the vault as a clerk.

The documents Johnson now sorted ordinarily arrived in large manila envelopes, often bearing red or blue wax seals. Some had laconic labels denoting special security classifications. Most of the security terms were meaningless to Johnson. But the KGB knew that the designations referred to sensitive cryptographic material, data about NATO strengths and strategies, and nuclear strike plans.

The KGB was concerned that the courier center might be equipped with a hidden alarm system set to sound a warning if any effort was made to open the vault during nonworking hours. Viktor showed Johnson illustrations, probably extracted from trade magazines, of various systems used in American banks, and ordered him to look for wiring or tiny boxes that would betray the presence of an alarm.

"You must examine the whole building centimeter by centimeter," Viktor said.

Johnson was able to comply by volunteering, on instructions from the Russian, to help paint the building. He reported that in his opinion it contained no alarm system. He was correct.

The most formidable and seemingly insuperable obstacles, of course, were the three locks. Viktor gave Johnson modeling clay in a cigarette pack and directed him to carry it at all times on the chance that he might be able to steal the vault key for a few minutes. Johnson protested that there would be no such chance because the key was always kept in the custody of an officer.

"We must not overlook any possibility," Viktor replied.

On a Monday morning early in 1962, a young lieutenant with whom Johnson was working complained of nausea. Suddenly ordering Johnson from the vault, he slammed the door shut, locked it and dashed outside to vomit. But, in his haste, he neglected to remove the key. Johnson grabbed it and quickly made an impression in the clay.

Two meetings later, Viktor told Johnson that the impression was too indistinct. The sergeant had bungled an opportunity that might not repeat itself, but there was no reproof in Viktor's words or tone, for Johnson was now too valuable to antagonize.

"Mistakes occur," Viktor said. "Let us hope there will be another opportunity."

One day, more in idle conversation than from curiosity, Johnson pointed to a small metal cabinet in the vault and asked the supervising officer, "What's in there?"

"Nothing," the officer replied, swinging open the unlocked cabinet. "It's empty."

Johnson saw that the cabinet was indeed empty except for a key in the corner—a spare key to the vault. Late that afternoon, he slipped it into his pocket and kept it overnight, carefully making three separate impressions in the clay. The next morning, while an officer was absorbed in a new batch of documents, he returned it unnoticed. Some three weeks later, a smiling Viktor handed him a shiny key made in Moscow. "You have a saying in America," he commented. "One down and two to go."

3. X-RAY MACHINE

JOHNSON NOW TRIED to memorize the combinations of the remaining two locks by watching officers while they opened them. Once an officer abruptly turned on him and snapped, "Stand back, Johnson. Don't hover over my shoulder when I'm doing this." The incident frightened Viktor more than Johnson.

"From now on, stay away when it is being opened; don't show any interest at all," Viktor ordered.

In accordance with routine security procedure, the Army changed the combination of one of the locks in June 1962. A captain who had been on leave telephoned another officer to ask for the new combination. The officer refused to release it over the phone, but after some argument consented to list numbers which, when appropriately added to the old combination, would yield the new. The captain recorded the numbers and performed the necessary addition on a slip of paper which he then carelessly discarded in his wastebasket.

"You are to be congratulated," said Viktor, after Johnson gave him the paper retrieved from the basket. "Now we must make certain this is the combination. It is time you volunteered for weekend work."

In addition to their regular duties, the clerical personnel took turns standing watch at the center when it was closed at night and on weekends. These were the only times the installation was protected by just one man. During weekday nights, however, couriers sometimes arrived at odd hours, making it necessary for the sentry to summon officers to reopen the center. Therefore, the KGB concluded that if the vault was ever to be penetrated, the attempt would have to be made on weekends, when couriers almost never came and the area was generally deserted.

With the pleasures of Paris only a few miles away, the lonely, boring weekend duty was universally unpopular. Most disliked of all was the shift lasting from 6 p.m. Saturday to 6 a.m. Sunday. In an effort to make it more palatable, the Army offered two weekdays off to anyone who volunteered for it. Still, there were few volunteers, and Johnson had no difficulty obtaining a permanent assignment to the Saturday-night watch. He explained that he needed a weekday free to take his wife to the doctor. The first night he stood guard, he waited until nearly 2 a.m. before testing the combination. "Two down," he thought, as the lock clicked open.

"Our scientists think they may have a way to figure out the combination of the other lock," Viktor confided in August. "But first we need many good close-up pictures of it from all angles. Use this Minox camera this weekend. I will receive the film from you on the way to work Monday at 0700." Holding up a map, Viktor pointed out a meeting site by a bridge along a country lane not far from Orly.

When Johnson halted his old Citroën by the bridge, he saw Viktor running out of the woods followed by a dark, slender man in an elegant blue suit. They both jumped into the car, and Viktor said, "Let me present my replacement, Feliks."

"Where are you going?" Johnson asked.

"I will still be here, working with you," Viktor replied. "However, we feel that two men are now required for our mutual success."

Indeed, the operation had assumed transcendent importance at KGB headquarters. Preparations for its decisive moments had grown so complex that many officers, both in Moscow and Paris, were now devoting themselves to it. The KGB needed at least two officers in Paris able to deal with Johnson, in case one should become incapacitated. In addition, to guard against enemy surveillance, it wanted an extra officer available to watch future meetings with Johnson.

Feliks Aleksandrovich Ivanov, who sometimes posed as a diplomat, sometimes as a United Nations official, knew Johnson well as a result of Viktor's briefings and his own study of the files. By nature Feliks was much more restless, authoritarian and intense than Viktor; yet he, too, treated Johnson considerately. He behaved like a patient tutor determined to extract the most from a dull and unstable pupil.

He met Johnson in early October at the Café L'Etoile d'Or, on the corner of the Boulevard Brune and the Rue des Plantes, to transmit critical instructions. "You must listen very carefully. If at any time you do not understand me, please say so," he began. "A special device soon will come from Moscow. It looks like this."

He unfolded a piece of onionskin paper bearing draftsman's designs and Russian lettering. One illustration showed a flat, circular metal plate about four inches in diameter and a thick metal cone perhaps nine inches long.

"You might call this a little X-ray machine," Feliks explained. "Once you place it over the lock, it will automatically X-ray the mechanism. Our scientists believe that from the X rays they can calculate the combination.

"As you can see, what you must do is simple. But there is danger. When in operation, the apparatus becomes radioactive. As soon as you place it over the lock, you must go to the farthest part of the room and wait 30 minutes. Is that clear?"

Along the same country lane where Johnson first met Feliks, the KGB delivered the device in two packages on a Friday night. Johnson stopped his Citroën just long enough for Viktor to pass one part through the window. About a mile down the lane, Feliks stepped from the woods and got into the front seat with the second part. Then he drilled Johnson once more in the procedures he was to follow.

In the courier center, at three o'clock Sunday morning, Johnson planted the plate and cone over the lock. They fitted perfectly, and instantly began to emit a barely audible humming sound. Johnson crouched in the darkness against a corner wall, continually checking his watch as the device did its work. After 30 minutes the hum ceased, and he replaced the cone and the plate in their respective boxes. Three weeks later, on November 30, Feliks handed him a slip of paper inscribed with a series of numbers. "That is it!" he said triumphantly.

"How do you know it's right?" Johnson asked.

"We know. There is no doubt," Feliks replied with a smile. "We have scheduled your first entry for December 15. There is much to do between now and then."

That night, Feliks drove Johnson in his gray Mercedes to Orly Field and turned onto a service road leading to the administration building, stopping on a bend near an overpass. "At 15 minutes past midnight, I will be standing here by my car," he said. "I will wave as you approach in your car. It will seem that I am seeking assistance. You will stop and give me the documents. We estimate that you will be away from your post less than five minutes."

From the airport, they traveled about five miles into the countryside, where Feliks parked his car on a dirt road by a forsaken little cemetery and said, "At 0315 hours I will return the documents to you here."

Feliks took two identical blue Air France flight bags from the trunk of his car. Giving one to Johnson, he said, "You are to place the documents in this bag. When you hand it to me near the overpass, I will give you this one in return. Look inside."

Inside the second bag were a bottle of cognac, four sandwiches, an apple and four white tablets.

Feliks explained that the cognac contained a drug that would quickly induce sleep. "Should anyone come to your post between our first and second appointments, give him a drink," he instructed. "Then you can safely leave to recover the documents from us. If it is necessary for you to drink also, take two of the tablets at once and the other two five minutes later. They will prevent the drug from affecting you."

The methodical rehearsals continued almost daily now, and they reflected the scope of the KGB's preparations. Feliks led Johnson 200 yards into a field off Highway D33. At the base of a tree he picked up a large rock and, as Johnson watched wonderingly, unscrewed it so that it formed two hollow parts.

"In an emergency, you will find here a Canadian passport with your photograph, personal credentials, money, instructions, a 1921 American silver dollar and an address in Brussels," Feliks said. "Make your way to Brussels. There, with a copy of the London *Times* in your left hand, come daily at 11 a.m. to the address. Our representative will approach you with a 1921 American silver dollar and ask if you dropped it. You will show your silver dollar and abide by his orders."

"How do you expect me to remember all that?" Johnson asked.

"We will practice until you can," Feliks calmly replied. "Now, let us begin the lesson again. . . ."

Feliks stressed that the KGB escape plan would automatically go into effect unless Johnson, after leaving the courier center on Sunday morning, signaled that all was well. To give the signal, he was to drop a pack of Lucky Strike cigarettes, with an "X" penciled inside it, by a certain telephone booth on his way home.

The final rehearsal was Friday night, December 14. Once more, Feliks drove Johnson to the bend on the Orly Field road near the overpass, then to the cemetery. "I will be waiting for you. Many people will be waiting," he said in parting. "Good luck."

The next night at the courier center, Johnson turned on a transistor radio and set his watch by the 11 p.m. time signal sounded by the U.S. Armed Forces radio network. In Paris, 24 miles away, Feliks did the same. Meanwhile, at the Soviet embassy in Paris, a team of KGB technicians, flown in from Moscow via Algeria, gathered in a small room on the third floor. They knew that they would have scarcely more than an hour to break the seal of the envelopes, photograph the contents, and reseal the envelopes in a manner that could not be detected.

Johnson took less than two minutes to open the three locks to the vault. Inside, he stuffed envelopes—some 11 by 13 inches, others 8 by 11—into the blue flight bag. Locking the vault and then the outer door of the Center, he ran to his Citroën and drove off to meet Feliks. All went precisely as rehearsed. At 3:15 a.m., Johnson recovered the envelopes at the cemetery and replaced them in the vault. By the time he reached home Sunday morning, a mass of American cryptographic and military secrets was already en route to Moscow.

The next Saturday night, December 22, Johnson again looted the vault without the least difficulty. This time he selected new envelopes that had arrived during the preceding two or three days.

The day after Christmas, Feliks greeted Johnson jubilantly: "On behalf of the Council of Ministers of the U.S.S.R., I have been directed to congratulate you on the great contribution you have made to peace. I am told that some of the material we sent was so interesting that it was read by Comrade Khrushchev himself. In appreciation, you have been awarded the rank of major in the Red army. I also have been authorized to give you a bonus of $2000. Take a holiday and go to Monte Carlo and live it up."

The rank of major represented a fictitious award bestowed by the KGB to boost Johnson's ego and motivate him further. But there is independent testimony to the effect that an excited Khrushchev did study the materials Johnson supplied. Yuri Ivanovich Nosenko, a KGB major who worked at headquarters in Moscow before fleeing to the West, states that the arrival of the first documents from the vault created a sensation. According to what he was told, copies were rushed to Khrushchev and certain Politburo members immediately after translation. Nosenko also heard that some of the stolen data disclosed numbers and locations of American nuclear warheads stored in Europe.

Clearly, the documents from the vault were extraordinary, not only because of their content, but because of their indisputable authenticity. Anyone studying them might as well have been admitted to the highest councils of the United States and been allowed to take notes. Some of the ultra-secret papers outlined major modifications or additions to the basic American strategic plan for the defense of Western Europe. No one document by itself provided an overall blueprint of the plan, but collectively they laid it bare. The Soviet Union could now identify with certainty strengths to be countered and vulnerabilities that could be exploited. Decisive battles have been won with less intelligence than these penetrations yielded. And this was only the beginning.

Indeed, the initial yield was so spectacular that the Soviet Union adopted further precautions to safeguard the operation. Nosenko says that all subsequent entries into the vault required direct approval from the Politburo, and that with the approach of each, an air of tension and excitement pervaded the KGB command.

This corresponds with instructions that Johnson received in January 1963 from Feliks, who advised that henceforth the vault would be looted only at intervals of from four to six weeks, and that each entry would be scheduled a minimum of 14 days in advance.

"We must bring people in from Moscow," Feliks said. "The arrangements are very complicated."

A team of technicians was required to process the documents that Johnson removed, but the KGB dared not station them permanently in Paris. It knew that French security would eventually recognize them as the specialists they were and realize that their presence signified a leak of considerable importance. The KGB also knew that the technicians probably would be detected if they shuttled in and out of Paris too often. Therefore, it chose to reduce the frequency of their journeys and to have them come to Paris individually and by various routes.

Additionally, the KGB recognized that, although Johnson had twice taken documents from the vault with ease, each penetration still entailed high risks. If anyone chanced to find him missing during the two crucial absences from the center, there was no way he could explain himself. The Russians did not bother to equip him with a cover story because they knew that any excuse would be futile. Moreover, although Johnson, by virtue of his position, had become a priceless agent, the KGB had no admiration for him as a person. It knew that if he was ever interrogated seriously he would soon collapse and confess.

The night was cold and mist-laden when Johnson met Feliks at 3:15 a.m. in late February to retrieve documents that he had passed three hours before. As usual, they shook hands and silently exchanged the blue flight bags. But when Johnson tried to drive away, the engine of his old Citroën refused to start.

"Let me try," Feliks insisted. Neither of them could make the weary car respond. Then they heard another automobile braking to a stop behind them. Both Feliks and Johnson jumped out and froze before the silhouette of a man approaching with a revolver. It was Viktor, who had been guarding the rendezvous from a distance. For 20 minutes—each second increasing the probability of disaster—they struggled to start the Citroën. Finally, after Viktor had pushed it nearly half a mile with his own car, the Citroën coughed and began to run. The next week, with money from Moscow, Johnson bought a used Mercedes.

One Sunday in March, after Johnson had successfully raided the vault, he left his apartment in the afternoon to buy bread. To his astonishment, he saw both Feliks and Viktor parked near the entrance of the building. When they spotted him, they quickly drove off. Johnson was puzzled—until he realized that he had forgotten to leave the cigarette package by the telephone booth to signal that he was safe.

"You can't imagine what trouble your negligence caused," Feliks said angrily at the Wednesday critique that regularly followed each theft of documents. "To prepare for your escape, we had to alarm people all the way from Paris to Moscow. I will have to waste two days now writing reports to explain."

"I'm sorry," Johnson replied. "I just forgot."

"Never let it happen again," Feliks warned. "This is the kind of carelessness that will put you in prison."

On April 20, 1963, Johnson entered the vault for the seventh time, intent on grabbing two envelopes that had arrived from Washington the day before. At 12:15 a.m. on April 21, Johnson handed the bagful of secrets to Feliks. But at 3:15 he failed to appear at the cemetery.

Feliks began a torturous wait. Possibly someone had come to the center, and Johnson had not yet succeeded in drugging him with the doped cognac. Perhaps he had had an accident en route, or maybe he had been caught and had already told about the Russian waiting on the road by the cemetery. Maybe, at this very moment, platoons of armed Americans were on their way.

About 5 a.m., Feliks realized that he could wait no longer. Soon dawn would break over Orly Field, and with daylight there would be no chance of replacing the documents. Johnson would be arrested, the great operation destroyed. Feliks took the only gamble he could. He drove to Orly and stopped his car about ten yards from the courier center. Leaving the engine running, he dropped the flight bag containing the documents into the front seat of Johnson's car. He left with little hope that his daring could overcome the catastrophe he was certain had befallen both Johnson and the KGB.

However, Johnson was not the victim of any misfortune. He simply had fallen asleep. Around 5:30, he woke in clear daylight. Frantically, he ran to the car. There was the bag. He had just shut the vault, and still had his hand on one of the locks to the outer door, when a corporal arrived to relieve him for breakfast.

Johnson could not force himself to admit to the KGB that he had been so stupid as to fall asleep. So he concocted a story that an officer had come at 3 a.m. to pick up documents for a special delivery and had decided to take a nap before departing.

"The s.o.b. stayed until after five," he told Feliks. "There was nothing I could do."

"I see," Feliks remarked. "It must have been a difficult time."

This reaction convinced Johnson that his lie had been accepted. It had not been. The KGB was aware that withdrawals from the center were never made on Sunday, and that, in any case, no officer could remove documents without submitting to inventory control by a second officer. Therefore, it knew that Johnson was lying. But it could not imagine why.

Thus in doubt, the KGB decided in May to retire temporarily from the the game while it still was a grand-scale winner. Much of the value of what the KGB had stolen depended upon keeping the United States ignorant of the thefts. Should the Americans find out, they could begin revising plans and redistributing forces. Thus, until it knew the real reason for Johnson's lie, the KGB wanted to take no more risks.

Feliks explained the suspension to Johnson by saying that, with the coming of summer, the nights would be too short.

4. CONFESSION

DURING THE SUMMER, THE KGB found no evidence that Johnson had compromised himself, and it prepared to resume operations in the fall. It was reassured when Johnson received a promotion in September. But, with the promotion came a transfer to the Seine Area Command in Sainte-Honorine. The vault had been rifled for the last time.

Then, in May 1964, the Army sent Johnson to the Pentagon to be near Hedy, who had been flown to Walter Reed Hospital for psychiatric treatment. Just before leaving France, Johnson dined with Feliks and Viktor in Paris. "Do you know what your duties will be at the Pentagon?" Feliks asked.

"More of the same, I guess," Johnson said. "Shuffling secret papers, hauling them around."

Both Feliks and Viktor beamed over such unbelievable luck. "Well, that could be a very interesting assignment," Viktor commented. They parted with an understanding that Johnson would meet a KGB man at La Guardia Airport in New York on December 1, 1964.

Johnson rented a pleasant brick house on a tree-lined street in Alexandria, Va., and Hedy joined him there after her release from the hospital, seemingly much better. Coming home from the Pentagon one afternoon in July, he stopped on Columbia Pike in Arlington to buy a pizza. While he stood in line, a man called to him from the doorway. "How are you, Bob?" They were the same words with which Mintkenbaugh had greeeted him in Berlin, in Las Vegas, in Orléans.

Reunited over beer and pizza that evening, Johnson and Mintkenbaugh recounted their espionage experiences since they had last seen each other. Mintkenbaugh had performed a variety of useful if unspectacular chores for the KGB. He lived six weeks in Canada collecting birth certificates and other documents for use by KGB illegals infiltrating the United States. Eventually he became a real-estate salesman in Arlington, which enabled him to supply the Russians with information about government employes looking for housing. During the Cuban missile crisis of October 1962, the KGB dispatched him on an emergency trip to report about a massive military mobilization in southern Florida.

"I'm going to see them again in December," Johnson confided. But he soon forgot about the Russians, his duties at the Pentagon and everything else. In September, Hedy's spasms of insanity and jealousy returned with such violence that fear of them obsessed him. Once, in a restaurant, she fancied that a woman at a nearby table was courting Johnson's attention. Suddenly, she jumped up, threw over the table and began pulling the woman's hair. In a supermarket she imagined that Johnson was flirting with a shopping housewife. She slipped up behind him and kicked him so hard that he stumbled forward, knocked over a display of canned goods and sprawled in the aisle on his face. So, on the afternoon of October 2, 1964, after failing to have Hedy committed at the hospital, Johnson chose to flee.

At the Old Dominion Bank in Arlington, he withdrew $2200 in savings, then drove aimlessly about until he saw a highway sign pointing to Richmond. There he abandoned his car, bought a bottle of whiskey and embarked on a drunken bus journey to Las Vegas via Cincinnati, St. Louis and Denver. In Las Vegas, he rented a dingy little room for $24 a month and began to gamble.

Thirty days after Johnson vanished, the Army classified him as a deserter and asked law-enforcement agencies to track him down. Two FBI agents called on Hedy in quest of routine information. Though obviously disturbed, she answered their questions more or less rationally. She acknowledged that she and her husband had been quarreling a lot, but professed concern about his disappearance and welfare. It looked like the most ordinary of cases—an Army sergeant off on a binge, in quest of respite from the nagging of a mentally ill wife.

In view of the available evidence, no one could have reproached the two FBI men if they had simply filed their report and considered their duty done. They chose, however, to explore the case further. Within a few days, they discovered that while being treated at Walter Reed, Hedy had called her husband a spy.

They returned for a second visit, asking Hedy if there wasn't something troubling her that she would like to talk about.

The three of them sat in silence for perhaps two full minutes while Hedy kept her head bowed and her hands over her face. "My husband, he's a bad man," she finally said. "And Hedy is a very bad girl."

"What do you mean, Mrs. Johnson?" an agent asked.

"He's a spy," she said. "And I know someone else who is, too."

The appalling narrative Hedy then offered was rambling and inherently incredible. She confused dates and places, and on occasion her memory failed entirely. Yet, deranged as she was, Hedy offered too many specific details to be ignored. Parts of her story were subjected to quick verification. They proved to be all too true.

Alarm multiplied the next morning when the FBI agents went to Mintkenbaugh's Arlington apartment. He, too, had disappeared. The FBI found him three days later hiding at an old address in northern California. Pale and trembling, he denied any involvement in espionage. But, on being confronted with specific allegations, he began to sob and confess. His confession continued for days, interrupted by tearful attempts to explain himself.

"I couldn't understand for a long time why I was doing it," he told the FBI. "Now I know that revenge got into me. You see, God makes mistakes, and I'm one of them. I wish I had died as a baby."

The accounts of Hedy and Mintkenbaugh conclusively demonstrated that Johnson was a spy. But neither she nor Mintkenbaugh knew about the looting of the vault. To the Defense Department and the FBI, the critical question remained: What had Johnson given the Russians? Only he and the KGB had the answer. FBI teleprinters advised field offices throughout the country that Johnson's apprehension was of urgent national importance.

While FBI agents and police watched for him at airports, rail and bus terminals, bars and hotels, Johnson, on the morning of November 25, 1964, awoke despondent and groggy from alcohol. He reached into his pocket and counted all the money he had left—four cents. Unshaven and bedraggled, he walked into a police station in Reno, identified himself as a deserter and surrendered.

The military police escorted Johnson to Washington, and eventually he confessed. He evinced not the least remorse or even any awareness that he had done anything wrong. It was not until an interrogator mentioned the possibility of execution that Johnson seemed to worry.

"Listen, you guys are going about this the wrong way," he said. "I can do you fellows a lot of good."

"What do you mean?" asked an FBI agent. "I can be a counterspy," Johnson answered seriously.

Two FBI agents and two Army officers present stared at him in disbelief, probably the same kind of disbelief with which KGB officers had regarded him 12 years before in Karlshorst when he proposed that he be made a commentator on Radio Moscow. During hundreds of subsequent interrogations, Johnson seemed to enjoy reliving his life as a KGB agent, and he supplied the FBI with mountainous details about it.

On July 30, 1965, in the federal district court at Alexandria, Johnson and Mintkenbaugh, who had pleaded guilty to charges of espionage conspiracy, were each sentenced to 25 years' imprisonment. From the brief proceedings, the public derived no intimation of the enormity of the losses the United States had sustained. In Moscow, meanwhile, Paula, Viktor, Feliks and at least four other KGB officers who participated in the Johnson-Mintkenbaugh operation were awarded the Order of Lenin, the highest decoration of the Soviet Union.

Because Johnson could not identify all the documents that he delivered to the KGB, the United States had to assume that the Russians had copied every one that passed through the courier center between December 15, 1962, and April 21, 1963. On grounds of national security, the Department of Defense declines to comment about the possibility that the documents enabled the KGB to break U.S. cipher systems.

"It is accurate to characterize our losses as enormous. Some are irreparable and incalculable," a Department of Defense spokesman has stated. "It is also impossible to reckon precisely in dollars the cost of repairing that damage which could be repaired. There is, however, a more fundamental consideration. Had we not discovered the losses, and and had there been war, the damage might have been fatal."

The consequences of Johnson's espionage did not end with his imprisonment. The widely read West German magazines *Stern* and *Der Spiegel,* in September 1969, published articles purportedly based on authentic copies of top-secret U.S. contingency plans. The contents of the alleged plans as reported by the magazines were enough to horrify friends and foes of America alike. They suggested that should Soviet forces overrun Western Europe, the United States intended to devastate the continent by waging bacteriological and nuclear warfare against the civilian population.

Circulation of the alleged documents bore some basic and familiar characteristics of a KGB "dis-information" operation. They earlier had been mailed to other European journals and first appeared in a publication in Italy, *Paese Sera,* to which no one paid any attention. Subsequently, the "documents" were mailed from Rome to the two German magazines by an unknown source. The "documents" were not originals but copies, and therefore not subject to technical tests that could prove them to be either authentic or bogus. *Der Spiegel* asserted that they were circulated as part of a KGB dis-information operation. Nevertheless, the reported American plans engendered alarm in Western Europe and doubtless sowed much mistrust of the United States.

In its issue dated February 1, 1970, *Stern* published an even more incendiary article ostensibly based on another top-secret U.S. document, *Handbook of Nuclear Yield Requirements.* Excerpts from this alleged document showed that the United States, in event of war, intended to blow up more than a thousand civilian targets in Egypt, Syria, Iraq and Iran, as well as in Western and Eastern Europe. Another understandable anti-American furor ensued.

U.S. authorities have usually been able to expose such Soviet forgeries by citing errors in style or terminology. But the "documents" that the KGB disseminated in 1969 and 1970 were almost perfect in form—because the Russians were able to pattern them after similar, authentic documents that Johnson had mined from the vault.

THE STORY OF ROBERT LEE JOHNSON finally ended in May 1972. Johnson and Hedy had a son, Robert, who ordinarily would not have been mentioned in this account. Events now require otherwise.

Over the years, Hedy's illness and Johnson's character defects made their home a hell, and young Robert was eventually placed with foster parents. He joined the Army at 19, and fought in Vietnam—and there he began to brood about his traitorous father.

Johnson must have been pleased when notified that Robert, back from Vietnam, wished to visit him on Thursday afternoon, May 18, 1972. Only once before had Robert come to see him—at the federal penitentiary in Lewisburg, Pa.—and he rarely wrote. Smiling, Johnson walked into the prison reception room and reached to shake hands with his son. Without a word, Robert plunged a knife deep into his father's chest. Johnson died within the hour. He was 52.

Robert, who is serving a ten-year sentence for manslaughter, has consistently refused to explain his action. To the FBI he will only say, "It was a personal matter."

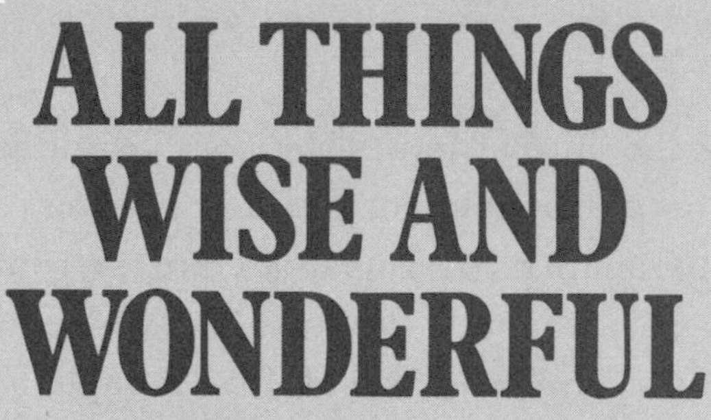

ALL THINGS WISE AND WONDERFUL

CONDENSED FROM THE BOOK BY

James Herriot

ILLUSTRATED BY GEORGE H. JONES

This is the third of James Herriot's beguiling accounts of his experiences as a practicing veterinarian in rural England. Here the young doctor tells of joining the Royal Air Force to serve his country in World War II. But, though the demands of military life are many, his mind constantly wanders back to the Yorkshire Dales and his professional practice.

The reader is presented with such unforgettable stories as that of Blossom, the old cow whose time has not quite come; of Cedric, the huge friendly dog with an unfortunate affliction; of Oscar, the cat who needed all of his nine lives.

1. REFLECTIONS

"MOVE!" BAWLED THE DRILL CORPORAL. "Come on, speed it up!" He sprinted effortlessly to the rear of the gasping, panting column of men and urged us on from there. "At the double, *qui-ick* march, 'eft, 'ight, 'eft, 'ight."

I was somewhere in the middle, jogging laboriously with the rest and wondering how much longer I could keep going. A country veterinarian, especially in the Yorkshire Dales, never had a chance to get out of condition; he was always on the move, wrestling with the big animals, walking for miles between the fellside barns; he was hard and tough. That's what I thought.

But now other reflections began to creep in. My few months of married life with Helen had been so much lotus-eating. She was too good a cook and I was too faithful a disciple of her art. Three days ago I was in Darrowby; half of me was still there, back with Helen.

And on this, my third day in the Royal Air Force, the whole thing was still a blur.

"Round again, lads!" the corporal yelled.

Bitter thoughts assailed me as I lurched forward again. You left a loving wife and a happy home to serve king and country, and this was how they treated you.

The night before I had dreamed of Darrowby. I was back in old Mr. Dakin's cow byre. The farmer's patient eyes in the long, drooping-mustached face looked down at me from his stooping height.

"It looks as though it's over wi' awd Blossom, then," he said, and rested his hand briefly on the old cow's back. It was an enormous, work-swollen hand. Mr. Dakin's gaunt frame carried little flesh, but the grossly thickened fingers bore testimony to a life of toil.

I dried off the needle and dropped it into the metal box where I carried my suture materials, scalpels and blades. "Well, it's up to you, Mr. Dakin, but this is the third time I've had to stitch her teats and I'm afraid it's going to keep on happening."

That was the worst problem for old cows. Their udders dropped so that when they lay down in their stalls the vital milk-producing organ was pushed into the path of the neighboring animals. If it wasn't Mabel on the right standing on it, it was Buttercup on the other side.

"Aye, well," Mr. Dakin said. "Ah reckon t'awd lass doesn't owe me anythin'. Ah remember the night she was born, 12 years ago. She was out of awd Daisy and Ah carried her out of this very byre and the snow was comin' down hard. Sin' then Ah wouldn't like to count how many thousand gallons o' milk she's turned out; she's still givin' four a day. Naw, she doesn't owe me a thing."

Mr. Dakin blew out his cheeks. "Well, there's nowt else for it. I'll tell Jack Dodson to pick 'er up on Thursday. She'll be a bit tough for eatin', but Ah reckon she'll make a few steak pies." He was trying a joke, but he was unable to smile.

It happened that I was called back to the farm for other work on the following Thursday and was in the byre when Dodson, the drover, called to pick up Blossom. "Aye, come on with ye!" shouted the dealer, poking his stick against the cow's rump.

"Doan't hit 'er!" barked Mr. Dakin.

Dodson looked at him in surprise. "Ah never 'it 'em, you know that. Just send 'em on, like."

"Ah knaw, Ah knaw, Jack, but you won't need your stick for this 'un. She'll go wherever ye want."

The old man and I stood watching as the cow made her way unhurriedly out of the barn and up the hill. The path wound behind a clump of sparse trees, and man and beast disappeared. But Mr. Dakin gazed after them, listening to the *clip-clop* of the hoofs on the ground.

When the sound died away, he turned to me quickly. "Right, Mr. Herriot, we'll get on wi' our job, then."

When my work was finished, the conversation died and the silence was almost oppressive as we opened the byre door. Mr. Dakin paused, his hand on the latch.

"What's that?" he said softly.

From somewhere on the hillside I could hear the *clip-clop* of a cow's feet. Then a cow rounded a rocky outcrop and came toward us.

It was Blossom, moving at a brisk trot, great udder swinging, eyes fixed purposefully on the open door behind us.

"What the hangment. . . ?" Mr. Dakin burst out, but the old cow marched past us into the stall she had occupied for all those years. Mr. Dakin stared after her. The eyes in the weathered face were expressionless, but the smoke rose from his pipe in rapid puffs.

Heavy boots clattered suddenly outside and Jack Dodson panted his way through the door. "Oh, you're there, ye awd beggar!" he gasped. "Ah thought I'd lost ye!" He turned to the farmer. "By gaw, I'm sorry, Mr. Dakin. She must 'ave turned off at t'top of your other path. Ah never saw her go." The drover grinned and moved toward Blossom. "Come on, lass, let's have ye out o' there again."

But he halted as Mr. Dakin held an arm in front of him. Dodson and I looked in surprise at the farmer, who continued to gaze fixedly at the cow. There was a pathetic dignity about the old animal as she stood there, her eyes patient and undemanding, a dignity that triumphed over the unsightliness of the upturned hoofs, the fleshless ribs, the udder almost brushing the cobbles.

"Ah'm sorry to waste your time, Jack, but you'll have to go without 'er. T'awd lass has come 'ome." He directed a look of flat finality at the drover. Dodson nodded and then shuffled from the byre.

"Ah've had an idea," the old man said to me. "I can put two or three calves on to 'er instead of milkin' 'er. The old stable is empty—she can live in there where there's nobody to stand on 'er."

I laughed. "You're right, Mr. Dakin. She'd be safe in the stable and she'd suckle three calves easily. She could pay her way."

"Well, after all them years she doesn't owe me a thing." A gentle smile spread over the seamed face. "Main thing is, she's come 'ome."

I COULD SEE THE CORPORAL's laughing face. The man was clearly a sadist. And as I launched myself into the final series of exercises, it came to me suddenly why I had dreamed about Blossom. I wanted to go home, too.

In the RAF my impression that I had been hurled into a coarser world was heightened at the beginning of each day. It wasn't the cursing and the obscene remarks which struck deepest; it was the extraordinary abdominal noises issuing from the dark rooms. They reminded me of my patient, Cedric, and in an instant I was back in Darrowby answering the telephone.

"Mr. Herriot . . . I should be grateful if you would come and see my dog." A woman was speaking, obviously upper-class.

"Certainly; what's the trouble?"

"Well" she said, ". . . he . . . er . . . he seems to suffer from . . . a certain amount of flatus."

"I beg your pardon?"

There was a long pause. "He has excessive flatus. . . . I suppose you'd describe it as . . . windiness." The voice had begun to tremble.

I thought I could see a gleam of light. "You mean his stomach. . . .?"

"No, not his stomach. He passes . . . er . . . a considerable quantity of . . . wind from his . . . his. . . ." A note of desperation had crept in.

All became suddenly clear, and I asked her address. "It's Mrs. Rumney, The Laurels."

Mrs. Rumney herself let me in and I felt a shock of surprise at my first sight of her. She would be around 40, but had the appearance of a heroine in a Victorian novel—tall, willowy, ethereal. And I could understand immediately her hesitation on the phone. Everything about her suggested fastidiousness and delicacy.

"Cedric is in the kitchen," she said. "I'll take you through."

I had another surprise when I saw Cedric. An enormous boxer hurled himself on me in delight, clawing at my chest. I tried to fight him off, but he kept at me, panting ecstatically into my face and wagging his entire rear end.

"Sit down, boy!" the lady said sharply and then, as Cedric took absolutely no notice, she turned to me nervously. "He's so friendly."

I finally managed to push the huge animal away and backed into a corner for safety.

"How often does this excessive flatus occur?" I asked.

As if in reply an almost palpable sulfurous wave arose from the dog and eddied about me. I was up against the wall and unable to obey my first instinct to run for cover, so I held my hand over my face for a few minutes before speaking.

It turned out that Cedric was getting rather a lot of meat, and I drew up a little chart cutting down on the protein and adding extra carbohydrates. I prescribed an antacid mixture to be given night and morning and left in a confident frame of mind. But a week later Mrs. Rumney was on the phone again.

I had a busy day and it was after 6 p.m. before I got around to The Laurels. There were several cars in the drive, and when I went into the house I saw that Mrs. Rumney had a few people in for drinks; people like herself—upper-class and of obvious refinement.

Mrs. Rumney was about to lead me through to the kitchen when the door burst open, and Cedric bounded delightedly into the midst of the company. Within seconds an esthetic-looking gentleman was frantically beating off the attack. He got away at the cost of a couple of vest buttons, and the boxer turned his attention to one of the ladies, but soon I became aware that a more insidious element had crept into the situation. The atmosphere became charged with an unmistakable effluvium, and it was clear that Cedric's unfortunate malady had most assuredly reasserted itself.

Most dogs suffer from this affliction occasionally, but Cedric did it all the time. And at each expulsion he would look around inquiringly at his back end, then gambol about the room as though the fugitive zephyr was clearly visible to him and he was determined to corner it.

After that night I threw myself into the struggle on Mrs. Rumney's behalf. I felt she desperately needed my help, and I made frequent visits and tried innumerable remedies. I consulted my partner, Siegfried Farnon, on the problem, and he suggested charcoal biscuits. Cedric ate them in vast quantities, but they, like everything else, made not the slightest difference.

Cedric had one admirer, at least. He was Con Fenton, a retired farm worker who did a bit of gardening three days a week at The Laurels. After one of my visits, the boxer romped down the drive as I was leaving, and the old man looked at him with undisguised admiration.

"By gaw," he said. "He's a fine dog, is that!"

"Yes, Con, he's a good chap, really." And I meant it. Cedric gave off a constant aura not merely of noxious vapors but of bonhomie.

"Look at them limbs!" breathed Con, staring at the dog's muscular thighs. "He's what Ah call a dog!"

As he spoke, it struck me that Cedric would be likely to appeal to him because he was very like the boxer himself; not overburdened with brains, built like an ox, with powerful shoulders and a big, constantly grinning face.

A few weeks later I called in at The Laurels. "Maybe you'll think it's none of my business," I said to Mrs. Rumney, "but I honestly don't think Cedric is the dog for you. I think you should get another in his place—something smaller."

"But, Mr. Herriot, I couldn't possibly have Cedric put down." Her eyes filled quickly with tears. "I really am fond of him despite . . . everything."

"No, no, of course not!" I said. "I like him, too. But I think I have a good idea. Why not let Con Fenton take him? He admires Cedric tremendously, and the big fellow would have a good life with the old man. He has a couple of fields behind his cottage. Cedric could run to his heart's content, and Con would be able to bring him along when he does the garden. You'd still see him three times a week."

Mrs. Rumney rang within a few days. Con had jumped at the chance of taking on Cedric, and the pair had apparently settled in happily together. She had also taken my advice and acquired a poodle puppy.

I didn't see the new dog until it was nearly six months old, when its mistress asked me to call. Con Fenton's cottage was less than half a mile away and, on my way home, on an impulse I pulled up at the door. I had hardly stepped into the tiny living room when a hairy form hurled itself upon me, and I had to battle my way to the broken armchair by the fireside. Con settled down opposite, and when the boxer leaped to lick his face he clumped him companionably on the head with his fist.

"Siddown, ye great daft bugger," he murmured with affection.

"Well, Mr. Herriot," Con went on as he cut up some villainous-looking plug tobacco and began to stuff it into his pipe. "I'm right grateful to ye for gettin' me this grand dog. By gaw, he's a topper. No man could ask for a better friend."

At that moment a familiar pungency rose even above the billowings from the pipe. Cedric was obviously working something off. Con seemed oblivious to it, but I found it overpowering.

"Ah, well," I gasped. "I just looked in for a moment to see how you were getting on together. I must be on my way." I rose hurriedly and stumbled toward the door.

As I passed the table with the remains of the old man's meal I saw what seemed to be the only ornament in the cottage, a cracked vase holding a bouquet of carnations. I buried my nose in their fragrance.

Con watched me approvingly. "Aye, they're lovely flowers, aren't they? T'missus at Laurels lets me bring 'ome what I want, and I reckon them carnations is me favorite. There's only one thing," the old man said pensively. "Ah don't get t'full benefit of 'em. When I were a lad, I 'ad a operation for adenoids and summat went wrong."

"You mean. . . ?" A light was beginning to dawn.

"Aye," the old man went on sadly. "I 'ave no sense of smell."

2. FIRST CHILD

OUR BREAKING-IN WEEKS WERE nearly over, and we waited for news of posting to Initial Training Wing where we would learn navigation, principles of flight and so on. The air was thick with rumors. We were going to Wales; then it was Cornwall; then someplace else. I wanted the north, for Helen was expecting our first child, and I hoped to be as near to her as possible. When the posting came, it seemed too good to be true. I was going to Scarborough, a seaside resort only a three-hour bus ride from home.

I suppose once you embark on a life of crime it gets easier all the time. Soon after arriving in Scarborough, I played hookey in order to see Helen. Now, a few weeks later, I was doing it again. Helen was expecting our baby momentarily, and I didn't see how I could sit there these few miles away and do nothing.

After the long bus ride, I hurried up to the doorway of her parents' home where she was now living, went inside and gazed disappointedly at the empty kitchen. Somehow I had been sure she would be standing there waiting for me. I shouted her name, but nothing stirred. I was still there, listening, when her father came through from an inner room.

"You've got a son," he said.

I put my hand on the back of a chair. "What. . . ?"

"You've got a son." He was so calm. "Few minutes ago. Nurse Brown's just been on the phone. Funny you should walk in."

As I leaned on a chair he gave me a keen look. "Would you like a drop of whisky? You've gone a bit white, lad."

"Sorry, I couldn't. Would you mind if I borrowed your car?"

I was still trembling a little as I drove away, and when I pulled up outside Nurse Brown's it still hadn't got through to me that I was a father. Nurse Brown opened the door herself and threw up her hands. "Mr. Herriot! It hasn't taken you long! Where did you spring from?"

Still in a dreamlike state, I followed her up the stairs into a small bedroom. Helen was there in the bed, looking flushed.

"Hello," she said.

I went over and kissed her. She nodded toward the cot beside her.

I took my first look at my son. Little Jimmy was brick-red in color, and his face had a bloated, dissipated look. As I hung over him, he twisted his tiny fists under his chin and appeared to be undergoing some mighty internal struggle. His face swelled and darkened as he contorted his features; then, from deep among the puffy flesh, his eyes fixed me with a baleful glare and he stuck his tongue out of the corner of his mouth.

"My God!" I exclaimed.

The nurse looked at me, startled. "What's the matter?"

"Well, he's a funny-looking little thing, isn't he?"

"What!" She stared at me furiously. "Mr. Herriot, how can you say such a thing? He's a beautiful baby!"

I peered into the cot again. Jimmy greeted me with a lopsided leer, turned purple and blew a few bubbles.

"Have you by chance got any others on the premises?" I said.

"Any other what?" Nurse Brown asked icily.

"Babies—new babies. I want to compare Jimmy with another one."

There was a long pause as she looked at me as though I was something new and incredible. "Well, there's Mrs. Dewburn in the next room. Little Sidney was born about the same time as Jimmy."

Mrs. Dewburn was the butcher's wife and I knew her well. The face on the pillow was hot and tired like Helen's. I looked in the cot. Sidney was dark red and bloated, too, and he, also, seemed to be wrestling with himself. The inner battle showed in a series of grotesque facial contortions culminating in a toothless snarl.

I stepped back involuntarily. "What a beautiful child," I said. "Thank you very much, Mrs. Dewburn. It was kind of you to let me see him."

Outside the door I took a long breath and wiped my brow. The relief was tremendous. Sidney was even funnier than Jimmy.

When I returned to Helen's room Nurse Brown was sitting on the bed, and the two women were clearly laughing at me. "I suppose you think all your calves and foals are beautiful right from the moment they are born?" the nurse asked.

"Well, yes," I replied. "I have to admit—I think they are."

On the bus journey back to Scarborough, a devilish scheme began to hatch in my brain. I was due for compassionate leave, but why should I take it now? Helen would be in the nursing home for a fortnight and there didn't seem any sense in my mooning round Darrowby on my own. The thing to do would be to send myself a telegram two weeks from now announcing the birth, and we would be able to spend my leave together. I wasn't scrounging anything extra, I told myself. I was just altering the time. On the following day I wrote to a friend in Darrowby and arranged about the telegram. But I wasn't such a hardened criminal as I had thought, because, as the days passed, doubts began to creep in.

When the fateful day arrived my roommates and I were stretched on our beds after lunch when a great voice boomed along the corridor. "Herriot! Come on, let's have you, Herriot!"

My stomach lurched. Somehow I hadn't reckoned on Flight Sergeant Blackett coming into this. Blackett was an unsmiling martinet of immense natural presence. It was usually the junior NCOs who dealt with our misdemeanors, but if Flight Sergeant Blackett ever took a hand, it was a withering experience.

I heard it again. The same bull bellow which echoed over our heads on the square every morning. "Herriot! Let's be having you, Herriot!" He gave me the news, then said, "Let me be the first to congratulate you." He held out his hand and as I took it, he smiled. Suddenly he looked very like Gary Cooper.

"You haven't far to go, anyway. Let's see—Darrowby—yes, there's a train out of here at 3:20." He looked at his watch. "You ought to make that if you get your skates on."

A deepening sense of shame threatened to engulf me when he spoke again. "This'll be your first 'un, of course? I've got three of 'em, meself. Getting big now, but I miss 'em like hell. I really envy you, walking in that door tonight and seeing your son for the first time."

Guilt drove through me in a searing flood, and I was convinced my shifty eyes and furtive glances would betray me. But he wasn't really looking at me.

"You know, lad," he said softly, "this is the best time of your life coming up. Give my regards to them both."

I had a wonderful time with Helen, walking for miles, discovering the delights of pram pushing, with little Jimmy miraculously improved in appearance. Everything was so much better than if I had taken my leave at the official time, and there is no doubt my plan was a success.

But I was unable to gloat about it. The triumph was dimmed and to this day I have reservations about the whole thing.

Being away from Darrowby and living a different life, I was able to stand back and assess certain things objectively. I asked myself many questions. Why, for instance, was my partnership with Siegfried Farnon so successful?

EVEN NOW, AS WE STILL JOG along happily after 35 years, I wonder about it. Maybe it is because we are opposites. Siegfried's restless energy impels him constantly to try to alter things, while I abhor change. A lot of people would call him brilliant, while not even my best friends would apply that description to me. I could go on and on—we are even opposite physical types—and yet, as I say, we get along.

This of course doesn't mean that we have never had minor clashes on various points. One, I recall, was over plastic injectors for calcium. They were something new, so Siegfried liked them and, by the same token, I regarded them with deep suspicion. My doubts were nourished by my difficulties with them. Their early troubles have now been ironed out, but at the beginning I found the things so temperamental that I abandoned them.

My colleague pulled me up about it when he saw me washing out my syringe by running water from the surgery tap through it.

"For God's sake, James, you're not still using that old thing, are you? Haven't you tried the new plastics?"

"I have." I trickled the last drop through the tube and slipped it into its case. "The last time I used one the calcium squirted all over. I had great white streaks down my coat."

Siegfried laughed incredulously. "That's crazy! They're childishly simple to use."

"I believe you," I said. "But, I haven't got a mechanical mind."

Siegfried assumed a grave expression. "It only needs a little application on your part, James, and I must stress that you are behaving in a reactionary manner by being stubborn. I put it to you seriously that we have to move with the times, and every time you use that antiquated outfit of yours it is a retrograde step."

We stood, as we often did, eyeball to eyeball, in mutual disagreement. Then Siegfried smiled. "Look, you're going out now, aren't you, to see that milk-fever cow I treated at John Tillot's. I understand it's not up yet. As a favor to me, will you give one of the new packs a try?"

I thought for a moment. "All right, Siegfried, I'll have one more go."

When I reached the farm I found the cow comfortably ensconced in a field, in the middle of a rolling yellow ocean of buttercups.

"She's had a few tries to get on 'er feet," the farmer said. "But she can't quite make it."

"Probably just wants another shot." I went to my car and took one of the plastic packs from the boot.

Mr. Tillot raised his eyebrows when he saw me coming back. "Is that one o' them new things?"

I said yes and assured him it was sterilized.

"Ah don't care what it is. Ah don't like it!"

"Why not?"

"Ah'll tell ye. Mr. Farnon used one this mornin'. Some of the stuff went in me eye, some went in 'is ear 'ole and the rest went down 'is trousers. Ah don't think t'bloody cow got any!"

Some of our disagreements were sharp and short. I was sitting at the lunch table, rubbing and flexing my elbow. Siegfried, carving enthusiastically at a joint of roast mutton, looked up from his work.

"What's the trouble, James—rheumatism?"

"No, a cow belted me with her horn this morning," I said. "Right on the funny bone."

"Oh, bad luck. Were you trying to get hold of her nose?"

"No, giving her an injection."

"Injecting her? Up there? That's rather a daft place. I always use the rump. The neck's too damn near the horns."

"Well, the rump is too damn near the hind feet."

"The neck is quite often thinly muscled," snapped Siegfried. "You haven't got a nice pad there to stick your needle into."

"No, and you haven't got a tail either," I growled. "It's all right if you have somebody holding it, but otherwise it's a menace, lashing about."

"James, I don't like to speak to you in these terms, but I am bound to tell you that you are talking the most unmitigated poppycock."

I gave him a sullen glare. "That's your opinion, is it?"

"It is indeed, James."

"Right."

"Right."

We continued our meal in silence.

But over the next few days my mind kept returning to the conversation. Siegfried has always had a persuasive way with him, and the thought kept recurring that there might be a lot in what he said.

It was a week later that I paused, syringe in hand, before pushing between two cows. The animals, divining my intent as they usually did, swung their craggy hind ends together and blocked my way. Yes, by

God, Siegfried had a point. Why should I fight my way in there when the other end was ready and waiting?

"Hold the tail, please," I said to the farmer, and pushed my needle into the rump. That lovely pad of muscle, the easy availability of the site—my colleague had been dead right and I had been a fool.

The farmer laughed. "It's a funny thing how you fellers all have your different ways."

"What do you mean?"

"Well, Mr. Farnon was 'ere yesterday, injecting that cow over there. Had savage good arguments 'gainst goin' near the rump. He injected into the neck."

Something in my expression must have conveyed a message to him. "Now, Mr. Herriot, ye mustn't let that bother ye." He touched my arm sympathetically. "You're still young. After all, Mr. Farnon is a man of great experience."

3. OLD ALBERT AND MICK

We were sitting in the flight hut. The young airman had been telling me about his job in civilian life, and when I described my own working hours and conditions, he had been incredulous. "You must have to be a bit of an idiot to be a country vet," he said.

There was one time I would have agreed with him wholeheartedly. I was driving home from a difficult calving, frozen-faced, with my skin chafing under my clothes and feeling as though a group of strong men had been kicking me from head to foot. I was almost drowning in self-pity when I turned into the tiny village of Copton.

In summer, Copton was idyllic. But tonight it was a dead black place with the rain sweeping against the tight-shut houses—except for a faint glow where the light from the village pub fell softly on the streaming roadway. I stopped the car under the swinging sign of the Fox and Hounds. A beer would do me good.

A pleasant warmth met me as I went into the pub. There were about a dozen men drinking from pint glasses, some of them playing dominoes. Their faces were all familiar, especially that of old Albert Close, a retired shepherd who sat in the same place every night at the end of the settle, hard against the fire.

He sat as always, his hands and chin resting on the tall crook that he had carried through his working days, his eyes blank. Stretched under the seat lay his dog, Mick, old and retired like his master. The animal was clearly in the middle of a vivid dream, reliving the great days; his paws pedaled the air spasmodically, his lips and ears twitched, and now and then he emitted a stifled bark.

And Albert himself. What lay behind those empty eyes? I could imagine him in his youth, striding the windy uplands, covering endless miles over moor and rock. There were no fitter men than the Dales shepherds, living in the open in all weathers.

And there was Albert now, a broken, arthritic old man gazing apathetically from beneath the ragged peak of an ancient tweed cap. I noticed he had just drained his glass and I walked across the room.

"Good evening, Mr. Close," I said.

He cupped an ear with his hand and blinked up at me. "Eh?"

I raised my voice to a shout. "Will you have a drink?"

"Aye, thank ye." He directed a trembling finger at his glass. "You can put a drop i' there, young man."

I beckoned the landlord. The old shepherd lifted the recharged glass and looked up at me. "Good 'ealth," he grunted.

I was about to return to my seat when the old dog sat up. As he turned and faced me, I felt a sudden sense of shock. His eyes were terrible. In fact, I could hardly see them as they winked painfully at me through a sodden fringe of pus-caked lashes. I put my hand on Albert's shoulder. "Mick's eyes. They're in a bad state."

"Oh, aye," the old man nodded. "He's got a bit o' caud in 'em. He's allus been subjeck to it ever since 'e were a pup."

"No, it's more than cold. He's got turned-in eyelids. It needs an operation to put it right."

"That's right, young man." He took a sip at his beer. "Just a bit o' caud. Ever since he were a pup he's been subjeck. . . ."

I returned to my seat. Ted Dobson, a burly cowman, looked at me inquiringly. "What was that about?"

"Well, it's a nasty thing, Ted. The eyelids are turned in and the lashes rub against the eyeball. Causes a lot of pain, sometimes ulceration or even blindness. Even a mild case is damned uncomfortable."

"Poor awd beggar," Ted said. "It'll be a costly job, Ah reckon?"

I smiled wryly. "We usually charge about a pound for it." A human surgeon would laugh at a sum like that, but it would still be too much for old Albert. A pound was two weeks of the old-age pension.

The cowman crossed the room to old Albert. "Did ye understand what Mr. Herriot was tellin' ye, Albert?" he shouted.

"Aye, aye. Mick's got a bit o' caud in 'is eyes."

Ted yelled in exasperation. "Ye daft awd divil! Listen to what Ah'm sayin'—ye've got to take 'im and. . . ."

But the old man was far away. "Ever since 'e were a pup. . . ."

Some days later, Ted came to town to see his sister for the evening. Now he stood leaning on his bicycle in the surgery doorway, his cheerful, scrubbed face gleaming. He came straight to the point. "Will ye do that operation on awd Mick, Mr. Herriot? T'lads at Fox and Hounds are seein' to it. We're takin' it out of the club money. We put in a bit each week for an outin' in summer. But we won't miss a quid." He paused. "Wednesday night be all right?"

When Wednesday night arrived it was clear that Mick's operation had become something of a gala occasion. The van borrowed by Ted was crammed with regulars from the Fox and Hounds, and others rolled up on their bicycles.

In the operating room, I peered around at the unusual spectacle of rows of faces regarding me with keen anticipation. Under the lamp I got my first look at Mick. He was a handsome, well-marked animal except for those dreadful eyes. As he sat there, he opened them a fraction and stared at me for a moment before closing them again against the bright light; that, I felt, was how he spent his life, squinting painfully and briefly at his surroundings. Giving him the intravenous barbiturate was like doing him a favor.

And when he was stretched unconscious on his side, I was able to carry out my first examination. "You know," I said, "this is a mess, but I don't think there's any permanent damage."

The men didn't exactly break into a cheer, but they chattered and laughed; when I poised my scalpel, it struck me that I had never operated in such a noisy environment.

Starting with the left eye, I cut along the full length parallel to the margin of the lid, then made a semicircular sweep of the knife to include half an inch of the tissue above the eye. I cut away less skin from the lower lid, then started on the right eye. I was slicing away happily when I realized that the noise had subsided; there were a few mutterings, but the laughter had died. I glanced up and saw big Ken Appleton, the horseman from Laurel Grove; he was six feet four and built like the Shires he cared for.

"By gaw, it's 'ot in 'ere," he whispered, and I could see he meant it, because sweat was streaming down his face.

I was engrossed in my work or I would have noticed that he wasn't only sweating but deadly pale. I was stripping the skin from the eyelid when I heard a yell: "Catch him!"

The big man's friends supported him as he slid gently to the floor. And there he stayed, sleeping peacefully, till I had inserted the last stitch. Then, as I cleaned up and put the instruments away, he began to look around him, and his companions helped him to his feet. Now that the cutting was over, life had returned to the party and Ken came in for some leg-pulling; but his was not the only white face.

They brought Mick back in ten days for removal of the stitches, but I didn't see the final results of my work for another month. I was again driving home through Copton from an evening call, and the lighted doorway of the Fox and Hounds recalled me. I went in and sat down among the familiar faces.

Things were uncannily like before: old Albert Close in his usual place, Mick stretched under the table, his twitching feet testifying to another vivid dream. I crossed the room and called to him. There was a long moment when I held my breath as the shaggy head turned toward me. Then, with a kind of blissful disbelief, I found myself gazing into the clear, bright eyes of a healthy dog. There was no inflammation, no discharge. I stroked his head, and as he began to look around eagerly, I felt a thrill of delight at the sight of the old animal exulting in his freedom, savoring the new world that had opened to him.

"Mr. Close," I shouted, "will you have a drink?"

"Aye, you can put a drop i' there, young man."

"Mick's eyes are a lot better."

The old man raised his glass. "Aye, it were nob-but a bit o' caud. Ever since 'e were a pup. . . ."

There was a lot of shouting in the RAF. The NCOs always seemed to be yelling at me or at somebody else and a lot of them had impressively powerful voices. But for sheer volume I don't think any of them could beat Len Hampson.

I was on my way to Len's farm and on an impulse I pulled up the car and leaned for a moment on the wheel. It was a hot, still day in the late summer. Then, although the farm was two fields away, I heard Len Hampson's voice. He wasn't calling the cattle home or anything like that. He was just conversing with his family as he always did.

I drove on to the farm. "Good morning, Mr. Hampson," I said.

"Now, then, Mr. Herriot," he bawled. "It's a grand mornin'."

The blast of sound drove me back a step, but his three sons smiled contentedly. No doubt they were used to it. I stayed at a safe distance. "You want me to see a pig."

"Aye, a good bacon pig. Gone right off, he has. It hasn't ate nowt for two days."

We went into the pigpen. Most of the occupants careered around at the sight of a stranger, but one stood quietly in a corner. The animal had the look of doom about it.

"Did this start suddenly or gradually?" I asked.

"Right sudden!" In the confined space, the full-throated yell was deafening. "He were as right as ninepence on Monday night and like this on Tuesday mornin'."

I felt my way over the pig's abdomen. "This pig has a ruptured bowel," I said. "They do it when they are fighting or jostling each other. The chances of recovery are small."

"Nay, Ah don't like that much! Ah allus like to 'ave to go. Isn't there summat we can do? Let's try!"

"All right," I shrugged. "I'll leave you some medicine." I handed over a packet of my sulfonamide powders. They had done great things for me, but I didn't expect much here.

It was strange that I should go straight from the chief shouter of the practice to the chief whisperer. Elijah Wentworth made all his communications *sotto voce.* I found him hosing down his cow byre and he turned and looked at me with his habitual serious expression.

"Mr. Herriot," he whispered, "I've got a real bad case." He spoke always as though every pronouncement was of the utmost secrecy.

"Fine big bullock, Mr. Herriot. Goin' down fast." He moved in closer till he could murmur directly into my ear. "I suspect TB." He backed away, face drawn.

The farmer crooked a finger and I followed him into a box. The bullock, a Hereford Cross that should have weighed over a thousand pounds, was gaunt and emaciated. I went over the animal carefully.

"I think he's got liver fluke, Mr. Wentworth," I said. "I'll take a dung sample and have it examined for fluke eggs, but I want to treat him right away."

"Liver fluke? Where would he pick that up?"

"Usually from a wet pasture."

Again, Elijah came very close, then scanned the horizon anxiously. He breathed the words into my ear. "Ah know who's to blame for this. It's me landlord. Won't do anything for me." He brought his face round and looked at me wide-eyed before taking up his old position by my ear.

"Been goin' to drain this field for years, but done nowt," he added.

I wanted to dose his bullock. I had some hexacloroethane in my car, and I mixed it with water and administered it to the animal.

It was about a month later, on a market day, and I was strolling among the stalls that packed the cobbles. In front of the Drover's Arms pub the usual press of farmers stood chatting among themselves, talking business with cattle dealers and corn merchants.

"Hey, Mr. Herriot!" There was no mistaking Len Hampson. He hove in front of me, red-faced and cheerful. "Remember that pig ye doctored for me?" He had clearly consumed a few market-day beers and his voice was louder than ever.

The packed mass of farmers pricked up their ears. There is nothing so intriguing as the ailments of another farmer's livestock.

"Yes, of course, Mr. Hampson," I replied.

"Well, 'e never did no good!" bawled Len.

I could see the farmers' faces lighting up. It is more interesting still when things go wrong.

"Naw, 'e didn't. Ah've never seen a pig go down as fast. Aye, flesh just melted off 'im!"

"Oh, what a pity. But, if you recall, I rather expected. . . ."

"Went down to skin and bones 'e did!" The great bellow rolled over the marketplace. I looked around uneasily. "Well, Mr. Hampson, I did warn you at the time. . . ."

"Ah don't know what those powders were you gave 'im. But they did 'im no bloody good! Finished up as dog meat, poor bugger! Well, good day to ye, Mr. Herriot." He turned and walked away.

With an uncomfortable feeling that I was the center of attention, I was about to retreat hastily when I felt a gentle hand on my arm. I turned and saw Elijah Wentworth.

"Mr. Herriot," he whispered. "About that bullock." I stared at him, struck by the coincidence. The farmers stared, too, expectantly.

"Yes, Mr. Wentworth?"

"Well, now, I'll tell you." He came very near and breathed into my ear. "It was like a miracle. He began to pick up straightaway after you treated him."

I stepped back. "Oh, marvelous! But speak up, will you? I can't hear you." I looked around hopefully.

He came after me again and put his chin on my shoulder. "Yes," he said. "I don't know what you gave 'im but it was wonderful stuff. I could hardly believe it."

"Do speak a little louder," I said eagerly.

"He's as fat as butter now." The almost inaudible murmur wafted on my cheek. "Ah'm sure he'll get top grade at the auction mart."

The farmers had heard nothing, and their interest evaporated. Then, as they began to talk among themselves, Mr. Wentworth confided softly and secretly into my private ear.

"That was the most brilliant and marvelous cure I 'ave ever seen."

4. SOLO

TODAY," SAID FLIGHT OFFICER WOODHAM, "we're going to try a few new things. Spinning, side-slipping and how to come out of a stall." His voice was gentle, and before he pulled on his helmet, he turned his dark, fine-featured face toward me and smiled. He was always like that on the ground. He was altogether different in the air. As we soared about the summer sky, his instructions appeared simple and easy to carry out. But soon a new tone set in.

"Didn't I tell you opposite rudder and stick to side-slip?" he bawled over the intercom.

"Yes, sir," was all I replied, instead of the more appropriate "That's just what I'm doing, you stupid bugger!"

The goggled eyes bulged in my mirror. "Well, why the bloody hell aren't you doing it?" His voice rose to a wild shriek. "Take her up. We'll try again. And for God's sake, keep your wits about you!"

It was the same with the spins and stalls. And, of course, the panic gradually crept in. "Keep your eye on that cloud! Watch your artificial horizon! Don't you know what the altimeter's for? I told you to keep at 1000 feet, but it's like talking to a bloody wall!"

I never seemed to make any progress—whatever I did was wrong, and I was losing heart. I was hoping to be graded pilot, but after every session with F. O. Woodham the idea of ever flying an airplane on my own seemed more and more ludicrous.

This day he was as quiet and charming as ever when I met him—till we got up into the sky and the shouting started again.

"Relax! For heaven's sake, relax!" or "Watch your height! Where the hell d'you think you're going?" or "Didn't I tell you to centralize the stick? Are you bloody deaf?" And finally, when we shuddered to a halt on the grass: "That was an absolutely bloody landing! Take off again!"

On the second circuit he fell strangely silent. And though I should have been relieved I found something ominous in the unaccustomed peace. It could mean only one thing—he had finally given me up as a bad job.

When we landed he climbed out of the rear cockpit. "Stay where you are," he said. "You can take her up now. See me in the flight hut after you've landed." He turned and walked away.

Panic-stricken though I was, I did not forget the cockpit drill which had been dinned into me so often—test the rudder, ailerons, elevator. Then the engine roared. I pushed the throttle full open, and the little plane began to bump its way over the grass. I pulled the stick back and we climbed smoothly into the air. I was gripped by exhilaration and triumph. At last I was up here on my own, really flying. The feeling of relief intoxicated me, so that for a long time I just sailed along, grinning foolishly to myself.

When I finally came to my senses I looked down happily over the side. It must be time to turn now but, as I stared downward, cold reality began to roll over me in a gathering flood. I couldn't recognize a thing in the great hazy tapestry beneath me. Dry-mouthed, I looked at the altimeter. I was well over 2000 feet.

And suddenly it came to me that F. O. Woodham's shouts had not been meaningless; he had been talking sense, giving me good advice, and as soon as I got up in the air by myself I had ignored it all. I hadn't lined myself up on a cloud or watched my artificial horizon or kept an eye on the altimeter. And I was lost.

It seemed that one way or another I was going to make a name for myself. Funny things had happened to some of the other lads—many had been airsick, one had gone through a hedge, another on his first solo had circled the airfield again and again—seven times he had gone round—trying to find the courage to land while his instructor sweated blood and cursed on the ground. But nobody had flown off into the blue and returned on foot without his airplane.

My visions of my immediate fate were reaching horrific proportions and my heart was hammering uncontrollably when, far away on my left, I spotted the familiar bulk of the big stand on Ascot race course. Almost weeping with joy, I turned toward it and within minutes I was banking above its roof.

And there, far, far below and approaching with uncomfortable speed was the belt of trees which fringed the airfield. But I was still way too high—I could never drop down there in time to hit that landing strip.

The ignominy of it went deep. They would all be watching on the ground, and some would have a good laugh at the sight of Herriot overshooting the field by several hundred feet and cruising off again into the clouds. But what was I thinking about? There was a way to lose height rapidly and, bless you, F. O. Woodham, I knew how to do it.

He had told me a hundred times how to side-slip and I did it now as hard as I could, sending the little machine slewing like an airborne crab down, down toward those trees.

And, by golly, it worked! The green copse rushed up at me and before I knew it I was almost skimming the branches. I straightened up and headed for the long stretch of grass. The undercarriage made contact with the earth with hardly a tremor. Then I taxied in, climbed from the cockpit and walked over to the flight hut.

F. O. Woodham was sitting at a table, cup in hand, and he looked up as I entered.

"Ah, Herriot, I'm just having some coffee. Will you join me?"

I sat down and he pushed a cup toward me.

"I saw your landing," he said. "Delightful, quite delightful."

"Thank you, sir."

"That side-slip." One corner of his mouth twitched upward. "Very good indeed, really masterly."

He reached for the coffeepot and went on. "You've done awfully well, Herriot. Solo after nine hours' instruction, eh? Splendid. But then I never had the slightest doubt about you at any time." He poised the pot over my cup. "How do you like your coffee—black or white?"

WHEN I LEFT DARROWBY, Helen had gone back to live with her father, and the little rooms in the house we shared with Siegfried and his brother Tristan, a student, would be empty and dusty now. But they lived on in my mind, clear in every detail. I could see the ivy-fringed window looking over the tumble of roofs to the green hills, our few pieces of furniture, the bed and side table and the old wardrobe which only stayed shut with the aid of one of my socks jammed in the door.

I could hear the bedside radio playing, my wife's voice from the other side of the fire and, on that winter evening, Tristan Farnon shouting up the stairs from the passage far below.

"Jim! Jim!"

I went out and stuck my head over the banister. "What is it, Triss?"

"Sorry to bother you, Jim, but could you come down for a minute?"

The upturned face had an anxious look. I went down the long flight of steps two at a time, and Tristan beckoned me through to the consulting room. A teen-age girl was standing by the table, her hand resting on a stained roll of blanket.

"It's a cat," Tristan said. He pulled back the blanket and I looked down at a large, striped tabby. He gently lifted one of the cat's hind legs and rolled the abdomen into view. There was a gash through which a coiled cluster of intestines spilled grotesquely onto the cloth. The girl explained that she had found the cat—it was not hers—and, seeing the dreadful wound, had brought the animal to us. He had almost been disemboweled, and his intestines were covered in dirt and mud.

"There's only one thing to do," I sighed. "Those guts are perforated in several places. It's hopeless."

Tristan didn't say anything, but he whistled under his breath and drew the tip of his forefinger again and again across the furry cheek. And unbelievably, from somewhere in the cat's scraggy chest a gentle purring arose.

The young man looked at me, round-eyed. "Do you hear that?"

"It's no good, Triss," I said gently. "It's got to be done. Pour a little ether onto the cloth. He'll just sleep away."

Tristan unscrewed the cap of the ether bottle and poised it above the head. And then we heard it again: the deep purring which increased in volume till it boomed in our ears like a distant motorcycle.

Tristan looked at me and gulped. "I don't fancy this much, Jim. Can't we do something?"

Two hours and yards of catgut later, everything looked tidy. "He's alive, anyway, Triss," I said as we began to wash the instruments.

The door opened and Helen came in. "You've been a long time, Jim." She walked over to the table and looked down at the sleeping cat. "What a poor skinny little thing. He's all bones." She stroked the little animal for a moment. "Is he badly injured?"

"I'm afraid so, Helen," I said. "We've done our best, but I don't think he has much chance." She left us and returned with an empty box.

"I can make a bed in this box and he'll sleep in our room, Jim."

Over the next days she spoon-fed him a succession of milk, beef essence, strained broth and baby foods.

"We shall call him Oscar," she said.

"Why Oscar?"

"I don't know."

One of the things I like about women is their mystery, and I didn't press the matter further.

Oscar's purr became part of our lives, and when he eventually left his bed, sauntered through to our kitchen and began to sample our dog's dinner of meat and biscuit, it was a moment of triumph.

Oscar had been established as one of the family for several weeks when I came in from a late call to find Helen waiting for me with a stricken face. "It's Oscar. I think he's run away." She had searched the yard, even walked around the town. "And remember," she said, her chin quivering, "he ran away from somewhere before."

Just then the front doorbell jangled. I galloped down the stairs and as I rounded the corner in the passage I could see Mrs. Heslington, the vicar's wife, through the glass. I threw open the door. She was holding Oscar in her arms.

"We were having a meeting of the Mothers' Union at the church house," she explained, "and we noticed the cat sitting there in the room, as though he were listening to what we were saying. It was unusual. When the meeting ended, I thought I'd bring him to you."

A few nights later, Oscar was missing again. I heard the doorbell at nine. It was the elderly Miss Simpson peering through the glass with Oscar prowling on the mat.

"Where . . . may I ask?"

"At the Women's Institute," said Miss Simpson. "He came in shortly after we started and stayed till the end. He mixed with the company, apparently enjoying the slides, and showed great interest in the cakes. He made his own way here. I merely rang your bell to make sure you knew he had arrived."

I mounted the stairs in record time. "I know about Oscar now," I said to Helen. "He's not running away—he's visiting. He loves people, and he's interested in what they do. He's a natural mixer."

Helen looked at the attractive mound of fur on her lap. "Of course . . . that's it . . . he's a socialite!"

"Exactly, a high-stepper!"

"A cat-about-town!"

5. THE PRODIGAL

When the blow fell, it was totally unexpected. I was finishing the evening surgery. I looked round the door and saw only a man and two little boys. "Next, please," I said.

The man stood up. He had no animal with him. He was middle-aged, with the rough, weathered face of a farm worker. He twirled a cloth cap nervously in his hands. "Mr. Herriot?" he said. "Ah think you've got ma cat. There's a cousin o'mine lives in Darrowby and Ah heard tell from 'im about this cat that goes around to meetin's. I 'ad to come. We've been huntin' everywhere."

We went upstairs where Helen was putting some coal on the fire. "Helen," I said, "this is Mr.—er—I'm sorry, I don't know your name."

"Gibbons, Sep Gibbons. These are our two youngest." The two boys, twins of about eight, looked up at us solemnly.

I wished my heart would stop hammering. "Mr. Gibbons thinks Oscar is his. He lost his cat some time ago."

Helen put down her little coal shovel. "Oh . . . oh . . . I see." She stood very still for a moment, then smiled faintly. "Do sit down. Oscar's in the kitchen. I'll bring him in."

She reappeared with the cat in her arms. She hadn't got through the door when the little boys gave tongue. "Tiger!" they cried. "Oh, Tiger, Tiger!"

The man's face seemed lighted from within. He ran his big work-roughened hand along the fur. "Hullo, awd lad," he said, and turned to me with a radiant smile. "It's 'im, Mr. Herriot. It's 'im aw right, and don't 'e look well! By gaw, we did miss 'im."

Helen said it for me. "Well, Mr. Gibbons." Her tone had an unnatural brightness. "You'd better take him." She cupped the cat's head in her hands and looked at him steadily for a few seconds. Then she patted the boys' heads.

"You'll take good care of him, won't you?"

I showed Mr. Gibbons to the door, and returned to our rooms.

It was my habit at that time in my life to mount the stairs two or three at a time, but on this occasion I trailed upward like an old man, slightly breathless, throat tight, eyes prickling. I cursed myself for a sentimental fool, but as I reached our door I found a flash of consolation. Helen had taken it remarkably well. She had nursed that cat and grown deeply attached to him, and I'd have thought an unforeseen calamity like this would have upset her terribly. But no, she had behaved calmly and rationally. You never knew with women, but I was thankful.

It was up to me to do as well. I adjusted my features into the semblance of a cheerful smile and marched into the room.

Helen had pulled a chair close to the table and was slumped face-down against the wood. One arm cradled her head while the other was stretched in front of her as her body shook with an utterly abandoned weeping. I had never seen her like this, and I was appalled.

I tried to say something comforting, but nothing stemmed the flow of racking sobs.

Feeling helpless and inadequate, I could only sit close to her and stroke the back of her head. Maybe I could have said something if I hadn't felt just about as bad myself.

You get over these things in time. After all, we told ourselves, it wasn't as though Oscar had died—he had gone to a good family who would look after him. In fact, he had really gone home.

It was a month after that shattering night and we were coming out of the cinema at Brawton at the end of our half-day off. I looked at my watch. "Eight o'clock," I said. "How about going to see Oscar? It's only five miles."

A smile crept slowly across Helen's face. "That would be lovely. But do you think they would mind?"

"No, I'm sure they wouldn't. Let's go."

A busy-looking little woman answered my knock. She was drying her hands on a striped towel. "I'm James Herriot, and this is my wife. We had your cat for a while."

The woman grinned and waved her towel at us. "Oh, aye, Ah remember. Sep told me about you. Come in, come in!"

Sep got up from his place by the fire, put down his newspaper, took off a pair of steel-rimmed spectacles and shook hands. He waved Helen to a sagging armchair. "Well, it's right nice to see you. Ah've often spoke of ye to t'missis."

It wasn't until the tea had been made and poured that I dared to raise the subject.

"How," I asked diffidently, "how is . . . er . . . Tiger?"

"Oh, he's grand," the woman replied briskly. She glanced up at the clock on the mantelpiece. "He should be back anytime now, then you'll be able to see 'im."

As she spoke, Sep raised a finger. "Ah think Ah can hear 'im now." He walked over and opened the door and our Oscar strode in with all his old grace and majesty. He took one look at Helen and leaped onto her lap.

"He knows me," she murmured. "He knows me."

I went over and tickled Oscar's chin, then I turned to Mrs. Gibbons. "It's after nine o'clock. Where has he been?"

She poised her butter knife and looked into space. "Let's see, now," she said. "It's Thursday, isn't it? Ah, yes, it's 'is night for the yoga class."

SADLY, BEFORE the war was over I had an operation which disqualified me for further military service and I had to be mustered out. I suppose I was an entirely typical discharged serviceman. They had taken away my blue uniform and fitted me with a "demob suit," a ghastly garment of stiff brown serge with purple stripes that made me look like an old-time gangster.

The last lap home was by bus—the same rattling little vehicle that had carried me to my first job years before. The driver was the same, too, and the time between seemed to melt away as the fells began to rise again from the blue distance in the early light and I saw the familiar farmhouses, the walls creeping up the grassy slopes, the fringe of trees by the river's edge.

It was midmorning when we rumbled into the market place and I read "Darrowby Co-operative Society" above the shop on the far side. The sun was high, warming the tiles of the fretted line of roofs with their swelling green background of hills. I got out, and the bus went on its way, leaving me standing by my case.

And it was the same as before. The sweet air, the silence and the cobbled square, deserted except for the old men sitting around the clock tower. One of them looked up at me.

"Now, then, Mr. Herriot," he said quietly, as though he had seen me only yesterday.

A lot had happened since that first day when I arrived in Darrowby in search of a job, but it came to me suddenly that my circumstances hadn't changed much. All I had possessed then was an old case and the suit I stood in, and it was about the same now. Except for two great and wonderful things. I had my wife, Helen, and my new son, Jimmy.

They made all the difference. I had no money, not even a house to call my own, but any roof that covered my wife and son was personal and special. They were outside the town and it was a fair walk from here, but I looked down at the blunt toes of my boots sticking from my trousers. The RAF hadn't only taught me to fly, they had taught me to march, and a few miles wouldn't bother me.

I took a fresh grip on my cardboard case, turned toward the exit from the square and set off, left-right, left-right, on the road for home.

REPORT FROM ENGINE CO. 82

CONDENSED FROM THE BOOK

BY DENNIS SMITH

ILLUSTRATED BY GORDON JOHNSON

There are more than 13,000 firemen in New York City. In a single year, some 8000 of them are injured in the line of duty—falling through floors, inhaling smoke and superheated air, being struck by a collapsing ceiling or wall—and on the average, eight are killed.

Why do these men perform this dangerous job? Why do they volunteer to work in some of the city's worst slums where the hostility of the people is often as much a hazard as the fires themselves?

Dennis Smith, a fireman for many years, provides one man's answers in his report from the firefighters' front lines.

1. A NIGHT'S WORK

MY NAME IS Dennis Smith, and I'm a New York City fireman—one of "New York's bravest." That's what the editorial writers call us. I'm part of Engine Company 82. The firehouse I work out of is on Intervale Avenue and 169th Street in an area called the South Bronx. Along with Harlem and Bedford-Stuyvesant, it is one of the three biggest ghettos in New York City.

Around the corner from the firehouse is the 41st Precinct House. It is the busiest police station in the city. There are more homicides per square mile in this precinct than anywhere else in the United States—also more drug traffic and more prostitution.

There are four companies working out of the firehouse on Intervale Avenue. Engine 82 and Engine 85 do the hose work in the district. Ladder Company 31 and Tactical Control Unit 712 do the rescue work, the ladder work and the ax work. These four companies average 600 runs a month. It's safe to say that ours is the busiest firehouse in New York—and probably in the world.

I live in a small town called Washingtonville. It is a pretty town located north of the city, and we have a house there because an old lady died a few years ago in Boise, Idaho, and left one of her unknown relatives—my wife, Pat—enough for a down payment.

I am sitting in the kitchen now, waiting for Pat to finish cooking a mushroom omelet. I wish I had time to hold her softly, and tell her I love her, and more. But I have to go to work, and only have time for an omelet and tea.

I have been on medical leave for the last two weeks for a scorched throat. My throat doesn't hurt anymore now, and I'm anxious to return to the firehouse.

Pat places the steaming omelet in front of me. She leans toward me. Her lips touch mine, and she begins our game. I can feel her soft lips moving as she asks, "How much?"

"This much," I say, extending my arms as far as possible.

She looks both ways to make sure both hands are open, and the fingertips stretched. "In money?" she asks.

"The Pope's treasury."

"In minerals?"

"A flawless diamond."

"In mountains?"

"Mount Everest, and Rolls-Royce in cars, and New York in cities."

I wrap my arms around her and end the game. Her slender frame wriggles, and finally she escapes.

"Your eggs will get cold," she says. Then she sits there and bites the inside of her lower lip, a habit she has when there is something on her mind. At first she denies anything is bothering her. But finally she comes out with it: "How many years are you going to work in the South Bronx? I never worried half as much when you used to work in Queens. At least then you came home to me with some life in your body. Now you come home dead tired—if you come home at all, if you're not tied up at some hospital getting stitched, or X-rayed, or burns patched. Even in Vietnam they send the soldiers home after a year, but you've been in Engine 82 over five years."

Every fireman's wife worries about her husband. Until now, though, Pat has had her anxiety under control. Today I can see that she is genuinely upset. Yet there is little I can say that will calm her fears. Am I working in the South Bronx because of some abstract moral commitment, a belief that poor people must have professional protection from fire? Am I crusading? Or am I just doing a job? I have never really thought about it.

I reach over the table and grasp her hand. "Listen, baby," I say. "I wish you wouldn't worry about it. I've told you before that if a fireman is going to get hurt, or even killed, it happens just as easily in Queens or Staten Island as it does in the South Bronx."

I realize I don't know how to justify my job except to say that I like doing it. I put my empty teacup into the sink, walk to where Pat is sitting and hold her pretty face between my hands.

"Just think," I say in a near whisper. "In 11 short years I'll be able to retire at half-pay. I'll only be 42 years old, and we can move to a quiet town in New England, to Ireland, back to New York City—anywhere we please. Life will be easy, relaxed. The children will be grown. We can travel or do whatever we want. Right now, though, I like what I'm doing. I'm pleased as a worker and as a man. I believe I have something to contribute."

It is 3:30 p.m.—time to leave for the firehouse. My son Brendan, seven, is off riding his bicycle; the two younger boys—five and four—come running from a neighbor's yard where they have been playing.

"Good-by, Dennis. Good-by, Sean. Say good-by to Brendan for me."

Both heads nod, and little hands blow kisses as I back down the drive. Pat is on the porch, her arms folded below her breast, and her long hair blowing in the cold wind.

"Good-by, baby. Love ya," I call.

She waves. I can tell she is not happy with my explanation, and the question of working in Engine 82 is left floating in the air.

IT'S 2:30 A.M. We're spraying 250 gallons of water a minute at a fire, and it seems like the wind is driving each cold drop back into our faces. We've been here over an hour. The fire is still burning freely. If we could go inside the building and get close to the heat—but the chief says it is too dangerous. The roof might collapse at any moment.

Icicles have formed on the protective rim of my leather helmet, and they break off as I move to reinforce my grip on the fighting hose.

"Do you want a blow on the line, Dennis?" Benny Carroll yells.

"Yeah, Benny, you take it a while," I say, and he grabs the hose.

As I walk down the street in search of a warm hallway, I hear a soft but distinct crashing noise, like someone dropping a steel safe onto a pile of balsa wood. A giant mushroom of fire surges toward the sky. Part of the roof has fallen, and the oxygen overhead acts like a magnet for the fire. The old, dying building is a three-story wooden structure called a Queen Anne. It has a series of peaked roofs, and many small rooms which are particularly difficult for firemen to work in.

Just a little over an hour ago, we were sitting in the firehouse. The radiators were hissing, and the coffee was steaming. We had already responded to 12 alarms since our tour of duty started at six o'clock. Two were mattress fires, one was a burning abandoned car, another a couch, and the rest were garbage fires or false alarms. Then the bells rang for this fire, and Engine 82 was assigned on the second alarm. (In March 1972, the Bronx switched to a voice alarm system, with all fires being reported and equipment dispatched from a central office over an inter-com system. Bells are now used only as a backup.) We could see the red glare in the sky as we left our firehouse and knew that we would be there for some time.

I can't find a warm hallway; they are all cold. I return to the building directly across from the fire. Several firemen from other companies have had the same idea as I, and are there in the lobby. They walk back and forth or jump up and down. It is much too cold to sit on the floor and try to relax.

"Bad night, Dennis, bad night!" says a man from Squad 2 as he takes off his rubber coat. Like all of our coats, it is frozen, and stands by itself against the wall.

I can't help thinking that in another place, another city perhaps, where fires are uncommon and exciting, apartments up and down the street would be opened, and residents would be serving coffee and biscuits, and offering the warmth of their homes to the firemen and victims of the fire. But we are in New York City, where neighbors sometimes don't even bother to find out each other's names.

I rest a while and return to the fire. Benny Carroll has the stream directed at the roof. The icicles hanging from his helmet look like tassels on a party hat. His face muscles are strained, and the veins in his neck are raised. The wind is howling fiercely now, and the water comes back like small particles of glass. Benny calls for relief, and Willy Knipps moves up to take the nozzle. I take my place behind two other men, grasp the 2½-inch hose with all my strength, and push forward to relieve the back pressure.

There is a loud cracking noise, and the sky before us is again filled with fire. The rest of the roof has come down, and the fire is let loose from its confinement. It won't last long, though; all the lines around the building are directed at the roof. The fire darkens quickly, and we know it will be over soon.

The chief orders us to get a $1\frac{3}{4}$-inch hose and take it to the top floor. We pass the companies working on the second floor, and pull the hose to the third. There is still a lot of fire here, but it is buried beneath the fallen roof and ceilings.

The smoke is heavy now. Our noses are running, and we have to keep our heads low. Heat and smoke rise, so a fireman usually stays as close to the floor as possible.

Bill Kelsey, who has the nozzle, is on his stomach, crawling through what was once a doorway. Lt. Tom Welch is beside him, directing the beam of his portable lamp before them. Kelsey pushes into the apartment rooms, slowly but progressively killing the fire as he goes. Suddenly he jerks up to his knees. He closes the nozzle, shoves it down his right boot and reopens it. The water spills over the boot top.

"What's the matter?"

"I must have got something down my boot," Kelsey answers. "It hurts like hell.'

He moves out, and Willy Knipps, the next in line, replaces him. Finally it is my turn, and I take the "nob." The real work, the real challenge in firefighting, lies with the man controlling the nozzle.

The rooms before me are hotter than I anticipated. I am on my knees, sitting on my heels. Lieutenant Welch is beside me in the same position, and Knipps is behind feeding the line to us. We advance slowly, moving our knees forward, inch by inch, as if we were on a holy pilgrimage. We have extinguished the fire in three rooms; there is only one more room left. We creep toward it on our stomachs. The room has lit up completely, and the fire is reaching out toward us. I can feel the heat sink into my face, like a thousand summer days at the beach.

I have my head down now, and the nozzle is directed at the ceiling. I don't have to look up. I know the fire is cooling because the smoke is banking down. Lieutenant Welch is next to me, saying, "Beautiful, Dennis, beautiful. Keep the stream on the ceiling; we've got it made. Let's move in another foot."

The fire in the room is out now, but the smoke is still heavy. There must be fire in the walls, or caught between the ceiling and the roof. A man from a ladder company arrives and pulls the ceiling down in huge chunks. Now we can see the fire. He backs out so I can hit it. Then we return to the other rooms to let loose a final bath. Our job is finished.

In the street, we hear that Bill Kelsey has a nasty burn on his leg.

"Anybody else hurt?" someone asks.

"Yeah, a guy from Engine 50 fell through the floor—a guy named Roberti, or Roberto, something like that."

It's all very impersonal. When a guy gets hurt at a fire, it's easier to remember the injury than the man's name. A guy got burned, he fell through the roof, he got cut by falling glass, a wall fell on him, he was overcome by heat or smoke. These injuries can't be prevented, not as long as the best way to put out a fire is to get close to it.

It's almost 5:30 a.m. as the truck backs into the firehouse. I am just changing into a dry pair of pants when the alarm bells come in again. "Damn it, give me a break," I think as I slide down the pole from the second floor to the apparatus floor. Fortunately, the box that has been pulled is only five blocks away. It is a false alarm. In ten minutes we have responded, made a search of the neighborhood and returned to the firehouse. We have two more false alarms before the day crew begins arriving at eight o'clock. It is nine o'clock before I start the long drive home to a good day's sleep.

2. MALICIOUS FALSE ALARM

THERE ARE 13,350 firemen in New York City, and last year 8600 of them were injured in the line of duty. Annually, an average of eight are killed. Last year the total was seven.

I had a friend named Mike Carr, an upstanding kind of guy. He was the union delegate of Engine 85. Anything that had the smallest benefit for firemen interested him, and he worked untiringly for us.

Then one day a nine-year-old boy reached up and pulled an alarm-box handle. Kids do this a lot in the South Bronx. His friends giggled, and they all ran up the street to watch the fire engines come. The box came in on the bells—2787—Southern Boulevard and 172nd Street. Mike pulled himself up on the sidestep of the apparatus. The heavy wheels turned up Intervale Avenue, the officer's foot pressing hard on the siren. At Freeman Street the apparatus turned right, and Mike lost his grip. He spun from the sidestep like a top.

Marty Hannon and Juan Moran jumped off the apparatus even before it came to a screeching stop. There was blood all over. They could see that Mike had stopped breathing. Marty cleared some of the blood away with a handkerchief and began mouth-to-mouth resuscitation. He told me that all he remembers of those agonizing minutes was the battalion chief's voice blaring over the radio: "Transmit 1092 Box 2787. Malicious false alarm."

The following day the Uniformed Firefighters Association offered a $1000 reward for information leading to the arrest of the person who pulled the alarm, and that afternoon the nine-year-old boy was led through the heavy iron doors of the 41st Precinct House. News spreads quickly in the South Bronx, and the boy's friends had told their parents, who called the cops.

While the boy was being questioned at the police station, people from a neighborhood action group painted the alarm box black and hung a sign around it. The sign was in two parts, the top half in Spanish, the bottom in English: "A Man Was Killed While Coming Here to a False Alarm." Before the paint was dry, another false alarm was pulled at the same box, and the men of Engine 85 took the sign down.

Mike had two sons, seven and nine—two brave and frightened boys now walking slowly on either side of their mother, behind a shining red fire engine that moves between rows of their school chums and hundreds of firemen. They look up at the flag-draped casket on top of the fire engine and feel proud that their daddy is the cause of all this ceremony, but they are frightened because they are old enough to realize that there is a tomorrow, and it is going to be different without him.

The young boy in the police station is frightened, too, but in a different way. He wonders why everyone is so upset. He came to this country from Puerto Rico five years ago, and the kids on the block taught him that you have to make your own fun in the South Bronx. You can play in the abandoned buildings, or on the trash heaps, or in the rat-infested cellars. Or you can pull the handles of fire-alarm boxes. Why is everyone so upset?

What do you do with a nine-year-old boy who has pulled a false alarm that has resulted in a death? In this case the boy was turned over to the social services for guidance care. I understand the sad conditions in which this child has been forced to live, but I have lost sympathy with the cry that poverty caused the crime, not the boy. Anyone found guilty of pulling a malicious false alarm should be sent to jail for a year or, if under 16, to a reform school. But in the nine years I have been a fireman, I have seen only one man jailed, and I have responded to thousands of alarms that proved to be maliciously false. In fact, in New York last year, firemen answered 104,690 false alarms—an average of 287 daily, or one every 12 minutes.

It is not just firemen who are victimized by this. Often while firemen are answering a false alarm at one end of their district, a serious fire breaks out at the other end. Time is the most important factor in fighting fires. A minute or two can mean life or death. In New York City fires last year, 292 people died. You can be sure that some of those deaths could have been avoided if firemen had not been answering a false alarm minutes before.

The day following Mike's death, the firehouse was busy with journalists and television-news camera crews. They decided to film an interview with Charlie McCarty, the biggest and toughest man in Ladder 31. Charlie had applied the mechanical resuscitator to Mike Carr as the ambulance sped to the hospital, and he stayed with Mike the whole time the doctors worked on him.

"He was a great guy," Charlie said in answer to a question. "It's a shame this had to happen, and . . . and . . ." He turned away, his shoulders shaking. When he turned back, tears were running from his eyes, and he said, "I'm sorry—I just can't do this," and the toughest guy in the firehouse walked away.

I GREW UP ON the East Side of Manhattan in a tenement much like the ones I now fight fires in. I guess I'll never escape from tenements—and cockroaches. The names and geography may change, but conditions are universal when people are without money. Mrs. Hanratty, who lived down the hall from us in my youth, has been replaced now by Mrs. Sanchez; the "O'Dwyer for Mayor" sticker on the vestibule wall now reads "Father Gigante for Congress." But the smells of garbage and urine haven't changed, though the vomit on the stairs is now mixed with heroin instead of ten-cents-a-shot Third Avenue whiskey.

Roaches are part of my past, and now part of my work. They are under me or on me as I crawl down long, smoked-filled halls. They scurry helter-skelter as I lift a smoldering mattress, just as they scurried between the tin soldiers on the battlefield of my living-room floor. More than anything, they represent poverty to me. They are the one facet of my youth that I was forced to accept—the ugly, brown, quick-darting companions of the poor. My mother cleaned and sprayed, but it didn't help much. The roaches were put in the walls years ago, she whispered, because the builders had a grudge against the Irish and Italians. I learned that the little creatures could be fought, but not defeated. They adapted, and so did I.

I was 21 when I filled in the blanks on the fireman's application form. I didn't know what the job was all about—I only knew that it was a mark of success for a neighborhood boy to become a fireman or a cop. They were secure jobs, and much respected by our elders, who had lived through the Depression. The nuns in the school I attended as a child never spoke to us about becoming doctors or lawyers—only about becoming President of the United States (which was our birthright) or a fireman or a cop.

After I passed the civil-service exam for firemen, I was investigated thoroughly, and my moral character ascertained. In the course of his work a firefighter goes into banks, jewelry stores and people's homes; an applicant with a criminal record is not considered for obvious reasons. I took strenuous physical and medical examinations. Flat feet, missing fingers, less than 20/20 vision or less than perfect hearing, an even slightly imperfect cardiogram were all automatic disqualifiers.

Next came the department's training school. Each morning for eight weeks we began with 45 minutes of push-ups, sit-ups, pull-ups, jumping and running. Then there were three hours of classroom work, learning about building codes, inspection procedures, fire laws, explosions, alarm systems, arson investigation and a hundred other subjects as difficult as any college course I've taken.

In the afternoons we had three hours of field work, stretching hose up stairs, up fire escapes, up aerial ladders; crawling past 55-gallon drums filled with burning wood scraps in the heat room, crawling through controlled smoke conditions, breathing the first whiffs of the poison that we would soon get to know as a doctor knows death; chopping through floors and doors with eight-pound axes, forcing locks with Halligan tools, ripping down ceilings with six-foot hooks; lowering ourselves down the outside of a five-story building with a rope and a life belt, jumping three stories into a net; carrying victims, searching in smoky rooms for a dummy well hidden by a diabolical instructor, bandaging forelimbs, splinting legs. We learned everything except what it is like to be in the uncontrolled madness of a real fire.

I was ecstatic that I would soon be a part of the gongs, clangs and siren howls. I would play to the cheers of excited hordes, climbing ladders, pulling hose and saving children—always saving children—from the waltz of the hot-masked devil.

Now, so many years later, the romantic visions have faded. I have climbed too many ladders and crawled down too many grimy hallways to feel that my profession is at all glamorous. I have watched friends die, and I have carried death in my hands. There is no glamour in that.

I hope that the young men joining the fire departments around the country are doing so out of some sense of commitment to the profession and to the people, not because of the excitement of the sirens and bells. Firefighting is a brutalizing business. There are rewards, but they are intangible. Each firefighter must seek them in his own way.

Many of the fires in the South Bronx have a strange twist to them. Like the one on Intervale Avenue near Kelly Street.

We can smell the smoke as the pumper turns down Intervale, and hands automatically start pulling boot tops to thighs, clipping coatrings closed, pulling on gloves. The pumper stops, and we're about to stretch the hose when there is a scream from inside the building. A boy is running out of the doorway, his shirt and hair aflame.

Ladder 31 is right behind us, and one of the laddermen goes rapidly to the boy's assistance. Willy Knipps takes the first folds of the hose and heads into the building. Benny Carroll and I follow, dragging the rest of the hose to the second floor.

There are four apartments on the floor, and three of the doors are open; the occupants of these apartments have fled. The fourth door is locked. The chief arrives and rushes into the adjoining apartment. He starts kicking through the wall with all his strength. The smoke rushes out the hole, darkening the apartment. Knipps and I are coughing, and have to lie on our bellies as we wait for the water to surge through the hose. Two other men start to work on the locked door with the point of a Halligan tool.

The hole in the wall is widened, and Captain Frimes enters. He crawls on the floor toward the front door, swinging his arms before him as if swimming the breaststroke. His hand is stopped by the bulk of a body, lying on the floor. It's a big frame, and Captain Frimes struggles to drag it toward the hole in the wall. He passes the body out to another fireman, who carries it to the street. It is a boy, 16 or 17, a strapping black youth. He is still breathing, but barely. The fireman knows that he has to get some oxygen into him if he is to live, and begins mouth-to-mouth resuscitation. Meanwhile, in the burning room, Frimes crawls to the locked door and opens it.

The hose comes to life with water, and we start inching down the hall. We reach the first burning room, and Knipps opens the nozzle. The room is filled with the crackling of fire, and as the water hits the ceiling the sound is made louder by falling plaster, steaming and hissing on the wet floor.

The fire darkens quickly, and the smoke banks to the floor. There is no escape from it. Willy Boyle moves up, breathing easily in his mask.

He is going to relieve Knipps on the line, but he trips in the middle of the room. He feels around, and his hands sink into another body. "I got a victim here!" he yells through the mouthpiece of the mask. Benny Carroll joins him quickly, and they carry the body out and lay it on the sidewalk, next to the boy.

This turns out to be a teen-ager, too, and his clothes are like charred bits of paper sticking to his skin. He is badly burned, and the flesh on parts of his face has opened so that it looks as if there are pink patches woven into his black skin. Boyle turns away and vomits as Benny plugs the facepiece connection into the regulator of the resuscitator. He holds the mouthpiece tightly with both hands to ensure a good seal. Boyle places one hand over the other on the boy's chest. And he pumps like a heart—60 times a minute. "He's as dead as a board," Boyle says.

"Yeah," Benny says. "But we have to try."

Engine 73 has stretched a line to the floor above the fire. One room is lost, but they have stopped the fire. Ladders 31 and 48 are pulling down ceilings and walls. One final washdown, and we'll take up.

An aide comes up to the chief. "What should I do with the gas cans?" he asks. A search of the rooms has turned up three gas cans.

"Just leave them here. The fire marshal will be here shortly."

"That's somethin', isn't it?" Vinny Royce says, grimacing in disgust and dejection. "These kids were probably torching the place, and it lit up on them." He means they were arsonists. "I know it sounds lousy to say, but if it happened more often, people would learn, and we wouldn't have so many torch jobs."

Two fire marshals arrive and begin to question the chief. Their job is essentially that of a police detective, but they are responsible only for crimes connected with fires. The marshals take down the information they think necessary and leave for the hospital. They want to see if the two teen-agers who are still living can answer some questions.

Vinny gives the rooms a last spray. We drain the hose, repack it, and head back to the firehouse. It is nearly 6 a.m. now, and the brightness of day begins to invade the South Bronx.

We're in the firehouse kitchen again. The men haven't bothered to wash up, and they sit before their steaming cups of coffee, with smoke- and mucus-stained faces. They are talking about the ironic justice of the fire, although they don't call it ironic justice but "tough s---."

None of us wants to see anyone killed, but there is a kind of "It's either you or me" feeling now. We remember all the obvious torch jobs we have been called out on, all the vacant buildings, the linoleum placed over holes in the floor so the firefighters would fall to the floor below, the people killed in rooms above a fire because the tenant below had a fight with his wife and lit the place up, and the burns, cuts and broken limbs we have suffered because of all these things. Any one of us could have been killed in today's fire. But it was the arsonists who were killed this time.

Some days later, we hear what the marshals have learned: the landlord wanted the building vacant, so he hired some guy to torch the place. The guy then hired three kids to light it up, and when they were in there spreading the gasoline, the place caught fire. The police are out looking for the guy now. The two kids in the hospital aren't going to make it.

Benny and I are talking about this in the kitchen, but the bells come in. And on the backstep of the pumper I begin to think that it wasn't ironic justice at all. It's what always happens in the South Bronx. The real devil gets away without a burn, and the children of the South Bronx are the victims.

3. THE VALUE OF LIFE

THE JULY SUN is directly over the firehouse, and I am lying on a bed thinking of the fire we have just come from. The tenement on Fox Street was recently abandoned, and the day's heat penetrated the garbage piled in the center hall so that the odor was worse than I had ever experienced. I couldn't hold my breath long enough as I climbed over it, dragging the hose behind, and the smell made my stomach turn. The fire was on the fourth floor—and routine. We soon had it out.

The garbage smell rose through the stairwell, and there was no escaping it on the trip down. In the street again, I felt a strange sense of freedom, like being released from years of penal servitude. I stood in front of the building, not knowing where to go or what to do, yet profoundly relieved that I was no longer where I had been. I felt curiously fresh in the hot, muggy air of Fox Street.

I was sitting on the fender of a derelict car, waiting for the order to repack the hose, when I saw Elena R. walking slowly toward me. It had been years since I last saw her, but her face was unmistakable. Unmarred dark skin and the delicate bones of an aristocrat. But her eyes didn't sparkle as they used to; drugs made the lids droop. They once radiated happiness, but that is all lost. She was wearing a short white nylon skirt that clung to her thighs, and a thin red polo shirt that fitted snugly around her breasts. In another time people would have said she was developing into a chic young woman. The only unbeautiful things about her were her eyes and her needle-scarred arms.

"Denise, Denise," she called, accenting my name. "How are you?" Her voice was dull and drawled, but genuinely happy. "Man, eet's good to see you." She brushed her long black hair away from her face, and put her hand on my arm with a simple, easy grace.

Elena R. is 18 years old. She was born in Puerto Rico, and came to this country with her mother and three sisters and four brothers when she was six. She rises at 11 each morning, searches out her "man," and hits him for a shot. The heroin is stabilizing, and her appetite builds. She then goes to Amillio's Bodega for a breakfast of Pepsi-cola and cupcakes, and back to her apartment where she watches the afternoon soap operas, and nods.

Then her day begins. Elena is a five-dollar trick, and lately she has been forced to go for four. Times are tough; even the whores feel the inflation bite.

We didn't talk long, but she kept her hand on my arm all the while she spoke. She told me she shared an apartment with two other girls and four kids. The four kids belonged to one of the girls, who was on welfare. She told me, too, that she had tried to kick the drugs, but it didn't work. Maybe someday. And she talked of shooting up with a pathetic resignation that convinced me she knew as well as I that the dope would kill her someday.

Benny Carroll and the others returned to the street, pulling the wet hose behind them. Elena took her hand from my arm and offered it to me to shake. "Good-by, Denise," she said. "I see you. Okay?"

I answered a positive "Okay," and Elena walked slowly away, nodding slightly. I called to her, saying, "Take care of yourself, Elena."

And now, as I lie here in the comfortable, secure, regimented confines of the firehouse bunkroom, I think of how stupid that must have sounded to her—"Take care of yourself." That's what she is doing. Elena is surviving in the best way she knows.

When I first met her four years ago, she was a shy, sensitive 14-year-old high-school freshman. She lived on Home Street then, with her family. Her little brother, Antonio, liked fire engines, and one day she brought him to the firehouse. I was there at the time, and I spoke kindly to her. I asked what school she attended and if she liked her studies. I played with her brother. After that, the two of them visited the firehouse regularly. She would ask for "Denise," and the guys would rib me about being the idol of the under-16 set.

She told me that she hated living at home with all her brothers and sisters, and she hated school, because she couldn't read very well, and she wanted a job so she could buy pretty clothes, but she wasn't old enough to quit school yet. She had the same problems as millions of other adolescents. She was growing up, and trying to become a person instead of another mouth to feed.

After two or three months, Elena stopped coming to the firehouse. I had forgotten her completely until she walked up Fox Street this morning. And I can't help but think of all the other people who must have forgotten her somewhere along the road, along the short road of three blocks from Home Street—then—to Fox Street—now.

It is the same day. Someone on the apparatus floor is hammering the fire bell on the chief's car, the signal that lunch is ready. I ditch my cigarette in a sand bucket, and slide the pole to street level. Cagey Dulland, the guy who steers the back wheels of Ladder 31's truck, has cooked roast beef.

The heat of the gravy steams across my face as I lean over the lunch, but I am hungry and I don't let it bother me. Willy Knipps is complaining to Cagey, though, that he should have had better sense than to cook a hot meal on a day like this.

"And for 85 cents," he says. That's the price we will pay for today's meal; it is figured out every day, according to what is on the menu. "I could eat roast beef in the Waldorf-Astoria for that price." Cagey just mutters a few words about inflation and lets it go at that. He knows that the guys are grateful that he took the time to cook and the wisecracks are as natural as the rising sun.

I am sponging the gravy from the plate with a piece of bread when the bells interrupt. "Westchester Avenue and Fox Street," the house watchman yells.

Box 2555. We were just there. "I bet it's that abandoned building again," Benny Carroll says. As we approach, we see that he is right.

The people of Fox Street have left the midday heat of their apartments and have gathered in the middle of the street to watch the fire. The mood is festive. The people cheer and shout as they make room for the pumper. Why can't the city tear these buildings down, I wonder, as we approach the same building we did earlier—the same abandoned tenement with its heap of rotting garbage in the hall. Whoever lit the place up this time didn't feel like climbing the stairs to the fourth floor, because the fire is jumping out all the windows on the second.

There is not much for me to do except hump the hose in. Lieutenant Welch and Knipps start to take the apartment on the left side of the hall, and the guys of Engine 94 push their way into the apartment on the right. The fire is extinguished quickly. Gasoline must have been used to create so much fire, but it hasn't been burning long enough to get through to the floors above. The smoke has cleared.

Much of the water we used has found its way down the stairs, and the cooled garbage in the hall doesn't smell nearly as bad as we return to the street. The police are on the scene now, and are trying to control the crowd. But there are too many people—and only three cops. Ladder 31's rig is covered with kids, but we are used to that. The truck is a mobile jungle-gym set in a parkless neighborhood.

Vinny Royce is on the sidewalk across from the abandoned building. He has put his gloves on the fender of a parked car and is getting ready to repack the hose. We are all hot and sweaty, but Vinny has just helped Bill Valenzio uncouple the 4½-inch connection from the hydrant, and he appears to be sapped of strength. Suddenly, as Vinny is removing his heavy rubber coat, a garbage can, hurled from a rooftop, hits the ground next to him with a deadly thump. It doesn't miss him by more than 12 inches. Vinny moves quickly to the security of a doorway. The people in the street scatter, and the kids jump off the truck and run down the block. The street is a valley, canyoned by six-story tenements from end to end; all our eyes turn toward the roofs.

Benny Carroll screams, "Look out!" and runs to join Vinny huddled in a doorway. A volley of two-inch iron balls hit the street, one shattering the windshield of Ladder 48's rig. Cops run into the buildings. They soon return. Whoever was on the roof has disappeared.

We look at the garbage can that flew from the roof. It is on its side; it had been filled with ashes. We all keep our eyes on the roofs as we pull the hose forward and onto the fire engine. Three squad cars come wailing into the block, and we feel a little safer. The hose is packed, and we drive quickly from Fox Street, never taking our eyes from the roofs.

In the firehouse, I run to the second floor and the air-conditioning. I remove my shirt and dry my arms and chest. I take a clean shirt from my locker and think of my wife as I look at the well-pressed sleeves.

Benny and Vinny come into the bunkroom. They wash, change their shirts and lie on beds on either side of me. We talk some about what has happened. We all agree that it is difficult to make any sense out of it.

Benny says it could be organized guerrilla warfare; Vinny says it is just part of the lawless times; I say it could be both of those, but that it is also due to a loss of respect for human life. The people on Fox Street may feel they have good reason to hate us, but that's not the issue. I hated plenty of people when I was a kid, but I never thought of killing them.

I used to believe that people who threw rocks at firemen were motivated by conditions and that people would stop throwing rocks if they had a decent place to live and were given equal educational opportunities. I don't believe that anymore. The disease is more pernicious than uncaring landlords, or bureaucratic, apathetic school officials. The malignancy lies in the guts of humankind. We have unlearned the value of a human life.

It is still the same day. There is now a serious fire at Brook Avenue and 138th Street, and shortly the call comes in for "all hands." That means it is a bad fire, but not yet worthy of a second alarm. It is not our assignment, so we stay put.

Soon another fire develops—this one at Hoe Street and Jennings. A short time later, the "all hands" is sounded. Again, it is not our fire, and we lie calmly listening to Engine 85, Ladder 31 and the chief roll out. We slide the pole to listen to the department radio. From the doors of the firehouse we can see a high spiral of smoke rising to the northeast.

A second alarm is sounded for 138th Street—and then a third. There are so many bells coming over the system that I stop counting them.

Bill Kelsey is on house watch, and suddenly yells, "Get out 82 and 712. Boston and Seabury."

It is probably a false alarm, I say to myself. But, as we approach, a young boy runs down Seabury, turning occasionally to make sure we are following. There is a large crowd beginning to gather in front of the Diaz Bodega.

I am the first to reach the spot, and I see a guy in a crimson-stained yellow shirt lying in a mess of thick blood spread over the sidewalk. I hear the faceless voices of the crowd saying in broken English, "Someone tried to off 'im, man. Who the man cut 'im? We gonna get 'im." It seems strange to hear the blacks' dialect spoken with a Spanish accent.

The man is lying on his side with his head on his forearm. He is about 35 years old. His eyes are open, and he seems to sense our presence. We can see now where it hurts. His right ear has been slashed and is swinging freely by its lobe. John Nixon opens the first-aid box, hands me a sterile sponge. I pick up the ear and place it where I think it belongs. I hold the sponge in place as John wraps a bandage under the chin and around the head.

It is 3:30 as the pumper backs into the firehouse. The sun isn't beating directly on us anymore, but the air is still, and the heat seems to radiate from the sidewalks. I go to the soda machine. But as I open the can of cola, the bells redirect me. Box 2743. We know that box well: Charlotte Street and 170th. We go to that intersection more often than any other—and it is usually a false alarm.

We arrive at Charlotte and 170th. Kids are playing in a puddle at the corner, and people walk aimlessly by. We make a search as we have done a thousand times before, and we give Lieutenant Welch the thumbs-down signal. He radios the dispatcher that it is a false alarm.

In the firehouse again, I take an ice tray from the refrigerator. The creases have fallen out of my clean shirt, and there are large sweat stains at the armpits. I put the ice in a cup, and pour the soda in after it. It fizzes to the top, and as I'm waiting for it to recede, the bells come in again. I have to leave the soda once more. Box 2555—for the third time today. Kelsey is screaming with all the power in his lungs: "Westchester Avenue and Fox Street. *Again!* The Bronx is burning. Get out 82 and 712. I bet the bastards set it up again. Get out."

As we head up Tiffany Street, we can see the smoke still rising above Hoe Avenue to the north, and as we look to the southeast we can see still another column billowing rapidly above Fox Street.

"You know," Benny says to me as he pulls his boots up, "Kelsey is right. The Bronx is burning up, and the sad thing about it is that no one knows it. This is an insane day for fires, but you won't read anything about it in the papers tomorrow, and you won't see anything about it on TV tonight. That's the real sad thing. Nobody knows about it."

The crowd in the street makes room for us to pass. There is fire playing out of the windows of the first, second and third floors, and we can feel the intense heat as we pull in front of the building. A small crowd of teen-agers is gathered across from the burning tenement singing, "Burn, baby, burn! Burn, baby, burn!"

"Give it a good dash from the street first," Lieutenant Welch says, and I direct the nozzle toward the first-floor window; 250 gallons per minute hit the flaming room, and the fire darkens quickly.

We go into the vestibule and over the pyramid of wet garbage. We go up five steps, and the fire meets us at the first floor. Lieutenant Welch says that we can move in, but slowly. I keep the nozzle directed at the ceiling, and I'm making circular motions with my arms as Benny and

Vinny hump the hose in. Suddenly, a heavy piece of plaster falls, and my helmet is knocked from my head. I feel a long, cutting pain across the back of my neck. I let out a yell, and Lieutenant Welch quickly grabs the nob. Benny Carroll moves up. "What's the matter?" they both ask.

"I got burned on the neck."

"Back out," Lieutenant Welch says.

The smoke is banking down now and rushing for the oxygen at the door. I start to cough and crouch low to get beneath it, but the smoke follows me down. What, I ask myself, am I doing here? I return to the street, and sit on the fender of the derelict car—just where I sat when I saw Elena R. this morning. Firemen are racing past me, either dragging hose or carrying hooks and Halligan tools. The street is filled with hose—like arteries on a highway map. Sirens are wailing the arrival of second-alarm companies.

I put my gloves in the pocket of my rubber coat and touch the back of my neck. Blisters have risen across the full length of my neck, and I can feel the rough surface of the paint still sticking to the swollen skin. It doesn't hurt at all, but it will be tough moving my head for a while. Now there is nothing to do but wait for an ambulance—and watch as the Bronx burns up.

4. AN INFERNO

It is some weeks later now. The sun is setting beyond the bulging tenements of the South Bronx. It is 6:30, and I am standing in front of the firehouse. The summer was frenzied. We did 30 to 40 runs a day during July and August, but now we have dropped down to 20 to 30.

My attention is drawn to a little girl about 11 years old, standing by the curb. She has a pretty, round Spanish face. Her head is lowered, but her eyes stare up at me apprehensively. She is holding a notebook in one hand, and in the other a pencil. She seems to want to say something to me, but is too shy to open her mouth. I walk closer to her, smiling.

"Hello," I say in a gentle tone. "Can I help you?"

Her head is still lowered in a way that reminds me of the self-consciousness and under-rated self-image of poor children.

"My name is Cynthia," she says quietly. "I have to write a report about firemen. Are you a fireman?"

"Yes, I am a fireman, and I'll be glad to help you."

She smiles and raises her head. "Are you a chief?"

"No, I'm not a chief, but I think I can help you anyway." I take her into the firehouse and show her the equipment we use. Cynthia questions everything as a star reporter would, and scribbles furiously in her notebook. She is a bright child, and her speech is flawless. She is the first child of her family to be born in the States.

"Are you responsible for other things besides putting out fires, or should I say, extinguishing fires?" she asks. I tell her about our various duties, and how we keep the firehouse clean. "Oh, we have a man in our school who does work like that," she says. "He's called the custodian. Why don't you hire a man like that for your firehouse?" The fact is that firemen do all of their own housekeeping: cooking, sweeping, cleaning the latrines. Rather than try to answer her question—one that I have been thinking about for as long as I have been a firefighter—I ask her, "What do you want to be when you finish school?"

"Oh," she begins, "I don't think about it very much. Right now I just think about getting into a good high school. Maybe I'll be a teacher or maybe a lawyer."

Cynthia completes her interview, puts her pencil and book in her left hand and offers her right hand to me.

"Thank you," she says. "You have been very helpful." Then she walks out of the firehouse with as professional an air as I have ever seen.

The subject of kids is usually a sad one for us, but my little talk with Cynthia makes me feel light and happy. I realize that there must be many children like her in the South Bronx, and she represents the future as I want to see it. Unfortunately, though, we don't get to see many Cynthias. We see kids in filthy clothes playing in filthy alleyways. Kids who jeer at us and throw things at us. We have been into their homes. We have seen the holes in their walls, the rats in their halls and roaches scrambling over their bedsheets. It is not difficult to understand why kids are a problem to us in the South Bronx. It simply cannot be expected that Cynthias will be nurtured in these environs. But at least they exist.

I can't help thinking about Elena, the girl on Fox Street, who is now a prostitute. I wonder if a school counselor ever talked to her, or a teacher. I remember that her mother was on welfare, and wonder if some social-services official knows she exists, or existed. Wasn't there ever one person with some sense who talked to this shy, sensitive young girl? Someone to tell her that there are ways to unravel the emotional entanglements that human beings experience as they grow? Wasn't there someone who knew at least something about guidance, goals, self-motivation, self-esteem?

But maybe that's not it at all. Maybe it has to do, simply, with living in a tenement. How do you talk of self-motivation to a child who has never known the privacy of a room, or the quiet of a home? How do you talk of goals to a child who has never experienced a new pair of shoes, or to a child whose only trip in life has been from Puerto Rico to America?

And I can't help thinking of Cynthia, and of all the Cynthias of the South Bronx. God protect them!

As I stood shaving at the bathroom sink this morning, my wife came and stood by the door. I was shirtless, and after watching me for a short while she put her hand on the long scar on the back of my neck—one of the reminders of the Fox Street fire. "That's an ugly scar, Dennis," she said. "Do you think it will ever go away?"

I smiled at her reflection in the mirror, and replied, "I doubt it, but a shirt collar hides it, so what does it matter?"

"It only matters as a warning for the next one," she said, pulling my face down and pressing her lips to my cheek. Then, her eyes wet with concern, she continued, "Because in Engine 82 there will always be a next one. Oh, I know, you'll tell me that somebody has to do it, and I'm even learning to accept that, but I worry about you all the time. It will be hard for me to sleep tonight, knowing that you might be in the middle of a fire, and as I lie there I'll be wishing that you were beside me like a normal husband. But at the same time, I'll be as proud of you as our boys are. They only know that their father rides on the back of a fire engine, and they're proud of that; but I know that you are doing what you think is right for all of us, and that's good enough for me."

At that moment I felt one of the rewards of my occupation. My wife was communicating to me that she understood the nature of my job. She was fearful of the future, yet she acknowledged the importance, the value, of fighting fires. I was so moved that all I could think to say was "I love you." It was enough.

There is nothing much to do but wait for the alarms to come in. I find a book of mystery stories and start to read, but my eyes are straining by the second paragraph. I put the book down, reflecting unhappily that my eyes are not as strong as they used to be. I am still a young man, but I am beginning to feel weary. This is a young man's job, but it's making me old. I am 31, and at times I feel 50.

I have grown to love the men I work with as much as any man can love another. We have been through a lot together, from being huddled on a floor, flames jumping in front and behind, and unsure if we would be able to fight our way out, to consoling each other in hospital emergency wards, to drinking hard in North Bronx bars, to picnicking with our families by a calm upstate lake. Between us there is a mutual admiration and concern that can be found only among men whose very lives depend on each other's quick, competent and courageous actions. It is a good feeling, this dependency—a proud feeling.

The clang of the bells makes me jump, and I listen for the count. "82 and 31, get out. 1280 Kelly Street."

We can smell the smoke as the pumper leaves quarters. Up Tiffany Street and down 165th. As we turn into Kelly, the smoke has banked down to the street, making it difficult to see even ten feet.

Engine 73 arrives and helps us stretch out the hose. Between the banks of smoke, we can see that the job is on the top floor, five flights up. There is enough manpower for the stretch now, so I drop the hose and head for the mask bin. Bill Valenzio has the pumper connected to the hydrant by the time I have donned the mask, and Jerry Herbert has the aerial ladder of the truck up by the top-floor fire escape. He is climbing up it as I enter the building.

The fifth floor is enveloped in smoke, and I can barely see ahead of me. Billy O'Mann and Charlie McCarty are working on the door of the burning apartment, but it is secured inside with a long steel bar stretched from one side to the other like the gate of Fort Apache. The smoke is brutal, and Billy-O has a coughing fit between ax swings. Charlie pulls on the Halligan with all his strength, as Billy-O hammers with the head of the ax. Finally, the door begins to move. Still coughing and choking, Charlie puts his shoulder to it, and it swings inward.

Charlie and Billy-O dive to the floor, for the fire lunges out to the hall. Willy Boyle has the nozzle. "Let's go," Lieutenant Welch says.

Boyle makes it about ten feet into the apartment, but it is an old building, and the plaster is falling from the ceiling in large chunks. Boyle's helmet is knocked from his head. Lieutenant Welch orders me to take the line. Boyle has to back out. It is unsafe to operate in an inferno like this without something protecting the head.

Meanwhile, Jerry Herbert enters from a front window. He can hear McCarty and Billy-O banging at the door. The whole apartment except the front room is burning, and the smoke and the fire are being drawn there by the open window. Jerry crawls along the floor, realizing that the room could go up in a second. He hears a slight moan, coming from the far side of the bed that stands in the middle of the room. The room is dark with smoke, and Jerry crawls to the sound, patting with his hand before him. He reaches the other side of the bed, and the fire begins to lap at the ceiling above him. The smoke has taken everything from him, but he knows he can't back out now.

His hand gropes in front of him until at last he feels the soft give of a woman's body. There is a baby by her side. Jerry picks the child up and hurries on his knees toward the window. As he nears it, he sees Richie Rittman enter and yells to him. Rittman takes the baby in his arms and climbs out of the apartment. Jerry knows that he is in trouble, for the fire is coming at him fast. He grabs the woman under the arms and pulls her to the window, keeping his head as low as he can. As he lifts her out to the fire escape, he hears the front door give way, and at that moment the room lights up completely in fire.

I swing the nozzle back and forth across the ceiling. The floor is cluttered with furniture, fallen plaster. It is difficult moving forward.

"Keep pushing, Dennis, keep pushing," Lieutenant Welch says.

"Give me some more line," I yell to him through the mask, and he yells back to Royce and Knipps. We reach the front room, and as I lift my leg to get a stronger stance, the floor gives way and my leg goes down, caught between the smoldering boards of the floor. Lieutenant Welch sees what has happened and calls Royce up to the nozzle.

Knipps helps pull me up, and I start to move out, but the way is blocked by the men of Ladder 31. They are kneeling around a small body. It's the baby. I go to a window and rip open my facepiece to get some air. The taste is horrible as my stomach empties.

Billy-O is sitting on the vestibule steps, waiting for the ambulance. The baby that Ladder 31 found is wrapped in a bedspread and lies like a little bundle in his arms.

I come down the steps and ask him, "What is it?"

"It's a little girl," he says. "She never had a chance."

"Did you give her mouth-to-mouth?" I ask.

"We couldn't. She was roasted so bad, the skin was burnt completely off her face. The poor little thing. She never had a chance."

I don't say anything further, nor does Billy. I look at his eyes. They are almost fully closed, but I can see they are wet and tearing—the light reflects from the watered surfaces, and they sparkle. I wish my wife, my mother, everyone who has ever asked me why I do what I do, could see the humanity, the sympathy, the sadness of these eyes, because in them is the reason I continue to be a firefighter.

Tinkerbelle

CONDENSED FROM THE BOOK

BY ROBERT MANRY

ILLUSTRATED BY NICK SLOVIOFF

On June 1, 1965, a 47-year-old Cleveland newspaper man, who described himself as "a copy-desk Walter Mitty," set out alone to sail the Atlantic from Falmouth, Massachusetts, to Falmouth, England, in his 13½-foot sailboat. He reached his destination 78 days and 3,200 miles later, and was astonished and not a little embarrassed when the feat was hailed as an nautical triumph.

Here in *Tinkerbelle,* Robert Manry tells of his voyage, not only with engaging modesty but with boundless enthusiasm for his little boat and the many faces of the sea.

1. SOLO VOYAGE

IN THE SUMMER OF 1958, my wife Virginia and I decided that at long last we could afford a small secondhand sailboat. I was a copy-desk man on the Cleveland *Plain Dealer,* and every night at 10:40, when first-edition copies came off the presses, I eagerly scanned the classified ads. Most boat listings were disappointing, but after weeks of search I found this ad:

SAILBOAT, 13½ ft. Old Town, needs some repair, cheap. EN 1-7298.

Getting the jump on the regular subscribers, who wouldn't see the ad for some hours, I phoned at once and arranged to see the craft next morning.

The owner, a charming old Greek, met me with a twinkle in his eyes. From the way he spoke I could tell he loved the boat, which was 30 years old, but my first glimpse of her was shocking. She was turned forlornly bottom up in his backyard, her multiple coatings of varicolored paint were peeling away, and I could see two enormous splits. Aside from this, however, the planking appeared healthy and strong.

Lying on my back, I pushed under the boat and studied her interior. I discovered that "needs some repair" was an understatement. Nearly two dozen ribs were broken, and half a dozen others were infected with dry rot, which also had decayed chunks of the mast step and centerboard trunk. The canvas deck was badly worn, and the sails were too mildewed and threadbare to use. Everything else, though, was basically sound.

The boat was large enough to accommodate Virginia and me with our seven-year-old daughter, Robin, and our four-year-old son, Douglas, and yet small enough to keep in the garage (thus avoiding dockage fees which, at that stage, would have bankrupted us). Her split planks appeared mendable, and when I weighed the price, $160, against the expense of repairing her and buying new sails, I finally decided that, dilapidated as she was, she was the boat for us.

Two days later, Virginia and I rented a trailer and came to collect the little craft that had now become ours. The owner greeted us, and everyone pitched in to get the boat right side up and winched onto the trailer. Virginia told me later that she saw tears in the old man's eyes, and that both he and his wife patted the boat with affectionate gestures of farewell.

It required $300 and all my free time for nine months to put the craft into shape. I tinkered with her so much that we decided to name her *Tinkerbelle* (after the fairy in *Peter Pan,* but with a final *e* to emphasize her femininity). It was all rewarding. I had sailed no more than five times in my whole life, but I had always been in love with sailboats, and *Tinkerbelle* did not disappoint me. When we began to sail regularly on Lake Erie, taking our vacations on her, she entered deeply into our hearts. She wasn't just a boat anymore; she was a trusted friend.

As our sailing skill increased, so did my ambition. I wanted longer and longer trips on *Tinkerbelle,* and to make this possible I finally reequipped her completely, spending a full year redesigning and rebuilding her superstructure.

At this point I received an exciting invitation. Early in 1964, a friend who owned a 25-foot cruising sloop proposed that we sail it across the Atlantic to England. He spoke half in jest, not knowing that I had dreamed of such a venture for three decades and that I would latch onto the idea with enormous enthusiasm and tenacity. Virginia and the children approved of the proposed voyage, which was scheduled for the summer of 1965; and when my boss at the *Plain Dealer* granted me a leave of absence for it, my joy knew no bounds.

I was on Cloud Nine for about six weeks. Then came a crushing blow. The prospective skipper backed out of the venture, persuaded by his wife, father and business associates that it was ill-advised and would require too much time. I was heartbroken. It was like dropping from paradise to purgatory at the flip of a switch.

As I regained composure, however, a thought struck me: Why not make the voyage alone in *Tinkerbelle?* The more I mulled over the idea the less fantastic it appeared, for *Tinkerbelle* had now been transformed into a proper little yacht, with a cabin, cockpit, running lights, a compass and other gear usually found only on much larger vessels. A movable 100-pound iron daggerboard keel had given her increased stability and, when all her hatches were battened down and sealed, she was as watertight and as seaworthy as a corked bottle.

So I began to prepare for the trip, telling no one except Virginia and the children of the change in plans. I did not want my wife to become needlessly upset by listening to the fears of people who knew nothing about the sea.

MY FIRST STEP WAS to determine as precisely as I could the hazards to be expected on a transatlantic voyage in so small a craft, and then to decide soberly whether or not they were surmountable. If they weren't, I'd simply have to go back to being a copy-desk Walter Mitty and forget the dream.

I wrote to the U.S. Weather Bureau in Washington for its forecasts, and I studied the marvelously informative charts of the North Atlantic issued by the U.S. Naval Oceanographic Office. From these it appeared that I had a better than 50-50 chance of encountering a storm during the summer, but I was confident that my little boat would acquit herself well. A small boat, being light and buoyant, will generally ride *over* the waves, whereas a big ship will usually offer immense resistance.

However, I took every precaution I could think of. To make *Tinkerbelle* virtually unsinkable, I filled all the spaces between her deck beams with polyethylene foam flotation material. I bought a special Air Force transmitter which, in case I did run into trouble, sent out SOS signals on two frequencies by cranking. If this failed, I'd have flares, dye markers and signaling mirrors.

The next biggest problem, the danger of being run down by a big ship while I was asleep, was disposed of more easily. I would stay away from the regular shipping lanes, all of which were marked on the charts. Where it was necessary to cross such lanes, I would stay awake, with the aid of pills if necessary, until I was safely into the untraveled sea beyond.

What about navigation? It was essential that I learn the rudiments of this science, but it was a subject whose very name filled me with dread. Fortunately, some wonderful, anonymous men had taken all the pain out of it by producing a book of logarithmic tables called *H. O. 214,* which reduced all the required calculations to simple addition and subtraction. Add and subtract I could—just.

So, armed with various books and charts and a secondhand sextant, I set out to teach myself to guide a boat from one port to another across the trackless, signless sea. I did it on our front porch. My first sight with the sextant put me somewhere in the middle of Hudson Bay, hundreds of miles to the north. That was a bit alarming, for if I couldn't do any better, I might as well rely on a Ouija board. But I improved in time. In the end, my sightings came within nine or ten miles of being right, and that was close enough.

One danger at a time, I tried to anticipate every conceivable misfortune. I put a lightning rod at *Tinkerbelle's* masthead and grounded it to a copper plate on her bottom. I rigged a lifeline to tie myself to the boat, in case a wave washed me overboard. I assembled a tool kit and a supply of lumber. I bought an inflatable life raft, a shortwave radio, a solar still for converting sea water into fresh, and replacements for every piece of equipment that was under strain. I got a sail-repair kit and spare sails, and I put together a set of emergency medical supplies.

In the summer of 1964, before the planning had gone very far, Douglas, then ten, and I took a 200-mile trial cruise on Lake Erie, the longest yet for *Tinkerbelle.* In a thunderstorm one day, she ran up against stiff, squally winds and the biggest waves she had ever encountered, white-crested rollers, six to eight feet high. The spirited way in which she rode them made me even more optimistic about the Atlantic venture.

In January 1965 I began to gather food supplies: dehydrated meat bars, Army C rations, canned white bread and fruit cakes, cereal bars, 28 gallons of water and numerous cans of fruit juice and carbonated drinks. I expected the voyage to take between 60 and 75 days, but to be on the safe side, I collected provisions for 90, not forgetting to include several can openers.

In the spring, when I finally broke the news of my solo voyage to the rest of the family, they took it calmly. "It is wonderful to see someone carry out his dream," one of my sisters wrote. "So few of us take a chance." Mother was a little more concerned. "Of course your letter made me catch my breath," she wrote. "But I can understand the urge within you to do this thing, and this will be your adventure of a lifetime!" Later, I learned that her greatest fear was that the loneliness of the ocean would drive me insane, a possibility that hadn't even occurred to me.

By May I was up to my neck in last-minute preparations. I had gathered all the necessary charts, pilot books, lighthouse lists and so on, but I still had to get a passport and smallpox vaccination, fill out a voyage plan for the Coast Guard and fit a bilge pump to *Tinkerbelle.* Every minute away from my job was spent attending to these details.

Meanwhile, my cohorts on the *Plain Dealer,* still believing that I was going with someone else in a much larger boat, offered all sorts of raucous advice. They ceremoniously presented me with a bottle of brandy with directions affixed: In case of emergency—1. Remove contents. 2. Insert message. 3. Launch.

One colleague, recalling the *Titanic* disaster, suggested that we take along a phonograph and a recording of "Nearer My God to Thee" to play if the appropriate occasion arose.

"You at least ought to write down the words of the hymn," said Ted Mellow, the news editor, "so you'll be able to sing it as you go down."

FINALLY, THE DATE WAS SET. *Tinkerbelle* and I would begin our transatlantic adventure on June 1, sailing from Falmouth, Mass., to Falmouth, England. Virginia and her brother John drove east with me, and on May 26 we lifted *Tinkerbelle* from her trailer and lowered her into Falmouth Inner Harbor.

It was her first taste of the sea, and she took to it proudly. She looked like a brand-new boat. Her white hull, red deck and cabin top, and varnished mast, cockpit seats and cabin sides gleamed in the sunshine. There was no disputing the fact that no other boat like her existed anywhere in the world.

The man who owned the marina we were using couldn't believe his eyes when he saw all the things we were putting aboard. "Where's he going?" he asked Virginia in bewilderment. "England?"

That evening we had a farewell dinner, and the next morning Virginia and John returned to Cleveland. Last-minute details occupied the next few days, and on my last night ashore I wrote to my friends at the *Plain Dealer,* revealing the facts of my voyage. I hoped that no one would mind my deception. I also telephoned home and said a final good-by to the family. Then I went back to *Tinkerbelle* and tried to get comfortable for the night, but sleep eluded me for a long while.

Both of us were tugging at our moorings, anxious to be off. *Tinkerbelle's* mooring lines were strong, of three-eighths-inch Dacron; mine were made of invisible stuff—the social conventions, habits, thought patterns and bonds of affection that held me to the life on shore. But in their own way mine were as strong as hers, maybe stronger. Why then was I here?

As every man does, I have searched for truth in life, and over the years I have collected a handful of miscellaneous chips from the Mother Lode. Few have approached the pure, unvarnished verity of what Water Rat says to Mole in Kenneth Grahame's delightful book, *The Wind in the Willows:*

"Believe me, my young friend, there is nothing—absolutely nothing—half so much worth doing as simply messing about in boats."

Of course, I'm being partly facetious, but, mind you, partly serious, too. And if anything can, these words explain why a 47-year-old, sober and presumably sane newspaperman was so intent on crossing the ocean alone. To whisk myself off on a "small planet," as Joseph Conrad once described a boat, to escape from the troubles and tensions ashore, was a sheer delight. But there was the challenge, too, the summons to master wind and water and bend them to my will, and to master myself when I was in a crisis, balancing on the edge of panic.

I was positive that no one in the world had as wonderful a wife as I. Virginia could have insisted that I behave as other "rational" men did and give up this "crazy" voyage. But she knew I was stepping to the music of a different drummer, and she granted me the invaluable boon of self-realization by allowing me to keep pace with the music I heard. Her quiet faith was a compliment and a gift such as few men receive.

2. UNDER WAY

THE ALARM CLOCK JARRED ME AWAKE. It was 9 a.m., and the sun was beating on the cabin roof. At about 10:30 I hoisted *Tinkerbelle's* red mainsail and white genoa jib, and she and I set forth on our great voyage. It was a beautiful day. The sky was blue; the weather was warm, and a gentle breeze caressed the sails. Fortune was smiling on us.

We beat down Vineyard Sound, passing Nobska Point and, beyond it, Woods Hole, in the early afternoon. We had the Sound to ourselves all afternoon except for one small trawler that hurried by in the opposite direction as we approached the Elizabeth Islands. It was pleasant, easy sailing, with a breeze of 10 or 12 knots, just enough to keep *Tinkerbelle* moving along contentedly without any fretting or straining. I knew that many rough, uncomfortable days lay ahead, but I felt sure that my preparations had been adequate. More important, I had tremendous faith in my companion and friend. A one-man voyage is in reality a duet, in which the boat plays the melody and the skipper the harmony. I was just there for the ride, and to keep *Tinkerbelle* pointed in the right direction.

Robert Manry

The day was dying in a blaze of red as we slipped out of Vineyard Sound into the open ocean. It was a singularly thrilling moment for me. I was on the threshold of fulfilling the ambition of a lifetime. Fortunate beyond measure, I was finding my way to Never-Never Land, where dreams come true.

I was steering a southeasterly course in order to get across and below the heavily traveled shipping lanes out of New York. Except for the approach to England, I expected this period to be the most dangerous of the voyage. In fact, it proved to be near-disastrous.

In my anxiety to cross the shipping lanes as quickly as possible, I sailed all night. As we sloshed and splashed into the dark immensity of the ocean, *Tinkerbelle* gave me my first view of the display put on by phosphorescent plankton. The water, ruffled by the boat's passage, glittered and shone with a starry fire. We appeared to be floating on a carpet of sparklers more brilliant than any I'd ever seen, and trailing behind was a luminescent wake resembling the tail of a comet.

When morning broke, no land was in sight. I ate a cold breakfast so I wouldn't have to stop to prepare anything, but shortly after noon the wind died down and we came to a halt anyway. Since we couldn't move, and I had had no sleep for more than 24 hours, I left the red mainsail up to render *Tinkerbelle* visible, and stretched out in the cockpit for 40 winks.

It was about 2:30 p.m. when I awoke and found, to my dismay, that we still had no breeze and, worse, that we were surrounded by fog so dense that a ship could run us down without even knowing it. I got out the oars to be ready to row for my life if I had to, hoisted the radar reflector to at least warn radar-equipped vessels of our presence, and also got out the compressed-gas foghorn and sounded it from time to time. There were no answers.

In an hour, a light breeze gave us just enough wind power to maintain steerageway. But the claustrophobic fog remained and, when I began to hear ships passing by, my nerves got jumpier. We were in an area where numerous accidents had occurred, notably the tragic collision of the *Andrea Doria* and the *Stockholm* in 1956. Some of the vessels throbbed by so close that I could hear their bow waves breaking and, if they were freighters traveling light, their propellers chopping the water. But I could see nothing—until suddenly a mammoth black hull slid out of the fog off our port quarter and, apparently sighting *Tinkerbelle's* red sail, let go with a tooth-rattling blast which so startled me that I nearly fell overboard. Moments later it passed astern and disappeared again into the mist.

That night, although a hard rain dispersed the fog, winds of 40 or 45 miles an hour whipped up ten-foot waves, bigger than any I had ever experienced. I got the sails down and the sea anchor out, then huddled in the cockpit, expecting any minute to be inundated. Not until dawn did the sea subside a bit.

By that time—this was the beginning of the third day—my need for rest was becoming acute. But I wasn't aware of it. The stay-awake pills I was taking made me feel wonderful. In point of fact, I was on the verge of collapse, and that afternoon I was caught in the grip of a severe hallucination. For hours I sailed aimlessly back and forth under the illusion that I had taken aboard a passenger and that I must drop him off at a nearby island. (There are no islands to be found in that part of the Atlantic.)

Finally, I had the wit to put out the sea anchor, strike the sails and crawl into my cabin. Lying down on a pile of my supplies and pulling a blanket over me, I dropped into unconsciousness as if I had been dealt a knockout blow.

When I awoke, completely rested, the sun was shining bright. Thus far I had been calculating my position by dead reckoning, but at noon I took my first sextant shot—and came up with a sun line which, if accurate, would have put me miles from where I should have been. Oh well, I thought, tomorrow I'll try again.

But the following morning, June 5, I discovered something quite unsettling. I was experimenting with different sea-anchor arrangements and had hitched a canvas bucket to a 150-foot line. When I pulled it up, it was filled with sand. Yet we were supposed to be in water more than a mile deep!

I got out the sextant again and took as accurate a noon sight as I could. From this and the shallowness of the water, I deduced that we were at the edge of Cultivator Shoal, a mere 90 miles east of Nantucket—little progress for four days. Worse, I had thought we were south of the shipping lanes, but somehow we had sailed back 30 miles north of them. Thus, I would have to enter and cross this dangerous area all over again.

The blunt exposure of my shortcomings as a navigator left me shaken. Had I bitten off more than I could chew?

I NAPPED AND AFTERWARD fixed myself a tasty dinner on my canned-heat stove. Then, as the sun dropped below the horizon, I set off. We sailed all night at a delightful wave-slapping pace, and soon after dawn we arrived smack dab in the middle of the shipping lanes. For a good part of the day there were seven or eight craft in sight, and as one disappeared in the distance another would take its place. But by midafternoon we were again alone.

That night I wrote in the log: "I still don't know exactly where I am. I'll take some sextant sights tomorrow and try to pinpoint it. The ocean is a vast, empty expanse. I'm beginning to find out what real loneliness is. My nose is sunburned, and the backs of my hands are getting raw from being wet so much. My big problem is my backside. I'm sore from the dampness and constant jostling. Sitting on the life-preserver cushion helps, but tomorrow I'll have to render some first aid. Otherwise I'm in good shape."

The next day was glorious, and nothing unusual happened. But, late in the afternoon, I sighted a ship to the north, which made me fearful that I was still too near the shipping lanes; so I turned south for a couple of hours. Then I hove to, to sleep.

I remember that night well. I was worried because it was fogging up, and my radar reflector, which would have warned ships away, had been blown off during the storm several days earlier. My fretfulness made it difficult to sleep for a long time.

Before I was fully awake the next morning, a strange sound insinuated itself into my senses. It seemed to be a chorus of men shouting. But that was absurd—I must have dreamed it. Squirming into a new position under my blanket, I tried to ignore the noise. Then, suddenly, I exploded into wide-eyed consciousness.

Ah-youuuuuga! Ah-youuuuuga!

This was no dream. It was a nerve-jangling synthesis of the wailing of banshees, the booming of thunder and the screeching of all the demons in hell. That dreadful sound could mean only one thing: my time on earth was up. And when I identified the accompanying roar as that of diesel engines, I was sure of it. Without a doubt, a big ship was bearing down on *Tinkerbelle.*

I must have been hitting Mach 3 as I threw open the cabin hatch and flew out onto deck ready to dive overboard. Fortunately, I was able to halt myself before plunging into the sea. We were not about to be run down after all, I discovered; but what I saw nearly made my eyes pop from their sockets.

Lying alongside *Tinkerbelle,* so close I could almost have jumped aboard her, was an enormous submarine. And on the bridge staring at me were three or four men.

I felt foolish. To be scared out of my wits in front of an audience was humiliating. I tried to salvage my pride by changing my expression of panic to one of nonchalant greeting, but I suspected that the men weren't a bit deceived.

One of them called out, "Do you need any help?"

In my startled condition I scarcely knew what to reply. "No, thanks!" I finally shouted back.

Whereupon we lapsed into numbed silence. We couldn't think of anything more to say. We just stood there looking blankly, unbelievingly, at each other as we drifted farther and farther apart. Soon we could not have made ourselves heard if we'd wanted to. As the sub's stern passed, I saw markings which told me it was an American craft, the *Tench.*

Later I learned that the *Tench* was engaged in a NATO exercise with several other ships and had left New London the day before. Spotting my mast, the captain had come alongside to investigate. He had hailed me first by megaphone—to no avail.

"The solution was readily available," wrote her skipper, Lt. Cmdr. James A. Bacon, some months later. "I reached over and gave a long blast on the ship's whistle, and there you were, leaping out of the cabin as if you thought you were about to be run down by the *Queen Mary.* I must admit that I found your reaction somewhat amusing.

"I thought at the time that you probably were a sailing enthusiast from Boston or from someplace in the Cape area. I am sincerely glad I did not know your destination. If I had, I would have had a guilty conscience on leaving you there."

3. MAN OVERBOARD!

ON JUNE 13, NEARLY TWO WEEKS out and approximately 480 miles east of Long Island, I arose to find a stiff breeze blowing, so—as I had done several times in the days since meeting the *Tench*—I tethered *Tinkerbelle* to her sea anchor. This was becoming a nuisance. Fearing a capsize, I did not sail in high seas. That made sense. But for the same reason I stayed out of the cabin and therefore could not use this idle time to sleep. If we didn't get cracking soon, it would take more than three months to reach England instead of the two I had estimated.

The wind abated a bit in the afternoon, so I set sail. And though it picked up again by nightfall, I pushed on impatiently. *Tinkerbelle* skipped along at seven knots, her top speed.

Far from being a racing machine, she was lamentably slow in light breezes, but her beamishness and flattish bottom gave her extra stability in hard blows. Earlier on Lake Erie, we had done some of our most enjoyable sailing when small-craft warnings were hoisted and few other sailboats ventured out.

Today she needed all her inherent stability. Every now and then a foaming wave-cap slammed into her starboard side, sending a geyser along the deck, half-filling her self-bailing cockpit. Under each blow she lurched like a wounded doe, dipping to leeward with a tense, stomach-churning heave. She told me through the tiller, by the way she wanted to point closer to the wind, that she was unhappy. But I forced her on, full tilt.

My teeth chattered, even though I had on four layers of clothing; my socks, shoes and the lower halves of my trousers were soaking wet. Yet I was exuberant.

"England, here we come!" I yelled at the stars.

Shortly before daybreak, the wind moved around to the west and blew from directly astern. For a while the sea was confused. Then the waves, by degrees, grew higher and steeper, flinging us forward at breakneck speed. Clutched in a welter of hissing foam, we surfed giddily down the forward slope of a breaking wave, paused for a moment in the trough as the wave raced ahead, and then repeated the maneuver. It was exhilarating—and dangerous.

The chief hazard was that we might broach—that is, slue around broadside to the waves. A breaker striking *Tinkerbelle* in that position could roll her over. It might dismast her or inflict other dire injuries. So, favoring discretion over sailing valor, I reluctantly put out the sea anchor again.

Tinkerbelle seemed to appreciate the change, and for a while her motion was less violent. But the waves continued to grow. I could see them clearly in the brightening dawn. They resembled rows of huge, snow-capped mountains marching toward us. Regularly one of the snowy tops would curve forward, fall—carumpf!—and send tons of water cascading into the valley. What if an avalanche like that rammed into *Tinkerbelle?* Oh, brother . . . !

I thought how wonderful it would be to crawl into the cabin, out of the wind, but I didn't have the courage to do it. So I remained outside in the pitching, yawing, reeling, gyrating cockpit, exposed to the merciless clawing of the gale.

At 4:30 the sun bobbed up, and so did my spirits. The red-gold rays burnished the mahogany of *Tinkerbelle's* cabin and sent waves of radiant relief deep into my chilled hide.

What happened next came so fast, I still don't have a clear picture of it. I remember that I was reveling in the sun when suddenly a foaming wall of water fell on *Tinkerbelle* from abeam, inundating her, and battering me into the ocean in a backward somersault. One moment I was sitting in the cockpit, and the next I was upside down in the water, headed for Davy Jones's locker.

Instinctively I flailed my arms and legs, fighting to gain the surface. But I rose slowly, held down by my clothes. My lungs were at the bursting point when my head finally broke out of the ocean. I expected to find *Tinkerbelle* floating bottom up—but, joy of joys, able craft that she was, she was riding the waves like a gull. I was connected to her by the lifeline tied around my waist, and we were no more than ten feet apart. I reached down, caught hold of the rope and hauled myself back. It was quite a struggle getting aboard in my wet garments, but finally,

I flopped myself into the cockpit and lay there clutching a handhold.

The situation could have been a lot worse. I was soaked through, but nothing really calamitous had happened. *Tinkerbelle* was still right side up and clear of water. Best of all, I now had evidence of how stable she was, and that one piece of empirically gained knowledge made the whole harrowing experience a blessing in disguise. There would be no more torturous nights in the cockpit; from now on I would sleep in the comfort of the cabin, even in the foulest weather, with the assurance that my faithful boat would ride out the storm.

About ten o'clock the next morning, my mind began to play tricks again. I knew that truck drivers who took pep pills sometimes thought they saw things on the highway. And Joshua Slocum, on his solo voyage around the world, was visited by an apparition who claimed to be the pilot of Christopher Columbus's *Pinta.* Nevertheless, my previous hallucination had left me feeling half fearful, half embarrassed, and I had not mentioned it in my log.

Now I gradually became aware that *Tinkerbelle* and I were accompanied by other people in other boats and that we were searching for a small community known as Ada's Landing. I didn't know why the other sailors had to find the place, but I was to meet my daughter Robin there and help her overcome some threatening, though unspecified, difficulty.

Under genoa jib alone, I began to hunt for the landing. We sailed and sailed and eventually got to a part of the ocean called the Place of the Sea Mountains. It was aptly named, for the waves were lofty. As we climbed and slid over them, the notion seeped into my mind that we were in a kingdom controlled by a crusty Scot named MacGregor, a man with scraggly white sideburns, plaid tam-o'-shanter, knobby knees showing below his kilt and a knobby cane in his hand. For some reason he was determined to do me in.

He had the help of a demonic choir of evil-faced cutthroats who could control the size of the waves by the loudness of their singing. And they were singing their lungs out, goaded by angry tongue-lashings from MacGregor. The waves grew bigger and bigger.

I did some of the fanciest sailing of my life, cutting around the edges of those huge swells. But I never seemed to get anywhere, least of all to Ada's Landing. And neither did the people in the other boats. We all seemed to be trapped in a maze.

At last, after hours of struggling, we came upon a little elfin character, and I asked him, "How do we get out of this place?"

He stood there on the water studying me impishly for a long time. Then he scratched his bald head and said, "Sir, the trouble is that you have been sailing clockwise. You must sail counterclockwise."

I put *Tinkerbelle* into a counterclockwise course. Amazingly, it seemed the correct maneuver. We came to a place where the sea descended in a gigantic staircase and went down it lickety-split. (What we were really doing, I guess, was surf-riding the waves, but because of my distorted vision they appeared to be great steps in the sea.)

I had no awareness of the danger I was in. Suddenly—wham!—we broached, and I was plopped into the ocean a second time. But because of the lifeline I wasn't flung far from *Tinkerbelle,* and I got back on board in a jiffy. Twice more that afternoon, as I went down the "staircase," I was knocked overboard. It was as exasperating as *Tinkerbelle's* self-righting abilities were gratifying. But finally we got to the bottom of the steps, and by sunset we came to the "regular" ocean—out of the Place of the Sea Mountains at last.

By now every cell in my body cried for sleep. I decided that I would have to find Ada's Landing in the morning, hoping that Robin could wait that much longer.

Just as I was dropping off to sleep, the boat jiggled violently, and I heard people whispering. Apparently some pranksters had swum out from the landing and were jostling the boat to keep me awake. I tried to control my temper, but when I heard my tormentors, in low voices, planning more trickery, I could hardly contain myself. They jiggled *Tinkerbelle* again.

"Cut that out!" I yelled.

Quiet returned for a few minutes; then the boat began to seesaw. Adrenalin gushed into my veins, and I stormed out of the cabin ready to beat my harassers to a pulp.

"Dammit! You're going to get it now," I roared.

I searched the night intently, but there was no one there. Baffled, I went back to bed.

It was a great relief in the morning to realize that the whole experience was a waking dream, that Robin wasn't in trouble, that there was no Ada's Landing, no MacGregor, that there were no nocturnal pranksters. But what about those duckings? Were they hallucinations, too? The clothing I'd worn the previous day was tucked away in a corner, and it was still sopping. It couldn't possibly have got that wet unless I had been in the sea. Hesitantly I wrote the recollections in my log, adding, "This was one of the most unusual days of my life."

By June 16 we had covered only 10 of the 65 degrees of longitude that our 3200-mile voyage would involve. At this rate it would take more than 100 days to reach Falmouth, and I was provisioned for only 90. But I wasn't worried because I was consuming my rations slower than anticipated, and I was confident that we would move faster as I grew better acquainted with the ocean and *Tinkerbelle's* performance.

The following day, in midafternoon, the rudder broke. Its fiberglass covering had cracked, and water had seeped into the plywood underneath, causing it to soften and finally snap. I thanked my stars that, foreseeing just such a mishap, I'd brought along a spare.

My expectation of making faster progress once I had my sea legs proved true. I crossed the next invisible marker—50 degrees west longitude—on June 28. Thus I covered in 12 days a distance which previously had taken 16.

By now I had a daily routine fairly well established. I usually awoke at about 4 a.m. and began the day in sheer luxury: I had breakfast in bed. In fact, I had dinner in bed, too, for *Tinkerbelle's* cabin was too small to permit dining any other way. My toilet was brief. I shaved every other week—all except my upper lip which soon sported quite a respectable mustache. Once a week I took a sponge bath with sea water, afterward rinsing in fresh water.

To get under way, I took the anchor light out of the rigging, hauled in the sea anchor and lashed it down, unstowed and hung the rudder and lastly hoisted the sails. In good weather this required about 20 minutes, but if the sea was rough it sometimes took twice as long. Then I sailed until the time came for my morning sextant shot. I took three such sun lines during the day, and from them I established my position with reasonable accuracy.

Ordinarily I sailed until well after darkness, stopping to sleep anywhere from 9 p.m. to midnight, though once in a while I continued all night. I slept in my clothes and, because of cramped conditions in the cabin, in a semi-reclining position. Usually I was so tired that I had no trouble whatever getting to sleep; the sea rocked me as though I were in a cradle (luckily I have never been bothered by seasickness). When the morning alarm went off, there I was, already sitting up in bed. All I had to do was reach over to the stove—and the new day began.

Early in July we encountered bad weather, but July 5 turned out sunny with a perfect breeze, and I commented to myself, "The only thing that could make this day better would be for a ship to come along and pick up my mail."

Twenty minutes later, as if in answer to a prayer, a vessel steamed over the horizon. She was the S.S. *Steel Vendor,* bound from India to New York. I had met a few other ships out this far, but had got no closer than hailing distance. This time we drew to within 50 feet of each other—the 13½-foot *Tinkerbelle* and the 492-foot freighter—and we could talk easily. Her master, Capt. Kenneth N. Greenlaw, inquired if I was lost. I assured him that I wasn't, but asked for a check on my navigation. He gave me my exact position. Then a line was heaved down to me. I tied a bundle of letters to it, and they were aboard the ship in a jiffy, on their way to family and friends ashore.

"Thanks!" I yelled. "Have a nice trip."

We waved, slowly drew apart, and in a few minutes I was alone once again.

4. A MESSAGE

JULY 11 WAS AN IMPORTANT DAY to me because sometime during it I expected to pass the meridian of 40 degrees west. This was a few degrees short of the halfway mark, but I considered it the point of no return. With the prevailing westerly winds, it would now be as easy to go on as to return. I was hoping to have a good long day of swift sailing.

The wind *was* strong, and the waves seemed huge (some of them, I thought, were 20-footers, the biggest yet), but I kept *Tinkerbelle* boiling along under genoa only.

My spirits were beginning to soar when—crack!—my *spare* rudder snapped. This was serious trouble and would mean a long delay, for now I would have to repair the damage. To cap everything, as I was collecting my wits after this mishap, a breaking wave caught *Tinkerbelle* beam on and knocked her down, plopping me into the ocean for the fifth time. The boat righted herself at once, and I scrambled back quickly, for by that time I had amassed considerable boarding experience. Then I threw out the sea anchor.

It was desolating not to be able to sail on such a fine day, but the gloomy fact had to be faced. I gathered together my tools and, with pieces of oak, brass bolts, fiberglass and waterproof glue, went to work.

Later in the afternoon I took a sun shot. It indicated that we were only three or four miles away from 40 degrees west, but the information cheered me scarcely at all. I knew I could fix the rudder, but the halt for repairs and the slowness of our progress made me melancholy.

By nightfall I had stewed myself into a state of severe depression. I missed Virginia and Robin and Douglas, and the thought of further delay and the concern I would cause them tormented me. But I had a way out. If the voyage became too difficult or fraught with hardships, I could cut it short by heading for the Azores. Now it seemed the best thing to do, once the rudder was fixed, to swing southeastward and call it quits.

But after dinner that evening, as I was writing up the day's events, I spotted the tip of a piece of paper sticking from the pages of the notebook that served as my log. It was a leaf from a booklet that only Virginia could have put there. It read:

"Charles A. Lindbergh, flying the Atlantic alone, came to the point where he could go no farther. He was exhausted. His hands were so tired they refused to obey his mind. Then he made this simple prayer: 'God give me strength.' From that moment, he declares, he sensed a third part of himself, 'an element of spirit' which took control of both mind and body, 'guarding them as a wise father guards his children.'"

Finding this message at that moment of utter dejection was a bit of a miracle, for I desperately needed something to snap me out of it. The content of the note in itself was helpful, but what did most to lift my sagging spirits was the realization of the loving devotion that had led Virginia to slip it into my log. That gave me strength and new determination, and before long I was back on an even keel.

After two days of drifting to the sea anchor while I worked on the rudder, we started sailing again. It was soon evident that the repair job would hold up.

The next two days were cloudy, but July 15 was wonderfully sunny, and my sextant sights revealed that we had passed 37 degrees west, the halfway point. That evening I celebrated by eating a plum pudding which I had brought along for the occasion. I felt that we were getting somewhere at last. It would be downhill the rest of the way.

As if to underline this fact, two days later *Tinkerbelle* made her best run of the voyage: she covered 87 miles from one noon to the next. To achieve this mark I kept her going all night. It was worth it, for it made the step from 40 degrees west to 30 degrees west, which we crossed on July 21, the briefest of the whole countdown—only nine days.

Soon after reaching this milestone we were becalmed for several hours. The ocean in a dead calm must be the quietest place on earth. Not a sound was to be heard except my breathing. There were no birds, no ships, not even a ripple to lap against the hull. The ocean was flat and round like a gigantic coin. It was peaceful, soothing, soul-refreshing. I reveled in it.

Though I had been at sea now for more than seven weeks, I still found every day fascinating. The ocean exhibited an endless variation of waves, cross-waves and counter-waves. Sometimes it was colored such a brilliant blue it seemed as though *Tinkerbelle's* white hull would be stained; at other times it was gray, gloomy, foreboding.

Even bad weather was a pleasure, for *Tinkerbelle's* cabin was a marvelous refuge, a world of cozy comfort and order. There I could wait out storms with ease, passing the time in reading, eating, letter writing, listening to the BBC and the Voice of America, or playing my harmonica. There, too, I could burst into song at top volume without fear of annoying a soul.

There was always something to see. We encountered whales, dolphins, terns, flying fish and countless Portuguese men-of-war. Once we almost rammed a nine-foot shark, lallygagging on the surface. I think he was sleeping. Interesting inanimate objects also floated by: a 50-gallon oil drum, tree trunks, mooring buoys. The most surprising item was an electric light bulb bobbing along.

While I was still becalmed on July 21, I saw three ships, two of them at the same time. There hadn't been more than one ship in sight since June 6, when I had seen two Russian trawlers. "Made the spot seem like Times Square," I wrote in the log.

I hoped now to reach Falmouth by August 15, and I pushed steadily on, sometimes in heavy seas. On July 28 I calculated that we were 750 miles off Land's End, the westernmost tip of England, and only a short distance from 20 degrees west.

We ran into a thunderstorm on August 1, and to help pass the time I decided to launch a bottle with a note inside it. I jotted down my position on the Atlantic, the date, and asked the finder to write me, promising him a reward of five dollars. I put this message into an empty plastic water bottle and tossed it into the ocean. To my surprise and delight, I was notified two months later that it had been found on September 25 at Sintra, Portugal. The finder was a stonemason named Francisco Maria Baleizao. I was pleased to send him the five dollars, plus a ten-dollar bonus.

As expected, I began meeting more ocean traffic. On the evening of August 6, I wrote in the log: "No ship for days, but about 5 p.m. the *Sirio* of Palermo went by. The crew gave us a hearty cheer." Later, I added: "Saw about five more ships. They're getting thick."

On August 8 we met the 556-foot, 18,000-ton tanker *Belgulf Glory,* of Antwerp. Her skipper, Capt. Emile Sart, stopped and hailed me.

"Do you need any provisions?"

I didn't really, but I gladly accepted what proved to be a real banquet: a whole roast chicken, hot potato croquettes, fruit, bread, chocolate and two bottles of beer.

Events began to move swiftly after that. Late the same afternoon, a Royal Air Force bomber roared over us three times, then made a pass so low I thought it was going to clip off the top of *Tinkerbelle's* mast. As it

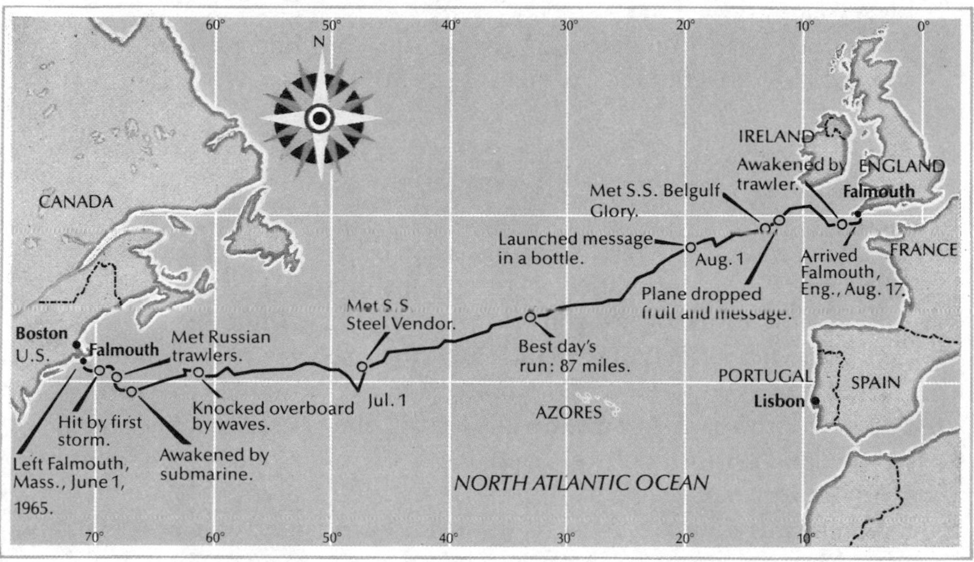

went by, it dropped two bright-orange canisters containing fruit and a message from Wing Cmdr. R. A. Carson:

"Welcome to British waters! You are 'big news,' and we shall be bringing gentlemen of the press to see you tomorrow." He topped off his note by giving me my exact location.

I didn't believe the business about being "big news," but that night, as I sat listening to a Voice of America broadcast in French, the announcer began talking about Robert Manry (only he pronounced it Row-bear Maw-ree), *navigateur solitaire.* I couldn't understand the rest of it but, when the newscast was repeated in English a few minutes later, it told all about me and *Tinkerbelle* and our voyage! It really bowled me over. I realized that despite my newspaper experience, I had failed to assess properly the obvious news value of my own story.

The next day a trawler, the *Roseland,* pulled up bearing the Cleveland television announcer, Bill Jorgensen, and his cameraman, who had obviously gone to enormous lengths and expense to find me. While Jorgensen was asking about the voyage, two R.A.F. planes returned, accompanied by a civilian plane which carried the "gentlemen of the press." After buzzing us again and again, one of the planes dropped a canister bearing a note from three of my *Plain Dealer* colleagues:

"Bob—You will see our boat somewhere out of Falmouth. Virginia and the children will be aboard with us. Keep sailing. Good luck, God bless you, and we'll see you soon."

That was a real bombshell. Virginia and the children were in Falmouth! How I wanted to see them.

5. REUNION

THE PLAIN DEALER'S PLANS for me had to be postponed. For, as I drew nearer to my destination, I got caught in a current which began pushing me north toward Ireland, no matter how I fought it. On August 12 my noon sextant shot indicated that we were only 65 miles off the coast of County Cork. Eventually, I corrected my course and got headed south again, but meanwhile R.A.F. planes had searched for me in vain, and it was widely reported that I was lost. Nobody knew where I was except me.

On the morning of August 16, however, I was roused by voices shouting, "Matey, wake up! Yank, are you there?" I jumped out of the cabin and saw an English trawler with four or five men at the rail calling out between cupped hands.

It turned out that the skipper of the boat, the *Trewarvenneth,* a Cornishman named Harry Small, was the brother-in-law of Capt. Ernest Hunter of the *Excellent,* which, with Virginia aboard, was scouring the ocean for me. Captain Small soon had Captain Hunter on the radiotelephone, told him he had found me and gave our position.

Three hours later, the *Excellent* was in sight, and soon afterward I got my first glimpse of Virginia. She looked great—tanned and fit, as though life at sea were agreeing with her. I don't remember what we said first. I was too dazed. But finally I called over to her, "Well, *Tinkerbelle* got you to England after all!"

"Yes," she said, "even before you."

When *Tinkerbelle* was secured alongside the *Excellent,* Virginia jumped down beside me and we hugged and kissed. It was marvelous to have her in my arms again, and she said she liked my mustache and didn't object to its tickling. The news photographers on the *Excellent* kept asking for further affectionate poses, but we didn't mind at all. We sat down in *Tinkerbelle's* little cockpit with our arms around each other and tried to talk. She had been flown to London on August 4, she told me, along with Robin, Douglas and several people from the *Plain Dealer.* They wanted to scoop the other papers with the story of our reunion, so everything had been hush-hush. Virginia and the children had been spirited to Falmouth on August 6, and soon afterward began searching at sea for me.

When Virginia's all too brief visit was over, the *Excellent* pulled away, and before long *Tinkerbelle* and I were alone once more. We kept going without letup all night before a southwest breeze, *Tinkerbelle* heeling pleasantly to starboard and scooting along gleefully, splashing ahead like a child stamping through puddles to see the droplets fly.

As dawn approached, the inky blackness of the sky changed to gray and then grew lighter and lighter with each passing minute. Up ahead, the Lizard Head Light flashed faithfully with its regular three-second rhythm. But it was not yet possible to tell how near it was.

Tinkerbelle headed straight for it, skipping joyfully over the waves in a manner that told me she was proud and happy. And she had every right to be. She had staunchly protected me from all the worst perils of the sea. She had never allowed herself to be turned bottom up, had righted herself after each knockdown, and had steadfastly kept herself watertight and buoyant.

There had been some scary moments, some moments of sharp loneliness and depression, but for the most part the voyage was a great, glorious, happy adventure. I wouldn't have missed it for the world. But what, I mused, had it accomplished?

For one thing, it had helped make an honest man of me. When I had asked Virginia to marry me, I had promised her two things: one, that we would travel; and, two, that although I might be a headache, I would never, never be a bore. Well, in 15 years of marriage we had hardly traveled anywhere. And, after 12 years on a newspaper copy desk, I was certainly becoming a crashing bore. But *Tinkerbelle* saved the day. She had banished boredom from our lives, and she had brought both of us to England, a country that Virginia had dreamed of visiting some day.

True, my landing there was to be far different from what I had imagined. I had thought that, since England was a maritime nation and had had her full share of adventurous sailors, little attention would be paid to *Tinkerbelle* and me. I had expected to sail into Falmouth almost unnoticed and go to a hotel for a nice bath and sleep. Then, in the morning, I would look for the Falmouth representative of the Associated Press, tell him that I had just sailed the Atlantic single-handed and my newspaper in the States might be interested in a story about it.

Now, it appeared, the arrival wasn't going to work out quite like that. The radio said that great excitement was building up in Falmouth, that a tremendous welcome was being planned, and that the mayor of the city had postponed his vacation so he could greet me. The impulse to duck away from the impending ordeal was strong, but I figured that I had better face the music.

Dawn was almost here now and, as more light filled the heavens, the outline of a steep headland could be distinguished. It was a breathtaking view, and I consumed it with my eyes, transported, enraptured. Land! Land at last!

This day, our 78th since leaving Cape Cod, promised to be momentous. There seemed to be a tingle in the air. I could feel goose bumps rising on my skin and spasmodic shivers running up and down my spine. I hoped I could live through what was coming.

I backed *Tinkerbelle's* jib and lashed down her tiller to heave to for breakfast. I also bathed, shaved, groomed my mustache and put on the cleanest clothes I had. Then I spruced up *Tinkerbelle,* with Old Glory flying from her stern and the Union Jack fluttering from her starboard shroud. She looked a gallant little lady with those flags snapping merrily in the breeze.

As we approached the fearsome Manacles, jagged rocks that reach out from the shore like the lower jaw and teeth of a gigantic monster, I thought that we were probably sailing over the same waters that the Spanish Armada had used more than 377 years earlier on its way to meet the British fleet off Plymouth. And no sooner had this possibility popped into my mind than another armada appeared, this one English and headed straight for *Tinkerbelle.* It came toward us fast, turned, and swept us up into its bosom to escort us the remaining few miles to Falmouth. A newsman estimated that there were 300 craft surrounding us. It was a fantastic sight.

Many of Falmouth's commercial craft were also ferrying people out to see us. They were jammed to the gunwales, and whenever one went by a chorus of "well dones" would fill the air. Then I'd call out, "Thank you," and we'd all wave happily to each other. I have never known more friendly, more warmhearted people than I met that day. And those Englishmen were no slouches when it came to business. Picture postcards of *Tinkerbelle* sailing along in the midst of that armada were being sold even before we reached the harbor entrance.

In all, there were only about 12 miles to cover, but by 6 p.m. we still had a couple to go, and the wind had fallen off to almost nothing. At length the harbormaster offered me a tow. I was reluctant to accept it, because I had hoped that we could sail in by ourselves. But I thought of those people waiting on shore to see us and how disappointed they might be, and I finally agreed.

Boats circled, crisscrossed and flocked all about us. Several times I thought we were going to be crushed. People cheered, gave me the victory sign, passed me things to eat. Others shouted, "Good show!" or, "Glad you made it, mate!"

As we moved past Falmouth's docks and on to the Custom House Quay, people were everywhere: standing along the shore, perched on window ledges, leaning out of doorways, crowded onto jetties, thronging the streets, clinging to trees. I heard later that 50,000 people had seen us complete our voyage.

When I moored *Tinkerbelle* at the stone quayside and stepped ashore, I almost fell flat on my face. The quay seemed to be shaking, and I staggered like a man who has had too much grog. I could see that it would take a few days to get back my land legs.

Every boat in the harbor let go with its whistle, and the sound shook the whole waterfront. R.A.F. bombers flew over with wing-wagging salutes, and a band struck up "The Star-Spangled Banner." After I had got together with Virginia, Robin and Douglas, I was greeted by Samuel Hooper, the mayor, who looked most impressive in his scarlet robes. When a newsman asked me what I thought of the reception, all I could say was, "I'm flabbergasted!"

If the occasion was triumphant, it was also sad. There had been peace out there on the ocean, amid the quiet and the challenge that brought out the best in a man and focused it on basic things. It was all over now, all behind us. I wanted at least to share the plaudits and the many "well dones" with *Tinkerbelle,* who had made the experience possible. I felt pricks of conscience at leaving her, but, as I looked back for her, she was hidden by the high side of the quay and by the crowd. I couldn't even see the tip of her mast.

Schaare

ALIVE

The Story of the Andes Survivors

CONDENSED FROM THE BOOK

by Piers Paul Read

ILLUSTRATED BY HARRY J. SCHAARE

The airliner had been chartered to carry a rugby team from Montevideo, Uruguay, across the Andes to Chile, where a match was to be played. With the members of the team went 25 friends and relatives to cheer them on. The flight was ill-fated. Beset by foul weather, the aircraft crashed high in the remote wastes of the Andean cordillera, a world of snow, rock, wind and subzero cold. Miraculously, few of the 45 persons aboard were killed in the crash. But in succeeding weeks, when all hope of rescue had vanished, many died from injuries and the bitter cold, and only a handful remained alive. They were too weak to attempt to escape across the imprisoning peaks, and soon there would be nothing left to eat. Just one slim chance for life remained—yet it meant violating a primitive taboo.

Piers Paul Read, a prizewinning English novelist, was selected by the 16 Andes survivors to write their story. He was the only one given a complete account of their agonizing ordeal and their unbelievable survival.

1. DEATH AND DESOLATION

THE FAIRCHILD F-227, a twin-engined turboprop of the Uruguayan Air Force, set off from Montevideo, Uruguay, for Santiago, Chile. The trip normally took about four hours, but reports of bad weather in the Andes brought the plane down in a small town on the Argentine side of the range. The pilots were worried about crossing the mountains, because the Andes, though less than 100 miles wide, rise to an average height of 13,000 feet, with peaks as high as 20,000 feet; one mountain, Aconcagua, which lay near their route, soars 22,834 feet, making it the highest mountain in the Western Hemisphere. The Fairchild's ceiling: 22,500 feet.

The next day, October 13, 1972, the skies cleared partially, and the Fairchild took off again, flying south to the Planchon Pass. The copilot, Lt. Dante Hector Lagurara, was at the airplane's controls. He set his course for Malargüe, a small town on the Argentine side of the pass. The plane climbed to 18,000 feet and flew with a tail wind of between 20 and 60 knots.

At Malargüe, the plane turned to fly over the cordillera, the curtain of brown and gray rock reaching toward the sky. Lagurara estimated he would reach Planchon—the point in the middle of the mountains where he passed from Air Traffic Control in Argentina to that in Chile—at 3:21 p.m. As he flew into the mountains a blanket of cloud obscured his vision of the ground, but visibility above the clouds was good, and with the high cordillera covered with snow, there would, in any case, have been nothing by which he could have identified Planchon. Only one significant change had taken place: the moderate tail wind had now changed to a strong head wind. Ground speed had therefore been reduced from 210 to 180 knots.

At 3:21, Lagurara radioed Santiago that he was over Planchon Pass and estimated arriving over Curicó—a small town in Chile on the western side of the Andes—in 11 minutes, at 3:32. Yet only three minutes later, the Fairchild once again made contact with Santiago and reported reaching Curicó. The plane turned at a right angle to its previous course and headed north. The control tower in Santiago, accepting Lagurara at his word, authorized him to begin a slow descent.

At 15,000 feet the plane entered a cloud and began to jump and shake about. Lagurara switched on the seat-belt and no-smoking signs and asked the steward to make sure that passengers did as instructed.

The plane had been chartered by 15 members of an amateur rugby team, most of whom were recent graduates of Stella Maris College in Montevideo. In addition, there were also 25 of their friends and relations aboard, traveling to see the team play a match in Chile.

The boys were all in high spirits; they had their rugby ball with them, and some were throwing it back and forth in the cabin. At the back of the plane a group was playing cards, and farther back, by the galley, the steward and the navigator had been playing *truco,* a kind of whist. As the steward returned from the cockpit to resume the game, he told the boys standing in the aisle to sit down.

"There's bad weather ahead," he said. "But don't worry. We'll be landing soon."

The plane entered another cloud bank and began to shake and lurch alarmingly. One of the boys took the microphone at the back of the plane and joked, "Ladies and gentlemen, please put on your parachutes. We are about to land in the cordillera."

At that moment the plane hit a strong downdraft and plummeted several hundred feet. Still, some of the boys had not fastened their seat belts when the plane hit a second downdraft and sank like a stone for another few hundred feet. A cry of *"Olé, olé, olé!"* went up from the boys—those, that is, who could not see out a window. Those that could stared in horror. For the second fall had brought the plane out of the clouds, and the view was not of the central valley of Chile but of the rocky edge of a snow-covered mountain no more than ten feet away.

There was a roar of engines as the Fairchild tried to climb again. It rose a little, but then came a deafening crash as the right wing hit the side of the mountain. The wing broke off, somersaulted over the fuselage and cut off the tail. Out into the icy air fell the steward, the navigator and their pack of cards, followed by three of the boys still strapped to their seats. A moment later the left wing broke away.

Without wings or tail, the plane hurtled toward the mountain. But instead of being smashed to pieces against a wall of rock, it landed on its belly and slid like a toboggan down the steep, snowy slope.

Two more boys were sucked out the back of the plane; the rest remained in the fuselage as it careered down the mountain. The force of deceleration caused the seats to break loose from their mountings and move forward, crushing the bodies of those in between and smashing the partition which separated the cabin from the forward luggage area.

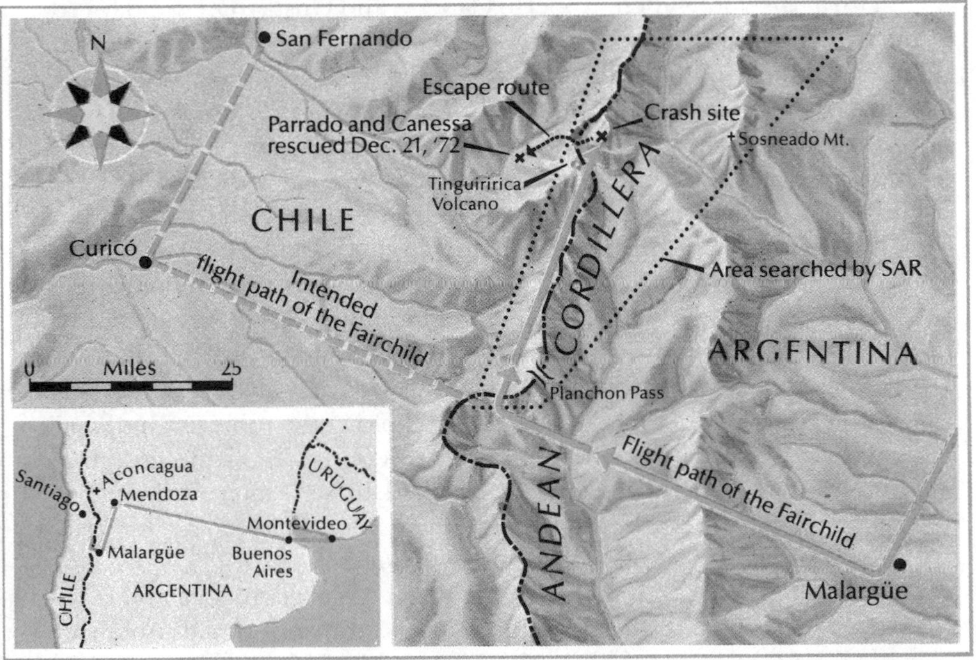

The few who still had their wits about them waited for the impact of fuselage against rock. It never occurred. One of the boys, Carlos "Carlitos" Páez, was saying his Hail Mary, begun when the wing had first touched the mountain. As he mouthed the last words of his prayer, the plane came to a stop. There was a moment of silence. Then, slowly, from all over the tangled mess within the cabin, came sounds of life—groans and prayers and cries for help.

Some of the younger boys, fearing that the plane might explode, jumped out the gaping hole at the back. All around them was snow and beyond, on three sides, the sheer gray walls of the mountains. The plane had come to a halt on a slight upward tilt, facing down the valley where the mountains were much farther away and now partly obscured by gray clouds.

In the fuselage, the first young men to move about thought initially that they were the only ones alive. But slowly others began to emerge from the wreckage. In fact, only three passengers still in the fuselage had been killed by the crash. One other, bleeding from a severed leg, died shortly afterward. But all around were cries for help from those who were injured.

Two of the young men, Roberto Canessa and Gustavo Zerbino, were currently studying medicine, and they treated those they could. They made bandages of the antimacassars from the backs of the seats, but for many of the injuries these were pitifully inadequate. One boy had had the calf of his right leg twisted around to cover the shin. The bone was entirely exposed. Zerbino took hold of the muscle, pulled it into its proper place, and then bound up the leg with a shirt.

Another boy, Enrique Platero, came up to Zerbino with a steel tube sticking into his stomach. Zerbino was appalled, but he remembered that a good doctor always instills confidence in his patient. Cheerfully he said, "Don't worry, you're strong. Come and give me a hand."

Platero seemed to accept this and turned toward the task of helping the others. As he did so, Zerbino grabbed hold of the tube, put his knee against Platero's body and pulled. The piece of steel came out, and with it almost six inches of what seemed to be Platero's intestine. Platero quickly bound himself up and then, under Zerbino's continued encouragement, went on helping the wounded.

They all felt sure that the plane had been reported missing and realized that rescue might be aided if they could transmit signals from the radio. The entrance to the pilots' cabin was blocked by the seats which had piled up at the front of the passenger compartment; but sounds of life could be heard from the other side, so one of the boys, Ramón "Moncho" Sabella, volunteered to reach the pilots from the outside.

It was almost impossible to walk on the deep snow, but Sabella discovered that he could use seat cushions as stepping-stones to the front of the plane. There he found both pilot and copilot trapped in their seats, the instruments of the crumpled plane embedded in their chests. The pilot was dead, but copilot Lagurara was conscious and begging for water. Sabella crammed snow into a handkerchief and held it to his mouth. He then tried to make the radio work, but it was dead.

Daylight was fading. By six the temperature had sunk far below freezing. It was clear that rescue would not come that day; and so, huddled in the plane, the 32 survivors prepared for the night.

The break at the back of the fuselage was jagged, leaving seven windows on the left-hand side of the plane but only four on the right. The distance from the pilots' cabin to the gaping hole at the rear measured only 20 feet, and most of this space was taken up by the knotted tangle of seats. The only floor space they had been able to clear before dark was by the hole. Here they laid the most seriously wounded.

They were able to stretch out almost horizontally, but they had little protection against the snow and the bitter wind that blew in from the darkness. The team captain, Marcelo Pérez, with the help of a hefty rugby player named Roy Harley, did his best to build a barrier against the cold with anything that came to hand—especially the seats and suitcases—but the wind was strong and their wall kept falling.

All night long there came from the dark the moans, screams and delirious ravings of the wounded, including faint cries from a despairing Lagurara. "We passed Curicó," he would say. "We passed Curicó."

In spite of the intense discomfort, some of the boys managed to drift off to sleep, but it was a long night. At one point Zerbino thought he saw the dim light of dawn through the improvised rampart. He looked at his watch: it was only 9 p.m. Later still, those in the middle of the plane heard a foreign voice at the entrance. For a moment they thought it was a rescue party, but then they realized that it was one of the wounded, praying in English.

The sun rose on the morning of Saturday, October 14, to reveal the hulk of the Fairchild half-buried in snow. It lay at about 12,000 feet, between the Tinguiririca Volcano in Chile and Sosneado Mountain in Argentina. In every direction rose walls of immense mountains. Occasionally, rough volcanic rock appeared through the snow, but at that altitude nothing grew—no bush, no scrub, no blade of grass.

Inside the plane Canessa and Zerbino began, once again, to examine the wounded. They discovered that three more had died in the night. As for the injured, there was little they could do. There were no drugs on the plane, and Canessa could only tell those with broken arms or legs to lay them on the snow to help bring down the swelling.

Zerbino examined the hole in Enrique Platero's stomach from which he had pulled the steel tube the day before. He unwound the shirt and there, just as he had feared, was a protruding piece of intestine. Zerbino tied it up with thread, to stem the flow of blood, disinfected it with eau de cologne, and then told Platero to push it back into his stomach and bind up the wound once again. This Platero did without complaint.

The two doctors were not without their nurse. One of the survivors was a married woman named Liliana Methol, and she was a natural source of comfort for the younger boys. Many of them were not yet 20; many of them, too, had been cared for throughout their lives by adoring mothers and sisters. Now, in terror and despair, they turned to Liliana, who spoke soft words to make their spirits strong.

All day Liliana and the doctors worked with the wounded. Their final tour of duty was to the pilots' cabin. Since early morning no sound had come from Lagurara, and when they forced their way in from the luggage compartment they found that he was dead.

With this death they had lost the one man who might have told them what they should do to facilitate rescue. The only surviving crew member, the mechanic, informed them that there were no emergency supplies or signal flares in the plane. Moreover, he said that the radio could only be made to work by the power of the plane's batteries, which had been stored in the missing tail.

Marcelo Pérez remained confident they would soon be rescued. It was agreed, all the same, that what food they had should be rationed, and Marcelo made an inventory of everything edible.

They had some wine and whiskey, but for solid food they had only 13 candy bars, some caramels which had been scattered over the cabin floor, some dates and dried plums, a packet of crackers, two cans of mussels, a tin of almonds, and a small jar each of peach, apple and blackberry jam. This was not a lot of food for 28 people, and since they did not know how long they would have to wait before being rescued, it was decided to make it last as long as possible. For lunch that day Marcelo gave each of them a square of chocolate and the cap from a deodorant can filled with wine.

Night came upon them more quickly than expected, but this time they were better prepared. They had cleared more space, and had built a better wall against the wind. And there were fewer of them.

On the morning of Sunday, October 15, those who came out of the plane found the skies clear and, in spite of the circumstances, they were impressed by the grandeur of their silent valley. The weather gave them reason to believe that they would be rescued that day, or at least spotted. In the meantime, there were certain problems. Their most pressing need was for water. The snow was difficult to melt in sufficient quantity to quench their thirst, and to eat it merely froze one's mouth.

It was Adolfo Strauch who invented a water-making device. Adolfo—or Fito, as he was called—was not a member of the rugby team. He had been persuaded to come to Chile by Eduardo Strauch, his cousin. Watching the sun melt the brittle crust of snow, it occurred to Fito that they might harness its heat to make water. His eye fell upon a rectangle of aluminum, which came from the back of a smashed seat. He bent up the sides so that it formed a shallow bowl and twisted the bottom to make a spout. He then covered it thinly with snow and turned the apparatus to the sun. Shortly, a steady trickle of water ran into the bottle that Fito had ready. Since every seat contained a rectangle of aluminum, there were soon several water makers at work.

On this day, too, another mouth was added to share rations. Fernando "Nando" Parrado, in a coma from a blow on the head since the crash, had been left for dead. Now, suddenly, he regained consciousness. His first thought was for his mother and sister, Susana, who had been traveling with him. He was told that his mother was dead, but his sister, though seriously wounded, was still alive.

SHORTLY AFTER NOON, the boys saw a jet flying directly overhead. It was high above the mountains, but all those out in the snow waved, shouted and flashed pieces of metal into the sky. Many cried with joy.

At midafternoon a turboprop flew over them from east to west, at a lower altitude, and soon after that another flew from north to south. Again the survivors waved and shouted, but the planes continued on their courses and disappeared.

Then, at 4:30, a small biplane appeared following a flight path which passed directly over them. Nothing now could stop the boys from believing what they wanted so much to believe, and some simply sat in the snow waiting for the arrival of helicopters. But shortly afterward it began to grow dark, and the bitter cold returned. And no helicopters appeared.

Parrado slept with Susana clasped in his arms, enveloping her with his tall body to give her all the warmth he could, aware of the irregular movement in and out of her lungs, broken by cries for her dead mother. Others, too, slept only fitfully, huddling under makeshift blankets made from torn-off seat covers.

Confined to a space measuring 20 by 8 feet, they could squeeze in only by lying together in couples, end to end, the feet of one resting on the shoulders of another. Any movement whatsoever caused agony to those with broken bones or injuries.

By Monday morning, the fourth day, some of the injured started to show signs of returning health. Nando Parrado's recovery was especially rapid, and Susana's condition did not make him despair. Quite the contrary. While most of his companions thought only of being rescued, Parrado began considering the option of getting back to civilization by his own efforts.

"Impossible," said Carlitos Páez. "You'd freeze to death."

"Not if I wore enough clothes."

"You'd starve. You can't climb mountains on a piece of chocolate and a sip of wine."

"Then I'll cut flesh from one of the pilots." Parrado said.

Although Carlitos did not take this seriously, he, too, was increasingly concerned at the time it was taking to rescue them. And he, too, began to think of leaving.

The difficulty facing them was that none of the boys had any real idea of where they were. From charts found in the cockpit, and the copilot's repeated references to Curicó, they were convinced that if they went west, they would soon reach green valleys and Chilean farmhouses. But the path west was blocked by gigantic mountains, while the valley in which they were trapped led east—back, they thought, into the middle of the cordillera.

Moreover, they had been able to walk away from the plane only until nine or so in the morning. After that, if there was any sun, the crust melted and they sank up to their thighs in the soft powder. Fito Strauch, their inventor, discovered, however, that if seat cushions were tied to their boots, they made passable snowshoes. Both he and Canessa immediately wanted to set off up the mountain, not only to see what was on the other side but to discover if any of their friends who had fallen in the tail had survived.

Carlitos Páez and Numa Turcatti were also eager to climb the mountain, and at 7 a.m. on October 17 all four set out. They walked for an hour, rested, then walked on. The air was thin and the going hard; as the sun rose, the crust melted and they had to tie on the cushions, which soon became sodden. None of them had eaten anything substantial for nearly five days, and before long Canessa suggested that they turn back. He was overruled, and they struggled on. But when Fito sank waist-deep in snow on the brink of a crevasse, it frightened them all. There were no suitcases to be seen and no sign of the tail.

"It's not going to be easy getting out of here," said Canessa. "Look how weak we've become without food."

"Do you know what Nando said to me?" Carlitos volunteered. "He said if we weren't rescued, he'd eat one of the pilots." After a pause, Carlitos added, "That hit on the head must have made him mad."

"I don't know," said Fito. "It might be the only way to survive."

Carlitos said nothing, and they turned back down the mountain.

2. FUTILE SEARCH

When Air Traffic Control at the airport in Santiago first lost contact with the Uruguayan Fairchild, they immediately telephoned the Servicio Aéreo de Rescate (Aerial Rescue Service). The commander of the SAR was away, so two former commanders were called in to direct the search-and-rescue operation—Carlos García and Jorge Massa.

That afternoon a DC-6 began to search the air corridor from Curicó to Santiago on a path starting from the last reported position of the missing aircraft. Finding nothing, they moved farther back along the supposed route of the Fairchild to the area between Curicó and Planchon. There was a snowstorm over Planchon itself, so nothing could be seen, and the DC-6 returned to Santiago.

The next day García and Massa analyzed more precisely the information they had. They concluded that the plane could not possibly have been over Curicó when the copilot reported this postion, but over Planchon, so that instead of turning toward Santiago, the Fairchild had flown into the middle of the Andes. They plotted a 20-inch square on their map, representing the area in which the crash must have occurred, then sent planes out from Santiago to cover it.

The difficulties were many. The mountains in the area rose to 15,000 feet. If the Fairchild had crashed anywhere among them, it would certainly have fallen into one of the valleys which lay around 12,000 feet and were filled with 20 to 100 feet of snow. Since the Fairchild had a white roof, it would be virtually invisible to an airplane flying above the level of the peaks. Nevertheless, there is an international convention that the country in which an accident occurs will search for the wreck for ten days; it was a duty the SAR had to perform.

The search continued until October 17, when heavy clouds and snow covered the area. Meanwhile, 22 relatives of the passengers had arrived in Chile, all clamoring to help.

The search by the SAR was resumed on October 19. It continued throughout the day and the next and into the morning of the 21st. At the same time, sorties were flown by Argentinian planes from Mendoza. There was no trace of the Fairchild.

From the very start the professionals of the SAR had little hope that anyone could have survived a crash in the middle of the cordillera. The temperature at that time of year went down at night to 30 or 40 degrees below zero F., so that if, by some quirk of fate, a few passengers had survived the crash, they would certainly have died of cold during the first night. Meanwhile, the lives of SAR men were being risked, and expensive fuel was being burned up.

At midday on the 21st, convinced that further effort was futile, commanders García and Massa announced that "the search for the Uruguayan aircraft is canceled because of negative results."

THAT NIGHT ON THE MOUNTAIN, Nando Parrado awoke and felt that Susana had grown cold in his embrace. At once he pressed his mouth to hers and, with tears streaming down his cheeks, blew air into her lungs. When exhaustion forced him to give up, Carlitos Páez took over. But to no avail. Susana was dead.

The survivors awoke on the morning of Sunday, October 22, to face their tenth day on the mountain. First to leave the plane were Marcelo Pérez and Roy Harley. Roy had found a transistor radio, and they were able to pick up scraps of broadcasts from Chile. But there was no news of any rescue effort.

Few of the other boys bothered to come out into the snow. Starvation was taking its effect. When they stood up they felt faint and found it difficult to keep their balance. They were cold, even when the sun rose to warm them, and their skin started to grow wrinkled like that of old men. It was clear to them all that they could not survive much longer.

Their minds turned to other sources of food. On some of the exposed mountain rock they found brittle lichens, which they scraped off and mixed into a paste with melted snow. The taste was bitter and disgusting, and as food it was worthless. Some thought of the seat cushions, but they were stuffed with nylon and foam rubber, not straw.

What remained was a ghastly prospect. Corpses lay in the snow around the plane, preserved by the intense cold. The thought of cutting flesh from those who had been their friends was deeply repugnant to them all, yet a lucid appreciation of their predicament led them, gradually, reluctantly, to consider it.

Finally, Canessa brought the horrible subject into the open. He argued forcefully that they were not going to be rescued; that they would have to escape themselves; that nothing could be done without food and that the only food was human flesh. He insisted that they had a moral duty to stay alive by any means at their disposal, and because Canessa was earnest about his religious belief—they were all Catholics—great weight was given to what he said.

"It is food," he argued. "The souls have left their bodies and are in heaven with God. All that is here are the carcasses, which are no more human beings than the flesh of the cattle we eat at home."

Others joined the discussion. "Didn't you see," said Fito Strauch, "how much energy we needed just to climb a few hundred feet up the mountain? Think how much more we'll need to climb to the top."

A meeting was called inside the Fairchild, and for the first time all 27 survivors discussed whether or not they should eat the dead to survive. Canessa and Fito Strauch repeated their arguments.

"But what have we done," asked Marcelo Pérez, "that God now asks us to eat the bodies of our friends?"

There was a moment's hesitation. Then Zerbino turned to his captain and said, "But what do you think *they* would have thought? If my dead body could help you to stay alive, I'd certainly want you to use it."

This argument allayed many doubts, for however reluctant each boy might be to eat a friend's flesh, all of them agreed with Zerbino.

Their discussion continued most of the day, and by midafternoon they knew that they must act now or not at all. Yet they sat inside the plane in total silence. At last a group of four—Canessa, Zerbino, Fito Strauch and Daniel Maspons—went out into the snow. With no exchange of words Canessa knelt, bared the skin of a body and cut into the flesh with a piece of broken glass. It was frozen and difficult to cut, but he persisted until he had removed 20 slivers the size of matchsticks.

The boys cowered silently in the Fairchild. Canessa told them that the food was on the roof, drying in the sun, and that those who wished should come out and eat. No one came, and again Canessa took it upon himself to prove his resolve. He prayed to God to help him do what he knew to be right and then took a piece of flesh in his hand. He hesitated. Even with his mind so firmly made up, the horror of the act paralyzed him. His hand would neither rise to his mouth nor fall to his side; the revulsion which possessed him struggled with his stubborn will. The will prevailed. The hand rose and pushed the flesh into his mouth. He swallowed it. He felt triumphant. He had overcome a primitive taboo. He was going to survive.

Later that evening, small groups of boys came out of the plane to follow his example. Zerbino took a strip and swallowed it as Canessa had done, but it stuck in his throat. He scooped a handful of snow into his mouth and managed to wash it down. Fito Strauch followed his example, then others.

The next morning Roy Harley switched on his radio and heard that the search for the Fairchild had been abandoned. As the word spread, the boys began to sob and pray—all except Parrado, who looked up at the mountains which rose to the west.

He wanted to set off at once, and it was only with great difficulty that the others restrained him. After all, ten days before he had been given up for dead. Instead, it was agreed that a group of the fittest should make the attempt, and little more than an hour later Zerbino, Turcatti and Maspons began the climb, watched by their friends.

The three young men left in such a hurry that they gave no thought to equipping themselves. They wore only sneakers or moccasins and shirts, sweaters and light jackets, with thin trousers covering their legs. Although expecting a short venture, they spent two days on the mountain, and during their one night they might as well have been naked. They were compelled to hit one another with their fists and feet to keep their circulation going, and none expected to survive.

The next day they continued, but the higher they climbed, the more hopeless is seemed. Every time they thought they had reached the summit, they would find they were on the top of a ridge; the mountain itself still towered above them.

At last they came upon some wreckage, and were able to account for all of the missing bodies. But they found no trace of the tail. Exhausted, they started back down the mountain. "I think," said Maspons, as they approached the plane once again, "that we shouldn't tell the others how bad it is."

There was no need. All three hobbled on frozen feet, and Zerbino was snow-blind. It escaped no one's attention that the brief expedition had almost killed three of the strongest among them.

On the evening of the 17th day, as Roy Harley settled in for the night, he felt a faint vibration and an instant later heard the sound of metal falling to the ground. He jumped up, but as he did so he was buried to his waist in snow. Looking around, he saw an appalling sight. The wall at the entrance to the plane had been toppled by an avalanche of snow; everything inside—blankets, cushions, sleeping bodies—was buried. Quickly, Roy burrowed for Carlitos, who had been sleeping nearby. He first uncovered Carlitos' face and then his torso.

Then, seeing the hands of others sticking out of the snow, he left him. He felt desperate; he alone seemed to be free to help. He uncovered Canessa and then went to the front of the cabin and dug out Fito Strauch. But the minutes were passing rapidly and many people remained buried.

Carlos Roque, the airplane's mechanic, and Juan Carlos Menendez had been killed almost immediately when the barricade at the entrance, and tons of snow, had fallen on them. Numa Turcatti and Alfredo "Pancho" Delgado were trapped under the curved emergency door, which had been built into the barricade, but they had air enough to breathe under its convex surface. They survived like this for six or seven minutes until others came to their rescue.

They all worked as hard as they could, retrieving one person after another. Some they uncovered only halfway, so they could breathe, before moving on. But when it was all over—when the living huddled together in the few feet of space that was left between the roof of the plane and the icy floor of snow—they found that some of their dearest friends lay buried beneath them. Marcelo Pérez, the captain, was dead. So, too, were Enrique Platero, whose stomach wound had healed at last; Gustavo Nicolich; Daniel Maspons, Ganessa's closest friend; Liliana Methol, who had helped them all; and Diego Storm. In all, eight had died under the snow.

As night set in, the survivors were wet, cramped and bitterly cold. They no longer had cushions, shoes or blankets to protect them, and there was barely room to sit or stand. They could only lie in a tangle, punching each other's bodies to keep the blood flowing, yet not knowing to whom the arms and legs they punched belonged.

The little air that was left in the plane became stale and stuffy, and some of the boys began to feel faint. Parrado took a steel pole, which was among the plane's auxiliary equipment, and poked it through the roof of the cabin. He worked by the light of five cigarette lighters as the boys around him watched anxiously, for they had no idea if the snow which covered them was one foot deep or 12. But after poking the bar through and working it up, Parrado felt it slide unimpeded into the fresh air.

Because the plane was tilted upward, the best route for escape to the outside seemed throught the cockpit. But when Roy Harley finally broke one of the front windows, he reported that a wild blizzard was blowing across the mountains.

A group of survivors outside the remains of the Fairchild

The snow continued for two more days. During this time they had nothing to eat. The bodies of those killed in the crash remained buried in the snow outside the plane, so at last they uncovered one of those who had been smothered in the avalanche and cut off the flesh before everyone's eyes. Previously the food had at least dried in the sun; now there was no alternative but to eat it raw. It was dreadful for them; indeed, for some it was impossible to eat gobbets of flesh cut from the body of a friend who two days before had been living beside them.

On November 1 it stopped snowing, and six of the boys climbed out onto the roof to warm themselves in the sun. Canessa and Zerbino dug the snow off the windows to let more light into the plane, and Fito and Eduardo Strauch and Daniel Fernández melted snow for water, while Carlitos smoked a cigarette and thought about his family, for it was his father's and his sister's birthday. He felt certain now that he would see them again. If God had saved him in both accident and avalanche, it must be to reunite him with his family. The nearness of God in the still landscape set a seal on his conviction.

In the days which followed, the weather remained clear. There were no heavy falls of snow, and the stronger and more energetic among the surviving 19 were able to dig a second tunnel out through the back of the plane. Then they set about removing from the cabin both the snow and the bodies buried beneath it. The snow was like rock; their tools inadequate. The corpses, frozen into the last gestures of self-defense, some with arms raised to protect their faces like the victims of Vesuvius at Pompeii, were difficult to move.

It took eight days for the plane to be made more or less habitable. But feeling that God would help them if they helped themselves, the survivors now set about planning for their ultimate escape.

3. OPERATION CHRISTMAS

A DECISION WAS MADE to pick a group of four expeditionaries. Several of the boys volunteered, but some were more obvious candidates than others. Parrado was so determined to escape that, had he not been chosen, he would have gone on his own. Turcatti, too, was emphatic that he should be picked; he had already made two shorter trips to prove his stamina. Canessa, who was known as "Muscles," felt it his duty to go because of his exceptional strength. The fourth volunteer was Antonio Vizintín.

Once chosen, they became a warrior class with special privileges. They ate more flesh than the others; they slept where, how and for as long as they liked. They were no longer expected to share the everyday chores. Prayers were said at night for their health and well-being, and all conversation in their hearing was of an optimistic nature.

The expeditionaries were not the leaders, but a caste apart. The three who actually governed the little community were Eduardo and Fito Strauch and Daniel Fernández (who was also a cousin of theirs). In the second echelon of power were Carlitos Páez, Pedro Algorta and Gustavo Zerbino. These three were the noncommissioned officers who received orders from Daniel Fernández and the Strauch cousins.

There were two among them who could play no part in the group: Rafael Echavarren and Arturo Nogueira. Echavarren was the boy whose calf had almost been torn off. His leg was now heavy with pus; also, his foot had frozen and black gangrenous flesh was spreading from his toes.

At first, Arturo Nogueira was in better physical condition, but he too had a septic leg wound, and he went rapidly downhill following the avalanche. Only after a week was it realized that he had not been eating his ration of food. After that Pedro Algorta would place small pieces of flesh in his mouth. But it did not help. Two days later Nogueira died as he slept in Algorta's arms.

Nogueira's death destroyed the thesis that those who had survived the avalanche were destined to live, and escape became more urgent. As the Andean spring drew nearer, the expeditionaries occupied themselves assembling the clothes they would wear. The only setback they suffered was that someone stepped on Turcatti's leg and the resulting bruise began to go septic. Numa dismissed it as insignificant, and at first no one was concerned. Their minds were more on which route to take. They knew, of course, that Chile was to the west. They also knew, however, that all water flows to the sea. Thus, they reasoned, the valley they were in, which ran east, must double back on itself and turn west. On this assumption, the expeditionaries planned to set off down the valley. The mountains to the west were simply too immense to climb.

The departure on November 15 was abortive. A snowstorm drove the expeditionaries back after a few hours and it continued to blow for two days. And in those days Turcatti's leg became worse. It was clear to all that he would only hold the others back.

On the morning of Friday, November 17, after five weeks on the mountain, they awoke to a clear blue sky, and before long Parrado, Canessa and Vizintín were on their way. But after walking two hours an event occurred which changed their plans, they discovered the plane's tail. It was like finding treasure, for here was most of their luggage, as well as the batteries which the mechanic had said could power the plane's transmitter.

They decided to return to the plane, remove the radio and bring it down to the tail. This decision was influenced by a second factor: from this position, it appeared that the valley did not turn, but continued eastward. They spent two days at the tail, then climbed back up to the plane, a sled and knapsacks loaded with clothes for the others.

They returned to a group that was bitter with disappointment and deep in despair. On the preceding day Echavarren had died.

MEANWHILE, NOT ALL of the parents had accepted the verdict of the SAR as final. On December 5, a group of fathers of the lost boys met with the commander in chief of the Uruguayan Air Force to ask that a Uruguayan plane be sent to search the mountains. The commander called for a subordinate officer who had been working with the SAR on an investigation of the accident. He reported that nothing could be done before February. That winter had seen the heaviest falls of snow in the

Andes for the past 30 years. The plane would be completely buried, and there was no possibility of survival.

The commander turned to the men who faced him, expecting them to accept this assessment. But though in their hearts they all agreed that a search would be hopeless, they insisted that it must take place. The commander's resolve weakened. "Gentlemen," he said, "the Uruguayan Air Force will arrange for a plane to be at your disposal."

On December 11, five of the fathers left for Santiago for their assault upon the Andes. They named it Operation Christmas.

THE ATTEMPT TO MAKE the plane's radio work failed. With only a screwdriver, a knife and pliers, the boys removed the earphones, microphone and transmitter from the cockpit and dismantled the sharkfin antenna from the roof. The job took several days. Then Canessa, Parrado and Vizintín, accompanied by Roy Harley, descended to the tail. In all, they were away eight days. Parrado and Vizintín making one trip back to the plane to get food.

Harley and Canessa made all the necessary connections between battery and radio and antenna, but still could not pick up a signal on the earphones. They thought that perhaps the antenna was faulty, so they tore out strands of cable from the electrical circuits, and made an aerial more than 60 feet long. When they connected it to their transistor radio, they could pick up many radio stations in Chile, Argentina and Uruguay. When they connected it to the Fairchild's radio, however, nothing came through.

As they continued to work they heard a bulletin on the transistor announcing that the search for them was to be resumed by a Uruguayan Douglas C-47. They decided to make a large cross in the snow by the tail with the suitcases that lay scattered all around. Then, before leaving, Vizintín removed the insulating material from around the Fairchild's heating system in the tail. It would make an excellent sleeping bag and solve the one outstanding problem which had beset them—how to keep warm at night without the shelter of the plane.

Returning to the Fairchild, Canessa was struck by the desolation of the scene. After eight days away he saw with some objectivity just how thin and haggard the bearded faces of his friends had become. He saw, too, with a fresh eye, the horror of the snow strewn with stripped carcasses and skulls, and he thought to himself that before they were rescued they must do something to tidy up the area.

They told the others what they had heard on their transistor. The boys were determined that this should not tempt the expeditionaries to abandon the idea of a further expedition. It soon became evident, however, that while the news of the C-47 in no way affected Parrado's determination to escape, it produced in Canessa a certain reluctance. "We should give them at least ten days and then, perhaps, set out," he argued. "It's crazy to risk our lives if it isn't necessary."

The others were thrown into a fury by this procrastination. They had not pampered Canessa for so long only to be told that he was not going. Nor were they optimistic that the C-47 would find them; they heard on the radio first that the plane had been forced to land in Buenos Aires with engine trouble, then that it had to have its engines overhauled in Los Cerrillos.

"Don't you realize," Fito said to Canessa, "that they aren't looking for survivors? They're looking for dead bodies. They'll take aerial photographs and then go back, develop them, study them. . . . It'll take weeks for them to find us."

December 8 was the Feast of the Immaculate Conception. To honor the Virgin, and to persuade her to intercede for the success of their journey, the boys decided to pray the full 15 mysteries of the rosary. Alas, soon after they had finished five, their voices grew thinner and fewer, and one by one they dropped off to sleep. They therefore made up the rest the next evening, which was also Parrado's 23rd birthday. To celebrate the occasion, the community gave Parrado one of the Havana cigars that had been found in the tail.

On December 10, Canessa still insisted that the expedition was not ready to leave. The sleeping bag was not sewn to his satisfaction, nor had he collected everything he would need. Yet instead of applying himself to what was still to be done, Canessa lay around "conserving his energy" or insisted on treating the boils that had developed on Roy Harley's legs.

The next morning the Strauchs rose early and set to work on the sleeping bag. They were determined that by evening there should be no excuse for further delay. But something happened that day that made their threats and admonitions superfluous.

Numa Turcatti had been getting weaker. His closest friend before the accident had been Pancho Delgado, and it was Delgado who took it upon himself to look after him, including giving him extra rations. But Turcatti continued to decline. He was intermittently delirious, and on December 11 he went into a coma. Delgado hurried to his side. Numa lay there with his eyes open, but he seemed unaware of Delgado's presence. His breathing was slow and labored. Delgado knelt and began to say the rosary. As he prayed the breathing stopped.

Turcatti's death persuaded Canessa that they could wait no longer. Roy Harley, José Luis Inciarte and Moncho Sabella were all weak and often delirious. A day's delay could mean the difference between their death or survival. It was therefore agreed by all that the expedition would set off the next day, due west to Chile.

At five o'clock the next morning, Canessa, Parrado and Vizintín prepared to go. First they dressed themselves in the clothes they had picked from the baggage of the 45 passengers and crew.

Parrado was typical. Next to his skin he wore a T-shirt and a pair of long woolen woman's slacks. On top of these he wore three pairs of blue jeans, and six sweaters. He put a woolen balaclava over his head, then the hood and shoulders that he had cut from his sister's fur coat and finally a jacket. Under his rugby boots he wore four pairs of socks which he covered with plastic bags to keep out the wet. For his hands he had gloves; for his eyes a pair of sunglasses; and to help him climb he held an aluminum pole.

Canessa liked to think that each garment he wore had something precious about it. One sweater had been given to him by a dear friend of his mother, another by his mother herself. One of the pairs of trousers he wore had belonged to his closest friend, Daniel Maspons, and his belt had been Panchito Abal's, killed in the crash. It had been given to him by Parrado with the words, "This was a present from Panchito, who was my best friend. Now you're my best friend, so you take it."

"Don't forget to book us hotel rooms in Santiago," one of the boys said. Then they embraced, and amid cries of *Hasta luego!* the three expeditionaries set off up the mountain. They took a reading on the plane's compass and started to climb due west up the side of the valley. It was heavy going. Not only were they faced with the steep slope, but the snow had started to melt and even in their improvised snowshoes they sank up to their knees. But they persevered, resting every few yards, and by the time they stopped by an outcrop of rocks for lunch they were already very high.

Their plan was to reach the top before dark, for it would be almost impossible to sleep on the steep slope. But, as they had already found out, distances were deceptive, and when the sun went behind the mountain they were nowhere near the peak.

Beginning to panic, they searched for a resting place. A little farther on they came to an immense boulder, beside which the wind had blown a trench in the snow; here they pitched camp and climbed into the sleeping bag.

When the sun came up from behind the mountains they started to climb again. The mountain now was so steep that Vizintín did not dare look down. What frustrated them all was that each summit they saw above them turned out to be a ridge of snow or an outcrop of rocks. By the middle of the afternoon they still had not reached the top.

They spent a second night on the mountain, and in the morning Canessa suggested that Parrado and Vizintín leave their knapsacks with him and the two climb a little farther up the mountain to see if they came to the top. Parrado set off at once, with Vizintín behind him.

The wall of snow was almost vertical, and Parrado could proceed only by digging steps for his hands and feet. Undismayed, he was driven on by all the excitement of a mountaineer whose triumph is at hand. As he climbed he told himself, "I'm going to see a valley, I'm going to see a river, I'm going to see green grass and trees. . . ." And then suddenly he was at the top.

His joy lasted only a few seconds; the view before him was not of green valleys running down toward the Pacific but of an endless expanse of snow-covered mountains. For the first time he felt that they were finished. He sank to his knees and wanted to curse and cry to heaven at the injustice, but no sound came from his mouth. As he looked up again, panting from his exertions in the thin mountain air, his despair was replaced once again by an elation at what he had done. "I've climbed this mountain," he thought to himself, "and I shall call it Mount Seler after my father."

As he studied the landscape before him he noticed that due west were two mountains whose peaks were not covered with snow. "The cordillera must end somewhere," he said to himself, "so perhaps those two are in Chile." He heard Vizintín calling him from below and shouted down in a buoyant voice, "Go back and fetch Muscles. Tell him it's going to be all right. Tell him to come up and see for himself!"

When Canessa reached the top, he looked aghast at the endless mountains stretching away to the west. "But we've had it," he said. "We've absolutely had it. There isn't a chance in hell of getting through all that."

Parrado pointed into the middle distance. "If we go down this mountain and along the valley it leads to a sort of Y. One branch of the Y must lead to those two mountains without snow."

Canessa followed the line of Parrado's arm. "Maybe," he said. "But it would take 50 days, and we have only enough food for ten days."

Parrado had considered this and made up his mind. Vizintín must turn back. That would leave them food for about 20 days, if carefully rationed, and after that—well, perhaps they would find something.

They retraced their steps down the mountain, reaching Vizintín around 5 p.m. Parrado told him of his decision. The next morning Vizintín split his supplies and some of his clothes with the others and made ready to descend.

"Tell Fito we've gone west," Canessa said. "And if you get rescued, make them come and look for us."

Vizintín went down sitting on a cushion like a sled. Though the ascent had taken three days, he reached the plane in 45 minutes.

4. VIEW OF PARADISE

At 9 a.m. on December 16, Parrado and Canessa set off once again for the top of the mountain. This time they were carrying their knapsacks which, with the departure of Vizintín, were even heavier than before. The air was very rarefied; their hearts beat fast and every three steps they had to rest, clinging to the precipitous wall of snow.

It took them three hours to reach the top. Then, after a short rest, they started down. The going was extremely difficult. The mountain was made up not of solid rock but of shale, and mostly they slid down on their backs and bottoms, sending small avalanches of stone cascading ahead of them. "You can make it tough, God," Canessa prayed, "but don't make it impossible."

At last they came to a point where the snow was still thick on the ground, and Parrado decided he would toboggan down on a cushion. He immediately began to fall faster, reaching a speed he estimated to be 60 m.p.h. He dug his heels into the snow, but they did nothing to stop him. Suddenly across his path he saw a wall of snow. "If there are boulders under that," he thought, "I've had it." An instant later he smashed into the wall and came to a stop, quite unharmed. Canessa caught up with him, and they both continued more cautiously down the mountainside, stopping at four in the afternoon.

The next day was the sixth of their journey, and at noon they reached the bottom of the mountain. They found themselves at the entrance to the valley which led to the Y. Although its surface was covered with deep, mushy snow, the slope was no steeper than 10 or 12 degrees. Nonetheless, Canessa began to fall farther and farther behind.

When Parrado remembered his companion, he would look around and see him several hundred yards back. Then he would wait and, when Canessa caught up, allow him to rest for four or five minutes. On one such stop they saw to their right a small stream coming down from the side of the mountain. Growing around the stream were some moss, grass and rushes. It was the first sign of vegetation that they had seen for 65 days, and Canessa, tired though he was, climbed up to the stream, picked some grass and rushes, and crammed them into his mouth.

They spent another night huddled on the snow and the next morning continued on. As they plodded along, the sound of their feet on the snow was slowly superseded by a roaring noise which grew louder and louder. Parrado walked faster, drawing 200 yards ahead of tiring Canessa, and suddenly found himself at the end of the valley.

The view which met his eyes was of paradise. The snow stopped, and from under its white shell a torrent of gray water tumbled down over boulders and stones to the west. More beautiful still, everywhere he looked there were patches of green—moss, grass, rushes, gorse bushes, and yellow and purple flowers. Both boys staggered forward off the snow and sank onto rocks by the river. There, amid birds and lizards, they prayed aloud to God, thanking him for having prized them from the cold and barren grip of the Andes.

The following day, the eighth of their journey, they found a rusted soup can and a horseshoe, incontrovertible evidence that they were approaching an inhabited area. Later, they came upon a small group of cows. Despite these encouraging signs, Canessa's condition worsened. By the next day he was staggering, and had to lean on Parrado's arm. That night they discussed ways in which they might kill a cow, for while the food supply remained adequate, it was beginning to suffer from the warmer temperatures. Parrado suggested climbing into a tree with a rock and dropping it on the head of one of the animals.

Tired in every limb, almost to the point of giving up, Canessa could still laugh. "You'll never kill a cow like that."

Parrado wandered away in search of brushwood for a fire. Canessa lay back and looked vacantly toward the other side of the river they were following. Suddenly, from the shadows, there came a moving shape, large enough to be a man on a horse. "Nando, Nando!" he shouted. "Look, there's a man! On the other side of the river!"

Both boys started toward the river, shouting and waving their arms. But when Canessa looked over the roaring torrent to the spot where he had seen the rider, he saw only a tall rock and its lengthening shadow.

"Come on," said Parrado, taking his companion by the arm. "We'd better get back and light a fire before it gets dark."

They had both faced back toward their camp when suddenly, over the splashing thunder of the river, they heard the sound of a human cry. They turned and there, on the other bank, they saw not one but three men on horses.

Immediately the two boys began to wave their arms and shout, but the noise of the river blotted out their words. "Help us!" they cried. "Help us!" And while Canessa's voice rose to a new pitch, Parrado sank to his knees and joined his hands in a gesture of supplication.

The horsemen hesitated. Then one of them reined in his beast and shouted some words across the gorge, the only one of which they could decipher was "tomorrow." And the men rode on.

Parrado and Canessa stumbled back to their camp. The one word they had heard was enough to give them enormous hope. At last they had made contact with other men.

The sun rose on the tenth day of their journey. At six both boys were awake, and looking across the river they again saw three men. One of them took a piece of paper, wrote on it, wrapped it around a stone, and threw it across to Parrado. It read: "There is a man coming later. Tell me what you want."

The man threw a pen across the river and with it Parrado feverishly wrote the following message: "I come from a plane that fell in the mountains. I am Uruguayan. We have been walking for ten days. In the plane are 14 injured people. We don't have any food. We are weak."

The Chilean unwrapped the message and signaled that he understood. Then he took from his pocket a piece of bread; threw it across the river, waved and turned to climb back up the gorge.

Two or three hours later they saw another man on horseback, this time on their side of the river. He greeted Parrado with reticence, concealing the extraordinary impression that must have been made on him by this tall, bearded, bedraggled figure. He introduced himself as Armando Serda, gave them some cheese and then went on up the valley to see to his cows. Canessa and Parrado ate the cheese and rested. Then, before Serda came back, they took what remained of the human flesh they had brought with them and buried it under a stone. It was Thursday, December 21, 70 days since the Fairchild had crashed.

The boys were taken down the valley to a cottage, fed and put to bed. While they slept, a man was sent to alert the police at a nearby town.

The officials there notified Santiago, where the news was received with surprise and skepticism by SAR commanders García and Massa. It was now dark and nothing could be done until morning.

The next day, despite a dense fog, three helicopters took off, carrying García and Massa, an air-force nurse, a medical orderly and three members of the Andean Rescue Corps. When they reached the cottage, they found that Canessa was still paralyzed from exhaustion, and the medics set to work caring for him. Parrado, however, refused medical attention and began to badger García and Massa to take off again for the Fairchild. Because of the fog it was impossible.

So they waited. Three hours after he had arrived García decided that the visibility had improved sufficiently for two of the three helicopters to make a rescue attempt. With them they took a medical orderly, the members of the Andean Rescue Corps and Parrado.

It was now around 1 p.m., the worst possible time for flying in the Andes because of turbulent air currents. Parrado was an excellent guide. He recognized all the spots in the valley where they had walked, and when they came to the Y he directed García to turn to the left and follow the narrower, snow-covered valley into the mountains.

Flying was difficult by now, but García noted that they were approaching 7000 feet. This, Parrado had told him, was the altitude registered on the Fairchild's altimeter. He felt confident that he could control his craft at that height.

"Where now?" he asked Parrado through the intercom.

"Up there," said Parrado, pointing to the sheer face of the mountain.

"But you can't have come down there."

"Yes, we did. It's on the other side."

García looked ahead, then up. What Parrado told him seemed incredible, but he had no alternative. He started to climb. Behind him came Massa in the second helicopter. As they rose the air became thinner and more turbulent, and the whole helicopter began to shake and vibrate. Still the mountain faced them; the peak was higher yet. The altimeter showed 12,000 feet, then 13,000; finally, at 13,500 feet, they reached the top. There the helicopters were hit by a strong wind from the other side which threw them back down. García made another run, but again the helicopter was thrown back.

He gave up the assault on the peak and guided the helicopter to a lower spot around the top of the mountain until, still buffeted by the violent currents, they found themselves on the other side.

"Go down now," said Parrado.

The helicopter descended, until at last Parrado saw far beneath him the tiny speck that he knew was the wreck.

"There!" he shouted. "There!"

The boys below began to wave and shout, and those in the plane tumbled out as the leading helicopter, rocking in the wind, came lower and circled above them. But the pilot seemed unable to land. The wind buffeted his craft so badly that every time he came lower the huge machine was in danger of being blown against the face of the mountain. Eventually, however, the first helicopter came so low that one of its skis touched the snow. Two packs were thrown from the open door, followed a second later by a medical orderly and a member of the Andean rescue team.

García did not dare land because of the slope and because the snow would not bear the helicopter's weight. He therefore hovered horizontally, afraid that the blades would touch the mountainside, and unable to turn onto an angle which would make it easier for the boys to climb in. The first to try was Fernández. He stretched up and was grabbed by Parrado, who pulled him in. Next, Alvaro Mangino managed to scramble on board, and the helicopter pulled up.

Massa then dropped two more Andean specialists and their equipment, and Páez, Algorta and Eduardo Strauch climbed on board. Behind them came Inciarte, and with these four Massa had his quota and rose into the air, leaving Delgado, Sabella, Roberto Francois, Vizintín, Javier Methol, Zerbino, Harley, Fito Strauch, the three Andean specialists and the medic.

The ascent of the east side of the mountain was no less terrifying than the climb up the other side. But at last they were over the top and speeding down the valley.

5. CONFESSION

BECAUSE THE AIR WAS so turbulent, García postponed the second rescue until the next day. The three Andean specialists had brought food with them, and, as it turned out, no one on the mountain was in imminent danger of death. Instead, the first eight survivors were flown on to a hospital in San Fernando.

They arrived shortly after 3 p.m. and were wheeled in on stretchers—all except Parrado, who insisted on walking himself, pushing his way through the crowd of nurses and visitors who were watching.

Once in the special area which had been cleared for them, Parrado refused to lie down and be examined by the doctors until he had had a bath. The nurses looked bewildered and went to ask the doctors, who shrugged their shoulders.

A bath was run, and then, at last, Parrado took off his stinking clothes and sank into the hot water. After the bath he felt magnificent, and at last allowed the doctors to examine him. They could find nothing wrong with him at all.

Of course, like the other seven, Parrado was severely underweight. He had lost more than 50 pounds, and the others corresponding amounts. In addition, Mangino had a fractured leg; Inciarte's leg was badly infected; Algorta had a pain in the region of his liver; and they all suffered from burned and blistered lips, conjunctivitis and skin infections. But it soon became clear to the doctors that the boys had been nourished on something more than melted snow. As he examined Inciarte's leg one of them asked, "What was the last thing you ate?"

"Human flesh," Inciarte replied.

The doctor continued to treat the leg without comment.

Fernández and Mangino also told the doctors what they had eaten on the mountain, and again the doctors made no response. But they issued strict instructions that no journalists be admitted to the hospital, and that no one be allowed to see the boys—not even the mothers of Páez and Canessa, who had already arrived from Montevideo.

One man, however, was made an exception to their rule. This was Father Andrés Rojas, the young curate in the parish church of San Fernando Rey. He was ushered to the private wing, and there he went into the room belonging to José Inciarte. It was a good choice, for no sooner was he identified as a priest than a gush of words poured out of Inciarte. He told Father Andrés about the mountain—not in the cold language of a detached observer, but in mystical words which more accurately conveyed what the experience had meant to him.

"It was something no one could have imagined. I used to go to Mass every Sunday, and Holy Communion had become something automatic. But up there, seeing so many miracles, being so near God, almost touching him, I learned otherwise. Now I pray to God to give me strength and stop me slipping back to what I used to be. I have learned that life is love, and that love is giving to your neighbor. There is nothing better than giving to a fellow human being. . . ."

As Father Andrés listened, he came to understand the exact nature of the gift to which Inciarte referred—the gift by his dead companions of their own flesh. No sooner did he realize this than the young priest reassured the excited youth that there was no sin in what he had done. It is the belief of the Catholic Church that anthropophagism (cannibalism) *in extremis* is permissible. "I shall be back this afternoon with Communion," he said.

"Then I should like to confess," said Inciarte.

"You have confessed," said the priest, "in this conversation."

The moment of reunion could not be postponed any longer. Graciela Berger, Parrado's married sister, incensed at being kept from him, pushed her way into his room, followed by the weeping figure of Seler Parrado. This poor man had had his hopes raised by a false list which had named his wife, daughter and son as survivors. Just before coming to see his son, he had been told the truth: only Nando was alive.

Farther along the corridor, Canessa suddenly looked up and saw his mother, father and fiancée. "Merry Christmas, Roberto," his mother said. Then she began to cry as she studied the wizened old man's face beneath the beard of her son. Canessa's father, too, burst into tears, and this torrent of emotion set Roberto crying until his parents offered to leave him. But he would not let them go, and when everyone was calmer he began to tell them about the accident and their survival, including the fact that they had eaten human flesh. Only his father started in shock before gaining control of himself. The two women seemed so happy to have Roberto back that they hardly cared what he said. But his father, who was a doctor, knew just what horrors his son must have been through and just what trials lay ahead.

The other eight survivors were brought out of the Andes the following day, most of them in surprisingly good condition. In fact, only four of the entire 16 were held briefly for further treatment.

By the evening of December 23, the whole party of Uruguayans who had come to Chile upon hearing the news of the rescue had settled in Santiago for a Christmas celebration—the survivors with their families in the Sheraton San Cristóbal Hotel; the parents and relatives of those who had died at the Crillon.

There, at the Crillon, the father of Gustavo Nicolich opened a letter that his son had written on the mountain before his death in the avalanche: "One thing which will seem incredible to you—it seems unbelievable to me—is that today we started to cut up the dead in order to eat them. There is nothing else to do." And then, a little later, the words: "If the day came and I could save someone with my body, I would gladly do it." This was the first intimation that any parent at the

Crillon had had that it was the bodies of their sons which had kept the 16 survivors alive, and Nicolich, already grief-stricken, recoiled still further at this grim information. Considering at that moment that the truth might never be known, he removed that sheet of the letter and concealed it.

The parents at the San Cristóbal Hotel had much the same reaction, but in addition they were in dread of the news breaking on the outside world. Their peace of mind was not assisted by the presence in the hotel of a mass of journalists asking incessant questions and taking pictures of the boys. In an earlier press conference at the hospital, when the survivors were asked what they had eaten, they answered that they had brought a lot of cheese with them and that herbs grew in the mountains. But clearly this would not satisfy the press for long.

The true story broke in a Peruvian newspaper and was picked up in Argentina, Chile and Brazil. The Santiago journalists fell once again upon the survivors. Confused, the boys continued to deny the cannibalism, but those who had betrayed their secret—the Andean rescue team—had furnished the proof. On December 26 the Santiago newspaper *El Mercurio* published on its front page a photograph of a half-eaten human leg lying in the snow against the side of the Fairchild.

The boys decided that, rather than talk to any particular newspaper, they would hold a news conference at Stella Maris College when they returned to Montevideo. This was a frail defense against the tornado that raged around them. The news merely whetted the appetite of the world's press, and the boys in the hotel were bombarded with questions. A Chilean magazine which usually specialized in pornography took two pages to print photographs of the limbs and bones which had lain around the Fairchild. Another Chilean newspaper printed the story under the headline: "May God Forgive Them." When some of the parents saw this, they wept.

With the atmosphere in Santiago poisoned by this clamor, the survivors chartered a plane and returned to Montevideo on December 28. At Stella Maris College everything was ready for their arrival. The large brick assembly hall had been laid out as for a prize-giving, with a long table on a podium and microphones and loudspeakers.

The conference began. The whole roon listened as, one after the other, the survivors told their tragic story, until it was Pancho Delgado's turn. He had been chosen to speak about the cannibalism. His eloquence—of little use on the mountain—now came into its own:

"When one awakes in the morning amid the silence of the mountains, and sees all around the snowcapped peaks—it is majestic, sensational, something frightening—and one feels alone in the world but for the presence of God. For I can assure you that God is there. We all felt it, inside ourselves, and not because we were the kind of pious youths who are always praying. Not at all. But there one feels the presence of God. One feels, above all, what is called the hand of God, and allows oneself to be guided by it. . . . And when the moment came when we did not have any more food, we thought to ourselves that if Jesus at his last supper had shared his flesh and blood with his Apostles, then it was a sign to us that we should do the same—take the flesh and blood as an intimate communion between us all. It was this that helped us to survive, and now we do not want this—which for us was something intimate—to be tainted or anything like that. In a foreign country we tried to approach the subject in as elevated a spirit as possible, and now we tell it to you, our fellow countrymen, exactly as it was. . . ."

As Delgado finished, it was evident that the entire company was deeply moved, and when the journalists were asked if they had any questions, there were none.

Twenty-nine of those who had departed in the Fairchild had not come back, and for the families of those 29 the return of the 16 meant the confirmation of their death. It was, moreover, a confirmation of a disturbing nature. Every member of every family confronted the knowledge that their husbands, mothers and sons were not only dead but might have been eaten.

It was a bitter admixture to hearts already brimful with sorrow, for however noble and rational the mind may have been in contemplation of this end, there was a primitive and irrepressible horror at the idea that the bodies of their beloved should have been used in this way. For the most part, however, they mastered this repugnance. The parents showed the same selflessness and courage as their sons had done and rallied around the 16 survivors.

Dr. Helios Valeta, the father of a boy who had been swept out of the tail, went with his family to the press conference. Afterward, he spoke to the newspaper *El Pais:* "I came here with my family," he said, "because we are sincerely happy to have these boys back among us. We are glad, what is more, that there were 45 of them, because this helped at least 16 to return. As a doctor I knew that no one could have survived in such a place and under such conditions without resort to courageous decisions. Now that I have confirmation, I repeat: Thank God that the 45 were there, for 16 homes have regained their children."

ROOTS

CONDENSED FROM THE BOOK

BY ALEX HALEY

ILLUSTRATED BY NOEL SICKLES

In the early 1960s, author Alex Haley embarked on an extraordinary personal adventure. At a time when black America had turned in anguish to confrontation and a new struggle for identity, Haley—a writer of distinction—decided to trace his family to its deepest roots, back to his African ancestors.

Like most black Americans, he had little to go on at first—only a few meager clues passed down over the years by word of mouth. But as he pursued his search, on three continents back through seven generations, the pieces of his ancient family puzzle began to fall into place.

The story that finally emerged portrayed not merely the agony of one man, the enslaved Kunta Kinte, and his descendants, but in a real sense, the epic journey of the American black.

Since its publication, *Roots* has found a vast audience and has become a classic of American literature. Through its eloquence, Alex Haley's passionate narrative speaks to all people and to all generations.

AUTHOR'S FOREWORD

MY EARLIEST MEMORY is of Grandma, Cousin Georgia, Aunt Plus, Aunt Liz and Aunt Till talking on our front porch in Henning, Tenn. At dusk, these wrinkled, graying old ladies would sit in rocking chairs and talk, about slaves and massas and plantations—pieces and patches of family history, passed down across the generations by word of mouth. "Old-timey stuff," Mama would exclaim. She wanted no part of it.

The furthest-back person Grandma and the others ever mentioned was "the African." They would tell how he was brought here on a ship to a place called "Naplis" and sold as a slave in Virginia. There he mated with another slave, and had a little girl named Kizzy.

When Kizzy became four or five, the old ladies said, her father would point out to her various objects and name them in his native tongue. For example, he would point to a guitar and make a single-syllable sound, *ko.* Pointing to a river that ran near the plantation, he'd say "Kamby Bolongo." And when other slaves addressed him as Toby—the name given him by his massa—the African would strenuously reject it, insisting that his name was "Kin-tay."

Kin-tay often told Kizzy stories about himself. He said that he had been near his village in Africa, chopping wood to make a drum, when he had been set upon by four men, overwhelmed, and kidnaped into slavery. When Kizzy grew up and became a mother, she told her son these stories, and he in turn would tell *his* children. His granddaughter became my grandmother, and she pumped that saga into me as if it were plasma, until I knew by rote the story of the African, and the subsequent generational wending of our family through cotton and tobacco plantations into the Civil War and then freedom.

At 17, during World War II, I enlisted in the Coast Guard, and found myself a messboy on a ship in the Southwest Pacific. To fight boredom, I began to teach myself to become a writer. I stayed on in the service after the war, writing every single night, seven nights a week, for eight years before I sold a story to a magazine. My first story in the Reader's Digest was published in June 1954: "The Harlem Nobody Knows." At age 37, I retired from military service, determined to be a full-time writer. Working with the famous Black Muslim spokesman, I did the actual writing for the book *The Autobiography of Malcolm X.*

I remembered still the vivid highlights of my family's story. Could this account possibly be documented for a book? During 1962, between other assignments, I began following the story's trail. In plantation records, wills, census records, I documented bits here, shreds there. By now, Grandma was dead; repeatedly I visited other close sources, most notably our encyclopedic matriarch, "Cousin Georgia" Anderson in Kansas City, Kan. I went as often as I could to the National Archives in Washington, and the Library of Congress, and the Daughters of the American Revolution Library.

By 1967, I felt I had the seven generations of the U.S. side documented. But the unknown quotient in the riddle of the past continued to be those strange, sharp, angular sounds spoken by the African himself. Since I lived in New York City, I began going to the United Nations lobby, stopping Africans and asking if they recognized the sounds. They listened to me, then quickly took off. I can well understand: me with a Tennessee accent, trying to imitate African sounds!

I sought out a linguistics expert in African languages. To him I repeated the phrases. The sound "Kin-tay," he said, was a Mandinka tribe surname. And "Kamby Bolongo" was probably the Gambia River in Mandinka dialect. Three days later, I was in Africa.

In Banjul, the capital of Gambia, I met with a group of Gambians. They told me how for centuries the history of Africa has been preserved. In the older villages of the back country there are old men, called *griots,* who are in effect living archives. Such men know and, on special occasions, tell the cumulative histories of clans, or families, or villages, as those histories have long been told. Since my forefather had said his name was Kin-tay (properly spelled Kinte), and since the Kinte clan was known in Gambia, they would see what they could do.

I was back in New York when a registered letter came from Gambia. Word had been passed in the back country, and a *griot* of the Kinte clan had, indeed, been found. His name, the letter said, was Kebba Kanga

Fofana. I returned to Gambia and organized a safari to locate him.

There is an expression called "the peak experience," a moment which, emotionally, can never again be equaled in your life. I had mine, that first day in the village of Juffure, in the back country in black West Africa.

When our 14-man safari arrived within sight of the village, the people came flocking out of their circular mud huts. From a distance I could see a small, old man with a pillbox hat, an off-white robe and an aura of "somebodiness" about him. The people quickly gathered around me in a kind of horseshoe pattern. The old man looked piercingly into my eyes, and he spoke in Mandinka. Translation came from the interpreters I had brought with me.

"Yes, we have been told by the forefathers that there are many of us from this place who are in exile in that place called America."

Then the old man, who was 73 rains of age—the Gambian way of saying 73 years old, based upon the one rainy season per year—began to tell me the history of the Kinte clan. It was clearly a formal occasion for the villagers. They had grown mouse-quiet, and stood rigidly.

Out of the *griot's* head came spilling lineage details incredible to hear. He recited who married whom, two or even three centuries back. I was struck not only by the profusion of details, but also by the Biblical pattern of the way he was speaking. It was something like, "—and so-and-so took as a wife so-and-so, and begat so-and-so. . . ."

The *griot* had talked for some hours, and had got to about 1750 in our calendar. Now he said, through an interpreter, "About the time the king's soldiers came, the eldest of Omoro's four sons, Kunta, went away from this village to chop wood—and he was never seen again. . . ."

Goose pimples came out on me. He had no way of knowing that what he told me meshed with what I'd heard from the old ladies on the front porch in Henning, Tenn. I got out my notebook, which had in it what Grandma had said about the African. One of the interpreters showed it to the others, and they went to the *griot*, and they all got agitated. Then the *griot* went to the people, and *they* all got agitated.

I don't remember anyone giving an order, but those 70-odd people formed a ring around me, moving counterclockwise, chanting, their bodies close together. I can't begin to describe how I felt. A woman broke from the circle, a scowl on her jet-black face, and came charging toward me. She took her baby and almost roughly thrust it out at me. The gesture meant "Take it!" and I did, clasping the baby to me. Whereupon the woman all but snatched the baby away. Another woman did the same with her baby, then another, and another.

A year later, a professor at Harvard would tell me: "You were participating in one of the oldest ceremonies of humankind, called 'the laying on of hands.' In their way, these tribespeople were saying to you, 'Through this flesh, which is us, we are you and you are us.'"

Later, as we drove out over the back-country road, I heard the staccato sound of drums. When we approached the next village, people were packed alongside the dusty road, waving, and the din from them welled louder as we came closer. As I stood up in the Land Rover, I finally realized what it was they were all shouting: "Meester Kinte! Meester Kinte!" In their eyes I was the symbol of all black people in the United States whose forefathers had been torn out of Africa while theirs remained.

Hands before my face, I began crying—crying as I have never cried in my life. Right at that time, crying was all I could do.

I went then to London. I searched and searched, and finally in the British Parliamentary records I found that the "king's soldiers" mentioned by the *griot* referred to a group called "Colonel O'Hare's forces," which had been sent up the Gambia River in 1767 to guard the then British-operated James Fort, a slave fort.

I next went to Lloyds of London, where doors were opened for me to research among all kinds of old maritime records. I pored through the records of slave ships that had sailed from Africa. Volumes upon volumes of these records exist. One afternoon about 2:30, during the seventh week of searching, I was going through my 1023rd set of ship records. I picked up a sheet that had on it the reported movements of 30 slave ships, my eyes stopped at No. 18, and my glance swept across the column entries. This vessel had sailed directly from the Gambia River to America in 1767; her name was the *Lord Ligonier;* and she had arrived at Annapolis (Naplis) the morning of September 29, 1767.

Exactly 200 years later, on September 29, 1967, there was nowhere in the world for me to be except standing on a pier at Annapolis, staring seaward across those waters over which my great-great-great-great-grandfather had been brought. And there in Annapolis I inspected the microfilmed records of the *Maryland Gazette.* In the issue of October 1, 1767, on page 3, I found an advertisement informing readers that the *Lord Ligonier* had just arrived from the River Gambia, with "a cargo of choice, healthy SLAVES" to be sold at auction the following Wednesday.

In the years since, I have done extensive research in 50 or so libraries, archives and repositories on three continents. I spent a year combing through countless documents to learn about the culture of Gambia's villages in the 18th and 19th centuries. Desiring to sail over the same waters navigated by the *Lord Ligonier,* I flew to Africa and boarded the freighter *African Star.* I forced myself to spend the ten nights of the crossing in the cold, dark cargo hold, stripped to my underwear, lying on my back on a rough, bare plank. But this was sheer luxury compared to the inhuman ordeal suffered by those millions who, chained and shackled, lay in terror and in their own filth in the stinking darkness through voyages averaging 60 to 70 days.

This book has taken me ten years and more. Why have I called it *Roots?* Because it not only tells the story of a family, my own, but also because it symbolizes the history of millions of American blacks of African descent. I intend my book to be a buoy for black self-esteem—and a reminder of the universal truth that we are all descendants of the same Creator.

1. THE STORY

EARLY IN THE SPRING OF 1750, in the village of Juffure, four days upriver from the coast of Gambia, West Africa, a manchild was born to Omoro Kinte and Binta Kebba. Forcing forth from Binta's strong young body, he was as black as she was, flecked and slippery with her blood, and he was bawling. The two wrinkled midwives, old Nyo Boto and the baby's paternal grandmother, Yaisa, saw that it was a boy and cackled with joy. According to the forefathers, who had followed Muhammad's teachings through hundreds of annual rains, a boy firstborn presaged the special blessings of Allah.

It was the hour before the first crowing of the cocks. The thin blue smoke of cooking fires went curling up, pungent and pleasant, over the small dusty village of round mud huts. The men filed briskly to the praying place where the *alimamo,* the village's holy man, led the first of the five daily Muslim prayers: *"Allahu akbar! Ashadu an lawilahala!"* ("Allah is great! I bear witness that there is only one Allah!") And afterward Omoro rushed among them, beaming and excited, to tell them of his firstborn son.

By custom, for the next seven days Omoro occupied himself with selecting a name for his son. It would have to be rich with history and promise, for the people of his tribe—the Mandinkas—believed that a child would develop seven of the characteristics of his namesake.

When the eighth day arrived, the villagers gathered in the early evening before Omoro's hut. As Binta proudly held her infant, a small patch of his first hair was shaved off, as was always done, and the women exclaimed at how well-formed the baby was. Then the village drummer began to beat his small *tan-tang* drums.

The *alimamo* said a prayer over the calabashes of boiled grain and *munko* cakes of pounded rice and honey brought as gifts by the villagers. Next he entreated Allah to grant the infant long life and the strength and spirit to bring honor to the name he was about to receive.

Omoro then walked to his wife's side, leaned over the infant and, as all watched, whispered into his son's ear the name he had chosen for him. Omoro's people felt that each human being should be the first to know who he was.

The drum resounded again, and now Omoro whispered the name into Binta's ear, and Binta smiled with pride. Then he whispered the name to the village schoolmaster, who announced: "The first child of Omoro Kinte and Binta Kebba is named Kunta!"

It was the name of the child's late paternal grandfather, Kairaba Kunta Kinte, who had come from his native Mauretania into Gambia, where his unending prayers for five days had saved the people of Juffure from a famine. He had married Yaisa, and had served Juffure honorably as the *alimamo* until his death. All the people proclaimed their admiration and respect for such distinguished lineage.

That night, under the moon and stars, Omoro completed the naming ritual. By the mosque of mud and thatch, he lifted his baby to the heavens and said: "Behold—the only thing greater than yourself."

In her hut each evening, Binta would soften her baby's skin by greasing him from head to toe with shea-tree butter, then carry him proudly across the village to the hut of Grandma Yaisa. The two of them would set little Kunta to whimpering with their repeated pinchings and pressings of his little head, nose, ears and lips to shape them correctly.

Sometimes Omoro would take his son away from the women to his own hut—husbands always resided separately from their wives—here he let the child's eyes and fingers explore his huntsman's bag, covered with cowrie shells, and the dark, slender spear whose shaft was polished from much use. Omoro talked to Kunta of the fine and brave deeds he would perform when he grew up.

When he was 13 moons, Kunta tried his first unsteady steps. Before long, he was able to toddle about without an assisting hand.

Three annual rains passed. Little Kunta spent his days romping under the watchful eyes of the old grandmothers who took care of what was called the first *kafo,* which included all the children under five rains in age. The boys and girls scampered about as naked as animals. Laughing and squealing, they played hide-and-seek and scattered the dogs and chickens, chasing them along the inside wall of the tall bamboo fence that enclosed the village.

But all the children would scramble to sit still and quiet when the telling of a story was promised by one of the grandmothers, especially the beloved Nyo Boto. Baldheaded, deeply wrinkled, as black as the bottom of an old cooking pot, her few remaining teeth a deep orange from the countless kola nuts she had gnawed on, Nyo Boto would settle herself with much grunting on her low stool and begin a story in the same way that all Mandinka storytellers began: "At this certain time, in this certain village, lived this certain person. . . ."

It was old Nyo Boto who told of the terrible time she remembered when there was not enough rain. Although the people prayed hard to Allah and the women danced the ancestral rain dance and sacrificed two goats and a bullock every day, still everything growing began to parch. Even the forest water holes dried up, and wild animals appeared at the village well. More and more people grew ill, and the old and weak began to die.

It was then, said Nyo Boto, that Allah guided the steps of Kairaba Kunta Kinte to the village. Seeing the people's plight, he knelt down and prayed to Allah—almost without sleep, and taking only a few sips of water as nourishment—for the next five days. And on the evening of the fifth day came a great rain, which fell like a flood and saved Juffure.

When she had finished her story, the other children looked with new respect at Kunta, who bore that honored name.

The seasons came and went. First, the planting season, when Binta and the other wives hurried to the dugout canoes on the banks of the village *bolong,* one of the many tributary canals that twisted inland from the Gambia River, and paddled to the fields where generations of Juffure women had grown their rice. In other fields the men had piled tall stacks of dry weeds and set them afire to nourish the soil; and now, as the first light rains began to fall, they put out their groundnuts and other seeds. And then the big rains came. And after that the harvest, and the long, scorching dry spell.

Kunta and his *kafo* mates began to feel older than their rains of age, which now ranged from five to nine. They envied the older boys of the third *kafo* their goatherding jobs and their *dundiko*—long cotton robes—and thought themselves too grown up to be made to go naked any longer. They avoided babies like Kunta's new brother Lamin and began hanging around adults in hopes of being sent off on an errand.

It was on the morning of the second day of the harvest, just as Kunta began to walk out the door of his mother's hut, that Binta said to him gruffly, "Why don't you put on your clothes?" Kunta turned around abruptly. There, hanging from a peg, he saw a brand-new *dundiko.* Struggling to conceal his excitement, he put it on and sauntered out the door. Others of his *kafo* were already outside—several, like him, dressed for the first time in their lives, leaping, shouting and laughing because their nakedness was covered at last. They were now officially of the second *kafo.* They were becoming men.

The next day, when Omoro handed Kunta a new slingshot, his breath all but choked off. He stood looking at his father, not knowing what to say, and Omoro spoke: "You are now second *kafo.* You will go to school and tend goats. You go today with Toumani Touray."

Kunta dashed away and joined his *kafo* mates. They clustered about the goat pens where the older boys were opening the gates for the day's grazing. With the help of *wuolo* dogs, they soon had the blatting goats hurrying down the dusty path. Kunta's *kafo* ran uncertainly behind.

Toumani Touray acted as if Kunta were some kind of insect. "Do you know the value of a goat?" he asked, and before Kunta could admit he wasn't sure, "Well, if you lose one, your father will let you know." And Toumani Touray launched into a lecture on goatherding. If a goat was allowed to stray into the forest, he said, there were lions and panthers which with a single spring from the grass could tear a goat apart. "And if a boy is close enough, he is tastier than a goat!"

The next morning, Kunta and his mates began their religious education. The schoolmaster, Brima Cesay, told them, "You are no longer children, but are of the second *kafo,* meaning you have responsibilities." With that evening's class he would begin to read to them certain verses of the Koran, which they must memorize. Now, between the goats all day, the schoolmaster after breakfast and late in the afternoon, and what slingshot practice Kunta could manage before darkness, there was little time for play. With the annual seven-day harvest festival less than a moon away, Kunta was also forced to tend his pesky little brother Lamin for several evenings, while his mother spun cotton which the men would weave for new clothes for the family.

The morning after the new moon, the big ceremonial *tobalo* drum sounded at dawn. The harvest festival began with dancing, and

Kunta's eyes widened as he saw his father join a throng of whirling, leaping bodies, some wearing horrifying costumes and masks.

Kunta had seen such ceremonies for many harvests, plantings, men leaving to hunt, and for weddings, births and deaths, but the dancing had never moved him as it did now. The beat of the *tan-tang* drums seemed to throb in his limbs. As if it were a dream, he felt his body begin to quiver and his arms to flail, and soon he was springing and shouting along with the others. From the very young to the very old, everyone danced on through the entire day.

The festival continued for six more days with parades, feasting, wrestling, trading, and storytelling by traveling *griots*. On the final day, Kunta was awakened by the sound of screams. Pulling on his *dundiko,* he went dashing out. Before several of the huts were half a dozen men in fierce masks, tall headdresses and costumes of leaf and bark. Kunta watched in terror as one man entered each hut and emerged pulling a trembling boy of the third *kafo,* a heavy white cotton hood placed over his head. When all of the older boys had been collected, the men, yelling and shoving, carried them out through the village gate.

Kunta knew that every five years the older boys were taken away from Juffure for their manhood training, but he had no idea it was like this. In the days that followed, he and his *kafo* mates could think of nothing but the frightening things they had learned of the training.

They all had heard that many full moons would pass before the boys returned. It was also said that they got beatings daily, and that they were sent out alone at night into the deep forest. But the worst thing—a knowledge that made Kunta nervous every time he had to urinate—was that during manhood training a part of his *foto* would be cut off.

Two rains passed, and Binta's belly was big again. Her temper was shorter than usual, and Kunta was grateful when goatherding and other tasks let him escape for a few hours. He couldn't help feeling sorry for Lamin, who was not old enough to go out of the house alone. So, one day he asked Binta if Lamin could join him on an errand.

After that, Kunta took his brother out nearly every day. He taught Lamin how to wrestle, how to whistle through his fingers, and showed him the kind of berry leaves from which his mother made tea. He cautioned him to take the big, shiny dung beetles they always saw crawling in the hut and set them gently on the ground, for it was very bad luck to harm them. To touch a rooster's spur was even worse luck.

Walking alongside, Lamin would ply Kunta with questions.

"Why does no one harm owls?"

"Because all our dead ancestors' spirits are in owls."

"What are slaves?" Lamin asked one day. Kunta did not know. And so, the next day, he questioned his father. Omoro was silent for a long while. Finally, "Slaves are not always easy to tell from those who are not slaves," he replied. He told Kunta that people became slaves in different ways. Some were born of slave mothers—and he named several who lived in Juffure. Others, facing starvation in their own villages during the hungry season, had come to Juffure and begged to become the slaves of someone who would provide for them. Still others had been enemies and had been captured.

"Even so," Omoro said, "their rights are guaranteed by the laws of our forefathers," and he explained that all masters had to provide their slaves with food, clothing, a house, a farm plot to work on half-shares, and a wife or a husband. Also, slaves could buy their freedom with what they saved by farming. If they married into the family that owned them, they were assured that they would never be sold or given away. But Kunta wanted to know more. Toumani Touray had told him about the hairy white men—the *toubob*— who sometimes burned villages and took people away. His father said nothing until, a few days later, he invited both Kunta and Lamin to go with him beyond the village to collect some roots.

Then he told them of a trip that he and his two brothers had taken many rains ago. They had trekked along the banks of the Gambia Bolongo, keeping carefully concealed.

At last they had come to a place where 20 great *toubob* canoes were moored in the river, each big enough to hold all the people of Juffure, each with a huge white cloth tied by ropes to a tree-like pole as tall as ten men. Many *toubob* were moving about, and *slatees*—black helpers—were with them. Small canoes were taking such things as dried indigo, cotton, beeswax and hides to the big canoes. More terrible than he could describe, however, said Omoro, were the beatings and other cruelties they saw being dealt out to those who had been captured for the *toubob* to take away.

"Some Mandinkas sell their slaves to *toubob,*" Omoro said. "Such men are traitors. A Kinte must never do this."

Kunta and Lamin sat frozen with fear. "Papa," asked Lamin, "where do the big canoes take the stolen people?"

"The elders say to *toubabo doo,*" said Omoro, "a land where slaves are sold to huge cannibals called *toubabo koomi,* who eat us. No man knows any more about it."

2. JOURNEY OF THE NEW MOON

ON A HOT, QUIET AFTERNOON a few days later, there suddenly came a sharp burst of drums from the village. Kunta dashed to the hut of Juffure's drummer: Others had already gathered there to hear the news. A messenger from the next village was speaking to Omoro. Five days of walking the way the sun rose, Kunta's uncles Janneh and Saloum Kinte were building a new village; their brother Omoro was expected for the ceremonial blessing of the village on the second next new moon. When the messenger had finished, Omoro gave his reply: Allah willing, he would be there.

Not many days before Omoro's departure, an idea almost too big to think about seized Kunta. Was it possible that Omoro might let *him* go, too? Now and then a boy was allowed to share a journey with his father, although never one so young as eight rains. Sensing that his mother would disapprove of his dream, Kunta knew that his only hope lay in asking his father directly.

Three days before Omoro was to go, the almost despairing Kunta saw his father leave Binta's hut. Abandoning his goats, he ran like a hare and came to a stop, looking up pleadingly at his father's startled face. Gulping, he couldn't remember a thing he had meant to say.

Omoro gazed at his son for a moment. Then, "I have just told your mother," he said—and walked on.

It took Kunta a few seconds to realize what his father meant. "Aiee!" he shouted. Dropping onto his belly, he sprang froglike into the air. Then, suddenly, he grew quiet with the knowledge that ever since the message had come his father had been thinking about him.

On the morning of their departure, first Omoro, then Kunta, took two steps into the dust outside Omoro's hut. Turning and bending down, they scraped up the dust of their first footprints and put it into their hunters' bags, thus ensuring that their footprints would return to this place. Binta watched, weeping, from her doorway. As they walked through the village, Kunta started to turn for a last look. But, seeing that his father did not turn, he kept his eyes front and quickly strode along, nearly trotting to keep the proper two paces behind Omoro.

After about an hour, Kunta's excitement had waned almost as much as his pace. His head-bundle began to feel heavier and heavier, the muscles below his knees ached, and his face was sweating. When the sun had covered nearly half the sky, Kunta began to think he wasn't going to be able to keep up. A short while later Omoro, who had neither spoken nor looked back, stopped and swung his head-load to the ground alongside a clear pool. There they sipped the cool spring water and roasted and ate four plump pigeons that Omoro had shot with his bow. Then they set out again.

"*Toubob* brings his canoes one day of walking from here," said Omoro when they had gone a good distance. "Tonight, my son, we must sleep in a village."

The orange ball of the sun was nearing the earth when Omoro and Kunta sighted a thin trail of smoke from a village up ahead. As they approached, they could tell that something was not right. No children came running out to meet them. As they passed by the village baobab tree, Kunta saw that it was partly burned. Most of the mud huts appeared to be empty, and the people of the village—many of them lying in the doorways of their huts—were all old or sick.

Several wrinkled old men weakly began to explain what had happened. Slave traders had taken or killed all of their younger people. "From your rains to his!" one old man said, pointing at Omoro, then at Kunta. "We old ones they spared."

For the next three days, Omoro and Kunta walked steadily on, bypassing villages, sleeping near the trail on beds of soft branches. It seemed to Kunta as if he had barely laid his head down before his father was shaking him awake in the early dawn.

On the fourth day, they came to a village where there was no one to be seen. Kunta waited in vain for Omoro to explain the mystery. It was the chattering children of the next village who finally did so. Pointing back down the trail, they said that the village's chief had kept on doing things his people disliked, until one night not long ago, as he slept, every family of that village quietly went away with all its possessions to the homes of friends and families in other places. They left behind an "empty chief," who was now going about begging his people to believe that, if they would return, he would act better.

At this second village, Omoro arranged for the village drummer to send the announcement of their arrival to his brothers. They would understand that Omoro would soon be there, though they did not

know that Kunta was with him. Kunta felt very proud that he had traveled so far with his father.

On the fifth day Kunta spotted smoke rising from a village not far ahead. Soon he began to hear the distant thunder of a *tobalo* drum, the throb of smaller *tan-tang* drums and the loud clapping of dancers. Then the trail made a turn—and there was the village.

Kunta's feet scarcely felt the ground. The pounding of the drums grew louder and louder, and suddenly dancers appeared, grunting and shouting in their leaf-and-bark costumes, stamping out through the village gate to meet the distinguished visitors. Two figures came pushing through the crowd. Omoro's head-bundle dropped to the ground, and he hurried toward them. Before he knew it, Kunta dropped his own head-bundle and was running, too.

The two men and his father were hugging and pounding one another. "And who is this? Our brother's son?" Both men lifted Kunta off his feet and embraced him. His uncle Saloum thumped his fist on

Kunta's head. "Not since he got his name have we been together. And now look at him. How many rains have you, brother's son Kunta?"

"Eight rains, father's brother," Kunta answered politely.

"Nearly ready for manhood training!" exclaimed his uncle.

Soon it was dark, and the village fires were lighted, and the people gathered around them. Then Janneh and Saloum walked inside the circle of listeners and told stories of their adventures. Before building this village, they had been travelers and traders. They spoke of strange, humpbacked animals. "They are called camels," said Saloum, "and they live in a place of endless sand."

Janneh unrolled a piece of tanned hide on which was a drawing. "This is Africa," he said, and his finger traced what he told them was a great sand desert, a place many times larger than their kingdom.

To the north coast of Africa, the *toubob* ships brought porcelain, spices, cloth, horses and countless things made by machines, said Saloum. Then men, camels and donkeys bore those goods inland to places like Sijilmasa, Ghadames and Marrakesh. The moving finger of Janneh showed where those cities were.

"Our own African goods are brought to many great cities," Saloum said, "gold, ivory, skins, olives, dates, cotton, copper and precious stones. As we sit here tonight, there are many men with heavy headloads crossing deep forests taking these things to the *toubob's* ships."

Looking as proud as his father beside him, Kunta listened with wonder, and then and there he vowed silently that someday he, too, would venture to such exciting places.

KUNTA REACHED HIS 12TH RAIN, and he and his *kafo* were about to complete the schooling they had received twice daily since they were five. When the day of graduation came, the parents of the boys seated themselves, beaming with pride, in the teacher's yard. Then Brima Cesay stood and looked at his pupils. He asked Kunta a question.

"What was the profession of your ancient forefathers, Kunta Kinte?"

"Hundreds of rains ago in the land of Mali," Kunta confidently replied, "the Kinte men were blacksmiths, and their women were makers of pots and spinners of cotton."

Next there were riddles, and then the students wrote their names on slates in Arabic as they had been taught. Finally, the teacher asked each graduate to stand, calling out his name. "Kairaba Kunta Kinte." With all eyes upon him, Kunta felt the great pride of his family, in the front row of spectators, even of his ancestors in the burying ground beyond the village. He read aloud a verse from the Koran. Finishing, he pressed it to his forehead and said, "Amen." When the readings were done, everyone broke into wild cheering.

The passing moons flowed into seasons until yet another rain had passed, and Kunta's *kafo* had taught Lamin's *kafo* how to be goatherds. A time long awaited now drew steadily nearer, for the next harvest festival would end with the taking away of the third *kafo*—those boys between 10 and 15 rains in age. Kunta did his best to hide the vivid memory of that morning, when he and his mates had been scared nearly out of their wits as they watched boys under white hoods being taken from the village by a band of masked, shrieking *kankurang* dancers.

The great *tabalo* drum soon sounded out the beginning of the new harvest, and Kunta joined the rest of the villagers in the fields. He welcomed the long days of hard work, for they kept him too busy and too tired to give much thought to what lay ahead. When the festival began, he found himself unable to enjoy the music and the dancing and the feasting as the others did.

On the night before the last day of the festival, Kunta was in Omoro's hut, finishing his evening meal, when his mother's brother walked in and stood behind him. From the corner of his eye, Kunta glimpsed his kinsman raising something white, and before he had a chance to turn, a long hood had been pulled down over his head. He felt a hand gripping his upper arm and urging him to stand up, then to move backward until he was pushed down onto a low stool.

He sat very still, trying to accustom himself to the darkness. He gulped down his fear, remembering that any boy who failed the manhood training would be treated as a child for the rest of his life, avoided, never permitted to marry lest he father others like himself.

Hours passed. The drumbeats and the shouting of the dancers in the distance ceased. He dozed, jerked awake with a start, and finally slipped into a fitful sleep.

When the *tobalo* boomed, he all but leaped from his skin. Now he could picture the morning's activities from the sounds his ears picked up—the crowing of the cocks, the barking of the *wuolo* dogs, the bumping of the women's pestles as they beat the breakfast grain. After a while, he heard the sound of people talking, louder and louder; then drums joined the din. A moment later, his heart seemed to stop as he sensed the sudden movement of someone rushing into the hut. His wrists were grabbed, and he was pushed out through the hut door into the deafening noise of drums and the bloodcurdling whoops of the *kankurang* dancers. The noise receded, only to rise again to a frenzied pitch every time another boy was dragged from a hut.

Kunta's ears told him that he had joined a moving line of marchers, all stepping to the swift, sharp rhythm of the drums. As they passed through the village gates the noise of the crowd began to fade. He knew that he was leaving behind more than his father and mother and his brothers and the village of his birth, and this filled him with sadness as much as terror.

But he knew it must be done, as it had been done by his father before him, and would someday be done by his son. He would return as a man—or not at all.

They must be approaching a bamboo grove, Kunta guessed. Through his hood he could smell the rich fragrance of freshly chopped stems. A few steps later, the pounding of the drums up ahead became muffled, as if they had entered an enclosure of some kind, and then the drums stopped and the marchers halted. For several minutes, everyone stood still and silent. Kunta remembered feeling like this once before, when his father, along the trail, had signaled for him to stand motionless until a pride of lions had passed them by in the dusk. He listened for the slightest sound that might tell him where they were, but all he could hear was the screeching of birds and the scolding of monkeys.

Suddenly, Kunta's hood was lifted. He stood blinking in the bright sun of midafternoon. Directly before Kunta and his mates stood stern, wrinkled Silla Ba Dibba, one of the senior elders of Juffure. His eyes scanned their faces as he would have looked at crawling maggots. Kunta knew that this was surely their *kintango,* the man in charge of their manhood training. Widening his gaze for a moment—careful not to move his head—Kunta saw that they stood in a compound dotted with thatch-roofed mud huts surrounded by a new bamboo fence.

"Children left Juffure village," said the *kintango* in a loud voice. "If men are to return, your fears must be erased, for a fearful person is a weak person, and a weak person is a danger to his tribe." He turned away, and as he did so, two of his helpers sprang forward and began to lay about among the boys with sticks, pummeling their shoulders and backsides as they herded the 23-boy *kafo* into the small mud huts.

Kunta and four other boys huddled in their hut for hours, not daring to speak. Just after sunset, as Kunta's belly was panging with hunger, the *kintango* helpers burst into the hut. "Move!" A stick caught him sharply across the shoulders as he rushed outside into the dusk. The *kintango* fixed them with a dark scowl and announced that they were about to undertake a night journey into the surrounding forest. At the order to march, the long line of boys set out along the path in clumsy disarray, and the sticks fell steadily among them.

It was almost dawn when the boys stumbled back into the *jujuo* compound. Every boy's feet bore big raw blisters. Kunta himself felt ready to die. He trudged to his hut, lost his footing, stumbled to the dirt floor—and fell asleep where he lay.

On the next few nights there were other marches, each longer than the last. The *kintango* showed them how men deep in the forest use the stars to guide them, and every boy of the *kafo* learned how to lead the group back to the *jujuo.*

Animals, the *kintango* told them, were the best teachers of the art of hunting. His helpers pointed out where lions had recently crouched in wait, showed the boys how to track antelope, and set the *kafo* to inspecting the cracks in rocks where wolves and hyenas hid. The boys were taught to imitate the sounds of animals and birds, and the air was rent with their grunts and whistles. Soon, every bite of meat they ate was either trapped by the boys or shot by their arrows.

But no matter how much they added to their knowledge and abilities, the old *kintango* was never satisfied. His demands and his discipline remained so strict that the boys were torn between fear and anger most of the time. Any command to one boy that was not instantly and perfectly performed brought a beating to the entire *kafo.* The only thing that kept Kunta and the others from giving that boy a beating of their own was that certain knowledge that *they* would be beaten for fighting. Among the first lessons they had learned in life—long before coming to the *jujuo*—was that Mandinkas must never fight among themselves.

3. MEN OF JUFFURE

IT CAME WITHOUT WARNING. One day, as the sun reached the noontime position, one of the *kintango* helpers gave what seemed to be a routine order for the *kafo* to line up in the compound. The *kintango* came from his hut and walked before them.

"Hold out your *fotos.*" he commanded. The time had come for that which Kunta dreaded: the *kasas boyo* operation which would purify a boy and prepare him to father many sons. Slowly they obeyed, each keeping his eyes on the ground as he reached inside his loincloth.

Then the *kintango* helpers wrapped around the head of each boy's *foto* a short length of cloth spread with a green paste made of a pounded leaf. "Soon your *fotos* will have no feeling," the *kintango* said, ordering them back into their huts.

Huddled inside, ashamed and afraid, the boys waited in silence until about midafternoon, when again they were ordered outside, where they stood watching as a number of men from Juffure—fathers, older brothers and uncles—filed in through the gate, Omoro among them. The men formed a line facing the boys and chanted together: "This thing to be done . . . also has been done to us . . . as to the forefathers before us . . . so that you also will become . . . all of us men together." Then the *kintango* sent the boys back inside their huts.

Night was falling when they heard many drums suddenly begin to pound, and they were ordered outside again. The fathers, uncles and brothers stood nearby, this time chanting, "You soon will return home . . . and in time you will marry . . . and life everlasting will spring from your loins." The *kintango* assistant called out one boy's name and motioned him behind a long screen of woven bamboo. A few moments later, the boy reappeared—with a bloodstained cloth between his legs. Another boy's name was called, and finally, "Kunta Kinte!"

He walked behind the screen. Here were four men, one of whom told him to lie down on his back. He did so—his shaking legs wouldn't have supported him any longer anyway. The men then leaned down, grasped him firmly, and lifted his thighs upward. Just before closing his eyes, Kunta saw the *kintango* bending over him with something in his hands. Then he felt the cutting pain. In a moment he was bandaged tightly, and his mother's brother helped him back outside. The thing he had feared above all else had now been done.

As the *fotos* of the *kafo* healed, a general air of jubilation rose within the *jujuo;* gone forever was the indignity of being mere boys in body as well as in mind. Now they were very nearly men.

"When your training is finished," said the *kintango* one evening, "you will begin to serve Juffure as its eyes and ears. You will be expected to stand guard over the village—beyond the gates—as lookouts for raiders and savages. You will also be responsible for inspecting the women's cooking pots to make sure they are kept clean, and you will be expected to reprimand them if any dirt or insects are found inside."

After that they would graduate, as the rains passed, to more important jobs. Men of Omoro's age—over 30—rose gradually in rank and responsibility until they acquired the honored status of elders and sat on the Council of Elders.

Still, hardly a day would pass without something new to make Kunta and his mates feel awkward and ignorant all over again. There seemed to be no limit to the things men knew that boys did not. It amazed them to learn, for example, that a rag folded and hung in certain ways near a man's hut would inform other Mandinka men when he planned to return, or that sandals crossed in certain ways outside a man's hut told many things that only other men would understand. But the secret Kunta found the most remarkable of all was *sira kango,* a kind of men's talk in which the sounds of Mandinka words were subtly changed.

Kunta remembered times when he had heard his father say something very rapidly to another man which Kunta had not understood, nor dared to ask about. And now Kunta himself was learning that secret talk of men.

For the next moon, Kunta and his mates learned how to make war. Famous Mandinka strategies were drawn in the dust by the *kintango,* and the boys re-enacted them in mock battles. Then the boys learned how to make barbed spears tipped with poison. After that it was wrestling, taught by the champion wrestlers of Juffure. And then came instruction in tribal history.

A *griot* arrived, so old that he made the *kintango* seem young. He told the boys, squatted in a semicircle around him, how every *griot* held, buried deep in his mind, the records of the ancestors. "How else could you know of the great deeds of the ancient kings, holy men, hunters and warriors who came hundreds of rains before us?" he asked. "The history of our people is carried in here"—and he tapped his gray head.

He thrilled them until late into the night with stories his own father had passed down to him—about the great black empires that had ruled over Africa hundreds of rains before.

"Long before *toubob* ever put his foot in Africa," the old *griot* said, "there was the empire of ancestral Ghana, in which an entire town was populated with only the king's court. Ghana's most famous king, Kanissaai, had a thousand horses, each of which had three servants and its own urinal made of copper. And each evening," said the *griot,* "when King Kanissaai would emerge from his palace, a thousand fires would be lighted, illuminating all between the heavens and the earth. And the king would sit on a golden porch, surrounded by his horses with their golden reins and saddles, by his dogs with their golden collars, by his guards with their golden shields and swords, and by his princeling sons with golden ornaments in their hair.

"But even Ghana was not the richest black kingdom," he exclaimed. "The very richest, the very oldest of them all was the kingdom of ancient Mali." Mali's enormous wealth came from its far-flung trade routes, its dealings in salt and gold and copper. Caravans of thousands of camels were common sights in such cities as Takedda and Niani, where huge ceremonies and pageants were held almost every day.

"Altogether, Mali was four months of travel long and four months of travel wide," said the *griot*. "And the greatest of all its cities was the fabled Timbuktu." Timbuktu, he told them, had 6000 dwelling houses and many rich mosques. The major center of learning in all Africa, it was populated by thousands of scholars, made even more numerous by a steady parade of visiting wise men seeking to increase their knowledge—so many that some of the biggest merchants sold nothing but parchments and books.

The next visitor to the compound was a celebrated *jalli kea,* a singing man, who led the boys in songs of great hunters and wise, brave and powerful Mandinka chiefs. Hardly had he left when a famous *moro*—the highest grade of teacher—arrived. He read to them from the Koran, and then from such unheard of books as the *Taureta La Musa* (the Pentateuch of Moses), the *Zabora Dawidi* (the Psalms of David) and the *Lingeeli La Isa* (the Book of Isaiah). When he had finished, the old man spoke to them of great events from the Christian Koran, which was known as the Holy Bible, of Adam and Eve, of Joseph and his brethren, of David and Solomon.

In his hut at night, Kunta lay awake thinking how nearly everything they learned tied together. The past seemed with the present, the present with the future, the dead with the living and those yet to live. All lived with Allah. He felt very small—yet very large. This, he thought, is what it means to become a man.

One night, when the moon was high and full in the heavens, the *kintango* helpers ordered the *kafo* to line up after the evening meal. Was this the moment for which they had waited? Kunta looked around for the *kintango.* His eyes searched the compound and finally found the old man standing at the gate of the *jujuo* just as he was swinging it open wide.

The *kintango* turned to them and called out, "Men of Juffure, you will return to your village!"

For a moment they stood rooted. Then they rushed up whooping, and grabbed and hugged their *kintango* and his helpers, who pretended to be offended by such impertinence.

When Kunta returned to the village, he found that his father had acquired a hut for him. Kunta would now live by himself, as would each of his *kafo.* Binta still cooked for him, however, and provided his new hut with a pallet, some bowls, a stool and a prayer rug. Kunta skillfully bargained for more household possessions, trading grain and groundnuts grown on a small plot of land assigned to him by the village elders. A young man who tended his crops well and managed his goats wisely could become a man of substance by the time he reached 25 or 30 rains, and begin to think about taking a wife and raising sons.

Every morning he took his prayer rug and fell in with his *kafo* as they walked with bowed heads behind the older men to the mosque. After prayers, Binta brought his breakfast. Then he joined his mates in undertaking their duties, which they performed with a diligence their elders found amusing.

The women could hardly turn around without finding one of the new men demanding to inspect their cooking pots for insects. Rummaging about outside the village fence, they found hundreds of spots where the state of repair failed to measure up to their exacting standards. Fully a dozen of them drew up buckets of well water, tasting carefully from the gourd dipper in hopes of detecting a saltiness or a muddiness or something else unhealthy. They were disappointed, but the fish and turtle that were kept in the well to eat insects were removed anyway and replaced with fresh ones.

At night, when it was his turn, Kunta made his way along the outside of the fence, past the sharp-thorned bushes piled against it and the pointed stakes concealed beneath, to a leafy hiding place that afforded him a view of the surrounding countryside. And here he guarded the village against whatever might threaten it. One night, a full rain since manhood training, Kunta left for the sentry post, taking with him not only his spear and bow, but an ax—for in the morning he intended to select and chop the wood that he would bend and dry into a frame for a drum for the village. Quickly, he climbed the notched pole in whose sturdy fork was built a platform eight feet above the ground.

During the first of his turns alone at these vigils, every shadowy movement of monkey, baboon, hyena or panther had seemed surely to be an enemy. But, after long nights on lookout, Kunta's eyes and ears became so highly trained that he could let them maintain vigilance almost on their own, while his mind explored private thoughts.

Since his new manhood, Kunta had begun to think of taking a very special trip. He meant to put his feet upon that place called Mali where, according to Omoro and his uncles, the ancient Kinte clan had begun, 300 or 400 rains ago. The school master had drawn a map for him, and estimated that the round trip would take about one moon. Since then, Kunta had many times drawn and studied his planned route on the dirt floor of his hut.

The sudden barking of the *wuolo* dog pushed the thought from his head. Standing on his platform, Kunta whooped and waved his arms at the dark hulks of baboons which had got up the courage to rush from the tall grass adjoining the fields and snatch up a few groundnuts before fleeing back into the bush. Twice more during the night they made forays, growing bolder as dawn approached.

At the first streaks of light in the east, Kunta gathered his weapons and ax, clambered stiffly down to the ground and began limbering up. Then he set off along the *bolong* toward a stand of mangrove trees to find the wood he wanted. He passed through the scattered first trees of the grove, for a thicker growth offered more choice. Leaning his weapons and ax against a warped tree, he moved here, there, his eyes searching for perfect trunks.

The sharp cracking of a twig mixed with a bird's squawk first registered as being merely the *wuolo* dog returning from a chase after a hare—then his reflexes flashed that no dog cracks a twig. Kunta whirled, and, comprehending the rushing, blurred pale face, knew two things that instant: *toubob* and *weapons beyond reach.*

Steal me . . . eat me. His foot, lashing up, caught the *toubob* in the belly, but a heavy object from behind grazed his head, then exploded pain in his shoulder. Glimpsing the kicked *toubob* doubling over, Kunta spun, fists flailing. He saw two black *slatee* men, and another *toubob* who was again jerking downward a short, thick club, which Kunta escaped by violently springing aside.

The blacks rushed him, and Kunta—his brain screaming for a weapon, any weapon—leaped into them, clawing, butting, kneeing, gouging. Then, as the three of them went sagging down, another club pounded against his back. A knee smashed over Kuntas's kidneys, rocking him with such pain that he gasped; his open mouth met flesh; his teeth clamped, cut and tore. His fingers found a face, and he clawed deeply into an eye as the club hit his head. Dazed, he heard the dog's sudden piteous yelp. Scrambling up, wildly twisting and dodging to escape more clubbing, with blood streaming from his head, he glimpsed one of the *toubob* standing near the brained dog.

Screaming his rage, Kunta went for the *toubob* and, almost choking on the awful *toubob* stink, tried desperately to wrench away the club. Why had he not heard them, sensed them, smelled them? For a split second he clearly saw his family and all the people of Juffure, his mind flashing that if a warrior died bravely, he became a noble ancestor. Raging at his own weakness, he knew he was fighting for more than his life—and then the *toubob's* heavy club squarely met his ear and temple.

4. TOUBOB'S CANOE

HE STRUGGLED BACK to consciousness to find himself gagged and blindfolded, with his wrists tightly bound behind him, his ankles hobbled. He was yanked to his feet, and sharpened sticks jabbed him as he stumbled along. Somewhere on the banks of the *bolong,* he was shoved into a canoe. When the canoe landed, he walked again, until finally that night they reached a camp where he was tied to a thick post and his blindfold removed. Kunta was then left alone. Dawn let him see other captives tied to posts—six men, three maidens and two children, their naked bodies bruised and bloody from being clubbed.

In wild fury, Kunta lunged back and forth trying to burst his bonds. A heavy blow from a club again rendered him senseless. When he woke again, he found himself also naked; his head had been shaved and his body smeared with red palm oil. Soon afterward, two new *toubob* entered the camp, one of them short and stout, his hair white. The *slatees,* now all grins, untied the captives and herded them into a line.

The white-haired one gestured at Kunta. Kunta screamed in terror as a *slatee* behind him wrestled him down to his knees, jerking his head backward. The white-haired *toubob* calmly spread Kunta's trembling lips and studied his teeth. Standing again, Kunta quivered as the *toubob's* fingers explored his eyes, his chest, his belly. Then the fingers grasped his *foto.* Two *slatees* forced Kunta finally to bend himself almost double, and he felt his buttocks being spread wide apart.

The white-haired *toubob* inspected the others, one by one—even the private parts of the maidens. Afterward he beckoned a camp *toubob* and jabbed his finger at four men—one of them Kunta—and two maidens.

Kunta howled with fury as again the *slatees* grabbed him, pushing him into a seated position with his back hunched forward. He could see a *toubob* withdrawing from a fire a long, thin iron. He thrashed and screamed as the iron burned into his back. The camp echoed with the screams of the others who had been selected. Then red palm oil was rubbed over the white *LL* shape that Kunta saw on each of their backs.

A few days later they were hobbling along tied together in a line, the *slatees'* clubs falling on anyone who balked. Kunta's back and shoulders were bruised and bleeding when, late that night, the captives were put in canoes and paddled through the darkness. When Kunta finally perceived the dark hulk looming up ahead in the night, he raged anew against his bonds. Heavy club blows rained down on him as the canoe bumped against the side of the dark object, and he heard above him the exclamations of many *toubob.* Helpless to resist the ropes looped around him, he was half pushed, half pulled up a rope ladder.

In the shadowy, yellowish light cast by lanterns, he glimpsed the short, stout *toubob* with the white hair calmly making marks in a book. Then Kunta was guided, stumbling, down narrow steps into a place of pitch blackness. He smelled an incredible stink, and his ears heard many men's moans of anguish. As he was shoved down, flat on his back, he felt that he was dreaming—and then lapsed into unconsciousness.

When he awoke, Kunta wondered if he had gone mad. He lay chained down naked between two other men in a pitch darkness full of heat and stink and a nightmarish bedlam of weeping, praying and vomiting. A rat's furry body brushed his cheek. As he lunged upward, his head bumped against a ceiling scarcely a foot above him. Gasping with pain, he slumped back, wishing that he might die.

I am trapped like a leopard in a snare! Kunta fought back panic. He guessed that many men must be shackled on the rough plank shelves in the foul darkness, and that some of them were down on another level below where he lay. They spoke in a babble of tongues—Fulani, Serere, Wolof and Mandinka. The man on his right, to whom he was shackled at wrist and ankle, muttered angrily in Wolof.

Kunta lay for a while, sobbing, his mind numbed. Though he could not get onto his knees, and he was unaware of which direction was east, he closed his eyes and prayed, beseeching Allah's help.

In the darkness of the big vessel, only the occasional opening of the deck hatch enabled Kunta to tell if it was day or night. Usually, when the hatch opened, four shadowy *toubob* figures would descend, two with lanterns and whips, the others pushing tubs of food along the aisleways. They would thrust tin pans of the food up onto the filth between the men shackled together. Kunta defiantly clamped his jaws shut, preferring to starve to death—until the aching of his stomach made his hunger almost as terrible as his other pains.

Shortly after feeding time, Kunta's ears picked up a sound vibrating through the planks over his head, as if many feet were dashing about. Then came the sound of some heavy object creaking slowly upward. Kunta sensed a slow, rocking motion. Then terror clawed into his vitals as he realized, "This place is moving. It's taking us away."

Abruptly, the men in the hold went into a frenzy of screaming, banging their heads against the planks, rattling their chains. "Allah," Kunta shrieked into the bedlam, "hear me! Help me!" And when his voice was gone from shouting, his mind screamed out in rage and helplessness, *"Toubob fa!"* ("Kill *toubob!*").

The next time the hatch rasped open, something the *kintango* had once said flashed into his mind: *Warriors must eat well to have great strength.* Weakness for lack of food would not let him kill *toubob.* And so this time when the tin pan was thrust up next to him, his fingers dipped into the thick mush of ground corn boiled with palm oil. He swallowed painfully until he could feel the food like a lump in his belly. Then he vomited—and vomited again.

As the days passed in the hold, vomit and feces gathered on the moaning, shackled men. In the filth, the lice multiplied by the millions until they swarmed all over the hold. Finally, eight naked *toubob* came down through the hatchway cursing loudly. Instead of food they carried long-handled hoes and large tubs. In teams of two they moved along the aisle, thrusting their hoes up onto the shelves and scraping the mess into their tubs. But when they had finished, there was no difference in the choking stench of the hold.

Not long afterward, many *toubob* descended. Kunta guessed that there must be 20 clumping down the hatch steps, some carrying whips and guns, the metal weapons of fire and smoke he had heard about when men spoke of *toubob* in Juffure. A knot of fear grew in Kunta's belly as he heard strange clicking sounds, then heavy rattlings. Suddenly, his shackled right ankle began jerking. He was being released. Why? Then the *toubob* started shouting and lashing with their whips.

One after another, pairs of men, still shackled at the wrists, went thumping off their shelves into the aisles. Kunta's long-unused muscles tightened with pain. He and his shacklemate were shoved and kicked along in the darkness toward the hatchway steps. As he stumbled up onto the deck, the sunlight hit him with a blinding force. Fumbling ahead, he opened his cracked lips, gulping in the salty air. Then he collapsed on the deck with the Wolof shacklemate.

In the light, the *toubob* looked even more wild and sickly pale than below, their long hair in colors of yellow or black or red, some of them even with hair around their mouths and under their chins. Some had ugly scars from knives, or a hand, eye or limb missing, and the backs of many were crisscrossed with deep scars from whips. A lot of the *toubob* were spaced along the rails, holding cutlasses or guns. Turning about, Kunta saw that a high barricade of bamboo extended completely across the width of the huge craft. Showing through its center was the black barrel of a cannon.

For the first time, Kunta observed his Wolof shacklemate in the light. Like himself, the man was crusted with filth, and pus was oozing from where the *LL* shape had been burned into his back. Looking about, Kunta saw more suffering men.

Now they were chained together by their ankle shackles in groups of ten and doused with buckets of sea water. *Toubob* with long-handled brushes then scrubbed the naked men. Kunta cried in agony as the salt water hit him, stinging like fire in his whip cuts, cried out again as the bristles tore the scabs from his back and shoulders. Bleeding from his wounds, Kunta and his shacklemates were herded back to the center of the deck, where they flopped down in huddled terror.

The sudden cries of women brought the chained men jerking upright. About 20 of them came running, naked and unchained, from behind the barricade. With a flooding rage, Kunta perceived all of the *toubob* leering at their nakedness. Then a *toubob* near the rail began pulling out and pushing in some peculiar thing in his hands which made a wheezing music. A second man beat on a drum. Other *toubob* began jumping up and down in short hops, keeping time to the drumbeats and gesturing that the men in chains should jump in the same manner.

"Jump!" shrieked the oldest woman suddenly, in Mandinka. "Jump now to kill *toubob!*" She began jumping up and down, her arms darting in the movements of the warriors' dance. When her meaning sank home, one after another shackled pair of naked men commenced a weak, stumbling hopping, their chains clanking and jangling against the deck. Kunta felt his legs rubbery under him, vaguely hearing the singing of the women. Then he became aware that in their singing the women were saying that the *toubob* took them into the dark corners of the vessel and made use of them. *"Toubob fa!"* they shouted, jumping up and down in a frenzy, while the grinning *toubob* clapped their hands with pleasure.

Chained back down in his place in the stinking hold, Kunta gradually noticed a low murmuring of voices in the darkness. He and his Wolof shacklemate had occasionally exchanged cautious whispers, picking up words in the other's tongue, much as toddling children of the first *kafo* learned their early words. But now that the men had actually seen each other in the daylight, there was a new quality to the whispers, as if there was between them a sense of brotherhood.

As their understanding improved, many questions were asked in the darkness. "How long have we been here?" brought a rash of guesses, until the question finally reached a man who had been able to keep a count of daylights through a small air vent. He said that he had counted 18 days since the great canoe had begun moving. Some asked if there were others in the hold from the same village. One day, Kunta nearly burst with excitement when the Wolof relayed the question, "Is one here from Juffure village?"

"Kunta Kinte!" he whispered breathlessly. He waited tensely during the hour it took for a response to return: "Yes, that was the name. I heard the drums—his village was grieving." Kunta dissolved into sobs, his mind streaming before him pictures of his family weeping and mourning their son, Kunta Kinte, gone forever.

How could the *toubob* on the big canoe be attacked and killed? How many were there? Days of questions and replies sought the answers. In the end the most useful information came from the women's singing as the men danced in their chains on deck. They said about 30 *toubob* remained on the craft, after five dead ones had been sewn into white cloth and thrown into the endless blue water.

Arguments arose as to how to kill the *toubob.* Some wanted to attack the next time they were allowed on deck. Others felt it would be wiser to watch and wait. Bitter disagreements grew in the stinking darkness, until one day the voice of an elderly man rang out: "Hear me! Though we are of different tribes and tongues, we must be together in this place as one village! And we must be as one behind our leader!" Murmurings of approval spread in the hold.

One fierce-looking Wolof led the argument that the *toubob* should be attacked immediately. On deck, everyone had seen this man dancing wildly in his chains while baring his sharply filed teeth at the *toubob,* who clapped for him because they thought he was grinning.

The group that believed in watchful preparation was led by a gloomy, whip-scarred Fula. Kunta had no doubt that the fierce Wolof could have led an army, but he joined in choosing the Fula as leader. Everyone knew that a Fula would spend years, even his entire life, bitterly avenging a serious wrong.

Soon they were herded on deck again, where, in obedience to the

Fula, they attempted to act happy in order to relax the *toubob's* guard.

One day on deck, Kunta stood rooted in astonishment, watching thousands of fish fly over the water like silvery birds, when suddenly he heard an animal-like scream. Whirling, he saw the fierce Wolof snatch a gun from a *toubob.* Swinging it like a club, he sent the *toubob's* brains flying. Then, bellowing in rage, he clubbed the others swarming toward him, until a cutlass flashed and the Wolof's head was lopped off. Then the big black barrel of the cannon exploded with a thunderous roar of heat and smoke just above the shackled men, and they screamed and sprawled on top of each other in terror.

Amid shouts, the *toubob* rushed the shackled men back toward the hatch with their guns and cutlasses. Almost before they realized it, the men found themselves again below, chained in their dark places as the hatch cover slammed down. For a long while, no one dared even to whisper. Bitterly, Kunta wondered why the signal to attack had not been given. From the gradually louder muttering sounds around him, it became evident that many men shared his thoughts. Soon word was passed from the Fula that the attack would come the next time they were all on deck being washed.

But, that night, Kunta heard a new sound from on deck. He guessed that strong winds must be making the great white cloths above flap more than usual. Then there was another sound, as if rain were pelting onto the deck. The big canoe began violently, jerkily rolling, and the men cried out in agony as their shoulders, elbows and buttocks, already festered and bleeding, were ground down on the rough boards beneath.

On the edge of consciousness, Kunta became dimly aware of the sound of water spilling down heavily into the hold. There was a clomping of feet, the sound of something like heavy cloth being dragged across the deck, and the noise of falling water lessened as the openings were covered. But now the heat and stench were trapped entirely within the hold. Gagging, Kunta gasped for breath.

That night, he revived on deck, jerkily breathing fresh sea air. By lantern light he saw *toubob* stumbling up through the open hatchway, slipping in vomit, dragging limp, shackled forms onto the deck and dumping them down near him. The great canoe was still pitching heavily, and the white-haired chief *toubob* had difficulty keeping his balance as he examined the bodies closely. Sometimes then, cursing bitterly, he would bark an order, and other *toubob* would drag a limp form over to the rail and dump it into the ocean.

These had died in the hell below. Kunta envied them.

By dawn, the weather had cleared. Looking dully around him, Kunta saw men lying on deck, many of them convulsing. The chief *toubob* was now moving among the chained men, applying salve and powder to their wounds. He opened the mouths of some of the men and forced down their throats something from a black bottle. When the *toubob* put grease on him, Kunta looked away. He would rather have felt a lash than the pale hands against his skin.

The next days were a twilight of pain and sickness. Lying below deck in his filth, Kunta did not know if they had been in the stinking belly of the *toubob* canoe for several moons, or even as long as a rain—for the man was now dead who had counted the days. Kunta's shacklemate had died, too. The *toubob* came, detached him from Kunta and dragged his stiff body away. Kunta lay limp with fear and shock: *"Toubob fa!"* he screamed into the darkness. But he was too sick and weak to care much about killing anyone anymore.

IT WAS AT FIRST ONLY A FEW of the men in the hold who began to make terrible new cries of pain. Their bowels had begun to drain a mixture of clotted blood and thick, yellow mucus. The *toubob* bringing the food, upon first smelling and glimpsing the putrid discharge, displayed great agitation. Minutes later, the chief *toubob* descended. Despite the camphor bag clamped between his teeth, he was soon gagging. Gesturing sharply, he had the newly sick men taken up through the hatch.

But it was of no use, for the contagion of the bloody flux moved swiftly. Severe pains in the head and back, a roasting fever and a shivering of the body were already in most of the men. When Kunta felt the awful, hot compulsion in his bowels, his cries of pain joined the increasing bedlam in the hold. In delirium he cried out the names of his father and grandfather: "Omoro—Omar the second Caliph, third after Muhammad the Prophet! Kairaba—Kairaba means peace!"

Each day now, the shackled sufferers were dragged up on deck into the fresh air, while *toubob* took down buckets of boiling vinegar and tar to fumigate the hold. Yet every day someone else died and was thrown overboard—sometimes a *toubob.*

One day when Kunta got up into the light and air, he dimly noticed that the great white sheets on the tall poles were drooping. It was hard to see; Kunta's once keen eyes were now gummy with some rheumy, yellowish matter—but the big canoe seemed to be almost motionless on a layer of gold-colored seaweed. The ship had entered the Sargasso Sea and was becalmed.

No more lashings now fell on the men's backs, and they were given more food and water. As much as 100 pounds of flying fish were lured aboard each night with lanterns, and the flesh added to the cornmeal. Still, the time finally came when Kunta could no longer even eat without help. The shreds of muscles in his arms refused to lift his hands for him to claw into the tin food pan. A *toubob* put a hollow tube into his mouth and poured gruel down his gullet.

At last the breeze freshened. Soon the big canoe was again cutting through the water with a foaming sound and, as the days passed, Kunta sensed a kind of excitement among the *toubob.* One morning they seemed particularly elated as they rushed into the hold and helped the crawling, scrambling men up through the hatch. Blinking in the early-morning light, Kunta saw the other *toubob* all wildly laughing, cheering and pointing. Between the scabbed, festering backs of the lice-encrusted men, Kunta kept squinting with his rheumy eyes—and then he was petrified.

Blurry in the distance, there was unmistakably some piece of Allah's earth again.

5. LAND OF TOUBABO DOO

CAPT. THOMAS DAVIES, with Cape Henry, Virginia, now in sight, retired to his cabin and began reviewing the whole voyage, his first as captain after years as a mate on slave ships. It was, moreover, the maiden voyage of his vessel, the *Lord Ligonier.* Built not quite two years before, in colonial New England, she was 68 feet long and 150 tons.

Drawing a document from his desk, he looked over his sailing orders: "We request the taking of only prime, able-bodied, well-formed, healthy, strong Negroes . . . and secondly any other items of cargo such as a lack of slaves may make room for."

Being as candid as possible with himself, the white-haired captain could find no major mistakes that he had made. The storm, the flux, the death of 42 Negroes and several crewmen, he could see but as the will of God. The 98 slaves remaining would bring a huge profit to the ship's owners. His personal salary called for $1200, plus a bonus of £6 for every slave delivered.

He had first sailed the *Lord Ligonier* from Annapolis to Gravesend, England, ballasted with a cargo of rum, which was easily sold. With part of the profits he bought 450 sets of wrist and ankle shackles; six dozen 20-foot lengths of thick chains; two branding irons with the ship's initials; and a plentiful supply of colorful, cheap goods for trading on the coast of Africa.

With additional crewmen, the *Lord Ligonier* sailed for Africa in July 1766. On her way, the ship was prepared to receive slaves. The carpenter raised ventilation openings on the deck and built long plank shelves in the hold. On these, with ruler and paint, he marked the 16-inch width allowed for each slave. The gunner made cartridges for the swivel guns; the mate plaited from strips of rawhide a supply of cat-o'-nine-tails. Sixty-eight days later—a disappointingly slow passage—Davies sighted land, entered the mouth of the Gambia River and paid a tax to the black King of Essau, who ruled the territory. Then he proceeded upriver and anchored off British-owned Fort St. James, which shipped up to 2000 slaves a year.

Before doing anything else, Davies sent men ashore to purchase mangrove thatching to build a barricade deckhouse. One wall would have an opening for mounting a swivel gun in case the slaves tried mutiny at sea. Then he visited some of the other ships in the harbor. Their captains warned him that prices were high—£25 apiece for prime slaves. And the black *slatees* would no longer take trinkets for their help; they demanded money. Captain Davies determined not to pay ransom prices for a quick cargo. He would patiently buy one black at a time, meticulously examining and selecting the individual Negroes who would bring top money in Annapolis.

Afterward he went to inspect some slaves. He bought two good specimens, a young male and female, endured their screaming as one of the new branding irons seared the identifying *LL* between their shoulders. In his log, when finally he put them on the ship, he made the traditional entry for the first male and female: "Adam and Eve on board."

Working with independent dealers, he began to acquire the slaves he sought. But, as the months passed, he increasingly had to turn to dealing with the larger, more expensive slave factories. There were 13 on the Gambia River, usually run by a degraded former ship captain and manned by *slatee* guards. The factories bought—at wholesale prices—entire coffles of slaves captured in village raids.

By the end of May 1767, he still had only 118 slaves. There was space for 200 on board—males in the hold, women and children in the barricade house. But a number of ships, arriving after the *Lord Ligonier,* had already departed with second-rate cargoes of slaves. Word of their quick round trip would travel fast. The captain knew his owners must be wondering what was keeping him so long. Finally, on July 5, having bought 22 more slaves and filled the ship's empty spaces with 1250 elephant's teeth, 3700 pounds of beeswax, 800 pounds of cotton and 32 ounces of gold, Captain Davies set sail. He reached Cape Henry the third week of September.

In his cabin, Davies continued figuring. The 98 slaves still alive should bring at least $600 apiece—a gross of about $58,000, since the children would bring less—and the incidental cargo another $1000. Even after paying off the crew (at $5 a month), sundry expenses and the cost of the ship, his owners would have $36,000 clear profit. He had not done badly for them. They should volunteer him a good bonus beyond what he was owed. A few more voyages and he could comfortably retire—God willing.

THE SMALL SHIP, the *Lord Ligonier,* arrived off the coast of Virginia in September 1767, and entered the strong current of Chesapeake Bay for the four-day journey to its home port of Annapolis. Belowdecks, in a misery of filth, lice and disease, was a cargo of 98 blacks, the weakened remnants of the 140 slaves who had been on board when the ship sailed from Gambia, West Africa.

Down in the stinking darkness, trembling with new fears now that they knew they were approaching the land of the *toubob,* the chained men did not open their mouths. Their silence let them hear more clearly the ship's timbers creaking, the muted *ssss* of the sea against the hull and the dulled clumpings of *toubob* feet on the deck overhead. During the two months and three weeks at sea, the ship's motions had rubbed the men's weight against the rough planking on which they lay until their buttocks and shoulders were ulcerated and seeping blood.

On the fourth day after land was sighted, the blacks were yanked roughly to the deck for a final scrubbing with coarse brushes, then were rubbed with oil until they shone. When the ship finally docked, the weak, sick, fear-numbed black men were driven under steadily cracking whips down the gangway onto the *toubob* earth. The impulse to escape surged wildly in Kunta, but *toubob* whips kept his chained line under tight control.

As they shuffled in single file alongside a gesturing, jeering crowd, he glimpsed finely clothed *toubob* watching the chained blacks with expressions of loathing. He saw incredulously what was surely a she *toubob,* with hair the color of straw. And he saw two black men, unmistakably a Mandinka tribesman and a Serere. They walked behind a *toubob,* their faces expressionless. Kunta's mind reeled: how could blacks docilely follow behind *toubob?*

The men were taken to a large square house of burnt mud with bars set into the few open spaces along the sides. In a large room, the wrists and ankles of Kunta and his mates were locked in thick iron cuffs, which were chained to bolts set in the walls. Terrified, Kunta huddled down on the cold earthen floor and beseeched Allah to save him.

After darkness fell—Kunta could see stars through one of the iron-barred spaces near him—he became more composed, and thoughts began to flicker through his mind like shadows in a dream. Although he did not wish to bring even their memory to this hated place, he could not help but think of his father, Omoro, and his mother, Binta, and his three younger brothers. And then he was sobbing.

It was nearly dawn, Kunta sensed, when there came into his head the sharp voice of his teacher, the *kintango:* "A man is wise to study and learn from the animals." Was this some message from Allah? Kunta was like an animal in a trap. The animals which he had known to escape their traps had not raged within, but quietly conserved their strength until a moment of carelessness gave them the chance to explode in flight. So, too, must Kunta appear to the *toubob* to have given up hope.

Through the small, barred space, Kunta counted six daylights and six nights. Three times each day a strange black man brought food. Kunta forced it down, knowing it would give him strength. Then, after the seventh morning meal, four *toubob* entered. Two stayed just inside the doorway, holding guns and clubs. The others unlocked the iron cuffs. In a chained line of six men, Kunta was shoved out into the bright sunlight.

"Just picked out of the trees! . . . Bright as monkeys!" A shouting man was standing on a low wooden platform, addressing a crowd. Kunta's nose rebelled at the heavy *toubob* stink as he and his mates were jerked through the mass of people. Then Kunta was unchained from the others and pushed toward the platform.

"Prime—young and supple!" The *toubob* was shouting again. Numb with terror. Kunta could scarcely breathe. Other *toubob* were moving in closely around him. With short sticks and whip butts they thrust apart his compressed lips, exposing his clenched teeth. They prodded him all over, on his back, his chest, his genitals. Then they stepped back and, amid the babbling of the shouting man, began to make their own strange cries: "Three hundred dollars!" "Three fifty!"

There were more strange sounds, and then Kunta heard, "Eight hundred fifty!" When no other calls came, the shouting one unhitched Kunta's chain and pulled him toward a *toubob* who had stepped forward. He then saw behind the *toubob* a black one with distinct Wolof-tribe features. *My brother, you come from my country.* . . . But the black one seemed not even to notice Kunta. He pulled hard on the chain so that Kunta came stumbling after him, and they began moving through the crowd. They stopped at a kind of box on wheels behind a large animal—the first horse Kunta had ever seen. The black one grabbed Kunta about the hips and boosted him onto the floor of the box.

Kunta heard the free end of his chain click into something at the front of the box. The black one and the *toubob* climbed up onto a seat, and the horse began pulling the box away, away from the big water which, far off, touched the land where Kunta had been born.

As the box creaked along, Kunta raised himself up and could see what he guessed were *toubob* fields. In one he recognized stalks of corn, the ears already picked; in another, he could distinguish the figures of black workers with a *toubob* standing over them. They passed a line of about 20 black men, chained together by wrist cuffs and guarded by a *toubob* on a horse.

At dusk, the rolling box turned off onto a small road and drew up before a large white house. Kunta saw several black people there, and hope surged in him when the *toubob* walked off toward the house. Would these black ones free him now? But they did nothing, and he wondered with a burst of rage what kind of blacks these were who acted as the goats of the *toubob.*

Kunta slept on the ground chained to a stake. In the morning, he had barely time to make his dawn prayer to Allah, bowing to the east, before they were on the road again. The sights and sounds were similar to those of the previous day. Twice more, always distant from the road, he saw large white *toubob* houses; nearby were mud and log huts where Kunta guessed the blacks lived.

After the sun set on the third day, the box turned off the main road. Through the moonlit darkness, Kunta could see the whiteness of another big house. Soon the box came to a stop. The *toubob* got down and went into the house. The box creaked on toward some small huts and stopped again. Kunta heard the click of the thing which had held his chain. The black one got down, came to the edge of the box and with one powerful arm levered Kunta up over the side to the ground.

In that instant the smaller Kunta exploded upward, his hands clamping about the black one's throat like the jaws of a hyena. The black one gave a hoarse sound; then he was pounding and clawing at Kunta's face and arms. Kunta's hands clamped tighter still until the man stumbled backward and went limp.

Springing up, Kunta fled wildly toward where he could see, in the moonlight, a distant forest. He kept low, his flailing legs crashing through frosted cornstalks. His long-unused muscles screamed with pain, but the cold, rushing air felt good, and he grunted with the pleasure of being free again. He reached the forest and plunged in, stumbling through brambles and vines, deeper and deeper, until suddenly he burst upon low brush. He saw with a shock that he had come to another wide field and another white house.

He ran back into the woods, his bare feet cut and bleeding. Then he crawled into deep undergrowth and passed the night there. As dawn came he kneeled and, facing the east, prayed to Allah.

Kunta first heard the deep baying of the dogs at a distance. The sound became louder and behind the baying he detected the shouting of men. Wildly, he went plunging through the brambles. But when he heard a *toubob* gun, he panicked and fell in the tangled briers.

Two dogs came crashing through the brush, snarling and biting at him. He tried to fight them off with his hands, at the same time sliding away from them like a crab. He heard men yelling from the edge of the thicket. Again the gun fired; the growling dogs backed off.

Several men with knives and clubs rushed toward him. Kunta recognized the black one whom he had choked. He looked murderous. Behind him were *toubob,* their faces reddish and sweating from exertion. The black one came forward, uncoiling a rope. A heavy blow to Kunta's head sent him into numbing shock. His arms were bound to his sides, and he was roughly hauled by a rope out of the forest and across a field to a tree. There the rope was thrown over a limb, and the black one pulled on it until Kunta's feet barely touched the ground. A *toubob* whip lashed against his back. He writhed under the pain, refusing to cry out, but each stroke felt as if it were tearing him in half. He began screaming, the lashing went on—and he passed out.

When consciousness returned, Kunta found himself spread-eagled, chained by his ankles and wrists to four stout poles in the corners of a small hut. The slightest movement brought excruciating pain, so he lay completely still, his face wet with sweat, his breath coming in gasps. He berated himself for not waiting longer—as the wise animal would have waited. He had failed because he had tried to escape too soon.

6. THE LOST TRIBE

ON THE FIFTH MORNING, shortly after the wakeup horn had blown, the black one entered carrying two thick iron cuffs connected by a short chain. Bending down, he fastened the cuffs around Kunta's ankles. Only then did he unfasten Kunta's other chains. Roughly jerking him to his feet, he began jabbing at Kunta's chest with his finger, uttering strange sounds: "You—Toby!" Kunta did not understand. He stared at him dumbly.

The black one tapped on his own chest. "I Samson!" he exclaimed. His finger poked at Kunta. "You To-by! Massa say you name Toby!"

His meaning slowly registered on Kunta, and he felt a flooding rage. He wanted to shout at the black one, "I am Kunta Kinte, the first son of Omoro, who is the son of the holy man Kairaba Kunta Kinte!"

The black one led Kunta outside to a large tin bucket that held water for him to wash in. Then he threw him some *toubob* garments to cover his chest and legs, and a hat of yellowish straw. Following the man called Samson, Kunta was taken on a quick tour of his surroundings. The blacks lived in ten huts, arranged in two rows, made of logs and chinked with a reddish mud.

In one of them he was given food by an old woman. Then Samson motioned with his head toward the distant fields. He walked off and Kunta followed, hobbling in his iron shackles. As they approached, he could see black men slashing down cornstalks while the women and younger men gathered them up.

In the field, a *toubob* rode up on his big horse and briefly exchanged words with Samson, who picked up a long, stout knife and slashed down about a dozen stalks. Turning about, he made motions for Kunta to pick them up. The *toubob* jerked his horse closer, his whip cocked. Enraged at his helplessness, Kunta began gathering the stalks.

In the days that followed, Kunta forced himself to do what was wanted of him. But behind his blank expression he missed nothing. He learned that he was in a place called Spotsylvania County, Virginia. The *toubob* who had brought him to this place was called "massa" by the black ones. In the big white house where the massa lived, there was a she *toubob* called "missis." Kunta had seen her once at a distance, a bony creature the color of a toad's underbelly. In the fields, Kunta learned, there was "corn," and when all the stalks had been cut and piled they then picked large round things the blacks called "punkins." They were put on a "wagon" and taken to a "barn."

But the thing which most interested and mystified him was the attitude of the other blacks. In the evenings, Kunta would sit down just inside the doorway of his hut with his legs stuck out to reduce the pain of the cuffs, while the other adults quietly seated themselves on wooden stools around a fire before the old cooking woman's hut. The sight filled him with a melancholy memory of the night fires in Juffure.

Usually the woman who cooked at the big house would speak first. She mimicked things said by the massa and missis, and Kunta heard the others all but choking to suppress their laughter lest it carry across to the big white house.

But then the laughter would subside, and the blacks simply talked among themselves. Kunta heard the helpless, haunted tone of some and the bitter anger of others, even when he could not know what they were saying. Finally the talking would die away as one of the women began singing and all joined in. Kunta did not understand the words, but he sensed deep sadness in the melodies.

They were heathen, pagan blacks—they even ate the flesh of the filthy swine—yet they did some things which were unmistakably African, and Kunta could tell that they were totally unaware of it themselves. All his life he had heard in Juffure the same sounds of spontaneous exclamations, punctuated with the same gestures and facial expressions. The way they moved their bodies was identical, and the way they laughed when they were together.

How had these people come to be in this place? Kunta could not fathom what had happened to them to so destroy their minds that they acted resigned, grinning at the massa and the "oberseer."

Perhaps it was because they had never known a home village in Africa. They had been born in this place. They were as a lost tribe.

Kunta reflected on all that he saw and heard and could neither understand nor accept it. And each night before sleep came he swore to his forefathers that he would escape; that he would die before he became like these black ones here.

Kunta's left ankle finally became so infected from the chafing of the iron that the overseer had the cuffs removed. With his iron bonds gone and unable to abide waiting, Kunta stole away that night, but Samson caught him only a short distance from his hut.

Kunta was pummeled and kicked, but not whipped or shackled. Soon he fled again after what the blacks called "snow" had fallen from the sky. The overseer caught up with him on one of the big farm horses by following the marks he made in the filmy whiteness. This time he was whipped and chained down. Yet he knew that as soon as the opportunity came, he would try again.

The moons went by, the fields were plowed, and spring planting began with seeds of various kinds, mostly of corn and something called "cotton." Kunta was unshackled, and he did what he was ordered to do, biding his time, chopping away weeds from the plants. As the harvesting began, Kunta noticed that wagons appeared more and more frequently on the distant roads, carrying the cotton to market. It came to him: the way to escape was to hide in a wagon.

His head burst with working out the details of the plan. He ruled out the cotton wagons of the farm on which he worked; someone was always watching. It must be one of the wagons moving along the main road.

One night, on the pretext of going to the outhouse, he studied the road. The flickering light of lanterns inching along told him that the wagons traveled in darkness as well as daylight. Another night he was able to kill a rabbit with a rock; he dried it as he had learned to do in Juffure. Then he honed to sharpness an old, rusty knife blade he had found and carved a wooden handle for it. He also made a *safo* charm. It had a cock's feather to attract the spirits, a horse's hair for strength and a bird's wishbone for success, all sewed inside a square of burlap.

One evening he pushed into a pocket the dried pieces of rabbit and tied the *safo* tightly about his upper right arm. Listening tensely through his hut's door, he heard the familiar night routine of the other blacks. Finally their mournful singing ended. When he was sure they were asleep, Kunta grasped his homemade knife and slipped out.

Seeing and sensing no one about, he bent low and began running. Where the farm road met the big road he huddled down into a thick growth of brush. Soon he heard a wagon. It seemed forever before its flickering light even came into view, but finally it was directly opposite Kunta. Two figures sat in front, but there was no rear lookout. Teeth clenched, Kunta burst from the brush, hunkered down behind the squeaking wagon and clawed over the tailboard.

The night was his friend, and he burrowed into the cotton and rode undetected. But when dawn touched the sky he left the wagon and quickly disappeared into the underbrush.

The dew that sprinkled him felt good, and he swung his knife as if it were weightless, working deep into what he assured himself was a large area of forest. In the afternoon he chewed a piece of the dried rabbit

with water. He plunged on until after sundown, when he made a bed of leaves and grass.

In the morning, he continued on. He did not know where he was or where he was going—only that he must escape. If he followed the way to where the sun rose, it should lead him back, in time, to the big canoe. And then? Kunta felt a growing uncertainty and fright. He prayed often to Allah and fingered his *safo.*

For four days Kunta traveled through the forest, hearing nothing but toads and birds and insects. But on the morning of the fifth day he was awakened by the sound he feared most—the baying of dogs. He sprang up and began running—then realized he had forgotten his knife. Dashing back, he searched among the vines and leaves, but could not find it. Steadily the baying came closer. He found a rock about the size of his fist and ran wildly, tripping, falling. The bloodhounds cornered him early the next morning. Too exhausted to run farther, he waited, with his back against a tree. His left hand clutched a stout branch, and his right was like a claw about the rock. The dogs stayed out of range of his makeshift club, baying and slavering, until two *toubob* appeared on horses. Kunta had never seen them before. They were professional slave catchers.

The older of the two men dismounted and walked toward him, a club in one hand, a whip in the other. As the *toubob* came closer, Kunta hurled the rock. He heard the *toubob* shout and saw blood running down his head.

Now both men approached him with guns and clubs. He knew from their faces that he would die and he did not care. They clubbed him nearly senseless, but still he writhed and shrieked as they tore his clothes off and roped him to a tree.

Then the bleeding *toubob* halted abruptly. A look came on his face, almost a smile, and he spoke briefly to the younger one, who grinned and nodded. The younger one went back to his horse, unlashed an ax from the saddle and gave it to his companion.

The bleeding one stood before Kunta. He pointed to Kunta's testicles, then to the hunting knife in his belt. He pointed to Kunta's foot, and then to the ax in his hand.

Kunta understood. He was being given a choice: his foot or his testicles. Something deep in his marrow shouted that a man, to be a man, must have sons. His hands flew down to cover his genitals.

The *toubob* were grinning. One of them pushed a log under Kunta's right foot, and the other tied the foot to the tree so tightly that Kunta could not free it. Then the bleeding *toubob* picked up the ax.

Kunta screamed and thrashed. The ax whipped up, then down, and severed the front half of his foot. As the blood spurted out, Kunta's body went limp.

7. A WOMAN NAMED BELL

WHEN HE REGAINED CONSCIOUSNESS, he was in some new place—a hut. He was tied down by the wrists and ankles, with his right foot propped against something soft.

A tall *toubob* came in carrying a small black bag. Kunta had never seen this one before. The *toubob* bent down alongside Kunta and did something that brought such spasms of pain that Kunta shrieked like a woman. "Bell!" the man called out, and a short, powerfully built black woman came inside bringing water in a tin container. The *toubob* took something from his black bag and stirred it into the water. The black woman kneeled and tilted the cup for Kunta to drink. It had a strange taste, and soon Kunta drifted into deep sleep.

When he awoke he knew that he was very ill. His whole right side felt numb, his lips were parched from fever, and his sweat had a sick smell. Involuntarily, he made an effort to flex his toes; it brought a blinding pain. The door opened, and the black woman came in again. Squatting down, she pressed a damp, cooling cloth against his forehead.

On her next visit she tried to get him to eat. He was even thinner now than he was the week before when Bell, serving the noon meal, was hurriedly called to help lift from a wagon the bloody heap. The sheriff had ordered the slave catchers to deliver it to Dr. William Waller, the brother of Kunta's owner. The doctor, who was Bell's massa, had been livid when he learned of the maiming.

Bell covered Kunta's bare chest with an acrid, steaming poultice of boiled elderberry leaves mixed with sulfur. Then she packed wet cloths over the poultice and covered Kunta with quilts.

When Kunta next awakened, he realized that his fever had broken. He wondered where the woman had learned what she had done. It was like the medicines of his mother, Binta, the herbs of Allah's earth passed down from the ancestors. His pain became less of an agony now, except for the tall *toubob's* daily treatment of his foot. One day Kunta was untied from the stakes, and he managed to prop himself on his elbows. He spent hours staring at the bandages over his foot stump. For most of his 18 rains he had run and climbed anywhere he wanted to go. It seemed monstrous that a *toubob* would chop his foot off.

He took out his rage and his humiliation on the black woman when she came in to feed him, snarling in Mandinka and banging down the tin cup after he drank. Afterward he lay, even more furious, reflecting that the woman's eyes had seemed to warm upon his show of anger.

After three weeks the *toubob* took off the bandages. Kunta almost screamed as he saw the swollen half of his foot covered with a thick, brownish scab. The *toubob* sprinkled something over it, bandaged it and left. Three days later he returned with two stout sticks with forked tops—Kunta had seen injured people walk with these in Juffure.

When the *toubob* had gone, Kunta painfully pulled himself upright and tried the sticks. He managed a few awkward, forward swings of his body. When Bell brought his breakfast the next morning, his glance caught the quick pleasure on her face at the marks the sticks had made on the dirt floor. Kunta glowered at her. He refused to touch the food until she left. But then he ate it hungrily, wanting its strength. Within a few days, he was hobbling freely about the hut.

In the evening on this farm the black ones gathered at the last hut in the row. It was occupied by a *sasso borro*—a man of about 50 rains who had brown skin, indicating that his father had been white. Listening from within his own doorway, Kunta could hear the brown one talking. Sometimes the others burst into laughter. At intervals, they barraged him with questions. Who was he, Kunta wondered.

One day as Kunta passed on his crutches, the brown one beckoned him to take a stool by his hut. Kunta sat down opposite the man.

"I been hearin' 'bout you so mad," the brown one said. "You lucky dey ain't *kilt* you! Law say anybody catch you escapin' can kill you; law say cut your ear off if white folks say you lied. Law 'gainst teachin' any nigger to read or write; law 'gainst nigger beatin' any drums—any of dat African stuff. . . ."

Somehow it did not matter that Kunta could not understand. An exhilaration gripped him that someone actually was talking to him directly. And the man simply loved to talk. If he had lived in Africa, Kunta thought, he would be a wandering *griot,* one who told the history of ancient kings and family clans.

Late that night, sleepless, his mind tumbling with inner conflicts, Kunta recalled something his father had once said when he had refused to let go of a mango so that his brother Lamin could have a bite. "When you clench your fist," said Omoro, "no man can put anything in your hand." Yet he also knew that his father would not want him to become like the other black people.

"Looka here!" the brown one said abruptly one afternoon. "You—you Toby!" Kunta's face flushed with anger. "Kunta Kinte!" he blurted aloud, astonished at himself. It was the first utterance to anyone in the more than a year since he had been in the *toubob* land.

The brown one frowned his disapproval. "You is *Toby!* You got to forgit dat African stuff! Make white folks mad and scare niggers." He looked around the room and picked up an oddly shaped wooden thing with a slender black neck. "Fiddle!" he exclaimed.

Kunta decided to repeat the sound. "Fiddle . . ." he said tentatively.

The brown one began pointing at other objects—"Bucket . . . chair . . . cornshucks"—and Kunta repeated the sounds. After they had gone through more than a score of words, the brown one grunted: "You ain't as dumb as you looks."

The lessons continued. In time Kunta was able not only to understand, but to make himself understood to the brown one, who wished to be called "fiddler."

One day, special shoes were brought to Kunta by a black man called Gideon, who made horse collars and shod the black people. One shoe's front half was stuffed with cotton. Kunta put them on. He felt stinging sensations in his right half-foot as he gingerly walked around his hut, but finally he put his full weight on it and did not feel undue pain. He had thought he would always have to walk with crutches.

That same week the fiddler heard from Luther, the black driver, that the *toubob* doctor now owned Kunta. He carefully explained the news to Kunta. "Luther say the massa got a deed to you from his brother who had you at first. Niggers here claim he a good massa," the fiddler continued, "an' I seen worse. But ain't none of 'em no good."

At about this time, Kunta began keeping a calendar by dropping pebbles into a gourd. He guessed he had spent 12 moons on the first *toubob* farm, so he dropped 12 pebbles into the gourd. Then he dropped in six more, making a total of 18 moons that he had been in the land of the *toubob.* Adding the 18 moons to his 17 rains when he was taken from Juffure, Kunta figured that he was now in his 19th rain.

Soon afterward, Kunta was told by an old black man who worked a small vegetable garden, "Massa put you to workin' with me." He showed Kunta how to hoe the weeds and pick off tomato worms and potato bugs. When the feeble old gardener became ill, Kunta tilled the garden alone.

The season of snow came, and the other blacks were caught up in an increasing excitement about some day called "Christmas." It had something to do with singing, dancing and eating. Kunta overheard talk that Christmas also involved the Allah of the *toubob* and the black ones. It made him ill at ease, and during the days of festivities he did not leave his hut even to visit the fiddler.

Spring came for Kunta, and then summer, in a sweating blur of days as he struggled to plow, plant and cultivate the garden, and supply vegetables to Bell, who was cook for the big house. At night he was too tired to do more than throw himself down on his cornshuck mattress, his clothes wet with sweat, and sleep. Sometimes he still thought of escape, but his impulse to flee was always tempered by the terrible memories of what had happened to him.

When the harvest was in and the fall chores were begun, there was talk of Christmas again. This Christmas, Kunta felt, Allah would have no objection to his merely observing the activities. But the Muslim Kunta was deeply offended when he watched the preparation of liquor from fermented apples. He thought it sickening when the young black ones amused themselves by holding dried hog bladders on sticks close to the fire until they burst. And he was particularly repulsed when Bell supervised the cooking of a large, black iron potful of hogs' jowls and black-eyed peas for the "New Years" of "Sebenteen Sebenty."

"Hog jowl an' peas is good luck!" the fiddler shouted at him, his mouth full. Kunta was disgusted. Sitting on his stool in his hut, he worried that he might find himself easing into an acceptance of the ways of the other blacks. Yet he wanted to know them better—the fiddler and the old gardener and the cook Bell.

One day, on an impulse, Kunta told Bell that she looked like a Mandinka. He meant it in a complimentary way, and he was astonished by her irate outburst: "What fool stuff you talkin' 'bout? Don' know how come white folks keep on emptyin' out boatloads of you black African niggers!"

Bell remained tight-lipped for days afterward. But one morning in March 1770, she came rushing out to the garden filled with excitement. "Sheriff jes' rid off! He tol' massa been some big fightin' up nawth somewhere called Boston! Massa sho' upset." Later Luther, the buggy driver, brought more information. "Dem Boston peoples got so mad at dat king 'crost the big water dey marched on his soldiers. Dem soldiers start shootin', an' first one kilt was a nigger name of Crispus Attucks! Dey callin' it de 'Boston Massacre.'"

From then on Luther brought regular news from slaves, stable hands and other drivers he talked to about the trouble with England. And scarcely a day passed when the field hands did not hear from an adjoining plantation, or a slave passing on a mule, a rising, lingering, singsong, "Yooo-hooo-ah-hoo! Don'tcha hear me callin' youuuu?" Then the nearest field hand would go running to pick up the latest report and would rush back to tell the others.

News of what was happening "up nawth" continued to come in fragments across the changing seasons. As Kunta dropped pebble after pebble into his gourd calendar, he tried to understand it all. It became increasingly clear to him that the *toubob* folks were moving toward a crisis with the *toubob* king. Kunta was especially interested in the thing called "freedom." As best he could find out from the fiddler, it meant having no massa, doing as one wanted and going wherever one pleased. But why would the white folks talk about freedom, he wondered.

The biggest excitement came with the news late in 1775 that Lord Dunmore, the Royal Governor of Virginia, had proclaimed freedom for slaves who would serve on his fleet of ships and help the *toubob* king. Not long afterward, Massa Waller called Bell to the living room. Twice he read slowly an item in the Virginia *Gazette.* He then ordered Bell to "read" it to the slaves, telling them what it meant. It said that the Virginia House of Burgesses had decreed ". . . death without benefit of clergy for all Negro or other slaves conspiring to rebel."

"What do it mean?" a field hand asked.

"It mean," the fiddler said dryly, "uprise, an' white folks won't call no preacher when they kills you."

The next summer there was more excitement when Luther returned from the county seat with the news that "all the white folks is carryin' on, hollerin' an' laughin' 'bout some Declaration of Independence."

The old gardener shook his head. "Ain't nothin' neither way for niggers to holler 'bout. England or here, dey's white folks."

In 1778 Bell brought the news that slaves were being promised their freedom if they would join the army as fifers or pioneers. Someone asked what "pioneers" meant. The fiddler replied, "It mean git stuck up front an' git kilt!" And when Bell reported later that two states—South Carolina and Georgia—would not let slaves enlist, the fiddler had a quick retort: "Dat's the only thing good I ever heard 'bout neither one of dem!"

In May 1781 came the astounding story that redcoats on horses had ruined Massa Thomas Jefferson's plantation. Then Luther reported that Massa George Washington's army was coming to save Virginia—"an' niggers aplenty is in it!" That October, the army attacked England's General Cornwallis at Yorktown, and soon came the news that set Slave Row shouting: Cornwallis had surrendered.

"War am ober! The freedom am won!" Bell told everybody. "Massa say gon' be peace now."

"Ain't gon' be no peace!" the fiddler said in his sour way. "Jes' watch what I tell you—it's gon' be worse'n it was—for niggers."

Shortly after the war ended, Luther helped a slave girl run away. He was found out and sold at auction. Kunta took Luther's place as buggy driver, and the new job vastly broadened his world. Taking Dr. Waller on his rounds, he visited plantations all over the countryside, he saw poor whites, he came into the nearby towns.

In the back yard of one big house he saw a very black woman, who appeared to be of the Wolof tribe. Both of her large breasts were hanging out, a *toubob* infant sucking at one, a black infant sucking at the other. When Kunta later described the sight, the old gardener said, "Ain't hardly a massa in Virginia ain't sucked a black mammy, or least was raised by one."

Speaking to Bell and the fiddler and the old gardener about such things, Kunta was astonished to learn that many white young'uns and black young'uns grew up together and became very attached to each other. The old gardener said that on his second plantation a *toubob* and black boy grew up together until finally the *toubob* young massa took the black one off with him to a William and Mary College.

"He say heap of times dey take dey niggers wid 'em to classes, den dey argue later on whose nigger learnt de most. Dat nigger we knowed couldn't jes' read an' write, he could figger, too, an' 'cite dem poems an' stuff dey has at colleges."

"Lucky if he ain't dead," the fiddler said. " 'Cause white folks is quick to 'spicion a nigger like dat be de first to hatch a uprisin' or revolt. Don't pay to know too much."

Sometimes Massa Waller invited a friend to ride with him, and then Kunta's rigid back belied that he heard every word. They talked as if he were not there. Whites seldom shared a buggy ride without expressing regional fears of slave conspiracies and revolts. "We should never have let them bear arms against white men during the war. Now we witness the result!"

Massa Waller went on to say that he had read that more than 200 slave outbreaks and revolts had occurred since the first slave ships came. "But beyond that," he added, "I've seen white deaths that, well, I'll not go into details—I'll just say I've thought them suspicious."

Kunta, in fact, knew as much, or more, of these matters. Black men often met secretly. Right in this county he had heard of black ones who had vowed to kill their massa or missis. He had knowledge of hidden muskets and had overheard whisperings of intended revolts.

Kunta's most consistent source of information, especially from faraway places, was when the massa happened to be in the Spotsylvania County Seat as a mail coach came whirling in. Minutes after the mail sacks and bundles of the Virginia *Gazette* had been dropped off, scores of massas, shopkeepers and other *toubob* men were gathered in clusters, talking and exclaiming, and usually Kunta was within hearing.

His ears filled with the *toubob* folks' fury and dismay at the increasing number of "Quakers" who, according to the *Gazette,* had been encouraging black ones to escape, and more recently had begun aiding, hiding and conducting such runaways to freedom in the north.

Returning home, Kunta told what he had seen and heard, with all of Slave Row gathered at the fiddler's cabin listening. Bell added that she had just overheard Massa Waller and some dinner guests bitterly discussing the news that slavery had recently been abolished in a northern state called "Massachusetts," and reports that other states near there would do the same. "What ''bolished' mean?" a field hand asked.

The old gardener replied, "It mean all us niggers gon' be free, one dese days!"

8. MORTAR AND PESTLE

IN THE SPRING OF 1788, Kunta WAS 38 rains of age. In Africa, he thought, he would have been married and have had three or four sons by this time. But the bride's proper age should be 14 to 16 rains, as in Juffure. He had not seen one black female of this age in the *toubob* land whom he had not considered preposterously giggly and silly.

In fact, the only woman he knew well at all was Bell, who was probably beyond 40 rains. She was also disrespectful of men, and she talked too much. But he remembered how, when he had lain near death, Bell had nursed and fed him, cleaned him when he soiled himself and broken his fever. And she did cook endless good things, grinding her corn by hand, although her stone mortar and pestle obviously did not grind as well as those carved from hard wood by the people of Juffure.

For days Kunta kept to himself, turning everything over in his mind. One evening when the horses were fed, he picked up an old, discarded hickory block, took it to his hut and began carving. He saw in his mind the mortar and pestle which Omoro had made, and which his mother had worn slick with grinding.

Whenever he had free time, he sat in his cabin, chopping carefully around the hickory block with a hatchet, making the rough shape of a mortar. Then he began to carve with a knife. Once finished with the block, he found a seasoned hickory limb, the thickness of his arm, from which he soon made a pestle, which fit snugly against the mortar's bottom. He smoothed the upper part of the handle, scraping it first with a file, next with a knife and finally with a piece of glass.

After the task was done, he took the mortar and pestle to Bell's kitchen door and set them down on the steps outside. Catching the thumping sound, Bell turned and saw Kunta limping away. She examined the painstaking carving and was deeply moved. It was the first time in her life that a man had made something for her with his own hands. Indeed, she was not even sure it was meant for her.

When Kunta returned in the afternoon, Bell blurted out, "What dat?" and gestured toward his gift.

In deep embarrassment, Kunta said, almost angrily, "For you to grind cawn wid."

For the next two weeks, beyond exchanging greetings, neither of them said anything. Then one day Bell gave Kunta a round cake of cornbread whose meal he guessed she had made with the mortar. Grunting, he took the bread back to his hut.

After that they saw each other oftener, and though Bell usually did all the talking, Kunta was drawn closer to her. The next summer he accompanied her and the other blacks to the annual Sunday camp meeting. Although he found the "O Lawd" religion repugnant, he recognized in the others' fervor many of the emotions of festivals back in Juffure. On the way home, with Kunta driving, the black ones began to sing: "Sometime I feels like a motherless chile . . . a long ways from home . . . a long ways from home—"

Kunta thought about the times when he had been driving the massa somewhere along a lonely road, and suddenly a sound would rise loudly; it would be some black one somewhere alone in the fields or the woods, who had opened his mouth and poured from his soul a single, echoing holler. The singing of the black ones, he thought, like his own silence, was a reflection of a terrible yearning.

One morning in August 1789, Bell invited Kunta to eat dinner with her in her cabin. He said nothing. But after work he scrubbed himself hard, using a rough cloth and a bar of brown lye soap. As he carefully put on his clothes he found himself singing softly a song from his village, "Mandumbe, your long neck is very beautiful . . ." Bell did not have a long neck, but it didn't seem to matter.

Bell's cabin was the nearest one on Slave Row to the big house. The room that he entered when Bell opened the door had a feeling of coziness, with its wall of mud-chinked oak logs and a chimney of handmade bricks. There were two windows and two rooms, one of them curtained off. On a table in the center of the main room there was a jar filled with flowers from Bell's garden. Over the fire, Bell heated some chicken and dumplings which she knew Kunta loved.

When Bell again asked Kunta to eat dinner, she cooked things which Kunta had told her also grew in the Gambia—black-eyed peas, and a stew made with peanuts, and yams baked with butter. As she ground up meal for hoecakes with the mortar and pestle he had given her, Kunta could envision her beating the breakfast grain in Juffure.

One evening, when he again came to dinner, Kunta presented Bell with a mat he had plaited from bulrushes with a bold Mandinka design in the center. "Ain't nobody gon' put dey feets on dat mat!" Bell exclaimed. She took it into her bedroom and soon came back. "Dese was to be fo' yo' Christmas, but I make you somethin' else. . . ."

Kunta took the gift. One of the finely knitted woolen socks had a half-foot, with the front part a soft woolen cushion. Neither he nor Bell seemed to know what to say. A strange feeling swept over Kunta; her hand sought out his. And for the first time in his 39 rains, a woman filled his arms.

With Massa Waller's permission, Kunta and Bell "jumped de broom" into slave matrimony on Christmas Eve, 1789. In the simple ceremony in Bell's cabin, with all of the people of Slave Row gathered, they locked arms and solemnly jumped together over a broomstick lying in the middle of the floor. That was all there was to it.

Afterward there was feasting and cheer. Kunta noticed uneasily that Bell was enjoying the wine and brandy which the massa had sent as his gift. Once he overheard her confiding to a woman friend, "Sister Mandy, been had my eye on 'im ten years!" He was mortified.

But Kunta got over that. And in the spring of 1790, when Bell announced that she was pregnant, he was overjoyed. In his mind he could see a small face—a manchild face—peering from a bundle on her back.

The baby came in September. Massa Waller was in the cabin with Bell for more than two hours. Kunta squatted just outside, hearing Bell's anguished moans rise into screams that ripped the quiet of Slave Row before there came an infant's sharp cries. Then Massa Waller emerged. "She had a hard time," he said. "But she'll be fine. You can go in now and see your baby girl."

Kunta's heart sank. A girl. But he limped through the doorway. Bell lay quietly, her drawn face managing a weak smile. Kunta kissed her, and for a long while he stared into the black infant's face. She definitely looked Mandinka. He thought to himself that he could not disappear for seven days, as a new father would in Juffure, to think of a meaningful name for the child; he must decide on one right away.

That night, as he walked the paths where he had first courted Bell,

he remembered Bell telling of her greatest grief. Before she was 20 she had been married. But her husband had been killed in an escape attempt, leaving her with two babies. Suspicious of her, her massa had sold Bell away—without the children. "Two li'l gals I ain't never seed since," Bell had said. "Ain't got no dream of where dey is even if dey's livin' or dead!"

Thinking of this, Kunta chose a name. In Mandinka it meant, "You stay here." He did not tell Bell the name, for by the tradition of his tribe, the baby must be the first ever to hear its name spoken.

The next night, over Bell's protests, Kunta carried his firstborn, snugly wrapped in a blanket, out into the crisp fall air. A short distance from Slave Row, he raised the baby up and whispered three times into her right ear: *"Ee to mu Kizzy leh."* ("Your name is Kizzy.") Lifting a corner of the blanket, he bared the small black face to the moon and stars and spoke aloud the words that once, in a village in Gambia, had been spoken to him: "Behold—the only thing greater than yourself!"

Bell was indignant when she heard the name. "Kizzy? Ain't nobody never heared of dat name! Ain't gon' do nothin' but stir up trouble." But Kunta explained its meaning, and she relented. The next day it was entered in Massa Waller's big black Bible: "Kizzy Waller, born September 12, 1790."

Kizzy was a bright and lively child; and as the years passed, Kunta began teaching her words in Mandinka. *"Fā!"* Kunta would say, pointing to himself, and was thrilled when the child finally repeated the word. As Kizzy grew, he taught her more involved words—his name, Kunta Kinte, and Kamby Bolongo (which was Mandinka for the Gambia River), and Juffure. And he told her about his father, Omoro, and his brothers, and of the Kinte clan as far back as the days of old Mali. Bell sometimes objected; such things would make trouble with the massa, but Kunta insisted.

Her father's gourd of pebbles had a fascination for Kizzy. Bell told her, "Don't never mess wid dem rocks," but Kunta was pleased at the child's interest. Now, each morning after a new moon, he would let her drop the pebble into the gourd.

He told Kizzy of how he had been captured and how he had been brought to this white folks' land. He would picture for her the village of Juffure. He told her story after story, drawing on long-forgotten incidents. She learned fast; she remembered well. Kunta was deeply pleased. "You will have children," he said. "They must know from you where they come from."

THE WORLD WAS CHANGING. When Kizzy was only three the cotton gin was invented, and by the time she was ten it was altering age-old patterns throughout the land.

By 1802, the gin had made large cotton plantations in the deep south more and more profitable. Slave traders roamed the roads inquiring of every owner if he had any slaves for sale, and coffles of slaves streamed south toward the black lands of Mississippi and Alabama. Bell reported to Slave Row that the massa said he would never sell any slave—unless that slave broke one of his rules. Kunta remembered Luther, the previous buggy driver. Now that he had Bell and Kizzy to live for, he did everything he could to stay out of trouble.

And yet in one year—1806, when Kizzy was 16—more than 20,000 blacks had been brought into just two states, Georgia and South Carolina. Slaves were selling for unheard of prices. Even a baby a few weeks old was worth $200.

And one morning in that year, the county sheriff visited Massa Waller. Bell, who was sent from the kitchen while the sheriff spoke to the massa, knew instinctively that something was wrong, and that it somehow involved her. Just before lunchtime, Massa Waller called her in.

His voice was strained and angry as he told Bell the sheriff's news. A young field hand had been captured after running away. Under beating, he had confessed that he had been helped by Kizzy. "You know my rules," he told Bell. "She will have to be sold." Bell fled screaming from the house to her cabin.

When Kunta returned from an errand in the buggy, Massa Waller led him into a small room in the big house. He told him what he had told Bell.

Kunta went to his cabin numbly. He could not really comprehend what the massa has said. His Kizzy—sold away? It was inconceivable. At the sight of Kunta, Bell began screaming. "Ain't gon' take my baby! Sell he, not my baby!" The truth sank in, and all the bitterness that had ever been in Kunta boiled in him anew, all that he had ever felt of *toubob,* all that he had never ceased to feel in this cruel land.

The sheriff returned in the middle of the afternoon with a slave trader. The trader went inside the house and emerged holding a chain attached to cuffs around the wrists of a weeping Kizzy. Bell charged from her cabin. "You done dis?" she shouted at Kizzy. Kizzy's face was an agony. It was plain that she had helped the black escape.

"Oh, Lawd Gawd, have mercy, massa!" Bell screamed. "She ain't meant to! She ain't! Please, massa, please! *Please!*"

Massa Waller spoke tersely: "Wrong is wrong. You know my rules. I have already sold her." He nodded to the slave trader who started to pull Kizzy toward his cart. Then Kunta sprang to his daughter, seizing her about the waist, hugging her as if he would crush her. "Save me, *Fā!*" she cried.

The sheriff's pistol butt came crashing down against Kunta's head, and he fell to his knees, dazed. Vaguely he saw the slave trader pushing Kizzy, her body thrashing, flailing, into the cart. The cart gathered speed; Bell went lumbering after it, and Kizzy was screaming.

Kunta rushed to where Kizzy had last stood. Bending, he scooped into his hands the dust of her footprints. The spirits said that if he kept that dust, her feet would return to that spot.

He ran with the dust toward the cabin in Slave Row. He must put it in some safe place. His eyes fell upon the gourd full of pebbles. He flung away the dust and, snatching up the gourd, banged it down against the packed-dirt floor. The gourd burst into pieces, and the pebbles which had been his record of the rains of his life went flying in all directions.

KIZZY WAS BOUGHT FROM the slave trader by a man named Tom Lea, who took her to a small plantation in North Carolina. Her new massa forced himself on her, and she bore a child named George. It bothered Kizzy that he was brown, but she learned not to think about it.

By the time he was four, George knew that his grandfather was African. Since few slave children on the Lea plantation even knew who their fathers were, George pestered his mother for more information about the man who had said his name was "Kunta Kin-tay," who called a fiddle or guitar *"ko,"* and a river "Kamby Bolongo."

"Where he from?" George would ask.

"He were a African, I tol' you!"

"What kin' of African, Mammy? Where 'bouts in Africa he from?"

Kizzy, remembering how her father had said she must tell her children where they came from, told George how Kunta Kinte had been not far from a village called Juffure, looking for wood to make a drum, when four men had captured him, put him on a ship, and taken him to a place called "Naplis."

In 1827, when George was 21, he "jumped de broom" with a girl named Matilda. Between 1828 and 1840 they had seven children. Each time one was born, George would assemble all the family in his cabin. With the new infant on his knee, the older children gathered about the hearth, he would implant in their minds the story of their great-granddaddy, "the African who said his name was 'Kin-tay,' who called a guitar *'ko,'* and a river 'Kamby Bolongo,' and said that he was out looking for wood for a drum when . . ."

The children of George and Matilda grew up, each one entering field work as he got old enough, all except the fourth child, Tom, who became a blacksmith, In 1856, Massa Tom Lea fell on hard times and had to sell his slaves. They all went to a tobacco plantation in Alamance County owned by Massa Murray.

There, in 1858, Tom, the blacksmith, married a half-black, half-Cherokee girl named Irene. As Irene had one child after another, Tom did what his father had done, and his grandmother Kizzy before that, telling his children about the African whose name was "Kin-tay." When the hard and bitter years of the Civil War were over, they became free. But they had no land and no place to go, so they stayed at the Murray plantation, the white Murrays and the black Murrays struggling on together.

Then, in 1872, George led a 29-wagon train of black families out of Alamance County, North Carolina, and through the Cumberland Gap to Henning, Tennessee. The last wagon was driven by his blacksmith son, Tom Murray, with his wife, Irene, and their seven children, the youngest a two-year-old girl named Cynthia.

That little girl was my grandma. At her knee I first heard the story of "the African," Kunta Kinte, which led to my search for roots.

Today the Haley family continues to reflect, in microcosm, the changing attitudes and opportunities of black America. Author Alex Haley's father, Simon, worked as a part-time Pullman porter while attending the Agricultural and Technical State University at Greensboro, N.C. In the summer of 1916, making the run from Buffalo to Pittsburgh, Simon Haley was befriended by R.S.M. Boyce, a retired executive of the Curtis Publishing Co. Boyce subsequently provided the funds that enabled Haley to graduate and go on to the New York State College of Agriculture and Life Sciences at Cornell University for a master's degree. Then, Simon Haley taught at small Negro colleges in the South.

Alex Haley's mother, Bertha, was a grammar-school teacher. He has two brothers, George W. Haley, an assistant director of the United States Information Agency; and Julius C. Haley, a Navy architect. Alex Haley himself, since retirement from the U.S. Coast Guard, has pursued an increasingly successful career as a writer of books, magazine articles and screenplays. To further the study of black heritage and genealogy, he and his brothers have established the Kinte Foundation, in Washington, D.C.

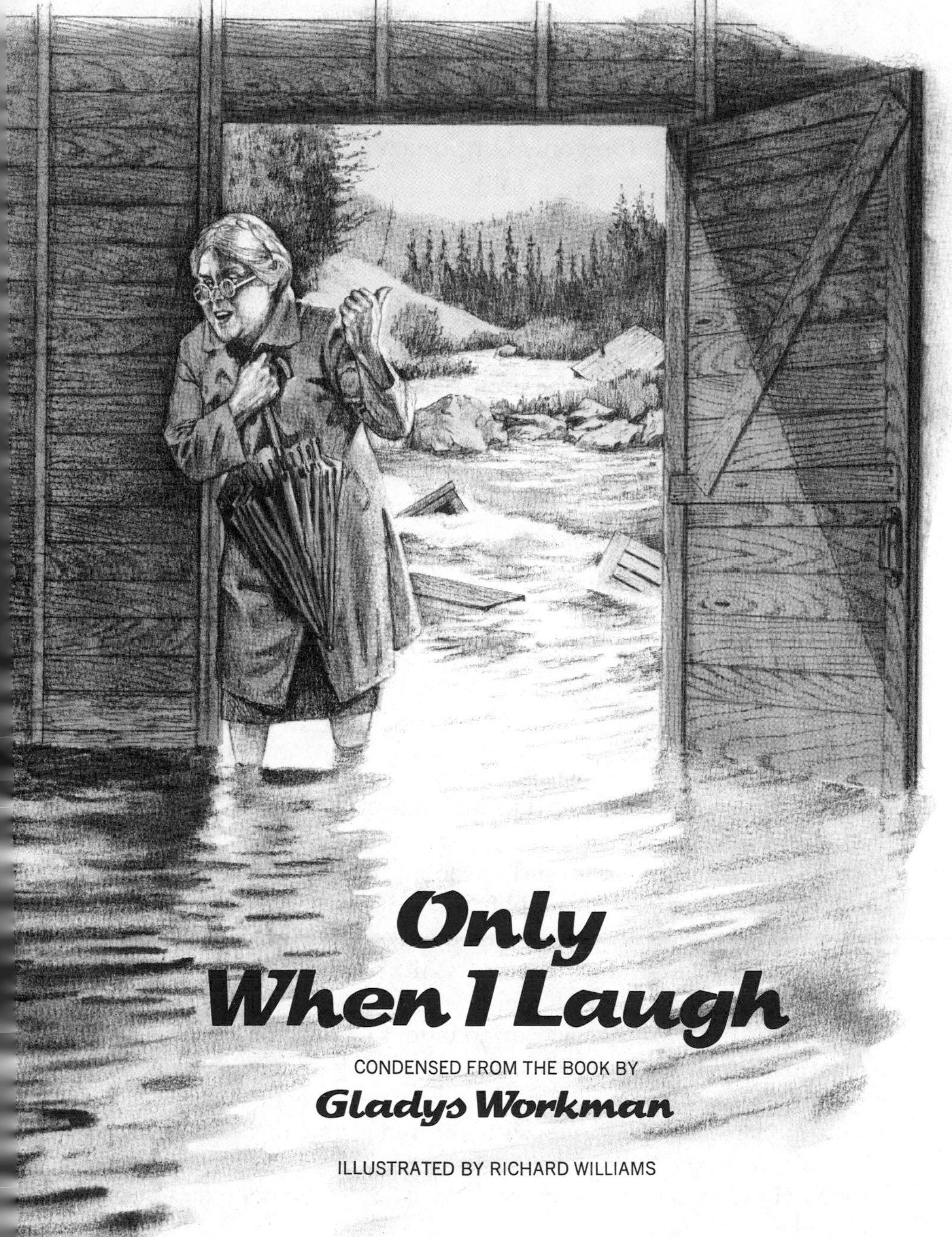

Only When I Laugh

CONDENSED FROM THE BOOK BY

Gladys Workman

ILLUSTRATED BY RICHARD WILLIAMS

The people of Oregon's Umpqua Valley are a breed apart. There is Old Abe, the hermit, who lives in a chicken house, happy in the company of ducks, goats and civet cats. And there are the loggers who can sit playing poker while invading floodwaters threaten to float them off their chairs. Whatever their personal quirks, these Old-Timers regard all newcomers with suspicion. Fortunately, newcomer Gladys Workman survived their distrust and became an Old-Timer herself. Her book *Only When I Laugh* is a high-spirited, walloping account of life in a region where conformity is unheard of.

1. OLD-TIMERS AND DRIFTERS

When we sold our suburban home in Rosemead, Calif., and moved 900 miles to an abandoned shack in Oregon's Umpqua Valley, I gaily told our friends to visit us any time. Since that would be like dropping in from New York to Chicago, I didn't expect many takers. I should have known better.

In spite of our primitive accommodations—applebox furniture, tin plates, blankets hung over poles where someday we would put a window and door—we were soon playing host to a stream of guests. One friend returned to California with the somewhat misleading news: "I've fished all over the West, but even at $25 a day I've never had such a time as I did with the Workmans." (That "$25" did not refer to us, of course; he was a guest.)

At first the visitors slowed down work on the shack that was to be our new home. My husband, Norman, and my nephew, "Young Norman"

Jackson, had started to build a porch, and when its walls were waist-high we felt we had passed a milestone. We were congratulating ourselves one evening when we heard a car stop outside the cabin. There was a knock at the wall. "See who's at the blanket," I said to Norman, but before he could reach it a young couple ducked in.

He was dressed like the compleat Abercrombie & Fitch sportsman, and he carried two suitcases and a variety of fishing rods. She was tall and willowy and wore a fur coat which she clutched tightly—to avoid contamination, I guessed.

"Here we are," said the young man cheerily. We chewed on that a while. There was no question about it, they *were* here. But we had never seen them before.

"Won't you have a cup of coffee?" I said brightly.

"Coffee?" She practically spat out the word. "We've driven all the way from San Francisco. I want food."

"I have some catfish," I offered.

"Catfish!" cried the man. "How about catching our own?"

I glanced at Young Norman. He grinned. "Come on," he said. "I'll show you a backwater where we always get them."

"You're not *going?*" wailed the girl. But he was already gone. Suddenly she sat on one of the suitcases, buried her face in mink, and began sobbing.

"It's so wild up here!" she bawled. "The woods are full of wolves."

"Nonsense," I said. "There aren't any wolves. There are a few bears here, but we *like* to have them around to remind us that the country is still country."

The poor thing was really frightened, but after a while she calmed down. "Could you show me to the bathroom?" she asked.

"I'm afraid we don't have one," I told her as gently as possible. "We—er—go outside."

She drew her mink tighter. "Then show me to my room," she snapped. "I'm going to bed."

"We don't have any room except the one we're in," I explained. "But we do have plenty of sleeping bags."

We waited uncomfortably until the men arrived with a dozen catfish. They fried a batch, and the lady sipped wanly at coffee. When we finished, Norman put the platter of leftovers on the porch. Then we all inserted ourselves in sleeping bags, and peace descended on the cabin.

About 3 a.m. the sylvan calm shattered into 10,000 jets of sound. One frightened cat can make a fantastic racket; we had five, and they made a screeching, howling maelstrom of noise. Our lady visitor screamed. We dashed for the porch. In their panic the cats tore around the walls, spinning higher and higher as they whirled by. When they reached the top they splayed out, hurled into the night by centrifugal force. Suddenly all was quiet. In the moonlight, we saw the cause of it all. A bear cub was sitting on the floor, holding a catfish in his paw like an icc-crcam conc.

"Bears!" I shouted.

My husband and Young Norman banged on pans to scare the cub away. But before I got a lamp lit, our visitors were packing. The girl was trembling so hard I thought she'd vibrate out of the mink she had put on over her nightgown. They raced for their car.

"Wait!" I cried, running up to the man. "Just tell me one thing. How'd you happen to stop here?"

"Some guy told us about you," he barked. "Now you tell me—where do you get the nerve to charge $25 a day for a dump like this?" The car roared out of sight.

In the shack, Norman handed me a cup of coffee. "You should have made them pay," he said. "Where else in the world could you buy a night like this for $25!"

THERE ARE TWO KINDS of people in the Umpqua Valley—the Old-Timers and the Drifters. We were Drifters.

"They'll get out in six months," said the Old-Timers, and for a while I was afraid they were right.

When we arrived in the valley, it was the Old-Timers against an outside world, a world they scarcely believed existed. They lived close to the soil and the rushing clouds; they knew the ways of the wind and the river. And they knew in harrowing detail everything about everybody—down to how long you wore a pair of socks, your standing with the bank and with God.

They did not much like what they knew about us. My husband and Young Norman were all right—but everyone knew that Norman Workman's wife was unfit for life in the valley. "Fool woman," they said. "Even a city woman ought to know you can't live in a shack like that and expect a sick man to make a living here."

Our decision to move from California started to form the day my husband collapsed at our home in Rosemead. When the doctor told us his blood had been poisoned from chemicals at the dye plant he managed, we knew we had to get him into the country for a long rest.

Finding a place was no problem. I'd lived part of my childhood in Oregon, and the Umpqua Valley remained in my mind as a green, enchanted land. But our friends were skeptical. "You're no spring chickens," they told us. "You're 46 and Norman's over 50. Where will you live?"

We found the answer on our first trip to Oregon. Friends of my childhood knew of some land for sale outside Scottsburg, so one day we drove up into the valley and stopped by a field near the Umpqua River. Scattered everywhere were wild apple trees, scarlet maples and huge firs. Not five yards from the road we saw five elk grazing at the line where forest fringed to field.

Paul Applegate, one of the few Old-Timers who offered to help us, pointed to an old cabin. "You could fix that up into a nice little house," he said.

The shack had a slight list and only one room, with windows (one broken) at each end. Rough two-by-fours supported the siding, and the floor tilted perilously. The place reeked of age and mustiness.

"What do you think?" I asked when we stepped outside again. Norman, soaking up the look and smell of the valley, smiled wistfully, and in that moment our decision was made. Before long our home on the Umpqua had started to become a reality.

In those first days I fought a losing battle with the wood stove we installed, and we ate most of our meals with Paul and Maude Applegate, who lived just down the road. One day Maude invited me on a shopping trip to Hedden's.

Hedden's was one of the early stores in this part of Oregon. As a child I'd heard of Cyrus Hedden, the old pioneer who once plodded through forests just ahead of a band of Indians, dragging a friend who'd been struck in the stomach by an arrow, and of his granddaughter Emma.

The store sat stolidly between Grange Hall and the community church. Across the street were a beer parlor and a few houses. That was the town of Scottsburg.

Hedden's could have been lifted from any TV western. A false front faced the highway, with big windows on either side of the door. Inside, shiny buckets gleamed from a high shelf. There were horsecollars, hammers, bolts of cloth and stacks of levis. A curl of flypaper spiraled down, coated with fossilized flies. The entire store smelled of leather and cookies and prunes and oil and bananas.

Emma Hedden was behind a row of post-office boxes when we arrived, a medium-sized woman with graying hair and small, old-fashioned glasses. After a brief greeting to me, she and Maude resumed a conversation which must have been running for years. Who was sick. Plans for a potluck. A baby had been born. There'd been a fight the night before at the beer parlor. Two women had kicked and torn at each other and then ganged up on the two-timing man. Emma had been summoned to break up the fight. "I sent them home to sleep off their beer," she snapped.

I felt a little queasy. What kind of place was Scottsburg anyway? I had pictured a quiet rural settlement, filled with happy descendants of rugged pioneers. Instead I heard Emma say, "There was a mess at the loggers' camp, too. I'll have to go down there and clean out the lot of them, you'll see."

We left the store. "Isn't there a policeman in Scottsburg?" I asked.

"No," Maude replied. "Emma's the only real policeman we have here. She can handle any drunk in the valley when she's got a sadiron in her hand."

We rode for a while, under the canopy of the forest.

"Golly, Maude, who makes all the trouble?"

"Oh, just Drifters," Maude said.

The Old-Timers, of course, could do no wrong. If one of the younger generation opened her bedroom to a new logger, the Old-Timers knew it almost as soon as the lucky fellow himself. But never a harsh word against the girl, if she came from an Old-Timer family. When Dud got drunk and ran his car into a bridgehead, strewing the highway with splintered guardrails, the Old-Timers chuckled. "Don't know how long the county can afford Ol' Dud," they'd say with a wink. "Those bridges are pretty expensive."

I WAS ENJOYING the valley—watching Norman get well and helping the cabin put on such elegances as new windows, curtains and doors—but I was making a name for myself. When friends arrived from outside the valley, I'd greet them as I always had, with a kiss. The valley, which could laugh juicily about the latest seduction downriver, was shocked. "Kissed that fellow right in front of Workman," they said. "If I had a woman like that, I'd beat the skin off her."

My first gesture toward being a good neighbor blew up in my face. There are some Old-Timers who still refer to it as "the night Gladys tried to kill us all."

One day Maude took me to Reedsport for some clamming. At Heyes' Wharf, she went off to see about a boat, and Old Man Heyes came up. "See that in the paper about the Red Tide?" he asked me.

"What's the Red Tide?"

"It's a time when the water gets all red," he said. "Don't know what causes it, but it makes the clams poisonous."

I laughed. "It looks like a nice blue today, so I guess we're safe." Just then Maude called me over to an outboard, and we chugged toward the sandbanks. In a few hours we had filled two sacks with big, juicy-looking clams.

The next night Norman and I threw a party to celebrate the completion of our home. The shack was now a neatly painted white house with bathroom, kitchen and screened-in porch. Besides the Applegates we had invited Jane and Ken Murphy, Dorothy and Walter Palmer, Maggie and Harry Burton and Rock Freyer.

Some time after the clams had disappeared, Maude leaned over to me. "Don't Rock Freyer look sort of funny?" she asked.

Rock's face, usually tan and ruddy, looked as gray as a pile of gravel. "I feel terrible," he moaned. "I've got the worst pain in my stomach I ever had."

The awful thought struck me: "The Red Tide!" I screamed, and told them what Old Man Heyes had said.

"We'd better give Rock something," said Norman. "I'll get some soda water." Rock downed five glasses of water mixed with baking soda. Then he walked, listing slightly, to the bathroom. I went to the phone and got Agnes Hudson, who ran the party line.

"Oh, Agnes," I wailed, "see if you can get us a doctor. I think we've all eaten poisoned clams."

That was the end of calm and dignity. The phone began to jangle. "Take hot salt water," someone said. "That'll make you throw up." Amid the clanging of the telephone, Paul Applegate turned green. "Maude, the poison's struck in on me!"

"I feel awful," cried Maggie Burton. "Whites of eggs!" screamed the phone. We had a new crate of 15 dozen eggs, and four of us started separating whites from yolks. Pansy Andrews rushed in the front door. "I got chittam bark to boil," she cried. "It'll clear out the bowels." "Mix the salt and the soda water," shouted the party line.

By now all of us were belting egg whites, soda and salt as fast as Norman could heat water.

The salt water was fantastically effective. It was explosive and uncontrollable. Our little cabin rocked as if under an artillery barrage. People were bent over the kitchen sink. People were bent over in the bathroom. People rushed to the privy in the back yard and dashed for the blackberry bushes that lined the road.

The hubbub slowly sloughed off, and eventually it was apparent that only Rock Freyer was still actually sick. Some of the men bundled him over to the hospital.

"Appendicitis," said the doctor to Rock. "I hope you haven't taken any laxatives."

"Well," said Rock, "I had nine glasses of hot salt water and about six of soda water. Then I drank some chittam juice and a couple of glasses of egg white."

The doctor laid his fingers over Rock's appendix. "Holy Christopher," he said softly. "By all the rules, she should have blown sky-high long ago."

2. THE LITTLE PIRATE

NORMAN WAS NOW almost completely well, and it occurred to us that we should have some means of support. Accordingly, he began scouting the valley for something to do. A few mornings later, I was feeding the two dappled fawns that always came into our yard for breakfast when Young Norman sidled around the corner of our house. "Aunt Gladys," he said, "Norman has bought three tons of daffodils. Paid $3000!" That was about every cent we had.

Just then Norman stepped up jauntily, put his arm around me and asked, "How does it feel to be the wife of a daffodil farmer?"

Norman knew nothing about farming, so he phoned an ad to the local newspaper: "Man wanted to manage small daffodil acreage." In answer we received a letter.

"I have been working in daffodils for the last eight years," it said. It was signed "V. Martin."

The next morning a pickup truck drove up to the cabin, and a little woman stepped out.

"My name is Val Martin," she said. "You lak Maxican, I'm Maxican. You lak Portuguese, I'm Portuguese. I don' care."

Val Martin was five feet tall, weighed 89 pounds, and looked like a tiny pirate. Her black hair was covered with a bright red bandanna, and she wore a pair of levis so tight they seemed painted on her little behind. She had a delightful grin, and her black eyes darted about, taking in everything.

I don't remember hiring Val formally, but she stayed with us for ten years. Under her direction, my husband and Young Norman tackled the art of daffodil farming. Norman leased a field and, with Val running alongside the tractor, he learned to plow, harrow and disk the furrows to receive the bulbs. The tractor had a tendency to wander a bit, much to Val's displeasure.

"Luke at the track you leave," she shouted at Norman. "She luke lak she left by a snake weeth the bellyache!"

When she got too bossy, Young Norman and the other men in the fields would pick her up and play catch with her, and Val would scream and laugh and cuss them.

One person who became a great favorite with Val was my mother, who had come to stay with us while the bulbs were being planted. "A nice ol' fat lady lak you should have a husban'," Val told her. (My father had died years before.)

"Who've you got in mind?" laughed Mama.

"Oh, I fin' somebody, you see," said Val. Every few days she nominated a candidate. Old Abe turned out to be her prize. "You should tak thees ol' guy," Val said. "He's got a couple of goats, and you can go into the cheese business. I tol' heem to come see you."

Old Abe came the next day. He is a typical hermit who loves all animals. He proved it by sharing his mountain cabin with his chickens, two turkeys, ducks, civet cats (which come daily), and his goats. He raised his hat politely at the back door, allowing a few spiky yellow hairs to escape the plastered-down mass on top of his head. His shoes, Army issue, were presentable, but his trousers carried the droppage of a hundred bachelor meals: egg spots, splotches of meat juice, souring milk, and jam.

"Wup, wup," he said as we asked him in, his weather-beaten face serious. "Beautiful day." (It was, in fact, raining hard.)

As we talked, about all we could make out of his part of the conversation was, "Oom-hoom, oom-hoom," with an occasional "wup." When he was leaving, I offered him some jam. "Wup, I love homemade jam. Right nice of you. Wup." He stepped into the rain and sloshed away, just as our phone rang.

"Heard Old Abe was at your place," said Paul Applegate. "Let me know when he leaves. Got to see he takes a bath today."

Since then Old Abe has dropped by about once a week. He doesn't read or write, but he's a good listener, and right there is an accomplishment rare enough.

The long, gray, featureless winter passed by. Just as Norman was girding himself for his first picking season in mid-February—the season on which our whole financial future hinged—the thermometer dropped and it snowed for two days. When we went out to the daffodil fields, my heart almost broke at the look on Norman's face. The long green leaves lay flat on the snow. The buds were prostrate. It was clear that our first daffodil crop was doomed.

"Don't worry," Val said that evening. "It don' make no deeference to them daffodeels eef eet snows." Norman just stared at her; hadn't he seen the daffodils lying lifeless in the snow? And yet the miracle happened. With all the hushed drama of a resurrection, the flowers raised their yellow buds a few hours after a warm rain and watery sunshine cleared the field.

In the first year of daffodil farming you plant a single bulb and it puts out a single flower. But while the bulb is in the ground it grows; the second year it might have two or three "noses" and each nose produces a flower.

By hiring pickers we took off nearly 90,000 buds that first year, and the market was good. When the bulbs were dug in the summer, the original three tons had increased to six and Norman sold the surplus to a flower house. We were in the daffodil business and prospering.

The first time I went to Scottsburg, I saw one man with no left arm, one with no left hand, another so stooped he could barely walk, and a fourth with a hook curling from one of his sleeves. Loggers, I was told, wearing the badges of their trade.

The valley people had lived with violence a long time and they actually enjoyed it, I believe. In a way this helped explain Emma Hedden to me. I'd look at Emma in her store, reading a letter for a man who couldn't read a word, and it was hard to imagine her in the role of a giant-killer. Now I know that she is one of the strongest women ever fabricated.

An Old-Timer told me about Emma and Blacky. The biggest man ever seen in the valley, Blacky was near six-feet-six and weighed close to 300 pounds. But, with all his strength, he was the gentlest fellow in the woods. Like an oversized St. Francis he would sit on a log and open his lunch pail to the whole forest. Deer, skunks, squirrels and jays would settle down for a meal. Even hummingbirds ate out of Blacky's hand.

This lovable giant was not above having an *apéritif* before dinner—maybe a dozen or so—of straight whiskey, and when he was drunk he was terrible to behold, because he always wanted to dance. Since there were no women at the camp, he'd insist on dancing with the men. The loggers never liked to refuse Blacky, but they didn't like to dance with him either, because he'd grab them so tight he'd break their ribs.

His last memorable drunk went according to pattern. In the loggers' bunkhouse he met three men. "Boys," roared Blacky, "I don't want to hurt you. But if you won't dance, I'll just have to throw you in the river." And one by one he looped them through the window and into the Umpqua.

Then he wandered outside, grabbed a loaded garbage can and whirled it about. "Let's shoot him," one of the loggers said darkly, "before he kills us all."

Suddenly a jeep slid to a stop and Emma Hedden got out. Blacky by then was lying happily in a pile of garbage. "Look, you hulk of a woodenheaded ox," said Emma, "you get up or I'll kick every tooth out of your stupid head!" For emphasis, she hauled off and kicked him as hard as she could.

Blacky staggered to his feet. As his face came within range, Emma belted him with the flat of her hand. "Now clean up this junk," she said. Without a word, Blacky obeyed.

Of all forms of violence in the valley, the most feared are fire and flood. We have seen both. *The* Umpqua Valley Flood was in 1861; *our* deluge is always referred to as a "freshet." I'm perfectly content that I was not present for The Flood.

The first fall rains were really little try-out showers that sluiced the dust from the gold and scarlet leaves and made the valley look radiant. Then the steady, plodding Oregon rain began. Before long the Umpqua clawed through willows and brambles, tumbling chicken coops and privies, overturning boats. At last it became a raging torrent almost a quarter of a mile wide.

Our house was high above the stream, but we knew of others that must be in danger. One night as we watched the river rise, Young Norman grabbed a flashlight and ran through the storm to warn some neighbors who were new to the valley. When he arrived at their house the river had reached the window level. He waded inside, flashed his light across the flooded room, and saw a baby asleep on a mattress, which was floating above the stove!

Upstairs the man and woman were peacefully asleep. He roused them and led the family safely to Emma's house, which was overflowing with refugees. Emma was about to leave.

"There's a bunch of drunken loggers playing poker in a shack by the river and they won't move," she said. She put on boots and raincoat, and trudged into the night. When she reached the shack, the river was washing around the feet of the players. "Hey, you guys," Emma said quietly. "Don't you have the sense God gave you? Get out before the place washes down the river."

"Don't get excited, Emma," said the host. "I got the damnedest winning streak I ever had, and I ain't going to quit now."

Emma stomped out, but she couldn't forget the drunks and a few hours later she waded back. The poker players were bleary-eyed, and the water was up to the seats of their chairs. "All right," Emma said, "get out of here right now."

"I'm going," said one of the players. "I'm tired of sitting with my hind end in cold water."

"I won so much I don't care what happens," said the host unsteadily. He shoved the table through the door and watched it float away. He threw a chair after it. "Let 'er go," giggled his wife. Piece by piece, they sent their furniture into the flood. Then they waded over to the bed—the mattress was about four inches above the water—and flopped down heavily.

Emma returned in the morning when the river had receded a bit and shook the two of them awake. The logger looked at the mud in the room. He looked at the river raging by a few feet from his door. "Wake up, old lady," he said to his wife. "We're almost drowned."

"They didn't even catch a bad cold," Emma sniffed.

3. THE PARTY LINE

YOU CAN HAVE the modern telephone and welcome to it. I know it's possible, in this miracle age, to dial coast-to-coast. The people at the telephone company brag about their gadgets. What they are hoping, obviously, is to make us forget how they shamefully murdered the party line, the finest tool ever perfected for human communication.

Nowadays you must be home to receive a call. Preposterous! When the valley had a party line, every ring was heard at every instrument and you could pick up your calls anywhere you happened to be.

Of course, people listened to conversations that were none of their business. Arguments raged over this pastime. One school said flatly that listening in was illegal. Some felt it was the only neighborly thing to do. Others said they didn't care—except that every receiver lifted from a hook sucked a bit more power off the line and, when too many nosy fools were listening, nobody could hear. That was certainly true, but there was a solution. The ones who *could* hear always were glad to relay the dialogue.

Our conversations were always popular because we received so many long-distance calls, and I soon learned to identify the eavesdroppers. One had a clock with a loud tick. Another rocked and *rocked* in a chair with a piercing squeak. But one night, when I was called from Chicago, there was a new entry, a fellow with a bad case of sniffles. I had a barely audible connection, and every time the newcomer sniffed we were drowned out completely.

At last I said, "For goodness sake, blow your nose! We'll wait, so you won't miss anything."

"Okay, Gladys," he said, and we waited. Soon he was back. "All set here," he announced, and Chicago and I went on.

In all our moods the party line tied us together, particularly during emergencies. One rainy afternoon Old Abe entered Emma's store, looking as desolate as the weather. "Wup, wup," he said. "My cabin burned down. Whole thing." He paused. "Saved the goats and chickens. Stove fell. Burned everything."

Emma lifted the receiver on the box telephone. "Who's on?" she asked. Several voices chirped up. All Emma said was: "Old Abe's cabin burned last night. Let's do something." For the next hour the phone bell rang constantly.

"Billy Hanson has a chicken house he doesn't use any more."

"We're going to put a couple of windows in the chicken house."

"Some of the fellows are making skids so we can move it."

Before nightfall, the party-liners had borrowed a tractor and dragged the chicken house to Old Abe's, and set it on a foundation of fieldstone. They whitewashed the walls, put up curtains, and installed a bed, rocking chair and small wood stove. They laid in a supply of flour, bread, preserves, cookies, bacon, potatoes and canned goods. They brought towels, washcloths and napkins.

A few days later Old Abe arrived in our yard. "Beautiful day," he said. "Wup, wup, you ought to see my new place. Bet the King of England ain't got no finer. Ain't letting the goats in *that* house!"

I was just a little girl when I first met Norman, and I think he still regards me as a child who should have her own way. He has survived and even enjoyed my alarms and whims. When I inadvertently became a professor of ceramics, he wavered in the shock, but he didn't break.

It started when a friend of mine, Stella Hardy, came up from Los Angeles bearing clay and paints. "Could we start a class?" she asked.

I got some girls lined up and we were soon launched on the first lesson. Unfortunately, Stella was called back to Los Angeles suddenly, and we had to abandon the project.

A few weeks later I discovered that some of Stella's ex-pupils were unhappy. I was at a church bazaar when a lanky young woman placed herself in front of me. She looked as big as a lady Paul Bunyan.

"So you're the jane who had those fancy classes?" she asked. "Those girls bought a whole lot of supplies. What are they supposed to do with them now?"

Another harpy, one of our daffodil pickers, spoke up. "You're going to find a lot of us won't show up to pick your buds."

I got mad. "Look," I said, "the classes have nothing to do with daffodils. But if you pick for us, I'll go to Los Angeles and take lessons, and I'll come back and teach you for free."

That is why I went to Los Angeles and plunged into a new and mysterious world of underglaze paint, potter's wheels and kilns. I learned how to cast clay in plaster molds; I learned how to fire greenware until it emerged as pure white bisque. I even learned how to make flowers almost as beautiful as our burgeoning daffodils.

At first, I did not take much time to think about ceramics beyond teaching the few who thought Stella had gypped them. But somehow, by the time everyone agreed all debts had been paid, I had been persuaded to start new classes. Soon the house and then the garage overflowed with supplies. We finally built a separate studio.

Still the students came. They ranged from backwoods ladies to a genuine refugee from Park Avenue. Somewhere in that first year we adopted the slogan "Ceramics for Fun," and along with fun some of the students turned out brilliant work.

One day as I started a new class I noticed an empty chair. "That's for Ruthie," a blond gal said, referring to a young woman who had just come to the valley as the bride of a logger. And at that moment Ruthie herself bounded into the room, her mouth turned down at the corners, her Dutch bob bristling with indignation.

"Ah think ah'm goin' to kill mah man!" she roared at the blonde.

The class froze in silence. "Last night," said Ruthie, "thet man never did show up. Round daylight, he come in all covered with mud. 'You been over to that redhead floozie's place?' ah asked.

"He says, 'Ah been gittin' a cat down the mountain.' Well, hale, thet's a lie. Mah man hates cats. 'Ah know where you been working,' ah said, 'an' ah'm goin' over an' pull ever' red hair off her floozie head.'"

Ruthie flashed us a quick, black look. "Ain't thet the dangdest lie?" she asked. "Up all night with a cat on a mountain?"

We didn't know whether to laugh or cry.

"Ruthie," said one of the loggers' wives, "he was talking about a Caterpillar tractor."

Ruthie was a constant delight. Once she returned from a Los Angeles holiday with a tale of her experiences on the freeways. "Kid," she reported. "you jest wouldn' believe how many cahs there is on them roads. Ah jest had to stop an' puzzle thangs out. A guy comes by slow an' hollers. 'Hey, what the hale you thank yore doin'?' He talked jest lak one of our loggers an' ah lakked thet.

"'Don' get your pants in an uproar, friend,' ah said.

"'Why the hale don' you git offen the freeway?' he hollered.

"'Freeway?' ah said. 'Effen ah knowed this was a freeway, ah'd ruther have *paid* a little an' stayed offen the damn thang.'"

Eventually our ceramics work attracted attention throughout the state. I started writing a regular column in the magazine *Popular Ceramics,* and extended my teaching to classes for the handicapped and mentally ill. Invitations to speak at hobby shows and garden clubs arrived from as far away as Chicago and Detroit. I accepted most of them, and once in a while someone in the audience would challenge me. I never minded, because I don't pose as an artist; all I claim to be is a sound teacher. Ruthie was with me when a woman rose to attack. "You know what I've heard about you?" she asked querulously.

"No telling," I replied.

"I heard you don't know any more about ceramics than a hog knows about holy water."

Ruthie was on her feet in an instant. "You got some nerve talking to Teacher lak thet," she said. She turned to the audience. "Don't pay her no mand," she said. "Her mouth ain't no prayer book, even effen it does open an' shet."

And *thet* took care of *thet.*

The Workman "Ceramics for Fun" spread throughout the entire state. At one time we were supplying more than 200 studios, most of which had been established by my students. Norman, who kept the books, astounded me when he announced we were doing a $40,000-a-year gross business.

I was so busy with my classes that I almost forgot we were also in the daffodil business—until Val Martin walked into the kitchen one day.

"I mus' tell you, my leetle peegeon," she said, "I don' theenk I come back any more."

"Is something wrong, Val?" I asked.

"Oh, no," she said, laughing. "But if you don' learn anything by now, I don' theenk you ever goin' to."

And, amid tearful good-bys, Val left us after ten wonderful years. She had taught us plenty. Recently we harvested a million blooms.

Norman by now was an expert daffodil farmer; indeed, he has made significant contributions to the bulb-growing industry in Oregon. He adapted machines which took much of the drudgery out of planting bulbs by hand, and he established a new system of marketing which raised the profits of all the growers in the valley.

THERE WAS ONE ANNOYANCE we never completely eliminated. Each year after the digging, there are a few bulbs left in the field which growers call by the expressive name of "bastards." These must be carefully removed to prevent random blossoms from popping up.

A man stopped at our door one day when Ruthie was holding the fort. "I'm not a bum," he said. "But I've been walking all morning and I can't find a place to eat. I've got money and I can pay."

"You willin' to do a little work?" Ruthie asked, and the man said he was. She handed him a shovel and pointed to where several men were clearing bastard bulbs from the field. "Take this thang an' git them bastards out of thet field."

"Kid," Ruthie told me later, "when ah rung thet dinner bell, this stranger was the only one thet showed up. Ah asked him where the others was at an' he said, 'Well, ma'am, you tol' me to git them bastards outten thet field an' I chased them dang near two miles up the road. Ah don' thank you'll have no more trouble with them.'"

The invitation to join the Grange, the white-steepled building in Scottsburg which served as the valley's social center, was our biggest triumph in the valley. It meant we were accepted at last, and the evening of our introduction was unforgettable. Jimmy Van Natta, a landscape architect who had entered the valley several years before, was our sponsor. That night he addressed the Old-Timers.

"I want to talk to you folks who own the original grants in this valley," he began. "You own your land clear and legal. But in another sense you cannot own it. Who can buy or sell the grace of a deer, or the strength of a salmon fighting up the river? Who owns the serenity we feel here watching the night creep over these mountains? These belong to God."

There was a stillness in the room as his listeners realized that Jimmy had found words for something they had all felt. Then he turned to us.

"These things involve you, too," he said, "because you have made your place in the community. It is good to welcome you as friends and neighbors."

Jimmy would have laughed if anyone had called him a poet, but his quiet speech that night remained in my memory as poetry. I decided that my success with ceramics was taking me too far from the life and the people we had come to love in the valley. Accordingly, I stopped much of my lecturing and teaching. Not that we wanted to quit ceramics altogether. We kept the studio as a small gift shop, and still have two kilns which are fired up from time to time.

The nicest thing about our semiretirement is that we have more time to spend with our neighbors and guests. Visitors still come from as far as Hawaii and New York to enjoy the serenity of the forest and the river, the sight of otters playing tag, and deer peering from the myrtlewood. But occasionally, some friends from the big cities ask me why we stay on the Umpqua. They are honestly puzzled to know what we find in this faraway corner of the United States. One friend from Los Angeles complained about the peace and quiet of our country life.

"I'm all packed and ready to go," she announced on the third day of one of her visits. We urged her to stay, for we knew that the zany, unpredictable side of valley life could erupt at any moment.

"No, I've just got to get back to some excitement," she said, climbing into her car.

At that moment, a speeding automobile missed the slight curve in front of our house, sailed gracefully down the slope and poked its nose through the shingles of the Applegate house, just between the twin beds in the bedroom. Our friend gazed at the dust settling around the Applegate manse. "I'm still going back to Los Angeles," she said. "The excitement is quieter there!"

Paul Applegate was resting on one of the beds when the car crashed into his room. Imperturbable as ever, he raised himself on one elbow and addressed the driver. "Hello, neighbor," he said. "What brings you here?"

As apprentice Old-Timers, we knew what *we* would have answered.

83 Hours Till Dawn

CONDENSED FROM THE BOOK BY

Gene Miller

IN COLLABORATION WITH

Barbara Jane Mackle

ILLUSTRATED BY JOHN THOMPSON

Thompson

The kidnapers came out of the night to seize their victim, a 20-year-old girl. They took her to an isolated wooded section where she was forced into a coffin-like box that had been sunk into the ground.

Stretched out with barely room to move, the girl heard the lid slammed down. Then came the sound of spadefuls of earth hitting the lid. After that—silence, terrifying silence.

That this dreadful crime did not end tragically is due not only to good police work but to a young woman who had the stamina and the courage to stay alive.

1. KIDNAPED

I DIDN'T KNOW what time it was, just that it was still night. Mother was talking to someone through our motel-room door.

"What's the matter?" I asked.

"There's a policeman outside," she answered, unbolting the latch.

I saw the gun before I saw the man. As Mother opened the door, the barrel poked through. Then the man flung the door wide, slamming Mother against the wall. He was big and husky. He had on a visored cap, leather jacket and dark pants. A boyish figure, wearing a ski mask, rushed past him into the room.

We thought that we were being robbed. "Take our money and jewelry and get out!" Mother cried angrily.

"Put your hands behind your back," the man said. "We're going to tie you up, but we won't hurt you." He held the gun against my temple.

The small figure—the one I thought was a boy—had Mother on the bed, first tying her hands behind her, then tying her ankles as well.

I put my hands behind my back. But the man said, "No. We're not going to tie you up."

For the first time I began to get scared. Mother was struggling. The boy was pushing her down, holding a rag to her face.

"It's a harmless anesthetic," the man said. Then he grabbed my arm, hauled me outside, and thrust me into the back seat of a station wagon. The boy jumped in beside me. "Chloroform her!" the man barked.

Very quickly I said, "That's okay. I'll put my head down. I don't want to see what you look like." And as the car pulled out I put my head in the boy's lap. I was shivering. All I had on was a nightgown, my panties, and a pair of woolen socks. Then the boy spoke—and it wasn't a boy's voice at all. It was a girl with a distinct Spanish accent.

We were going fast. I felt the car turn hard left, jolt over railroad tracks, bump along a short distance, and stop. The whole ride hadn't taken 15 minutes. "Keep her head down so she doesn't see the house," the man said. Then he left the car. They're going to put me in a house, I thought. But presently the man returned. "Jake and the boys dug the hole too deep," he said.

That's when I thought they were going to kill and bury me. I said to myself, "I'm going to get away from here. I'll run." I straightened up and there he was, right at the window. He tied my hands and feet and shined a flashlight in my eyes.

"I suppose you know you're being kidnaped?" he said.

"Uh-huh," I replied.

"We're asking quite a bit of money," he went on with a sort of chuckle. "But I'm sure your father can get it. Now listen carefully. I'm going to give this to you once and only once.

"We're going to put you into an underground room. It is big enough to walk around in. But you can only get your air by using a battery. This battery will run seven days. You have a light down there, but if you use the light, the battery will run out in five days."

He kept right on talking. An underground room? A battery? I couldn't understand it.

"You will be under water," he said. (I might have misunderstood. Maybe he said under the water table.) "There is a pump in there. If the water comes in, turn the pump on. A light will go on in the house."

He went into all kinds of detail about the pump and a ventilation fan, but I couldn't understand it all. Then the girl gave me a shot with a hypodermic needle. "It'll make you feel so you don't care what happens," the man said. He insisted on chloroform, too, and when I resisted the girl, he pushed the rag to my nose. I felt dizzy and woozy.

He pulled me out of the car. I was completely limp, and he had a hard time carrying me. I felt some branches brush across my shoulders. We were in a woods. Abruptly, he put me down in a sitting position with my feet dangling in a hole. "Slide down in there," he said, pressing hard on my shoulders.

My feet went in first, and then I was half sitting. I remember thinking, this is too small to be a room. Well, maybe it is a passageway, and the room is down lower. But when I tried to straighten out, my feet wouldn't go all the way. There was a light, and I saw that this wasn't a passageway. It was a box.

I was terrified. "No, no, no!" I cried. "You can't do this!"

I was still woozy, but I knew I had to get out. Let them kill me, but I had to get out. I was just getting up when suddenly the top of the box came down with a thud. I pushed against it as hard as I could. It didn't do any good. I guess I was screaming, sort of: "Wait, wait! I have to tell you something important!"

I could hear him screwing down the lid. And then I heard the dirt. I could hear it falling. There are no words to describe it. The first shovelfuls were very loud. After a while they became muffled. I was screaming, "No! Don't do this! Be reasonable! Listen to me!"

"Barbara!" It was the girl. "Don't worry, Barbara. We'll be back every two hours to check." Desperately, I wanted to believe her.

"Please come back!" I cried. "Just to talk to me."

I heard the man laugh. "All you want is human contact," he said.

"Yes," I said. "I do, I do."

That was the last I heard. I started pushing against the top. "Oh, God," I begged. "You can't leave me here!" I'd talk, then wait for an answer, then talk. And there was nothing. Only silence.

UNAFFECTED BY THE chloroform, Jane Mackle looked up just in time to see the two intruders leave with her 20-year-old daughter. Oh, my God, she thought, they are going to rape Barbara.

Frantically, her hands and feet tightly bound, she rolled over the bed to the phone, knocked the receiver off the hook and started to scream. There was no response. It was necessary to dial for the night clerk, and she could not. Struggling to her feet, she hopped across the room and, oblivious to the 24-degree cold, hobbled outside in her nightgown. "And I screamed and screamed and screamed."

Of the motel's 120 rooms, 71 were occupied that night. But no one came to find out what was wrong.

The horn, she thought suddenly. Barbara's green Pontiac was unlocked and parked close by. Still screaming, Jane Mackle hopped toward it. At the right front door she fell, staggered to her feet, fell again. A third time she fell, toppling backward onto the asphalt. But she kept trying. Bruised, bleeding, her lips dry and sore from the chloroform, she finally backed carefully toward the door and pressed the latch. It opened easily, and she plopped down on the front seat, put her chin on the horn, and pressed hard. "And I didn't let up."

The night desk clerk, a methodical man who had worked in hotels for 16 years, locked the lobby and made his way cautiously to the parking area. "Hey, lady," he shouted. "Shut up! You'll wake the guests!"

"For heaven's sake, help me," Mrs. Mackle gasped. "They took my daughter." But the clerk just stood there and "fussed at me." She had to bully him into untying her, and even then she had to call the police herself. Her call was logged by the DeKalb County, Georgia, police dispatcher at 4:11 a.m., December 17, 1968.

When two police officers pulled into the Rodeway Inn Motel minutes later, they found Jane Mackle standing alone outside her room. She was near hysteria, pacing back and forth. "When I realized that they hadn't robbed me, I knew that they were after Barbara. All I could think of was rape, and I just nearly died." The officers tried to calm her and learn her story, but she kept imploring them to do something. "Isn't there somewhere you can look?" she begged. "I'm so scared."

Her daughter Barbara, she explained, was a student at Emory University in Atlanta. In the midst of examinations for the fall quarter, she had caught the Asian flu, which was then sweeping the country. There had been no room for her in the Emory infirmary, already overcrowded with flu victims, so Jane Mackle had flown up from her home in Florida to look after Barbara herself, checking into this motel four days earlier. She had opened her door in the small hours of the morning to a man wearing a visored cap, and he had taken her daughter away.

Privately, both officers wondered if Barbara had left of her own free will. Could this be an elaborate college prank? Had she run off with a boyfriend? They were unaware that her father, Robert Mackle, was a millionaire real-estate developer in Coral Gables, Fla. To them, Barbara was just another coed, who had vanished from a motel room.

Soon a detective arrived to take over the questioning, and the officers left to search dead-end streets, lovers' lanes, and all the local "cracks," as they called them, where a rapist might take a victim. By now Jane Mackle had been joined by a family friend, who immediately placed a call to Barbara's father at the Key Biscayne Hotel and Villas, one of the Mackle family's many holdings.

It was still dark when Robert Mackle picked up the phone, but he snapped into abrupt wakefulness at the news.

"Call the FBI immediately and tell them to come right out," he said. "I want to put a lid on this. I don't want any publicity until we can find out what's going on."

I GUESS IF THERE WAS a peak of terror, it was right after they left. I started screaming and pounding to try to get out. I lost control completely. I was panting hard and could hear my heart beating.

Then everything just sort of hit me. It became real and I started thinking, now look, Barbara, calm down. This screaming will get you nowhere. Daddy will get the money. And they'll be back in two hours.

I was still scared, of course, but now I started looking around. I got the cord off my hands easily, and switched the fan on. I could hear it in a compartment behind my head, and I was thankful for the noise. To hear nothing was horrible.

I tried to reach the cord to untie my feet and I couldn't. The box lid was 12 or 14 inches above my face. If I rose up, I bumped it. Finally I turned on my side and sort of folded up, and got my feet undone.

Next I found a sofa pillow and three pages of instructions typed in capital letters. "Do not be alarmed," I read. "You are safe. You are presently inside a fiberglass-reinforced plywood capsule buried beneath the ground near the house in which your kidnapers are staying.

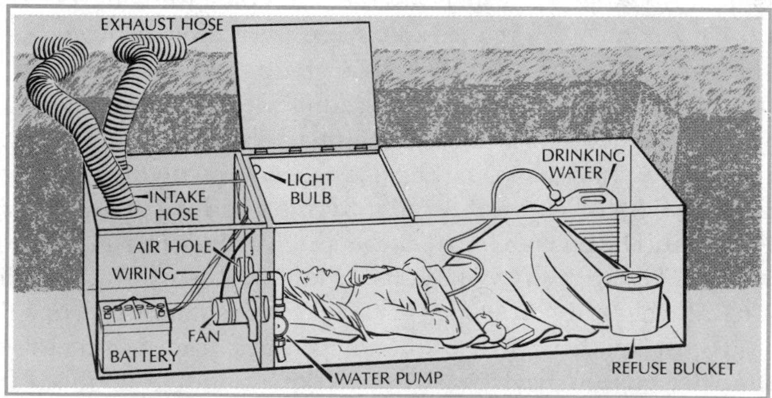

Diagram of the box in which Barbara Mackle was imprisoned

The capsule is quite strong. You will not be able to break it open." The instructions repeated much of what the man had already told me. They warned that continuous use of the light and pump would run the battery down more quickly and "your life expectancy will be cut." There was a detailed description of the capsule's contents: among other things a chemically treated refuse bucket, a jug of drinking water, candy, apples, blankets, and tranquilizers for aid in sleeping.

The document concluded: "We're sure your father will pay the ransom we have asked in less than one week. Should he fail to pay, we will release you, so be calm and rest—you'll be home for Christmas one way or another."

I read it and still I couldn't quite comprehend. It was awfully hard to believe. I wondered, God, am I going to die? Do people feel they are going to die before they do? Or is it the same feeling I have now? And they don't know it?

I began to think about Mother. Had they hurt her? In my mind I reconstructed the telephone call from Mother to Daddy. I saw Mother dialing, saw Daddy reacting when he first heard. I thought he might have tears in his eyes. But he wouldn't cry. He would calm down and get everyone working on it.

Oddly enough, I wasn't worried at all about drowning. I didn't believe that business about being under the water. But I *was* getting wet. Everything was damp. I pulled a blanket up over me. It was damp, too. I was cold.

I remembered the warning: "Use of the light when not necessary will cut your battery safety margin substantially." The light was white, about the size of a Christmas-tree bulb. I turned it off.

Immediately I got scared, real scared. As a little girl I'd always been afraid of the dark, and now I couldn't help myself. I started to tense up. I was angry at myself, but I had to turn the light back on. It didn't help. I could feel the panic building up anyway, getting worse and worse. I've got to get out of here.

The pump! The pump! That's it! The big man had told me it would turn on a red light and a buzzer in the house. I switched on the pump, and it made such a loud noise I actually jumped. It sounded like a broken Mixmaster going off in my ear. But I kept turning it on and off, and in my mind I could see the light and hear the buzzer responding in the house. Then I turned off the pump and fan so I could listen for their footsteps. But there weren't any.

I left the fan off. The panic subsided. The box began to get a little stuffy and warm, and I felt drowsy. This is great, I thought, I'm going to sleep. Then I began wondering about getting enough air. I turned the fan on, and it started getting cold again.

From the beginning I was waiting for those two hours to end. So I decided to count seconds. Sixty seconds for 60 minutes. That's 3600 seconds; doubled, that's 7200. I counted slowly, pronouncing each individual number in full. When I reached 7200 I turned off the fan and listened. Absolute silence.

Well, I thought, maybe I counted wrong. I started again at 6000. When I passed 7200 once more, I knew it had been more than two hours. That's when I realized that what they said wasn't true. The pump didn't turn on a light or a buzzer. There wasn't any house. And there was nobody there. "They are not coming back," I said. "They are not ever coming back. Ever."

2. REQUEST FOR RANSOM

ROBERT MACKLE immediately realized that kidnap for ransom was the likeliest explanation for Barbara's abduction. His wealth made him far more vulnerable to the greed of a criminal than the average man. Together with his brothers, Frank and Elliott, he operated the Deltona Corporation, home builders and land developers, with assets listed at $127,887,537.

A large, deeply tanned man of 57, with direct blue eyes and a smudge of gray in his black hair, Mackle looked the picture of a successful executive. Almost instinctively he now reacted as he had to hundreds of lesser crises in his business life: Keep calm. Get the facts. His first step was to telephone Billy Dale Vessels, a Deltona executive and former football great, and ask him to come at once to the Mackles' home in Coral Gables.

Next he called his brother Frank in New York City, and Frank, in turn, alerted the older Mackle brother, Elliott. Then, leaving word to have his phones at the Key Biscayne Hotel covered, Robert Mackle drove to his house to meet Vessels. Again, he arranged to have someone stand by the phones, and at 7:15 a.m. Mackle and Vessels flew to Atlanta. Said a family friend: "Robert was terribly upset, but he was tracking straight. There was no panic."

At the phone in the Mackles' den, Elliott Mackle and William F. O'Dowd, a Deltona executive, kept a tense vigil. The phone rang several times, but all were routine calls. Then, at 9:10, the bell jingled again. O'Dowd grabbed the instrument nervously.

"Robert Mackle?" asked a man's voice.

"No," said O'Dowd. "He's on his way to Atlanta."

There was a long pause. "Well, tell him to look under a palm tree at the northeast corner of the house, under a rock, about six inches down."

O'Dowd scrawled furiously on a pad. "Don't go so quickly," he said. "I can't take it down."

"That's all," the voice said, and the connection was broken.

Elliott Mackle's voice cut in on the extension. "Don't do anything," he said. "Wait for the FBI. They're on their way over."

When the agents arrived, they examined the Mackle garden closely. In the northeast corner there was a clump of Phoenix palms. Here the men found a single coral rock, the size of a man's fist. They began digging, and on the second shovelful unearthed a broken bottle containing a ransom note, typewritten on three rolled sheets of paper. It described Barbara's underground prison and demanded a $500,000 payment, in $20 bills.

When the money was ready, an ad was to be placed in Miami-area newspapers: "Loved one—please come home. We will pay all expenses and meet you anywhere at any time. Your family."

Detailed instructions for the ransom payoff would be relayed in a phone call "after midnight" following the ad's first appearance. "Should you catch the messenger we send to pick up the ransom," the message warned, "we will simply not say anything to anyone and Barbara will suffocate. Should you catch all of us, we would never admit to anything, as to do so would be suicide and, again—Barbara would die. As you can see, you don't *want* to catch us."

News of the ransom note was relayed to Atlanta, where by midmorning Robert Mackle was doing his best to comfort his wife. For the time being, the details of their daughter's underground imprisonment were withheld. Then, shortly after 4 p.m., FBI Inspector Rex Shroder arrived at the Rodeway Motel.

"Mr. Hoover has sent me personally," he told the Mackles. "He wants you to know that the weight of his organization is in back of this investigation. I assure you it is going to have a happy ending."

"He was the first person to say what I wanted to hear," Jane Mackle recalls. "He was so convincing, so sure." Shroder made the same impression on her husband. There was no doubt in Mackle's mind that this was the FBI's "first team."

Shroder had brought a copy of the ransom note, which Mackle now saw for the first time.

"Well," he said, when he had finished reading it, "my reaction to this is terror—but on the other hand I feel a lot better. I think we are dealing with some highly intelligent person and not some maniac who will chop somebody up."

"We feel exactly the same way," Shroder said, adding, "Did you notice there is $500,000 ransom?"

Mackle's face betrayed no concern. "My brothers have had this note for some time, I take it?" he said.

"Yes, since this morning."

"Then the money will be taken care of."

I BEGAN TO THINK about the kidnaper. If he was going to let me die, he wouldn't have gone to all this trouble. This box and this fan and everything. He would have just killed me, right? That's how I felt. Maybe he won't come back, but he'll tell somebody.

But what if something happened to him? What if a policeman stopped him and he got scared and clammed up and just forgot the whole kidnap and left me here? So many things could happen.

I tried to make myself laugh. Whenever I sing, I laugh—my voice is so terrible. So I started to sing "Jingle Bells" and "Deck the Halls With Boughs of Holly."

I had turned off the light to save the battery. I had been scared, but then I had thought, why should I be afraid of the dark? Nobody is going to get me in here. In fact, I wished someone would!

And then it happened. You know how a light bulb flickers just before it goes out? That's what it did. I had the light out and I reached up to turn it on. It flickered and went out.

"No!" I said. My hands were shaking. This was the worst possible thing that could have happened. I couldn't see anything. I sort of cried aloud, "O, God, you can't do this to me!"

Then in the darkness I remembered the tranquilizers mentioned in the man's note. I remembered there was a paper bag and I felt for it. Inside were apples, some bread and chewing gum. I felt a piece of candy, unwrapped and tasted it. It was a caramel, but I wasn't hungry at all. I kept feeling around for those tranquilizers and I couldn't find them. Well, I thought, this is just something else he lied about.

I was very thirsty. I recalled my brother Bobby saying once that anyone can live without food for a long time but that water is more important. The kidnaper had told me that a rubber tube in the box led to a water container. I found the tube and sucked hard. The water tasted terrible.

I remembered a teacher I had in seventh grade. He told us a story about a man who was in a prison camp undergoing mental torture. Whenever they tried to break him down, he would slowly build a house in his mind, brick by brick. Every time they started to get to him, a brick would fall, but he would just methodically pick it up.

I didn't think about building a house. I thought about decorating our Christmas tree. I decorated it in my mind three or four times. The bulbs and ornaments have been around for years, and I thought of each one specifically. I also wrapped presents in my mind and then invented all sorts of versions of the ransom payoff.

Some of them were pretty corny, I guess. I didn't think much about the amount of money. Maybe $5000. Honestly, I've never thought of ourselves as having money.

Anyway, they put the money in a cardboard box and wrapped it up. I thought of Daddy dropping it at the Atlanta airport. It was dark, and Daddy was scared. I imagined a dark shadowy figure picking it up. I pictured Mother and Daddy and Bobby sitting around the Rodeway waiting for the phone call from the kidnaper. Then they had to go buy a shovel. And I was thinking, it is about time now. The car is pulling up just about now. I was listening for their footsteps. And I turned off the fan so I could hear.

And I couldn't hear a thing.

So I started inventing delays. The airplane was late; the weather was real bad. I had Dad's car having a flat tire. That was another delay. I always gave them plenty of time and took them right up to when they would arrive to dig me out. Not quite to the point where they would get me out, but almost. But after a while I knew something had happened. I gave them so much time. . . .

3. PIECES OF THE PUZZLE

By noon the day of the kidnaping William O'Dowd had arranged to borrow $500,000 from Miami's First National Bank. At closing time, 85 bank officers stayed behind and began thumbing through packet after packet of notes. Working in two-man teams, they recorded serial numbers, and copied and verified more than six million digits on

25,000 bills that weighed 75 pounds when packed into the ransom suitcase. The job took almost six hours. That night the ad informing the kidnaper that the money was ready went to the newspapers.

Robert and Jane Mackle had returned to their Coral Gables home with Inspector Shroder. Jane, still unaware that Barbara was buried underground, lay asleep under heavy sedation. By now, the story had leaked to the press. It was front-page news, and the FBI had assigned more men to work on the case.

So far the only potential clue to the kidnapers' identity had come from one of Barbara's professors, Marshall Casse. He had seen two strangers asking for Barbara on the Emory campus the previous Saturday. One was a tall, heavy, bearded man. The other was a petite, short-haired girl. Professor Casse had seen them get into a blue foreign-built station wagon—he thought it was a Volkswagen—with Massachusetts plates.

Had the kidnaper shaved off his beard? Had Mrs. Mackle mistaken a masked girl for a young boy? Soon computers were working to trace all Massachusetts-registered blue station wagons of foreign make. But it was only a beginning—and in the meantime the Mackles sat and hunted desperately for other clues.

They were still up at 5:30 the next morning when Wednesday's paper plopped against the front porch. There was the ad: "Loved one—please come home." Despite the initial leak to the press, the ransom negotiations remained under tight security. Now Robert Mackle faced the long wait until the kidnaper telephoned "after midnight."

Just past noon a young Catholic priest walked up the drive through a crowd of television and press reporters and rang the doorbell. His name was Father John Mulcahy, he told the men who ushered him in, and he wanted to speak to Robert Mackle alone. "It's about Barbara."

"These are FBI agents, Father," Robert Mackle said. "I'd like them to be present."

Mulcahy told his story. He had just received a call at the Church of the Little Flower—the Mackles' church—from a man claiming to be the kidnaper. The caller said he knew the Mackle home was "full of cops, detectives and FBI men." He described Barbara's "coffin" and mentioned that two days of the battery's life had already gone. He instructed Father Mulcahy to tell Mackle that Barbara was okay—but to stress that "when the battery runs out, she runs out!" At the end of his account, Father Mulcahy asked, "Do you think he was for real?"

"Yes," said Shroder flatly. "You talked to the kidnaper."

He immediately requested and received permission to monitor Father Mulcahy's telephone.

The phones in the Mackle home were already being monitored, and arrangements had been made to trace all calls. This is an extremely difficult task in a large metropolis. Most of the Bell System's equipment is designed so that the calling party controls the system. The dialer sets off a series of impulses that race electronically toward any given number. Once the phone is answered, the apparatus locks and an experienced technician, knowing where to look, can figure out where the call originates, but only so long as the caller remains on the line. Obviously, a kidnaper would not waste any time.

However, by means of a little clothespin-like device called a "diode trap," the process can be reversed, provided the party receiving the call doesn't hang up. This works easily enough within a single exchange; for example, from one MOhawk number to another. But calls from different exchanges are much more complicated because the diode traps are needed for all incoming trunks. In Miami, that meant installing nearly 500 traps at 14 offices, and the city did not have that much equipment. An emergency call went out, and traps were delivered from as far away as Orlando.

In addition to this tight telephone surveillance, the FBI was determined to keep Robert Mackle's Lincoln automobile under discreet observation from the moment it set out to make the ransom payment. Most of the 150 FBI agents assigned to the Miami office were now scattered throughout the area in unmarked patrol cars. With them were FBI secretaries and girls from the steno pool who were acting as decoy "dates."

The agents were under explicit instructions not to intervene. Under no circumstances were they to get close enough to Mackle's Lincoln to arouse a breath of suspicion. There would be no attempts to arrest anyone: the kidnapers would be allowed to pick up the suitcase and leave unhindered. Regular police agencies in the Miami area had not been notified of the FBI's plans; that would have meant alerting an additional 400 men and would have increased the risk of a leak about the ransom delivery.

FBI technicians had installed a one-way radio transmitter in the Lincoln, its microphone hidden in the air-conditioner vent. Whatever Robert Mackle said in the car would now be heard in his den. But at Mackle's insistence the FBI had abandoned a scheme to replace him in the driver's seat with a look-alike agent. They had also been persuaded not to conceal a husky shotgun-wielding agent in the Lincoln's trunk.

The ransom note had declared, "We will call you at your home after midnight to advise you where you must go to deliver the money." Now everyone was keyed to the hour of 12. As soon as the phone rang, young Bobby Mackle would take the suitcase of money, go out to the garage and place it on the back seat of the Lincoln. An FBI agent would roll up the sliding overhead door. Road maps were out to pinpoint the site for Robert before he left. Mackle himself, following one of the kidnapers' stipulations, had changed to a white shirt and a new pair of white trousers. All was ready.

At 3:47 the telephone rang at last. "Robert Mackle?"

The voice was cold. Instantly, Mackle knew he was talking to the kidnaper.

The man said, "You'll go to Fair Isle Street. You know where it is? It is on the right off Bay Road."

"Right off Bay Road?"

"And you go to the—as far as you can go, up Fair Isle Street to the right toward the bay, and you'll come to a wall. If you look down the causeway, the bridge, over the wall, you'll see a blinking white light. You'll put the money in the box, which will have a light on it, and close the lid, and you'll turn around and leave. Is that clear?"

"Yes," Mackle said nervously. But it wasn't clear at all. Bay Road? Did the kidnaper mean South Bayshore Drive?

"And I go down which way on 27th Avenue, south or—"

"You take a right?"

"And down Fair Isle till I run into a dead-end street? I'm trying not to . . . I'm trying to get it . . . to a dead-end street."

The instructions were not good. For a frantic, hectic moment after the kidnaper hung up, Mackle tried to study a map.

"Oh, there it is," he said, as someone pointed. Then he hurried out to his car.

Speed was all-important. "We will not meet you," the kidnaper had warned, "if you fail to show within the time limit—which is only a short time longer than you will require to drive to the pickup site." Alone in the Lincoln, haunted by the kidnaper's threats, Mackle swung onto U.S. Route 1, radioing his movements to the listening agents as he went. So strong was the hidden transmitter that the car's blinking turn signal sounded like a plucked banjo string in the Mackle den.

Fair Isle lay 3¾ miles due east of the Mackle home, and the kidnaper's instructions, which reflected the most logical street approach by car, measured just under five miles. Mackle followed the directions as best he could. At last he reached an area which connected to a strip of beach known as Dinner Key. He was a mile too far south and he didn't know exactly where the bridge to Fair Isle was. The kidnaper's directions had been far from clear, and he himself had been under great emotional pressure. He turned right. It was the wrong way.

At Dinner Key he saw a couple of fishermen about to board a boat. "Is there a bridge over to an island around here?" he asked.

"Yeah," said one of the men. "But you can't get to it from this side; you have to go over that way." He sounded as if he knew what he was talking about. He did not. He was pointing in the wrong direction.

Acutely aware of passing time and bewildered by the many streets intersecting from the bay side, Mackle drove back onto South Bayshore Drive. He kept trying to read the signs through the darkness. At the end of one street he came to a pier, and suddenly, heart pounding, he realized his tires were off the sidewalk and into sand. In a panic he reversed, and his tires touched pavement again. But where was the bridge? Time was running out.

"I can't find the place!" he cried, his voice cracking. Once again he turned and sped back toward Dinner Key, where he knew a bait-and-tackle shop that stayed open all night. "Ain't but one island around here that's got a bridge to it," the man said. "It's up that way." He pointed northward, exactly where Robert Mackle had been.

"I'm desperate!" Mackle's voice crackled into the den of his house. "Somebody has to come help me!"

Billy Vessels could take no more. He and FBI Agent Edward Putz ran out of the Mackle front door and seconds later were screeching down U.S. 1 in Elliott Mackle's red Cadillac. With no radio equipment aboard, they were out of contact both with Mackle and the 20 or so FBI cars lying in wait around the general area of the pay drop.

At about this time FBI Agent Warren Walsh, accompanied by a secretary "date," was driving north on South Bayshore Drive when he saw what looked like a Ford with a man driving and a woman beside him. It had Massachusetts plates.

Cruising in the same area, Agent Ralph Hill also spotted the car. Its driver, seemingly looking for something, slowed and made a U-turn. Back in the Mackle den, agents were convinced the car was following Barbara's father. Obviously, if Vessels and Putz came racing onto the scene right now, the payoff would never take place. So they gave orders to stop Billy Vessels: "If you can't intercept him, ram him!" But unexpectedly the Massachusetts car dropped out of the picture, and the order was quickly countermanded.

Meanwhile, Vessels and Putz were carefully noting each street sign along South Bayshore Drive. They had one advantage over Robert Mackle: they had had plenty of time to study the map. There it was, a double sign: FAIR ISLE ST.—S. BAYSHORE LA. Then, up ahead, Vessels saw the Lincoln's headlights. He waved frantically, but Mackle went by without seeing him, still trying to identify the side streets.

The next time the Lincoln swung onto Bayshore, Vessels crossed the white center lane and stopped directly in its path. Leaping from the Cadillac, he threw himself into the back seat of Mackle's car. "Get going!" he said. Then, calmly, Vessels directed Mackle to the double sign and down Fair Isle Street, which narrowed between two houses and descended into a low retaining wall.

"Billy, I've already been here," protested Mackle.

"This is it! Take the damn thing! Get rid of it!" Vessels whispered.

Mackle got out with the heavy suitcase, deliberately leaving the front door open. He wanted the inside light on so that anyone looking would think he was by himself.

He walked to the wall. There was no box with a light, as the kidnaper had described. "I couldn't see any flashing lights anywhere. I couldn't see a bridge. I lifted the suitcase and gingerly let it down until I felt it rest on something solid."

For a second he stood there. Then he pivoted and walked hurriedly back to the Lincoln. Shortly after 4:30 he was home again.

Around 7 a.m. Mackle and Vessels, followed by FBI agents, drove back to the site of the pay drop to make sure the money had been picked up. It had. Mackle was immensely relieved. But suddenly an agent heard a *blurp* on his car radio and walked over to find out what the chattering was about. What he heard stunned him.

"There's been a shoot-out!" he called. "The money has been recovered. It's at the police station!"

"Oh, my God," sobbed Mackle. "My God, my God! They're going to kill my daughter!"

PACKED WITH $20 BILLS, the suitcase lay on a desk in Miami's downtown police headquarters. The officers responsible for bringing it in, Paul Self and William Sweeney, felt they had done a good night's work. Neither had been formally apprised of Barbara's kidnaping. What little they knew came only from press, radio and television.

Self, a sheriff's deputy from Dade County, was on night patrol when he saw a car parked in a blocked-off residential street at about 4 a.m. Ever since a nearby home had been burglarized, Self had made a point of checking out strange cars in the area, and he knew this one "didn't belong there." It was a 1966 blue Volvo station wagon. The doors were locked. Self noted the license plates—P72-098, Massachusetts, 1968—and called Dade County to see if the vehicle was wanted. They had no record on it. Self asked Dade County to notify the city police.

Within a few minutes, Officer Sweeney of the Miami police pulled up. He, too, checked the Volvo's number: it was not wanted by the city police either. The two men then idled away an hour in conversation.

Suddenly Deputy Self pointed. "Hey, look," he said. "There's somebody!" Both officers could see the figure of a man on the median strip of the highway about 500 feet away. The figure seemed to be walking toward the Volvo.

"Let's check him out," said Sweeney. As the officers hopped into their cars and headed for the man—bearing down on him from both sides of the median strip—he bolted into the darkness between a hedge and the far side of a house. He seemed to be carrying something, Sweeney recalled, and was "running like hell." Moments later Sweeney spotted him, attempting to scramble over a wire-link fence.

"Stop or I'll shoot!" Sweeney yelled.

Slowly the man pivoted. Sweeney thought he was surrendering, then saw the man was raising a carbine as he turned. Sweeney fired two quick shots and flung himself to the ground, expecting return fire. None came. When Sweeney looked up, the man was gone.

Returning to the Volvo, Sweeney saw some luggage sitting on the median strip where he and Self had first glimpsed the man. There was a duffle bag, with the name "Ruth Eisemann" stenciled on it in white paint, and a large suitcase. By this time other police cars were arriving on the scene, and Sweeney was joined on the median strip by Matthew Horan, a colleague from the city police department.

Together they opened the suitcase. Money spilled out. "Wow!" said Sweeney, and stuffed the bills back.

"It's got to be a hit on an armored car!" Horan gasped. Carefully, they locked the suitcase and duffle bag in the trunk of Sweeney's car and drove to headquarters.

They had no idea what they were holding. But the moment Miami Police Inspector Francis Napier reported for duty at 7 a.m. and saw the suitcase, he knew. He immediately called the FBI.

"Can you freeze it?" asked the agent who took the call, hoping the information could be kept secret.

Napier couldn't. Practically everyone in the station knew, and there was a newspaper reporter standing in the doorway looking straight at the open suitcase.

BILLY VESSELS and Robert Mackle drove back from Fair Isle Street in pit-bottom despair. "It's all over," Mackle wept. "I've bungled it."

At his house he told the FBI, "I don't care about the money. We've got to get another contact. We've got to let them know we had nothing to do with it. We have to tell them it was completely accidental, and that I have the money and that I'm ready to deliver it."

Not long afterward, a plea signed by Robert Mackle was issued to the news media. In the next 24 hours it was read repeatedly over television and radio and printed in all the newspapers.

"I regret that you did not get the money," the message ran, "because my only interest is the safety of my daughter. I did everything you told me to do, and I had nothing to do with the accidental appearance of the Miami police on the scene.

"Please contact me again through any channel. I will do anything you ask so my daughter will be freed."

Within hours of the morning's shoot-out, the FBI knew exactly whom it wanted for the kidnaping.

The Bureau's Boston office had quickly established ownership of the Volvo. It belonged to a George Deacon, a former employe of the Massachusetts Institute of Technology and now apparently employed as a research assistant by the University of Miami's Institute of Marine Sciences. Among other things found in the Volvo were a key to a room at the Rodeway Inn Motel, some blank paper showing distinct typewritten indentations of the very words used in the ransom note, and a bankbook in the name of George Deacon. In a black purse, FBI agents discovered papers identifying Deacon's "boy" accomplice as Ruth Eisemann-Schier, a native of Honduras and a graduate student at the Marine Institute. Also in the car were photographs of the two kidnapers (Deacon was big, beefy and bearded, as Professor Casse had noted), and a Polaroid photo of Barbara Mackle. A sign lettered KIDNAPED was under her chin. Her eyes were closed.

Agents immediately began following up all leads found in the car, and slowly the backgrounds and personalities of Deacon and Eisemann-Schier began to surface. At the Marine Institute, for example, they learned that Deacon had worked in Alaska until 1960. He was married and the father of two small boys. He had met Ruth at the Institute, and she had openly become his mistress. Deacon's wife was now living in California.

The FBI learned that Deacon was considered likable by some, but that others found him aggressive and arrogant. He wanted to be thought of as intelligent, even a genius, and he often gave the impression of being a "know-it-all."

Later that day the FBI discovered that George Deacon was an alias: the kidnaper's real name was Gary Steven Krist. FBI files in Washington produced the information that Krist, born in 1945 in Aberdeen, Wash., had been arrested three times for car theft and once for burglary, and had escaped from reformatories twice. At present he was wanted for unlawful interstate flight to avoid confinement.

The response to Robert Mackle's plea came at 5:15 p.m. Father Joseph Biain of the Church of the Epiphany in Miami received a call assuring Mackle that he was not being blamed for the local police interference, and urging him "not to be so nervous." The kidnaper then promised he would call Father Biain again at 11 p.m. with further instructions.

The Mackles were elated. The $500,000 had been re-counted for the second pay drop. Inspector Shroder had reestablished a command post in the Mackle den. As darkness fell, the vigil began again.

At the Church of the Epiphany, Father Biain also waited anxiously. But the call, when it came, was at 10:35, and it was not to Father Biain but to Father Mulcahy. Mulcahy immediately relayed the kidnaper's instructions for the second payoff to the Mackles. "This time they were pretty clear," Robert Mackle recalls.

But what if they delivered the money as instructed only to have someone else call the Church of the Epiphany at 11? Could they be dealing with two men—one the real kidnaper, the other an enterprising crook who knew that a suitcase containing $500,000 was up for grabs? Cautiously, they decided to let 11 p.m. go by—there was no second call—before making the delivery.

This time Billy Vessels drove the Lincoln, with Agent Lee Kusch hiding under a blanket in the back. Following instructions to the letter, Vessels headed west out of town on the Tamiami Trail until he reached a little dirt road on his left. He swung into it, and "all of a sudden there was this car in front of me, 12 or 15 yards ahead, its lights out. I hit the brakes hard and just stared for three or four seconds."

He turned off the engine, leaving the headlights on, and got out with the suitcase. As instructed, he put it down in the middle of the road, broadside to the Lincoln's headlight beams.

He walked back to the car. "The package is dropped!" he shouted into the microphone. "I'm heading home!"

At 12:30 a.m. the FBI dispatched another car to the site. The report came back moments later: "The package is gone."

4. A TALK WITH GOD

I THOUGHT ABOUT dying again. Three or four times I thought, this is going to be my casket. I wondered who would find my body. Maybe it would be a farmer, or someone building something. In 10 years? In 20? I wondered how I'd look and how I'd be identified.

When things got really bad, I'd say, I don't want to wait, I want to die now. And I'd turn off the fan. It would start getting hot and stuffy. Then I would get hold of myself. What if they found me and I'm already dead? Daddy is going to pay the money, Daddy will find me.

I thought about suffocating regardless of what I did. I knew there had to be an air intake above the ground and I thought, what happens if a squirrel or a small animal gets stuck in it? I had plenty of time to think of kidnaping in general, too. The logical thing in a kidnaping, of course, is just to kill the victim. And especially in a case like mine where I could identify the kidnapers. So why not just leave me here forever?

In my mind I constructed the ransom payoff again. This time I decided the kidnapers would want a little more money, $10,000. I sure was naïve. I decided something had gone wrong on Tuesday, the first night. I kept saying to myself, today is Wednesday, and the payoff will take place tonight. I kept building up to the point where they should arrive. But I heard nothing.

I kept thinking I should be hungry. I took three or four bites of an apple and that was enough. I'm sure I slept some, but I can't remember how much. Most of all it was cold and wet. The dripping almost drove me crazy. I wanted to stretch, but the box was too confining.

The time came when I started to talk to God. I don't generally pray. But when I was there, buried alive, I prayed. I just started talking, as if God were there beside me. And I said, "God, I know You are not going to let me die. Even if no one else knows where I am, You know." And I found this comforting. I know there is a God. And I know He heard me.

"WITHIN 12 HOURS after you deliver the money, you will receive another phone call advising you of your daughter's whereabouts," the kidnap note had said. Now 12 hours had come and gone, with no call.

That morning Inspector Shroder returned to his headquarters, vowing he'd be back "for the family reunion." Robert Mackle wanted desperately to believe him. Inevitably, though, it occurred to him that the kidnaper might make a run for it after collecting the ransom, forgetting all about Barbara. At one point he voiced everyone's fears by saying, "When they get her out, she'll be a vegetable. *If* they get her out."

At the switchboard of the FBI's Atlanta office, pretty Trisha Poindexter was just about ready to go to lunch. It was 12:47, Friday, December 20. Ever since the kidnaping, she had received scores of calls from people who wanted to be helpful.

"FBI," she answered, as another call came in.

"I want to give you some information on the Mackle girl," a man's voice said.

"Just a minute," said Trisha. "I'll give you an agent."

"No," the man answered emphatically. "I want to give you directions on how to find the capsule. I'll give this to you one time."

Trisha had no idea what he was talking about, but she began to write out the message.

"Out on I-85," the caller began. "Buford Highway. To Norcross. Stoplight at Buford and Tucker. Proceed 3.3 miles from intersection. Small white house on a hill. Turn left. Dirt road a mile on right. Go up there about 100 feet in the woods. Do you have that?"

"Yes," Trisha said, not at all certain that she had taken everything down correctly.

The caller hung up.

Still thinking about getting away for lunch, Trisha looked up as Agent Don Tackitt walked by. "Hey," she called, "this guy just called in and gave me some directions on how to find a capsule. . . ."

Capsule!

Moments later Trisha was in the office of Jack Keith, acting agent in charge, reading her notes. A dozen or so FBI agents had been scattered around Atlanta in anticipation of this call, and Agent Keith immediately ordered all units to head for the intersection and stoplight mentioned by the kidnaper.

"Proceed 3.3 miles." But in which direction? Four roads led away from the intersection, and there was a fifth nearby. Any of them could be the right one. Agents hurriedly began to check them out. Almost exactly 3.3 miles down one of them, they found a white house on a hill, but the only turnoff was to the right, not the left, and there was no dirt road a mile farther on. Off another of the roads they again found a white house on a hill at about the right distance. A two-lane blacktop went to the left, and about 1.1 miles along it a dirt road turned right.

"This has got to be it," said Keith. Leaving four agents to comb the area, he headed back to set up a command post at the crossroads. But he was far from optimistic. It was approaching four o'clock, and there was not much daylight left. He knew that every piece of rolling equipment the FBI owned in Atlanta would soon be there—but it might not be enough. They *had* to find the girl. She could be dying right now. If they could find her—now—they could save her.

Back at the dirt road, Agents Vincent Capazella and Robert Kennemur pushed their way into the underbrush. The dirt road ended some 130 feet from the blacktop at a junkpile near the foundation of a torn-down house. Beyond the trash and flattened beer cans littering the site, they discovered the faint traces of a path leading down a wooded hillside. Following it, they reached a point some 300 feet from the dump. Suddenly Capazella stopped.

"I hear a noise," he said. He kicked the undermat of fallen leaves and pine needles and saw red clay, the fresh red earth of Georgia.

I HEARD A LITTLE RUSTLE. It was the first time, absolutely the first time, that I'd heard anything. I turned off the fan and held my breath, straining to hear it again. Nothing.

But it had to be something. I just knew it. I clenched my fists and pounded as hard as I could. Once more I stopped to listen, and I didn't hear anything. I started pounding again. By this time I didn't think anyone was there. And while I was pounding I heard footsteps and then a man shouting: "Barbara Mackle! This is the FBI!"

Agent Capazella scuffed the red earth again. Both he and Kennemur heard three distinct knocks. Frantically, they clawed dead leaves, twigs and branches aside. "I'll radio for help," said Capazella.

Within minutes Jack Keith and other agents were racing to the scene. In the junkpile one agent found an old bullet-riddled bucket, once used for target practice, and gouged and scooped at the tightly packed earth. Another ripped a branch from a small sweetgum tree and dug at the mound Capazella had uncovered. Other agents tore away with tire irons or their bare hands. Still others had received radio instructions to bring shovels.

Digging feverishly, they heard the fan's faint hum, but didn't know what it was. Agent William Colombell had the terrible thought that Barbara would die before they could reach her. Another thought kept recurring to Kennemur. Would she be stark-raving mad?

One end of the box was uncovered; with the aid of a tire iron, the agents tore off the top. It was the wrong end, a section partitioned off to hold a battery, pump and ventilation fan. It took another four or five minutes to uncover a trapdoor-like lid attached with four hinges and tightly screwed down. It was 4:32 p.m. But for Barbara Mackle it was dawn. It had been 83 hours till dawn.

I HEARD THE PRYING. They were right over my head. The box was shaking. And then finally they opened the lid and the dirt was falling and I heard a loud *creeeeek*.

It was so bright I blinked. I saw hands reaching in for me. There was a whole lot of men, all of them looking down at me. They were all smiling, too, and I could see tears in their eyes, tears and sweat.

They pulled me out and asked how I was. I said, "Fine," and tried to stand up. My knees gave way; they caught me, and one of the men said, "She can't walk."

And there I was, grinning. I know I looked ridiculous, wet and dirty and everything. I asked, "How is my family?" and they said, "Fine, fine." Then one of them picked me up and carried me through the woods to their cars. "What time is it?" I asked.

Someone said around four o'clock, and I said, "In the morning?" and he said no.

Another guy asked, "How long have you been here?"

"Just as soon as they got me."

"Wasn't there anyone with you?"

"No," I said. "Nobody came back after me."

He didn't say anything. No one said anything. I could tell they were angry. They put me in a car, in the back seat, and the man on my right had tears running down his face. I really didn't think he was crying for me. I said, "Is there something wrong?"

And he said no and sniffed and looked out the window, and then it dawned on me and I felt bad for even mentioning it. So I said, "You are the handsomest men I've ever seen." And they all laughed.

The man in the front seat said, "Well, now we know something is wrong with you," and I laughed.

In the Mackle game room 669 miles south of Atlanta, Agent Lee

Kusch impatiently picked up the telephone. "Get off the line, please," he began, then stopped in mid-sentence. "I'm sorry," he said, and handed the phone to Frank Mackle.

"I heard a male voice," said Frank. "Someone said, 'Mr. Hoover is coming on the line.' "

Frank braced himself. In a second he would know.

"This is Edgar Hoover," said the director of the FBI in a quick, staccato voice. "I have good news. Barbara is alive and well."

"She is alive and well!" Frank shouted, and saw everyone stare at him, stunned, immobile. "It was a second and a half before anyone reacted," he recalls. "And then everyone was coming at me. I could see Robert running for Jane. And the whole house went crazy."

The trackdown of Gary Steven Krist was swift. Just before 4 p.m. the same day that Barbara was found, a West Palm Beach boat dealer reported selling a 16-foot-outboard motorboat to a man answering Krist's description. The man had aroused his suspicions by paying in cash with $20 bills taken from a brown paper bag. He had asked if the craft would get him to Bimini without running out of gas.

Thirty minutes later, the first Coast Guard helicopter was searching for Krist between Fort Lauderdale and Bimini. The hunt lasted until nightfall. Then someone began wondering whether Krist was really headed for the Bahamas—or whether he could be using the Okeechobee Waterway to cross Florida and emerge in the Gulf of Mexico.

Calls to locks along the waterway produced the information that Krist had indeed chosen this escape route. At 10:30 the next morning FBI agents aboard a Coast Guard airplane spotted him near the Gulf and kept him under constant watch.

Knowing he had been found, Krist ran his boat aground on the sandflats of Hog Island, a swampy bit of tidal land covered with dense vegetation. He leaped ashore and disappeared inland. But the island was a trap. The only way to leave on foot was across a narrow, easily patrolled sandflat. Eighty-five agents and more than 150 local police converged on the spot, and around midnight Krist was captured as he crouched in a tangle of mangrove roots. All of the money, except for $3000, was recovered. Krist had held onto it for just 48 hours.

Ruth Eisemann-Schier took longer to catch. Separated from Krist by the shoot-out that had marred the first ransom payoff, she had panicked and left Miami that afternoon. Not until March 5, 1969, did the FBI locate her in Norman, Okla., working as a carhop at a drive-in called the Boomerang, under an assumed name.

Krist's trial opened on May 19, 1969, in DeKalb County, Georgia. It moved swiftly, the prosecution showing that Krist had minutely planned the kidnaping: he had chosen Barbara Mackle as a victim after a careful study of the Miami social register, and had spent months building her capsule—made of plywood and fiberglass and measuring eight feet long by two feet wide and high. He had used materials from the workshops of the Marine Institute. After less than four hours of deliberation, the jury brought in a verdict of guilty with a recommendation of life imprisonment. (Krist could have received the death penalty.) Three days later, Ruth Eisemann-Schier pleaded guilty to her role in the kidnaping and drew a seven-year sentence.

THE ONE QUESTION everyone always asks about me is "How is she, *really?*" Mother kids me about it. "Now, Barbara," she says, "if you ever do anything odd during the rest of your life, everyone is going to say, 'I knew it. I knew it all along.'"

But I'm fine. I haven't seen a psychiatrist. I don't think I need one.

I don't think about the kidnaping very much. I still wake up occasionally, startled and afraid, not knowing where I am for a few seconds. But it goes away quickly. When I think about the kidnaping now, it is usually about my family. Coming home. Meeting Dad. Seeing Mother and Bobby. Their faces. I could see the mental agony in their faces.

The kidnaping, I know, has changed my life in some ways forever. I never truly understood how profoundly other people could care about someone they didn't know. We had so many letters to answer. I answered all the personal ones to me, and Mother and Daddy and Bobby and my uncles answered all theirs. I even have a Czechoslovak Fan Club. We had to have a secretary to help with some of the others, and she was so overcome by emotion she couldn't type.

You hear so much about the insensitive nature of many today, and I was amazed that so many thousands of persons identified themselves with our family. People who cared. I am convinced that compassion is a basic part of man's nature.

I have no hatred for either Krist or Ruth. I just don't. Perhaps I would have felt differently if anything had happened to Mother or Daddy—if they had had a mental breakdown or anything like that. But we've all come out all right.

Every once in a while I think I could still be there. And I thank God. We all take life so much for granted.

Carrying the Fire:

AN ASTRONAUT'S JOURNEYS

CONDENSED FROM THE BOOK BY

Michael Collins

PHOTOGRAPHS COURTESY OF NASA

The first landing on the moon has rightly been called one of man's greatest adventures. The daring enterprise is described in this book, not by one of the pair of astronauts who actually set foot on the lunar surface, but by the third member of the Apollo 11 team, Michael Collins. His job was to pilot the command ship, *Columbia,* round and round the moon and be in position to pick up his companions after the completion of their mission—a task Collins did perfectly.

Yet this book is more than a report of that eventful day in July 1969. It is the story of what it took to be an astronaut.

1. OUTWARD AND UPWARD

Carrying the Fire is simply what I feel space flight is like, when limited to three words. Of course, in Greek mythology it was a god (some say Apollo) who carried the fiery sun across the sky in a chariot, but beyond that—how would you carry fire? Very carefully, that's how, with lots of planning and at considerable risk. It is a most delicate cargo, and the carrier must constantly be on his toes lest it spill. I carried the fire for six years, and now I would like to tell you about it, simply and directly as a test pilot must, for the trip deserves the telling.

The rumor was out. NASA (the National Aeronautics and Space Administration) was hiring astronauts again. They had, of course, already picked seven in 1959—the *Original* Seven, who were all military test pilots. These men had been exposed to greater public scrutiny than any group of pilots, engineers, scientists, freaks, or what-have-you in recorded history. And the reaction had been uniformly good. All of them came through as Gordon Goodguy, steely resolve mixed with robust good humor, waiting for whatever hazards might be in store for them "up there." The nation loved them.

Except for the "old heads" at Edwards Air Force Base in California, where I was a test pilot myself. Some of these veteran pilots were disgruntled because they had not been selected, but others had avoided the program like the plague. They were here to *fly,* not to be locked up in a can and shot around the world like ammunition. Not having accumulated sufficient credentials to be so snooty, the new boys like myself watched and wondered. For me, the clincher came on February 20, 1962, with John Glenn's magnificent three-orbit flight aboard Friendship 7. Imagine being able to circle the globe once each 90 minutes, high above all clouds and turbulence!

NASA's announcement, when it came in April 1962, was encouraging. The agency was sticking with test pilots. A degree in one of the biological sciences or engineering was also required, and candidates could not be more than six feet tall or over 35 years old. My application was in before the ink was dry on the announcement.

The first hurdle was a real one—a five-day physical exam at Brooks Air Force Base, Texas. Monday morning you arrive, fasting, and are greeted by a lab technician who takes what seems to be a quart of blood. You then breakfast on a large beakerful of glucose, sickeningly sweet, and are punctured with more needles. Cold water is poured into one of your ears; your body is taped with electrocardiograph sensors; you blow into a bag; your lower bowel is violated by the "steel eel."

Then the shrinks take over. Thrust and parry. What are inkblots supposed to mean anyway? I want to fly to the moon, badly, and I will describe the card they give me in any way that will please them. Perhaps I see a great white moon on it, or a picture of Mother and Dad—with Dad a little larger than Mother.

More tests and interviews followed in Houston. By now our group had been pruned to the point that, out of nearly 300 candidates, only 32 were left. The interviewing was getting to the serious stage, and I wasn't very confident, mainly because, with barely one year's experience in flight testing, I knew my credentials were marginal.

In Houston we were shown two movies, one a grand tour of our solar system, the second a series of underwater shots of reef life. Then we took out paper and pencil and described, as best we could, each planet visited and each fish glimpsed.

Then came the main course—the technical interview. The questions required answers of substance and precision. In some cases I felt I gave satisfactory answers; in others I clearly did not.

Back at Edwards, the really tough part—the waiting—began. Of the nine Air Force finalists, six were stationed at Edwards, and we warily kept tabs on each other, on the lookout for any behavior that might indicate someone had heard good news from NASA.

In mid-September, the word arrived in a letter to me from Bob Gilruth, the director of Houston's Manned Spacecraft Center:

> The impression that you made on our Selection Committee was favorable. Overall, however, we did not feel that your qualifications met the special requirements of the astronaut program as well as those of some of the other outstanding candidates.

My failure was, of course, quite a blow, even though I had never really expected to make it. Certainly I had nursed no childhood dream of flying to the moon—or anywhere else.

I took my first plane ride as a boy in Puerto Rico, where my father, a career Army officer, was then stationed. But my love affair with the airplane, unlike that of many young Americans, was neither all-consuming nor constant. However, I did enter West Point and, as graduation approached, I had to decide whether to stick with the Army or strike out in a new direction with the Air Force.

The airplane as a career posed problems. One could—25 percent did—wash out of pilot training, and one could be killed practically as easily in peacetime as in war. Then, too, I had a personal problem. My father's younger brother was Army Chief of Staff at the time; my father had retired as a two-star general; another uncle had been a brigadier; my brother was a colonel; my cousin a major—all in the Army. I felt I had a better chance to make my own way in the Air Force.

After six months in Mississippi learning the basics, I moved on to Texas for instrument and formation flying and jet indoctrination. At graduation I was among the few chosen to go to Nellis Air Force Base, which was then the sole channel to Korea, where our F-86 Sabrejets were battling the MIGS so successfully.

At Nellis we really learned to fly—a concentrated, aggressive course designed to weed out anyone who might be a marginal performer. It was a brutal process. In the 11 weeks I was there, 11 people were killed.

There followed assignments in California (the Korean War was over) and France. I began to think about how I might progress beyond my present station. My brother-in-law, a Naval aviator, had recently completed the Navy's test-pilot school in Maryland, and I was fascinated by the brief glimpses of his flying which I gleaned from his letters. So, after returning to the States in 1957, I lost no opportunity to fly whatever airplanes I could, sweet-talking strange operations officers, making myself available nights and weekends, and taking trips that no one else wanted. In this way I finally built up my flying time past the magic 1500-hour mark needed to apply to the test-pilot school at Edwards. I immediately fired off my application.

There must have been thousands like me. Therefore I could not have been more pleased when I was assigned to "Class 60-C, commencing 29 August 60, course duration 32 weeks." *This was the place.* Here the first American jet had been tested; here Capt. Chuck Yeager had broken the sound barrier on October 14, 1947; here Capt. Mike Collins was going onward and upward.

The place was also dry, hot, windy and isolated, not at all what a proper Bostonian—my wife—would expect as a nursery for our firstborn. But at least we were in for a long and stable assignment. And God knows Pat deserved it: in less than four years of marriage we had lived in four houses, four apartments and what seemed like 44 motels.

I was soon immersed in the theoretical and analytical intricacies of testing new aircraft. We learned to control airspeed to the nearest knot; we learned to observe, remember and record every last movement of a bucking, heaving, spinning plane; we learned to organize our tasks so that not one minute of practice flight test time was wasted.

Our great fear was that we would be sent off to the bush leagues, assigned to fly endless circles in the sky while an engineer in the back of the plane twiddled with the dials of some new electronic box. The majority of our class would fill these quasi-test-pilot positions, while the *real* test pilots would be assigned to Test Operations (Fighter Branch, of course). We waited and we worried.

Finally, the word arrived. By what alchemy I shall never know, the only available slot in Fighter Ops went to Mike Collins. And for almost a year it seemed the best job in the world. Then gradually it lost its larger-than-life quality. For I got to know people in Houston, and I envied them.

SPECIAL REQUIREMENTS? If I didn't have them, could I get them?

With NASA growing by leaps and bounds, the Air Force became increasingly edgy about the role it might be assigned in the exploration of this new medium grandly called Space. As a result, the Experimental

Flight Test Pilot School was renamed the Aerospace Research Pilot School (ARPS), and a couple of "postgraduate" classes were introduced. In these, selected graduates of the test-pilot course were brought back for six months of additional instruction. Anything which would qualify me for the next NASA selection was worth a try, so I took a six-month leave from Fighter Ops, and in October 1962 reported to ARPS.

We students had some interesting flying to do, centering on the F-104. Built by Lockheed in the mid-1950s, the Starfighter was the first Mach 2 (twice the speed of sound) plane in our inventory.

The F-104 was our toy at ARPS. We pretended it was a spacecraft and tried to do spacecraft-like things with it. We dressed up in pressure suits, climbed to 35,000 feet, got it going as fast as was legal, and then pulled back on the stick and zoomed upward as high as it would go, until we floated over the top of a lazy arc in a not-so-bad simulation of the weightlessness of space. At 90,000 feet, the sky overhead is so dark blue as to be almost the pure black of space; the weather—indeed, practically all the atmosphere—is below you. So near, yet so far away!

We spent time indoors, too, some of it crushingly boring, some fascinating. Consider the rendezvous problem, with one vehicle behind another and the laggard wishing to catch up. In an airplane, the answer is simple: increase the speed and approach from the rear. This simply will not work in a spacecraft: adding thrust toward the target puts one into a higher orbit, and higher orbits are slower; so, instead of catching up, one falls behind. No, against all instincts, one must apply thrust away from the direction of the target, drop down into a lower, faster orbit, and then transfer back up into the original orbit at precisely the right point.

Our class entered the homestretch amid rumors about another NASA astronaut selection, which were confirmed on June 5, 1963. Fortunately, I was still under the age limit (by 16 months) and I met all the other requirements; on the other hand, as NASA had broadened the field to include non-test pilots, I had no idea what my chances were.

The selection process followed the pattern established the previous year: by mid-July, NASA had screened 271 applicants and reduced their number to 34. After another round of medical screenings, I went back to Houston in September for interviews. This time I carried with me a sense of finality; the moment of truth was coming in my attempts to convince NASA that it couldn't fly to the moon without me.

Unconvinced myself, I quietly resumed my life in Fighter Ops at Edwards, pretending that all was well. The weeks became a month and more. Finally, on October 14, I was called to the phone, and on came the gravelly voice of Deke Slayton, of the Original Seven. Never one to use a paragraph when a phrase would do, Deke allowed as how he was ready to hire me, if I still wanted to come to work for NASA. I don't have any idea what I said, but it must have been intelligible, for Slayton grunted, told me to be in Houston on October 18, and hung up.

2. TRAINING

AT THIS TIME in Houston, a lot of answers still had to be provided before any rational person could assess the chances of reaching the moon. Where to begin, what to study, how to take the first step on the proverbial thousand-mile journey? Thoughtfully, NASA had provided a tidy little course of classroom instruction for us, divided into fairly predictable categories: astronomy, rocket propulsion, navigation, digital computers and so on. Everything on the list seemed in balance. That is, until the last item: geology—58 hours. Geology?

Apparently, we were not only going to fly to the moon, we were expected to act as prospectors once we got there. (How could I have known that $[Fe^{2+},Mg]Ti_{2}O_{5}$ would be discovered at Tranquillity Base in 1969; and that this new mineral would be called "armalcolite," after Armstrong, Aldrin and Collins?) We had to learn a whole new way of looking at rocks. "Gray and lumpy" would not suffice; it was now "hypidiomorphic granular, porphyritic, with medium-grained gray phenochrists."

Next came a survival course, designed to teach us what to do if the spacecraft landed unexpectedly in a remote part of the world. So we were off to Panama, to the Air Force's tropical survival school, where we spent a couple of days in the classroom followed by a couple of days living off the land.

Fortunately, no spacecraft has yet come down in an area where survival training has been needed. Thus, as in the case of so much astronaut training, the information has never really been used. But such preparation has been one of NASA's wisest investments.

Little by little, our group, the Fourteen, edged toward accreditation as "real" astronauts. Both Gemini and Apollo missions were in the formative stages, but it was still early enough to change designs, based on what potential crew members had to say. Each astronaut was given a slice of the technological pie. Among the slices were mission planning, communications, guidance and navigation, and mine—pressure suits and extra-vehicular activity (EVA).

There is a kind of love-hate relationship between an astronaut and his pressure suit: love, because it is an intimate garment protecting him 24 hours a day; hate, because it can be extremely uncomfortable. Each crew member has three suits tailored to his individual measurements. The first, called the training suit, was worn in simulators, centrifuges, zero-G airplanes—whenever the realism of having the crew suited was required. It got battered and beaten by several hundred hours of hard use. The second suit was the flight suit, the third the backup. Both were generally worn just enough (perhaps 20 hours each) to break them in.

First and foremost, a pressure suit must be airtight, so that it can be pumped up (pressurized) to protect the astronaut from the vacuum of space. Without gas pressure around him, the fluids inside his body would vaporize—his blood would literally bubble. So we must begin with a gas bag, or bladder, which can be pressurized to 3.7 pounds per square inch. To prevent ballooning, there must then be a restraint layer, which still allows the suit to bend as the astronaut bends, twist as he twists and, in general, act as a tough extra layer of skin.

Inside an airtight bladder, the astronaut would dissolve in a pool of sweat, so a complex array of ventilation tubes had to be added to torso, helmet, arms and legs. In addition, there was an electrical system which provided a path for radio signals to reach earphones. Biomedical information was routed from four sensors (taped to the chest) into the same electrical connector.

Gloves and helmet added another host of design problems. The gloves had to be thin and flexible to allow manipulation of delicate controls even when pressurized. The helmet had to be strong, light, comfortable, contain earphones and microphones, and provide excellent vision.

If things seem to be getting complicated, remember that all we have done so far is to allow a man to operate in a vacuum. Now we must add the other hazards of that vacuum: the blinding energy of the sun, the subfreezing temperature of any object shielded from the sun, and the possible penetration of the suit by tiny projectiles called micrometeorites. Fortunately, the problems of heat, cold and micrometeorites had a common solution—a thick cover layer of a felt-like material which would be a superb thermal insulator, and a tough nylon outer covering to provide protection against high-velocity impacts.

To test the suits, we took to the zero-G airplane—a KC-135 (essentially a Boeing 707) with all the seats removed and the interior padded. The pilots would dive steeply, pull up sharply and then push the plane over the top at exactly the right rate to keep our bodies suspended between ceiling and floor in the aft cabin.

The first time I had flown it, back in 1963 at Edwards, it had been a simple indoctrination flight, and our ARPS class piled on board with great enthusiasm, dressed in thin cotton flying suits. We laughed ourselves silly trying to drink water out of paper cups (in zero G you really can't do it; the water floats up out of the cup in great spherical blobs before you can get it into your mouth), and did a hundred other foolish things not possible here on earth.

The zero-G airplane I later learned to hate was altogether a different matter. First, we were there to work, not play. Second, we nearly always wore pressure suits, meaning we were hot to begin with and got hotter yet. Third, we always had more things to find out than we had time to do, so we worked frantically during each parabola—and we flew so many parabolas!

In addition, I was reintroduced to that diabolical device known as the centrifuge, whose job is to imitate the acceleration one experiences riding a rocket into space or the deceleration caused by re-entering the earth's atmosphere. It does it by swinging a small gondola, or imitation cockpit, around in a circle, on the end of a 50-foot arm. As the arm spins faster and faster, centrifugal force pushes the occupant deeper and deeper into his seat or couch. Seven Gs were routinely reached during the Apollo lunar return, and if your angle was slightly steeper than normal, it could easily soar to 10 or 15. Hence, 15 Gs was our limit on the wheel, and it was no fun at all.

At anything over eight Gs, I start feeling pain centered below my breastbone. By ten Gs the pain has increased and breathing is nearly impossible; in fact, an entirely different breathing technique is needed at high Gs. If you breathe normally, you find you can exhale just fine, but when you try to reinflate your lungs, it's just as if steel bands were tightly encircling your chest. So you have to keep your lungs almost fully inflated at all times, and give rapid little pants "off the top."

All this has a kind of sinister fascination the first time through, but once is enough. After that it becomes most unpleasant work, with a lingering hangover that can last a day or two, sometimes accompanied by dizziness when the head is turned suddenly. So I wasn't too happy going back to the centrifuge, especially since, with three suits, I had to go through all the tests three times.

NINETEEN SIXTY-FIVE was the year for Gemini. After two successful unmanned shots, Gemini 3 was ready by March 23; then came 4, 5, 6 and 7. The purpose of Gemini was to test EVA and rendezvous-in-space techniques and, even more important, to discover if a crew could sustain eight days of weightlessness—the time it would take to get to the moon and back. In general, all went well.

Late in June, I learned that I would be part of the Gemini 7 backup crew—and a prime crew member for Gemini 10. John Young, who had flown on Gemini 3, was also chosen for 10, and by the time 6 and 7 were back on earth, we had started to train in earnest. We were sobered by the magnitude of the job asked of us. In three days, we were to conduct two rendezvous with two different Agenas (target vehicles) in two different orbits; two EVAS, each quite different from the other; and 15 scientific and technical experiments.

As 1966 began, my life assumed an urgency I had never felt before. I kept a 7-by-10-inch notebook divided into six sections: (1) Schedule, (2) Systems Briefings, (3) Experiments, (4) Flight Plan, (5) Miscellaneous, and (6) Open Items. Section 6 meant problems of which I became aware as we went along and which were duly listed by number. I reviewed them periodically and bugged the appropriate people for answers. As each was solved, I drew a line through its number. By the morning of launch, I had 138 items, and all 138 had been crossed out.

The spacecraft spent most of its time in St. Louis inside a special room—a room kept meticulously clean, painted white, with filtered air. Everyone was dressed in white smock and cap, and white booties. The white room ran on a 24-hour schedule and usually had three or four spacecraft in it, mounted vertically as they would be on the launch pad. Hour after hour, John and I lay on our backs with our legs above us, lazily flicking Gemini 10's switches as we ran through a variety of tests. Each test had a script, a huge volume listing the role of every supporting technician in the drama of make-believe flying. Some sequences were straightforward; others required a complex interrelationship between the test conductor, his supporting crew of equipment operators and the crew in the cockpit. We perused the volume ahead of time and red-lined any notation referring to our participation. Then, precisely at the correct instant in the test sequence, we would activate the right switch for exactly the right interval. If we or anyone else on the team goofed, the test was repeated, sometimes three or four times.

No one who has never seen a Gemini can fully appreciate what it's like being locked inside of one. It is so *small,* smaller than the front seat of a Volkswagen, with a large console between the pilots—sort of like having a color-TV set in a VW separating two adults. You cannot get out of the seat because there is no place to go. I couldn't sit in the Gemini on the ground more than three hours at a stretch. What made long flights possible was weightlessness, which allows the astronaut to float free of the seat, restoring circulation and preventing bedsores.

When it was not the spacecraft, it was the simulator—the very heart and soul of the NASA system. Learning geology is commendable; jungle living is amusing; the centrifuge hurts; the spacecraft ground tests are useful. But one does not fly until the simulator says he is ready.

The St. Louis simulator specialized in rendezvous. Day after day, we sat in this infernal machine, watching a light on a darkened screen (the Agena) surrounded by other lights (the stars). Sometimes we caught the Agena without difficulty; at other times, we arced wildly through the skies, missing the Agena entirely, or catching it only after our fuel tanks had theoretically run dry.

As the flight nears, a crew balances the time remaining against training objectives not yet attained, and a point is reached where you must admit that everything is not going to get done. At least that's the way it was on Gemini 10—but we had arranged priorities so that items left unstudied were in the "nice to know" rather than the "need to know" category. In my case, the pace of training had been building for months and peaked about three days before the flight. At that point I simply said, "The hell with it! If I don't know it now, I never will."

3. A RAMBLE IN SPACE

THE FAMILIAR pressure suit is there waiting for me, in a modified house trailer where we will dress. It is not far from Pad 19, where our rocket stands. A medical technician shaves a clearing in my chest hair and tapes his disk-shaped sensors to my skin.

Then I climb into cotton underwear cinched up with a special built-in belt, which will amplify my heartbeat for relay to Mission Control; next I get into the suit. Finally, the helmet is gently, almost reverently, lowered onto the neck ring until satisfactorily aligned. Then it is brutally shoved downward, locks snapping into place. The transition into space begins when the visor is lowered and locked. From now on, no air will be breathed, only pure oxygen; no human voice will be heard, unless electronically piped in. Out to the launch pad now and into the cockpit with willing hands making the necessary assist, shoving a bit, connecting oxygen hoses and finally lowering the hatches gently upon us. We are isolated at last, in our own little world, with only the crackle of the intercom and the hiss of oxygen for company.

Days have turned to hours, hours to minutes. No simulation this, no ride back down on the elevator, no debriefing over coffee. The excited voice on the radio reaches the end of its message: 10—9—8 . . . grab the ejection D-ring between your legs with both hands; one jerk and our seats will explode free of this monster . . . 7—6—5 . . . it's really going to happen . . . 4—3—2—1 . . . engines should be starting—IGNITION—pay attention to those gauges—LIFT-OFF!

A barely perceptible bump, and we are airborne. Fairly high noise level, but we feel the machine, rather than hear it. There is absolutely no sensation of speed, and only a moderate increase above one G as we are gently pushed back into our contoured seats. In 50 seconds we pass our ejection-seat limit and I loosen the death grip on my D-ring.

As we reach orbit, I get my first manifestation of weightlessness: tiny bits of debris—washers, screws, dirt particles—are floating aimlessly about the cockpit. In an hour or so they will be gone, sucked into the inlet screen of the ventilation system, but for the time being they are an amusing oddity as well as a sober reminder that this machine had been assembled by fallible hands which drop things that find their way into inaccessible and possibly dangerous crevices.

At two hours and ten minutes we fire our thrusters briefly to get in proper phase with our first Agena target; at 3:48 we ease into a course 15 miles below it. The ground has coached us on all these maneuvers. At 4:34 we make a move on our own, using our radar and computer to calculate an intercept trajectory. Everything looks good as Agena grows from a flashing light to a discernible cylinder. Then, suddenly, something is wrong. We are off to one side and turning, but not getting any closer. It's a mistake we'd made in the simulator, correctable, but only by using extra fuel.

Finally, we are parked next to our Agena, right on time (with only 36 percent of our fuel remaining instead of the 60 percent we should have at this stage). For the second time in history—Gemini 8 was first—one spacecraft docks with another, as John smoothly and expertly guides our nose into the docking collar on the front of the Agena. The Agena has its own engine, and we will use it now to boost us to its brother—the Gemini 8 Agena somewhere up there above us.

The first step in this overtaking process will lift John and me higher than man has ever ventured—475 miles. The purpose of the maneuver, however, is not to set a new altitude record, but rather to establish the proper timing of our orbit relative to 8 Agena's orbit. We need to slow down a bit, and that means we must go higher. The operation goes without a hitch.

My first EVA comes on Day 2; it is designed to get ultraviolet signatures of selected hot, young stars. Since the spacecraft windows do not transmit ultraviolet light, I must operate the camera while standing in the open hatch. We dump cabin pressure by opening a small valve. Like letting water out of a bathtub, it takes a while, and we don't dare open the hatch until the pressure gauge reads zero.

As I cautiously emerge, waist-high, it is pitch-black. The stars are everywhere, on all sides. Down below, the earth is barely visible, as the moon is not up, and the only light comes from an occasional lightning flash along a row of thunderheads. We are gliding across the world in silence, with absolute smoothness; a motion of stately grace which makes me feel godlike as I stand erect in my chariot cruising the sky.

EVA No. 2, on the third day, is more difficult. John is flying in formation with the 8 Agena. I am to go over to it and remove a package that has been measuring micrometeorite impacts for the past three months. I am tethered to the Gemini by a 50-foot umbilical cord carrying oxygen and communications. I have a nitrogen "gun," which fires bursts of gas to control my movements.

Gently, gently, I push away from Gemini. It's not more than three or four seconds before I collide with my target, the docking adapter on the end of the Agena. I grab the slippery lip of the docking cone with both hands and start working my way around it counterclockwise. It takes about 90 degrees of handwalking in stiff, pressurized gloves to reach the package. Now I must stop; I am falling off! I have built up too much momentum, and the inertia in my torso and legs keeps me moving; first my right hand, then my left feels the Agena slither away. I see absolutely nothing but black sky for several seconds; then the Gemini heaves into view. I am up above it looking down at John's window.

With my gun I fly behind the Gemini, a location I have never intended to explore. "I'm back behind the cockpit, John, so don't fire any thrusters."

My approach to the open hatch isn't exactly graceful, but I snag it with one arm and it slows me practically to a stop. Time for another try. Up I glide and plunge my right hand down into the recess between the docking adapter and the main body of the Agena. I find some wires to cling to. I'm not going to slip off this time! Finally, I make it around to the meteorite package and retrieve it. I come home the easy way, hand over hand on my umbilical, but slowly to avoid going fast enough to splat up against Gemini.

BEING THE 17TH AMERICAN to fly in space is a small distinction, and in a small way it changed my life. My name didn't become a household word, but I was a real, or "flown," astronaut now. I began a lifetime of explaining "what it was like up there" in a press conference and at technical debriefings. I put in my travel voucher for the Gemini flight (three days at $8 per diem: $24), took two weeks at the beach to get reacquainted with Pat and our three children, and returned to my desk, available for the Apollo program.

It seemed to be just the right time. Gus Grissom was talking about getting Apollo 1 (then labeled 012) airborne before the end of the year, and it was hoped that the lunar landing might be possible as early as 1968. Therefore, I was delighted when Frank Borman told me I was assigned to his crew.

On Friday, January 27, 1967, we had just started a staff meeting in Deke Slayton's office (he was away at the time), when the red crash phone on Deke's desk rang. Don Gregory, Deke's assistant, snatched it up and listened impassively. Finally, he hung up and said very quietly, "Fire in the spacecraft."

That's all he had to say. There was no doubt about which spacecraft (012) or who was in it (Gus Grissom, Ed White, Roger Chaffee) or where (Pad 34, Cape Kennedy) or why (a final systems test) or what (death, the quicker the better).

My God, such an obvious thing, and yet until right now we hadn't considered it. We worried about engines that wouldn't start, we worried about leaks, we even worried about how cabin pressure might be lowered to stop a fire in space. But right here on the ground, we put three guys inside an untried spacecraft, strapped them into couches, locked the hatches behind them and left them no quick way of escaping.

As we sat stunned, we began to think about the crew's families. I called the astronaut office and got Al Bean, who said he would organize the notification of the wives while I stayed near the red telephone. Within a few minutes, Al had found astronauts and wives to go to the Grissom and White households, but he had not been able to find an appropriate person to notify Martha Chaffee. With a sinking feeling in my stomach, I told Al that I would tell her, and slowly drove the mile and a half to her house, three doors down from ours.

Martha was left with a folded flag and two children to raise, and all the other wives were left with the knowledge that space flight, just like the airplane, *did* kill. Always before it had been a possibility, but it had never happened. How many astronauts would decide now that they hadn't signed up to be incinerated, and would quit? How many wives would quit if their husbands didn't? The answer, of course, is that no one quit; but how many close calls there were, no one can say. I know I never discussed it with Pat in any but the most superficial way. I suppose I was afraid to measure the depth of hostility toward this Apollo which held us both captive.

In the dismal early months of 1967, it became increasingly obvious that the fire in 012 was not simply a one-time freakish occurrence but a sign of generic weakness. That meant new materials, new mechanisms, and all these things took time. In the aftermath of the fire, our hopes for getting three manned flights off in 1967 quickly evaporated. A year's delay at least, said the smart money, to fireproof the interior. It ended up being closer to two.

Meanwhile, work throughout the Apollo program continued without let-up. My own personal hair shirt was the Apollo guidance-and-control system, with its on-board computer, a telescope, a sextant, and a three-gimbal inertial platform. The basic idea was simple enough. It all began with the stars, whose position in space was well known and unchanging. The wizards at M.I.T. had decreed that the astronauts' computer should be given the celestial coordinates of 37 selected stars. The astronaut, peering through telescope or sextant, finds one of the chosen few, superimposes a cross hair on it and pushes a button at the instant of perfect alignment. He then tells the computer which star it is, by number. Repeating this process on a second star allows the computer to determine which way the spacecraft is pointing.

It took me many days of suffering through "simple" explanations of the system by M.I.T. experts, but by 1968 I found myself writing memos in M.I.T.-ese ". . . MSFN computes external AV maneuver. MSFN updates state vector, using LM state vector locations. Crew transfers the MSFN vector from the LM to CSM locations in the computer. . . ."

At about this time, however, another concern started intruding more and more forcibly into my consciousness. It began with an awareness during handball games that my legs didn't seem to be functioning normally. Occasionally, when I was walking downstairs, my left knee would buckle and I would nearly fall. My left leg felt strange, tingling in some places and numb in others. Worse yet, the abnormal area was spreading.

With great reluctance, I visited the NASA flight surgeon, who sent me to a neurosurgeon. X rays showed that a bony growth between my fifth and sixth neck vertebrae was pushing against my spinal cord. The pressure had to be relieved by surgically removing the spur; then the two vertebrae would be fused together with a small dowel of bone removed from my hip. I entered the hospital on July 22, 1968.

The operation went well. After a week of physical therapy, I went home for a month's convalescent leave. During this time I received a delightful surprise. Apollo 8, as my flight was now called, was probably going to fly around the moon. Of course, I had been dropped from the crew. Instead, as the December lift-off approached, I became one of the three capsule communicators (CAPCOMS) for the flight—a spokesman for the crew within Mission Control, and a spokesman for Mission Control when talking to the crew. And Lord knows we would have plenty to talk about. As Jerry Lederer, NASA's safety chief, pointed out, "Apollo has 5.6 million parts. Even if all functioned with 99.9-percent reliability, we could expect 5600 defects."

When Apollo 8 finally plopped gently into the Pacific three miles from the *USS Yorktown* shortly before dawn on the seventh day, pandemonium filled the normally staid Mission Control room. People waved miniature American flags and slapped one another on the back and the traditional cigars were broken out. None of our worries had materialized; our planning had been sound, our simulations accurate. We could have destroyed Apollo 8 in a thousand different ways, but we had instead nurtured and guided it through the most far-ranging week in the history of man.

For me personally, the moment was a conglomeration of emotions and memories. I had helped this flight evolve into an epic voyage. I had two years invested in it—it was my flight. Yet it was not my flight; I was but one of a hundred packed into a noisy room. I could wave my flag and smoke my cigar and finger my surgery scar, but that was about all. For some reason I felt like crying, but I couldn't do that in Mission Control, so I clapped a few good working troops on the back and left.

Apollo 8 splashed down on December 27, and the names of the Apollo 11 crew were announced on January 9. If everything worked out, Apollo 11 would land two men on the moon. The crew was Neil Armstrong, Buzz Aldrin and Mike Collins.

4. MARCHING ORDERS

ARMSTRONG AND ALDRIN. Not only were they near the top of the alphabet; they were highly thought of within our tight little astronaut group. Neil was the most experienced test pilot, and Buzz the most learned, especially when it came to rendezvous. I considered myself fortunate to be joining them.

In the six months remaining before our launch date, July 16, I was busier than I had ever been in my life. The NASA center at Langley, Va., had conducted an extensive study of the problems of docking the lunar module (LM) and command module (CM); they had full-scale replicas of the two vehicles hanging from wires in their huge hangar, which I had to inspect and "fly." Then I drew my own conclusions as to possible docking problems when the two real machines met for the first time. (The LM had never flown with a crew on board. Apollo 9 and 10 would, we hoped, supply all the hard facts we needed, except for those pertaining to making the moon landing itself.)

My training problems as CM pilot could be divided into two piles: those which Apollo 11 would be facing for the first time and for which there were no pat answers; and those which had been faced before, but which, through sloth, inattention or inability, I simply didn't understand well enough. One in the latter category was the mechanism that linked the CM and LM together, the probe and drogue.

When the CM (subsequently christened *Columbia*) first docked with the LM (*Eagle*), it placed its probe inside the LM's drogue and three tiny little prongs snapped into place. Then the probe was retracted into the CSM, pulling the LM's tunnel in to abut the CM's tunnel, at which point 12 mechanical latches were triggered. Now the pilot (me) left his seat, and assumed the mantle of master mechanic. The probe, inside the tunnel, was in the way and had to be removed, as did the drogue, so that people could pass back and forth between the two machines.

But before that could take place, there was an incredible checklist to perform, full of mysterious notations such as "Preload handle-torque counterclockwise to engage Extend Latch (red indicator not visible)." If the thing refused to budge, I was supposed to get out the tool kit and dismantle it. Me, who couldn't repair the latch on my screen door!

As the days before lift-off grew short, it seemed to me that my ability to concentrate and absorb increased. Having gone through much of this before, during Gemini days, was a tremendous help. But there were some profound differences. On Apollo 11 we three were our nation's envoys. We would be watched by the world, including the unfriendly parts of it, and we must not fail. There was pressure to plan, to study, to concentrate, to explore each nook and cranny of my mind for some fatal flaw, something overlooked, something ill-conceived, something I was supposed to do which I simply could not.

To make it worse, only those of us inside the program knew the opportunities we had to fail. A broken probe, a cracked engine nozzle, an electrical short, a crew lapse of attention, a jillion other things—and we would never make it. I don't know about Neil and Buzz, because we never discussed these things, but I really felt this awesome sense of responsibility weighing me down. By flight time, I had tics in both eyelids (which went away as soon as we got airborne).

Physical conditioning, physiological conditioning, mental conditioning: nothing left to do. I took Tuesday, July 15, off and browsed around crew quarters. I talked to Pat in Houston, and read and reread her last-minute note, which included the following poem, obviously not a last-minute thought:

I could have sought by wit or wile
Your bright dream to dim. And yet
If I'd swayed you with a smile
My reward would be regret.

So, for once, you shall not hear
Of the tears, unbidden, welling;
Or the nighttime stabs of fear.
These, this time, are not for telling.

Take my silence, though intended;
Fill it with the joy you feel.
Take my courage, now pretended—
You, my love, will make it real.

THE NEXT MORNING we don our suits and are taken to the launch-tower elevator. This elevator ride, this first vertical nudge, marks the real beginning of Apollo 11, for we cannot touch the earth any longer. I am treated to one more view, however, as I stand on a narrow walkway 320 feet up, ready to board. On my left is an unimpeded view of the beach below, unmarred by human totems; on my right, the most colossal pile of machinery ever assembled. If I cover my right eye, I see the Florida of Ponce de León, and beyond it the sea which is mother to us all. I am the original man. If I cover my left eye, I see a frightening array of wires and metal. I am but one technological adolescent in an army that has received its marching orders.

Neil has entered the spacecraft. I am next.

The approach of lift-off is signaled by the traditional backward count toward zero. Launch directors have this penchant for increasing the drama surrounding an event. Why don't they just hire a husky-voiced honey to whisper, "It's time to go, baby"? Be that as it may, my adrenalin pump is working fine as the monster springs to life. Shake, rattle, and roll! Noise, yes, lots of it, but mostly motion, as we are thrown left and right against our straps in spasmodic little jerks. The rocket is steering like a nervous lady driving down a narrow alley, and I just hope it knows where it's going. . . .

We are climbing like crazy—35,579 feet per second. In nine hours, when we are scheduled to make our first mid-course correction, we will be 57,000 miles out. It's hard to believe we are on our way to the moon less than three hours after lift-off. I'll bet the launch-day crowd down at the Cape is still bumper to bumper, straggling back to the motels. . . .

Out from behind the shadow of the earth, we are into the constant sunlight. In a way, there is constant darkness as well, for it depends on which way one looks. Toward the sun, nothing can be seen but its blinding disk; down-sun there is simply a black void. The stars are there, but cannot be seen.

If we hold any one fixed position, the side of the CM pointing at the sun will become too hot, and the side in the shade will become too cold. To prevent either, we must rotate slowly, like a chicken on a spit.

The moon doesn't appear to be getting much bigger, but the earth is shrinking very noticeably. As bedtime approaches, home scarcely fills one small window. What it lacks in size, however, it makes up in brilliance. We humans are accustomed to watching the moon and thinking of it (when it's full at least) as being very bright; the earth is four times brighter.

I remember last December, during the flight of Apollo 8, my five-year-old son had one specific question: Who was driving? Was it his friend Mr. Borman? One night when it was quiet in Mission Control, I relayed this concern to the spacecraft, and Bill Anders promptly replied that no, not Borman, but Isaac Newton was driving. A truer or more concise description of flying between earth and moon is not possible. The sun is pulling us, the earth is pulling us, the moon is pulling us, just as Newton knew they would. Up until now the earth's influence has been dominant, but by late tomorrow, the third day, the moon will take over. In the meantime, we have to correct our course slightly. For the three brief seconds of engine firing, Mike Collins will be driving instead of Sir Isaac Newton. Three seconds' worth! . . .

I wonder at the lack of communication, or at least the strange form of communication, among the three of us. Neil and Buzz don't confide in me, nor I in them; we have enough technical trivia to fill our quota of words as the days go by, and no one seems inclined to share anything more than that. It has been that way through our preflight training, and I expect that the same pattern will continue after the flight. . . .

Day 4 has a decidedly different feel to it. Our first shock comes as we swing ourselves around to bring the moon into view. It is *huge,* completely filling our window. The belly of it bulges out toward us in such a pronounced fashion that I almost feel I can reach out and touch it. It hangs there ominously, a formidable presence without sound or motion, issuing us no invitation to invade its domain. . . .

As we ease on around the left side of the moon, I marvel at the precision of our path. We have missed hitting the moon by a paltry 300 nautical miles, at a distance of nearly a quarter of a million miles from earth—and don't forget that the moon is a moving target. When we launched the other day, it was nearly 200,000 miles behind where it is now, and yet those big Houston computers didn't even whimper while belching out their super-accurate predictions. I hope. . . .

THE EAGLE HAS WINGS! Neil and Buzz, in the LM, are swooping down farther and farther below me. Their terse conversation sounds like a ground-controlled approach into fog, and Buzz calls out altitude and velocity to Neil, who has his eyes glued on the scene out the window. "Six hundred feet, down 19 (feet per second)." "One hundred feet, down 3½." "Forty feet, down 2½, kicking up some dust." "Thirty seconds," says Houston. That's how much fuel they have left. Better get it on the ground, Neil. "Contact light!" sings out Buzz. They have arrived! "We copy you down, *Eagle,*" says Houston, half question, half answer. Neil makes it official. "Houston, Tranquillity Base here, the *Eagle* has landed." Whew! . . .

I know from preflight press questions that I will be described as a lonely man, but, far from feeling lonely or abandoned, I feel very much a part of what is taking place on the lunar surface. I know that I would be a liar or a fool if I said that I have the best of the three Apollo 11 seats, but I can say with truth that I am perfectly satisfied with the one I have. This venture has been structured for three men, and I consider my third to be as necessary as either of the other two.

I don't mean to deny a feeling of solitude. It is there, reinforced by the fact that radio contact with the earth abruptly cuts off the instant I disappear behind the moon. I am alone, truly alone, and absolutely isolated from any known life. I am it, and I feel this powerfully—not as fear or loneliness, but as awareness, anticipation, satisfaction, confidence, almost exultation. I like the feeling. . . .

The Apollo II insignia shows an American eagle landing on the moon, with an olive branch symbolizing peace

Today is rendezvous day, and that means a multitude of things to keep me busy, with approximately 850 separate computer key strokes to be made, 850 chances for me to foul something up. Of course, if all goes well with *Eagle,* then it doesn't matter too much, as I merely retain my role as base-camp operator and let them find me. But if . . . if . . . if any one of a thousand things goes wrong with *Eagle,* then I become the hunter instead of the hunted.

When the instant of lift-off from the moon arrives, I am like a nervous bride. I have been flying for 17 years, but I have never sweated out any flight like I am sweating out the LM now. My secret terror for the last six months has been the thought of leaving Neil and Buzz on the moon and returning to earth alone; now I am within minutes of finding out the truth. If they fail to rise from the surface, or crash back onto it, I am not going to commit suicide; I am coming home, forthwith. But I will then be a marked man for life.

Hold it! Buzz is counting down. Off they go! Their single engine seems to be doing its thing, but it's scary nonetheless. One little hiccup and they are dead men. It seems I am holding my breath for the entire seven minutes it takes them to get into orbit.

Things look good! I can look out through my docking window and see the LM get bigger and bigger as they drive down that final approach path. For the first time since I was assigned to this incredible flight six months ago, I feel that we really *are* going to carry this thing off.

As soon as we are engaged by the three little capture latches, I flip a switch to pull the two vehicles together. Then I hustle on down into the tunnel and remove hatch, probe and drogue, so Neil and Buzz can get through. Thank God, all the claptrap works beautifully. The first one through is Buzz, with a big smile on his face. I grab his head, a hand on each temple, and am about to give him a smooch on the forehead, but then, embarrassed, I think better of it and grab his hand, and then Neil's. . . .

An old fighter-pilot friend of mine used to say after every flight, "Well, I cheated death again." The first couple of times I heard him, I was shocked at his sarcasm, his brashness, his cynicism, his honesty. But what the hell, why not say it! Twice is enough; I am going to spend the rest of my days catching fish, and raising dogs and children, and sitting around on the patio, talking to my wife. Another drink? Yes, thank you, I believe I will. Are the steaks on? Grand!

FIVE AND A HALF YEARS after Neil and Buzz touched the face of another heavenly body, I look back on the event with a mixture of pride, incredulity and smugness. I am optimistic about the present and future state of the world and Mike Collins. In my own case, I have found a postastronaut job to my liking, as has Neil. I am now director of the Smithsonian Institution's National Air and Space Museum in Washington, and Neil is professor of engineering at the University of Cincinnati. Buzz, on the other hand, has had a more difficult time of it, suffering bouts of depression severe enough to require hospitalization. Being an astronaut is a tough act to follow, as all three of us have discovered.

I find that my two space flights have changed my perception of the earth. Of course, Apollo 11 changed my perception of the moon, too.

But the moon is so scarred, so desolate, so monotonous, that I cannot recall its tortured surface without thinking of the infinite variety the delightful planet earth offers: misty waterfalls, pine forests, rose gardens, blues and greens and reds and whites.

And yet if I could use only one word to describe the earth as seen from the moon, I would ignore both its size and its color and search for a more elemental quality, that of fragility. From space there is no hint of ruggedness to it; smooth as a billiard ball, it seems delicately poised in its circular journey around the sun, and above all it seems fragile.

Flying in space has also changed my perception of myself. For one thing, my threshold of measuring what is important has been raised. Part of this stems from having received a number of terrestrial honors, and part from having been privileged to see the earth from a great distance. The three of us have been entertained by kings and queens; we have received the Presidential Medal of Freedom and many others; we have addressed a joint session of Congress and a hundred lesser audiences. Through it all, the earth continues to turn on its axis; I can see it doing so, and I am less impressed by my own disturbance to that serene motion.

Outwardly, my life-style has not changed as much as I would have guessed. By and large, one brings back from the moon the same limitations of imagination, taste and pocketbook that one took on the trip, and one is stuck with them.

But although I may feel that I am basically the same person, I am different, too. I have dangled from a cord 100 miles up; I have seen the earth eclipsed by the moon; I have seen the sun's true light unfiltered by any planet's atmosphere; I have seen the ultimate black of infinity in a stillness undisturbed by any living thing. I have not been able to do these things because of any great talent I possess; rather, it has all been the roll of the dice. Army career or Air Force? Ground officer or test pilot? Edwards or Houston? In my life so far, I have been lucky, very, very lucky.

It is perhaps a pity that my eyes have seen more than my brain has been able to assimilate or evaluate. But, like the Druids at Stonehenge, I have attempted to bring order out of what I have observed, even if I have not understood it fully.

I have no intention of spending the rest of my life looking backward—there is magic aplenty for me here on earth. But I do have this secret, this precious thing, and I will carry it with me always.

N. ENGLE
AWS

Jonathan Livingston Seagull

CONDENSED FROM THE BOOK

by Richard Bach

ILLUSTRATED BY NITA ENGLE

For most seagulls, it is not flying that matters, but eating. Jonathan was different. For him, it was not eating that mattered, but flying.

"Why don't you *eat?*" his mother would plead. "You're nothing but bone and feathers!"

And Jonathan would answer, "I don't mind being bone and feathers, Mom. I just want to know what I can do in the air and what I can't, that's all. I just want to know."

But this is more than a story of a gull who liked to talk and lived to fly. It is a parable. And the lesson it draws is as wondrous as flight itself.

The idea for this extraordinary book came to the author one night when he was taking a lonely walk. Several years were to pass before the story was finally completed and published. At first, it went almost unnoticed by reviewers. Then, suddenly, like Jonathan, the book was a soaring success.

The reason is in the reading.

1. BREAKTHROUGH

It was morning, and the sun sparkled gold across the ripples of a gentle sea. A mile from shore a fishing boat chummed the water, and the word for Breakfast Flock flashed through the air, till a crowd of a thousand seagulls came to dodge and fight for bits of food.

But way off alone, out by himself beyond boat and shore, Jonathan Livingston Seagull was practicing. A hundred feet in the sky he lowered his webbed feet, lifted his beak and strained to hold a painful twisting curve through his wings. The curve meant that he would fly slowly, and now he slowed until the wind was a whisper in his face. He narrowed his eyes in fierce concentration, held his breath, forced one . . . single . . . more . . . inch . . . of curve. Then his feathers ruffled, he stalled and fell.

Seagulls, as you know, never falter, never stall. To stall in the air is for them disgrace and dishonor.

But Jonathan Livingston Seagull, unashamed, stretching his wings again in that trembling hard curve—slowing, slowing and stalling once more—was no ordinary bird.

Most gulls don't bother to learn more than the simplest facts of flight—how to get from shore to food and back again. For most gulls, it is not flying that matters, but eating. For this gull, though, it was not eating that mattered, but flight. More than anything else, Jonathan Livingston Seagull loved to fly.

This kind of thinking, he found, is not the way to make oneself popular with other birds. Even his parents were dismayed as Jonathan spent whole days alone, making hundreds of low-level glides, experimenting.

He didn't know why, for instance, but when he flew at altitudes less than half his wingspan above the water, he could stay in the air longer, with less effort. His glides ended not with the usual feet-down splash into the sea, but with a long flat wake as he touched the surface with his feet tightly streamlined against his body. When he began sliding in to feet-up landings on the beach, then pacing the length of his slide in the sand, his parents were very much dismayed indeed.

"Why, Jon, *why?*" his mother asked. "Why is it so hard to be like the rest of the flock? Why don't you *eat?* You're nothing but bone and feathers!"

"I don't mind being bone and feathers, Mom. I just want to know what I can do in the air and what I can't, that's all."

"See here, Jonathan," said his father, not unkindly. "Winter isn't far away. Boats will be few, and the surface fish will be swimming deep. If you must study, then study food, and how to get it."

Jonathan nodded obediently. For the next few days he tried to behave like the other gulls; he really tried, screeching and fighting with the Flock around the piers and fishing boats, diving on scraps of fish and bread. But he couldn't make it work.

It's all so pointless, he thought, deliberately dropping a hard-won anchovy to a hungry old gull chasing him. I could be spending all this time learning to fly. There's so much to learn!

It wasn't long before Jonathan Gull was off by himself again, far out at sea, hungry, happy, learning. The subject was speed, and in a week's practice he learned more about speed than the fastest gull alive.

From a thousand feet, flapping his wings as hard as he could, he pushed over into a blazing dive toward the waves, and learned why seagulls don't make blazing steep power dives. In just six seconds he was moving 70 m.p.h., the speed at which one's wing goes unstable on the upstroke.

Time after time it happened. Careful as he was, working at the very peak of his ability, he lost control at high speed.

Climb to a thousand feet. Full power straight ahead, then push over, flapping, to a vertical dive. Then, every time, his left wing stalled on an upstroke, he'd roll violently left, stall his right wing recovering and flick like fire into a wild, tumbling spin. Ten times he tried, and each time, as he passed through 70 m.p.h., he burst into a churning mass of feathers, out of control, crashing down into the water.

The key, he thought at last, dripping wet, must be to hold the wings still at high speeds—to flap up to 50 and then hold the wings still.

From 2000 feet he tried again, rolling into his dive, beak straight down, wings full out and stable from the moment he passed 50 m.p.h.

It took tremendous strength, but it worked. In ten seconds he had blurred through 90 m.p.h. Jonathan had set a world speed record for seagulls!

But victory was short-lived. The instant he began his pullout, the instant he changed the angle of his wings, he snapped into that same uncontrolled disaster, and at 90 m.p.h. it hit him like dynamite. Jonathan Seagull exploded in midair and smashed into a brick-hard sea.

When he came to, it was well after dark, and he floated in moonlight on the surface of the ocean. His wings were ragged bars of lead, but the weight of failure was even heavier on his back. He wished, feebly, that the weight could just be enough to drag him gently down to the bottom and end it all. As he sank low in the water, a hollow voice sounded within him. There's no way around it. I am a seagull. I am limited by my nature. If I were meant to learn so much about flying, I'd have charts for brains. If I were meant to fly at speed, I'd have a falcon's short wings, and live on mice instead of fish. My father was right. I must fly home to the Flock and be content as I am, a poor limited seagull.

The voice faded, and Jonathan agreed. The place for a seagull at night is on shore. From this moment forth, he vowed, he would be a normal gull. It would make everyone happier. He pushed wearily away from the dark water and flew toward the land, grateful for what he had learned about work-saving, low-altitude flying.

But no, he thought. I am done with the way I was; I am done with everything I learned. I am a seagull like every other seagull, and I will fly like one. So he climbed painfully to 100 feet and flapped his wings harder, pressing for shore.

He felt better for his decision to be just another one of the flock. There would be no ties now to the force that had driven him to learn; there would be no more challenge and no more failure. And it was pretty, just to stop thinking and fly through the dark toward the lights above the beach.

Dark! The hollow voice cracked in alarm. *Seagulls never fly in the dark!*

Jonathan was not alert to listen. It's pretty, he thought. The moon and the lights twinkling on the water, throwing out little beacon-trails through the night, and all so peaceful and still. . . .

Get down! Seagulls never fly in the dark! If you were meant to fly in the dark, you'd have the eyes of an owl! You'd have charts for brains! You'd have a falcon's short wings!

There in the night, 100 feet in the air, Jonathan Livingston Seagull blinked. His pain, his resolutions, vanished.

A falcon's short wings!

That's the answer! What a fool I've been! All I need is a tiny little wing; all I need is to fold most of my wings and fly on just the tips alone. *Short wings!*

He climbed 2000 feet above the black sea and, without a thought of failure and death, brought his forewings tightly into his body, left only the narrow swept daggers of his wingtips extended into the wind, and fell into a vertical dive.

The wind was a monster roar at his head. Seventy m.p.h., 90, 120 and faster still. The wing strain, now at 140 m.p.h., wasn't nearly as hard as it had been before at 70, and with the faintest twist of his wingtips he eased out of the dive and shot above the waves, a gray cannonball under the moon.

He closed his eyes to slits against the wind and rejoiced. One hundred and forty m.p.h.! Under control! If I dive from 5000 feet instead of 2000, I wonder how fast. . . .

His vows of a moment before were forgotten, swept away in that great swift wind. Yet he felt guiltless, breaking the promises he had made himself. Such promises are only for the gulls that accept the ordinary. One who has touched excellence in his learning has no need of that kind of promise.

By sunup, Jonathan Gull was practicing again. From 5000 feet the fishing boats were specks in the flat blue water and the Breakfast Flock was a faint cloud of dust motes, circling.

He was alive, trembling with delight, proud that his fear was under control. Then without ceremony he hugged in his forewings, extended his short, angled wingtips, and plunged directly toward the sea. By the time he passed 4000 feet, he had reached terminal velocity; the wind was a solid beating wall of sound against which he could move no faster. He was flying straight down, at 214 m.p.h. He swallowed, knowing that if his wings unfolded at that speed he'd be blown into a million tiny shreds of seagull. But the speed was power, and the speed was joy, and the speed was pure beauty.

He began his pullout at 1000 feet, wingtips thudding and blurring in that gigantic wind, the boat and the crowd of gulls tilting and growing meteor-fast, directly in his path.

He couldn't stop; he didn't know yet how to turn at this speed. Collision would be instant death. And so he shut his eyes.

It happened that morning, then, just after sunrise, that Jonathan Livingston Seagull fired directly through the center of the Breakfast Flock, ticking off 212 m.p.h., eyes closed, in a great roaring shriek of wind and feathers. The Gull of Fortune smiled upon him this once, and no one was killed.

By the time he had pulled his beak straight up into the sky, he was still scorching along at 160 m.p.h. When he had slowed to 20 and stretched his wings again at last, the boat was a crumb on the sea, 4000 feet below.

Terminal velocity! A seagull at 214 m.p.h.! It was a breakthrough, the greatest single moment in the history of the Flock, and in that moment a new age opened for Jonathan Gull. Flying out to his lonely practice area, folding his wings for a dive from 8000 feet, he set himself at once to discover how to turn.

A single wingtip feather, he found, moved a fraction of an inch, gives a smooth, sweeping curve at tremendous speed. Before he learned this, however, he found that moving more than one feather at that speed will spin you like a rifle ball . . . and Jonathan had flown the first aerobatics of any seagull on earth.

He spared no time that day for talk with other gulls, but flew on past sunset. He discovered the loop, the slow-roll, the point-roll, the inverted spin, the gull-bunt, the pinwheel.

When he joined the Flock on the beach, it was full night. He was dizzy and terribly tired. Yet in delight he flew a loop to landing, with a snap roll just before touchdown. When they hear of it, he thought, of the Breakthrough, they'll be wild with joy. How much more there is now to living! Instead of our drab slogging forth and back to the fishing boats, there's a reason to life! We can lift ourselves out of ignorance; we can find ourselves as creatures of excellence and intelligence and skill. We can be free! *We can learn to fly!*

The years ahead hummed and glowed with promise.

The gulls were flocked into the Council Gathering when he landed, and apparently had been so flocked for some time. They were all, in fact, waiting.

"Jonathan Livingston Seagull! Stand to Center!" The Elder's words sounded in a voice of highest ceremony. Stand to Center meant only great shame or great honor. Stand to Center for Honor was the way the gulls' foremost leaders were marked. Of course, he thought—the Breakfast Flock saw the Breakthrough this morning! But I want no honors. I have no wish to be leader. I want only to share what I've found, to show those horizons ahead for us all.

He stepped forward.

"Jonathan Livingston Seagull," said the Elder. "Stand to Center for Shame in the sight of your fellow gulls!"

It felt like being hit with a board. Jonathan's knees went weak, his feathers sagged, there was roaring in his ears. Centered for shame? Impossible! The Breakthrough! They can't understand! They're wrong!

". . . for his reckless irresponsibility," the solemn voice intoned, "violating the dignity and tradition of the Gull Family. . . ."

To be centered for shame meant that he would be cast out of gull society, banished to a solitary life on the Far Cliffs.

". . . one day, Jonathan Livingston Seagull, you shall learn that irresponsibility does not pay. Life is the unknown and the unknowable, except that we are put into this world to eat, to stay alive as long as we possibly can."

A seagull never speaks to the Council Flock, but it was Jonathan's voice raised. "Irresponsibility? My brothers!" he cried. "Who is more responsible than a gull who finds and follows a higher purpose for life? For a thousand years we have scrabbled after fish heads, but now we have a reason to live—to learn, to discover, to be free! Give me one chance, let me show you what I've found."

The Flock might as well have been stone.

"The Brotherhood is broken," the gulls intoned together. With one accord they solemnly closed their ears and turned their backs on him.

2. OUTCAST

JONATHAN SPENT THE REST of his days alone, but he flew out way beyond the Far Cliffs. His one sorrow was not solitude. It was that other gulls refused to believe the glory of flight that awaited them; they refused to open their eyes and see.

He learned more each day. He learned that a streamlined, high-speed dive could bring him to find the rare and tasty fish that schooled ten feet below the surface of the ocean: he no longer needed fishing boats and stale bread for survival. He learned to sleep in the air, setting a course at night across the offshore wind, covering a hundred miles from sunset to sunrise. With the same inner control, he flew through heavy fogs and climbed above them into dazzling clear skies—in the very times when every other gull stood on the ground, knowing nothing but mist and rain. He learned to ride the high winds far inland, to dine there on delicate insects.

What he had once hoped for for the Flock, he now gained for himself alone; he learned to fly, and was not sorry for the price he had paid. Jonathan discovered that boredom and fear and anger are the reasons that a gull's life is so short, and with these gone from his thought, he lived a long, fine life indeed.

They came in the evening, then, and found Jonathan gliding peaceful and alone through his beloved sky. The two gulls that appeared at

H. ENGLE

his wings were as pure as starlight, and the glow from them was gentle and friendly in the high night air. But most lovely of all was the skill with which they flew, their wingtips moving a precise and constant inch from his own.

Without a word, Jonathan put them to his test—a test that no gull had ever passed. He twisted his wings, slowed to a single mile per hour above stall. The two radiant birds slowed with him, smoothly, locked in position. They knew about slow-flying.

He folded his wings, and dropped in a dive to 190 m.p.h. They dropped with him, streaking down in flawless formation.

At last he turned that speed straight up into a long vertical slow-roll. They rolled with him, smiling.

He recovered to level flight and was quiet for a time before he spoke. "Very well," he said. "Who are you?"

"We're from your Flock, Jonathan. We are your brothers. We've come to take you higher, to take you home."

"Home I have none. Flock I have none. I am Outcast. And we fly now at the peak of the Great Mountain Wind. Beyond a few hundred feet, I can lift this old body no higher."

"But you can, Jonathan. For you have learned. One school is finished, and the time has come for another to begin."

As it had shined across him all his life, so understanding lighted that moment for Jonathan Seagull. They were right. He *could* fly higher, and it *was* time to go home.

He gave one last long look across the sky, across that magnificent silver land where he had learned so much.

"I'm ready," he said at last.

And Jonathan Livingston Seagull rose with the two star-bright gulls to disappear into a perfect dark sky.

So this is heaven, he thought, and he had to smile at himself. It was hardly respectful to analyze heaven in the very moment that one flies up to enter it.

As he came from Earth now, above the clouds and in close formation with the two brilliant gulls, he saw that his own body was growing as bright as theirs. True, the same young Jonathan Seagull was there that had always lived behind his golden eyes, but the outer form had changed.

It felt like a seagull body, but already it flew far better than his old one had ever flown. Why, with half the effort, he thought, I'll get twice the speed, twice the performance of my best days on Earth!

His feathers glowed brilliant white now, and his wings were smooth and perfect as sheets of polished silver. He began, delightedly, to learn about them, to press power into these new wings.

At 250 m.p.h. he felt that he was nearing his level-flight maximum speed. At 273 he thought he was flying as fast as he could fly, and he was faintly disappointed. There was a limit to how much the new body could do, and though it was much faster than his old level-flight record, it was still a limit that would take great effort to crack. In heaven, he thought, there should be no limits.

The clouds broke apart. His escorts called, "Happy landings, Jonathan," and vanished into thin air.

He was flying over a sea, toward a jagged shoreline. A few seagulls were working the updrafts on the cliffs. Way off to the north, at the horizon itself, flew a few others.

New sights, new thoughts, new questions. Why so few gulls? Heaven should be *flocked* with gulls! And why am I so tired, all at once? Gulls in heaven are never supposed to be tired, or to sleep.

Where had he heard that? The memory of his life on Earth was falling away. Earth had been a place where he had learned much, of course, but the details were blurred—something about fighting for food, and being Outcast.

The dozen gulls by the shoreline came to meet him, none saying a word. He felt only that he was welcome and that this was home. He turned to land on the beach, beating his wings to stop an inch in the air, then dropping lightly to the sand. The other gulls landed, too, but not one of them so much as flapped a feather. They swung into the wind, bright wings outstretched; then, somehow, they changed the curve of their feathers until they had stopped in the same instant their feet touched the ground. It was beautiful control, but now Jonathan was just too tired to try it. Standing there on the beach, still without a word spoken, he was asleep.

In the days that followed, Jonathan saw that there was as much to learn about flight in this place as there had been in the life behind him. But with a difference. Here were gulls who thought as he thought. For each of them, the most important thing in living was to reach out and touch perfection in that which they most loved to do, and that was to fly. They were magnificent birds, and they spent hour after hour every day practicing flight, testing advanced aeronautics.

For a long time Jonathan forgot about the world that he had come from, that place where the Flock lived with its eyes tightly shut to the joy of flight. But now and then, just for a moment, he remembered.

He remembered it one morning when he was out with his instructor, while they rested on the beach after a session of folded-wing snap rolls. "Where is everybody, Sullivan?" he asked silently, quite at home now with the easy telepathy that these gulls used instead of screes and gracks. "Why aren't there more of us here? Why, where I came from, there were . . ."

". . . thousands and thousands of gulls. I know." Sullivan shook his head. "The only answer I can see, Jonathan, is that you are pretty well a one-in-a-million bird. Most of us came along slowly. We went from one world into another that was almost exactly like it, forgetting right away where we had come from, not caring where we were headed, living for the moment. Do you have any idea how many lives we must have gone through before we even got the first idea that there is more to life than eating or fighting, or power in the Flock? A thousand lives, Jon, ten thousand! And then another hundred lives until we began to learn that there is such a thing as perfection, and another hundred to get the idea that our purpose for living is to find that perfection and show it forth. The same rule holds for us now: we choose our next world through what we learn here. Learn nothing, and the next world is exactly the same as this one, all the same limitations and lead weights to overcome."

He stretched his wings and turned to face the wind. "But you, Jon," he said, "learned so much at one time that you didn't have to go through a thousand lives to reach this one."

In a moment they were airborne again, practicing. The formation point-rolls were difficult, for through the inverted half Jonathan had to think upside down, reversing the curve of his wing, and reversing it exactly in harmony with his instructor's.

"Let's try it again," Sullivan said over and over. "Let's try it again." Then, finally, "Good." And they began practicing outside loops.

One evening the gulls that were not night-flying stood together on the sand, thinking. Jonathan took all his courage in hand and walked to the Elder Gull who, it was said, was soon to be moving beyond this world. "Chiang . . . ," he said, a little nervously.

The old seagull looked at him kindly. "Yes, my son?" Instead of being enfeebled by age, the Elder had been empowered by it; he could outfly any gull in the Flock, and he had learned skills that the others were only gradually coming to know.

"Chiang, this world isn't heaven at all, is it?"

The Elder smiled in the moonlight. "You are learning again, Jonathan Seagull," he said.

"Well, what happens from here? Where are we going? Is there no such place as heaven?"

"No, Jonathan, there is no such place. Heaven is not a place, and it is not a time. Heaven is being perfect." He was silent for a moment. "You are a very fast flier, aren't you?"

"I . . . I enjoy speed," Jonathan said, taken aback but proud that the Elder had noticed.

"You will begin to touch heaven, Jonathan, in the moment that you touch perfect speed. And that isn't flying a thousand miles an hour, or a million, or flying at the speed of light. Because any number is a limit, and perfection doesn't have limits. Perfect speed is being there."

Without warning, Chiang vanished and appeared at the water's edge 50 feet away, all in the flicker of an instant. Then he vanished again and stood, in the same millisecond, at Jonathan's shoulder. "It's kind of fun," he said.

Jonathan was dazzled. He forgot to ask about heaven. "How do you do that? What does it feel like? How far can you go?"

"You can go to any place and any time that you wish," the Elder said. "I've gone everywhere and everywhen I can think of." He looked across the sea. "It's strange. The gulls who scorn perfection for the sake of travel go nowhere, slowly. Those who put aside travel for the sake of perfection go anywhere, instantly. Remember, Jonathan, heaven isn't a place or a time, because place and time are so very meaningless. Heaven is . . ."

"Can you teach me to fly like that?" Jonathan Seagull trembled to conquer another unknown.

"Of course, if you wish to learn."

"Tell me what to do," Jonathan said, and a strange light glowed in his eyes.

"To fly as fast as thought, to anywhere that is," Chiang said, "you must begin by knowing that you have already arrived."

The trick, according to Chiang, was for Jonathan to stop seeing himself as trapped inside a limited body that had a 42-inch wingspan and performance that could be plotted on a chart. The trick was to know that his true nature lived everywhere at once across space and time.

Jonathan kept at it, fiercely, day after day, from before sunrise till past midnight. And for all his effort he moved not a feather-width from his spot.

"Forget about faith!" Chiang said it time and again. "You didn't need faith to fly; you needed to understand flying. This is just the same. Now try again."

And one day Jonathan, standing on the shore, closing his eyes, concentrating, all in a flash knew what Chiang had been telling him. "Why, that's true! I *am* a perfect, unlimited gull!" He felt a great shock of joy.

"Good!" said Chiang, and there was victory in his voice.

Jonathan opened his eyes. He stood alone with the Elder on a totally different seashore—trees down to the water's edge, twin yellow suns turning overhead.

"At last you've got the idea," Chiang said, "but your control needs a little work. . . ."

Jonathan was stunned. "Where are we?"

Utterly unimpressed with the strange surroundings, the Elder brushed the question aside. "We're on some planet, obviously, with a green sky and a double star for a sun."

Jonathan gave a screech of delight. "It works!"

"Well, of course it works, Jon," said Chiang. "It always works, when you know what you're doing. Now about your control . . ."

By the time they returned, it was dark. The other gulls looked at Jonathan with awe in their golden eyes, for they had seen him disappear from where he had been rooted for so long.

"We can start working with time if you wish," Chiang said, "till you can fly the past and the future. And then you will be ready to begin the most difficult, the most powerful, the most fun of all. You will be ready to begin to fly up and know the meaning of kindness and love."

A MONTH WENT BY, or something that felt about like a month, and Jonathan learned at a tremendous rate. He always had learned quickly, and now, as the special student of the Elder himself, he took in new ideas like a streamlined feathered computer.

Then the day came that Chiang vanished. He had been talking quietly with them all, exhorting them never to stop their learning and practicing and striving to understand more of the perfect invisible principle of all life. As he spoke, his feathers went brighter and at last turned so brilliant that no gull could look upon him.

"Jonathan," he said, and these were Chiang's last words, "keep working on love."

When the gulls could see again, Chiang was gone.

As the days went past, Jonathan found himself thinking time and again of the Earth from which he had come. If he had known there just a tenth, just a hundredth, of what he knew here, how much more life would have meant! He stood on the sand and fell to wondering if there was a gull back there who might be struggling to break out of his limits, to see the meaning of flight beyond a way of travel to get a breadcrumb from a rowboat. Perhaps there might even be one made an Outcast for speaking his truth in the face of the Flock. And the more Jonathan practiced his kindness lessons, and the more he worked to know the nature of love, the more he wanted to go back to Earth. For in spite of his lonely past, Jonathan Seagull was born to be an instructor, and his own way of demonstrating love was to give something of the truth that he had seen to a gull who asked only a chance to see truth for himself.

Sullivan, adept now at thought-speed flight and helping the others to learn, was doubtful.

"Jon, you were Outcast once. Why do you think that any of the gulls in your old time would listen to you now? You know the proverb, and it's true: *The gull sees farthest who flies highest.* Those gulls where you came from are standing on the ground, squawking and fighting among themselves. Stay here. Help the ones who are high enough to see what you have to tell them." He was quiet for a moment, and then he said, "What if Chiang had gone back to *his* old worlds? Where would you have been today?"

Sullivan was right. *The gull sees farthest who flies highest.*

Jonathan stayed and worked with the new birds coming in, who were all very bright and quick with their lessons. But the feeling returned, and he couldn't help but think that there might be one or two gulls back on Earth who would be able to learn, too. How much more would he have known by now if Chiang had come to him on the day he was Outcast!

"Sully, I must go back," he said at last. "Your students are doing well. They can help you bring the newcomers along."

Sullivan Seagull laughed in spite of himself. "You crazy bird," he said kindly. "If anybody can show someone on the ground how to see a thousand miles, it will be Jonathan Livingston Seagull." He looked at the sand. "Good-by, Jon, my friend."

"Good-by, Sully. We'll meet again." And, with that, Jonathan held in thought an image of the great gull flocks on the shore of another time, and he knew with practiced ease that he was not bone and feather but a perfect idea of freedom and flight, limited by nothing at all.

3. BEGINNING

FLETCHER LYND SEAGULL was still quite young, but already he knew that no bird had ever been so wrongly treated by any Flock.

"I don't care what they say," he thought fiercely, as he flew out toward the Far Cliffs. "There's so much more to flying than just flapping around from place to place. A *mosquito* does that! One little barrel-roll around the Elder Gull, just for fun, and I'm Outcast! Are they blind? Can't they see? Can't they think of the glory that it will be when we really learn to fly?

"I don't care what they think. I'll show them what flying is! I'll be pure Outlaw, if that's the way they want it. And I'll make them so sorry. . . ."

The voice came inside his own head, and though it was very gentle, it startled him so much that he faltered and stumbled in the air.

"Don't be harsh on them, Fletcher Seagull," said the voice. "In casting you out, the other gulls have only hurt themselves, and one day they will know this, and one day they will see what you see. Forgive them, and help them to understand."

An inch from his right wingtip flew the most brilliant white gull in all the world, gliding effortlessly along, not moving a feather, at what was very nearly Fletcher's top speed.

There was a moment of chaos in the young bird. "What's going on? Am I mad? What is this?"

Low and calm, the voice went on within his thought, demanding an answer: "Fletcher Lynd Seagull, do you want to fly?"

"Yes, I want to fly!"

"Do you want to fly so much that you will forgive the Flock, and learn, and go back to them one day and work to help them know?"

There was no lying to this magnificent being, no matter how proud or hurt a bird was Fletcher Seagull. "I do," he said softly.

"Then, Fletch," the bright creature said to him, "let's begin with Level Flight. . . ."

Jonathan circled slowly over the Far Cliffs, watching. This rough young Fletcher Gull was very nearly a perfect flight student. He was strong and light and quick in the air—but far and away more important—he had a blazing drive to learn to fly.

Here he came this minute, a blurred gray shape roaring out of a dive, flashing past his instructor. He pulled abruptly into another try at a 16-point vertical slow-roll, calling the points out loud.

". . . 8 . . . 9 . . . 10 . . . see-Jonathan-I'm-running-out-of-airspeed . . . 11 . . . I-want-good-sharp-stops-like yours . . . 12 . . . but-blast-it-I-just-can't-make . . . *aaakk!*"

Fletcher's whipstall at the top was all the worse for his rage and fury at failing. He fell backward, tumbled, slammed savagely into an inverted spin, and recovered at last, panting, a hundred feet below his instructor's level. "You're wasting your time with me, Jonathan! I'm too stupid! I try and try, but I'll never get it!"

Jonathan Seagull looked down at him and nodded. "You'll never get it for sure as long as you make that pull-up so hard. Fletcher, you lost 40 m.p.h. in the entry. You *have* to be smooth! Firm but smooth, remember?" He dropped down to the level of the younger gull. "Let's try it together now, in formation. And pay attention to that pull-up."

By the end of three months Jonathan had six other students, Outcasts all, yet curious about this strange new idea of flight for the joy of flying. Still, it was easier for them to practice high performance than it was to understand the reason behind it.

"Each of us is in truth an idea of the Great Gull, an unlimited idea of freedom," Jonathan would say in the evenings on the beach, "and precision flying is a step toward expressing our real nature. Everything that limits us we have to put aside."

And his students would be asleep, exhausted from the day's flying. They liked the practice, because it was fast and exciting, but not one of them, not even Fletcher Lynd Gull, had come to believe that the flight of ideas could possibly be as real as the flight of wind and feather.

"Your whole body, from wingtip to wingtip," Jonathan would say, "is nothing more than your thought itself, in a form you can see. Break the chains of your thought, and you break the chains of your body, too." But no matter how he said it, it sounded like pleasant fiction, and they needed more to sleep.

It was only a month later that Jonathan said the time had come to return to the Flock.

"We're not ready!" said Henry Calvin Gull. "We're Outcast! We can't force ourselves to go where we're not welcome, can we?"

"We're free to go where we wish and be what we are," Jonathan answered, and he lifted from the sand and turned east, toward the home grounds of the Flock.

There was brief anguish among his students, for it is the Law of the

Flock that an Outcast never returns, and the Law had not been broken once in 10,000 years. The Law said stay; Jonathan said go; and by now he was a mile across the water. If they waited much longer, he would reach a hostile Flock alone.

"Well, we don't have to obey the Law if we're not a part of the Flock, do we?" Fletcher said, rather self-consciously. "Besides, if there's a fight, we'll be a lot more help there than here."

So they flew in from the west that morning, eight of them in a double-diamond formation, wingtips almost overlapping. They came across the Flock's Council Beach at 135 m.p.h., Jonathan in the lead, Fletcher smoothly at his right wing, Henry Calvin struggling gamely at his left. Then the whole formation rolled slowly to the right as one bird, . . . level . . . to . . . inverted . . . to . . . level, the wind whipping over them all.

The squawks and grockles of the Flock were cut off as though the formation were a giant knife, and 8000 gull eyes watched without a single blink. Now, one by one, each of the eight birds pulled sharply upward into a full loop and flew all the way around to a dead-slow, stand-up landing on the sand. Then, as though this sort of thing happened every day, Jonathan Seagull began his critique of the flight.

"To begin with," he said with a wry smile, "you were all a bit late on the join-up. . . ."

IT WENT LIKE LIGHTNING through the Flock. Those birds are Outcast! And they have returned! And that . . . that can't happen! Fletcher's predictions of battle melted in the Flock's confusion.

"Well, sure, okay, they're Outcast," said some of the younger gulls, "but hey, man, where did they learn to fly like that?"

It took almost an hour for the Word of the Elder to pass through the Flock: Ignore them. The gull who speaks to an Outcast is himself Outcast.

Gray-feathered backs were turned upon Jonathan from that moment onward, but he didn't appear to notice. He held his practice sessions directly over the Council Beach, and for the first time he began pressing his students to the limit of their ability. "Martin Gull!" he shouted across the sky. "You say you know low-speed flying. You know nothing till you prove it! *Fly!*"

So, quiet little Martin William Seagull, startled to be caught under his instructor's fire, surprised himself and became a wizard of low speeds. In the lightest breeze he could curve his feathers to lift himself without a single flap of his wing from sand to cloud and down again. Likewise, Charles-Roland Gull flew the Great Mountain Wind to 24,000 feet, came down blue from the cold, thin air, amazed and happy, determined to go still higher tomorrow.

Fletcher Seagull, who loved aerobatics like no one else, conquered his 16-point vertical slow-roll and the next day topped it off with a triple cartwheel, his feathers flashing white sunlight to a beach from which more than one furtive eye watched.

Every hour Jonathan was there at the side of each of his students, demonstrating, suggesting, pressuring, guiding. He flew with them through night and cloud and storm, for the sport of it, while the Flock huddled miserably on the ground.

When the flying was done, the students relaxed on the sand, and in time they listened more closely to Jonathan. And gradually, in the night, another circle formed around the circle of students—a ring of curious gulls listening in the darkness for hours, not wishing to see or be seen, fading away before daybreak.

It was a month after the Return that the first gull of the Flock crossed the line and asked to learn how to fly. In his asking, Terrence Lowell Gull became a condemned bird, labeled Outcast, and the eighth of Jonathan's students.

The next night from the Flock came Kirk Maynard Gull, wobbling across the sand, dragging his left wing, to collapse at Jonathan's feet. "Help me," he said quietly, speaking in the way that the dying speak. "I want to fly more than anything else in the world."

"Come along then," said Jonathan. "Climb with me away from the ground, and we'll begin."

"You don't understand. My wing. I can't move my wing."

"Maynard Gull, you have the freedom to be yourself, your true self, here and now, and nothing can stand in your way. It is the Law of the Great Gull, the Law that Is."

"Are you saying I can fly?"

"I say you are free."

As simply and as quickly as that, Kirk Maynard Gull spread his wings, effortlessly, and lifted into the dark night. The Flock was roused from sleep by his cry, as loud as he could scream it, from 500 feet up: "I can fly! Listen! I can fly!"

By sunrise there were nearly a thousand birds standing outside the circle of students, looking curiously at Maynard. They didn't care whether they were seen or not, and they listened, trying to understand

Jonathan Seagull. He spoke of very simple things—that it is right for a gull to fly, that freedom is the very nature of his being, that whatever stands against that freedom must be set aside, be it ritual or superstition or limitation in any form.

"Set aside," came a voice from the multitude, "even if it be the Law of the Flock?"

"The only true law is that which leads to freedom," Jonathan said. "There is no other."

"How do you expect us to fly as you fly?" came another voice. "You are special and gifted and divine, above other birds."

"Look at Fletcher! Lowell! Charles-Roland! Judy Lee! Are they also special and gifted and divine? No more than you, no more than I. The only difference is that they have begun to understand what they really are and have begun to practice it."

His students, save Fletcher, shifted uneasily. They hadn't realized that this was what they were doing.

The crowd grew larger every day, coming to question, to idolize, to scorn.

4. THE CLIFF

It happened just a week later. Fletcher was demonstrating the elements of high-speed flying to a class of new students. He had just pulled out of his dive from 7000 feet, a long gray streak firing a few inches above the beach, when a young bird on its first flight glided directly into his path, calling for its mother. With a tenth of a second to avoid the youngster, Fletcher Lynd Seagull snapped hard to the left, at something over 200 m.p.h., into a cliff of solid granite.

It was, for him, as though the rock were a giant hard door into another world. A burst of fear and shock as he hit, and then he was adrift in a strange sky, forgetting, remembering, forgetting; afraid and sad and sorry, terribly sorry.

The voice came to him as it had in the first day that he had met Jonathan Livingston Seagull. "The trick, Fletcher, is that we are trying to overcome our limitations in order—patiently. We don't tackle flying through rock until a little later in the program."

"Jonathan! What are you doing here? The cliff! Didn't I . . . die?"

"Oh, Fletch, come on. Think. If you are talking to me, then obviously you didn't die. What you did manage to do was to change your level of consciousness rather abruptly. It's your choice now. You can stay here and learn on this level—which is quite a bit higher than the one you left—or you can go back and keep working with the Flock. The Elders were hoping for some kind of disaster; they're startled that you obliged them so well."

"I want to go back to the Flock, of course. I've barely begun with the new group."

"Very well, Fletcher. Remember what we were saying about one's body being nothing more than thought itself . . .?"

Fletcher shook his head and stretched his wings and opened his eyes at the base of the cliff, in the center of the whole Flock assembled. There was a great clamor of squawks and screes from the crowd when first he moved.

"He lives! He that was dead *lives!*"

"Touched him with a wingtip! Brought him to life! He's a devil! *Devil!* Come to break the Flock!"

There were 4000 gulls in the crowd, frightened at what had happened, and the cry *devil* went through them like the wind of an ocean storm. Eyes glazed, beaks sharp, they closed in to destroy.

"Would you feel better if we left, Fletcher?" asked Jonathan.

"I wouldn't object too much if we did. . . ."

Instantly they stood together a half-mile away, and the flashing beaks of the mob closed on empty air.

"Why is it," Jonathan puzzled, "that the hardest thing in the world is to convince a bird that he is free, and that he can prove it for himself if he'd just spend a little time practicing? Why should that be so hard?"

Fletcher still blinked from the change of scene. "What did you just do? How did we get here?"

"You did say you wanted to be out of the mob, didn't you?"

"Yes! But how did you . . ."

"Like everything else, Fletcher. Practice."

By morning the Flock had forgotten its insanity, but Fletcher had not. "Jonathan, remember what you said a long time ago, about loving the Flock enough to return to it and help it learn?"

"Sure."

"I don't understand how you manage to love a mob of birds that has just tried to kill you."

"Oh, Fletch, you don't love that! You don't love hatred and evil, of course. You have to practice and see the real gull, the good in every one of them, and to help them see it in themselves. That's what I mean by love. It's fun, when you get the knack of it. I remember—I remember well—a fierce young bird, for instance. Fletcher Lynd Seagull his name was. Just been made Outcast, ready to fight the Flock to the death, getting a start on building his own bitter hell out on the Far Cliffs. And here he is today building his own heaven instead, and leading the whole Flock in that direction."

Fletcher turned to his instructor, and there was a moment of fright in his eyes. "*Me* leading? What do you mean, *me* leading? You're the instructor here. You couldn't leave!"

"Couldn't I? Don't you think there might be other flocks, other Fletchers, that need an instructor more than this one, which is on its way toward the light? You don't need me any longer. You need to keep finding yourself—that real, unlimited Fletcher Seagull. He's your instructor. You need to understand him and to practice him."

A moment later, Jonathan's body wavered in the air, shimmering, and began to go transparent.

"Don't let them spread silly rumors about me, or make me a god. Okay, Fletch? I'm a seagull. I like to fly, maybe . . ."

"Jonathan!"

The shimmering stopped. Jonathan Seagull had vanished.

After a time, Fletcher Gull dragged himself into the sky and faced a brand-new group of students, eager for their first lesson.

"To begin with," he said heavily, "you've got to understand that a seagull is an unlimited idea of freedom, an image of the Great Gull, and your whole body, from wingtip to wingtip, is nothing more than your thought itself."

The young gulls looked at him quizzically. Hey, man, they thought, this doesn't sound like a rule for a loop.

Fletcher sighed and started over. "Hm. Ah . . . very well," he said, and eyed them critically. "Let's begin with Level Flight." And, saying that, he understood all at once that his friend had quite honestly been no more divine than Fletcher himself.

No limits, Jonathan? he thought. Well, then, the time's not distant when I'm going to appear out of thin air on *your* beach, and show you a thing or two about flying!

And though he tried to look properly severe for his students, Fletcher Seagull suddenly saw them all as they really were, just for a moment, and he more than liked, he loved what he saw. No limits, Jonathan? he thought, and he smiled. His race to learn had begun.

MY MOBY DICK

CONDENSED FROM THE BOOK BY

WILLIAM HUMPHREY

ILLUSTRATED BY P. HENDERSON LINCOLN

The trout was enormous, more than 40 inches in length and weighing close to 30 pounds. From the moment the author first spotted old One-Eye lurking in the shadowy waters of the small New England stream, he became obsessed with catching the giant fish.

"I logged his comings and goings," writes William Humphrey, "like an assassin establishing his victim's routine."

The pursuit of the wise old fish turned into a season-long duel which, finally, came to a surprising climax. *Newsweek* called this beguiling tale "Altogether charming."

1. THE BIG ONE

CALL ME BILL. Some years ago—never mind how long precisely—I thought I would go fishing. It is a way I have of driving away the spleen and, after a winter spent in the Berkshire Mountains of Massachusetts, I had a whale of a swollen spleen. Whenever I find myself snarling at little children; whenever I stop being grateful that my bottle is half full and start grumbling that it is half empty—then I account it high time to go fishing as soon as I can.

I do not mean that I am tormented by an itch for places remote, that I feel the lure of distant seas and mysterious monsters of the deep. Not for me marlin in the Gulf or swordfish off Patagonia. Such fishing costs money, and if I have been saved from evil it is by never having had much of the root of it all.

As for big fish, all is relative. Every species has its prodigies. T. S. Hudson got his name in the record book, where it has stood for a generation, by catching a $4\frac{3}{4}$-pound bluegill. To land it must have taken fully five minutes. Which is the pan-fishing equivalent of the three-day battle between the whale Moby Dick and the crew of the *Pequod.*

For me fishing is an act as private as prayer. I am particular about fishing, requiring that it be cheap, nearby yet uncrowded, in a mountain stream or a meadow brook; and since it is fishing more than fish that I am out for, I want a fish that is finicky, wily and skittish, hard to lure, game when hooked. I want one that is not merely edible but delicious, and, while I am at it, one that does not have to be scaled. "Is that all!" you may say. "Why the fish you would have must be as rare as white whales—if not as big." I *am* hard to please; but there is, among all the many kinds of fish, just one that fulfills all my requirements.

I am not alone in my monogamous—even monotheistic—devotion to the trout. There are many fishermen like me—far too many, as far as I am concerned—and I am sure the others all feel that way, too.

But I am getting away from my story. As I said, I had spent that winter in the Berkshires. Not far from my house there was a stream, a tributary of the Housatonic, that is of literary-historical interest only. This little creek originates in Stockbridge Bowl, the big lake below Tanglewood, summer home of the Boston Symphony Orchestra, and meanders down to Stockbridge, where it joins the big river. All that grim, gray winter, I rode alongside it on my way to and from the library in Lenox, where I went to get the volumes of Nathaniel Hawthorne and Herman Melville that sustained me until spring. It was intriguing to read *The House of Seven Gables* in these surroundings, because the Hawthornes had lived in a little red cottage near the stream—"Shadow Brook," they called it—during the year the book was written.

To that cottage, mounted on his horse, Melville, himself busy that same year of 1850 writing *Moby Dick,* rode from Pittsfield to visit, and to tell, in young Julian Hawthorne's words, "tremendous stories about the South Sea Islands and the whale fishery," looking, "when the narrative inspiration was on him, like all the things he was describing—savages and sea captains, even the terrible Moby Dick himself."

Remembering Shadow Brook more than half a century later, Julian Hawthorne wrote: "It was clear brown, with glancing gleams of interior green, and sparkles diamond white; tiny fishes switched themselves against the current with quivering tails; the shaggy margins were flecked with sunshine. Fragments of rock and large pebbles interrupted its flow and deepened its mellow song; above it brooded the twilight of the tall pines and walnuts, responding to its merriment with solemn murmurings." By my time, a century later, it was largely unchanged.

Boys were fishing in the stream—in a pool just below a bridge—one day in July when I, on my way home from the library, had a flat there. I watched them from the road bank as I rested after changing tires. They were catching pan fish. But they were neither keeping them nor throwing them back. Whenever a boy landed one he stepped on it to keep from getting finned while he unhooked it. When he had baited his hook again he left the fish to flop on the bank. Very intent they all were, yet no boy bothered to string or even keep track of his catch. Maybe they meant to gather them all when they had enough and have themselves a fish-fry. They ought to kill them quickly, though, not leave them to flop on the ground until they died.

I was withdrawing my eyes from the scene when I noticed something lying in shallow water near the bank downstream from the boys. A log, probably. Or a long, narrow rock. To nobody but a nut on the subject, like me, would any other possibility have occurred. I got my binoculars from the car. What they showed me was a trout 30 feet long. It could not be included in the glasses' field of view; it had to be scanned, section by section. The spots on it were as big as those on a dappled horse, and gave to it the look of a submarine hull painted in camouflage.

My binoculars being eight power, the fish was actually between three and four feet long. I skipped a breath. I was being shown—I put it that way because I had a strong sense of having been chosen—one of nature's prodigies. Not in the remote, unpeopled wildness of Labrador, but here in this little roadside pool, where cars whizzed at my back and from the houses clustered all around came the mood music of daytime TV serials, lived one of the world's biggest trout. Few men—I mean by that, say, half a dozen—had ever seen one anywhere near as big.

Seeing me with my binoculars trained on them, the boys all quit fishing and, leaving their fish, clambered up the bank and fled on their bicycles as though they had been apprehended poaching.

I went down to the water's edge, treading softly so as not to spook the big trout. Some of the bluegills abandoned on the bank were still giving an occasional feeble flounce, others were dead and dry; all had had their eyes gouged out. I could account for this barbarity no better after finding a tangle of line with a hook baited with a fish's eye. In addition to being atrocious, it seemed senseless. Catch a fish and pluck out its eyes to catch another fish with, and all only to throw the fish away? This—to say the least—unsporting behavior seemed all the more shocking and saddening in this setting: in the same pool where a truly noble fish lived. One thing I understood: the boys' flight. They knew that what they were doing was wicked.

The big trout lay almost touching the bank. I crept up on him cautiously. I need not have. It was to protect himself where he was unguarded that he lay so close to the bank. His eye on that side, his right, was blind. It was opaque, white, pupil-less, like the eye of a baked fish. That, too, was saddening. One hates to see a splendid creature impaired in any way.

An explanation for those boys' behavior now dawned on me. It was pretty farfetched, enough to make me wonder whether I was not a little touched, but I could think of none other to account for the presence together there of the half-blind trout and the blinded fish. The boys were not fishing for the bluegills, only for their eyes to use as bait. With these they were fishing for the trout. I theorized that they credited the trout with an appetite for fishes' eyes because of resentment over the loss of that one of his. I may have been overinfluenced by the literary associations of the place. Or I may just have been reading too much Melville. A one-eyed Ahab of trout?

Whatever, something that has given me much pleasure—fly fishing—I owe to the two things that came together there at that little pool in Shadow Brook: that big fish and those boys. I had once tried fly fishing for a whole year. In search of pleasure, I had spent the most frustrating, humiliating and unhappy season of my life, before converting my fly rod into a spinning rod and, thereupon, catching, with a worm, my first trout. But I always felt inferior to a true fly fisherman.

Now I was going to fish for the fish, and without reproach to myself that I had trespassed upon the boys' prior claim to him. They had forfeited all right to that trout. It was my revulsion at that ugly business of theirs that made me forswear all live bait, and determined me to try again to learn to fish with artificial flies. Nothing but the most sporting of methods was worthy of that once-in-a-lifetime fish.

2. DEEP AND MURKY WATERS

MEASURING YOUR FISH before you catch him is counting your chickens before they hatch; but as I did not much expect to catch that big one-eyed trout, I measured him first. It was possible to do this because he always lay at his feeding station with his blind side almost touching the bank. I went to the pool at break of day the morning after discovering him, carrying with me a carpenter's folding rule. I stretched it, and myself, upon the bank. In addition to the rule, I took with me my wife, and while I do not expect to be believed myself, I trust that no one is unchivalrous enough to doubt her word. She too was stretched upon the bank, and she is ready to affirm that the fish measured 42-and-a-fraction inches. I did not attempt to tape-measure his girth, but I have measured that of my own thigh, to which it corresponded. When the length and the girth of a fish are known, its weight can be roughly estimated. I estimated old One-Eye's to be 30 pounds, give or take five.

He could never have attained such size in that little pool. He must have come down, and not very long before, from Stockbridge Bowl, perhaps been washed down in a flood. Nor could he have attained that size half-blind. The loss of his eye, too, had to be fairly recent.

Now, a fish that big cannot be caught. That he has not been is all the proof needed that he cannot be. He is too wise. The allotted life-span of the trout—which only the tiniest fraction of them attain—is seven years, by which age the average one is 22 inches long. Cyclops was just under double that; had he likewise doubled the normal life-span? He must in his time have seen—and seen through—all the 3000 patterns of artificial flies that are said to exist. Considering the odds against it, his survival to that age made him a Hercules, a Solomon of trout.

On the other hand, a fish that big is too big *not* to be fished for. What happens is that the fish hooks the fisherman.

I knew how dangerous a sport fly fishing for trout can be. It has wrecked men's marriages, their careers; when begun early enough in life it has prevented them from ever getting around to either marriage or a career and turned them into lifelong celibates and ne'er-do-wells. Theodore Gordon, the hermit saint of trout fishing, who floated the first dry fly in the New World in 1890, threw up his job at an early age, sponged off his relatives, remained a lifelong bachelor, neglected his old, dying mother, and did nothing but two things with himself: fish for trout and, out of season, tie flies to fish through the coming one. The danger of becoming that kind of addict not only scared me, it appalled me. I both pity and despise any person who makes a passion out of a pastime. I am a firm believer in moderation.

That is my belief—in practice I am excessive in everything I do, and I had long suspected that my failure to master fly fishing had been a blessing in disguise. Now providence had placed in my path a fish that was enough to unbalance a stabler man than I, and had restricted my method of angling for him by putting those boys there, committing a crime against nature that nothing less than the purest and most high-minded method, one I had tried, failed at and forsworn, could make up for. I wanted that fish and I wished I had never laid eyes on him. I had not lost a leg to him, as Captain Ahab had to Moby Dick, but he had certainly taken a big bite of my brain.

I needed instruction, but I had no one to instruct me. I sought help in books—no other sport has spawned so many. The salesclerk guided me to volumes that he said were "the latest thing." Innocent that I was, I supposed that one manual on fly fishing, updated periodically, would suffice for all time, the same as one on sex. I learned now that if you were to compete with crowds now on the streams you needed to be a physicist, an entomologist, a limnologist, a statistician, a biometrician.

To solve that most basic of problems, which artificial fly to offer the fish, one of my authorities, the one I called The Efficiency Expert, counseled approaching the stream with a net, a bottle of formaldehyde, and the highest-power microscope you could conveniently carry. Plant your net in the stream like a seine stretching from bank to bank, go upstream and turn over some rocks on the creek bed, go back to your net, pick off the little nymphs that have washed down against it, get out your microscope and identify them; then, with your handy streamside fly-tying kit of hooks in 20 different sizes, tinsels, threads of all colors, feathers and furs, from all the world's feather- and fur-bearers, tie artificials to match—or to match not the nymphs themselves, if you were a dry-fly purist, like me, but their winged-adult stage. *Oh, Cyclops!* I thought. *Into what deep and murky waters you have led me!*

From The Entomologist I learned that when the fish are being finicky—"selective" is the word—about the fly they are feeding on, the angler must match it. When, for example, it is *Ephemerella subvaria* that they are all eating like peanuts, then you must show them the Hendrickson fly, not the Quill Gordon, which was all they would look at last week when *Iron fraudator* was in season.

I closed that volume as though slamming down the lid on Pandora's box. Demented I might be, but that way lay madness maddened.

It was I, alone, unaided, who solved my problem. I hit upon a solution which, though I say so myself, was brilliant. It was elementary, of course; every brilliant stroke is—after somebody has had it! The problem: I needed a mentor. The predicament: I knew no one, could trust no one. As long as I kept thinking of my preceptor as a fisherman, I got nowhere. Once I thought of him as a fish—*eureka!* Who knew more about the ways of trout than the world's greatest trout? Here I had him in a fishbowl of a pool, and he was blind on one side; without his seeing me, I could study his every move, every mood.

I went to the pool. When I got there I found those wicked boys up to their tricks. I had forgotten about them. Now there they were, one of them yanking a bluegill onto the bank, another stepping on his fish, still another with his bloody little paws busy at their grisly task. As soon as I showed up, of course, they skulked away. And they made themselves scarce for however long I stood guard, defending One-Eye against them and against his own savage proclivities.

My time to learn was short—what was left of this season. He was too old to survive another Berkshire winter. He could not live long in this little pool. No scope for his bulk here. He was home from sea, passing his decline in this sailors' snug harbor.

I logged his comings and goings like an assassin establishing his victim's routine. When I had fixed the hours at which he issued from his lair beneath the bridge, then I was there, on the bank beside his spot. He was unfailingly punctual in keeping the appointments with me that he never knew he had. Almost cheek to cheek with his sworn enemy he lay. And though he was a prodigy of his kind and I merely representative of mine, yet nature had given to me a dubious superiority which made me pity him: unlike me, he did not know that he must die.

Such a jittery creature he was, ever alert, ever fearful, as though he understood that he lived his life in a medium that exposed to hostile view his every movement. The fleeting shadow of a cloud passing over him was enough to send him darting for safety underneath the bridge. Old and big and wise in his way as he was, he could never for an instant relax his lifelong vigil; indeed, he must redouble it, for now he had but one eye with which to be twice as watchful.

It might be expected that such a monster, such a freak, would be clumsy, muscle-bound, weak, but the fish's great bulk was no impediment to his grace, his agility, his might. From dead still, he could, when alarmed, accelerate with a speed that amounted to vanishing on the spot—a magician's trick: now you see it, now you don't.

His mastery of his element was total. Without the movement of a muscle he could maintain himself as stationary as a stone. By inflating and deflating his air bladder, he surfaced and sounded like a submarine. He would sight his prey as it entered the pool. Then, light as a bubble he rose, his dorsal fin broke water like a periscope, his huge streamlined snout silently dimpled the surface, and into that great maw of his a grasshopper or a caterpillar or a late-hatching mayfly drifted, borne helplessly on the current. Mission accomplished, he sank soundlessly from sight.

My studies were not confined to the fish. It was equally important that I familiarize myself with his immediate surroundings, that small dining area of the pool in which, if at all, he was to be taken unawares.

That the little feeder stream that served up the fish's food to him was scarcely two feet wide, that it was slow and unruffled, and that my fly would float on its surface, above any obstructions, might seem to make my task easy. Not so. The very narrowness of the channel would demand a cast of pinpoint accuracy, and the very stillness of the surface meant that my fly must fall upon it so unnoticeably as to seem to have hatched from under it.

And there was still another worry.

There were—there always are, in even the narrowest stretch of flowing water—more currents than just one. This is what, sooner or later, always causes drag. The fisherman's fly must ride the current that ensnares the live insects and carries them to the lurking fish. Meanwhile, the leader to which the fly is attached lies across the adjacent current, or currents. No two currents of a stream, however close, flow at the same speed. One of them will carry the leader at a rate faster than that of the fly. After a while the leader bellies in the current downstream of the fly, dragging the fly faster and faster as it lengthens. Nothing could be more unlike the free float of the natural insect, and trout are all born knowing this. The fisherman's time to deceive and hook the fish is that brief interval between the alighting of his fly upon the water and the commencement of drag. Drag a fly over a wise, wary old trout, and you might as well move on.

I would have yet another problem. The field of view of a normal trout is just 97.6 degrees. Within that narrow compass the fisherman's fly must be presented; if the fish is to take it, he must see it. Only half that would I have in which to attract and deceive old One-Eye. To put down a fly, from a distance of some 40 feet, on that small target would be about like asking a bombardier to hit a one-lane bridge from five miles' altitude.

It was not that familiarity had bred contempt for him in me that made me decide the time had come to take him on. I had just wakened to the realization that it was late August. The fishing season was fast running out. Now or never, I must get up off my belly and into the water with him.

3. OLD ONE-EYE

I THEN LEARNED that we were not alone, my fish and I. While I had been observing him, I was being observed myself.

"After that big old trout?"

I was crawling backward away from the bank. Looking over my shoulder, I saw a towheaded little boy, as freckled as a trout. I spent another minute on my hands and knees searching for the thing I was pretending to have lost.

"Trout?" I inquired, giving up my search and getting to my feet. "What trout?"

The boy stepped around me and started down the path to have a look for himself. He knew where to look.

"Don't go too near!" I said. "You'll scare him."

"Scare him? What's he got to be scared of? Hell, he's bigger'n I am. You're wasting your time fishing for that big old one-eyed trout."

The boy watched as I rigged my rod. From a pocket of my vest I took one of my many fly boxes and selected a fly.

"What's that?" the boy asked.

I showed him the Hairwing Coachman, size 10, that I had chosen.

"What is it?" he asked.

"An artificial fly. A hook with feathers tied around it to look like a live insect."

"What's it for?"

"It's my bait."

"That? You think you're going to catch a fish with *that* thing?" To him my foolishness was monumental. "Mister," he said, "there's just one bait you might get that fish there to bite. Know what it is?"

"I suspect I know what you think it is," I said.

"It's. . . ."

"Never mind! You do things your way, I'll do them mine."

With a shrug the boy gave up on me. He had done his best.

I waded into the water behind the fish. I dared approach him no nearer than 35 feet. I flicked my line back and forth in false casts, adding to its length. When I judged it to be the proper length, I let it drop. It touched water just where I wanted it to and, so it seemed to me, touched softly. Nevertheless, the fish bolted for the bridge, much to the enjoyment of the boy on the bank.

What I had done was disregard the first and most famous dictum of fly fishing, that of one of the earliest writers on the subject, Charles Cotton: "Fish fine and far off."

In fly fishing, the lure being weightless, it is the weight of the line that the fisherman casts. This makes it far too heavy and conspicuous a thing to fool even the most foolish fish. To get "fine and far off" the fisherman is forced to interpose between the line and the fly an additional piece of tackle. This is the leader, the translucent terminal addition to the fisherman's line to which is attached the fly.

A leader's diameter is measured with a micrometer, in thousandths of an inch. It tapers from butt to tippet, going from about the size of carpet thread down to something that looks as though it were spun by an anemic spider. In fishing for trout, a leader nine feet long is generally the shortest used; anything less than that puts the heavy and highly visible line too near the fish. The maximum length? There is none. It is whatever the fish demands. Late in the season, with the water slow-moving and clear, and with big, wise, wary old fish, the leader grows ever longer, ever finer, with the fisherman hoping to stop at the point where the leader is fine enough to fool the fish but still strong enough to land him.

In the eastern United States nowadays a two-pound trout is a big one. My Cyclops was 15 times that size and surely to the 15th point wiser. Thus, paradoxically, the biggest of fish was to push me to use the lightest of leaders. I had begun with a nine-foot leader terminating in a tippet of .011-inch diameter with a dead-weight breaking strength of nine pounds. This the fish not only disdained, he let me know it was a gross insult to his intelligence.

As, over the succeeding weeks, I grudgingly added length to, and subtracted from, my leader—and as I learned to cast the clumsy thing, I had the satisfaction, and the anxiety, of seeing a growing change in the response of my adversary.

Conscious that my time was short, I applied myself closely, and under the fish's strict tutelage I was becoming a better fisherman. He demanded nothing less than perfection. A careless cast, one that missed its aim by an inch or that landed with the least disturbance, and he was gone. How fatuous of me it seemed then ever to have thought I was going to catch that wonder of the world—a feeling unfailingly seconded by the freckle-faced little boy on the bank.

I was improving steadily, and all the same I remained as far short as ever of the mastery needed to entice the phenomenon of a fish into taking my fly. Steadily forcing me to yield to him in the battle of the lengthening leader, he now had me down to one 18 feet long, spidery thin. With that I could see I was beginning to interest him. So big was he that even at my distance from him I could detect that rippling of his spots which denoted that he was tensing, readying himself to pounce upon his approaching prey.

But at the last moment he always had second thoughts, sank back and let my fly drift past. I alternated between cursing him for his invulnerability and feeling that I had been uniquely privileged to have made the acquaintance of so remarkable, so rare a creature. He was giving me incomparable training in how to catch trout—lesser trout than himself, that is—and I should have been content with that. I was not. He himself was the fish I wanted to catch, and, forgetting now that I owed my betterment all to him, I grew more and more confident that I could. Right up to the season's closing day I continued to believe that.

"Closing day," my small companion announced as we met at poolside. "Still using them artificial flies, I see. Ever get him to bite one of them yet?"

"Can't say I have."

"Then what makes you think he's going to now?"

"Don't think he's going to; just hoping he might."

But the truth was, the boy had dashed my hopes. At midnight the Massachusetts Division of Fisheries and Wildlife would extend protection over its most venerable trout, and he would live out his pensionage in this little pool. It was only to round out the fitness of things that I waded into the water. I owed him his total triumph over me.

As often happens, now that I had lost confidence and, with it, the compulsion to perform, I excelled myself in my casting that day. Four times running I placed my fly over the fish without rousing his suspicions. My fifth cast would have alighted in the same spot, some four feet in front of the fish, as the others had. It never did. Exploding from the water, the fish took it on the wing, a foot above the surface. Why that cast and none of the countless others, nobody will ever know. Instantly, he felt the barb.

Out of the water he rose again—out and out, and still there was more to him, no end to him. More bird than fish he seemed as he hovered above the water. His gleaming wetness gave an iridescent glaze to him, and as he rose into the sunshine his multitudinous markings sparkled as though he were studded with jewels. At once both weighty and weightless, he rose to twice his own length. Then, giving himself a flip like a pole-vaulter's, down he dived, parting the water with a wallop that rocked the pool to its edges.

The next moment I was facing in another direction, turned by the tug of my rod. Nothing remotely resembling his speed and power had I ever experienced.

Straight up from the water he rose again, higher than before. There was exuberance in his leap, joy of battle, complete self-confidence, glory in his own singularity. I believed now that he had taken my fly for the fun of it. I was quite ready to credit that superfish with knowing this was the last day of the season, even with knowing it was his last season and wanting to show the world what he was capable of.

Another unrestrainable run, then again he leaped; for this one the former two had been only warm-ups. He must have a drop of salmon in his blood! Up and up he went until he had risen into the bright sunshine, and there, in defiance of gravity, in suspension of time, he hung. He shook himself down his entire length. The spray that scattered from him caught the light and became a perfect rainbow in miniature. Set in that aureole of his own colors, he gave a final toss of his head, breaking my leader with ease, did a flip and re-entered the water with a splash.

"Dummy!" cried the boy on the bank. "You had him and you let him get away!"

Even so worldly a man as Jonathan Swift could write late in life, in a letter to his friend Alexander Pope, "I remember when I was a little boy, I felt a great fish at the end of my line, which I drew up almost to the ground, but it dropped in, and the disappointment vexes me to this day." Sick with disappointment at losing my once-in-a-lifetime fish, I was sure I would never get over it.

But now I wonder, would I really rather have that fish hanging on my wall than to see him as I do in my memory, flaunting his might and his majesty against that rainbow of his own making? Many times I have rerun that vivid footage photographed by my eyes and been cheered that that was my last view of him. He is the one fish of my life that has not grown bigger in recollection.

Fishing stories always end with the fish getting away. Not this one. This, reader, has been the story of a fisherman who got away. For old One-Eye made a changed man of me. No fish since him has been able to madden me. I have hooked and lost some big ones in that time, but to each and all I have been able to say, "Go your way. I have known your better, and there will never be his like again. You, however big you may be, are a mere minnow compared to my Moby Dick."

THE FIRST FOUR YEARS

CONDENSED FROM THE BOOK BY

Laura Ingalls Wilder

ILLUSTRATED BY DAVID BLOSSOM

Laura Ingalls was born in 1867 in a log cabin in the Wisconsin wilderness. With her family she traveled by covered wagon to Kansas, then to Minnesota and finally to the Dakota Territory. There, at 18, she married Almanzo (Manly) Wilder. In the 1930s and '40s she chronicled her early years in what have become widely hailed as the Little House books.

After her death in 1957 at age 90, a brief pencil-written manuscript was found among her papers. In it she described the pioneer hardships and simple joys of her first four years of marriage. The story was published just as she wrote it.

1. THE FIRST YEAR

IT WAS A HOT AFTERNOON with a strong wind from the south, but out on the Dakota prairie in 1885 no one minded the hot sunshine or the hard winds. They were to be expected: a natural part of life.

The swiftly trotting horses drawing the shining black-top buggy swung around the corner of Pierson's livery barn, making the turn from the end of Main Street to the country road.

Looking from a window of her Pa's three-room claim shanty a half-mile away, Laura saw them coming and just had time to put on her hat and pick up her gloves. Laura made a pretty picture at the door of the shanty, the brown August grass under her feet and the young cottonwoods standing in their square around the yard. Her pink dress with its small sprigs of blue flowers just cleared her toes. The sage-green, rough-straw bonnet lined with blue silk softly framed her cheeks and her large blue eyes with the bangs of her brown hair above them.

Manly said nothing of all this; he helped her into the buggy and tucked the linen lap robe carefully about her to keep off the dust. Then he tightened the reins and they dashed away for an afternoon drive.

"Can't we be married soon?" Manly said. "If you don't want a big wedding, and you would be willing, we could be married right away. Harvest is coming, and I'd like us to be settled first."

Laura twisted the bright gold ring with its pearl-and-garnet setting around and around.

"I've been thinking," she said. "I don't want to marry a farmer. I have always said I never would. I do wish you would do something else. There are chances in town now while it is so new and growing."

There was a silence; then Manly asked, "Why don't you want to marry a farmer?"

And Laura replied, "Because a farm is such a hard place for a woman. There are so many chores for her to do. Besides, a farmer never has any money. The people in towns tell him what they will pay for what he has to sell and then they charge him what they please for what he has to buy."

Manly laughed. "Well, as the Irishman said, 'Everything is evened up in this world. The rich have their ice in the summer but the poor get theirs in the winter.'"

Laura refused to make a joke of it. She said, "I don't always want to be poor and work hard while the people in town take it easy and make money off us."

"But you've got it all wrong," Manly told her seriously. "Farmers are the only ones who are independent. I have 50 acres of wheat this year. It is enough for me but if you will come live on the farm, I will break the ground this fall and sow another 50 acres next spring. You see, on a farm it all depends on what a man is willing to do."

There was a skeptical silence on Laura's part, broken at last by Manly, who said, "If you'll try it for three years and I haven't made a success in farming by that time, I'll quit and do anything you want me to do. I promise."

Laura enjoyed the freedom and spaciousness of the wide prairie. Two quarter sections of this land, each with 160 acres of rich black soil, would be theirs, for Manly had already proved up* on a homestead and he also had a tree claim on which he was growing the ten acres of trees required by law to get title. Between the two claims lay a school section

*He had fulfilled the requirements for receiving a patent for government land.

where anyone could cut the hay, first come, first served. It would be much more fun living on the land than on the town street with neighbors so close on each side.

"The house on the tree claim will be finished in a couple of weeks," Manly was saying. "Let's be married the next week. It will be the last week in August before the harvest begins."

There seemed to be no other way than to be married suddenly because of the help it would be to have a home and a housekeeper in the rush of fall work coming on. It would be thought the right way to do it by the neighbors and friends, for they were all engaged in the same struggle to establish themselves on the new prairie land.

And so on August 25, at ten o'clock in the morning, the quick-stepping brown horses and the buggy drew up at the little claim house in its hollow square of young cottonwoods. Laura stood at the door, her Ma and Pa on either hand, her two sisters behind her. They threw kisses and waved their hands. Bright green leaves of the cottonwoods waved too in the wind and there was a choke in Laura's throat, for they seemed to be saying good-by, and she saw her Ma brush her hand quickly across her eyes.

The preacher lived on his homestead two miles away and it seemed to Laura the longest drive she had ever taken, and yet it was all over too soon. Once in the front room, the ceremony was quickly performed. Laura and Manly were married for better or worse, for richer or poorer. Then, away to the new home on the other side of town. The first year was begun.

The house had been built on the tree claim, looking forward to the time when the small switches of trees should be grown. Already Manly and Laura seemed to see it sitting in a beautiful grove of cottonwoods and elms and maples. The hopeful little trees stood in the half-circle of the drive before the house. Surely, if they were tended well, it would not be long before they sheltered the house from the summer's heat and the winter's cold and the winds that were always blowing.

The first breakfast in the new home was a hurried affair, for Manly must go to the Webbs' for the threshing. All the neighbors would be there. Since they would expect Mr. Webb to give them a good day's work in exchange, as their turns with the threshers came, no one could afford to hold up the gang at Webb's place.

Laura was alone for the day, but there was much to do putting the house in order. It was a bright and shining little house, and it was really all theirs, Laura thought. It belonged to just Manly and her. Oh, she did hope Manly was right, and she smiled as she repeated to herself, "Everything is evened up in this world."

Manly was late home, for threshers worked as long as there was daylight to see by. Supper was on the table when he came in from doing the chores, and as they ate he told Laura the threshers would come next day, would be there at noon for dinner. Now Laura had always been a pioneer girl rather than a farmer's daughter, always moving on to new places before the fields grew large, so a gang of men as large as a thresh-

Laura and Almanzo the winter after they were married

ing crew to feed by herself was rather dismaying. But if she was going to be a farmer's wife that was all in the day's work.

Early next morning she began to plan and prepare the dinner. She had brought a baking of bread from home, and with some hot corn bread there would be plenty. Pork and potatoes were on hand and she had put some navy beans to soak the night before. There was a pieplant (rhubarb) in the garden; she must make a couple of pies. The morning flew too quickly, but when the men came in at noon from the thresher, dinner was on the table.

There was plenty of food, though something seemed to be wrong with the beans. Lacking her Ma's watchful eye, Laura had not cooked them enough and they were hard. And when it came to the pie—Mr. Perry, a neighbor of Laura's parents, tasted his first. Then he lifted the top crust and spread sugar thickly over his piece. "That is the way I like it," he said. "If there is no sugar in the pie, then every fellow can sweeten his own as much as he likes without hurting the cook's feelings."

Mr. Perry made the meal a jolly one. He told tales of when he was a boy in Pennsylvania. His mother, he said, used to take five beans and a kettle of water to make bean soup. The kettle was so large that after they had eaten all the broth and bread they could, they had to take off their coats and dive for a bean if they wanted one. Everyone laughed and talked and was very friendly, but Laura felt mortified about her beans and her pie without any sugar. How could she have been so careless?

The wheat turned out only ten bushels to the acre, and wheat was selling at 50 cents a bushel. Not much of a crop. It had been too dry, and the price was low.

Manly was determined to double his acreage next year. He was early in the field, plowing, and Laura was busy all day with cooking, baking, churning, sweeping, washing, ironing and mending. The washing and ironing were hard for her to do. She was small and slender but her hands and wrists were strong and she got it done. Afternoons, she always put on a clean dress and sat in the parlor corner of the front room sewing, or knitting on Manly's socks.

Sundays they went for a buggy ride and as Skip and Barnum trotted along the prairie roads Laura and Manly would sing the old school songs. Their favorite was "Don't Leave the Farm, Boys."

You talk of the mines of Australia,
They've wealth in red gold, without doubt;
But, ah! there is gold on the farm, boys—
  If only you'll shovel it out.
  Don't be in a hurry to go!
  Don't be in a hurry to go!
Better risk the old farm awhile longer,
  Don't be in a hurry to go!

IT WAS GROWING LATE in the fall. The nights were frosty and soon the ground would freeze. The breaking of the new 50-acre field was nearly finished. There were no Sunday-afternoon drives now. Skip and Barnum were working too hard at the plowing to be driven. They must have their day of rest. Instead, there were long horseback rides—often

20 miles over the open prairie before breakfast, Manly on his saddle pony, Fly, and Laura on hers, Trixy.

It was a carefree, happy time, for two people thoroughly in sympathy can do pretty much as they like. To be sure, now and then Laura thought about the short crop and wondered. Once she even saved the cream carefully and sent a jar of fresh butter to town for sale, thinking it would help pay for the groceries. With the butter, she sent five dozen eggs, for the little flock of hens were laying wonderfully well. But Manly brought the butter back. Not a store in town wanted it at any price and he had been able to get only five cents a dozen for the eggs.

A few days later Manly butchered his fat hog and Laura had her first experience making sausage, headcheese and lard all by herself. Laura found working alone very different from helping Ma. But it was part of her job and she must do it, though she did hate the smell of hot lard, and the sight of so much fresh meat ruined her appetite for any of it.

One blustery day Manly started early for town, leaving Laura alone. She was used to being the only person on the place and thought nothing of it, but the wind was so cold and raw that she had not opened the front door. In the middle of the morning, busy with her work, Laura looked out the window and saw horsemen coming across the prairie. She wondered why they were not traveling on the road. As they came nearer she saw there were five of them, and they were Indians.

Laura had seen Indians often, without fear, but she felt a quick jump of her heart as they came up to the house and without knocking tried to open the front door. She was glad the door was locked, and she slipped into the back room and locked the outside door there.

Seeing Laura through the windows, the Indians made signs for her to open the door, indicating that they would not hurt her. But Laura shook her head and told them to go away. Likely they only wanted something to eat, but still one never could tell. It was only three years ago that the Indians nearly went on the warpath a little way west, and even now they often threatened the railroad camps.

She watched them as they jabbered together. Why didn't they go away! Instead, they were going to the barn—and her new saddle was hanging in the barn and Trixy was there. . . .

Laura was afraid; in the house there was comparative safety. But now Laura was angry, too, and as always, she acted quickly. Flinging the door open, she ran to the barn, and standing in the doorway, ordered the Indians out. One of them was feeling the leather of her beautiful saddle and one was in the stall with Trixy.

The other Indians were examining Manly's saddle and the buggy harness with its bright nickel trimmings. But they all came and gathered around Laura just outside the barn. She stormed at them and stamped her foot. Her head was bare and her long brown braids blew out on the wind while her eyes flashed fire as always when she was excited. The Indians only stared for a moment; then one of them grunted an unintelligible word and laid his hand on Laura's arm. Quick as a flash she slapped his face with all her might.

It made him angry and he started toward her, but the other Indians laughed, and one who seemed to be the leader stopped him. With signs, pointing to himself, his pony, and then with a sweep of his arm toward the west, he said, "You go—me—be my squaw?"

Laura shook her head, and stamping her foot again, motioned them all to their ponies, telling them to go. And they went, riding their running ponies without saddles or bridles.

But as they went, their leader turned and looked back at Laura where she stood, with the wind blowing her skirts around her and her braids flying, watching them go away across the prairie into the west.

WILD GEESE WERE FLYING SOUTH, the leaders calling and their followers answering until the world seemed full of their calls. Even at night the lonely, wild cry sounded through the darkness, calling, calling. It was almost irresistible. It made Laura long for wings so that she might follow. Manly said, "The old saying is that 'everything is lovely when the geese honk high,' but I believe we will have a hard winter, the geese are flying so high and in such a hurry. They are not stopping to rest on the lakes nor to feed. They are hurrying ahead of a storm."

For several days, the wild geese hurried southward; and then one still afternoon a dark cloud line lay low on the northwest horizon. It climbed swiftly, higher and higher, until the sun was overcast, and with a howl the wind came and the world was blotted out in a blur of whirling snow.

Laura was in the house alone when the wind struck the northwest corner with such force the whole house jarred. Quickly she ran to the window but she could see only a wall of whiteness beyond the glass. Manly was in the barn, and at the sudden shriek of the storm he, too, looked out a window. Then, although it was only midafternoon, he fed the horses and cows for the night, and shutting the barn door tightly behind him, started for the house.

As soon as he was away from the shelter of the barn, the full force of the storm struck him. It seemed to come from every direction at once. Whichever way he turned his head he faced the wind. He knew the direction in which the house lay. He could see nothing but a blur of white. It had grown intensely cold and the snow was a powdered dust of ice that filled his eyes and ears; he felt smothered. After taking a few steps he could not see the barn. He was alone in a whirling white world.

Keeping his face in the right direction, Manly went ahead; but soon he knew he had gone far enough to be at the house, yet he could not see it. A few steps more and he stumbled against an old wagon that had been left some little distance south of the house. In spite of his guarding against it, the wind had blown him south of his way.

Again setting his face in the right direction he went on. Again, he knew he should have reached the house but had not. If he should become hopelessly confused he might not find it at all but wander out on the open prairie to perish, or he might even freeze within a few feet of the house. No shout of his could be heard above the wind.

Well, he might as well go on a little farther; no use standing still. Another step, and his shoulder lightly brushed something. He put up his hand and touched the corner of a building. The house! He had almost missed it and headed out into the storm.

For three days and nights the blizzard raged. Before Manly went out again, he rigged the long rope clothesline from the house to the barn. After that he cared for the stock once a day.

Laura kept the fire going from the store of coal in the storm shed. She cooked from the stores in her pantry and cellar and she sang at her knitting in the afternoon. Old Shep and the cat lay companionably on the rug before the cookstove and there was warmth and comfort in the little house standing so sturdily in the midst of the raging elements.

Late in the afternoon of the fourth day the wind went down. The sun shone again with a frosty light and huge sundogs stood guard on each side of it. And it was *cold!* Laura and Manly went outdoors and looked over the desolate landscape.

Next day Manly drove to town to get a few supplies and to learn the news. When he came home he was very sober. A man south of town, caught at his barn by the storm as Manly had been, had missed the house going back. He had wandered out on the prairie and had been found frozen to death when the wind went down.

Range cattle had drifted before the storm for a hundred miles. Blinded and confused they had gone over a high bank of the Cottonwood River, the later ones falling on top of the first, breaking through the ice of the river and floundering in the water and loose snow until they had smothered and frozen to death. Men were dragging them out of the river now, hundreds of them, and skinning them to save the hides.

The holidays were near and something must be done about them. Christmas presents were hardly to be thought of, the way the crops had turned out, but Manly made handsleds for Laura's little sisters, and they would buy Christmas candy for all.

For themselves, they decided to buy a present together, something they could both use and enjoy. After much studying of Montgomery Ward's catalogue, they chose to get a set of glassware. They needed it for the table and there was such a pretty set advertised, a sugar bowl, spoon-holder, butter dish, six sauce dishes, and a large, oval-shaped bread plate. On the bread plate raised in the glass were heads of wheat and some lettering which read "Give us this day our daily bread."

When the box came from Chicago a few days before Christmas and was unpacked, they were both delighted with their present.

With work and play, in sunshine and storm, the winter passed. The wild geese were coming back from the southland. Manly was getting his plows and harrows in order for working the land. The wheat for seed was stored in the claim shanty on the homestead, for there was no granary on the tree claim. At the shanty, Laura held the grain sacks while Manly shoveled the wheat into them. Watching the plump wheat kernels slide into the open mouth of the sack made Laura dizzy. And then she heard Manly saying, "Sit down a minute! You're tired."

She sat down, but she was not tired. She was sick. The next morning she felt much worse and Manly got his own breakfast. For days she fainted whenever she left her bed. The doctor told her to lie quietly. He assured her she would feel much better before long, and that in a few months, nine to be exact, she would be quite all right. Laura was going to have a baby.

Laura missed the drives over the greening prairie in the freshness of early spring. She missed the wild violets that scented the air with their fragrance, but when wild rose time came in June she was able to ride behind Skip and Barnum along the country roads, where the prairie roses made glowing masses of color from pale pink to deepest red and the air was full of their sweetness.

On one such drive she asked abruptly out of a silence, "What shall we name the child?"

"We can't name it now," Manly replied, "for we don't know if it will be a boy or a girl."

And after another silence Laura said, "It will be a girl and we will call her Rose."

It rained often that spring. It rained through the summer. And, oh, how the wheat and oats did grow! The days went by and by and the wheat headed tall and strong and green and beautiful. In just a few days more the crop would be safe. Even if it turned dry now there would be a good crop, for the stalks would ripen the wheat.

Laura did a little mental arithmetic—100 acres at 40 bushels to an acre would be 4000 bushels of wheat. Four thousand bushels at 75 cents a bushel would be $3000. Why, they would be rich!

Perhaps she could have someone to do the work until the baby came. Then she could rest; she needed rest, for, not being able to retain her food for more than a few minutes, she had not much to live on and was very emaciated.

Manly cut the 50 acres of oats. He was jubilant at night. It was a wonderful crop and early tomorrow he would begin on the wheat.

But, the next morning, when Manly had cut twice around the wheatfield, he unhitched and came back to the barn with the team. The wheat would be better for standing a couple of days longer.

As the afternoon passed it grew hotter and there was no wind, which was unusual. It left one gasping for breath and feeling smothered. About three o'clock Manly came in from the barn and said it was going to rain for sure. He was glad he had not been cutting the wheat to have it lie in a rainstorm before he could get it shocked. The sunshine darkened, and the wind sighed and then fell again. The wind rose a little, and it grew lighter, but the light was a greenish color. Then the storm came. It rained only a little; hailstones began to fall, at first scattering slowly, then falling thicker and faster while the stones were larger, some of them as large as hens' eggs.

In just 20 minutes the storm was over, and when they could see as far as the field, the wheat was lying flat.

"It's got the wheat, I guess," Manly said.

But Laura could not speak. The storm left a desolate, rain-drenched and hail-battered world. Leaves and branches were stripped off the young trees and the sun shone with a feeble, watery light over the wreck. The wreck, thought Laura, of a year's work, of hopes and plans of ease and pleasure.

She was muttering to herself. "What's that?" Manly asked.

"I was only saying," Laura answered, "that the poor man got his ice in the summer this time."

Though plans are wrecked, the pieces must be gathered up and put together again in some shape. Winter was coming. Coal must be bought. That would cost between $60 and $100. Seed grain would have to be bought for next spring's sowing. There were notes on the machinery coming due. There was also the $500 still due on the building of the house.

"Five hundred dollars' debt on the house!" Laura exclaimed. "Oh, I didn't know that!"

"I didn't think there was any need to bother you," Manly said.

But something must be done, and he would go to town and see if he could raise money with a mortgage on the homestead. That was proved up, thank goodness. He couldn't mortgage the tree claim. That belonged to Uncle Sam until Manly had raised those trees.

He found that he could renew all his machinery notes for a year by paying the interest. He could sell all the wild hay he had for $4 a ton delivered at the railroad in town. But he could not raise money with a mortgage on the homestead unless they were living on it. If they were living on the homestead he could mortgage it for $800. He had found a renter for the tree claim on shares; Manly would furnish the seed.

An addition would have to be built on the homestead claim shanty before they moved, but they could make do with one new room and a cellar underneath through using the original shanty for a storeroom.

So, Manly dug a hole in the ground for the cellar, and over it he built the one-room addition to the claim shanty. It was narrow (12 feet by 16) but it was all very snug and pleasant, and the stock were comfortable in their new barn. Manly built the frame of a barn, cut slough hay, and when it was dry, stacked it around the frame to make a hay barn. Sheltered from the north and west by the low hill and facing the south, it would be warm in winter.

Manly and Laura moved to the homestead the day after the barn was finished. It was the 25th of August. And the winter and the summer were the first year.

2. THE SECOND YEAR

As soon as breakfast was over on the day after the moving, Manly hitched Skip and Barnum to the mowing machine and began cutting hay. Laura left her morning's work undone and went with him to see the work started and then because the air was so fresh and the newcut hay so clean and sweet, she wandered over the field, picking the wild sunflowers and Indian paintbrush.

So the nice weather passed. The haying was finished. In November, the snow came and covered the ground, making good sleighing. Manly and Laura, well bundled up and covered with robes, went often for sleigh rides on sunny afternoons. Because Laura felt so much better outdoors, Manly made a sled and a breast-collar harness for old Shep.

On pleasant days Laura hitched Shep to the sled and let him pull her down the hill to the road. Then together they would climb the hill, Shep pulling the sled and Laura walking beside him to take another ride down until she was tired from the walking and the fun. Shep never got tired of it, and at times when the sled tipped against a drift and Laura rolled into the snow he seemed actually to laugh.

The sun was shining on the morning of December 5, but it looked stormy in the north. "Better play outdoors all you can today, for it may be too stormy tomorrow," Manly said.

So after breakfast Laura hitched Shep to the sled and took the day's first ride down the hill. But she stayed out only a little while. "I don't feel like playing," she told Manly when he came from the barn. "I would rather curl up by the stove." After the dinner work was done she sat idly by the stove in her rocking chair, which worried Manly.

Along in the afternoon Manly went to the barn and came back with the horses hitched to the sleigh. "I'm going for your Ma," he said. "Keep as quiet as you can until we come."

It was snowing hard now as Laura watched him drive down the road with the team trotting their best. She thought that the pace would have won them the prize at the Fourth of July races.

She walked the floor or sat by the stove until Manly came back with her Ma.

"My goodness!" Ma exclaimed, as she warmed herself by the fire. "You should not be up. I'll get you to bed right away."

Laura made no objections and only vaguely knew when Manly drove away again to fetch a friend of her Ma's from town. Mrs. Powers was a friendly, jolly Irishwoman. The first Laura knew of her being there was hearing her say, "Sure, she'll be all right, for it's young she is. Nineteen, you say? The very age of my Mary. But we'd better have the doctor out now, I'm thinking."

Laura was being borne away on a wave of pain. A gust of cold, fresh air brought her back and she saw a tall man drop his snowy overcoat by the door and come toward her in the lamplight. She vaguely felt a cloth touch her face and smelled a keen odor. Then she drifted away into a blessed darkness where there was no pain.

When Laura opened her eyes, the lamp was still shining brightly over the room. And in the bed by her side was a little warm bundle.

"See your little daughter, Laura. A beautiful baby, and she weighs eight pounds," Ma said.

Rose was such a good baby, so strong and healthy that Ma stayed only a few days. Then the three, Manly, Laura and Rose, were left by themselves in the little house atop the low hill with the sweep of the empty prairie all around it.

A hundred precious dollars had gone for doctor bills and medicine and help through the summer and winter so far; but after all, a Rose in December was much rarer than a rose in June, and must be paid for accordingly.

The rest of the winter passed quickly. Spring came, with the singing of meadowlarks and the sweetness of violets and new grass as the prairie turned a soft green. On all the farms seeding was begun. Laura put Rose in a clothes basket with her tiny sunbonnet on her head and set the basket nearby while she and Manly planted the garden.

The old dog Shep was gone. He never had become reconciled to Rose but always was jealous of her. One day he went away and never came back, and his fate was never known. But a friendly stray, a huge black dog soon named Nero, came to the house and was adopted in Shep's place. Nero seemed to think his special job was to watch over Rose, and wherever she was, there he would be curled around her or sitting up close against her.

The cookstove was moved into the storeroom, leaving the other room cooler for the hot weather, and in the summer kitchen Laura worked happily, with Rose and the big black dog playing on the floor.

There could be no horseback riding safely with a baby, but Laura did not miss it so much, because Manly fastened a dry-goods box in the front of the road-cart, leaving just enough room for Laura's feet at the end where the driver sat. When the work was done after dinner, Laura would hitch Barnum to the road-cart and with Rose in her pink sunbonnet sitting in the box would drive away wherever she cared to go. Sometimes they went to town; more often to see her Ma and the girls.

With housework, garden work, caring for and driving with Rose, the summer soon passed and it was haying time again. Laura and Manly both liked to stay out in the sunny hayfield, and leaving Rose asleep with the big dog watching over her, Laura sometimes drove Skip and

Barnum on the mowing machine while Manly raked hay with Fly and Trixy.

The yield on the grain was not nearly so much as it should have been. The season had been too dry. And the price of wheat was only 50 cents a bushel. Still there was enough money to pay all the interest and some of the smaller notes, those for the mowing machine and horse rake and for the sulky plow, and the first payment was made on the harvester. There were still the wagon note and the $500 due on the house and the $800 mortgage on the homestead. Seed must be kept for the next sowing, taxes must be paid, the coal must be bought and they must live until after the next harvest.

There would also be the hay again, and this year there were two steers to sell. They were nice large two-year-olds, and they would sell for $12 each; $24 would help buy groceries.

They hadn't done so badly, considering the season.

The 25th of August had come again, and this winter and summer were the second year.

3. THE THIRD YEAR

THOUGH THE WEATHER was cold that third winter there were no bad blizzards and the winter was slipping by very pleasantly. Laura's Cousin Peter had come up from the southern part of the territory, and was working for the Whiteheads, neighbors who lived several miles to the north. He often came to see them on Sunday.

To surprise Manly on his birthday Laura asked Peter and the Whiteheads to dinner, cooking and baking in the summer kitchen. It was a pleasant day and warm for winter and the dinner was a great success.

But in spite of the warm day Laura caught a severe cold and had a touch of fever so that she must stay in bed. Ma came over to see how she was and took Rose home with her for a few days. Instead of getting better, the cold got worse and settled in Laura's throat. The doctor when he came said it was not a cold at all but a bad case of diphtheria.

Well, at least Rose was out of it and safe with Ma. But there were several anxious days, while Manly cared for Laura, until the doctor reported that Rose had escaped the disease.

But then Manly came down with it, and the doctor ordered him to bed with strict orders to stay there. He said he would send someone out from town to help them. So both in the same room, with the crudest sort of care, Manly and Laura spent the miserable, feverish days. Laura's attack had been dangerous, while Manly's was light.

At last they were both up and around again, but the doctor had given his last warning against overexertion. Laura and Manly, well wrapped, spent a day in the summer kitchen while the sickroom was fumigated. Then after a few days longer, Rose was brought home. She had learned to walk while she had been away and she seemed to have grown much older. But it was pleasant to have her taking her little running steps around the room, and most of all, it was good to be well again.

Laura thought the trouble was all over now. But that was not to be for many a day.

Manly—disregarding the doctor's warning—had worked too hard, and one cold morning he nearly fell as he got out of bed, because he could not use his legs properly. They were numb to his hips and it was only after much rubbing that he could get about with Laura's help. Together they did the chores; after breakfast, Laura helped him hitch up the wagon and he went to town to see the doctor.

"A slight stroke of paralysis," the doctor said, "from overexertion too soon after the diphtheria."

From that day on there was a struggle to keep Manly's legs so that he could use them. Some days they were better and again they were worse, but gradually they improved until he could go about his usual business if he was careful.

In the meantime spring had come. Sickness with its doctor bills had been expensive. There was no money to live on until another harvest. The renter on the tree claim was moving away and Manly in his condition could not work both pieces of land. The tree claim was not proved up and the young trees must be cultivated to hold it.

Something must be done. And in this emergency a buyer for the homestead came along. He would assume the $800 mortgage and give Manly $200. And so the homestead was sold and Manly and Laura moved back to the tree claim one early spring day.

The house was in bad order, but a little paint, a few fly screens and a good cleaning made it fresh and sweet again. Laura felt that she was back home, and it was easier for Manly to walk on the level ground to the barn than it had been for him to climb up and down the hill on the homestead.

He was gradually overcoming the effect of the stroke but still would fall down if he happened to stub his toe. He could not step over a piece of board in his way but must go around it. His fingers were clumsy so he could neither hitch up nor unhitch his team, but he could drive them once they were ready to go.

So Laura hitched up the horses and helped him get started and then was on hand to help him unhitch when he drove them back.

The rains came as needed and the wheat and oats grew well. If it would only keep on raining often—and not hail.

There were three little calves in the barn lot and two young colts running all over the place, plus a third colt they had bought when the school board had paid Laura for the teaching she had done before her marriage. He was now a three-year-old and grown out nicely. The little flock of hens were laying well. Oh, things weren't so bad after all.

It was a busy summer for Laura, what with the housework, caring for Rose and helping Manly whenever he needed her. But she didn't mind doing it all, for slowly Manly's paralysis was wearing off. He was spending a great deal of time working among the young trees. It had been too dry for them to grow well the summer before and they were not starting as they should this spring.

Some of them had died. The dead ones Manly replaced, setting the new ones carefully. He pruned them all, dug around their roots, and then plowed all the ground between.

And the wheat and oats grew rank and green.

"We'll be all right this year," Manly said. "One good crop will straighten us out and there was never a better prospect."

Cousin Peter came one Sunday to tell Manly and Laura that Mr. Whitehead wanted to sell his sheep, 100 purebred Shropshires.

A Presidential election was coming and it looked as though the Democrats were due to win again. If they did, Mr. Whitehead, being a good Republican, was sure the country would be ruined. Peter was sure the sheep could be bought at a bargain. He would buy them himself if only he had a place to keep them.

"What would you have to pay?" Manly asked.

Peter said he could buy them for $2 apiece since Mr. Whitehead was feeling particularly uneasy about the election. "And the sale of the wool next spring ought nearly to pay for them," he added. Peter had $100 due him in wages. That would be half of the money needed.

"But the other $100?" Laura asked doubtfully.

Manly reminded her of the colt they had bought with her school money, and said he believed he could sell it now for $100. She could buy half the sheep if she wanted to gamble on them. And so it was decided. A few days after the colt was sold, Peter came driving the sheep into the yard that had been built for them. There were 100 good ewes and six old ones that had been thrown in for nothing.

The rains came frequently. It even seemed as though the winds did not blow as hard as usual, and the wheat and oats grew splendidly.

The days hurried along toward harvest. Just a little while longer now and all would be well with the crop. Fearful of hail, Manly and Laura watched the clouds. If only it would not hail.

As the days passed bringing no hailstorm, Laura found herself thinking: everything will even up in the end. When she caught herself at it, she would laugh. If only they could harvest and sell this crop, it would mean so much. Just to be free of debt and have the interest money to use for themselves would make everything so much easier.

At last the wheat was in the milk and again Manly estimated that the yield would be 40 bushels to the acre. Then one morning the wind blew strong from the south and it was a warm wind. Before noon the wind was hot and blowing harder. And for three days the hot wind blew.

When it died down at last the wheat was dried and yellow, absolutely shriveled. It was not worth harvesting as wheat but Manly hitched Skip and Barnum to the mowing machine and mowed it and the oats, to be stacked and fed without threshing to the stock.

As soon as this was done, haying was begun, for they must cut the hay on the school section ahead of anyone else. Laura and Rose went to the hayfield again. Laura drove the mower while Manly raked the hay cut the afternoon before. And a neighbor boy was hired to herd the sheep while Peter helped Manly stack the hay. They stacked great ricks of hay all around the sheep barn and on three sides of the sheep yard, leaving the yard open on the south side only.

And the 25th of August came and passed and the third year of farming was ended.

4. A YEAR OF GRACE

MANLY SAID HE WOULD have to get another team, for he wanted to break the 60 acres of sod and have the whole 160 acres ready to seed in the spring. "But the three years are up. Do you call this farming a success?" Laura objected.

"Well, I don't know," Manly answered. "It is not so bad. Of course, the crops have been mostly failures, but we have four cows now and some calves. We have the four horses and the colts and machinery and there are the sheep. . . . If we could only get one crop. Just one good crop, and we'd be all right. Let's try it one more year. Next year may be a good crop year and we are all fixed for farming now, with no money to start anything else."

It sounded reasonable, as Manly put it. There didn't seem to be anything else they could do, but as for being all fixed—the $500 still due on the house worried Laura. Nothing had been paid on it. The binder was not yet paid for and interest payments were hard to make. But still Manly might be right. This might be when their luck turned, and one good year would even things up.

In December Laura again felt the familiar sickness. The house seemed close and hot and she was miserable. But the others must be kept warm and fed.

On a day when she was particularly blue, the neighbor to the west, a bachelor living alone, stopped as he was driving by and brought a partly filled grain sack to the house. When Laura opened the door, Mr. Sheldon stepped inside, and taking the sack by the bottom, poured its contents out on the floor. It was a set of the Waverley Novels.

"Thought they might amuse you," he said. "Don't be in a hurry! Take your time reading them!" And as Laura exclaimed in delight, Mr. Sheldon opened the door and was gone.

And now the four walls of the close, overheated house opened wide, and Laura wandered with brave knights and ladies fair beside the lakes and streams of Scotland or in castles and towers, in noble halls or lady's bower, all through the enchanting pages of Sir Walter Scott's novels.

She forgot to feel ill at the sight or smell of food, in her hurry to be done with the cooking and follow her thoughts back into the book. When the books were all read and Laura came back to reality, she found herself feeling much better.

It was a long way from the scenes of Scott's glamorous old tales to the little house on the bleak, wintry prairie, but Laura brought back from them some of their magic and music and the rest of the winter passed quite comfortably.

Spring came early and warm. By the first of April a good deal of seeding had been done and men were busy in all the fields. The morning of April 2 was sunny and warm and still. Peter took the sheep out to graze on the school section as usual, while Manly went to the field. It was still difficult for him to hitch up the team, and Laura helped him get started. Then she went about her morning's work.

Soon a wind started blowing from the northwest, gently at first but increasing in strength until at nine o'clock the dust was blowing in the field so thickly that Manly could not see to follow the seeder marks. So he came from the field and Laura helped him unhitch and get the team in the barn.

In the house they could only listen to the rising wind and wonder why Peter didn't bring the sheep in.

"He couldn't have taken them far," Manly said.

Dust from the fields was blowing clouds so dense that they could see only a little way from the windows, and in a few minutes, Manly went to find Peter and the sheep.

He met Peter about a quarter-mile from the barn. Peter was on foot, leading his pony and carrying three lambs in his arms. He and the dog were working the sheep toward their yard. The sheep could hardly go against the wind but they had to face it to get home.

They had not been sheared and their fleeces were long and heavy. If a sheep turned ever so little sideways, the wind would catch under the wool, lift the sheep from its feet and roll it over and over, sometimes five or six times before it could stop. It took them both over an hour to get all the sheep into the yard.

After that they all sat in the house and let the wind blow. Their ears were filled with the roar of it. Their eyes and throats smarted from the dust that was settling over the room even though the doors and windows were tightly closed.

The wind reached its peak about two o'clock, then slackened gradually. It died away as the sun went down, and was still.

Rose lay asleep with her tired, dusty little face streaked with perspiration. Laura was prostrated with exhaustion, and Manly and Peter walked like old men as they went out to the barn to see that the stock was all right for the night.

There was nothing to do but to reseed the fields, for the seed was blown away or buried in the drifts of soil around the edges of the plowed land. So Manly bought more seed wheat and oats in town, and at last the seeding was finished.

As spring turned the corner into summer, the rains stopped and the grain began to suffer for lack of moisture. Every morning Manly looked anxiously for signs of rain, and seeing none, went on about his work.

And then the hot winds came. Every day the wind blew strongly from the south. It felt on Laura's cheek like the hot air from the oven when she opened the oven door on baking day. For a week, the hot winds blew, and when they stopped, the young wheat and oats were dried brown and dead. The trees on the ten acres were nearly all killed too. Manly decided there was no hope of replanting to have the trees growing to fulfill the law for the claim.

What was it she had read the other day? "The wheel goes round and round and the fly on the top'll be the fly on the bottom after a while." Well, she didn't care what became of the top fly, but she did wish the bottom one could crawl up a little way. She was tired of waiting for the wheel to turn. And the farmers were the ones at the bottom, she didn't care what Manly said.

If the weather wasn't right they had nothing, but whether they had anything or not they must find it somehow to pay interest and taxes and a profit to the businessmen in town on everything they bought, and they must buy to live.

She hated the farm and the stock and the smelly lambs, the cooking of food and the dirty dishes. Oh, she hated it all, and especially the debts that must be paid whether she could work or not. But she'd be darned if she'd go down and stay down or howl about it.

It was time to prove up and Manly could not. There was only one way to save the land. He could file on it as a pre-emption.* If he did that he must prove up in six months and pay the United States $1.25 an acre. The $200 cash at the end of six months would be hard to find, but there was no other way.

So Manly pre-empted the land. There was one advantage: he did not have to work among the trees anymore. Here and there one had survived and Manly mulched those with manure and straw from the barn. The cottonwood tree before Laura's pantry window, being north of the house, had been protected from the full force of the hot winds and from the sun. It was growing in spite of the drought. Laura loved its green branches that waved just the other side of the glass as she prepared food on the shelf before the window and washed the dishes there.

The weather continued hot and dry, and August 5 was especially warm. In the afternoon Manly sent Peter to bring Laura's Ma, and at four o'clock he sent Peter again to town, this time for the doctor. But their son was born before the doctor could get there.

Laura was proud of the baby, but strangely she wanted Rose more than anything. Rose had been kept away from her mother for the sake of quiet, and a hired girl was taking indifferent care of her.

Then, one day, Laura heard the hired girl refuse Rose a piece of

---

*The government allowed settlers on land in the public domain to purchase it at a fixed price.

bread and butter, speaking crossly to her, and that Laura could not bear. Calling from her bed, Laura settled the question in Rose's favor.

Laura felt she must hurry and get her strength back. Rose shouldn't be meanly treated by any hired girl; and besides, there were the wages of $5 a week. They must be stopped as soon as possible.

Laura was doing her own work again one day three weeks later when the baby was taken with spasms, and he died so quickly that the doctor was too late.

To Laura, the days that followed were mercifully blurred. Her feelings were numbed and she wanted only to rest—to rest and not to think.

But the work must go on.

Manly and Peter were putting up hay on some land two miles away a week later. Laura started the fire for supper in the kitchen stove. The summer fuel was old, tough, long, slough hay, and Manly had brought an armful into the kitchen and put it down near the stove.

After lighting the fire and putting the teakettle on, Laura went back into the other part of the house, shutting the kitchen door.

When she opened it again, a few minutes later, the whole kitchen was ablaze: the ceiling, the hay, and the floor underneath and wall behind. As usual, a strong wind was blowing from the south, and by the time the neighbors arrived to help, the house was in flames.

Laura had thrown one bucket of water on the fire, and then, knowing she was not strong enough to work the pump for more water, taking the little deed-box from the bedroom and Rose by the hand, she ran out and dropped on the ground in the drive before the house. Burying her face on her knees, she screamed and sobbed, saying over and over, "Oh, what will Manly say to me?" And there Manly found her and Rose, just as the house roof was falling in.

Mr. Sheldon had gone in through the pantry window and thrown all the dishes out through it toward the trunk of the little cottonwood tree, so the silver wedding knives and forks and spoons rolled up in their wrappers had survived. Nothing else had been saved from the fire except a few work clothes, three sauce dishes from the first Christmas dishes, and the oval glass bread plate around the margin of which were the words, "Give us this day our daily bread." And the young cottonwood stood by the open cellar hole, scorched and blackened and dead.

Mr. Sheldon needed a housekeeper and gave Laura and Manly houseroom in return for board for himself and his brother. Now Laura was so busy she had no time for worry through the rest of the haying and while Manly and Peter built a long shanty, three rooms in a row, near the ruins of their house. It was built of only one thickness of boards and tar-papered on the outside, but it was built tightly, and being new, it was very snug and quite warm.

The September nights were growing cool when the new house was ready and moved into. The 25th of August had passed unnoticed, and the year of grace was ended.

Was farming a success? "Well, it all depends on how you look at it," Manly said when Laura asked him.

They had had a lot of bad luck, but anyone was liable to have bad luck even if he wasn't a farmer. There had been so many dry seasons now that surely next year would be a good crop year.

They had a lot of stock to sell, and by building the new house so cheaply, they had money left to help pay for proving up on the land.

"Everything will be all right, for it all evens up in time. You'll see," Manly said, as he started for the barn.

As Laura watched him go, she thought, yes, everything is evened up in time. The rich have their ice in the summer, but the poor get theirs in the winter, and ours is coming soon.

Winter was coming on, and in sight of the ruins of their comfortable little house they were making a fresh start with nothing. Their possessions would no more than balance their debts, if that.

It would be a fight to win out in this business of farming, but strangely she felt her spirit rising for the struggle.

The incurable optimism of the farmer who throws his seed on the ground every spring, betting it and his time against the elements, seemed inextricably to blend with the creed of her pioneer forefathers that "it is better farther on"—only instead of farther on in space, it was further on in time, over the horizon of the years ahead instead of over the horizon to the west.

She was still the pioneer girl and she could understand Manly's love of the land through its appeal to herself.

"Oh, well," Laura sighed, summing up her idea of the situation in a saying of her Ma's. "We'll always be farmers, for what is bred in the bone *will* come out in the flesh."

And then Laura smiled, for Manly was coming from the barn and he was singing:

You talk of the mines of Australia,
They've wealth in red gold, without doubt;
But, ah! there is gold in the farm, boys—
If only you'll shovel it out.

FEVER!

CONDENSED FROM THE BOOK BY

BY JOHN G. FULLER

ILLUSTRATED BY DAVID BLOSSOM

The threat of plague has always been a terrifying one, but in modern times the threat has seemed distant, even unreal. Yet in the hinterlands of South America and Africa, and in certain other remote regions, lurk lethal viruses, each capable of triggering a worldwide calamity.

In the winter of 1969, an unknown disease, later named Lassa fever, burst from hiding in Nigeria. It proved to be untreatable and a vicious killer. Unless a handful of medical researchers could track it to its source, the disease might easily travel undetected aboard jet airliners to New York, London, Paris, Moscow, to cities and countries all over the globe in an incredibly short space of time.

John G. Fuller in *Fever!* tells one of the most dramatic and terrifying detective stories in the field of modern science.

1. DEADLY PUZZLE

A RAP ON THE DOOR shortly after 3 a.m. brought Laura Wine awake. She was needed at the hospital immediately. After dressing, she moved quickly along the path toward the lights of the Lassa Mission Hospital, where she was head of obstetrics. As she walked, she realized that a recent pain in her back was much worse.

Lassa, a village of thatched-roof mud huts with some 1000 inhabitants, is typical of the remote towns in northeast Nigeria. Lying at the base of the mountains that separate Nigeria from the Cameroons, it is practically inaccessible for half the year when the rains come. Here, in the 1920s, the Church of the Brethren had built a mission to serve the Hausa, Fulani, Margi, Higi and other tribes.

Soon after dawn, a baby was born to a village woman, and Laura Wine returned to her house to rest. At 65 she had retired as a nurse near Chicago, and had spent the four years since in the Nigerian bush. Ordinarily she moved with a sprightliness which belied her age, but now the nagging pain in her back was slowing her.

To the surprise of her friends, she did not attend church that morning, Sunday, January 19, 1969. But, afterward, John and Esther Hamer—he was the only doctor at the mission station—were relieved to see her walking toward their house for her usual Sunday meal with them. Halfway through dinner, word came that a Margi tribeswoman had just delivered a baby alongside a dusty road leading to Lassa. Laura rose from the table, but the pain in her back forced her down into her chair again. Esther Hamer insisted on taking the assignment, and urged her friend to go home. Uncharacteristically, Laura agreed.

By that evening, Laura felt somewhat better and nearly everyone attributed the trouble to a touch of arthritis. Next morning, she went

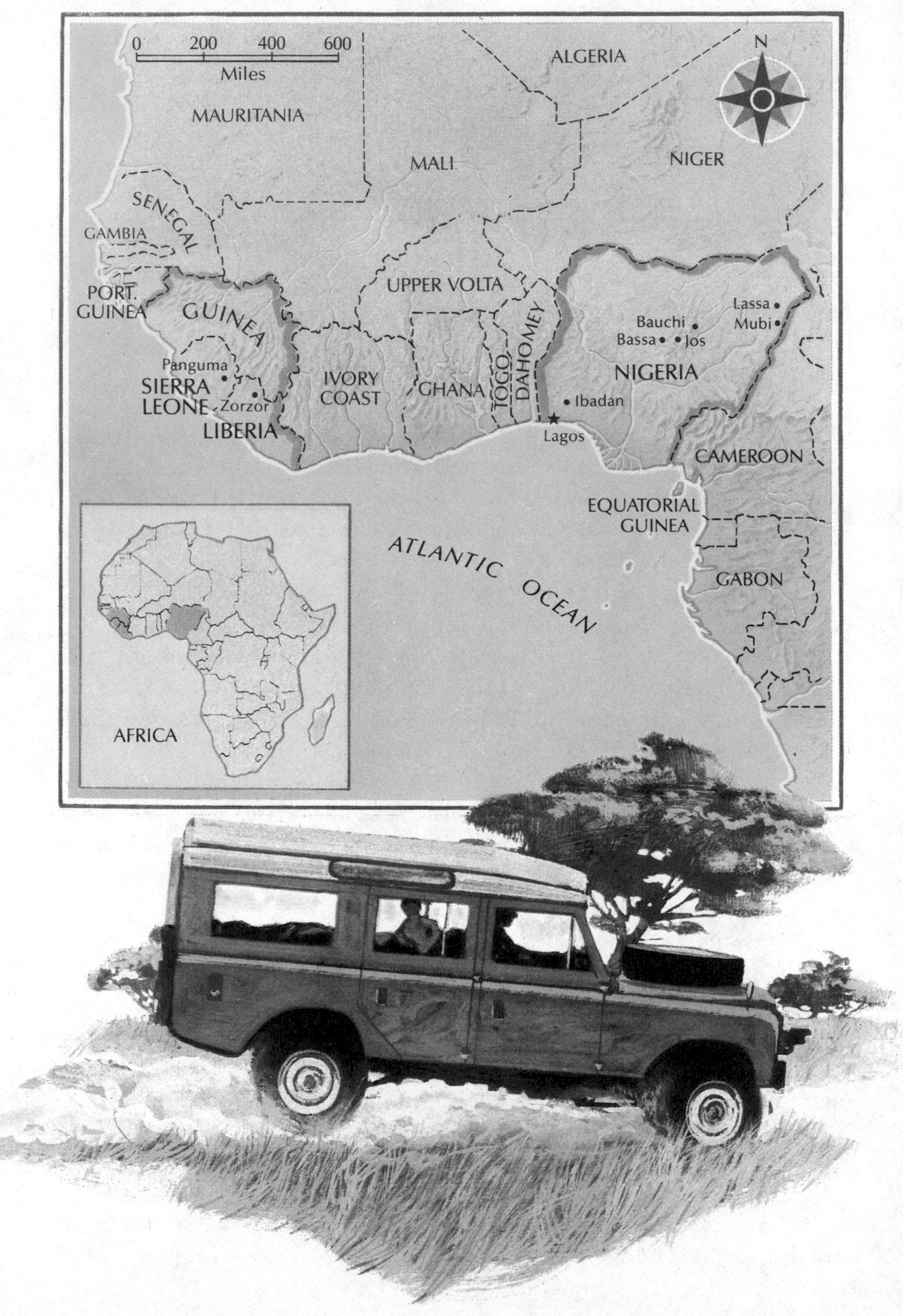
0 200 400 600
Miles
N
ALGERIA
MAURITANIA
MALI
NIGER
SENEGAL
GAMBIA
PORT. GUINEA
GUINEA
UPPER VOLTA
DAHOMEY
TOGO
Lassa
Mubi
Bauchi
Bassa
Jos
NIGERIA
Panguma
SIERRA LEONE
Zorzor
LIBERIA
IVORY COAST
GHANA
Ibadan
Lagos
CAMEROON
EQUATORIAL GUINEA
ATLANTIC OCEAN
GABON
AFRICA

to the shortwave radio in the hospital office and took her turn monitoring and reporting the bulletins from the mission stations of the Church of the Brethren scattered throughout northeast Nigeria.

Her voice was noticeably weaker as she annunciated the usual: "Brethren Lassa, calling Brethren Jos. Over to Jos . . ." Later, she mentioned to Esther Hamer that she had a sore throat. Dr. Hamer took a look, but saw nothing abnormal. Tuesday morning, Dr. Hamer checked her again. Far back in her throat and on the inside of her cheeks were groups of yellowish ulcers with halos around them. Her temperature was just over 100 degrees. Dr. Hamer prescribed procaine penicillin and chloroquine, an anti-malarial drug.

By Wednesday, January 22, there was no improvement, and Hamer decided to get at the root of the illness. He took a blood smear, plus urine and stool specimens. A high white blood count would be evidence of bacterial infection. Instead, the count was low, a condition known as leukopenia, which occurs in many diseases. The urine test was likewise inconclusive. The low volume, however, was disturbing, and Dr. Hamer urged Laura to drink as much fluid as she could.

That evening, her temperature nudged up over 101 degrees, and a small, purple-blue mark, which indicated bleeding under the skin, appeared on her left arm. John Hamer was baffled.

On Friday morning, he got up before dawn and pored through a back file of medical journals. As the sun came up, he began to think more and more about the possibility of an unusually stubborn virus. By noon, Laura's speech was extremely difficult to understand. There seemed to be a kidney shutdown; her urine output had dwindled to almost zero. She could barely swallow; her mouth was dry and caked.

Dr. Hamer decided to move her to a better-equipped hospital at Jos. But Jos was 400 miles away over terrible roads, and so he arranged to have her flown out by small plane from Mubi, 50 miles distant.

They set off early Saturday morning in the mission Land Rover. Dr. Hamer would drive, while Esther attended Laura in the back of the car. Laura was now having extreme difficulty in breathing. As they moved her to the Land Rover, she convulsed, and her skin suddenly turned blue. Not enough oxygen was getting to the blood. Quickly Dr. Hamer brought an oxygen mask to her face, and she recovered. As they lifted her into the car, she went into convulsions again, and once more the oxygen mask was put to her face. There now appeared to be signs of cardiac failure.

John Hamer drove as fast as he dared, trying to dodge the enormous potholes. But, at any speed, it was impossible to keep the Land Rover from pitching and yawing over the rough road. In the rear, Esther and her patient tossed back and forth.

The Land Rover pulled into the Mubi airstrip at 11, and soon Laura was aloft. She was conscious, but unable to speak. There was practically no oxygen left in the bottle, and little could be done in the crowded cockpit if she convulsed again.

As the plane bearing Laura approached Jos, a bed for her in the Bingham Memorial Hospital was being prepared by Dr. Jeanette Troup, then the only full-time hospital doctor. Dr. Jeanette, as she was called, met the plane and brought Laura to the hospital, administering oxygen all the way. Once they were there, lab tests were begun immediately. The signs now suggested massive internal hemorrhaging.

Esther Hamer was beside her the next morning when Laura stirred restively in her bed. Sunday services had begun, and the hymn "A Mighty Fortress Is Our God" sounded across the courtyard.

A wan smile appeared on Laura's face. Without opening her eyes, she said to Esther: "Oh, I'm *so* glad the hymns are in English today!" Then, realizing that in distant Lassa the services were always in Hausa or Margi, she asked, "But where am I?"

She convulsed again that afternoon. There was no more urine output. She went into shock, and by 9:30 p.m. she was dead. On Monday afternoon, she was buried in a remote mission compound.

The effect of her death was ultimately to be far different from that of countless others who have died serving in foreign lands. Laura Wine's death would soon reach from Africa across the Atlantic to the United States in a series of mysterious and frightening incidents.

CHARLOTTE SHAW, a nurse in her 40s, worked at the Bingham Memorial Hospital in Jos. The morning of Laura Wine's arrival, she had been in her flower garden, cutting a bouquet of roses to take to the hospital with her that evening. Reaching high for a particularly striking blossom, she punctured her finger on a thorn. She went back to her house, washed the wound off and dabbed it with antiseptic. It soon clotted, and she promptly forgot about it.

That night, though hardly able to speak, Laura Wine had complained about discomfort in her throat, and Charlotte went to a nearby cabinet for a gauze swab. She wrapped it around her finger and gently cleansed the ulcerated throat. As the fluid soaked through the gauze, she became aware of a slight stinging sensation in her forefinger, and suddenly remembered the rose prick. She disposed of the gauze, flooded her finger with water and soap, dabbed it with more antiseptic and put a bandage on it.

Eight days after Laura Wine died, Charlotte began to notice severe back and leg pains. When she began to feel chills, she decided that she was coming down with malaria, common on the Jos plateau. Reluctant to bother anyone with her problem, she went to the hospital pharmacy and took three anti-malarial tablets. She was certain that by the next morning she would get back to her usual routine.

But in the morning there was no improvement. Her temperature was 102 degrees. Another nurse, stopping by on the way to the hospital, persuaded Charlotte to enter the hospital at once as a patient.

Penny Pinneo, the head nurse, assisted Dr. Jeanette as she gave the patient a thorough examination and took the necessary specimens for laboratory tests. Charlotte's fever had now risen to 103, and one thought was on everyone's mind. But when Charlotte told them about the small wound on her finger and the stinging sensation she had felt when swabbing Laura Wine's throat, they reassured her that there was nothing to worry about.

It is always easy to jump to conclusions in diagnoses, especially when gun-shy from a particularly dramatic and mysterious case. On the other hand, Charlotte Shaw showed no signs of an ulcerated throat, and there was no difficulty in breathing, no subsurface hemorrhaging. So, without being unduly alarmed, Penny Pinneo concentrated on giving Charlotte the best possible attention, and left the rest to the Lord. But Charlotte did not improve. Seven days after she had become ill, her temperature had risen to 104.8 degrees, and indications of the strange ulcers from which Laura Wine had suffered, now appeared in her throat.

By the evening of February 12, Charlotte's face and neck were swollen, and she experienced difficulty in breathing. By midnight, the blue discoloration of the skin set in. At 3:45 a.m. on February 13, she died. It was the 11th day of her illness—whatever it had been.

One hope for enlightenment would come from sending tissue specimens and blood samples of the two victims to New York for analysis. Therefore, an autopsy had to be done quickly. Shortly after midnight the next day, Penny Pinneo and Dr. Jeanette put on their gowns and gloves, and prepared for the unwelcome job. Neither saw any need to wear a gauze mask.

The major incision was made by Dr. Jeanette, as Penny assisted.

One by one, the organs of the chest and abdominal cavity were removed and biopsies taken. The body cavity was abnormally filled with amber fluid. Penny sponged this out, squeezing it into a bowl. There had obviously been massive internal hemorrhaging. There was lung, liver and kidney damage. Yet there was no specific clue to the killer.

A week later, on the eve of her 52nd birthday, Penny Pinneo began to run a fever.

The news that a third mission nurse was laid low with strange and undiagnosable symptoms caused major concern. Dr. Jeanette held several conferences with two newly arrived doctors. They agreed to set Wednesday, February 26, as a deadline: If the fever did not abate by that day, they would make immediate arrangements to send Penny to New York.

On the day of the deadline, Dr. Jeanette wrote in her medical report: "It would seem as if the illness is following the same pattern as that of the last patient whom she cared for."

The logistics of getting a patient to New York were imposing. A Sudan Interior Mission plane would have to fly from the Jos plateau to Lagos, nearly 450 miles away. A plywood stretcher would have to be fitted into the plane in place of the front seat. Customs and immigration clearances would have to be arranged in Lagos. Permission would have to be obtained from Pan American World Airways in New York for transporting a stretcher case, necessitating the purchase and removal of four first-class seats and the installation of special curtains to screen off the patient. The accompanying tissue and blood specimens from Laura Wine and Charlotte Shaw would have to be iced and put in containers so that whatever virus might be lurking in them would withstand both the Nigeria and transocean flights.

On the 27th, Penny Pinneo was flown to Lagos on the Nigerian coast. There she had to wait four days for the flight to New York. She spent them in the sweltering heat of the Lagos Pest House, a crumbling structure set aside for contagious diseases, her sheets wet with sweat, her dehydration increasing.

Antibiotics were continued, but if the villain was a virus, it would remain untouched. Unfortunately, what works against bacteria does not work against viral infections.

At last, on March 3, Penny was put aboard a jet for the 13-hour flight to New York. Her fever was high; she appeared acutely ill, exhibiting severe dehydration. It was her 12th day of sickness. If death was to come, it would come soon.

Meeting the plane was Rose Pinneo, Penny's sister, herself a nurse, together with a mission official and Dr. John Frame, a specialist in tropical diseases from the Columbia-Presbyterian Medical Center. He had been alerted by Dr. Jeanette.

Before Penny could be put into a wheelchair to be carried off the plane, John Frame wanted to take a blood specimen. Immediately he drew ten cc's of blood from her arm. Then he picked up the large vacuum jug full of the iced tissue and blood specimens from all three victims and headed for his car. Suddenly, he changed his mind. He headed instead for the washroom in the terminal, where he scrubbed hard. He wouldn't be worth much if he were unable to follow this enigma to the end.

2. THE SEARCH BEGINS

IN 17 YEARS OF PRACTICE with missionaries, Dr. Frame, a lean, graying man, had on several occasions been mystified by reports of unidentified fevers, many of them fatal, among his adult missionary patients. In times past, these localized "African fevers" were not considered much of a threat to other areas. But in the jet age, such diseases could be transported around the world in a matter of hours.

In 1965, Frame expressed this fear to Dr. Wilbur Downs, head of the Yale University Arbovirus Laboratory Unit in New Haven, Conn. (Arboviruses are viruses transmitted by insects.) Downs shared his concern, and Frame agreed to begin collecting blood specimens from returning missionaries who had reported unusual fevers in their past. Yale would analyze and catalogue them and build up a file that might reveal fresh information on both known and unknown viruses.

In 1968, Frame decided to step up his program and happened to ask Dr. Jeanette Troup, who was going back to Jos at the time, to draw blood from unusual fever patients there. With the outbreak of fever at Jos itself, Dr. Jeanette had alerted Dr. Frame and he, in turn, had telephoned the Yale Arbovirus Lab. The sobering question: Had they unexpectedly come upon a killer virus?

Soon after Penny Pinneo arrived, Dr. Downs came to Frame's office in New York and collected the other jug of blood and specimens. He returned to New Haven late that afternoon, and within minutes was on the seventh floor of the high-rise building of the Yale Public Health and Epidemiology Department. Most of his staff was waiting for him.

He prefaced his remarks by laying down strict rules. First, everyone working on the project in any way was to wear mask, gown and gloves, just as the staff was doing at Columbia-Presbyterian, where Penny had been hospitalized. Second, no one in the organization who had small children at home would be permitted close to the research. He said it very simply: "You people will not *touch* the stuff!"

The only individuals allowed to handle the specimens would be Spanish-born Dr. Jordi Casals, a highly respected Rockefeller Foundation pathologist and microbiologist; Dr. Sonja Buckley, originally from Zürich, whose research in tissue cultures had made her internationally famous; and himself. The work would begin right away.

The isolation of a virus is a complex task. It involves hundreds of laboratory animals, an exasperating length of time for signs that disease is incubating, careful preparation of tissue cultures, painstaking statistical correlation of data and electron-microscope observations.

Nothing that the Yale lab could do would be of immediate help to Penny Pinneo. These men and women were trying to identify the enemy. Only then could they counteract it by the development of a vaccine or plasma containing antibodies. Further, if the carrier of the virus could be found, measures could be developed to wipe it out. But all this might take months or years.

The infectious material brought to New Haven was for the most part blood serum and fluid from the chest cavity. There was some doubt that the suspected virus had survived its long trip, but the Yale scientists could only go forward on the basis that it had.

Sonja Buckley immediately began preparing a series of tissue cultures in large Roux bottles, shaped something like hip flasks. Inside each was a red nutrient fluid carpeted with living animal cells which she would try to kill in various controlled ways with the infected serum. Buckley began pouring off the cells into smaller two-ounce bottles and test tubes filled with a nutrient jelly. When she had finished, nearly 200 cultures sat in rows of tubes and bottles, like a regiment of soldiers on review. The cells would be allowed to grow in their new environment for several days.

The task facing Downs and Casals was different. They were going to inject the blood and fluid specimens directly into the brains of a colony of mice. No racehorses had been bred with more care. The mice all had to be identical, or the tests would vary. And obviously they had to be free of other diseases.

The animals were individually housed in metal containers which resembled large breadboxes. To reduce the danger of spreading infection should a mouse kick up disease-laden dust, each box had its own ventilating system which drew the air out into an incinerator.

Realizing that one slip of a hypodermic needle could be fatal to themselves, Downs and Casals put their first batch of mice under deep ether anesthesia so they couldn't wriggle unpredictably. Then Downs took a syringe with 2/100 milliliters of the suspect, straw-colored serum, picked up a mouse, and plunged the needle into its cranium. Casals did the same.

When they finished their first injections, Downs said, "It might be a good idea, Jordi, not to tell your wife about this project."

Jordi Casals nodded.

At Columbia-Presbyterian Hospital, Penny Pinneo's temperature soared to 107 degrees. That high a fever in an adult is usually the threshold of death; few can survive such an inner furnace. The doctors and nurses packed her in ice and placed her in an oxygen tent. They gave her aspirin; they continued intravenous fluids. There was not much else that could be done.

Slowly, her temperature fell, but in the wake of fever came pneumonia, bringing with it a flooding of the lungs and a racking cough. This was followed by inflammation of the brain. An incessant ringing in her ears developed, along with deafness and dizziness. There was internal bleeding. Her heart, kidneys and other organs were affected. But she was still alive, and she had now survived longer than either of her stricken colleagues.

At Yale, on March 10, Sonja Buckley went to her lab to begin the assault on the tissue cultures. She sucked out the old nutrient fluid from each bottle, using a glass pipette as she would a soda straw. The pipettes were plugged with cotton to prevent the fluid from coming up into her mouth, but at this point there was nothing to worry about because there was no serum containing viruses in the bottles.

Then she added a new solution which would maintain the tissue cultures in good health, but would not cause them to grow. Finally, the critical step. Sucking up the infected blood serum into a pipette, she dropped 1/10 of one milliliter into each of a series of bottles. For a matching control group of bottles, she added only a nutrient broth without the diseased serum. Then Sonja Buckley put all the bottles aside to incubate.

Meanwhile, Downs and Casals were looking for results. But their mice still appeared normal and healthy. If they stayed that way, it would be very doubtful that the blood samples contained a deadly virus. However, it was too soon to tell; some laboratory mice survived virus injections for nine or ten days. But by Tuesday morning Jordi Casals was pessimistic about the outlook.

Disgruntled, he came into Sonja Buckley's lab and asked how she was doing. She replied that she had nothing to report. Apparently it was still too soon.

That afternoon, as Buckley was working with her cultures, Dr. Max Theiler, a Nobel laureate who had been given the award in 1951 for his work in developing the yellow-fever vaccine, dropped by for an informal visit. He, too, asked how the research was going, and Sonja took a look at the bottles.

She could hardly believe what she saw. Every single carpet of cells in the infected group was covered with plaques—white spots or holes that looked as if the carpet were covered with chicken pox. A virus was eating away with a vengeance.

Yet it was strange that her tissue cultures should have responded before the mice, which had been inoculated three days earlier. Possibly her bottles had been contaminated by some other virus. She decided to make a second try at the whole process.

By the following Tuesday, March 18, she had her answer. Every single infected bottle again showed the telltale "moth holes." She knew then for sure that she was working with an "agent," an unknown virus of great potency.

Wil Downs and Jordi Casals were elated at her results, but puzzled by the continued health of their mice. Then a rather obvious thought occurred to them. They had used baby mice, thinking they might be more susceptible to disease. But there are strange variations in the nature of viruses. What if they tried tougher, adult mice? They began work with an adult colony.

The following day, Jordi Casals went to his cages, not really expecting anything. He picked up an adult mouse by the tail. He was startled to feel a faint tremor coming from the mouse into his hand. Going from box to box, he found that practically all the mice infected with the African serum showed the same tremors. But his control group showed none at all.

A few days later, practically all of the infected mice were dead.

Jordi Casals now began a series of new tests. Was this "new" virus only a duplicate of others already identified in South America and

Africa? How powerful was it? What was its size? Could it be seen and identified under the electron microscope?

The answer to these questions would involve intimate work with the infected material and, even if the lab people used extreme caution, disasters could still happen. As just one example, they were mindful that 25 percent of the early Rockefeller Foundation yellow-fever researchers, in the era before the vaccine, had been killed as a result of their laboratory work.

The overwhelming power of the new African virus was obvious; to find its exact strength, Casals and Buckley independently went about a process called titering.

Since virus particles cannot be counted, even under an electron microscope, it is necessary to have some scale on which to judge their potency. The titering process provides a means of doing this. Basically, both Sonja Buckley and Jordi Casals followed the same methods.

Casals used ten test tubes. He took a pipette, sucked up the infected serum, and dripped it full strength into the first test tube. In the second tube, he dropped the same serum, but diluted it 10 to 1. In the third test tube, he put serum diluted 100 times; in the fourth tube, the serum was diluted 1000 times—and so on.

Casals and Buckley then took their weakest solutions—in this case as thinly diluted as one part infected serum to 100 million parts of fluid—and inoculated either a group of ten mice or ten tissue cultures with it.

If none of the mice died or none of the tissue cultures were destroyed, they would try a stronger solution. The idea was to continue this process until a strength was reached which destroyed roughly 50 percent of the animals or tissue cultures. The weaker the solution that killed 50 percent of the animals—which scientists call Lethal Dose 50—the stronger the virus was.

One serum specimen taken from Penny Pinneo destroyed 50 percent of the tissue cultures at a dilution of 1 to 10 million. This was terrifyingly lethal, and all the precautions the laboratory was taking were reinforced.

Next, Sonja Buckley went about the complicated job of preparing some of Penny Pinneo's infected serum for observation under an electron microscope. She made sure first that her specimen was infectious by again testing it in her bottles. She next incubated the sample for five days, and transferred it to a centrifuge, where the cells were spun until they were hard and dry.

She was then able to slice them tissue-thin so that they could be stained and observed.

Bob Speir, a specialist in electron microscopy, took over the process here. He mounted the specimens and got them ready for the electron microscope, which would magnify the image more than 100,000 times. (If a dollar bill were enlarged this much, it would cover nearly one fourth of a football field.)

Speir zeroed in the electronic lens. The virus was there: a fuzzy tennis ball, with black polka dots on its surface, and spike-like protuberances jutting out. It was ugly, ominous—and, though dead, it seemed to be staring back at him from the microscope's viewing screen.

One of the most important jobs facing the Yale scientists was to find and create antibodies for the new virus. It is thought that there is at least one antibody for any viral invader. An antibody can clamp onto and neutralize a virus because its shape is an exact negative cast of the virus it's designed to fight; thus the two fit together and, locked in a fatal embrace, are swept unceremoniously out of the body as waste.

Because antibodies can be found in an animal or human that has successfully recovered from a virus disease, Wil Downs had already cabled the Virus Research Laboratory of the University of Ibadan in Nigeria, asking scientists there to investigate the outbreak at Lassa and Jos. Perhaps Nigerian villagers could be found who had survived the new disease. If so, their blood should contain antibodies. He also asked that the wildlife of the region—especially rodents—be bled and tested in hopes that the carrier of the virus might be found.

Meanwhile, the course of Penny Pinneo's illness had taken a turn for the better. Her temperature had continued downward, and after March 20 it never rose above 99 degrees. On May 3, nine weeks after she entered the isolation ward at Columbia-Presbyterian, she was released. Her hearing was far from normal, and she had lost 28 pounds and most of the hair on her head. But she was alive.

Her apparent recovery gave Jordi Casals another potential weapon against "Lassa fever," as John Frame and his colleagues had now labeled it. For if antibodies showed up in Penny's blood serum, it would be possible to make a crude anti-serum from it.

The practice of injecting serum containing antibodies into someone who has contracted a virus disease is an old one, used mainly before the techniques of modern vaccine production were perfected. It is dangerous. For one thing, the serum may contain hidden live virus. It may cause serum hepatitis, or in some cases induce complete kidney shutdown and thus kill a patient who otherwise might have recovered. But, in an emergency, when there is no vaccine available, it is about the only technique that can be used.

Casals's tests were positive: serum taken from Penny Pinneo on the 28th day of her illness was packed with Lassa-virus antibodies.

Casals than set out to establish how long the virus could persist after clinical recovery of a victim. He was startled to find that, although none of his baby mice had ever shown any signs of illness, live Lassa virus was present in their urine some 45 days after they had been injected with infectious serum. Apparently the virus could hide in the kidneys for a long period—in rodents at least.

This finding indicated a strong similarity between Lassa virus and certain deadly South American viruses. The working hypothesis was this: infant rodents became infected with the disease at birth, and carried it without damage to themselves; but they could transmit it through their urine to humans.

Such a supposition dovetailed neatly with an unusual custom of the Nigerian bush. During the dry season, village youngsters, armed with clubs, would move out to the deeper savanna, set fire to the grass, wait at the edges for the rats to rush out in panic, club them and take them to their compounds and cooking fires. A high percentage of the protein of the tribesmen came from this source. Of course, when the rats were caught, they were frightened; and when they were frightened, they urinated.

Early in June, sitting at his laboratory bench, Jordi Casals felt a chill go through him. He ignored it and continued working. But it persisted. He took two aspirin and went back to his bench. In line with the tradition of his profession, he refused to allow himself to think that his symptoms might be serious. That would only lead to hypochondria, a fatal obsession in his kind of work.

On the following day, Sonja Buckley saw him sitting in his lab with both a thick gray sweater and a tweed jacket on under his white lab coat. To her, his face looked almost as gray as his sweater; and he was shivering. "What in the world is the matter with you?" she asked.

"I have a cold," Casals replied. Buckley told him to go home to bed until it cleared up. Casals said he would think about it.

Six days later, racked by excruciating pains in his thighs, burning with fever, he was taken by ambulance to the Isolation Unit of Columbia-Presbyterian Hospital.

3. MOUNTING TERROR

THAT EVENING, John Frame and his wife, Veronica, were celebrating her birthday with family and friends at their home on Long Island. Thc phonc rang. It was Wil Downs.

"John," Downs said, "I'm at Columbia-Presbyterian. Jordi Casals is in Isolation." He quickly summarized Casals's clinical picture. It was ominously like that of the three mission nurses. He did not need to give his diagnosis; it was too obvious. "Do you know where Penny Pinneo is?" he asked.

Frame thought she was upstate with her sister. He managed to reach her by phone the next morning. She was shocked at the news. Frame asked whether she would consider letting them take blood serum from her to give Jordi Casals. And was she up to the trip?

"Try and stop me," she replied. By midafternoon she was aboard a jet en route to New York.

At the Yale Arbovirus Laboratory, Jordi Casals's colleagues gathered to try to conjure up some kind of solution to the dilemma they faced. One by one, the dangers of giving Casals the anti-serum were considered. They were serious. Yet if they did nothing, they might just be letting their friend sink into a crisis that would kill him.

They now knew that Casals's symptoms were following an all-too-familiar pattern: dehydration; low white-blood-cell count; signs of internal hemorrhaging. They were all convinced that Jordi had Lassa fever, and the speed with which the virus moved did not allow much time for vacillation. Charlotte Shaw had died on the 11th day of illness. Casals, they figured, had had the virus for seven.

All through the next day, Casals sank lower. While Dr. Downs was with him, Casals's wife, Lynn, was permitted to don mask, gown and gloves to see her husband. She was appalled, on the verge of tears. When her time was up, she moved automatically toward her husband and leaned down to kiss him through her mask. Downs yelled sharply and grabbed her away. Lassa fever did not allow a margin for affection.

On Wednesday morning, with the news that Jordi Casals was going downhill rapidly, another meeting was held at Yale. His colleagues were troubled by the fact that they had no real proof that Jordi had Lassa fever; giving him Penny's serum might infect him with a fatal disease he did not have. Before the meeting, Downs put through a phone call to a leading international virologist, Dr. Karl Johnson, who was in Panama working on the deadly Bolivian hemorrhagic fever, one of the South American diseases which so closely resembled Lassa fever. Johnson listened attentively as Downs spelled out the clinical course of Jordi Casals's sickness. When Downs had finished, Johnson said firmly, "Wil, give that serum!"

Dr. Edgar Leifer, Dr. Casals's physician, and the medical staff at Columbia-Presbyterian Hospital had also been holding repeated conferences. This word tipped the balance in favor of using the anti-serum.

That night, the anti-serum began flowing, drop by drop, into Jordi Casals's veins. In the morning, there was little change. All through the day, the scientists at Yale and Columbia wondered if they had done the right thing.

The next morning, Sonja Buckley examined the tissue cultures which she had infected with serum from Jordi Casals. Every cell carpet was ravaged by the Lassa virus. He had the disease.

That morning, he took a definite turn for the better. His temperature fell. After June 26 there was no fever. The relief at Yale and Columbia was immense. Dr. Robert Shope, one of the Yale experts, visiting Casals at the hospital, used an expression that Casals will always remember. Shope said: "Jordi, we were very frightened." Scientists don't use those words often.

On hearing the news about Casals, the New York office of the U.S. Public Health Service called John Frame. They were worried. It was one thing for a mission nurse to get Lassa fever in Africa, quite another when the disease was contracted in the United States. Would the Lassa virus now move out of the hospital and into the streets?

Dr. Frame shared this concern, and together they improvised a procedure to be put into effect at international airports. Travelers returning from Nigeria would be questioned extensively. If there was any indication whatsoever of illness, they would be required to get in touch with Frame for a thorough examination.

The Center for Disease Control of the Public Health Service in Atlanta joined in the alert. A new $2.5-million "hot" lab had just been completed there, and Lassa virus became its first assignment. Dr. Shope shipped live virus from Yale by special messenger with a note warning Atlanta of its long life and potency.

In the new facility, specimens were untouched by human hands. Conveyer belts brought them into the lab through long tunnels and fed them into airtight "isolators"—large steel tanks with thick glass windows for visibility. In the windows were portholes opening into arm-length rubber gloves. The scientists placed their arms in the gloves to work on animal or tissue cultures inside the isolators.

The building had special air locks and filters. Anyone entering the inner chamber to work on material in the isolators had to change his clothes in a special room, don disposable garments and, on leaving, take a shower and stand in front of ultraviolet light. No materials came out of the building without being sterilized or incinerated.

Yale, redoubling its safety measures, continued its own studies. After convalescing, Casals returned to his job. In New York, John Frame pursued a hunch that Lassa-fever antibodies, far from being confined to Nigeria, might well be found in the blood of missionaries who had recovered from "African fevers" in other countries of the vast Sudan. He began following up several cases from his files that sounded suspiciously like Lassa fever. In Africa, the search for a possible carrier continued. But, despite the alert, Lassa fever suddenly seemed to vanish. Throughout that summer of 1969, no new cases were reported.

Instead, in October, yellow fever broke out in Jos and surrounding areas. It was a tragic epidemic, taking several months to run its course, with thousands of cases and uncounted deaths. Work on the Lassa virus continued without let-up against the chilling prospect of what a virus can do to an unvaccinated population in a short time.

Thanksgiving brought a welcome respite from the research at the laboratory. Jordi Casals finished several jobs on the Wednesday before the holiday, and he was glad to have the time off, for he still tired more easily than previously. As he went down the hall toward the elevators, he said hello to Juan Roman, a young lab technician who, with his wife, was working on other projects. Roman was planning to drive to York, Pa., with his wife for a family visit. They wished each other a happy holiday, and went their separate ways.

On Monday, the Romans did not return. Sonja Buckley, who had been teaching Roman's wife to be an assistant in tissue cultures, thought this curious. Then, just before lunch, a doctor called her from York to say that Juan had been confined to bed with a mild virus infection.

After she had hung up, the possibility of Lassa fever crossed Sonja's mind. She immediately dismissed the thought, chiding herself for being paranoid. Juan's job had nothing to do with the Lassa virus. He worked in an entirely separate lab.

But by the end of the week, Juan Roman and his wife still had not returned to Yale. The following week, another call came. Roman was in the hospital. His condition was not critical, but puzzling. Jordi Casals decided he had better have a look at his colleague.

By the time Casals reached the hospital, Roman was in critical condition with typhus-like symptoms. Casals took a blood sample and hurried back to Yale to get it checked out on tissue cultures and mice.

But nothing that came out of the tests would be of any use to Juan Roman. Within two days, he was dead. A few days later, the results of the test were determined: Juan Roman's system had been riddled with Lassa virus.

The news stunned everybody involved. The exact channel of infection was impossible to trace. Juan Roman had never touched anything remotely connected with Lassa virus. He had never entered Casals's special isolation room.

The reaction was swift and unequivocal. All research at Yale involving live Lassa virus stopped, and all live Lassa specimens were shipped to the hot lab in Atlanta. All remaining materials and equipment used in the live Lassa-virus research were incinerated or thoroughly sterilized. Any worker in any part of the laboratory was to report the first sign of any illness, regardless of how minor or trivial. Bulletins were sent from the lab to medical and public-health officials throughout the world. No new specimens suspected of harboring Lassa virus would be accepted at Yale.

On Christmas Day, the Christians in the village of Bassa, 20 miles from Jos, prepared a parade featuring drums and chanting. Tamalama Sale looked forward to seeing it, but that morning she was burning with a fever and had to remain in bed. Soon she was very ill, and on December 30 her family took her to the hospital at Jos, along with her infant son and three-year-old daughter. Her brother registered her under a fictitious name and village, for it is a long-standing superstition among the plateau tribes that the evil spirits of disease cannot then follow the patient home when he is cured and plague him again.

Tamalama Sale remained in the hospital for ten days. There were times when it seemed as if she would not survive, but eventually she pulled through and returned to Bassa. Within three days, her mother and both her children came down with a searing fever. The mother and the baby boy gradually recovered. Her three-year-old daughter died.

Shortly after Tamalama was dismissed from the hospital, two other Nigerian women developed symptoms similar to hers. Within four days, one of them was dead. Then three more patients were admitted with high fevers.

Dr. Jeanette and Hal White, the calm, quiet doctor who headed the medical-assistants school affiliated with the hospital, hesitated to discuss their fears. They simply could not believe that Lassa fever had returned. Yet the new cases could not be diagnosed as yellow fever, or any of the conventional diseases, and the symptoms were strikingly like those that had afflicted the three mission nurses almost exactly a year before. Leaving nothing to chance, they drew serum specimens to send to the University of Ibadan for analysis.

Several more Nigerians were hospitalized. There had now accumulated, with alarming suddenness, a total of 12 suspicious cases; four of them were members of the hospital staff. On Sunday, January 25, two of the staff members died. The news of the second death was announced during the middle of a Bible-study meeting. For a moment there was a stunned silence. Then Dr. Jeanette, whose composure in crisis after crisis during the terrible yellow-fever epidemic had been so constant, burst into tears and wept openly.

Later, her composure seemingly regained, she performed the autopsy on the body of Maigari, who had been a male scrub nurse. The scalpel moved down through his chest, exposing the rib cage, then down to the abdomen to get at the viscera. Carefully Dr. Jeanette reached in with the scalpel to free one of the ribs, but as she did so the scalpel slipped. It sliced cleanly through the rubber glove on her other hand and into her finger. Blood spurted from the wound.

Quickly she jerked her hand out of the bloody chest cavity, went to the scrub sink and took her slashed rubber glove off. She ran water freely over the cut. Then she scrubbed it with surgical soap, flooded it with antiseptic and bound it carefully with gauze. She put on a new rubber glove and went back to the autopsy.

After making rounds, Hal White stopped by the operating room to see if he could help with the autopsy. But the job was finished, and Dr. Jeanette was alone. "Hal," she said, "I've been in Africa for 16 years. I've made an awful lot of stupid mistakes in that time. The Lord has had to cover them up for me. And I just made another one." She held up her bandaged finger and asked him not to alarm the staff by saying anything about it.

The next morning, Dr. Jeanette sent a letter and a large vacuum jug of iced specimens to Don Carey, director of the Virus Research Laboratory at the University of Ibadan. The letter was matter-of-fact, but

Carey knew Dr. Jeanette too well to be fooled by its understatement. Frankly alarmed, he immediately cabled news of the outbreak to Yale, asking if it was possible to get a shipment of two units of Jordi Casals's serum with its antibodies as quickly as possible. Then, with Graham Kemp, one of his best virologists, he began setting up tissue cultures.

New cases continued to arrive at the Jos hospital, all with the same ominous symptoms. The list had now grown to 19. Ten had died. There were no facilities for real isolation. Even if there had been, the staff was too small and overburdened to follow complex isolation procedures.

In Jos, there was mounting terror. Meetings were canceled. Social engagements dwindled. Air traffic into the city thinned to a trickle. Travelers would speed through the town, windows rolled up regardless of the heat. Water was boiled for an hour, rather than the usual 20 minutes, then filtered twice. Great caution was taken to avoid mice or other rodents. Anyone coming down with flu or a sore throat was convinced he had Lassa. Jos was a besieged city.

On the evening of February 3, Dr. Jeanette went to bed with a severe chill. Her muscles ached, and her back was particularly painful. The next morning, feeling feverish, she got up, dressed, and made the rounds of the wards, checking the charts. She avoided going near any of her patients and colleagues. Then she went home and rested.

A week after her first symptoms appeared, her temperature rose to nearly 104 degrees. Hal White insisted that she go to the hospital. He put her in a private room, and ordered that no one was to enter without cap, gown and mask. It was the closest thing to an isolation unit that could be improvised.

4. THE FIRST CLUE

THE INFORMATION reaching New York about the outbreak in Jos was fragmentary, but obviously the situation was deteriorating. Both Penny Pinneo and Jordi Casals were alerted. They were prepared to leave for Jos at a moment's notice, but with the chaotic political situation caused by the civil war in Nigeria, neither had been able to obtain a visa. Meanwhile, both had been bled, their serum centrifuged and refrigerated. Jordi Casals also had some dead Lassa-virus specimens that he hoped to take directly to Ibadan so that Don Carey could make a positive, on-the-spot identification of the virus. The news of Dr. Jeanette's illness had not yet reached them.

The Casals/Pinneo immune plasma and samples of dead Lassa virus arrived at Ibadan on February 15. Though unaware of this, Hal White had decided the same day to fly Dr. Jeanette to Ibadan. But, quite unexpectedly, her temperature dropped from 103 degres to normal. Dr. White felt a surge of relief. After talking the matter over with Dr. Jeanette, he decided that the trip would be unnecessary.

The next morning, Dr. Jeanette's temperature plunged to 94.6 degrees, critically below normal. Urine output was distressingly low, and her white-blood-cell count soared.

White tried to get in touch with Ibadan, but was unsuccessful. Still knowing nothing of the Casals serum, he now faced a difficult decision: whether or not to give Dr. Jeanette serum from the blood of Raphael, the only hospital worker to have survived the virus. Unfortunately, the presence of antibodies in Raphael's blood had not been confirmed. Moreover, the proper equipment was not available. Without a centrifuge, Dr. White would have to let the red blood cells in Raphael's blood settle by gravity, then draw off the serum with a syringe.

White went to Dr. Jeanette's room and told her he was going to give her the serum. She agreed weakly: "You're the doctor, Hal." He drew the blood, separated the serum—about a third of a pint—and injected it intravenously.

Dr. Jeanette did not respond. On February 18, her respiration became labored, and external cardiac massage was attempted. She was still conscious, however, and in the late afternoon she reached out her hand to Comfort, a tall Nigerian nurse who had been at her bedside every chance she could get. Taking the nurse's large, strong hand in hers, she said, "You've done everything for me, Comfort. God bless you." Comfort's face mask was wet with tears.

At 4:30 p.m., Dr. Jeanette was dead.

In a sad anticlimax, the visas for Jordi Casals and Penny Pinneo came through in the latter part of February. But, with the arrival of the two in Nigeria, the cases of Lassa fever began disappearing as mysteriously as they had first appeared. Only two new cases entered the hospital after Dr. Jeanette's death. The vicious virus had gone back into hiding. The problem now was to find it before it came out to kill again. It was all-important to find the *initial* case, and through it the original source of the disease.

Don Carey, Graham Kemp, Jordi Casals and Penny Pinneo began the search. At Jos, they pored over the case histories of 23 victims and questioned survivors who were located. It soon became clear that Lassa fever had been hospital-transmitted, at least among the first 17 patients. But, as they checked and rechecked the flow of patients, visitors and staff, they could not find a single case which could have infected *all* the primary patients in the outbreak.

Then Kemp came across Tamalama Sale's case history, which was registered under her fictitious name. At first, she didn't seem a promising lead, since her illness had not been diagnosed as Lassa fever. But gradually a clear and incriminating picture began to emerge. Three of the first recorded victims of the virus had been in A Ward while Tamalama was a patient; in fact, all of the primary cases had been patients, workers or visitors when Tamalama was under treatment. What evolved in theory was that Tamalama had brought Lassa fever into the hospital and passed it on to the first patients known to have the fever. They, in turn, passed it on to their families and friends.

To confirm this theory, Tamalama would have to be found and a sample of her blood taken to see if it contained antibodies. If it did, Kemp would trap and bleed as many animals as possible in her village in an attempt to find Lassa's source. The problem was: Who and where was Tamalama?

About the only thing Graham Kemp could do was to run ads in the Jos newspaper describing the little he knew about Tamalama and appealing for help in locating her. One lead came in. Someone thought that she might be the wife of a truck driver known as "King of the Railroad," that her name was something like Soulé, and that she was supposed to live in Bauchi, some 600 miles by road from Ibadan.

Kemp took off on the punishing 1200-mile round trip. No one in Bauchi seemed to know of a woman named Soulé, but by an incredible stroke of luck he was referred to a woman named Sale. She turned out to be the divorced wife of Mallam Sale of Lagos. She had never been in the hospital at Jos. She did not know if Mallam Sale had remarried.

Lagos, the capital of Nigeria, is a sprawling city of half a million people. Before plunging into its teeming labyrinth, Kemp sent out inquiries to people in the area. Finally, he received another clue. He was told that the Hausa term for "King of the Railroad" also meant "King of the Motor Park," a logical place for a truck driver.

He spent his first day in Lagos roaming the dusty streets looking for "motor parks," large outdoor parking lots for semi-trailer trucks where the drivers congregated between trips to drink beer and palm wine. No one seemed to have heard of his quarry. But the next day his luck changed, and he was guided to the Tawaz Trucking Company, where

Mallam Sale, "King of the Motor Park," was working as a mechanic. It didn't take long to find out that he was from Jos and his wife from the nearby town of Bassa. The house they occupied in Lagos was within walking distance.

After much persuasion, Tamalama Sale allowed Kemp to take a blood sample. Then he pressed her for information. Had she been ill a year ago? Yes, she had—and slowly the vital information came out.

The test results on the blood sample showed Tamalama's blood to be full of Lassa antibodies. She could be assumed to be the "index case" for the Jos outbreak. But Kemp's job was far from completed. Soon after the blood tests, he set out for Bassa, armed with dozens of Vacutainers for bloodletting and animal traps for rats, bats and birds that might carry the disease.

In Bassa, he took more than 70 human-blood samples and hired local hunters to set out the traps. Each night he filled his station wagon with animal corpses, tagging them, wrapping them, packing them in ice and sending them off to Atlanta. The job extended over many weeks while Kemp waited for the results of the tests.

When they did come, there was cause for some elation. Antibodies existed in many of the Bassa villagers. But, unfortunately, the source of the virus remained a mystery. None of the animal specimens trapped in the area showed any signs of Lassa.

An article about the Jos epidemic, appearing in a medical journal, reflected a quiet despair. No doctor reading it had any illusions about the probability that Lassa virus could spill out again without warning. Indeed, in New York, John Frame was sure of it. He was convinced that one of the ways to forecast new epidemics lay in the study of past cases of "African fevers" that had never been properly diagnosed. With the help of the Yale Arbovirus Laboratory, he had extended his blood-sampling programs to include 80 sub-Sahara hospitals.

Curiously, only five of the more than 700 blood specimens that he received from West Africa showed Lassa antibodies—but four of these came from Guinea. In November 1970, Frame cautioned a group of virologists that Guinea, or neighboring Sierra Leone, were logical targets for a Lassa-fever outbreak.

Months passed with no new signs of the disease. Then, in March 1972, Dr. Frame was having dinner in New York one evening when his phone rang. It was a call from a ham radio operator, who informed him that he had Penny Pinneo on his wireless from Africa and would try to patch the call in for a three-way telephone conversation.

Penny told Frame that she was on her way from Jos to Liberia to help with what looked like an outbreak of several new cases of Lassa. They were occurring in the village of Zorzor, on the Guinea border, only a few miles from one of the locations that Frame had singled out as a potential disease area.

The lab in Atlanta had also been notified, and had instructed its personnel in Liberia to meet Penny Pinneo and Tom Monath, a quiet, soft-spoken Atlanta virologist on loan to Ibadan University, when they arrived with immune serum.

At Zorzor, Monath found the mission and the hospital personnel subdued and depressed. The cases at the hospital totaled 11, with four dead. It was becoming impossible to get enough staff to work in the improvised isolation ward. For all practical purposes, the hospital was closed to everyone except suspected Lassa cases. Monath sat down with Dr. Paul Mertens and other members of the staff and worked out a plan of attack. They would follow generally the same procedure carried out in Bassa. The emphasis would be on finding the index case and trapping animals in the area.

Monath hired 20 village hunters, and with their help set out traps and strung up fine-meshed nylon to snag bats. In eight nights, he collected 164. At an improvised laboratory, he extracted blood from the hearts. He then cut the animals open, snipped out sections of the internal organs and packed them in iced containers for shipment to Atlanta.

No more cases of Lassa showed up, and the outbreak died quickly. Like the one at Jos, it seemed to stop at the termination of the "secondary" cases. Only the first, or index, case appeared to be wildly contagious. At Jos, there were many people, patients and hospital workers alike, who were exposed in one way or another to Tamalama, the index case. The secondary cases seemed to come only out of direct close family relationship to those who had been infected from the index case. And then the disease stopped. The same was true at Zorzor.

A theory began to emerge: Maybe the virus mutated when it passed through a human carrier. This, in fact, is the principle behind the production of vaccines. The virulence of the virus is softened by passing it through several animals until it no longer has the power to infect but does have the ability to produce antibodies.

The suspicion remained strong that a rodent or bat was the source. The new reports from Atlanta on Monath's bats and rats still showed no virus, however. Meanwhile, precious quotas of immune plasma were distributed to Ibadan, Jos and Zorzor in case of another emergency—although in any real crisis it would be woefully inadequate.

Then, three months after the terror had died down in Zorzor, several suspicious fever illnesses began developing in the Panguma Catholic Hospital in Sierra Leone, some 100 miles from Zorzor. The patients had drifted in slowly over a period of many months. A number of deaths had been reported.

In Atlanta, Tom Monath cabled Panguma that there was a possibility it might be Lassa, although it was not typical for the disease to move so slowly. But Lassa fever seemed to be able to make its own laws. He requested serum-blood specimens and drew up a contingency plan with others at the lab. In the event the specimen tests confirmed Lassa, a team of doctors and scientists that included Monath, Casals and Kemp would be flown to the stricken area.

When the tests were completed, they clearly showed Lassa, and the team left for Africa, arriving at Panguma to find that 64 cases had occurred, with 23 deaths. The outbreak appeared to be more dangerous than previous ones, for it was not just hospital-transmitted. The disease passed from village to village, and probable cases began showing up in other hospitals in the region.

Among the animals being caught there were many types of rodents, which villagers chased out of the bush and ate. Suspicions began growing, and a special effort was made to get as many as possible.

Cases continued to appear in Sierra Leone, but the crisis was over. Tom Monath returned to Atlanta to help with the complex tests that he hoped would establish a specific rat as the carrier. A preliminary finding had indicated that one type of rodent might indeed be the culprit. He brought each sample, wrapped in a sealed plastic bag, into the laboratory through a "dunk" tank filled with chlorine bleach. Then, inside the steel-and-glass isolator, his hands punched into the long rubber gloves, he proceeded with the awkward work demanded by the hot-lab routine. None of the tests, however, produced conclusive findings.

Monath was discouraged, but determined to keep going. The hot lab could handle only about 50 specimens a week at best, and there were hundreds still to be tested. He would have to be selective.

His mind went back to the harrowing case of Hawa Foray, a Sierra Leone housewife. She had been a classic Lassa-virus case, confirmed by both her blood specimen and the liver cells he had extracted from her body after she died. He remembered the eight wild rats of the *Mastomys natalensis* species that had been trapped in her household after her death. This rodent was common in West Africa, but it usually stayed in the bush. Only when the larger and more ferocious house rat abandoned the premises did it venture into the villages. He decided to test it.

He and his technicians took snips of tissue, ground them with mortar and pestle in a fluid, inoculated rows of tissue cultures—and waited.

The tissue cultures were soon riddled with cell damage. Despite the possibility of a false lead, the researchers worked with fresh enthusiasm. Monath did not want to admit it, but for some reason he felt confident that they had reached the end of their search. Perversely, he bet one of his technicians $10 that the final tests would not reveal Lassa.

This time there was no disappointment. The tests showed, unmistakably, that seven of the eight rats had carried Lassa fever. There was no longer any doubt about the animal reservoir. The lair of the vicious, malignant speck with its spiky, polka-dotted overcoat that had eluded the virus hunters for so long had at last been found.

There was still much to be done, but at least there would be no more blind stumbling. The problem would now shift to control of the rodent carrier, and the long, involved process of developing a vaccine. None of this would be easy.

Word of the breakthrough reached Jordi Casals at Yale through a phone call from Tom Monath in Atlanta. Casals was elated, and went down the hall to Sonja Buckley's lab bench to tell her the news. She said very simply, "That's great. It makes sense." She remembered Jordi's struggle with death and her own struggle with her cell cultures. There was no champagne, no celebration. Just a feeling of immense relief, coupled with a desire to get on with the job of combating any new, threatening agent that might spring up in the virus universe, just as had been done with the mysterious challenge of Lassa fever.

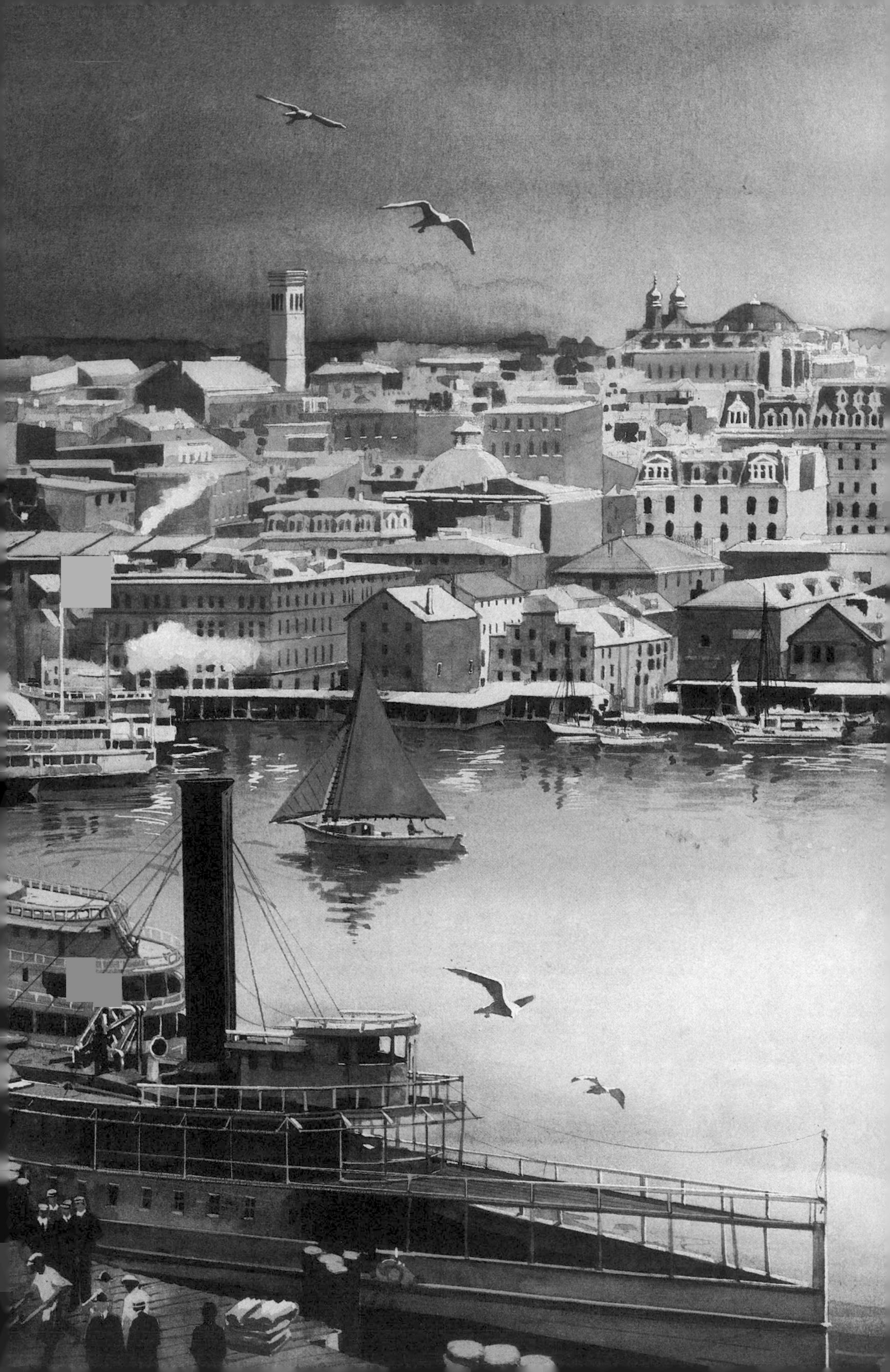

The Watermen

CONDENSED FROM THE BOOK
"CHESAPEAKE" BY

James A. Michener

ILLUSTRATED BY
JIM BUTCHER

The locale of James A. Michener's novel *Chesapeake* is that teeming body of water on America's Atlantic coast, the Chesapeake Bay. The Bay was a principal breeding place of the American experience: the growing cities of Philadelphia, Williamsburg, Baltimore and Washington, D.C. Here passed John Smith, founder of Jamestown, the pirates of the Spanish Main, the carriers of the slave and rum trade, the warships of the Revolution and the Civil War—and the watermen who worked the oyster beds in season.

In the selection condensed on these pages, the time is the 1880s and the principal characters are Jake Turlock and Tim Caveny. Ordinary people, with common weaknesses and simple strengths, they are The Watermen, engaged in a constant struggle with the sea to survive. It is the story of their friendship, their rivalry and their fierce resistance to any intrusion on their territory.

1. THE FEUD

THE GOLDEN AGE of the Eastern Shore came in that four-decade span from 1880 to 1920 when the rest of the nation allowed the marshy counties to sleep undisturbed. True, in these years the world experienced panics and wars, revolutions and contested elections, but these had almost no impact on the somnolent estuaries and the secluded coves.

There was, of course, excitement, but it rarely arrived from the outside world. One of the adventures that caused most excitement came in 1887 when a ship commanded by Capt. Thomas Lightfoot docked at Patamoke with a cargo of ice sawed from the freshwater ponds of Labrador. When the sawdust had been washed away, and the blue-green cakes were stored in icehouses along the riverfront, Captain Lightfoot announced: "I've somethin' extra for you. Before it appears I wish to inform you that it is for sale, ten dollars cash."

A moment later, one of his black stevedores appeared on deck leading by a leash one of thc most handsome dogs ever seen in Maryland. He was jet black, sturdy in his front quarters, sleek and powerful in his hind, with an intelligent face. His movements were quick, his dark eyes following every development nearby, yet his disposition appeared so equable that he seemed always about to smile.

"He's called a Labrador," Captain Lightfoot said. "Finest huntin' dog ever developed."

"He's what?" Jake Turlock snapped.

"Best huntin' breed known. They can smell ducks, and they've never been known to lose a cripple."

"Can't touch a Chesapeake retriever," Turlock said, referring to the husky, reddish-brown dog bred especially for Bay purposes.

But this new animal captivated Tim Caveny. The black dog displayed intelligence that showed promise of further development. Caveny said, "I'd like to see him."

Captain Lightfoot turned the Labrador loose, and with almost a psychic understanding that his future lay with this Irishman, the dog ran to Caveny, leaned against his leg and nuzzled his hand.

Tim's heart was lost, and he said, "I'll take him."

"Mr. Caveny, you just bought the best Labrador ever bred."

Tim paid ten dollars, then reached down and patted his new hunting companion. "Come on, Lucifer," he said.

"That's a hell of a name for a dog ," Turlock growled.

"He's Old Testament black," Tim said. And to Captain Lightfoot's surprise he recited, "How art thou fallen from heaven, O Lucifer, son of the morning!"

"To me he looks like horse manure," Jake Turlock said.

"He what?" Caveny demanded.

"I said," Turlock repeated, "that your dog looks like a horse turd."

Tim handed the leash he had been holding to a bystander. With a mighty swipe he knocked Turlock to the wet and salty boards of the wharf. Caveny then leaped across the planking and kicked Turlock in his left armpit, lifting him well into the air. When Turlock landed, his hand fell upon some lumber stacked for loading onto Captain Lightfoot's ship. After he had quickly tested three or four clubs he found one to his liking and with it delivered such a blow to Caveny's head that the new owner of the Labrador staggered back, tried to control his disorganized feet, and fell into the Choptank.

In this way the feud between Irishman Tim Caveny, owner of a black Labrador, and Englishman Jake Turlock, owner of a red Chesapeake, began.

The first test of the two dogs came in the autumn of 1888 at the dove shoot on the farm of old Lyman Steed. Each hunter was allowed to bring one dog to the shoot. The animal had to be well trained, because the birds came charging in at low altitude, swerved and dodged in unbelievable confusion and, when they were hit, fell in unpredictable spots. The only practical way for the hunter to retrieve his dove was to have a dog trained to leap forward when he saw a bird fall and find it no matter where it dropped—swamp, field or brambles.

Jake Turlock's Chesapeake was a large, surly, well-trained beast named Hey-You. Tim Caveny's Lucifer was an unknown quantity. He had never before participated in a dove shoot.

The field contained about 20 acres and had recently been harvested, so that it provided a large, flat, completely open area. It was surrounded by a marsh on one side, a large blackberry bramble on another, and a grove of loblollies covering a thicket of underbrush on a third. The doves would sweep in over the loblollies, drop low, hear gunfire and veer back toward the brambles.

The men took their positions. It was half after one in the afternoon. From the woods came six doves, flying low in their wonderfully staggered pattern, now swooping in this direction, now in that. Jake Turlock, taken by surprise, fired and hit nothing. "Mark!" he shouted at the top of his voice. Tim Caveny fired and hit nothing. "Mark!" he bellowed. The doves dived, swirled and twisted, and three other hunters fired at them to no avail.

On the next flight Tim got no chance to shoot, but Turlock did, and this time he hit a bird that fell into brambles. "Fetch the dove!" Jake told his Chesapeake, but the bushes were too thick. The bird was lost.

Now another dove flew into Tim's range, and when he fired, this one also fell into brambles. "Fetch the dove," Tim said calmly, his heart aching for a good retrieve.

Lucifer plunged directly for the fallen bird but could not penetrate the thick and thorny briars. Unlike Turlock's Chesapeake he did not quit, for he heard his master calling softly, "Circle, Luke! Circle!" And he ran in wide circles until he found a back path to the brambles. But again he stopped, and again his master cried, "Circle, Luke!" This time he found an entrance that allowed him to roam freely. But with so much ranging, he had lost an accurate guide to the fallen bird. Still he heard his master's voice imploring, "Circle, Luke!" and he knew that this meant he still had a chance.

So, in the depth of the bramble patch, but below the reach of the thorns, he ran and scrambled and clawed and finally came upon Caveny's bird. He gave a quiet yup, and when Tim heard this his heart expanded. Lucifer had passed his first big test. On the way out of the patch, the dog retrieved Turlock's fallen bird as well.

When he laid the two doves at Tim's feet, the Irishman wanted to kneel and kiss his rough black head, but he knew that all the hunters in his area were watching, so in a manly way he patted the dog, then prepared for his moment of triumph.

It was a custom that if a hunter downed a bird that his dog could not retrieve and another man's dog did fetch it, the second hunter was obligated to deliver the dove to the man who had downed it.

Proudly Tim Caveny walked the hundred-odd yards to where Jake Turlock was standing. Lucifer started to follow, but Tim cried sharply, "Stay!" and the dog obeyed. The other hunters took note of this, then watched as Tim gravely delivered the bird, but at this moment another hunter shouted, "Mark!" and a whole covey flew over.

Automatically, Jake and Tim fired, and two birds fell. Jake's Hey-You was on the spot, of course, and proudly ran out to recover the dove his master had knocked down. Lucifer, far distant from where his master had shot, was so obedient to the earlier command, "Stay," that he did not move. When Tim shouted, "Fetch the dove," he leaped off his spot, rushed directly to the fallen bird, and carried it not to where Tim was standing, but back to his assigned location.

The hunter next to Tim called, "You got yourself a dog, Tim."

The day was a triumph. Luke hunted in marshland as well as he had in brambles. He proved he had a soft mouth. He circled well in woods, and on the open field he was superb. And with it all he displayed the bland, sweet disposition of the Labradors.

The final test came in November. As four men and their dogs holed up in a blind at the Turlock marshes, Jake reminded them: "Geese ain't so plentiful now. Can't afford any mistakes, man or dog." He was right. Once, the Choptank and its sister rivers had been home for a million geese; now, the population had diminished to less than 400,000 and bagging them became more difficult. Jake, a master of the goose call, tried from dawn till ten in the morning to lure the big birds down, but failed. The hunters had a meager lunch, and toward dusk, when it seemed that the day was a failure, nine geese wheeled in, right at the blind. Guns blazed and, before the smoke had cleared, Jake's Chesapeake had leaped out of the blind and retrieved the goose his master had killed. Lucifer went into the water too, but many seconds after Hey-You, and he was both splashy and noisy in making his retrieve.

"Sure doesn't like cold water," Jake said contemptuously.

"Neither did yours when he started," Tim said.

"A Chesapeake is born lovin' water, colder the better."

It became obvious to the hunters, after eight mornings in the blind, that while Tim Caveny's new dog was exceptional with doves on warm days, he left much to be desired as a real hunter in the only form of the sport that mattered, goose on water. He displayed a discernible reluctance to plunge into cold waves, and they began to wonder whether he would go into ice at all.

The Patamoke hunters were a suspicious clan. The most important thing in their lives, more important than wife or church or political party, was the totality of the hunting season: "You got to have the right gun, the right mates, the right spot, the right eye for the target and, above all, the right dog."

Tim had faith. He talked to Lucifer constantly, encouraging him to leap more quickly into the cold water. He showed what ice was like, and how the dog must break it with his forepaws to make a path for himself to the downed goose. Using every training trick the Choptank had ever heard of, he tried to bring his dog along step by step.

He failed. In January, when real ice formed on the river, the men went hunting along the banks of the Bay itself, and when Jake Turlock knocked down a beautiful goose, it fell on ice about 200 yards from the blind: "Hey-You, get the bird!"

And the big Chesapeake showed what a marvelous breed he was by leaping into the free water, swimming swiftly to the edge of the ice, then breaking a way for himself right to the goose. Clutching the big bird proudly in his jaws, he returned to the blind, entering it with a mighty, water-spraying leap.

"That's what I call a dog," Jake said proudly, and the men agreed. Lucifer did not perform so well. He retrieved his goose all right, but hesitantly and almost with protest.

"He did get the goose," Jake admitted condescendingly, and for the rest of that long day the two dogs performed in this way, with Hey-You doing as well as a water dog could and Lucifer just getting by.

Tim never spoke a harsh word. Lucifer was his dog, a splendid, loving, responsive animal; if he didn't like cold water, that was a matter between him and his master. Toward dusk, the dog found an opportunity to repay Tim's confidence. Jake had shot a big goose that had disappeared into a marsh from which Hey-You failed to extract it. In the meantime, Lucifer remained in the blind trembling with eagerness. Tim realized that his Labrador knew where that goose was. After Hey-You had returned with nothing, Tim said softly, "Luke, there's a bird out there. Show them how to get it."

Like a flash the black dog leaped into the water, splashed his way through the semi-ice into the rushy area and swam in noisy circles until he found the goose. He grabbed it in his gentle mouth, and swam back to the blind. But as he was about to place the goose at Tim's feet, the Irishman said, "No!" The dog was so attentive to his master that he froze, wanting to know what he had done wrong. "Over there," Tim said, and Luke took the goose to Jake, placing it at his feet.

The feud between the two watermen never ended. The men at the general store fired it with unkind comments about Lucifer's deficiencies, but once or twice Caveny caught a hint that their animosity was weakening for, at some unexpected moment, a man would see in Tim's dog a quality that made him catch his breath. The way in which Lucifer stayed close to Tim, anxious to detect any nuance in the Irishman's mood, tantalized the others. All they would grant openly was: "Maybe Tim's got somethin' in that black dog." But Jake Turlock would not admit even that: "What he's got is a good lap dog, and that's about it. As for me, I'm interested solely in huntin'."

Aside from this disagreement over dogs, and a fistfight now and then, the two watermen maintained a warm friendship. They hunted together, fished together and worked the oyster beds in season. But it was the big gun that cemented their partnership, giving it substance and allowing it to blossom.

2. THE BIG GUN

IN THOSE DECADES when the Eastern Shore flourished, the city of Baltimore also flourished. Some considered it the best city in America, combining the new wealth of the North with the old gentility of the South. The city offered additional rewards: a host of German settlers who gave it warmth. But for most observers, its true excellence derived from the manner in which its hotels and restaurants maintained a tradition of savory cooking: southern dishes, northern meats, Italian spices and German beer.

In 1888, the noblest hotel of them all opened, the Rennert, eight stories high. It became immediately noted for the luxuriance of its cuisine: "Eighteen kinds of game. Fourteen ways to serve oysters. And the best wild duck in America." To dine at the Rennert was to share the finest the Chesapeake could provide.

Jake Turlock and Tim Caveny had never seen the new hotel, but it was to play a major role in their lives. Its black chefs demanded the freshest oysters, and these were delivered daily during the season by Choptank watermen who packed their catch in burlap bags, speeding them across the Bay by special boat. When the boat was loaded with oysters, the captain could usually find space on deck for a few last-minute barrels crammed with ducks: mallards, redheads, canvasbacks and the juiciest of all, the black. By providing these ducks to the

Rennert, Jake and Tim began to acquire a little extra money, which they saved for the larger project they had in mind.

One night at the store, Jake said, "I know me a man's got a long gun he might want to dispose of."

Tim Caveny was excited: "If you can get the gun, I can get me a couple of skiffs."

Turlock replied, "Suppose we get the gun and the skiffs. I know me a captain who'll ferry our ducks to the Rennert. Top dollar."

Caveny added, "We put aside enough money, we can get Paxmore to build us our own boat. Then we're in business."

So the pair sailed upriver to the landing of a farm owned by old Greef Twombly. Twombly rocked back and forth, then led them to a monstrous gun, 11 feet, 6 inches long, about 110 pounds in weight, with a massive stock.

"You ever fire one of these?" the old man asked.

"No, but I've heard," Turlock said.

The old man explained, "You charge it with three quarters of a pound of black powder in here, no less or she won't carry. Then you pour in a waterglassful of No. 6 shot, plus one fistful. You tamp her down with greasy wadding, like this, and you're ready. Trigger's kept real tight so you can't explode the charge by accident, because if you did, it would rip the side off'n a house."

When the two watermen struggled with the preposterous weight of the gun, the old man said, "It ain't for boys."

He accepted the gun into his 14-foot skiff, dropped its barrel between the chocks and flipped a wooden lock that secured it. He then deftly fitted the heavy butt into a socket made of burlap bagging filled with pine needles.

"What you do," Twombly said, "is use your big paddle to ease you into position, but when you come close to the ducks you stow it and take out your two hand paddles, like this." And with the two paddles that looked like whisk brooms, he silently moved the skiff about.

"When you get into position, you lie on your belly, keep the hand paddles close by, and sight along the barrel of the gun. You don't point the gun. You point the skiff, and when you get 70, 80 ducks in range, you turn your head away to protect your eyes, then you slap this trigger, and . . ."

The gun exploded with a power that seemed to tear a hole in the sky. The kickback came close to ripping out the stern of the skiff, but the pine needles absorbed it, while a cloud of black smoke curled upward.

CAVENY PRODUCED the two skiffs he had promised, and their mode of operation became standardized: as dusk approached, Jake would inspect his skiff to be sure he had enough pine needles in the burlap to absorb the recoil; he also cleaned the huge gun, prepared his powder, checked his supply of shot; Tim in the meantime was preparing his own skiff and feeding the two dogs.

Duck hunting with a big gun was an exact science best performed in the coldest part of winter with no moon. When the ducks were located, vast collections huddling in the cold, Turlock took command. Slowly, slowly he pointed the nose of the skiff at the heart of the congregation. When he had satisfied himself that the muzzle of the gun was pointed correctly, he brought his short paddles in and took a series of deep breaths. Then, with his cheek close to the stock but not touching it, he poised his hand to hit the heavy trigger and waited. Slowly the skiff would drift, and when everything was in line, he turned his head aside and slapped the trigger.

He was never prepared for the magnitude of the explosion that ripped through the night. It was monstrous, like the fire of a cannon, but in the brief flash it produced, he could see ducks being blown out of the water as if a hundred expert gunners had fired at them.

Now Caveny became the focus. Paddling furiously, he sped his skiff through the dark water, the two dogs quivering with desire to leap into the waves to retrieve the ducks. But he wanted to bring them much closer to where the birds lay, and to do so he enforced a stern discipline: "No! No!" That was all he said, but the two dogs obeyed.

"Fetch!" he shouted, and the dogs leaped into the water and began hauling the ducks to the two skiffs, Hey-You always going to Turlock's and Lucifer to Caveny's.

As soon as the two skiffs reached Patamoke, the watermen packed their catch in ventilated barrels that they handed over to the captain of the boat running oysters to the Rennert, and at the end of each month they received from the hotel a check for their services.

So their pockets filled with dollars, and they began to think seriously about acquiring a real boat with which they could branch out.

"There's a man on Deal Island got hisse'f a new kind of boat," Turlock said one morning as they were packing their ducks. "Made especially for drudgin'."

Time out of mind, watermen of the Chesapeake had used two words with unique pronunciation. There was no such thing as an oyster, never had been. It was an arster and to call it anything else was profanation. And a man did not dredge for arsters, he drudged them. Jake and Tim proposed to become arster drudgers, and the boat they had in mind was ideal for their purpose.

It put into Patamoke one day and Turlock ran to the Paxmore Boat Yard and asked Gerrit Paxmore to join him in inspecting it. The Quaker boat builder analyzed what the Deal Island men had done.

"Very shallow draft, so it can go anywhere on the flats. Single mast far forward, but look how it's raked. Gives them a triangular sail. More room on deck. Also allows the tip of the mast to hang over the hold, so that they can drop a line and haul cargo out. Enormous boom to give them drudgin' power. Very low freeboard, so they won't have to hoist the arsters too far."

But then his practiced eye saw something he definitely did not like. "She has a retractable centerboard, which accounts for her shallow draft. But to insert a centerboard, you've got to penetrate the keel. At Paxmore's we never touch the keel." He looked at an old boat tied to the wharf, its backbone arched out of shape. "Our boats don't do that." He would not discuss the new craft any further.

Over the winter Turlock and Caveny became convinced that they must have the new boat, and that if Paxmore would not build it, then some other builder would. Paxmore, the descendant of generations of Quaker ship carpenters, understood that argument and relented, accepting a contract to build his first skipjack—named after the fish that skips over the water.

As the ducks flew north, he finished the job, and when the craft was launched he told the two watermen, "This boat will sail better than any in the Bay." Turlock and Caveny were prepared to believe this, but they were taken aback when the Quaker added, "I've kept thy money in our office. I'm prepared to hand it back, because thee doesn't have to take this boat . . . if thee doesn't wish."

"Why wouldn't we?" Turlock growled.

"Because," Paxmore said quietly, "I've done something with the centerboard."

The three men went aboard and down into the hold to inspect the bottom of the boat, and there Turlock and Caveny saw the damnedest thing their eyes had ever met. Instead of placing the centerboard in the middle of the keel—cutting a slim hole 14 feet long right through the heart of the oak, then building around it what boatmen called the trunk to keep out the water—Paxmore had left the keel untouched, as the tradition of his family required, but had cut a hole parallel to it, thus offsetting the boat's centerboard some eight inches to starboard.

"You fool!" Turlock shouted. "It's off center. It'll never . . ."

"Friend," Paxmore said gently, "thy deposit is waiting."

"To hell with our money! We want our boat."

"Thee is not obligated . . ."

"What we might do," Tim suggested, "is take her for a trial." Turlock did not want to do this, lest he like the results, but Paxmore encouraged the idea. Tim had an additional thought: "Suppose we do accept it, damaged though it is. How much reduction in cost?"

"Not one penny," Paxmore said. "This is the finest boat on the Bay, and if truth were told, thee should pay me an extra two hundred."

"Let's give it a trial," Tim pleaded, and he began to haul the mainsail. Every pulley, every rope worked so perfectly that he said, "They're right. A sail like this does raise easier."

No man in his right mind would build a boat with the mainmast so far forward, yet it worked. It was a curious mast: it not only rose from the innards of the boat at a severe angle, so that it appeared almost to be leaning backward, but its top bent forward, producing an arc that seemed certain to break it. The mast thus fought against itself, leaning backward but curving forward, and it was this tension that made it so powerful; from it hung one of the largest sails ever used on a small boat.

They raised the jib, too, then swung the gigantic boom, two feet longer than the boat that supported it, and they could feel the power of the canvas overhead. There was a good breeze, so Caveny and Paxmore moved the skipjack into the middle of the Choptank—Turlock wouldn't touch sail or wheel. She began to lay over to starboard, and the water broke white, and seagulls followed the new craft, and after a long while Turlock muscled his way aft and shoved Caveny away from the wheel.

They christened her the *Jessie T* after Jake's mother, and before she took her first trip oystering, the conventions governing skipjacks were installed: "No color of blue ever to board this boat. No red brick ever to be used as ballast. No walnuts to be eaten. No hatch cover ever to be placed on deck upside down." And because of the extremely low railing and the massiveness of the boom, larger by far than that on any other type of vessel sailing the Chesapeake: "Above all, when you work on deck, mind the boom!"

The *Jessie T* was worked by a crew of six: Capt. Jake Turlock in command of the craft and responsible for her safety; First Mate Tim Caveny, who took care of the money; three Turlocks who manned the oyster dredges; and the most important member, the cook. From the day the boat was planned to the moment when the three Turlocks were hired, there had been only one candidate for cook: a remarkable black man renowned along the Choptank.

Big Jimbo was an unusually tall Negro, son of the slaves Cudjo and Eden Cater. From his father he had learned to read and from his mother to carry himself with fierce pride. He was a gentle man, given to humor, and because of his rare ability with a ship's stove he knew that he was as good as the captain and better than the crew.

He resolved one possible difficulty the instant he came aboard. On a skipjack the three crewmen slept forward in cramped quarters. The captain, cook and mate—in that order—divided the three good bunks aft among themselves, and it had become traditional for the captain to choose the extra-long bunk to the starboard, the cook to take the next best one to port, with the mate getting the somewhat less convenient bunk across the back of the cabin. But on the *Jessie T* things worked out a little differently: one of the Turlocks who should have slept forward was a close cousin of Jake's and he announced that he would sleep aft, because he was sure "the nigger" wouldn't mind berthing in the smaller quarters.

So when Big Jimbo came aboard he found his bunk taken. Without even a second's hesitation, he politely lifted the gear out, placed it on deck and said, "Cain't no man cook if'n he sleeps forward."

He had made a mistake, and a serious one. The gear he had thrown out of the aft cabin was not the intruder's, but Tim Caveny's, the co-owner of the skipjack. When the Turlock had decided to move aft, Tim had seen a chance to promote himself into a better bunk, so he had preëmpted the cook's and had diverted Jake's cousin into the shorter aft bunk. When Tim saw his gear thrown on deck, he started to raise hell, but Big Jimbo said, "Mister Tim, if'n that's yours, I do apologize," and he was more than polite in returning it to the cabin, placing it not in the bunk that Tim had preempted, but in the aft one.

"I sort of thought I'd sleep here," the Irishman said tentatively, pointing to the cook's longer bunk.

"Cook sleeps here," Big Jimbo said, and used his words so sweetly that even the displaced owner was disarmed. Then, before any ill feelings could develop, Jimbo assembled the crew on deck and said, "I brung me some milk and some cream, so we gonna have the world's best arster stew. You want she-stew or he-stew?"

"You cain't tell a she arster from a he," one of the Turlocks said.

"I ain't talkin' about the arsters. I'se talkin' about the eaters." He smiled at the watermen and asked, "What's it to be, she or he?"

"What's the difference?"

"That ain't for you to ask."

"We'll take he."

"Best choice you ever made," Jimbo said, and he disappeared down the hatch to his wood stove.

Jimbo's "she-stew" was the traditional one served throughout the Chesapeake: eight oysters per man, boiled ever so slightly in their own liquor, then simmered in milk and thickened with flour, flavored with a bit of celery, salt and pepper. It was a great opening course but somewhat feeble for workingmen.

A "he-stew" was something quite different and Big Jimbo mumbled to himself as he prepared it: "First we takes a mess of bacon and fries it crisp." As it sizzled he chopped eight large onions and two hefty stalks of celery, holding them back till the bacon was done. Deftly he whisked the bacon out and put it aside, tossing the vegetables into the hot oil to sauté. Soon he withdrew them, too, placing them with the bacon. Then he tossed 48 oysters into the pan, browning them to implant a flavor; quickly he poured in the liquor from the oysters and allowed them to cook until their gills wrinkled.

Now Big Jimbo did the two things that made his he-stew unforgettable. From a precious package purchased from the McCormick Spice Company on the dock in Baltimore, he produced first a paper canister of tapioca powder; taking a small pinch, he tossed it into the milk. Then he added the oysters and vegetables, and crumbled the bacon between his fingers, throwing it on top.

From the McCormick package he next brought out saffron, which he blended into the stew, giving it a golden richness, augmented by the half-pound of butter he threw in at the last moment. This melted as he brought it to the table, producing one of the richest, tastiest stews a marine cook had ever devised.

"Do we eat this good every day?" Caveny asked, and Big Jimbo replied, "You brings me the materials, I brings you the dishes."

Big Jimbo rang his bell, and the men moved below, all but the youngest Turlock; he watched the wheel, standing in front of it as the captain had done.

As in most skipjacks, no one moved a spoon until the cook had taken his place at the small table and reached out his large black hands to grasp those of Captain Turlock and Mate Caveny, whose free hands sought those of the two crewmen. The circle thus having been completed, the five watermen bowed their heads while Captain Turlock uttered the Protestant grace. Then it was Tim Caveny's responsibility to intone the Catholic grace. "Amen," the watermen whispered, and spoons dipped into the golden stew.

3. SHANGHAIED

DREDGING OYSTERS was hard work. The season was divided into halves, October to Christmas when the oysters were plentiful, and January to the end of March, when they were more difficult to harvest. Skipjacks manned by local crews left Patamoke each Monday morning, stayed on the beds all week, returning Saturday night for church services on Sunday. But those boats that had to be staffed by outside crews dared not risk desertions over the weekend; they remained in the Bay three months at a time, living miserably and eating like animals. These boats sold their oysters to larger boats that roamed the Bay, flying empty bushel baskets from their masts to indicate that they were buy-boats, eager to purchase the day's catch for shipment to Baltimore.

When Captain Jake felt that the *Jessie T* was properly positioned over the beds, he ordered Caveny and the three Turlocks to drop the two dredges, one port, one starboard. After these iron-pronged collectors had bounced over the bottom long enough, he tested the wires holding them, calculating whether the load was adequate. When satisfied, he ordered the dredges hauled aboard.

Now the muscle-work began. Port and starboard stood two winches, powered by hand, and around the drum of each, the wire leading to its dredge was wound. Then the men, two to a winch, began turning the heavy iron handles; as the drums revolved, the lines holding the submerged dredges were hauled aboard. Danger came when the iron prongs of the dredge caught in rock, reversing the handle and knocking out men's teeth or breaking their arms. Few watermen ever worked the oyster bars without suffering some damage from reversing handles.

When the dredges finally came aboard, dripping with mud and weed, their cargo was dumped on deck, except when the load was simply too dirty to work; then the men engaged in a maneuver that almost jerked their arms from their sockets. Alternately lowering the dredge into the sea a few feet, and yanking it back, they sloshed the great net up and down until the mud washed free.

Quickly the dredges were emptied onto the deck, then thrown back for another haul. As soon as they were back in the water, the watermen knelt on the deck to begin the sorting; with deft hands well scarred by the sharp edges of oysters, they picked through the mass of dead shell and weed, isolating the living oysters that represented their catch.

Toward the end of each day, Captain Jake began to look for the buy-boat; when it came alongside, the men aboard the *Jessie T* had to work double-fast. Into the iron measuring bucket dropped onto their deck by a boom from the buy-boat they shoveled their catch. Each time the iron bucket rose in the air and returned to the buy-boat, depositing their oysters into its hold, Tim Caveny at the railing would cry, "Tally one!" "Tally two!" and so on until the fifth bucket, when he would shout "Mark one!" Then he would begin again with "Tally one!"

The *Jessie T* worked on shares. The skipjack itself received one third, divided evenly between the two owners, Jake and Tim, but they had to pay for the food, the cordage, the dredges. The captain received a third, which again he had to split with Caveny, who could just as easily have served as leader. And the four crewmen split the remaining third among them, except that Big Jimbo was recognized as such a superior cook that he received a little extra from everyone.

The extraordinary contribution of Big Jimbo was demonstrated one gray February morning when the men were at breakfast, with the youngest Turlock at the wheel. The skipjack was heeling to starboard so that the dishes on the crowded table were sliding, and Captain Jake called up through the cabin door, "All okay up there?"

"All's fine!" the man at the wheel shouted back, but soon thereafter he cried in some alarm, "Cap'm! Very dark clouds!" And then, immediately, "I need help!"

Captain Jake started for the ladder, but Ned Turlock, one of the three sailors, beat him to it. With a hearty bound, the young man leaped up the four steps and made the deck just in time to be struck in the face by the flying boom that had been swept across the deck by a change in the storm's direction. Ned was knocked into the turbulent water and was soon far aft of the skipjack without a lifebelt. Captain Jake, taking command of the wheel, swung the boat about while everyone worked the sails to regain control.

As soon as the skipjack steadied and was on a course that might bring her near the thrashing waterman, Big Jimbo tied a rope about his waist, then asked Tim Caveny to lash smaller ropes about his shoulders as a kind of harness. Then the big cook plunged into the deep, icy waters. His arms thrashed wildly as he tried to stabilize himself, and one of the Turlocks cried, "Hell, he cain't swim neither."

Big Jimbo, kicking his feet and flailing his arms, caught the exhausted man, clutched him to his bosom in a giant embrace and pressed water from his lungs as the men aboard the *Jessie T* pulled on the ropes to drag the two men aboard. At supper that night, when the oysters had been sold and the profits calculated, the six watermen joined hands as Caveny poured out their thanks.

With the near-drowning of Ned Turlock, the suspicion that *Jessie T* might be a bad-luck boat gained so much credence that Captain Jake found it difficult to keep a crew.

When an Eastern Shore skipjack found itself shorthanded, as Jake did after the departure of two Turlocks, it was traditional for the captain to make the decision Captain Jake now made: "Caveny, we sail to Baltimore." With only Big Jimbo to help, they headed across the Bay, past Fort McHenry, where the Star-Spangled Banner had flown that troubled night, and into one of the finest small anchorages in the world, Baltimore's inner harbor.

As the *Jessie T* approached her wharf, Captain Jake warned his companions to be especially alert.

"We may have to pull out of here in a hurry," he said. "Jimbo, you guard the boat while Tim and me goes ashore to tend our business."

As Turlock and Caveny swaggered toward the row of saloons, Jimbo called out, "Good luck, Cap'm. I be waitin'."

There was one saloon, The Drunken Penguin, at which captains on the prowl often had success, so it was natural that the two watermen should head there. "What a fine sign!" Caveny exclaimed, as he saw for the first time the besotted penguin leering at him. Turlock, ignoring the art criticism, banged into the swinging doors with his shoulder and smashed his way into the darkened bar, standing for a moment to survey the familiar scene. When he moved to a table at the rear, two young men who recognized him as an Eastern Shore skipper quietly rose and slipped out a side door.

Later, an Englishman about 24 years old, bleary-eyed, underfed, came in with just enough money for a beer, which entitled him to gorge on the free lunch. Turlock, noting his ravenous appetite, nodded to Caveny, who moved to the bar.

"From the city of Dublin, I'm sure."

"London," the Englishman said.

"None finer in the world, I always say. Would you be offended if I suggested another beer?"

The young man was not disposed to argue about such an invitation, but when the drink was paid for, and the glass stood empty on the bar, he discovered the heavy cost of this courtesy: suddenly he was grabbed from behind by the strong arms of a man he could not see, and his generous friend Timothy Caveny from Dublin was bashing him in the face. When he revived he found himself bound hand and foot in the cabin of a strange boat, with a very large black man standing guard.

Jake and Tim returned to The Drunken Penguin, resumed their seats and waited. After dark, a young man from Boston, waiting for his ship to arrive from New Orleans, came into the bar. The sailor ate two beets, took three gulps of drugged beer and fell flat on the floor. "Grab his feet!" Captain Turlock ordered, and watchers at the bar, who had seen this operation before, stepped back as Jake and Tim lugged their second hand to the *Jessie T.*

The impressed seamen had to work like slaves. They threw the dredges into the water, they pulled them up, they sloshed them when there was mud; they stayed on their knees hours and days at a time picking through the haul; and when the buy-boat came, it was they who shoveled the oysters into the metal buckets.

"When can we go ashore?" the Englishman asked.

"You mean, when can you leave our boat?"

"In a manner of speaking, yes."

"At Christmas, you have my solemn promise," Turlock said. And then, to make the deal binding, he added, "Mr. Caveny will attest to that, won't you, Tim?"

"As sure as the moon rises over Lake Killarney," Caveny assured him, "you'll be off this boat by Christmas."

Two days before that holiday, when the last buy-boat had loaded itself with oysters, Captain Turlock convened his crew in the galley and said brightly, "Jimbo, if one of the lads could fetch you some milk at Deal Island, could you make us a mess of he-stew?"

"I like to," the big cook said, and Turlock studied the two shanghaied crewmen. "You go," he said to the Bostonian. Then, as if changing his mind for some deep philosophical reason, he said to the smaller Englishman, "Better you take the pail. I want to talk wages with this one." So the Englishman grabbed the pail and went on deck.

Caveny, Jimbo and Ned Turlock maneuvered the *Jessie T* into the dock at Deal Island, so that the Englishman could step ashore. While this was underway, Captain Turlock engaged the Boston man in conversation about the money due him.

On deck the others understood why the captain was keeping the Bostonian below, for when the Englishman stepped ashore with his pail, Caveny yelled, "The house at the far end," and as the young man headed toward the village, the Irishman gave a signal, and Ned Turlock at the wheel swung the skipjack away from the dock.

"Hey!" the young man shouted as he saw his boat, and his wages, pull away. "Wait for me!"

There was no waiting. Relentlessly, the oyster boat left the island and the young man standing with his empty pail. He was beached, "paid off with sand," as the watermen said of this common practice, and if he was lucky he could straggle back to Baltimore at the end of two or three weeks, without any chance of ever recovering his wages.

Tim Caveny, watching him standing by the shore, said to his two companions, "I told him he'd be ashore by Christmas."

When the abandoned Englishman could no longer be seen, Captain Turlock bellowed from below, "Mr. Caveny, come down here and pay this man!"

When Caveny appeared in the galley, Turlock said forthrightly, "This man has honest grievances. Calculate every penny we owe him and pay him in full. I want him to remember us with kindness." And he went on deck, where he took the wheel.

With all the Irish charm he could command, Caveny reached for his account books, spread them on the table and assured the Bostonian, "You've worked hard and you've earned every penny," but as he was about to start handing over the cash there was a wild clatter on deck. Noises that could not be deciphered shattered the air and from them came Captain Turlock's agonized cry: "On deck. All hands."

The young sailor from Boston leaped automatically up the companionway, not noticing that the paymaster remained stolidly at the table. Bursting through the cabin door and leaping forward to help in whatever emergency had struck, he arrived on deck just in time to see the massive boom sweeping down on him at incredible speed. He thrust his hands before his face, failed to break the blow and screamed as the thundering boom pitched him wildly into the muddy waves.

Now the four Patamoke men lined the railing and shouted instructions: "You can make it to shore. Just put your feet down and walk."

They were distressed when he flopped and flailed, too terrified by his sudden immersion to control himself. "Just walk ashore!" Captain Turlock bellowed. "It's not deep!"

At last the young fellow understood what the men on the disappearing boat were trying to say. Stumbling and cursing, he gained his footing and started the cold march to Deal Island.

"It's a Christmas he'll never forget," Tim Caveny said as the sailor struggled to safety.

There were now only four to share this season's riches.

4. SHOWDOWN

THE NEXT SEASON, the *Jessie T* crew included a giant German, Otto Pflaum, also shanghaied in The Drunken Penguin. The men of the *Jessie T* came to appreciate how lucky they were to have found big Otto Pflaum when they were confronted by their ancient enemy: boatmen from Virginia encroaching on Maryland waters, even though a compact between the two states clearly reserved those oyster beds for Eastern Shore watermen.

The Virginia men had three advantages: they were more numerous; their boats were bigger than the skipjacks; and they were allowed to use fueled engines while Marylanders were restricted to sail.

They also carried rifles and were not afraid to use them; two Patamoke men had already been killed.

In spite of the fact that Patamoke boats sailed under a constant threat of open warfare, Captain Turlock had been reluctant to arm the *Jessie T.* When the armed Virginia boats began to encroach, he withdrew, content to work the smaller beds inside the Choptank. But his retreat merely emboldened the invaders, and before long they were brazenly aprowl at the mouth of that river.

The Virginians were led by a daring boat whose arrogance was infuriating. It was a large bateau named *Sinbad,* distinguishable for two features. For her figurehead she carried a large, carved roc, the legendary bird with great talons, and the entire boat was painted blue, a color forbidden to skipjacks. The *Sinbad* was formidable.

This winter she challenged the *Jessie T,* almost running her down on a sweep across the beds. "Stand clear, idiot!" the Virginia captain bellowed as he bore down.

"Run into him!" Ned Turlock shouted to his uncle, but the *Sinbad* was much too heavy a boat for such tactics, and prudently the *Jessie T* retreated.

Otto Pflaum had had enough. Storming into the cabin at dusk he shouted: "You don't go into Patamoke, you afraid I jump ship. You don't buy us rifles, you afraid of *Sinbad.* By God, I not no duck, let them others fire at me, bang-bang. I want a gun!"

He got one. Next afternoon, when the *Jessie T* tied up to a Baltimore buy-boat, Captain Jake asked if it had any extra guns for sale, and five were procured, so that on the following morning when the blue-hulled *Sinbad* bore down with her engine at top speed, she found Otto Pflaum standing forward with a repeating rifle that blazed.

Gunfire became commonplace, and Captain Jake was inclined to retreat to protect his boat, but Otto Pflaum and young Ned Turlock would not allow it to be taken off station.

The *Jessie T* became a target for the *Sinbad.* "Move back, you bastards!" the captain of that vessel bellowed as he brought his engine to full speed.

"Don't alter course!" Pflaum shouted.

The skipjack held fast, as Pflaum and Ned Turlock stayed in the bow, blazing away at the invader.

It posed a problem of morality when the time approached to throw Otto overboard. It was a gray day with the wind blowing, as it did so often, from the northwest. The Bay threw muddy spray, and the dredges were stowed port and starboard, having crawled across the bottom for three unbroken months. The oystermen were heading home to divide their spoils.

"All hands!" Captain Turlock shouted as a tremendous clatter echoed on deck.

Later, Caveny confessed: "It could of been my fault. You see, I knew the call was comin', so I didn't react. In a flash Otto saw I had no intention of goin' on deck. So he give me a look I'll never forget, and you know what happened when he reached the deck."

What happened was that Otto knew the boom would swing in upon him; he was ready when it came, grabbed it with his left arm, swung far out over the Bay as it swept past, and with his right hand produced a pistol, which he aimed right at Captain Turlock's head. When he drew even with Jake he said, "I stay in cabin. Alone. You take this boat to harbor. Quick."

Whatever slight reputation the *Jessie T* might have earned by her good oystering was destroyed when Otto Pflaum loudmouthed it in the Patamoke bars that Captain Turlock had tried to drown him and that he, Pflaum, had been forced to capture the skipjack and hold it against five opponents for more than a day.

"Jake botched it," the other watermen said, and none but Ned and Big Jimbo would sail with him.

Normally, Turlock and Caveny would have sailed to Baltimore to shanghai a crew, but they were afraid that Pflaum might be lurking there, so they swallowed their pride and permitted Big Jimbo to sign up some of his friends. Thus the *Jessie T* became the first Patamoke boat to sail with three whites and three blacks; it was a cohesive crew, for Big Jimbo disciplined his recruits, warning them: "You do right, they gonna be lots of black watermen. You mess around, no niggers never gonna see inside of a skipjack."

Soon afterward, two skipjack captains sailed into Patamoke with the superstructures of their boats chopped up: "We was drudgin' proper in our waters off'n Oxford when the Virginians swept in, *Sinbad* leadin'. They like to shot us clean outa the water."

On Monday morning the *Jessie T* sailed out of Patamoke with a grim crew. All six men were armed, and Big Jimbo assured Captain Jake that his two black sailors were first-class squirrel hunters. If there was to be battle, the skipjack was ready.

But she was hardly prepared for what the Virginians did. Four of their power-driven boats lay off the point of Tilghman Island, and as the *Jessie T* moved down the Choptank, these adversaries, led by the *Sinbad,* moved in upon her, judging that if they could knock Jake Turlock out of the river, they would have little trouble with the rest of the fleet.

It was a most uneven fight. Captain Jake stayed at the wheel, while his five crewmen, including Big Jimbo, stationed themselves along the rail. The Patamoke men fought well but the invading boats were too swift, the gunfire too concentrated.

On one pass, bullets ripped into the stern of the *Jessie T,* and Captain Turlock would have been killed had he not dropped ignominiously to the deck. Infuriated, he bellowed for Ned to take the wheel, while he crouched behind one of the dredges to fire at the *Sinbad.*

At this moment one of the Virginia boats swept in from the port side and rained a blizzard of bullets at the skipjack. Jake, kneeling behind the dredge, saw one of Big Jimbo's men spin in the air, lose his rifle overboard and fall in a pool of blood.

"Christ a'mighty!" Jake cried, forgetting his own safety and rushing forward, but as he did so, sailors from the blue *Sinbad* fired at the wheel, thinking to gun down the captain. Instead, they hit Ned Turlock, who fell to one knee, clutched at the wheel, sent the skipjack turning in a circle and died.

GLOOM WAS DEEP upon the Choptank as its watermen studied what they must do to repel the invasion from Virginia.

It was crafty little Tim Caveny who devised the tactic whereby they could punish the *Sinbad,* and it was so bizarre and daring that when Jake heard it, his jaw dropped: "You think we could handle it?"

"Positive," Tim said.

The two watermen fell silent as each reviewed the strategy and finally Jake said, hesitantly, "What we really need . . ."

"Don't tell me," Caveny broke in. "Otto Pflaum."

"The same. And I'm gonna swallow my pride and go fetch him."

They crossed to Baltimore, going straight to The Drunken Penguin.

"Otto, sit down and talk with us," Caveny pleaded.

"You want to hire me again?"

"Yes!" the Irishman said eagerly.

"Same wages as before? A swingin' boom?"

"Otto, you misunderstood . . ." Caveny was eager to explain that a failure in communication had been responsible.

"We need your help," Turlock said. "The Virginians. They're drivin' us from the Bay."

Turlock had said the only words that could have excited this giant. Pflaum had seen the arrogant *Sinbad* and had fought against her, so he relished the prospect of renewed combat.

"This time, no boom?"

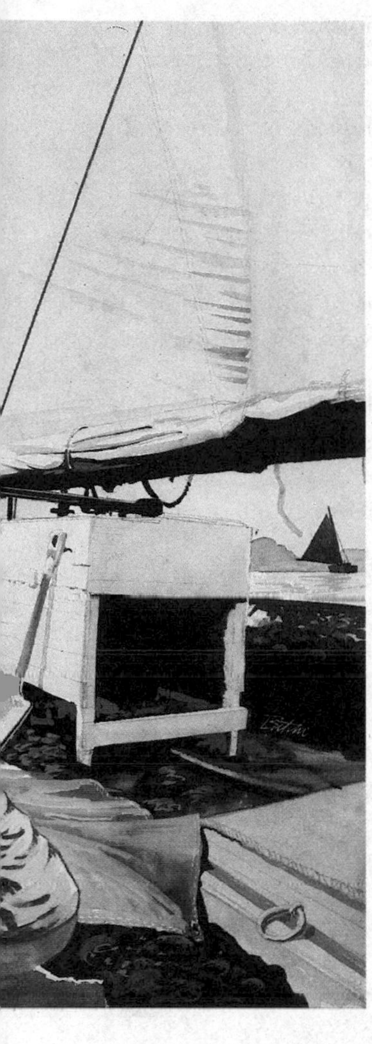

"There was none last time," Caveny said gravely. "A sudden wind."

"This time, I want my pay before I leave Baltimore."

This was agreed, and the *Jessie T* returned to Patamoke for the unusual fitting out that Jake and Tim had contrived.

When Otto Pflaum saw the magnitude of the big gun that Jake proposed for the bow he was staggered: "That's a cannon." Jake said nothing, merely pointed to the small cannonballs intended for the gun, and before Pflaum could comment, Jake showed him three more long guns, several kegs of black powder, and larger kegs of lead pellets. He also showed him three batteries of seven shotguns each that Tim Caveny had linked together so they could be fired nearly simultaneously.

"What you tryin' to do, destroy the *Sinbad?*" Otto Pflaum asked.

"Exactly," Jake said grimly.

"Should I aim at the cabin?"

"Aim at the waterline," Jake said. "I'm going to sink her."

Two days passed without incident. On the third day the ominous blue *Sinbad* entered the Choptank. As expected, the Virginia boat drove the smaller skipjacks off, then came directly at the *Jessie T.*

The first fire came from the *Sinbad.* When its crew saw that the *Jessie T* was not going to back off, their captain cried, "Give them another whiff." Shots ricocheted about the deck.

"Not yet!" Jake called, and his men stood firm while the *Sinbad* grew careless and moved closer. Jake caught the eye of Otto Pflaum, finger on the great gun once owned by the master hunter, Greef Twombly.

"Now!" he shouted, and from the entire port side of the skipjack a blaze of powder exploded, sending a devastating rain of lead across the decks of the *Sinbad* and punishing her at the waterline. Those Virginians who were not knocked down were so confounded that they could not regroup before Tim unleashed another shotgun volley at them, while Otto Pflaum leaped to a second long gun and fired it right at the gaping hole opened by his first.

The *Sinbad,* mortally wounded, started to roll on its port side and its crew began leaping into the water and shouting for help.

With grand indifference the *Jessie T* withdrew from the battle.

It was a triumphal return, such as few naval centers have witnessed, for the victorious vessel came to the dock laden with oysters, and, as Tim Caveny called out details of the battle, Otto Pflaum counted the iron buckets as buyers on dock hauled them ashore: "Tally three! Tally four! Mark one!"

But the *Jessie T* had earned more that day than 198 bushels of oysters. It had won the right to say that the riches of the Choptank would be harvested in a responsible manner.

The victory of the Choptank men led to a series of events that no one could have imagined even four years earlier.

The fact that Captain Turlock used three whites and three blacks meant he could make up the crew locally and berth each weekend at Patamoke. This allowed him and Tim Caveny to go duck hunting with such results that the two watermen accumulated surplus income in the local bank.

Since Jake Turlock had grown sick and tired of hearing the men at the store downgrade his boat, he decided to get rid of her and buy the partnership a real boat with its centerboard where it ought to be.

When the contract between Paxmore and the Turlock/Caveny partnership was drawn—"a first-class skipjack with centerboard trunk through the keel, $2815"—Gerrit Paxmore asked the owners of the *Jessie T* what they intended doing with their present skipjack, and Turlock growled, "I suppose we'll find a buyer somewheres." Paxmore replied, "I think I can take it off thy hands," and Caveny asked, "You got a buyer?" and Paxmore replied, "I think so," but he would not divulge who it was.

The new skipjack was superior in every way to the *Jessie T.* After a couple of trial runs out into the Bay, Jake and Tim concluded that they had bought themselves a masterpiece.

But when Jake went to Frog's Neck to advise Jimbo that the new skipjack would be sailing on Monday, he found to his dismay that the big cook would not be assuming his old place.

"Why not?" Jake thundered.

"Because . . ." The tall black was too embarrassed to explain, and

Turlock heckled him, charging cowardice because of the gunfight, a lack of loyalty to his crew mates and ingratitude. Big Jimbo listened impassively, then said in a soft voice, "Cap'm Jake, I'm takin' out my own skipjack."

"You're what?"

"Mr. Paxmore done sold me the *Jessie T.*"

The information staggered the waterman. "You buyin' my boat?"

"Yes, sir. From the day I could walk, my daddy tol' me, 'Git yourse'f a boat. When a man got his own boat, he free.'"

"Hell, Jimbo, you don't know enough to captain a skipjack."

"I been watchin', Cap'm Jake. I been watchin' you, and you one o' the best."

Jake slapped his flank and said, "All the time you was on deck, doin' extry work to help the men, you was watchin' ever'thing I was doin'." He burst into laughter. "But you got to change her name."

Big Jimbo had anticipated him. When he and Captain Jake went to Paxmore's to inspect the refitted *Jessie T,* they found the old name painted out and in its place a new board with the simple letters *Eden.*

In October 1895 the skipjack *Eden* out of Patamoke made its first sortie on the oyster beds.

When the black crew began to unload huge quantities of oysters into the buy-boats, the Bay might have been outraged but not really surprised. Then Randy Turlock, a nephew of Captain Jake's, signed up as a member of the *Eden's* crew, which now consisted of five blacks and one white.

On shore, relations between whites and blacks did not duplicate what prevailed in the skipjacks. When oyster dredging, a waterman was judged solely on his performance. But when he stepped ashore this camaraderie stopped. The black oysterman could not join the circle at the store, nor send his children to the white man's school, nor pray in a white church.

The permanent relationship between the two races was underlined at the start of the century when a gang of venal Democratic politicians in Annapolis proposed an amendment, aimed at blacks, to the Maryland constitution. Under the provisions of the amendment, not only was a literacy test required, but eligibility to vote was based on whether a person had voted before 1869, or was a lineal descendant of someone who had.

Residents along the Choptank were almost universally opposed to black franchise, and this illustrated a singular change that was modifying Eastern Shore history: during the Civil War well over half the Choptank men who had served did so in the Union Army, but now when their descendants looked back upon that war they claimed that well over 95 percent had fought with the Confederacy. The reasons behind this self-deception were simple: "No man could have pride in havin' fought for the North, side by side with niggers. My pappy was strictly Southern." Patamoke families were proud if an ancestor had marched with Lee or ridden with Jeb Stuart; ashamed if he had served with Grant, and it became common for families to lie about past affiliations. Because of this selective memory, the Eastern Shore converted itself into one of the staunchest Southern areas and people were apt to say, "Our ancestors had slaves and fought to keep 'em. Emancipation was the worst evil ever to hit this land." It was these belated Southerners, egged on by plantation families whose ancestors had honestly sided with the South, who now united to keep blacks from their schools and churches; they joined in mobs to discipline them when they became fractious; and gleefully they combined to adopt this amendment that would rescind the right to vote. The only people who opposed the new law were the Quaker Paxmores and recent immigrants, alarmed that it would deprive them also of their franchise. In the end, the proposal lost. Blacks could continue to vote.

In August 1906, when the two watermen were in their grizzled 60s, Caveny came running to the store with exciting news: "Jake, I think we got us a contract to haul watermelons to Baltimore." This was important news, for oystermen spent their summer months scrounging for commissions that would keep their skipjacks busy; the shallow-drafted boats carried too little freeboard to qualify them for entering the ocean.

So the watermen prayed for a cargo of farm produce to Baltimore and a load of fertilizer back or coal to Norfolk, or pig iron from the blast furnaces north of Baltimore. Best of all was a load of watermelons from far up some river, for then, with a crew of three, the skipjack could earn real money, passing back and forth across the oyster beds it had worked during the winter.

With their windfall profits, the two watermen trekked to the Rennert for a duck dinner, then visited Otto Pflaum and his wife, loaded up with fertilizer and sailed for home. As they quit the harbor they chanced to find themselves at the center of a triangle formed by three luxurious Bay steamers, now lighted with electricity, and they admired the scintillating elegance of these fine vessels as they set out to penetrate the rivers coming into the Bay.

"Look at 'em go!" Jake cried as the vessels went their individual ways, their orchestras sending soft music over the water. For most of an hour the Choptank men regarded them almost enviously.

The oystermen could not have imagined that the large, gaudy steamers would one day disappear entirely from this Bay. But not the quiet little skipjack. It would endure when everything on the Bay that night had gone to rust, for it was generic, born of the salt flats and heavy dredging, while the brightly lighted steamers were commercial innovations useful for the moment but bearing little relation to the timeless Bay.

"They disappear mighty fast," Caveny said as the lights merged with the waves.

Now the watermen were alone on the Bay, and before long the low profile of the Eastern Shore began to rise in the moonlight, a unique configuration of marshland and wandering estuaries. "We really have the land of pleasant living," Turlock mused as his skipjack drifted in the night air, but when they approached Devon Island he fixed his gaze at the western end of the island, where a multitude of trees lay wallowing in the tide.

"I never noticed that before," he said. "That island's gonna wash clean away, one of these storms."

The watermen inspected the erosion, and Caveny said, "I read in a book that all our land on the Eastern Shore is alluvial."

"What's that?" Turlock asked suspiciously.

"Land thrown here by the Susquehanna, when it was 50 times as big. You know, Jake, I think long after we're dead there ain't gonna be no Eastern Shore. The land we know will wash into the ocean."

"How soon?" Jake asked.

"Ten thousand years."

Neither man spoke. They were sailing over oyster beds for which they had fought, beds whose icy catch had numbed their hands and cut their fingers, bringing blood to their frozen mittens. Beyond that spit barely visible in the night, the *Laura Turner* had capsized, six men lost. Over there the *Wilmer Dodge* had foundered, six men gone. Around the next headland, where ducks rafted in winter, they had driven off the invaders from Virginia.

Softly the skipjack entered the Choptank. Jake's third-generation Chesapeake patrolled the bow ready to repel invaders, but Caveny had a Labrador that lay prone on the deck, close to Tim's ankle, dark eyes staring up at the Irishman in boundless love.

THE LUSITANIA

CONDENSED FROM THE BOOK BY

COLIN SIMPSON

ILLUSTRATED BY C. G. EVERS

On May 7, 1915, the British ocean liner *Lusitania,* the largest and fastest passenger ship of her time, was torpedoed by a German submarine off the south coast of Ireland. The great vessel, described as a floating palace, sank within 20 minutes. Of the 1198 persons who lost their lives, 128 were Americans, among them millionaire Alfred Gwynne Vanderbilt and producer Charles Frohman. The sinking triggered a storm of indignation in the United States and became a major factor in hastening America's entry into World War I.

Was the *Lusitania* an "unarmed" passenger ship as claimed? Or was she not only armed but carrying a cargo of munitions and contraband for Britain and therefore a legitimate war target?

Here is the startling truth about one of the most fateful of all disasters of the sea.

"Simpson has peered long and deep into murky waters . . . for a book that clamors to be read," reported the *London Observer.*

1. GREYHOUND OF THE SEAS

THE OLD HEAD OF KINSALE is a steep and rocky promontory which juts aggressively into the Atlantic Ocean from the southwest coast of Ireland. On its crest are a lighthouse, a coast-guard station and the ruins of an early Celtic settlement. For 2000 years it has been an essential landmark for those at sea. Behind it lies the sleepy fishing port of Kinsale, swollen each summer by tourists and yachtsmen. There is little to do there but talk, and any conversation eventually turns to the British liner *Lusitania,* torpedoed nearby during World War I with the loss of 1198 lives. Equally inevitable is the legend that the great liner, which now lies 300 feet down on the granite and current-swept bottom of the Atlantic, 12 miles south of the Old Head, was loaded with bullion.

My first inquiries into the *Lusitania* disaster stemmed from the mistaken notion that here was a classic tale of sunken treasure. The obvious starting point was to discover the manifest of the *Lusitania's* last cargo. There had been two formal inquiries into the disaster, first in London, then in New York, and at each the manifest would have been an exhibit. A third manifest was held by the Cunard Line. I located all three of these documents, and found all three to be different. The problem was: What did the original manifest say?

A carbon copy of the original was found among the private papers of the late President Franklin D. Roosevelt, and I obtained a duplicate. That discovery and the circumstances as to how and why President Roosevelt had obtained the document proved the starting point of this book. I did not tell either the British Admiralty or the U.S. State Department that I had it, but asked them for access to all their records relating to the *Lusitania.* They courteously gave their permission.

Both sets of archives contain meager information, and have substantial differences of fact. In many cases it is difficult to accept that the files relate to the same vessel. However, the two collections of documents both agree in their conclusions. These form the basis of the official or authorized version of the *Lusitania* affair, which was published as a small booklet in October 1915. It would be unjust not to quote from it:

"Ever since 1840, the Cunard Steam Ship Company Limited has been intimately associated with the British Government. In 1902, the Company arranged to build two large steamers, to hold at the disposal of the Government the whole of its fleet and to remain a purely British undertaking. The outcome of this agreement was the building of the world-famous ocean leviathans, the *Lusitania* and *Mauretania.*

"On September 7, 1907, the *Lusitania* sailed from Liverpool to New York on her maiden voyage; and it is no exaggeration to say that never before had such widespread interest been taken in the first sailing of any liner. Fully 200,000 people witnessed her departure. Her reception on the other side of the Atlantic was just as hearty, a whole fleet of tugs and pleasure steamers greeting her.

"From the first, the *Lusitania* became a great favourite with Atlantic travelers, and no wonder, for in addition to her speed, she was so luxuriously appointed that her passenger accommodation was the acme of comfort, and well merited the description of a 'floating palace.'

"On her second westbound trip she averaged 24 knots, and reduced the passage between Liverpool and New York to well under five days, bringing back to the British mercantile service the 'Blue Riband of the Atlantic'. . . .

"And now we come to the last phase of her career. Although the War broke out in August 1914, and the British Government, according to its agreement with the Company in 1902, could have requisitioned the *Lusitania,* she was never actually in Government Service but maintained her regular place amongst Cunard sailings.

"On May 1, 1915, the *Lusitania* left New York for Liverpool. Prior to the sailing, threatening statements were published in the American Press by German authorities foretelling the sinking of the liner; but in the words of Lord Mersey, who subsequently conducted the Inquiry into the loss of the vessel: 'So far from affording any excuse, the threats serve only to aggravate the crime by making it plain that the intention to commit it was deliberately formed, and the crime itself planned before the ship sailed.'

The largest ship afloat arrives in New York on her maiden voyage in 1907

"On 7th May, the Irish Coast was sighted, and at 2:10 p.m. the liner was within 8 to 10 miles of the Old Head of Kinsale. Without the slightest warning, the wake of a torpedo from a German submarine was seen approaching the ship, and she was struck between the third and fourth funnels. There was evidence that a second, and perhaps a third, torpedo was fired, and the great ship sank within 20 minutes.

"It is impossible to satisfactorily draw a pen picture of the heart-rending scenes which followed. Men, women and children, caught like rats in a trap, were vainly fighting for their lives amongst wreckage of every description. The doomed liner's S.O.S. was answered within a few hours of the call, and 761 lives were saved. Still, the Hunnish pirates had performed their task, proving to the civilized world that the whole gamut of barbarism had been exhausted in the interest of German Kultur. The Belgian atrocities, poisoning of wells, and asphyxiating gases—all these dwarfed to insignificance in the face of the foulest act of willful murder ever committed on the high seas.

"It was only to be expected that the enemy would attempt to justify his heinous work by proclaiming that the vessel was armed. By wireless, and through his own newpapers, the enemy made this foul and diabolical charge. This was proved to be totally unfounded. . . . Another German lie exposed!

"The *Lusitania* today lies at the bottom of the sea—her name will be a lasting monument to the atrocities of a race steeped in savagery, and whose lust for blood knew no bounds."

STRIPPED OF ITS bellicose statements, this account accurately reflects the public beliefs of the British Admiralty and the American State Department as to what did happen and why—beliefs that they share to this very day.

But now six years of sifting the accumulated records have convinced me that the "official" version contains remarkable gaps, omissions, contradictions and inaccuracies. There is, in fact, evidence that the whole *Lusitania* incident sparked a monumental exercise in political cynicism, motivated at the outset by arrogance and ignorance, and after the disaster by a desire for personal and political survival. It is important to remember in this regard that on her last voyage the *Lusitania* carried among her passengers 197 Americans. Most perished with her. The disaster therefore concerned neutral United States as well as belligerent Britain. It was, in fact, the first and most dramatic of the events which led to eventual U.S. entry into World War I.

The *Lusitania* was built to be the largest and fastest ship of her time, and her design had a great deal to do with the ultimate tragedy. For some 100 years the Admiralty had subsidized the major passenger-ship companies, and in return had the right in wartime to call up certain vessels for use as transports or auxiliary cruisers. In the case of the *Lusitania* and *Mauretania,* the Admiralty agreed to finance the building costs, plus an annual operating subsidy of £75,000 each, if the Cunard Line would construct two ships which could achieve a constant 25 knots in moderate weather and be capable of mounting substantial armament. (At that time the fastest transatlantic ship ever built was the German liner *Kaiser Wilhelm II,* with engines of 38,000 h.p. producing 23½ knots. To generate the extra knot, the *Lusitania* would require an additional 30,000 h.p.—68,000 h.p. in all.)

Thus, the requirements that the Cunard directors presented to Leonard Peskett, their chief designer, were formidable. He had to fulfill the Admiralty specifications without deviation. The ship would carry more than 2000 guests and a staff of about 800. Yet, to obtain the needed speed, Peskett had to fit everything into a waterline length of 760 feet and a maximum beam of 88 feet. This narrow beam entailed building higher than anyone had ever built a ship before.

All engines, boilers, fuel and vital controls had to be placed below the waterline, as was standard practice in warships. Each of four vast boiler rooms was built as a separate watertight compartment; to give the buoyancy desired, a watertight compartment was fitted down each side of the ship, flanking the boilers and machinery.

Since engines, boilers and the two longitudinal watertight compartments totally filled the below-water-line space, no place was left for the 6600 tons of coal needed to power the ship from Liverpool to New York. To meet the Admiralty specifications, and because no one at the time knew any better, it was decided that the longitudinal compartments would be used to store the coal.

But with coal in the watertight compartments, openings had to be cut into their bases for access to the fuel. These apertures were fitted with watertight hatches which were controlled by the stokers. Anybody who has ever drawn coal from a domestic coal bunker will know the extreme difficulty of closing the hatch: the weight of the coal inside, plus the accumulation of dust and fine scraps of coal, precludes an efficient closure.

Peskett made a series of calculations, and found that with one bunker hatch open to the sea the ship would list seven degrees. With two hatches open, she would list at least 15 degrees. With more than two flooded, she was unlikely to float.

By modern standards, this inherent instability would never be acceptable, but there were even more compromises to be made. Peskett had been forced to build high. On top of the "power platform" he raised six decks—A to F, reading from top to bottom. The ship's lifeboats were suspended above deck A. When swung out for lowering, they cleared the edge of the deck by 18 inches. It apparently did not occur to anyone that if the ship listed even slightly, it would be impossible to launch the boats on the "high" side, short of sliding them down the *Lusitania's* side.

Less sinister, but equally worrying, was that the boats on the "low" side would swing outward from the side, and with the same slight list would hang seven feet from the edge of the deck, with a sheer drop of 60 feet to the water below.

But criticism with the benefit of hindsight is doubtless unfair. The *Lusitania's* size inspired confidence from the start. She was longer than the Capitol in Washington, D.C., and a stroll around the promenade (B) deck was marginally over a quarter of a mile. This height, length and distinctive narrowness of beam inspired the description "Greyhound of the Seas," and for several years the *Lusitania* and *Mauretania* were *the* crack liners of the North Atlantic seaway.

2. THE LIVE-BAIT SQUADRON

On February 19, 1913, Alfred Booth, Cunard's chairman, presented himself on request to the Board of Admiralty. The First Lord, 38-year-old Winston Churchill, left Booth in no doubt that there was likely to be a war with Germany soon. Therefore, he expressed a wish that the *Lusitania* and *Mauretania* be modified forthwith so that if hostilities should break out, they could, without any delay, take up their role as armed cruisers.

Under strict secrecy, the *Lusitania* entered dry dock at Liverpool on May 12. Cunard announced that she was being temporarily withdrawn from service to have the latest design of turbines installed. What actually was done is well documented in the Cunard archives. Between two of the decks—for a height of 14½ feet—the entire length of the vessel was double-plated. A reserve coal bunker was converted to a magazine, and special shell racking and handling elevators were installed. Two revolving gun rings for 6-inch quick-firing guns were mounted on the forecastle and two on the afterdeck. Deck C was adapted to take four 6-inch guns on either side, making a total complement of 12 guns. All that remained was to lower a gun onto each ring and secure 12 bolts.

The *Lusitania* returned to the New York service on July 21, and on March 16, 1914, a proud Churchill announced to the House of Commons that 40 British merchant ships had been defensively armed.

Britain declared war on Germany on August 4, 1914—just as the *Lusitania* was about to leave New York. Immediately on her arrival at Liverpool she was handed over to the Admiralty and moved into dry dock to have her guns installed. On September 17 she entered the fleet register as an armed auxiliary cruiser, and was so recorded on the Cunard ledgers.

But on the same date circumstances suddenly overturned the Admiralty's plans. Just as the ship became operational, Churchill went to visit the Grand Fleet, which was moored at Loch Ewe, a remote but magnificent anchorage in northwest Scotland. There he had an opportunity to talk informally with Commodore Roger Keyes, one of the navy's most promising officers.

Keyes was extremely concerned about the Royal Navy's *Bacchante*-class cruisers, which had unarmored longitudinal compartments much like the *Lusitania's*. A month earlier, the Admiralty had ordered that any warships so constructed were on no account to be exposed to submarine attack or to play offensive roles without suitable escorts. And yet, Keyes pointed out, no fewer than four of the *Bacchante* class were steadily patrolling the North Sea and had been doing so every day since the outbreak of war. They were in a most exposed and dangerous situation. The fleet, he informed the First Lord, had christened them "the Live-Bait Squadron."

Churchill was horrified. The following day, on his return to the Admiralty, he promptly ordered the patrol discontinued. However, the Admiralty war staff took its time and, pending the transfer of the *Bucchante* squadron, sent three of the cruisers to patrol close to the Dutch coast.

September 21 saw Churchill in Liverpool. The *Lusitania* was alongside the dock. Churchill and Peskett, the ship's designer, looked at her towering above them. Churchill mentioned the shortcomings of the *Bacchante* class, and questioned Peskett closely on the Cunarder's bulkhead layout and stability. Peskett reassured him: "The navy hasn't anything like her."

Churchill mumbled a reply which was to haunt him. "We have. To me she is just another 45,000 tons of live bait.

Shortly after dawn the following day, one of the three *Bacchante*-class cruisers off the Dutch coast was torpedoed by a German submarine. She capsized almost immediately and sank in 25 minutes. Chivalrously her companions steamed to the scene, and both suffered immediate and similar fates: more than 1400 men were drowned.

The *Bacchante*-class disaster dramatically reversed the Admiralty's attitude toward submarines. Hitherto, Churchill and many of the senior staff of the Admiralty had tended to disregard the U-boats. Now it became plain that if a submarine could sink a cruiser, she could play havoc with vital British trade routes.

The Admiralty had always considered that a merchant vessel should be treated by a submarine in exactly the same way as by a marauding cruiser. Briefly: it was correct practice to halt an unarmed merchant ship by a shot across the bow, search it and, if it were a neutral, let it go.

If it were a belligerent, both the crew and passengers would become hostages, and the cargo and ship would be taken as prizes. These principles, known as the Cruiser Rules, had been accepted with minor modifications by all maritime powers. They applied, however, to *unarmed* merchantmen.

Churchill's action in arming British merchant ships in 1913 stripped them of the right to expect such treatment. Belatedly, it was realized that no submarine would now dare to undertake the dangerous practice of surfacing and ordering an armed ship to halt and submit to search. Even if a submarine were to do this successfully, what was it to do with the crew, passengers and prize?

The first thought for submarine defense was a boom designed to stretch across the Channel, hung with nets and festooned with mines. It was a costly failure and abandoned. The only answer was intensive patrolling and the use of mines, and so a new system was devised which spoke only too eloquently of a navy which had not seen a major action since Trafalgar.

A coastal yacht and motorboat patrol was established, and teams of two swimmers were put aboard each launch. One man carried a black bag, the other a hammer. If a periscope was sighted, the boat would cruise as near to it as possible; then the swimmers would dive in, seize the periscope, and after one man had placed the black bag over it, the other would attempt to shatter the glass with his hammer. Another brainstorm was to attempt to train sea gulls to defecate on periscopes, and for a short while a remote corner of a harbor in Dorset was littered with dummy periscopes and incontinent gulls.

Churchill, for all his love of the unorthodox, was among the first to diagnose that booms, black bags and sea gulls were not an effective counter to the submarine. Instead, he devised an ingenious and subtle strategy. In his autobiographical account of World War I, *The World Crisis,* he wrote: "The maneuver which brings an ally into the field is as serviceable as that which wins a great battle."

Essentially, the problem facing the Admiralty was that the only maritime power in the world of any account not engaged in the conflict was the United States, which day by day became more indispensable as a bountiful source of supply. And so from October 1914 onward a steady stream of inflammatory orders was issued to the masters of British merchant ships. At their discretion, masters could engage a threatening U-boat, either with their armament if they possessed it, or by ramming if they did not.

The World Crisis identifies the strategy: "The submerged U-boat had to rely increasingly on underwater attack and thus ran the greater risk of mistaking neutral for British ships and of drowning neutral crews and thus embroiling Germany with other Great Powers."

To encourage such mistakes, the Admiralty advised all British ships to paint out their port of registry, and when in British waters to fly a neutral flag. On the orders sent to Cunard is the manuscript annotation, "Pass the word around that the flag to use is the American."

British naval vessels were also ordered to treat the crews of captured U-boats as felons, and not to accord them the status of prisoners of war. The introduction of "mystery" or Q-ships—seemingly unarmed merchantmen carrying concealed armament and a naval crew dressed as civilians—was planned in September 1914. By February 1915, Churchill had endorsed the policy, and "mystery" ships went into operation. He personally drafted their orders, and those that related to prisoners were symptomatic of his ruthless policy designed to escalate and inflame the war at sea. "Survivors," wrote the First Lord, "should be taken prisoner or shot—whichever is the most convenient."

Meanwhile, to keep the trade routes open, the role of the armed liners was altered. They offered a swift method of bringing crucial supplies from the United States, and with their speed and armament should be immune to the unforeseen peril of the U-boat.

The new plan for the *Lusitania* was explained to Alfred Booth by the Secretary of the Admiralty, Sir William Graham Greene, in the smoking room of the Reform Club on the evening of October 3, 1914. Cunard, Booth was told, would be required to operate the *Lusitania* and other ships on a high-speed service between Liverpool and New York. The *Lusitania's* guns would be removed, but her cargo space was to be held at the disposal of the Admiralty. Any cargo space—or accommodation—not required by the authorities could be utilized by the company but, in the case of eastbound cargo, only with the permission of the Admiralty staff stationed in New York.

Booth was flabbergasted. He was later to write to his cousin, George Booth: "In essence, Sir William took me into *my own club* and ordered me to be a high-grade 'contrabandist' in the National Interest."

ON JANUARY 30, 1915, the German submarine U-21 appeared off the Lancashire coast, and in one afternoon sank three unarmed merchant ships. No lives were lost, as in each case the U-21 surfaced, challenged the ships, gave the crew ample time to take to their boats and then destroyed the ships by placing bombs on board. Aboard the third victim, the 3000-ton merchant ship *Ben Cruachan,* the U-21 captured a complete set of Admiralty orders, including the instructions to ram and to fly a neutral flag.

This discovery sparked an immediate backlash. Several submarines had narrowly escaped disaster from attempts to ram, and feelings among the U-boat commanders were running hot. The German officers prepared a memorandum urging that U-boats also abandon Cruiser Rules and attack all Allied merchantmen without giving any warning.

German public and press opinion also demanded retaliation against British measures, including the naval blockade, begun early in the war, whose effects were starting to be felt. In fact, rationing of cereals, milk and flour had been introduced just the previous week.

On February 4, the German government formally announced its decision: "The waters surrounding Great Britain and Ireland including the whole English Channel are hereby declared to be comprised within the war zone." (The North Sea had been so declared by the British three months previously.)

When this proclamation was formally presented to the U.S. State Department, Secretary of State William Jennings Bryan was away on a speaking trip, and the German note was received in his absence by his deputy, Robert M. Lansing.

Lansing, tall, urbane, ambitious, clearly favored England and the Allies in the war; he habitually wore tweeds and took elocution lessons to develop an English accent. Despite the United States' publicly declared policy of "strict neutrality," he had already been instrumental in helping to obtain loans from American banks on Britain's behalf.

He reacted belligerently to the German proclamation, and produced a draft reply. It did not respond to a German suggestion that the American government should warn Americans not to seek passage on Allied ships, and Secretary Bryan, on his return, protested angrily at this omission. Nonetheless, Lansing's opinion prevailed.

To maintain a semblance of impartiality, a sharp note went to Britain simultaneously with the reply to Germany, complaining of the use by English ships of the American flag. The British Foreign Office blandly replied that neither the government nor the Admiralty had sanctioned such action. This was the diplomatic lie direct, and Lansing must have known it, since the German proclamation had enclosed photographs of the Admiralty instructions that the U-21 had captured. He had ignored them and had not mentioned them to either Bryan or President Wilson.

The American note to Germany contained this passage:

"If the commanders of German vessels of war should act upon a presumption that the flag of the United States was not being used in good faith and should destroy on the high seas an American vessel or the lives of American citizens, it would be difficult for the government of the United States to view the act in any other light than as an indefensible violation of neutral rights." In such a situation, Germany would be held to "a strict accountability."

This concept that any Allied ship, even an armed munitions carrier, should be immune to attack if it carried a single American aboard was in fact a warning to Germany that such an attack risked war with the United States—a view that astounded the Germans as much as it delighted the British. Churchill's policy of embroiling Germany with neutral powers was obviously succeeding.

In the next few weeks, U-boats sank 25 merchant ships. Sixteen of these were torpedoed without warning, and 52 crewmen (out of 712) lost their lives. But the 25 doomed ships also carried 3072 passengers, and not one of them was killed.

Then on March 28, acting under Cruiser Rules, the U-28 stopped the cargo and passenger liner *Falaba.* Two extensions of the time limit for disembarkation were granted. An armed British trawler, summoned by the *Falaba,* came to the scene. The U-28 promptly put a torpedo into the *Falaba,* and her cargo, which included 13 tons of high explosives, blew up. Among the casualties was an American citizen.

The American press reacted with fury. The public version of events was that little or no warning had been given and that the torpedoing had been a cold-blooded and wanton act of destruction. The true nature of the cargo was vigorously denied.

Lansing insisted that a hard line be taken with Germany. Bryan, after investigating, disagreed, and the President decided that in this case a hard line was "perhaps not necessary." But the handwriting was on the wall.

In New York, a group of worried German-Americans met. "Sooner or later," said George Viereck, editor of the pro-German, English-language newspaper *The Fatherland,* "some big passenger boat with Americans on board will be sunk by a submarine; then there will be hell to pay."

One of the men asked the departure date of the next great English passenger liner. It was the *Lusitania,* due to sail in ten days, on May 1.

Viereck shouted, "Then publish a warning before she sails!"

Viereck left the meeting authorized to insert a suitable notice in any 50 newspapers of his choice. He planned it to appear on Friday, April 23, to give it at least a week's exposure before the *Lusitania* sailed. Seven days' publicity and debate, he believed, would allow passengers ample time to change their minds about traveling on the ship. He drafted the wording in his office and, when he had finished, telephoned Capt. Franz von Papen, military attaché at the German embassy in Washington, to explain its import.

Von Papen approved the text and unofficially suggested that, instead of signing it "The German Committee of New York," it should be signed "The Imperial German Embassy." He explained that under U.S. law the advertiser could be subject to damages for libel and for causing loss of business to British shipping companies. But if the German embassy could deny that it was the real author of the text, then all would be well.

The advertisement, together with an appropriate check, went that night to each of the 50 papers Viereck had selected, and was delivered by hand to the New York papers so that it would not miss the April 23 deadline. The advertisement read:

> NOTICE!
>
> Travellers intending to embark on the Atlantic voyage are reminded that a state of war exists between Germany and Great Britain; that the zone of war includes the waters adjacent to the British Isles; that vessels flying the flag of Great Britain, or of any of her allies, are liable to destruction in those waters and that travellers sailing in the war zone on ships of Great Britain or her allies do so at their own risk.
>
> IMPERIAL GERMAN EMBASSY
> WASHINGTON, D.C.

The advertisement reached the New York *Sun* shortly before midnight and, since the advertising department was closed, the envelope, marked URGENT, was brought to the night news editor. Scenting a story, he telephoned the State Department for advice. The duty officer there suggested that the *Sun* verify the text with the German embassy the next morning. So that his rivals should not scoop him, the editor then telephoned United Press and asked them to inform all newspapers subscribing to their service that the State Department had contacted the *Sun* and ordered that no advertisement should be carried by any publication for any belligerent embassy without the authorization of the State Department or its attorneys. Of Viereck's original 50 selections, only the Des Moines *Register* carried the advertisement on April 23.

In the meantime, the advertisement became a talking point among many American journalists. A British naval attaché heard about it on April 21, and cabled the text to Naval Intelligence in London. As a result, officers of the Dover patrol and units at Liverpool, Dartmouth and Queenstown (now called Cobh), on the south coast of Ireland, were warned that submarine attacks were to be expected on very large transports. Extra vigilance was urged. At this time, the *Lusitania* was at sea on her way to New York.

Somehow the German Admiralty heard of these moves and, in turn, ordered three U-boats of the third submarine flotilla to set out and "await large English troop transports coming out from west and south coasts of England."

George Viereck spent Monday, April 26, in Washington, asking the State Department why his advertisement had not been published. Eventually, he managed to obtain an interview with Secretary Bryan. Viereck pointed out to Bryan that on all but one of her wartime voyages the *Lusitania* had been carrying munitions. Technically, this was legal if the transaction took place between one individual and another, but such cargo was still contraband and subject to seizure on the high seas. To disguise it, the British had discovered a loophole in the regulations of the port of New York which allowed them to issue partial cargo manifests on which no munitions appeared, then supplement them with more accurate information four or five days after sailing. The New York collector of customs knew of the ruse and countenanced it because he was avidly pro-British.

Viereck now produced copies of these supplementary manifests, which were open to public inspection at the customs collector's office. More important, he informed Bryan that no fewer than six million rounds of ammunition were due to be shipped on the *Lusitania* the following Friday, and could be seen on Pier 54 in New York.

Bryan picked up the telephone and at once cleared publication of the advertisement. He promised Viereck that he would also endeavor to persuade the President publicly to warn Americans not to travel. No such warning was issued, but there can be no doubt that Wilson was told of the character of the cargo destined for the *Lusitania.* He did nothing, but was to concede on the day he was told of her sinking that this foreknowledge had given him many sleepless hours.

3. FLOATING POWDER KEG

AFTER DOCKING IN NEW YORK on April 24, the *Lusitania* had six days of coaling, reprovisioning and cargo loading. There were to be more passengers than usual for a wartime voyage, and the volume of cargo was larger, too. But the main problem was hiring seamen. It took 77 to work the ship, but in the end the *Lusitania* sailed with only 41. This was a ratio of just under one seaman per lifeboat.

On this trip, almost the entire cargo was to be contraband. In the lower orlop hold (a small, below-water-line space between the foremost boiler room and the bow), above a load of 1639 copper ingots, were 1248 cases of what the Cunard waybill described as shrapnel—small pieces of metal with which to load shells. However, the shipping note of the Bethlehem Steel Co., which supplied it, specifies "1248 cases of three-inch shrapnel shells filled; weight 51 tons."

Stowed on top of the lethal load were 74 barrels of fuel oil, 3863 packages of cheese, 600 cases of canned goods, 696 tubs of butter, several hundred cases of sundries and 329 cases of lard. Only the sundries and lard showed up on the manifest. The reason for omitting the copper and the shells is quite obvious, but the omission of the food is significant. Unlike the modest shipments of butter and cheese stowed elsewhere in the ship, this "cheese" and "butter" was consigned to the Liverpool box number of the superintendent of the Naval Experimental Establishment.

Just above, the main orlop hold was devoted to 76 cases of brass rods, plus 4927 boxes of .303-caliber cartridges, 1000 rounds per box—net weight 173 tons. Since each cartridge was fitted with a fulminate-of-mercury cap, the weight of explosives in this consignment was marginally over 10½ tons.

Above was F deck, sometimes used for carrying troops, this time marked on the Cunard stowage plan as empty. However, a crewman later reported that the deck's two forward sections were filled with cargo. There is no doubt what that cargo was. Two days after the disaster, in answer to his London-office query as to where "the ammunition" had been stored aboard the *Lusitania,* Cunard's New York manager cabled that it completely filled the orlop holds, plus the trunkways and passages of F deck.

Among the items stowed on E deck were a mystifying 280 bales and

33 cases of raw furs shipped by a man who has been identified as a tool of the British, a bankrupt American rogue living off his wits. Three clues suggest that the furs were not what they purported to be: 1) They were insured for $150,000, but no claim was ever made. 2) Shipping documents show that they came from Hopewell, Va.—not a fur-storage depot, though it had a branch of E. I. du Pont de Nemours & Co., a major supplier of munitions. 3) They were consigned to a Liverpool cotton firm, whose records show they never had business with the shipper, never dealt in furs and in 1915 imported nothing at all.

At dusk on April 30, with loading almost complete, 200 additional tons of cargo were transferred to the *Lusitania* from another liner. At least part of this was also ammunition. The Remington Union Metallic Cartridge Co. wrote a letter to its agent asking him to load 2000 cases of .303-caliber ammunition onto the *Queen Margaret;* coupled to it later was a Cunard receipt for the cases, with the name *Queen Margaret* canceled and *Lusitania* written across it.

The *Lusitania* completed loading shortly after 9 p.m. on April 30. The loading manifest totaled 24 closely written pages but clearance to sail was applied for on a manifest which filled one page, listing only a few carefully selected items. Clearance was automatically granted.

At 8 a.m. the following day, the *Lusitania's* two masters-at-arms stood by the main gangway with a bevy of the ship's staff. On the pier, passengers were joined by a crowd of reporters and a newsreel team. The Senior Third Officer thought some very famous person indeed was about to embark and whispered behind his hand, "Who's the quality traveling with us?"

The purser replied with the condescension of pursers and hotel managers everywhere. "We have no quality, just moneyed people."

The presence of the reporters was explained when one of them showed a ship's officer the morning New York *Tribune,* folded open to the German warning. The newsman asked to see the captain. Instead, the manager of Cunard's New York office, Charles Sumner, was summoned to come to the pier, where he spoke to the press.

Sumner cast scorn on the advertisement. The *Lusitania,* he said, was the fastest ship on the Atlantic, and no German warship or submarine could catch her. (In fact, in order to economize, Cunard had reduced the engine-room crew by 83, and so was able to fire only 19 of the 25 boilers, cutting the cruising speed from 24 knots to 21.)

Many passengers boarding the ship had not seen the German warning, but news of it spread quickly. There was none of the usual pre-sailing party spirit. Travelers stood expectantly around the purser's office, eyeing each other, saying nothing. Many asked cabin staff not to unpack their clothes. Everyone seemed to be waiting for someone else to have the courage to cancel his passage.

Shortly before noon, Capt. William T. Turner appeared and stalked down the gangway in a determined hurry. He was on his way to collect the sailing orders. He fully expected the departure to be delayed or canceled and to see the passengers shifted to the American liner *New York,* sailing the same day almost empty from Pier 62. However, his orders were to proceed and, in the absence of any special instructions from the Admiralty, to take the same course as last time. The cruiser *Juno* would rendezvous with him near the Fastnet Rock, off the southwest tip of Ireland.

"Bowler Bill," as Turner was known because of his habit of wearing a bowler hat at all times except when on the bridge, was a martinet who had first gone to sea before the mast. He was immensely broad, chunky-faced, with a legendary reputation for personal strength and ability. He loathed the social side of a captain's life and made sure he took most meals on the bridge so as to avoid passengers who clamored to sit at his table.

As he boarded the *Lusitania* again, an American passenger asked the question that was on everyone's lips: "Is there any danger?"

"There is always a danger," Turner replied. "But the best guarantees are the *Lusitania* herself, and the fact that your safety is in the hands of the Royal Navy."

The great ship sailed at noon. Meanwhile, one of the three U-boats ordered to intercept "large troop transports" was playing havoc off England's western coast. The U-30 had already sunk six ships in four days when, at noon on May 1, some 45 miles northwest of the Scilly Isles, it halted a Dutch steamer to inspect her papers. Alerted, two British patrol vessels, *Filey* and *Iago,* headed for the position. On their way, they stopped the American oil tanker *Gulflight* and, suspecting her of illicitly fueling the marauding U-boat, ordered her into the nearest port.

Just before 1 p.m., the U-30 surfaced ahead of the three craft and commanded the little convoy to stop. Since the *Filey* was flying a Royal Navy ensign, the U-boat skipper took the tanker to be British as well. When the *Filey* attempted to ram him, he crash-dived, and fired a torpedo into the *Gulflight.* It caused only superficial damage. However, two of the tanker's crew panicked, jumped overboard and drowned.

Later that night, the *Gulflight's* master suffered a fatal heart attack.

For the second time, American citizens had died as a result of U-boat action, and the accounts published in both Britain and the United States were of a murderous, unprovoked, piratical attack. Predictably, Lansing gave Bryan a memo saying that the United States was being forced to the breaking point in its relations with Germany. He urged immediate, vigorous protest. The laying of the powder train that was to be ignited when the *Lusitania* arrived in these waters was complete.

By 8 a.m. on May 5, Churchill and his First Sea Lord, Admiral of the Fleet Lord John Fisher, were closeted in the Admiralty. The twin energies of these two strong, clever men had provided the Admiralty's main impetus. But now their working relationship had soured. Churchill saw his role in an untraditional way and, unlike previous First Lords, was not content to leave day-to-day operations to the professionals. His vigor and vision had done much to shape up the service, but his actions were deeply resented and had earned him a reputation for irresponsible meddling.

The post had first attracted him because of its possibilities for personal glory. Now, realizing that the war had become one of attrition, in which the navy had a largely passive role, he was looking for a graceful exit—preferably transfer to a senior command in the field. To achieve this, he had built up a strong personal relationship with Field Marshal Sir John French, Commander-in-Chief of the British Expeditionary Force in France, which necessitated frequent unofficial visits to the Field Marshal's headquarters. Among his staff, these visits were unkindly referred to as "trips to the French mistress."

Meanwhile the strain of events, the eternal disputes over the navy's failing Dardanelles campaign, had taken a heavy toll on Fisher. There were increasing signs that the 74-year-old admiral was losing his judgment, if not his reason. Indeed, Clementine Churchill had tried to dissuade her husband from going to France, telling him that the septuagenarian admiral could not bear the strain. Thus, in the Admiralty that morning Fisher was tired, and Churchill's mind undoubtedly was elsewhere. He had a train to catch to Paris. The discussions were brief, the decisions faulty.

One pressing item on the agenda was the realization that U-boats were coming around the north of Scotland and the west coast of Ireland. The Admiralty had believed that they lacked the range, and could reach England's western waters only by penetrating the Straits of Dover. Hence the western approaches were of least priority for antisubmarine defense, and several patrol cruisers there were not suitable for exposure to submarine attack. To avoid another *Bacchante* disaster, their deployment must be revised immediately.

Churchill, Fisher and some of their staff went down to the great operations room of the Admiralty to study the situation. One wall of this room was (and is) covered by a 20-by-30-foot chart of the world. Plotted on the map was the current position of almost every German and Allied naval unit, plus important merchant ships. (For months, British Naval Intelligence had been able to decipher almost every German naval message, and through direction-finding stations to pinpoint its source.)

Churchill had to ensure that in his absence Fisher knew exactly what was going on. Fisher did not want the responsibility. He chided Churchill for going. It was therefore a somewhat sullen old admiral, at his desk since dawn, who now had to listen to the decisions of a First Lord 35 years his junior who characteristically was instructing him on how to conduct a navy at war.

Vice Admiral Henry Oliver, Chief of the Naval War Staff, dealt with each operational area on the chart in turn. When he got to the western approaches, he pointed out that the U-30, now well north of Ireland, was on its way home. But there was a new submarine present, the U-20, sighted at 9 a.m. a few miles northwest of the Fastnet Rock. Also in this vital southwestern area was the ancient patrol cruiser *Juno,* designated to rendezvous with the *Lusitania.* Well out to the west loomed "the Greyhound" herself, swiftly closing on the Fastnet. If U-20 remained stationary, the two would meet at dawn the next day, with the *Juno* close by.

However, the briefing officer drew Churchill's attention to the fact that *Juno's* bulkhead design—longitudinal—made her unsuitable for exposure to submarine attack without escort, and suggested that destroyers be sent out from Milford Haven.

At this juncture, the decision was taken that was to be the direct cause of the disaster. Everyone present knew that grave danger now threatened the liner. Yet, shortly after noon on May 5, the Admiralty ordered the *Juno* to abandon her escort mission and return to Queenstown. The *Lusitania* was not informed that she was now alone and drawing closer every minute to the U-20.

It was an incredible decision by any standards. No one alive today knows who took it, but Churchill and Fisher must share the responsibility. Either they were too preoccupied with the Dardanelles campaign and personal affairs to appreciate the full extent of the danger, or this was the pinnacle of Churchill's strategy of embroiling U-boats with a neutral power.

One of the officers present was Cmdr. Joseph Kenworthy of Naval Intelligence. He left the meeting disgusted by the cynicism of his superiors. In 1928, he wrote a book, *The Freedom of the Seas.* "The *Lusitania.*" he said then, "steaming at half-speed straight through the submarine cruising ground on the Irish coast, was incontinently sunk." (The original manuscript stated, ". . . was *deliberately sent.*" The phrase was deleted by the publishers at the request of the Admiralty.) Their Lordships, Kenworthy concluded at the time, had decided to let the international legality of Germany's submarine offensive be tested in the court of world opinion.

Kapitänleutnant Walter Schwieger, commanding the U-20, cleared Fastnet shortly after 2 p.m. and set an eastward course paralleling the Irish coast some 20 miles away. On his last voyage Schwieger had had to crash-dive to avoid a ramming attempt. He had escaped but had been forced to limp home with a badly damaged periscope and water leaking in through the joints whenever he submerged. He had been ordered back to sea along with the U-30, but repairs to the periscope caused several days' delay. Hence, he was arriving in the area just as the U-30 was leaving.

Toward evening, scrupulously observing Cruiser Rules, Schwieger stopped a schooner and sank it, in full view of several Kinsale fishing smacks and a small steamer. At dusk, he attacked another ship 12 miles east of Kinsale. The vessel escaped into the fog, and Schwieger retired out to sea.

Both attacks were promptly reported to Vice Admiral Sir Henry Coke, in command of this patrol area, at his headquarters in Queenstown. Coke relayed word to the Admiralty.

By 1 p.m. on May 6, two more British ships had gone to the bottom—the *Candidate* and the *Centurion.* Schwieger torpedoed the second one without warning, but it did not sink at first. Even after an additional torpedo was fired at pointblank range, the *Centurion* took 80 minutes to go down.

German torpedoes sometimes failed to explode, and the damage could be insufficient to sink the ship. Against a ship with longitudinal bulkheads and properly secured watertight hatches, Schwieger noted in the log, his torpedoes were next to useless.

By 6 p.m., fog had cut visibility to 30 yards. Once again Schwieger headed for the open sea, to charge his batteries on the surface overnight. He had only three torpedoes left and intended to keep at least two for his long return trip.

The Admiralty was informed of the U-20's further attacks, but it still took no countermeasures. Hitherto, escorts had been rushed out even to protect cargoes of mules, or ships had been diverted into a safe harbor.

Admiral Coke at Queenstown was forbidden to initiate any instruction to any ship not under his command without recourse to the Admiralty, or to send any specific information over his radio. Nevertheless, the *Lusitania* situation appeared so grave that he had to do something. At 7 p.m., he studied the day's reports of submarine sightings, and decided to warn the *Lusitania* to the best of his ability.

His message reached Captain Turner at 7:50 p.m., just as Turner was about to go down to dinner and then to the first-class passengers' concert in the smoking room. It read: "Submarines active off south coast of Ireland."

Turner's hands were tied as well. He was not allowed to divert from his course without specific instructions. However, he anticipated meeting the *Juno* around dawn the following morning, and expected her to order him either north around Ireland or into Queenstown if the threat persisted.

Earlier, the *Lusitania* had heard a general Admiralty instruction reporting: "Submarines off Fastnet." Turner accordingly reduced his speed slightly so that he rounded the Fastnet during darkness. Many lifeboats were swung out on their davits, their canvas covers removed, their oars and provisions checked. Double lookouts had been posted; all watertight doors and bulkheads not essential to the working of the ship had been closed. The stewards had been ordered to black out all passenger portholes and the passengers themselves had been asked not to show any unnecessary lights.

In the smoking room, Captain Turner stood up and faced his passengers. It was customary on an occasion such as a concert for the captain to make a short speech, but this evening was different. Every passenger had watched the swinging out of the boats, the sudden blackout of their cabins, and they had all felt the *Lusitania* slow down. What, they asked the captain, was happening?

Turner explained that there had been a submarine warning, and that he had reduced speed to cross the Bar at Liverpool in early dawn.

He stressed that these were just routine precautions, and that in the morning they would find a cruiser alongside which would shepherd them into Liverpool on schedule.

"On entering the war zone tomorrow," he told the passengers, "we shall be securely in the care of the Royal Navy."

4. FATED MEETING

TURNER WAS ON the bridge at dawn the next morning, Friday, May 7. Visibility was a mere 30 yards. He slowed to 15 knots and began sounding his foghorn. The *Juno* was by now 100 miles to the east, closing on Queenstown. One hundred and twenty miles ahead, Schwieger stood in the conning tower of the U-20 while his batteries were charging and the fog swirled around him. If it had not cleared by the time the charging was finished, he would set course for home.

At 11 a.m., Schwieger submerged after sighting one of Coke's patrols just off the entrance to Queenstown harbor. He decided to stay submerged until noon and then take a quick periscope look around. To the west the fog cleared, and Captain Turner increased his speed from 15 to 18 knots. Anxiously he scanned the horizon for the *Juno,* but there was no ship in sight. The coast of Ireland was still an indistinct blur on the horizon, and he ordered a modest change of course to draw a mile or so closer so that he could establish his precise position.

In Queenstown, Coke studied his plot with growing concern and checked his forces and their locations. He found that he had a total of 13 fishing boats of the Auxiliary Patrol, three motorboats and three yachts dispersed over an area of almost 200 miles. One of these, the *Scadaun,* was on detached duty escorting the auxiliary tug *Hellespont* from the area of the Fastnet to Queenstown. Unlike most of the patrol, the *Hellespont* had a radio. Coke decided to detach the *Scadaun* from the tug and send her to search the area between the Fastnet and Queenstown for submarines.

Around 11 a.m., he later claimed, he also spoke with the Admiralty. There is no record of what was said, but Coke has stated that he asked for permission to divert the *Lusitania* and could not get a firm decision.

The tug *Hellespont* was a merchant-fleet auxiliary, as was the *Lusitania,* and both were referred to in signal parlance as MFAs. Thus the *Lusitania,* like the *Hellespont,* had the call sign MFA. Coke wished to inform the tug that her escort *Scadaun* was to search for submarines while she herself was to come to Queenstown as quickly as possible. The message was sent, and was received by the *Lusitania.*

The Admiralty, for its part, categorically denies, and has done so before four courts of law—and over 58 years—that any message, coded or otherwise, was sent to the *Lusitania* at 11:02 a.m. on May 7. Fortunately, a certified copy of the transmission log of the naval station at Valentia has survived, and this clearly shows that the *Lusitania* received a 12-word message in naval code addressed to MFA at 11:02 G.M.T., which was acknowledged.

The message was taken to Captain Turner. To the end of his life he was adamant that it instructed him to divert into Queenstown. Thus the *Lusitania* was diverted, probably by accident, possibly because it was Coke's way of trying to ensure her safety.

At noon, Schwieger heard the throb of propellers above him, and a few moments later he came up to periscope depth and saw the *Juno* heading away from him into Queenstown. He also noticed that the sun was fully out, the fog had cleared. After a 20-minute delay, he surfaced and headed back toward Fastnet at full speed.

Forty miles away was the *Lusitania;* Captain Turner had finished decoding Coke's MFA signal a few moments before. At 12:15 G.M.T., he swung the *Lusitania* to port so violently that several passengers lost their balance and chaos was created in the galleys below. The *Lusitania* headed for the shore.

At 1:20, Schwieger saw a smudge of smoke on his starboard bow, then soon saw the four funnels of a steamer some 14 miles ahead. He promptly submerged and set a course that would take him abreast of his target should it turn to starboard and head toward Queenstown. Such a course would give him a perfect flank shot. In the meantime he sang out to his pilot as the crew went to attack stations: "Four funnels, upward of 25,000 tons, speed about 22 knots." The pilot replied, "Either the *Lusitania* or the *Mauretania,* both armed cruisers used for trooping." Schwieger believed that he had found the target he had been sent to sink.

As the *Lusitania* closed to the coast, Turner could make out a lighthouse on the top of a high bluff. He reasoned correctly that it was the Old Head of Kinsale and promptly ordered a change of course to starboard which would take him into Queenstown. He was now ten miles offshore and 25 from safety. Ever a cautious man, he ordered the officer of the watch to take a series of four bearings on the lighthouse to help him establish his precise position before he navigated his way into port without either tugs or pilot. The course change led him directly into Schwieger's trap.

The log of the U-20 relates what happened then with a professional simplicity:

> The steamer turns starboard, takes a course to Queenstown and thus makes possible a drawing near for the firing. Ran at high speed in order to get a position up-front.
>
> Pure bowshot at 700 meters range. Shot strikes starboard side right behind the bridge.

Schwieger had little faith in his torpedoes, and his log reflects his awed surprise at what happened next. The first indication of a hit was a waterspout rising slightly forward of the front funnel. His account, dictated to the pilot standing beside him as he watched through the periscope, continues:

> An unusually heavy detonation takes place, with a vast explosion cloud (far beyond front funnel). Explosion of the torpedo must have been followed by a second one (boiler or coal or powder?). Superstructure above the point of impact and the bridge are torn asunder, fire breaks out, smoke envelops the high bridge. The ship stops and heels over to starboard quickly, immersing simultaneously at the bow. It appears as if the ship were going to capsize very shortly. Great confusion is rife on board. Some boats, full to capacity, are rushed from above, touch the water stem or stern first, and founder immediately.

The torpedo struck between the lower orlop hold and the reserve coal bunker, exploding into both. The force of the blast blew down the entire length of the longitudinal bunker, almost empty by now, and water soon poured into the forward boiler rooms through the "watertight" coal hatches.

The torpedo failed to blow in the inner bulkhead of No. 1 boiler room, but just farther forward *something* blew out most of the bottom of the *Lusitania's* bow. It may have been the shrapnel shells, the six million rounds of rifle ammunition, the highly dubious contents of the bales of "fur" or the 40-pound boxes of "cheese." Divers who have been to the wreck unanimously testify that the bow was blasted by a massive internal explosion, and large pieces of plating, buckled from the inside, lie some distance from the hull.

Whatever the cause, it was the second explosion that did most damage. The result of Schwieger's torpedo was the flooding of the starboard coal bunkers and a 15-degree list. The result of the second explosion was the sinking of the *Lusitania.*

Turner was standing on the bridge when a lookout shouted that a torpedo was approaching from starboard. As he looked in that direction, he saw a streak of foam and the torpedo struck. Within ten seconds the ship took such a list that it was almost impossible to stand on the deck.

Turner shouted to the quartermaster to come "hard-a-starboard," and scanned the indicator showing which bulkheads were secure and which compartments had fire or flooding. At this moment, according to Turner, "there came a second, rumbling explosion, and the 'telltale board' indicators went berserk for most of the forward compartment." In that moment, Turner knew he had lost his vessel. As the bow dipped into the water, he gave the order to prepare to abandon ship.

For a minute or two the list stabilized at 15 degrees, but then the *Lusitania* began to heel still farther to starboard. It was obvious to Turner that within minutes the *Lusitania* was going to capsize. Ten minutes had now gone by, and already the foredeck was completely under water. The sea was pouring into the ship through the forward hatches and over the bulkheads. Turner tried to turn her toward the Old Head of Kinsale, tantalizingly close in the afternoon sun. But the bow, now invisible below the surface, would not come around. Unknown to him, the rudder was almost out of the water.

Down below, the initial list had put the E-deck portholes under water; soon those on D deck were submerged as well. Survivors' statements show that at least 74 portholes were open, and water poured through each one at the rate of $3\frac{3}{4}$ tons a minute. Turner signaled that, despite the still appreciable headway, it was time to launch the boats.

At 2:23 the quartermaster called up to Turner that the list was now 25 degrees. "Then save yourself," Turner answered. The officer picked up a lifejacket, was washed off the bridge, and "had to go where the tide took me."

Turner was now alone, high up on the port side of the navigation bridge. He stood gazing at the boat decks, rearing above him as the *Lusitania's* stern rose higher out of the water. As the propellers came clear, the headway diminished. Seconds later, the bow struck the granite ocean floor. The *Lusitania* was now literally standing on her head at a 45-degree angle. Ever so slowly, she began to settle, at the same time turning over onto her starboard side. The bulkheads into the boiler rooms finally gave way and No. 3 boiler exploded, blowing off No. 3 funnel. When the steam cleared, the *Lusitania* was gone. It had sunk in 18 minutes.

Schwieger closed down his periscope and headed out to sea.

The *Lusitania* carried 48 lifeboats. Twenty-two were the conventional wooden type suspended from launching davits, and 26 were collapsibles with canvas sides, most of these being stored beneath the wooden ones. Each had a capacity ranging from 50 to 70 persons.

After the torpedo struck, Junior Third Officer Albert Bestic, in charge of stations 2, 4, 6, 8 and 10 on the port side, ran to make the boats ready. Many of the lowering crews had not yet arrived, but every

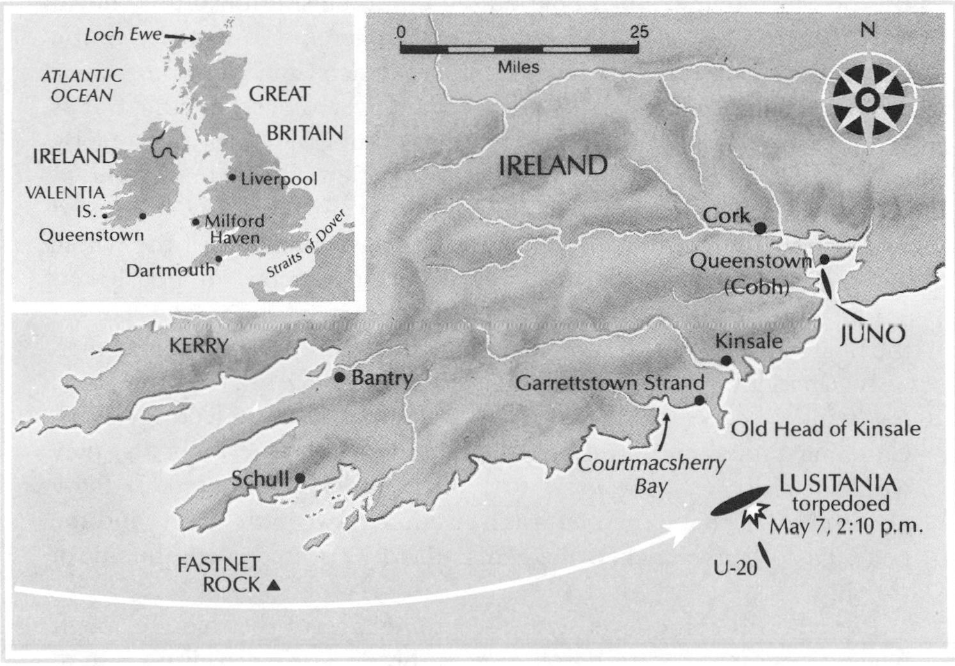

one of the suspended lifeboats was already full. Bestic hoisted himself onto the stern davit of No. 2 to see what was going on and to try to bring order out of the confusion which was only too evident.

As he climbed, he realized that the ship's list would preclude the boat's being lowered clear of the side, and that the lifeboat, already heavy with passengers, would swing inboard the moment tension on the snubbing chain was released. (This was a canvas-covered chain linking the edge of the deck and the inboard gunwale of the lifeboat; it was designed to damp down the boat's outward swing and act as a buffer on the inboard side.)

Bestic shouted for men to push the boat outward so it would clear the ship's side. But as willing hands clambered up to carry out his order, he heard a clang as someone knocked out the pin of the snubbing chain. No. 2 boat crashed inward, crushing the passengers on the collapsible beneath it. Then both boats slid forward along the slanted deck toward the bow, carrying other passengers before them and pinning them against the bridge superstructure. Each of the lifeboats, unladen, weighed five tons.

Determined to stop a recurrence, Bestic climbed up to No. 4 station. But he was too late. No. 4 boat crashed in, then slid inexorably down onto the wreckage of No. 2. Weeping with anger and frustration, Bestic desperately fought his way to No. 6 boat, which Staff Captain Anderson was trying to empty so it could be maneuvered over the side. But as fast as people vacated their places, others climbed aboard. And one by one, as Bestic watched, Boats 6, 8 and 10 suffered the fate of 2 and 4. His station looked as though a cyclone had hit, with the splintered boats piled on top of each other and the passengers—and the whole awful heap sliding farther forward as the liner's bow lurched lower.

On No. 12 station, Anderson managed to restore some order. He got the boat emptied, manhandled over the ship's side, reloaded, and then he began to lower away. The *Lusitania's* list was now almost 20 degrees, her flank a slope studded every few inches with projecting rivets. Catching under the lower edges of the planks of the lifeboats, they would rapidly tear the craft to pieces. Anderson shouted to those aboard No. 12 to use their oars as a cushion between the rivets and the boat. The order was acknowledged, and No. 12 grated down the side of the ship.

But when it came level with the promenade of the deck below, it began to swing inboard. Passengers on this deck tried to climb into it, while those aboard pushed them off. Someone shouted to the lowering crew, invisible above, to "lower away," but one of the davitmen lost control and No. 12's stern dropped suddenly, throwing all aboard into the ocean. For a moment, the boat hung by the bow rope; then that rope parted, and No. 12 slid down the rivets and onto the passengers beneath.

No. 14 fell straight down onto the wreckage of No. 12 and slowly sank. It was by now impossible to push the remaining boats over the side, but nevertheless everyone went on trying. As they did so, the water crept up toward them, driving them ever higher toward the stern.

On the starboard side, the boats swung out six feet clear of the ship, so far that it was difficult and dangerous to climb aboard. W snubbing chins were released, the gap increased to ten feet. A the deck listing toward the water, the davitmen had trouble obtaining purchase. Nevertheless, except for one wrecked by falling debris from the explosions, almost all the boats on this side were lowered into the water—though passengers were tumbled into the sea from one, and the sinking *Lusitania* took two more to the bottom, apparently held fast by unreleased snubbing chains.

Boat 13 was lowered safely with 65 passengers, and Boat 15 with more than 80. When Boat 1 was found floating empty, half of the people aboard No. 15 transferred to it, and then both boats pulled back to the ship to collect swimmers.

Meanwhile, back on the port side, Boat 18 hung in its davits, packed with passengers. A seaman stood on the gunwale with an ax, ready to cut the fall ropes as soon as the sea came level with the boat. But passenger Isaac Lehmann of New York did not know of this.

Remorsefully, Lehmann explained later: "I ran down to my room on D deck to get my life preserver, but someone had already taken it. So—I don't know what ever possessed me—I got my revolver and rushed up to A deck. I stood up on one of the collapsible boats and asked why the lifeboat was not being put into the water. A seaman with an ax in his hand said, 'Captain's orders.' My reply was, 'To hell with the captain! Don't you see we are sinking? Launch this boat or I shoot to kill.' And I drew my revolver."

The seaman obeyed. The boat, loaded with people, fell onto the collapsible and then—like the others—rolled down the steeply inclined deck, scything a path through the crowd of passengers struggling up it. Lehmann saw at least 30 people crushed to death close to him, and he himself suffered a severely injured leg. This was just before the ship went completely under, with what Lehmann, who found himself in the water alongside, remembered as "a terrible moan."

5. LIFEBOAT FIASCO

ONLY SIX OF THE *Lusitania's* 48 lifeboats were afloat. The water was dead calm, and there was not a rescue ship to be seen. Junior Third Officer Bestic was surprised to find the sea so warm.

After his desperate attempt to launch the portboats, he had gone into the liner's great entrance hall, where a number of first-class passengers stood, seemingly unconcerned that they had only seconds in which to save themselves. Millionaire Alfred Vanderbilt and the prominent theatrical producer Charles Frohman were tying lifejackets to a series of Moses baskets in which, after lunch, many of the infants aboard had been sleeping in the ship's nursery. (Since the nursery was right under the bridge, many parents were unable to reach their children after the torpedo struck.) Bestic tried to alert the men to the danger, but Vanderbilt merely shrugged. As the waters rose higher, Frohman allegedly said, "Why fear death? It is the most beautiful adventure in life."

A rush of water then swept Bestic out the doors, over the rail and into the sea. Lying on his back in the middle of wreckage, he heard the wails of the babies in their wicker baskets as they floated around him. The hastily tied lifejackets did not survive the turbulence caused by the wreck settling far below. One by one the cries ceased, and Bestic found himself alone. He could not forget the fiasco of the lifeboats, and until Bestic died in 1969 the memory of those 18 minutes was almost impossible to live with.

About 2:15 p.m., Queenstown received the *Lusitania's* S.O.S., which said, "Come at once—big list," Admiral Coke immediately ordered the *Juno,* which still had steam up, to the scene. Minutes later, word came that the *Lusitania* had sunk. Coke reported this to the Admiralty. Admiral Fisher took the news calmly, reacting only when he heard the the *Juno* was on her way. He ordered her recalled at once. He wanted no recurrence of the "live-bait" tragedy.

The cruiser was in sight of survivors in the water when she received the recall order and turned back. As a result, almost two hours elapsed before the first rescue ships started picking up survivors.

All that remained in the water drifted westward on the tide, to be set gently ashore on the sands of Garrettstown Strand and the mudflats of Courtmacsherry Bay. At dawn the next morning, beachcombers from these two villages picked up a grisly harvest of more than 200 bodies. Farther west at Schull, Bantry, and below the rocky headlands of the Kerry Coast, searchers scoured the jetsam of successive tides spurred on by financial incentives offered by the Cunard Line and anxious relatives. An ordinary body earned £1, an American £2, and a jackpot of £1000 was offered for the remains of Alfred Vanderbilt.

Because of censorship of telephone and telegraph cable, the bare announcement of the *Lusitania's* sinking did not reach London newspapers, Cunard and the American embassy until 4 p.m. Recipients believed that all passengers had been saved—late-evening London papers and New York papers printed this reassuring news.

The American ambassador in London went ahead with a big dinner he had planned. Only when guests were arriving did he receive a first casualty bulletin, telling of almost 1000 victims, including at least 100 Americans. The dinner continued as planned, but it was a macabre occasion. It was universally accepted that the United States would now enter the war. This feeling was shared by much of the U.S. press and by the American ambassadors in Berlin and Brussels who immediately began making preparations to close their embassies.

President Wilson was told the news just after a Cabinet meeting, and the next day Bryan ordered Lansing to check on the *Lusitania's* cargo. By noon, he had a detailed report from customs that "practically all her cargo was contraband" and listing great quantities of munitions. Lansing and Wilson realized that if it became public that more than 100 American lives had been lost because of the Administration's lax interpretation of neutrality, they would not survive the inevitable political holocaust.

Though the East Coast press was thundering for war, Wilson stopped short of a diplomatic break, saying, "There is such a thing as a man being too proud to fight." This drew biting criticism. In England, the United States and its President were seen as craven cowards. Whenever the word "America" was mentioned in a theater the audience would boo and hiss. In Flanders, an unexploded shell or dud was nicknamed "a Wilson." One result of this backlash was that when Wilson's Cabinet met on the morning of May 11 to discuss a note of protest to Germany, it was obvious to all present that for domestic political reasons, at least, it would have to be abrasive.

So truth was suppressed and an uncompromising note of protest to Germany was drafted. It echoed the phrase "strict accountability" and stressed that the *Lusitania* was "unarmed." To the Germans' countercharge that the *Lusitania* carried munitions and contraband, the President and Lansing replied: "The Imperial German Government has been misinformed." Bryan refused to sign this note, and when the President would not hear his protests, he resigned, hoping that by doing so he would give the public a glimpse of what was going on.

The Admiralty also hoped to conceal the decisions which had hazarded the ship and passengers in dangerous waters. Following the disaster, Adm. Henry Oliver, Chief of the Naval War Staff, and Capt. Richard Webb, director of the Trade Division, worked through the night and the weekend, initiating a stream of signals. One of the first asked Admiral Coke to "ensure that bodies selected for the inquest had not been killed or mutilated by means we do not wish made public."

With no time for legal niceties, agreement was secured at once for an official Board of Trade inquiry—thus, under British law, effectively silencing press speculation as to the causes of the sinking. (Reporters were already mentioning the second explosion, and quoting passengers' statements about ammunition aboard.)

After Oliver had signaled Churchill, he and Webb labored to prepare a memo for his return. It is a report striking for its studied omissions and blatantly anti-Turner attitude. Using convenient, edited extracts from the dozens of frequently contradictory advices and instructions issued since hostilities had begun, they charged that he had consistently disobeyed orders and even suggested that he had been "got at by the Germans."

Admiral Fisher grasped at this straw and violently underlined the latter suggestion, adding in the margin: "Fully concur." Churchill agreed, later noting, "We shall pursue the captain without check."

Lord Mersey, the eminent jurist who had conducted the inquiry into the sinking of the *Titanic,* also conducted this one. He was briefed by Admiralty officers, the inquiry was limited strictly to very carefully tailored questions, and he was bluntly told: "It is considered politically expedient that the master of the *Lusitania* be most prominently blamed for the disaster."

No mention was made of the withdrawal of the *Lusitania's* expected escort. Turner was alleged to have disobeyed instructions and flagrantly risked his ship by coming within ten miles of shore (the wreck was 12.2 miles offshore). The message which he believed had ordered him into Queenstown was suppressed. The timing of other Admiralty advices was misrepresented. Of the many crewmen and passengers who wished to be heard, only a selected few were allowed to testify. And the U.S. note to Germany was accepted as evidence that the U.S. government had "enforced its statutes with scrupulous vigilance," that the *Lusitania* was "unarmed," and her cargo as innocuous as manifested.

Captain Turner answered most questions in monosyllables. Besides the after-effects of losing his ship and spending three hours in the water at age 60, he was miserably unhappy. A whispering campaign had started against him. On the first day of the hearing some militant female handed him a white feather. His wife gave him no support. In fact, he never spoke to her again or saw his two sons after the hearing.

Whatever the original reasons for the breach, the *Lusitania* disaster made it permanent.

Ironically, Turner owed his survival in the inquiry to Lord Mersey's belated but profound respect for English law, which surfaced dramatically toward the close of the hearing. Mersey suddenly became aware of discrepancies between certain Admiralty documents being used in the case. He reached across and took a bundle of papers from an admiral assisting him. Among the papers was the master log of the Valentia radio station—which had not been entered in evidence—recording that a message in naval code had gone to the *Lusitania* at 11:02 the morning of the disaster. It was obvious to Mersey that he was being deliberately misled by the Admiralty.

In the end, he stated that Turner had "exercised his judgment for the best and ought not, in my opinion, to be blamed." But, as a whole, his verdict assisted the government. He castigated a passenger who claimed that the second explosion was caused by a cargo of munitions, found that all the *Lusitania's* portholes had been closed in time, and that there had been no explosion of anything except torpedoes, at least two of them.

Two days later, Mersey wrote formally to the prime minister, waiving his fee for the case and requesting that "henceforth I be excused from administering His Majesty's justice." He was more forthright to others. "The *Lusitania* case," he reportedly told a few close to him, "was a dirty business."

One item that might have been expected to appear in evidence but never did, either in London or at a court case three years later in New York, was the *Lusitania's* original manifest. The manifest had been given to President Woodrow Wilson by the New York customs collector. Wilson sealed the papers in an envelope, marked it, "Only to be opened by the President of the United States," and consigned it to the Treasury archives.

The documents remained there until January 1940, by which time Britain and America stood in a relationship almost identical to that of May 1915. President Franklin D. Roosevelt—who had been Under Secretary of the Navy in 1918—knew of the existence of the envelope, and now asked that it be brought to him. After he had opened and read the packet, he had the manifest bound in a leather case and placed in his own personal collection of naval manuscripts, where it is to this day. It is, of course, the carbon copy of the original, which went down with the ship.

Lindbergh Alone

CONDENSED FROM THE BOOK BY

by Brendan Gill

ILLUSTRATED JOHN T. McCOY

N-X-211
RYAN
NVP

Half a century ago, a 25-year-old American became the first person to fly alone across the Atlantic Ocean, nonstop from New York to Paris. It was a daring feat and brought Charles Augustus Lindbergh fame, fortune and, later, deep tragedy.

But this book is less an account of that flight than it is of the man who made it, and who—dramatically, irrevocably—changed not only his own life but the lives of all of us forever.

With the cooperation of the Lindbergh family Brendan Gill has written an arresting memoir of this famous flier who died in 1974.

1. THE BIG FLIGHT

THE DAY AFTER which nothing would ever be the same for him was Friday, May 20, 1927. That morning, alone in a little plane powered by a single engine, Charles A. Lindbergh took off from a muddy runway on the outskirts of New York. If everything went according to plan—and from earliest childhood he had taken pains to see that everything always went according to plan—he would become the first person in history to fly nonstop from New York to Paris.

For a number of years, Raymond Orteig, a Frenchman who had enjoyed a prosperous career as a hotel proprietor in New York, had been offering a prize of $25,000 to "the first aviator who shall cross the Atlantic in a land or water craft (heavier than air) from Paris or the shores of France, to New York, or from New York to Paris or the shores of France, without stop."

Less than two weeks before Lindbergh took off, two celebrated

French aviators had set out from Paris and had vanished somewhere over the sullen Atlantic. Other aviators, starting from the American side, had suffered one grievous misadventure after another, some of which ended in death. In the world's eyes, though not in his own, the odds against Lindbergh were tragically high; from the moment the "Spirit of St Louis" started down the runway, lurching under the burden of more gasoline than it had ever been called upon to carry, Lindbergh was reckoned to be in desperate danger.

Nowadays, it is all but impossible for us to imagine the heavy weight of unlikelihood borne by Lindbergh's attempt to win the Orteig Prize. The feat of flying nonstop to Paris has long since diminished into so commonplace a passing of a few idle hours aloft that it would never occur to us to mention its being nonstop. What Lindbergh was the first to do, by an act of superb intelligence and will, millions of us accomplish regularly with the expenditure of no more intelligence and will than are required to purchase a ticket and pack a bag.

Fifty years or so later, we are statistically no doubt in graver danger driving to Kennedy Airport than we are in flight. In an immense projectile decorated like the lounge of some not very exclusive suburban country club, we are flung through the sky at many hundreds of miles an hour, tens of thousands of feet above the earth.

What has this to do with flying as Lindbergh experienced it in his youth and, in after-years, exultantly wrote about it: an encounter on the highest pitch of consciousness between an individual with his assortment of hard-won skills and some impersonal, unknowable God in nature? For as he grew older and thought more deeply about his past, Lindbergh came to believe that the world is riddled with divinity, and to him this divinity manifested itself most openly in the isolation of flight, least openly in the mindless, imposed fraternity of crowds.

By an irony that was to be repeated many times throughout his life, the example he set for the rest of us almost always proved to have consequences radically at odds with his intentions. That first New York-to-Paris flight, with its awesome risks coolly faced and outwitted by a single valorous young man, has led to an ever-increasing traffic in the sky above the Atlantic and an ever-decreasing awareness of awe and risk on the part of the army of non-fliers who have followed him. His valor is hard to keep fresh in our minds when the most that we are asked to face and outwit above the Atlantic is boredom.

Lindbergh traveled a great deal in the 1950s and the 1960s. He traveled first-class only when there was no room in economy, and his baggage consisted of as much as he could carry aboard unchecked. Flight for him, as for most of us, had become simply a means of saving time.

Those hours in the air would have been a vexation if he had not discovered a way to keep them fruitfully occupied. As soon as he went aboard, he would hunch down in his seat—a white-haired, balding man, no longer recognizable by elderly strangers as the slender "Lindy" of their youth—and give himself up to that labor of writing which had become for him the best means of shutting a door in the face of the world, and the best means of opening a door into himself.

Except for an occasional catnap, Lindbergh would rarely lift his eyes from the page as the words flowed on in his strong, legible hand. He was writing his *Autobiography of Values.* The manuscript amounted to many hundreds of pages, but he was in no hurry to bring it to an end. For a long time, he had been putting in order the matter-of-fact affairs of his outward life and now he was putting in order the affairs of his inward life as well. He wrote in his 70s that old age provided a vantage point from which to look back upon the accumulated values of a lifetime—"with health, one is still close enough to life to keenly feel its surgings and close enough to death to see beyond one's passions." Almost at the moment of writing those words, he came down with a series of illnesses that proved to be the masks of a fatal cancer.

When death neared, in the summer of 1974, Lindbergh was as ready for it as any man could be. He saw it as a test to be taken and passed with honor—the last but not necessarily the hardest of a long lifetime of tests. He was cheerful and reassuring. He said that he had been close to death many times, and he felt no fear of the moment of passage, or of what might befall thereafter. He would meet death as he had always met life, according to plan.

Of all the ironies that make up Lindbergh's life, none is more startling than the fact that, at the time of his birth, aviation—the means by which he was to become the most famous man of the 20th century—had yet to exist. As a boy growing up in Little Falls, Minn., Lindbergh never saw a plane; even automobiles were comparative rarities in the small towns of Minnesota in those days.

Lindbergh in age was haunted by the number of changes he had experienced at firsthand in the comparative brevity of a single lifetime. His paternal grandmother, whom he knew well, vividly recalled to him her terror during the desperate Sioux uprising of 1862, when hundreds of Minnesota settlers were massacred. Still further back in time were the stories he heard and cherished about his paternal grandfather, who, before he emigrated to the New World, was an influential member of the Swedish *riksdag* and a close friend of the king, Charles XV.

What a brave man that old August Lindbergh had been! Once, stumbling against the blade of a saw in a mill in Sauk Centre, he had so mutilated his left arm that it had had to be amputated. The operation had been performed without an anesthetic, and the family story was that August hadn't uttered so much as a single groan. Later, he had rigged up a harness, by means of which he was able to chop wood, cut hay, and carry out other farm tasks as ably as any two-armed man.

The life that August Lindbergh led in the fields and pastures of Minnesota was not unlike the life that his ancestors had lived in Sweden for centuries before him—a life close to nature and obedient to its laws. It was a life that young Charles caught the last unselfconscious echoes of when he lived on the farm—a life without electric lights, or telephones, or any sort of mechanical device except a gasoline pump for drawing water up out of a well. And the man who knew that life knew also, only a few decades later, the life of Cape Canaveral blastoffs and astronauts puttering about in big boots on the gravelly moon.

Lindbergh's childhood on the banks of the Mississippi, roaming the pine and oak woods, swimming and fishing and hunting (he had his own .22-caliber rifle at the age of six and a 12-gauge shotgun when he was eight), seems to our eyes to be scarcely of the 20th century at all. Yet when he flew the Atlantic in 1927, he became in our eyes the avatar of a new breed of American—one who seemed cheerfully at ease, as most of the rest of us were not, with the intricate technical wonders pouring daily from our laboratories and factories. He had a thrilling gospel to preach and he preached it in good faith to millions of people throughout the world, both by uttering it in brief speeches and by the example of his little plane in flight. Aviation was an intrinsic good, which would prove a valuable servant to mankind.

If it is ironic for a man to be older than his métier, it is still more ironic for him to live long enough to wish that the métier had never come into existence. For years, Lindbergh served as a consultant to the Secretary of the Air Force, and in the course of his duties he helped to reorganize the Strategic Air Command. "Although I could find no wise alternative," he wrote in his *Autobiography of Values,* "each year that I worked on weapons development left me more concerned about our future. It appeared to me that our civilization involved a negative evolution for life, and that the security we were building for today and tomorrow led toward eventual catastrophe. Still more disturbing was my growing realization that even a catastrophic war was probably not the greatest danger confronting man. Civil technology vied with military technology in breaking down the environment. Every day, increasing numbers of bulldozers cut into mountains, slashed through forests, left far greater scars on the earth's surface than those created by bombs. Gases from civil vehicles polluted our atmosphere. Wastes from civil factories poisoned our rivers, lakes and seas. Civil aircraft laid every spot on earth open to the ravages of commerce. What was the prospect for mankind?"

Plainly, for Lindbergh the prospect seemed dark indeed, but he had learned something as a young aviator that caused him to square his shoulders and face the darkness instead of retreating from it. Barnstorming throughout the West and, later, flying the mail from St. Louis to Chicago, he had reached the conclusion that the best way to cope with danger was to keep in continuous, intimate contact with it.

The slender young man who had urged more air routes, more airports, more international trade was now the aging man who urged us to be content with less of everything—fewer babies, fewer cars, fewer weapons, fewer luxuries. It was remarkable, he said, what you could learn to live without. In 1974, a few weeks before his death, he wrote in the solemn cadences of a last testament: "I do not want to be a member of the generation that through blindness and indifference destroys the quality of life on our planet."

2. THE ALL-AMERICAN BOY

WHERE HAD HE SPRUNG FROM, this extraordinary man? The question began to be answered with increasing irresponsibility the day the newly finished "Spirit of St. Louis" took off from San Diego. The plane had been designed by Donald A. Hall, the chief engineer of Ryan Airlines, Inc., according to specifications drawn up by Lindbergh.

No plane like it existed anywhere in the world; it was a beautiful, silvery toy, just under 28 feet long and with a wingspan of 46 feet. It had a nine-cylinder Wright Whirlwind engine, estimated to be able to run for 9000 hours without a breakdown. (Lindbergh was figuring that he might need as much as 40 hours to cover the 3600 miles between New York and Paris; as far as the engine was concerned, the margin of safety seemed ample.)

Lindbergh made a record-breaking, nonstop flight east from San Diego to St. Louis and, the very next day, a second record-breaking flight from St. Louis to New York. Until then, he had been merely a name, often misspelled, in items about Byrd, Chamberlin, and the other well-known fliers competing for the Orteig Prize. When he touched down at Curtiss Field, on Long Island, the news of the sensationally speedy little plane and its blue-eyed, tousle-haired young pilot had already caught the imagination of the public. As Lindbergh was later to write in *The Spirit of St. Louis,* "Somebody shouts my name, and immediately I'm surrounded by a crowd. Even at the hotel, newspapermen fill the lobby and watch the entrance so carefully that I can't walk around the block without being followed. There's never a free moment except when I'm in my room."

As for "Lucky Lindy," how he hated to be called that! Never in his life had he depended upon luck for anything; for that matter, never had he been called "Lindy." It was a nickname based on the need in newspaper headlines for a catchy brevity.

Day after day, with a hit-or-miss recklessness that nobody would ever take the trouble to examine, reporters fumbled their way toward a Lindbergh whom the public would be eager to read about—a Lindbergh who would sell papers. The task was made easier for them because they had so little to go on. Lindbergh was tall and slender, with a pleasing seriousness of manner which could be instantly transformed into playfulness by a radiant smile. Although he was 25 and on several occasions had faced death both on the ground and in the air, he struck almost everyone who met him as an unmarked boy.

The boylike quality was something deeper than mere boyishness; it sprang in large part from the indubitable purity of his character. He neither smoked nor drank, and it was impossible to imagine him as a womanizer. Looking up into those clear eyes, listening to that unguarded voice, one felt sure that here was someone who would never cheat, or lie, or take unfair advantage. He was assuredly the All-American Boy, and then something more. It was the something more—the proud and passionate inner man, bent on self-fulfillment at whatever cost—that the press got wrong and continued to get wrong.

Lindbergh thought he knew what the reporters were after in those long, watchful May days of 1927, and he marveled at their professional slovenliness. When facts were so abundant, why did they not make some slight effort to ascertain them? Writing in the present tense in *The Spirit of St. Louis,* more than a quarter of a century later, he tells of his incredulity: "Depending on which paper I pick up, I find that I was born in Minnesota, that I was born in Michigan, that I was born in Nebraska; that I learned to fly at Omaha, that I learned to fly at Lincoln, that I learned to fly at San Antonio.

"The way the tabloid people acted when my mother came left me with no respect for them. Did she know what a dangerous trip her son was undertaking? they asked. Did she realize how many older and more experienced aviators had been killed in its attempt? They wanted her to describe her sensations for their readers. They demanded that we embrace for their cameras and say good-by. When we refused, one paper had two other people go through the motions, and substituted photographs of our heads for theirs."

At Curtiss Field, a few days before he took off for Paris, Lindbergh made a couple of test flights. On the last of these the tail skid of the "Spirit of St. Louis" was broken. The accident happened because a number of photographers ran out onto the field and got in Lindbergh's way. "The most annoying thing," he wrote, "was that, instead of having a penalty to pay for violating the field regulations, the cameramen got a more valuable picture—and the reporters had 'a better story.' As far as I could tell, the fact that I damaged my plane to keep from hitting somebody didn't bother them a bit. Most reporters omitted that from their accounts. 'So terrific was his speed in landing that he slightly damaged the machine's tail skid. Undismayed by the accident, which he considered trivial, Lindbergh hopped out wearing a broad smile: "Boys, she's ready and rarin' to go!" he said.' That's how one of the next day's articles went. These fellows must think I'm a cow-puncher, just transferred to aviation."

LINDBERGH TOOK seriously the Platonic dictum that the unexamined life is not worth living; still, there were times when he found the principle easier to respect than to follow. What was surely the single most important event in the forming of his character—the early breakup of his parents' marriage—he glanced at again and again throughout his life, always to turn away from it in filial distress. Well into old age, he cherished a hope that somehow they had gone on caring for each other.

Charles A. Lindbergh, Sr., was almost as remarkable a man as Charles, Jr. By merit, he made his way up from extreme poverty into the landowning middle class. He met and married a leading belle in Little Falls and had three daughters by her; one died, and then his wife suddenly died, at 31, of an inoperable cancer.

In the slang phrase of the day, C.A., as the senior Lindbergh was always called, was a catch, but his grief was genuine and it was some years before he consented to be caught. The girl who caught him was herself a catch—a welcome stranger in every way to the stolid Swedish conventionalities of Little Falls. She had a degree as a Bachelor of Science from the University of Michigan, and at 24 she had come to Little Falls to teach chemistry in the local high school. She was said to have been the prettiest girl of her time at the university and she was very spirited. Her name was Evangeline Lodge Land, and her father, Dr. Charles H. Land, was a celebrated dentist and inventor in Detroit; her mother was the daughter of a prominent Detroit physician.

Evangeline and C.A. were married at her parents' home in March 1901, and they honeymooned in California. In May, they returned to Little Falls and set about building a considerable mansion on a bluff above the Mississippi. C.A. had owned the property for several years—120 acres of gently rolling woodland, with scattered pastures and fields. They called the property Lindholm, an approximate Swedish abbreviation of "Lindbergh house."

The main house was a wooden structure, three stories high, containing 13 rooms. It had a cavernous, stone-wall basement, a ground floor with living room, dining room, study, kitchen and laundry and, on the two upper floors, seven bedrooms and a billiards room. Among the outbuildings were a caretaker's cottage, a barn and an icehouse, and paths led down to the grassy bank of the Mississippi on one side and, on the other, through tall pines and oaks to Pike Creek.

While the house was under construction that summer, C.A. and Evangeline roughed it in a temporary cabin. She was pregnant by then and proud of herself; this was the happiest time that she and C.A. were ever to know together. The baby was born on February 4, 1902. He was named Charles Augustus, Jr., without discussion; luckily, his first name also served to pay homage to Grandfather Land.

One of little Charles' earliest memories was of the fire that destroyed Lindholm. It happened on an August day in 1906; he was playing with his father in the parlor when he was suddenly thrust into his nurse's arms. She ran with him to the barn—a distance of several hundred yards—in order to keep him from watching the house go up in flames.

The next day, he and his mother stand looking over the ruins of the house. Smoke still rises out of the blackened basement. His mother says, "Father will build us a new house," but somehow the child knows better—"my toys, and the big stairs, and my room above the river, are gone forever." For something has happened not only to the house but to his parents' marriage; the new house is only half the size of the old, and there is an air of makeshift about it. It is not to give parties in, not to raise a big family in. It may be that Evangeline and C.A. will go on loving each other, but they are no longer in love. And the child knows.

Like his father, C.A. was a stoic; there was scarcely any test of mental or physical anguish that he could not meet and pass. It was remembered of him in Little Falls that he was out duck-hunting with a group of men on a particularly cold fall day. They brought down a number of ducks, which fell into a lake so icy that none of the hounds accompanying the hunters dared venture into the water. Lindbergh immediately stripped off his clothes, swam out and retrieved the birds.

Almost from Charles' birth, C.A. taught him to face pain and danger as he did. Although he was middle-aged when Charles was born, C.A. was in excellent physical condition, and he was a close companion to the boy. He taught him how to fish and hunt and hike and make fires and pitch tents and paddle a canoe. As Charles was to write many years later, "He'd let me walk behind him with a loaded gun at seven, use an ax as soon as I had strength enough to swing it, drive his Ford car anywhere at 12. Age seemed to make no difference to him. My freedom was complete. All he asked for was responsibility in turn."

Charles learned to swim one day in the usual Lindbergh fashion. Wading out from shore, he found himself unexpectedly beyond his depth. In terror, he looked to his father for help and he saw that he was still on the shore and laughing at his son's plight. The son began frantically to paddle and splash and within a few seconds had discovered that he was capable of remaining afloat. In describing this episode, he reveals no hint of distress at his father's conduct: it is how fathers are meant to behave. "You and I can take hard knocks," the father told the boy. "We'll get along no matter what happens."

When the marriage deteriorated, Evangeline felt a sense of being unjustly imprisoned, and C.A. had no intention of setting her free. He was running for Congress for the first time, and a divorce would have meant an end to his political career. He would give her no grounds for a divorce. When she asked for a legal separation, he refused.

We catch few glimpses of how the child behaved in the course of the long and increasingly bitter détente. He was handed back and forth between the parents, loving them both and looking up to them both and striving not to take sides. Lindbergh was always to speak of his childhood as idyllic, and it is plain that he achieved that view of it in part by his mother's taking care to conceal from him far more than she ever told. By an act of remarkable discipline she kept most of her rancor to herself. In only one way—and a way thoroughly unexpected—did she appear to punish the child indirectly for her unhappiness, and that was in regard to his schooling.

3. RELUCTANT STUDENT

NOT UNTIL HE WAS nearly 20 did Lindbergh ever complete a school term. He was constantly being transferred from school to school, in accordance with his parents' needs. He would be now in Little Falls, now in Detroit or Washington, and sometimes he would be in temporary residence in some such unexpected place as Redondo Beach, Calif., where he and his mother spent a few months in 1916. Little Falls was where he liked best to be, but even there he found school unsympathetic. Without the assurance that his classmates felt as they moved in an orderly fashion from term to term toward graduation, naturally he did less well than his obvious intelligence argued that he ought to be able to do.

In Little Falls he had the enjoyment of his beloved woods and fields and streams. And in the course of his and his mother's often protracted visits to Detroit he had the companionship of his lively grandfather to look forward to—they would tinker together in the grandfather's smoky laboratory, or take jaunts out into the nearby countryside. But in Washington he not only disliked going to school, he disliked the city itself. Living in a small apartment, a country-bred boy could find hardly any enterprise worth undertaking.

Not that he didn't enjoy having a Congressman for a father—C.A. was reckoned a distinguished man on the Hill and his little blond son was often to be seen scooting around the Capitol grounds on roller-skates or accompanying his father to the House chamber. Once, when he was 13, he went with C.A. to the White House to meet President Woodrow Wilson. The President shook hands with Charles and asked him civilly how he was and Charles replied with equal civility, "Very well, thank you." That evening, he informed his mother that he had not been unduly excited by the encounter; the President, after all, was a man like any other. On landing in Paris and being feted by innumerable presidents, prime ministers, and other heads of state, Lindbergh manifested a social grace that people marveled at in a callow country boy. But they were misreading him, in the way that he was nearly always being misread; he had been of the country, but he was certainly no hayseed.

His failure as a student was painful enough; still more painful was his failure to become a member of any group. A boy who starts a school term late is probably doomed to find himself at the bottom of the traditional school pecking order. That was often Lindbergh's situation, and he made matters all the more awkward for himself by a laconic manner and a seeming lack of concern for how he was treated. He didn't seek attention by kowtowing to others, he didn't volunteer answers in class and he rarely attempted any of the competitive sports—baseball, football, basketball—that form the foundation of group activities in school.

Nothing could sum up more poignantly the loneliness of the types of excellence that Lindbergh pursued than this: that they were always activities which required him to compete not against others but against himself. The flight to Paris was only the most extreme example of this loneliness.

In the light of how little interest Charles had in his studies, it was just as well that a quirk of history ensured his graduation from high school. The United States entered the World War in 1917, and as a part of the national effort to raise more food, it was decreed throughout Minnesota that any boy who worked full-time on a farm would be given credit for having passed a successful year in school. Charles was delighted. Much of his senior year he spent turning the hitherto "pretend" farm of Lindholm into a real one. It was as an authentic dairyman and farmer that Charles graduated with the class of 1918 from the Little Falls High School. He was convinced that he would make his way in the world as his Swedish forebears had done, cultivating the land.

As far as one can tell, both parents were content with Charles' decision, and it is curious thay they should have been. C.A. had struggled hard to lift himself up out of the muck of manual labor on his father's farm, and the means of C.A.'s deliverance had been education. He as a lawyer and Evangeline as a schoolteacher were both conspicuous embodiments of the advantage of going to college, and yet between them they contrived a life for their son that rendered the prospect of a college education for him improbable.

When they denied Charles the opportunity to pursue an ordinary school career, did they do so out of innocent selfishness, or were they unconsciously using Charles as a means of punishing each other

Charles Lindbergh, eight years old, with his father, C.A.

Charles and his mother, Evangeline, just before his daring flight

through him? Was C.A. too busy and too often absent from home to see, or did he see and choose to ignore, the consequences of Evangeline's plucking Charles out of school to go on visits here and there, little by little making sure that she could retain possession of him in isolated Lindholm?

Once, after Charles had become famous, Evangeline was accused in print of having considered herself so superior socially to her neighbors in Little Falls that she had refused to let Charles play with their children. Charles protested in private on her behalf that, on the contrary, she had sometimes paid the neighbors' children small sums for the very purpose of making sure that he had someone to play with. But the defense is more bewildering than the accusation, for why should any such payment have been necessary? How had it come about that this appealing boy had no close friends? With a charm that was one day to be responded to instantly throughout the world, how did he manage to pass almost unnoticed among his generation of boys and girls in Little Falls?

When reporters descended upon the town in the summer of 1927, seeking information about Lindbergh's past, few of the townspeople could remember much of anything about him, except that he had a mechanical bent, liked to ride a motorcycle, and never dated. Little as she may have been aware of it, Evangeline's need to sequester and dominate her son was very strong. Charles was hers, and the evidence is that for 27 years no other woman came within touching distance of him. Few mothers have held the absolute fealty of their sons for so long.

Throughout the course of the war, Charles worked the farm, but by 1919 farm prices began to fall and it was clear that no matter how stubbornly he and his hired man might labor, Lindholm was too small to compete against the large-scale farms in the neighborhood. Charles would later write:

> In 1919 I turned the farm over to tenants in preparation for going away to college. It was a difficult and rather heartbreaking procedure, giving up the stock and machinery and seeing my methods and hopes give way to the methods and hopes of others. I spent a good deal of time selecting the college of I wanted to enter and finally chose the University of Wisconsin. That ended all my close contacts with our farm.

His parents had been pleased by his decision to take a chance on going to college. Best of all from Evangeline's point of view was the fact that she wouldn't be losing him. On the contrary, she moved with Charles, rented a flat for them near the university and secured a position for herself as a teacher of science in a local junior high school. She would never again live at Lindholm, never again be in C.A.'s shadow; her long domestic imprisonment was ended.

Charles drifted through the first year of college with low grades and, to his mother's dismay, sank to still lower depths in his second year. In February 1922, she received the following communication from Charles' adviser, who was not in so intimate an advisory position as to have mastered his first name:

> The record made by Carl in the first semester is very discouraging.
>
> Machine Design I..Failure
> Mathematics 52..Failure
> Physics 51..Incomplete
> Shop 6..88
> Shop 13..88
>
> On account of the above poor record the Sophomore Adviser Committee decided on February 2 that Carl should be dropped from the University.

"When I was a sophomore at the University of Wisconsin, I decided to give up my course in mechanical engineering and learn to fly." Determined truth-teller though he was, in writing *The Spirit of St. Louis* some 30 years after the event, Lindbergh was able to bring himself to say only that he had left college, not that he had been dismissed. But it is the end of the quoted sentence that is of great importance, for from the moment that he undertook to learn to fly, his whole life changed utterly.

It was as if Lindbergh in taking to the air had immediately acquired some preternatural capacity for self-fulfillment that ordinary mortals lacked. It was a capacity that was bound to put him at a distance from most of his contemporaries and, even before the Paris adventure, would cause him to be placed in the category of hero. Lindbergh was distressed and irritated whenever he was described by that term; still, when he was a gypsy flier barnstorming around the West in 1922 and 1923, wingwalking and giving exhibition parachute jumps, and when, some time later, on several occasions he had to bail out of a plane in order to save his life, his coolness in the face of danger struck others as having the indisputable stamp of the heroic upon it.

Both Evangeline and C.A. were skeptical of the feasibility of flying. When Charles first spoke to them about the possibility that, on graduating from high school, he might try to earn a living as an aviator, they shook their heads in disapproval. C.A. put it to him bluntly: flying was extremely dangerous and he was their only son; they couldn't afford to lose him.

His failure at the university made it possible for Lindbergh to announce to his parents that, whether they liked it or not, he had made up his mind to fly.

The occasion on which he broke the news to his mother is described in *The Spirit of St. Louis:* "I was so anxious to get into aviation that I scarcely realized what parting meant to her. 'All right,' she said. 'If you really want to fly, that's what you should do.' 'You must go,' she told me later. 'You must lead your own life. I mustn't hold you back. Only I can't see the time when we'll be together much again.' Her prophecy came true. Hundreds of letters and packages have gone back and forth between us, but I haven't been home for more than a few days at a stretch since then. But we went barnstorming together in southern Minnesota in the summer; and she's flown back and forth between Chicago and St. Louis with me on the mail route, riding on the sacks."

The "hundreds" of letters that Lindbergh mentions must have been more like thousands; Evangeline had always been an industrious correspondent, and as soon as Charles went off to fly she began to pepper him with letters. When he gave up barnstorming and enrolled in the Army Air Service, his fellow cadets at Brooks Field and Kelly Field assumed from the volume of mail he received that an infatuated girl friend was in feverish pursuit of him.

He begged his mother to spare him embarrassment by writing less often. She replied that she would address envelopes to him in a number of different hands. There! she said, in effect—now they will envy you because they will think that you have a lot of girl friends, and it will really be only me.

Luckily for Charles, Evangeline was an entertaining correspondent. She reported the latest jokes that were circulating in school and she ticked off with accuracy the idiosyncrasies of her students and colleagues. There was a sufficient openness between them for her to be slangily robust in her language and for Charles to be able to tell her an anecdote about a drunk who took off with him on a $5 ride and who kept trying to climb out of the cockpit in flight, bawling at the top of his lungs, "I have to take a p---!"

Two things emerge from Charles' letters of this period. One is his delight in playing practical jokes; the other is his passage from being a mediocre student to being a brilliant one. Lindbergh confessed to being a master of the art of squeezing toothpaste into the open mouth of a sleeper, of putting scorpions and grasshoppers between people's sheets, and of hiding needed clothing and gear on barracks roofs and other inaccessible places.

Although Lindbergh had full confidence in his flying ability, he was alarmed by what might befall him in the classroom. He was conscious of the fact that throughout the years cadets would be "washed out" at a steady rate, with perhaps a fifth of the class managing to receive its wings upon graduation.

As usual, Lindbergh looked a difficult situation in the face and sought to master it by putting it as nearly as possible under his total control. A year before he died, he looked back in his *Autobiography of Values* upon that moment of decision.

"I concluded," he wrote, "that the surest way of passing all 70-plus examinations would be to strive not just for passing but for the highest marks I could get. I began studying as I had never studied before—evenings, weekends, sometimes in the washroom after 'bed-check,' far into the night. When I graduated in March 1925, I had the highest standing in my class."

4. HERALDED

AMBASSADOR MYRON T. HERRICK, writing from the U.S. embassy in Paris in June 1927, pointed out the practical value of Lindbergh's flight in helping to mend the uneasy relations that existed between the United States and France. This was, however, only a fortunate by-product of what the ambassador felt to be an authentic spiritual experience for both nations and, indeed, for the world. With heartfelt Victorian eloquence, Herrick compared Lindbergh's arrival in Paris to the French victory at the Marne, in the First World War:

> Just before the Battle of the Marne I was standing on the river embankment. A great harvest moon was rising over the city near Notre Dame. The French flag was blowing steadily across its face. In the fleeting moments while this spectacle lasted, people knelt on the quay in prayer. I inquired the meaning of these prayers. The answer was that there is a prophecy centuries old that the fate of France will finally be settled upon the fields where Attila's hordes were halted and driven back, and where many battles in defense of France have been won. And pointing up the Seine to the French flag outlined across the moon, people cried: "See! The sign in Heaven! It means the victory of French arms! The prophecy is come true as of old and France is once more to be saved on those chalky fields."
>
> Now when this boy of ours dropped unheralded from the skies and circling the Eiffel Tower came to rest as gently as a bird on the field of Le Bourget, I was seized with the same premonition as those French people on the quay that August night. I felt that his arrival was far more than a fine deed well accomplished, and there glowed within me the prescience of a splendor yet to come. Lo! It *did* come and has gone on spreading its beneficience upon two sister nations which a now-conquered ocean joins.

"This boy of ours" was certainly unheralded, but to look back upon Lindbergh in the light of history is to perceive many signs of that splendor which was to come. Lindbergh was radically exceptional both in his ancestry and in his upbringing, and from the moment of his enlistment in the Army Air Service he was radically successful in his career.

At 23, having graduated from the Army Flying School and having received his commission as a second lieutenant in the Army Air Service Reserve, Lindbergh accepted a position as chief airmail pilot for the

Robertson Aircraft Corp., in St. Louis. He was probably earning as much money in his early 20s as any aviator in the country. Moreover, by the time Lindbergh was getting ready for the New York-to-Paris adventure, he had made four emergency parachute jumps from planes that he had been forced to abandon. No other man in the country had made so many.

The first of these jumps is of lasting interest because it marked the first time than anyone had ever survived the collision of two planes in the air. Lindbergh's official report of the accident was remarkable not alone for the facts it contained but for the skill with which it was written. Eventually, the report made its way into *Aviation* magazine, and then into the New York *Evening World*, and was reprinted and used in schools as a model of unadorned narrative style.

The text of the report goes as follows:

> Report by cadet C.A. Lindbergh on the collision in air at about 8:50 a.m. March 6th, 1925, approximately ten miles north of Kelly Field.
>
> A nine-ship SE-5 formation, commanded by Lieutenant Blackburn, was attacking a DH4B, flown by Lieutenant Maughan at about a 5000-foot altitude and several hundred feet above the clouds. I was flying on the left of the top unit, Lieut. McAllister on my right, and Cadet Love leading. When we nosed down on the DH, I attacked from the left and Lieut. McAllister from the right. After Cadet Love pulled up, I continued to dive on the DH for a short time before pulling up to the left. I saw no other ship nearby. I passed above the DH and a moment later felt a slight jolt followed by a crash. My head was thrown forward against the cowling and my plane seemed to turn around and hang nearly motionless for an instant. I closed the throttle and saw an SE-5 with Lieut. McAllister in the cockpit a few feet on my left. He was getting ready to jump.
>
> Our ships were locked together with the fuselages approximately parallel. My right wing was damaged and had folded back slightly. Then the ships started to mill around and the wires began whistling. The right wing commenced vibrating and striking my head at the bottom of each oscillation. I climbed out past the trailing edge of the damaged wing, and jumped backward as far from the ship as possible. Fearing the wreckage might fall on me, I did not pull the rip cord until I dropped several hundred feet. The parachute functioned perfectly.
>
> I saw Lieut. McAllister floating above me and the wrecked ships pass about 100 yards to one side, continuing to spin to the right and leaving a trail of lighter fragments along their path. I watched them until, still locked together, they crashed in the mesquite about 2000 feet below and burst into flames several seconds after impact.

I was drifting in the general direction of a plowed field which I reached by slipping the chute. Although the impact of landing was too great for me to remain standing, I was not injured in any way. During my descent I lost my goggles, a vest-pocket camera which fitted tightly in my hip pocket, and the rip cord of the parachute.

What is most startling about this report, especially to the non-flier, is how little startling the episode itself appears to have been to Lindbergh. For him the air had become so nearly his natural element that an astounding accident taking place a mile up in the sky was perhaps less cause for alarm than if two automobiles had collided at top speed on the ground. The only note of distress in the report has to do with the loss of his goggles and camera and the parachute's rip cord; fliers who forgot to hold on to their rip cords when they jumped were subjected to a prolonged razzing. "What? You threw away your rip cord? And *you* want to be a flier?"

A stumbling block to all biographers of Lindbergh is that the central event of his life—the event that pitched him headlong into history overnight—has been described with such verve and particularity by Lindbergh himself that no one can hope to better it. One races through the pages of *The Spirit of St. Louis* as if it were a series of stop-press newspaper bulletins—as if, hour after hour, the outcome of that unprecedented flight were still in doubt.

And what makes Lindbergh's accomplishment even more impressive than it is commonly reckoned to be is that the flight was, except for a single mischance, so easy. Easy? It is an unlikely word for an attempt that, up to then, had nearly always ended in death, and yet it is one of the underlying themes of the book that Lindbergh and Donald Hall, the designer of the plane, had anticipated every contingency so well that in mechanical terms nothing of importance *did* go wrong.

In their view, once the plane was off the ground and headed in the direction of Paris, there was no reason whatever that it wouldn't eventually get there. For on the way to the drawing board the problem had been a simple one to state: design a plane that at takeoff could lift gasoline enough to fly 4000 miles. After that, everything depended on the pilot.

In a few seconds on the morning of May 20, 1927, it turned out that Lindbergh and Hall had provided such a plane. The weather on the flight was foul, but it was no worse than the weather Lindbergh had often encountered flying the mail between St. Louis and Chicago. The Great Circle route that Lindbergh had laid out in 100-mile "takes" looked, on his crudely inked chart, like the handiwork of a child; nevertheless, it proved so accurate that, coupled with his superb navigation, the "Spirit of St. Louis" made landfall almost exactly on target at Dingle Bay on the southwest coast of Ireland. (Illustrated on pages 610–611.) Lindbergh had estimated that he might reach Europe as much as 400 miles off-course; that was why he had asked for a range of 4000 miles. Landing in Paris, he could not resist boasting that the gas remaining in his tanks would have carried him as far as Rome.

The main text of Charles Lindbergh's *The Spirit of St. Louis* ends abruptly, with an exclamation—"But the entire field ahead is covered with running figures!"

Lindbergh had arrived at Le Bourget assuming that, because he was ahead of schedule, there would be no one there to meet him. He would identify himself to the authorities, arrange (by sign language, if necessary) for his plane to be placed in a hangar, and then ask for assistance in making his way to Paris and securing accommodations at some inexpensive hotel. He had concentrated hard on the flight itself and had ignored its consequences.

The crowd at Le Bourget stunned Lindbergh. Unbeknownst to him, word of his approach along the valley of the Seine had been reaching Paris by telegraph and telephone from the moment he had been sighted over Cherbourg. It appeared that all Paris had set out for the field to welcome him, leading to the greatest traffic jam in Paris history. He touched down at 10:22 p.m. Paris time, and while he was still taxiing across the field thousands of cheering people began to press in around the plane.

Ambassador Herrick fell at once under the young man's spell. He invited Lindbergh to "come home" with him to the embassy, and Lindbergh accepted. From the moment that he fell asleep, wearing a pair of pajamas borrowed from the ambassador, Lindbergh was never to occupy the world of his youth again. A signal of his crossing from one world to another was the tender and whimsical telegram that Herrick dispatched to Evangeline Lindbergh in Detroit: "Warmest congratulations. Your incomparable son has honored me by becoming my guest. He is in fine condition and sleeping sweetly under Uncle Sam's roof."

When Lindbergh woke early in the afternoon of the 22nd of May, he found Blanchard, the ambassador's valet, standing by his bedside. A bath, Blanchard announced, had been drawn. The room, Lindbergh thought at once, was like those he had seen in movies: a room in a palace, different from any he had ever encountered in real life. Blanchard held out a bathrobe, and to Lindbergh the gesture was again movie-like, fantastic. He had never owned a bathrobe; he had considered it a totally superfluous article of clothing.

"As an individual, I was astonished at the effect my successful landing in France had upon the nations of the world. To me, it was like a match lighting a bonfire. I thought therefore that people confused the light of the bonfire with the flame of the match and that one individual was credited with doing what, in reality, many groups of individuals had done." He wrote those words in his 60s, not in the least out of false modesty. The 33½ hours he had spent in the air between New York and Paris had not changed him by an iota—they had only intensified in him the very characteristics that had prompted him to undertake the flight—but the first 33½ hours of his stay in Paris threatened to bestow on him a new and not necessarily welcome career. He would have to act fast in order to prevent simple good manners from amounting, in the world's eyes, to an unprotesting acceptance of that career.

To that end, Lindbergh set about externalizing his superb adventure; at every opportunity, he drew attention to the bonfire and not the match. Whenever speeches were given in his honor, whether at first in Paris and Brussels and London, or later in Washington and New York and St. Louis, and he was called upon to make a reply, he would speak not about himself but about international goodwill and the future of aviation. People praised him for his modesty, and he deserved their praise, but he was also setting strict limits upon the use to which he was willing to be put: this far would he go and no further.

5. THE GRAND TOUR

THE WELCOME that Lindbergh was given in New York has never been rivaled. It lasted for four days, and on every day there was an unbroken succession of parades, luncheons, dinners, and private and public receptions. On the morning of the first day, on the traditional drive up Broadway, a couple of tons of ticker tape and confetti were showered upon his motorcade from the windows of the skyscrapers in the financial district. This next morning, the New York *Times* devoted its first 16 pages to Lindbergh; in the eyes of the editors, he was plainly the greatest single event in American history.

From New York he flew to St. Louis for two days of incessant celebrations which he shared with the nine backers of the flight. From St.

Louis, Lindbergh made a quick flight to Dayton, Ohio, where he hoped to enjoy a quiet visit with Orville Wright. So many thousands of well-wishers turned up at Wright's house and clamored to see Lindbergh that Wright's gardens were soon trampled into dust and the house itself was threatened with serious damage.

Lindbergh returned to New York in late June to start work on a book about the flight. He broke off all pending engagements and, settling down at the country place of a newly acquired friend, he undertook the task of writing, in longhand and with remarkable rapidity, the little book called *We.* Lindbergh's host was Capt. Harry F. Guggenheim, president of the Daniel Guggenheim Fund for the Promotion of Aeronautics, and a Naval aviator in World War I.

The Guggenheim estate, "Falaise," at Sands Point, Long Island, provided Lindbergh with the privacy required to write his book, protected from hero-worshiping crowds and a press that pursued him even when he had no news to impart. Moreover, there was a horse pasture on the property that served admirably as an airstrip. It was at "Falaise" that he took Anne Morrow up in a rented plane on the first of the three dates they had before they became engaged.

Meanwhile, Lindbergh was making plans for a new adventure. While writing *We,* he had received hundreds of requests for personal appearances. Now it occurred to him that he could honor those requests and, at the same time, assume a role that he believed in and that the success of his Paris flight had more or less imposed on him—the role of chief spokesman for the new world of commercial aviation. In behalf of that cause, he would undertake a tour of cities from coast to coast, demonstrating that when it came to maintaining regular schedules, planes were already approaching the reliability of trains (a demonstration that, at the time, probably no one but Charles Lindbergh was capable of making).

Starting in July and ending in October, Lindbergh flew well over 22,000 miles in 260 flying hours. He made scheduled stops in 82 cities and dropped messages on innumerable other cities at designated hours. He devoted 147 speeches to the general topic of aviation.

As usual he had little to say about himself and in interviews he refused to answer any personal questions; when asked whether he preferred blondes or brunettes, he would say curtly, "What has that to do with aviation?"

A total of 30 million people were estimated to have seen Lindbergh and the "Spirit of St. Louis" in the course of the tour, and there was no doubt whatever that the tour greatly increased the public's interest in both air travel and airmail.

This formidable demonstration of flying skill was matched by the nonstop flight he made in December between Washington, D.C., and Mexico City, which proved in some respects more difficult and no less dangerous than the flight to Paris. Dwight W. Morrow, the U.S. ambassador to Mexico, was chairman of a committee appointed by President Calvin Coolidge to investigate the state of American aviation. Morrow invited Lindbergh to fly to Mexico on a goodwill visit.

"The ambassador's invitation gave me an opportunity to accomplish several objectives on a single flight," Lindbergh later wrote in *Autobiography of Values.* "In addition to the gesture of friendship he desired, I could demonstrate still more clearly the capabilities of modern aircraft. After the visit was over, I could fly on to South America, thereby helping to link together the continents of our Western Hemisphere by air."

Ambassador Morrow was upset when he learned that Lindbergh intended to fly nonstop to Mexico. He protested that he didn't want Lindbergh to do anything hazardous on his behalf, and Lindbergh smilingly rejoined that the ambassador was to stop worrying and leave the flying to him.

The account of the takeoff in the New York *Times* is a fair specimen of how Lindbergh was written about in the press in those days.

> Intent, cool, clear-eyed and clear-headed, under conditions requiring supreme moral and physical courage and consummate skill, America's young viking of the air lifted his gray plane from a puddle-bespattered morass into an underhanging fringe of threatening mists just before noon today, pointed its nose southwestward, and was off again on a new, hazardous adventure to a foreign land—personifying again in the hearts of his people their unofficial ambassador of goodwill.

Lindbergh flew south all day over Virginia, the Carolinas and Georgia, dodging heavy squalls, and then on through the night. At about nine in the morning he reached Tampico, Mexico. The squalls and fog and dense clouds were behind him. The sky was blue and the visibility unlimited; he assumed that he had endured the worst of the flight. And then to his astonishment he made an unpleasant discovery: he was lost.

The best maps of Mexico that Lindbergh had been able to obtain in the States showed few details—straightish black lines, representing railroads, occasionally crossed wavy blue lines, representing rivers, but looking back and forth between the maps on his knees and the terrain below him he could make nothing match. He followed a railroad westward, hoping that it would intersect with another railroad and thereby form an angle that he could recognize. No such angle appeared.

Next he tried a method that he had commonly employed in his barnstorming days. Strung out along the railroad line were villages and hamlets, each of them with a railroad station. Back in the States, every such station would have fixed to its end walls black-painted signs giving the name of the town. He had often "shot" such stations in order to check on his route; now he began to "shoot" the little Mexican stations, dropping to within 50 feet of the ground.

He saw a sign, "Caballeros," but he could find no town of that name on the map. Another town and again the sign "Caballeros." And again and then again, maddeningly. He had been over 25 hours without sleep and his responses were slowing down; at last it dawned on him that the word on the signs indicated not the name of the town but the presence of toilet facilities. So there he was, lost in broad daylight, in perfect flying weather, and the time at which he had promised to arrive in Mexico City was long since past.

He landed two hours and 40 minutes late, and profoundly embarrassed. He was also aware of the humor of the situation. In his account of the flight, which appears as a dispatch to the New York *Times,* he wrote, "Something went wrong, and it must have been me."

During the next six weeks, Lindbergh flew to 14 Latin American countries, as well as to the Canal Zone, being welcomed everywhere as some sort of divine apparition dropping benignly out of the skies. On his 26th birthday, he flew from Puerto Rico to Santa Domingo; by then, he was already making plans to bring his "public" life to an end. His tour, which had covered over 9000 miles, ended in St. Louis, in February 1928, and a few weeks later he made his last flight in the "Spirit of St. Louis." The Smithsonian Institution, in Washington, had asked for the plane in order to put it on permanent exhibition next to the Wright Brothers' "Kitty Hawk." Lindbergh loved flying the "Spirit of St. Louis" and would be sorry never to be able to do so again, but he had been in constant apprehension of its being torn to pieces by admiring crowds. He flew from St. Louis to Washington on April 30, 1928, and turned the "Spirit of St. Louis" over to officials of the Smithsonian. Many times during the next half-century, he would stroll into the Smithsonian and, with a hat shadowing his face, at a distance from any crowd, he would stare up at the little single-engine airplane hanging there alone in space.

Lindbergh assumed that when he announced a return to private life his fame would begin to subside as spontaneously as it had arisen. Nor was he naïve or disingenuous in making this assumption. We have a tradition in this country of creating famous figures overnight, using them up, and then discarding them. Unfortunately, far from having used him up, the public wanted more of him, and yet more, and so an unseemly tug of war began between the press and him, which ended only with his death.

The greatest flier in the world would be busy over the next few years laying out commercial air routes within the United States and between North America and other continents, and from time to time he would be flying faster, or higher, or longer than any other human being had ever flown, and those feats were as nothing compared to the scoops, true or false, that sold papers. Again and again the black headlines would blazon forth a fiction about his latest girl friend, his latest illness, his latest accident, his latest death.

The happiest event of Lindbergh's life was certainly his falling in love with and marrying Anne Morrow, but their courtship and honeymoon were made harrowing by reporters who pursued them night and day and whose constantly reiterated question to Lindbergh whenever they succeeded in running him to earth was, "What about it, Lindy? She pregnant?" The saddest event in Lindbergh's life was the kidnapping of and murder, in 1932, of his infant son and namesake. The press turned the event into a sideshow.

When the Lindbergh's second son, Jon, was born, he had to be guarded around the clock not only from potential kidnappers—scores of threatening letters were received after his birth—but also from reporters and photographers. Their hope was to get a close-up that could be featured on the front page of papers from coast to coast—the very picture that the Lindberghs with good reason were bending every effort not to have taken. Once, a car in which Jon was being driven to kindergarten was forced up onto the curb by another car; out jumped some photographers, who thrust their cameras full in the face of the frightened child. There were many such incidents, and in 1935 the Lindberghs felt obliged to leave the United States, taking a secluded house in the English countryside.

By then, Lindbergh had added to his brilliant career in aviation a scarcely less brilliant career as a medical technician. Ever since 1930, he had been working with Dr. Alexis Carrel, at the Rockefeller Institute for Medical Research in New York City on the development of a pump for perfusing living organs. Carrel and Lindbergh made the first announcement of the pump in the magazine *Science,* in 1935, and three years later they jointly published a book, *The Culture of Organs.*

Carrel was some 30 years older than Lindbergh, and he had a profound effect upon the young man's intellectual development. "He believed in the supernatural realm," Lindbergh wrote. "He was always searching for bridges between the physical and the mystical. He studied developments in the new field of psychosomatic medicine, listened intently to accounts of mental telepathy and clairvoyance, and was convinced of the efficacy of prayer."

In 1938, the Lindberghs, with Jon and a new baby, Land Morrow, moved to a tiny island called Illiec, off the coast of Brittany. It was only a few minutes by boat or, when the tide was low, on foot to the somewhat larger island of St. Gildas, where Carrel and his wife made their summer home. The composer Ambroise Thomas had owned Illiec in the late 19th century and had built a substantial stone manor house there. Living conditions were primitive and consequently very much to Lindbergh's taste; he felt primordial forces lingering among the wizened, wind-racked trees and he rejoiced at the great storms that would send sea boulders flying over their stout slate rooftops.

That life was soon to be interrupted by the Second World War. In 1939, the Lindbergh's reluctantly abandoned Illiec and rented a country place on Long Island. It was from there that Lindbergh embarked on another career—one that took from him most of his popularity without markedly diminishing his fame. At first on his own, and then under the auspices of the America First Committee, he argued vehemently against America's entry into the war. In the course of a running debate with the Roosevelt Administration, he felt obliged to resign his commission as a colonel in the U.S. Army Air Corps.

His career as a polemicist was ended by Pearl Harbor. Lindbergh at once volunteered his services to the Air Corps, and it was conveyed to him that if the White House were to permit his commission to be restored to him, he must first publicly admit that he had been wrong. Lindbergh, of course, refused. His contribution to the war effort would have to be made as a civilian. It was galling, but his pride was intact.

In 1944, as a civilian "observer" and therefore flagrantly against all the rules, Lindbergh flew no fewer than 50 combat missions, dropping bombs on gun emplacements and, on one occasion, engaging a Japanese pilot, whom he shot down somewhere over South Borneo. He would have been bitterly disappointed not to have had these tastes of combat; he rejoiced to pit his flying skills against other people's, and no wonder—by common consent he was the greatest flier that ever lived. After the war, Lindbergh shouldered a score of tasks, some of them for the Air Force, others for one or another of the philanthropies in which he took an increasing interest. He worked hard and traveled often, but at last, and for the first time in their married lives, the Lindberghs had a fixed point of departure and return—their country place in Darien, Conn. There they had come into possession of one of the few certain blessings: the merriment and distraction of a big old house filled with handsome, energetic children: three boys—Jon, Land and Scott—and two girls, Anne and Reeve.

The children grew up and scattered and married, and the first of the grandchildren began to arrive. All his life, Lindbergh had been haunted by the way in which the generations of a family are able to bind themselves together through time; now he thought of his grandmother, who had known many people born in the 18th century, and of his grandchildren, who would live well into the 21st century, and he saw that he served as a bridge between them.

He wished that there were more sheer volume of information that could be carried back and forth across the bridge. He would do his best to see that nothing of value was lost. He would tell his grandchildren stories, as his grandmother had told him. Some of them were fine stories for children, because they contained just the right mixture of the frightening and the bizarre.

He would tell them, for example, the story of how his grandfather August, having had his arm amputated, asked that it be brought to him in its pine box. Old August shook the lifeless fingers at the end of the amputated arm and said slowly, in broken English, "You have been a good friend to me for 50 years. But you can't be with me anymore. So good-by. Good-by, my friend."

The children themselves were the occasions for stories. It was Land who, as a child in school, was asked by one of his classmates, "Didn't your father discover America?" Land replied, "Yes, and he flew across the ocean, too."

With the children grown, the Lindberghs sold the house in Darien, reserving a portion of the property as a site for a smaller house. They lived part of the year in Darien, part in a chalet near Vevey, Switzerland, and part in Maui, Hawaii.

Lindbergh's favorite house was in Maui. As soon as the doctors in New York told him that he was dying, that was where he wanted to be.

He was wearing an oxygen mask when he began to die, and at first he thought that something had gone wrong with the apparatus feeding air into the mask. It was always his first thought to test his equipment; he reached out as if to take off the mask and then Anne saw in his eyes that he knew that it was not the mask.

ONCE, FROM A height of 2000 feet, he sighted the rocky little island of St. Gildas—the summer home of the Carrels, where he was about to make his first visit. As he glided down and circled over the main house, the Carrels came out to wave at him. He had timed his arrival for the ebb tide, so he would be able to walk across the sea bottom from the mainland to St. Gildas. He wrote on a slip of paper that he would be back as soon as he could arrange for the care of his plane. He tied the slip of paper to a cloth streamer, weighted the streamer with a stone he had brought along for the purpose, and dropped it over the side of the cockpit.

On the mainland, he had difficulty finding a place to land. After more than an hour's search, he glided down onto an airfield near the city of Dinan, about 70 miles southeast of St. Gildas. It would be close to midnight, with the tide high, by the time he got back to the coast. Moreover, he was unable to communicate with the Carrels, because they had no telephone. He hired a driver and car and tossed the emergency rubber raft from his plane into the car, along with his luggage.

The north coast of Brittany was in total darkness when they drove into the little village opposite St. Gildas. He could see the island glimmering vaguely at sea, under a few pale stars. He unloaded his gear on a concrete ramp running down into the sea, pumped up the raft, jointed its oars together, stowed his luggage, shoes and socks, and set out for the island.

Each dip of the oars left phosphorescence swirling in its wake. Phosphorescent jellyfish floated at different depths around him. He lost all sense of time and space. His modern world had vanished; he felt as if he had rowed backward through a million years.

He made landfall at St. Gildas on a beach of round stones. His feet slipped as he stepped out into the velvety dark. Since the Carrels had had no idea that he would be crossing the water at night, no one had waited up to welcome him. He hung his raft on his shoulder, picked up his luggage, and began feeling his way toward the still invisible house. He felt utterly alone and exultant.

ACKNOWLEDGMENTS AND CREDITS

Acknowledgments

MADAME SARAH by Cornelia Otis Skinner, *Reader's Digest,* Apr. 1967. Cond. from the book. Copyright © 1966 by Cornelia Otis Skinner. Reprinted by permission of Houghton Mifflin Company and International Creative Management. KING TUT'S TOMB: THE UNTOLD STORY by Thomas Hoving, *Reader's Digest,* Jan. 1979. Cond. from *Tutankhamun: The Untold Story.* Copyright © 1978 by Hoving Associates, Inc. Reprinted by permission of Simon & Schuster, a division of Gulf & Western Corporation. MY FRIEND FLICKA by Mary O'Hara, *Reader's Digest,* Jan. 1942. Cond. from the book. Copyright 1941, renewed 1969 by Mary O'Hara. Reprinted by permission of Lippincott & Crowell and Mary O'Hara. TRAVELS WITH CHARLEY by John Steinbeck, *Reader's Digest,* June 1964. Cond. from the book. Copyright © 1961, 1962 by The Curtis Publishing Co. Copyright © 1962 by John Steinbeck. Cond. by permission of Viking Penguin, Inc. Reprinted by permission of William Heinemann, Ltd. GOOD POPE JOHN by Lawrence Elliott, *Reader's Digest,* Dec. 1972. Cond. from *I Will Be Called John,* copyright © 1972 by The Reader's Digest Association, Inc., and published by the Reader's Digest Press. IN ONE ERA AND OUT THE OTHER by Sam Levenson, *Reader's Digest,* Oct. 1973. Cond. from the book. Copyright © 1973 by Sam Levenson. Reprinted by permission of Simon & Schuster, a division of Gulf & Western Corporation. NIGHT ON FIRE by John Evangelist Walsh, *Reader's Digest,* July 1978. Cond. from the book. Copyright © 1978 by John Evangelist Walsh. Reprinted by permission of McGraw-Hill Book Co. ON HIGH STEEL by Mike Cherry, *Reader's Digest,* Feb. 1975. Reprinted by permission of Times Books, a division of Quadrangle/The New York Times Book Co., Inc., from *On High Steel: The Education of an Ironworker* by Mike Cherry. Copyright © 1974 by Mike Cherry. Also reprinted by permission of Curtis Brown, Ltd. THE SERGEANT WHO OPENED THE DOOR by John Barron, *Reader's Digest,* Jan. 1974. Cond. from *KGB: The Secret Work of Soviet Secret Agents,* copyright © 1974 by The Reader's Digest Association, Inc., and published by the Reader's Digest Press. ALL THINGS WISE AND WONDERFUL by James Herriot, *Reader's Digest,* Oct. 1977. Copyright © 1976, 1977 by James Herriot. Cond. from the book. Reprinted through special arrangement with St. Martin's Press, Inc. Also published by Michael Joseph Ltd. REPORT FROM ENGINE CO. 82 by Dennis Smith, *Reader's Digest,* July 1972. Adapted from the book. Copyright © 1972 by Dennis Smith. Reprinted by permission of the publisher, E. P. Dutton. TINKERBELLE by Robert Manry, *Reader's Digest,* July 1966. Cond. from the book. Copyright © 1966 by Robert Manry. Reprinted by permission of Harper & Row, Publishers, Inc., and William Collins, Sons & Co., Ltd.

ALIVE: THE STORY OF THE ANDES SURVIVORS by Piers Paul Read, *Reader's Digest,* Aug. 1974. Cond. from the book. Copyright © 1974 by Piers Paul Read. Reprinted by permission of Lippincott & Crowell and the Alison Press/Martin Secker & Warburg, Ltd. ROOTS by Alex Haley, *Reader's Digest,* May and June 1974. Cond. from the book. Copyright © 1976 by Alex Haley. Used by permission of Doubleday & Company, Inc., and Hutchinson & Co. (Publishers), Ltd. ONLY WHEN I LAUGH by Gladys Workman, *Reader's Digest,* Apr. 1962. Cond. from the book. © 1959 by Prentice-Hall, Inc. Published by Prentice-Hall, Inc., Englewood Cliffs, New Jersey 07632. 83 HOURS TILL DAWN by Gene Miller in collaboration with Barbara Jane Mackle, *Reader's Digest,* Dec. 1971. Cond. from the book. Copyright © 1971 by Barbara Jane Mackle and Gene Miller. Used by permission of Doubleday & Co., Inc. CARRYING THE FIRE: AN ASTRONAUT'S JOURNEYS by Michael Collins, *Reader's Digest,* Jan. 1975. Cond. from the book. Reprinted with the permission of Farrar, Straus and Giroux, Inc. Copyright © 1974 by Michael Collins. JONATHAN LIVINGSTON SEAGULL by Richard Bach, *Reader's Digest,* May 1972. Cond. from the book. Copyright © 1970 by Richard D. Bach. Cond. by arrangement with Macmillan Publishing Co., Inc. Reprinted by permission of Turnstone Books, London. MY MOBY DICK by William Humphrey, *Reader's Digest,* Sept. 1979. Cond. from the book. © 1978 by William Humphrey. Reprinted by permission of Doubleday & Co., Inc., and Chatto & Windus, Ltd. THE FIRST FOUR YEARS by Laura Ingalls Wilder, *Reader's Digest,* Dec. 1976. Cond. from the book. Text copyright © 1971 by Roger Lea MacBride. Reprinted by permission of Harper & Row, Publishers, Inc., and Lutterworth Press, London. FEVER! by John G. Fuller, *Reader's Digest,* March 1974. Cond. from the novel of the same title. Copyright © 1974 by John G. Fuller. Used by permission of International Creative Management. Reprinted by permission of Granada Publishing, Ltd. THE WATERMEN by James A. Michener, *Reader's Digest,* Oct. 1978. Cond. from the book *Chesapeake* by James A. Michener. Copyright © 1978 by Random House, Inc. Also published by Martin Secker and Warburg, Ltd. © 1978 by James A. Michener. THE LUSITANIA by Colin Simpson, *Reader's Digest,* Nov. 1973, *The Truth About the Lusitania.* Cond. from the book *The Lusitania.* Copyright © 1972 by Colin Simpson. Reprinted by permission of Little Brown and Co. and Penguin Books, Ltd. LINDBERGH ALONE by Brendan Gill, *Reader's Digest,* May 1977. Cond. and reprinted by permission of Harcourt Brace Jovanovich, Inc. Copyright © 1977 by Brendan Gill. Extracts from *The Spirit of St. Louis* by Charles A. Lindbergh, reprinted by permission of Charles Scribner's Sons; original publisher, John Murray, Ltd. Copyright 1953 Charles Scribner's Sons. Extracts from *We* by Charles Lindbergh. Reprinted by permission of G. P. Putnam's Sons. Copyright 1927 by Charles A. Lindbergh; renewed copyright © 1955 by Charles A. Lindbergh.

Illustration Credits

Pages 8–9, Petit Palais Museum, Paris. 44 *inset* Photography of Egyptian Expedition. Metropolitan Museum of Art. 61, Lee Boltin. 138–139, Yale University Art Gallery, The Mabel Brady Garvan Collection. 314, Jean-Pierre Laffont Sygma. 453, NASA. 499, Laura Ingalls Wilder Home and Museum, Mansfield, Missouri. 581, Brown Brothers. 623 *left* Charles Lindbergh Papers, Yale University Library; *right* Wide World Photos. 44, 47, 149, 293, 303, 412, 522, 601, George Buctel (*maps and diagrams*).